DOUBLE EAGLE AND CRESCENT

Vienna's Second Turkish Siege and Its Historical Setting

**The Real Heroes of the Siege of Vienna:
The Austrian Infantryman and Cuirassier of 1683**

The foot-soldier carries a Montecuccoli-model, matchlock-flintlock musket, an old style bandoleer, and "swyne's feather"; see Chapter Six, footnote 53.

(Vienna, Army Historical Museum)

Double Eagle and Crescent

VIENNA'S SECOND TURKISH SIEGE
AND ITS HISTORICAL SETTING

Thomas M. Barker

Obverse of a commemorative coin minted in Hamburg, after
a Viennese model, by Hermann Lüders, probably in late 1683.
The double-headed eagle gazes both at the sunlike, radiant
eye of God (above) and the Ottoman crescent sinking behind
a cloud bank (below). The orb, which its claws clutch, is engraved with the profile of Vienna. The three inner inscriptions read: "Under the shadow of thy wings He united the
rays of succor and drove the vanquished into the shadows."
The outer label says: "He interposes the wall of the Empire
within the realm of Austria." (See O. C. Gaedchens, *Ham-
burgische Münzen und Medaillen*, Vol. II, Hamburg, 1854,
pp. 11–12.)

STATE UNIVERSITY OF NEW YORK PRESS

Printed in the United States of America

To
Guy Earl Mack
(1877–1949)

Preface

The abortive Turkish siege of Vienna in 1683 is usually mentioned as one of the premier incidents of European history. Many writers emphasize the intervention of King John Sobieski of Poland, who was, undeniably, the most romantic figure to participate in the relief of the Danubian fortress. In fact, the Polish ruler has often been depicted, largely because of his own publicity efforts, as the savior of Christianity and of Western civilization without much credit being given to anyone else.[1] While it is hardly possible to maintain such a view after considering overall conditions during the late seventeenth century and, more particularly, after examining individual events and human actions, 1683 was nevertheless an unusually critical year in the history of continental Europe. The siege and the great battle that ended it also have a great deal of appeal on their own account. The characters are colorful, their actions dramatic, and the military problems of no little significance.

I decided to begin the present study after preparing a class lecture some years ago, having discovered that standard references in English provided only meager information and that there was nothing else. The little that was available was marred not only by varying degrees of Polish nationalist bias but also by contradictions. Even the most recent account in a foreign language, Reinhold Lorenz' *Das Türkenjahr 1683* (third ed., Vienna, Braumüller, 1944), while brilliant, left much to be desired because of a Srbik-school, Pan German orientation. Moreover, it seemed that the time was ripe for a new synthesis because the period following the Second World War had witnessed the appearance of definitive editions of two more or less unexploited sources[2] as well as a series of fine, archivally-based articles. After my manuscript was well advanced, the English author, John Stoye, published his *Siege of Vienna* (London, Collins, 1964). This gracefully written book has helped me focus certain ideas more sharply, for its viewpoints are substantially different from my own.

The learned reader will find a relatively limited use of unprinted materials in this volume. There is a double reason for this: the inherently fascinating nature of the topic not only impelled numerous witnesses to write for the literate public of their own day; it also caused professional historians, from the very dawn of systematic disciplinary research in the nineteenth century, to comb depositories thoroughly for items that had somehow remained buried. In short, the range of readily available sources for the *res gestae* of 1683 is probably greater than is normally the case. Right at the start of my own work in Vienna well-initiated archivists told me that there was little chance of my discovering anything really new. I could expect to unearth fresh data only in Simancas (Spain) —advice which did prove modestly rewarding. Nevertheless, I have personally examined all the presumably relevant fascicles and cartons in the Austrian State Archives. While I have been able to retrieve a few lesser details, it does in fact seem unlikely that much else is left. To be sure, since only a fraction of some three million documents has been individually catalogued, there is at least a theoretical possibility of additional revelations some day.

Clearly it has been impossible to read all the publications concerning the second siege of Vienna that have appeared in the course of 280 years. Walter Sturminger's bibliography, a monument of love and an indispensable time-saver for all future researchers, alone lists 2547 titles.[3] My presentation is based simply upon a broad survey and selective exploitation of the sources as well as upon a perusal of all the serious scholarly efforts of the last hundred years.

Although my original motive in undertaking research did not involve any penchant for philosophic speculation, the pursuit of so broad a project has unavoidably led to reflection on the meaning of the past. A great number of contemporary historians would probably hold that the forces which condition change are infinitely manifold and would consider their outlook eclectic. The author is no exception. Still, it is hard not to yield to the temptation of stressing certain causal factors over others. In this book four seem particularly intrusive. The influence of evolving military technology and, concomitantly, of tactical and strategic innovation stands out sharply. The significance of geographic relationships is also very evident. Chance, as might be expected, has its rôle to play. Finally, the old thesis that men make history finds much support in the events of 1683, for the judgments made by a handful of personalities strikingly affected the outcome of the second great assault upon Vienna. The failure of the enterprise was not inevitable unless one holds that the figures had to act as they did, their own psyches having been molded by circumstances more distantly removed.

If one must be concerned with whys and wherefores, equally important —but less complex—is the question of results. There has never been much doubt that the repulse of what proved to be the last major Ottoman endeavor to subdue the Christian West set off in turn a chain of events, at the end of which the Casa d'Austria had won the territorial basis and the physical means with which to become a great power outside of Germany, that is, a state in its own right. While a Turkish victory could scarcely have inhibited the complex process of "decay" within the sultan's own realm, a Habsburg defeat could have crippled the dynasty and thus have prevented the rise of the Austrian Empire of the nineteenth and twentieth centuries.

The siege of Vienna and the subsequent War of the Holy League are of abstract interest in another respect also. In the past two decades or so there has been a growing concern for the study of warfare as a primary social phenomenon. While the conflicts of seventeenth century Central and Western Europe have received considerable attention, little has been written about those in the East. Certainly the story of 1683 is not complete without noting, albeit briefly, the unique character of the struggle between Christian and Turk.

Throughout the volume I have replaced historical German and Magyar place names with their proper modern equivalents. The former are included in parentheses on the occasion of the first reference only. While in most cases the nationality in political control in the 1960's has always enjoyed numerical superiority, cultural underdevelopment prevented the spreading of indigenous forms to the rest of Europe, and thus cities, towns, and natural features became known by words often entirely strange to the bulk of the local inhabitants. For that matter, the terms used by the two dominant nationalities also frequently differed from one another (e.g., Raab for Győr, Gran for Esztergom); in such cases the German usually prevailed. Since the reader is well advised to turn to supplementary maps or to an atlas and since contemporary geographers, almost without exception, base themselves upon current nomenclature, I conclude that the historian, too, ought to renounce outdated designations. The only logical deviation from this practice would seem to be the continued use of terms such as the "Diet of Pressburg" and the "Peace of Karlowitz" (instead of speaking of a "Diet of Bratislava" or a "Peace of Sremski Karlovci"). The German forms are so imbedded in English writing that the substitution of native counterparts would have a stilted and awkward effect. Another deviation, of course, is the use of specifically English forms where they happen to exist ("Belgrade" for "Beograd," "Warsaw" for "Warszawa"). I realize, of course, that no attempt to solve problems of this nature is entirely without disadvantage.

A brief explanation of political terminology likewise seems in order. Certain of my usages reflect seventeenth-century sources and the strange, confused constitution of the Holy Roman Empire. The adjectives "Austrian" and "Imperial" refer to organs of the Habsburg dynasty and to its own, immediate subjects. "German" is an unavoidably ambivalent word. In some cases it has the above meaning even though Slavs, Magyars, and Romanics stood shoulder to shoulder with German-speaking Austrians. However, depending upon the context, "German" may also indicate: (a). German adherents of the Archhouse together with *Reichs-deutsche* or "Empire Germans" (i.e., persons from the non-Habsburg principalities of Germany) —a frame of reference primarily cultural and ethnic; (b). German *and* non-German Austrians when allied with territorial Germans; "Austro-German" says the same thing more clearly. The appellations "Austro-German" (or "Austrian German") as understood by the later Pan German movement and "Austrian" and "German" in their mid-twentieth century senses are, of course, largely irrelevant here.

Translations are mostly my own. However, in instances where the grammar and the vocabulary seemed to be fairly simple, I have left quoted passages in the original tongue in an attempt to preserve something of the flavor of the seventeenth-century environment. A special note is necessary regarding Turkish words and not yet really consistent Turkish orthography. Generally, for simplicity's sake, I have used the singular form of nouns in an English plural context. However, in one instance (Chapter Two), following my source, the proper indefinite plural suffix "lar" as well as the English "s" seemed more appropriate. As for spelling, I have tried, for the most part, to conform to the most modern standards.

The broad scope of the first part of the book has a particular purpose. It seems to me that students and, possibly, teachers with more general interests may find some value in an introduction to the overall period. The idea, in short, is to place the somewhat restricted events of 1679–1683 in perspective. Specialists, nevertheless, may wish to skip this portion. Another feature of the volume is detail with respect to locations in and around Vienna. I have included this material especially for the benefit of the many English-speaking persons (including old friends and colleagues) who have become acquainted with the city since 1945. For others, the addition of a number of maps, both seventeenth century originals and my own, should prove to be a mitigating factor. Whoever lacks a taste for the details of diplomatic history will probably wish to skim through Chapters Four and Five.

Finally, I should like to acknowledge my indebtedness to all the persons and institutions that have aided me in one way or another although naturally I alone bear responsibility for the defects of my work. I carried out the basic research in Vienna during the academic year 1961–1962 and made further visits there during the summers of 1965 and 1966. (I have also inspected most of the battle sites of 1683.) I was able to utilize the almost perfect collection of the understaffed and overcrowded Austrian National Library as well as the less complete holdings of the Vienna City Library and the University Library. I am particularly grateful for the consideration shown me by the officials of the last two establishments, especially by Herrn Bibliothekar Hugo Alkar and Herrn Wilhelm

Belinski of the *Universitätsbibliothek*. I should also like to express my appreciation to Professors Reinhold Lorenz and Otto Forst de Battaglia, to Herrn Ministerialrat Walter Sturminger, to indefatigable Frau Maria Schönbauer, to Dr. and Mrs. Alexander Ritschny, Herrn Fritz Baer, Dr. Wilhelm Schlag, and to Herren Norbert Weyss and Herbert Anschütz of Viernheim (Hessen). My obligation to Oberrat Dr. Walter Hummelberger of the Vienna Municipal Historical Museum and to Dr. Richard Kreutel, Austrian *chargé d'affaires* in Kabul (Afghanistan), is very great. Dr. Christiane Thomas and Countess Anna Coreth of the *Haus-, Hof- und Staatsarchiv*, Archivar Dr. Kurt Peball of the *Kriegsarchiv*, and the staffs of the *Institut für österreichische Geschichtsforschung*, the *Forschungsinstitut für den Donauraum*, and the Army Historical Museum also afforded valuable assistance. The personnel of the *Archivo General de Simancas*, the French Foreign Ministry Archives, the *Bibliothèque Nationale*, and the New York Public Library provided further indispensable services. My brother-in-law, Mr. Richard Duncan of London, kindly procured me otherwise inaccessible data from the British Museum. For assistance with interlibrary loans in the United States I am most thankful to Miss Margaret Wardell of Western Illinois University and Misses Eleanor Streun and Margaret Wagner of the State University of New York at Albany. For help with archaic Spanish, florid Baroque Latin, and Turkicized Greek I must mention my indulgent colleagues, Professors Xavier Fernández and Hans Pohlsander. My ignorance of Polish was overcome by Frl. Anja Wengorz of Berlin, Mlle. B. Zoltówska of Montréal and my colleague, Professor Alicja Iwańska. Professors John B. Wolf and Arthur May made a number of excellent suggestions drawn from their vast store of experience. Professor Kendall Birr has also shown much kindness. In the days before the Xerox revolutions's spread to Austria, my wife, Fritzi, spent many wearisome hours in the Viennese libraries making excerpts for me from rare volumes. Mrs. Virginia Cornell did a superb job of typing an unusually difficult manuscript. The appearance of the volume has been much expedited by the receipt of a fellowship and an expense grant from the Research Foundation of the State University of New York. Lastly, I am beholden to the Vienna Municipal Historical Museum, the Austrian National Library, the Austrian Army Historical Museum, and the Hamburg Historical Museum for supplying illustrations and permitting their reproduction.

THOMAS M. BARKER

Albany, New York
December 15, 1966

Contents

Facies Europae
1648–1679

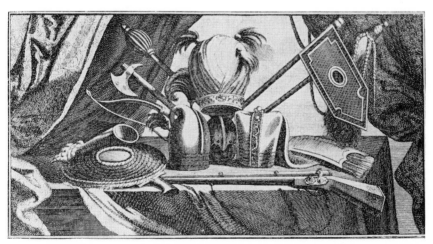

(from Luigi F. Marsigli, *Stato militare Ottomano,* The Hague, 1732. New York Public Library.)

CHAPTER ONE

The Habsburg Monarchy

Vienna can arouse in men an intense, enduring love in a way equalled perhaps only by Paris. Among the Danubian city's varied attractions are a deliberately preserved, Imperial Habsburg aura, mundane, sophisticated manners, a deep commitment to artistic and intellectual values, and, surely best known, the outlying girdle of mountain, forest, and river. Nevertheless, even the most extravagant admirer, will have to concede that the place does have certain negative features—an admission that may seem shocking to the non-Austrian, who most likely envisages an atmosphere in which insouciance and gaiety predominate. The town's principal physical disadvantage is its climate, objectionable even in summer. By July one can see humid heat undulating from the dull, gray cobblestones. The sultry air, plus an affection for countryside and nature common to many Viennese, causes a great exodus, especially of the leisured classes, which flee to the gilt hostelries of Carinthia's modish Wörthersee, to the chalets of Tyrol's equally fashionable Kitzbühel, or to the strands of the Adriatic.

In a former age, however, the materially-privileged were wont to retire to stuccoed, yellow and cream-colored, Baroque villas and to geometrically patterned gardens not too far from their mansions within the capital's walls. The weather of July, 1683, was apparently just as disagreeable as usual. Indeed, according to some accounts, it was even worse. Leopold I, by God's grace, King of Germany, Holy Roman Emperor Elect, King of Bohemia, Hungary, and Croatia, Archduke of Austria "and so forth," spent several days at the beginning of the month on an estate and game farm near Perchtoldsdorf, a Gothic village at the base of the Vienna Woods. The stags, boars, and bears inhabiting this Imperial property probably afforded their owner some distraction as he was an impassioned devotee of the hunt. In Perchtoldsdorf itself were rather unique playing fountains (*Wasserkünste*), in the cool shade of which the bemused sovereign lingered for some time after the exertions of the chase, listening to a music ensemble, sipping wine, and nibbling sweetmeats.[1] Yet the hour was hardly appropriate to such diversions. For, at the very same time, the Emperor's crack, aristocratic cavalry was being covered by the dust of its own retreat from the Hungarian Alföld, while his peasant-bred infantry was taking shelter in the swampy Danubian islands just to the southeast of Bratislava (Pressburg, Poszóny).

The 30,000 man Habsburg field army was well-equipped and more or less intact, but its commanders realized that there was little chance of its withstanding the cumbrous, conglomerate Ottoman horde, which, according to some reports, counted as many as 300,000 Islamic warriors. Throughout Central Europe the clergy, fearing for the survival of Christendom, set church bells, the so-called *Türkenglocken,* a-pealing in order to urge the faithful to recite prayers of intercession. For weeks the responsible civil and military authorities in Vienna had been laboring to close the gaps in the city's only partly prepared defenses. Leopold, apparently sensing the full gravity of his situation, returned to the capital. Not wishing, so it was claimed, to arouse further fears among the burghers already perturbed by all manner of terrifying rumor, he tarried for another twenty-four hours in the Hofburg, the dynasty's venerable and tradition-crusted town residence. By July seventh there could no longer be much doubt about the goal of the Turkish steamroller, and thus early in the evening the heavy, ornate Imperial carriages trundled onto the flagstone pavement of the ancient Schweizerhof, the core of the palace. Trunks of valuables, hastily packed, were thrown aboard. Greater foresight had already assured the removal from Bratislava of the Crown of St. Stephen, which had been whisked off by a troop of horse, led by Count Erdödy, one of few Magyar magnates still loyal to the House of Habsburg.

At eight p.m. the ruler, his third wife, Eleanora, seven months with child, "their young Lordships" (his earlier progeny), and a retinue of high officials, foreign diplomats and courtiers ascended the waiting vehicles. The caravan had no choice but to proceed through the city's streets,[2] arousing, as it passed, howls of dismay from the hysterical common rabble, swollen by flocks of atrocity-tale-bearing refugees now more or less safe behind the bastions and courtine. The basically kind-hearted Emperor ordered his 300 man cavalry guard to be less vigorous in driving off the proletarians who seemed at times to be blocking the carriages' progress. The line of conveyances debouched at the Rothenturm Gate, crossed the drawbridge over the shallow Danube Arm (the "Canal" of today), rumbled through the Leopoldstadt (the present Second District), from which the monarch had expelled the Jews some years previously, rolled past the normally inviting Augarten, and clattered across the brace of wooden bridges which spanned the then multi-channeled main Danube. Progressing slowly over a road jammed with fellow fugitives, the Imperial party reached Korneuburg, nine miles from the Gate, only at midnight. The embittered local peasants showed open hostility. They cursed the Catholic clergy, whose persecution of Hungarian Protestantism they believed to be the cause of Austria's current plight. They even heckled the Emperor to his face. The sovereign and his companions were unable to make their way to any inn. The evening's repast consisted only of a few boiled eggs, snatched perhaps from some unattended hen house, and the

only beds available were garment-bedecked piles of straw in some now
unremembered hovel. On the horizon the flickering of burning farm-
steads could be perceived, and it was known that vicious Tatar raiders,
mounted on swift ponies, were not far away and might even traverse the
river.[3]

Such was the immediate overture to the second Turkish siege of
Vienna. Not since the time of the tragic Maximilian had any head of the
house of Austria been forced to flee his realm's metropolis in like igno-
miny. One may legitimately ask what historical circumstances had joined
together to bring about this flight in the swelter and torpor of early
summer.

A. Emperor Leopold I

Since the Emperor was at least partly responsible for his own predicament, the question naturally arises, what kind of a person was he? As the
younger of Ferdinand III's two sons, Leopold was not originally expected
to succeed to his father's office, for his elder brother did not die until he
himself was fourteen. The future monarch's schooling thus commenced
with the presupposition of a clerical career. Since the victory of the
Counter Reformation, all education in the Habsburg domains lay in the
hands of the Society of Jesus, which imparted to learning a strongly
devotional, moralistic tone. It might consequently be supposed that the
child was artificially marked with the imprint of Roman Catholicism.
It seems, however, that his nature was inherently religious. He delighted
in prayer at an age when most other boys appear more interested
in outdoor games. He actually played at being a priest. He was
especially fervent in his veneration for the Blessed Virgin, a characteristic
aspect of Baroque piety.[4] As an adult he is said to have heard three
Masses daily.[5] He surrounded himself with clerical confidants and advisers. In short, his whole life was associated in one way or another with the
precepts of the Church or the counsel of its representatives.[6]

STRENGTHS AND VIRTUES

The physical appearance of the man who came to govern a vast,
polyglot empire seemed somewhat absurd to one penetrating, although
not entirely unprejudiced, contemporary, the Marquis de Sèbeville, envoy
extraordinary of the King of France to the Habsburg Court:

> All in all there is nothing pleasing about him although he has good
> color, very attractive eyes and a well-cut nose. The trouble is that his
> underlip hangs down so much that it is impossible to accustom one's
> self to his visage. Nor can one become used to his grave and serious, or
> rather prideful and timid manner. He is always afraid that people will
> laugh about him and laughs rarely himself.[7]

Diuo Leopoldo Cæsari August: ac Germaniæ Hungariæ Bohemiæ Regi.
Archiduci Austriæ &c: *Domino suo Clementijsimo subiechjsimus Chens Joannes Vldalricus Mejr Dedicat*
Matthæu Kusell sculp

Emperor Leopold I

The short, somewhat stocky, organically healthy monarch clothed his thin, weak legs in scarlet stockings, cultivated a curled mustache and Vandyke beard, and wore over his long, black hair a wig and a broad hat with a red or black feather. A large chain of the Order of the Golden Fleece was often draped about his cloak.[8] While descriptive accounts of Leopold concur and while one might suppose that he looked the complete fool, his solemnity and dignity contributed a great deal toward compensating for his physical flaws. He was a good rider and thus more impressive on horseback than on foot. He did not lack a certain degree of majesty.[9]

Although outwardly dissimilar to the naturally regal Louis XIV, the Habsburger was his counterpart in other respects. Like the Sun-King, Leopold was devoted to work although his dedication may have come more from an inculcated sense of responsibility than from natural disposition. In any case, the Emperor kept so regular a schedule that one could almost set a watch by his comings and goings. His Court was every bit as hospitable to culture as that of France even though Germany itself fell short of Gallic intellectual attainments at that time. Baroque music— orchestral, choral and operatic—was performed regularly. In fact, the Western world owes the Habsburgs much for having imported musical drama from Italy and for guiding it into new paths of development. (A particularly important patron was Leopold's Mantuan-born stepmother, Eleanora of Gonzaga.) By the end of the reign more than 400 productions had been given. A luxurious theater ("Das Komödienhaus"), the demolition of which was one of the sad necessities of the Turkish siege, arose next to the Burg Courtine. Clavicymbals—an instrument which Austria's ruler played with expertise—could be found throughout the Palace. The All Highest was, moreover, a competent composer, the author not only of a large number of musical works in a variety of forms, including even German hymns, but of ballets as well. He also designed stage settings and often took over the conductor's baton. One of his more famous—and more costly—undertakings was a sumptuous equestrian ballet, in which the talents of human artists complemented the skills of Lippizaner stallions from the Spanish Riding School. The Emperor likewise dabbled in painting, was interested in alchemy, numismatics, and Roman antiquities. He loved books and, together with his renowned curator, Lambeccius, spent many an hour in the *Hofbibliothek,* the core of the present Austrian National Library.[10] Leopold was, in short, of a scholarly bent although certain of his efforts were dilettantish and his intellect marred by susceptibility to superstition (itself characteristic of his age and milieu). He demonstrated taste, finesse, and sensitivity. Loud, vulgar-mouthed people were unwelcome at court. His impeccable sexual morals contrasted sharply with Louis XIV's. The Austrian was considered an ideal spouse, and the fact that he had three wives—the lovely, blonde Margareta Theresa of Spain, immortalized as a child by Velasquez; the pert and saucy Claudia Felicitas of the Innsbruck branch of the dynasty; and the somewhat less pulchritudinous Eleanora of Pfalz-Neuburg—was due, it appears, only to the high mortality rate of the era. He further manifested tact and skill in managing his womenfolk.[11] It cannot be said, however, that the Emperor was exclusively dedicated to esthetic and familial pleasures. Like later members of his House, he was, as indicated, inordinately fond of the hunt, taking delight in carefully staged mass slaughters. At least so it seemed to the French envoy.[12]

Despite a relative lack of ingenuity and an inability to grasp quickly intricate political situations and other people's personalities, the Emperor possessed a respectable intelligence: somewhat slow but basically sound, methodical and mature. He had a retentive memory, which was already apparent in early childhood and which continued to impress foreign representatives throughout his adult years. He showed real linguistic talent. He knew Latin, in which his style was held to be especially felicitous; French, which he preferred not to speak because of political enmities; Italian, the favored court tongue, which, according to the Venetian ambassador, Leopold spoke like a native; and Spanish. His German was excellent, a noteworthy point in view of that language's degenerate status at that time and, as his Protestant, north German biographer remarked, considering the fact that he himself was an Austro-German. Leopold also wrote poetry (in Italian) and was an impressive public speaker.[13]

His good mind was complemented by a stolid emotional make-up, conditioned by religious faith. "L'imperturbilita dell'animo è la virtú, ch'in più, eminente grado possede."[14] Throughout all the ups and downs of his career, in success and in failure, stability of behavior was characteristic of the man. While he was not immune to depression and discouragement, he never seems to have been actually seized by panic, even in the headlong flight from Vienna. Linked with his psychological steadiness was a tenacity of purpose, for which his whole reign is the witness. He might make decisions slowly, but, once made, he held to them rigorously.[15]

PERSONALITY DEFICIENCIES

Alongside such merits were disturbing weaknesses, serious enough, it seems, for history to reject the cognomen "Great" accorded him by early writers. His overly-scrupulous conscience, his excessive, religiously-induced humility were obstacles to statesmanship. It was believed that his Jesuit mentors and confessors had bent him so much in the direction of moral self-questioning that he had become incapable of making decisions independently.[17] One Venetian ambassador wrote home:

His great intelligence and his very perspicacious mind cause him . . . to remain all the more perplexed. . . . He does not act without letting himself be guided by his ministers' opinions and has little faith in his own. If an appeal is made against His Majesty, he almost rejects his conclusions in order to follow those of others. Such diffidence and modesty are an heroic virtue in private persons, but pestiferous in a prince.[18]

A later ambassador again stressed this character flaw and added:

If through . . . an heroic effort of will, he would take upon himself the burden of decision and would follow his own opinions; and if he would pass over the widespread web of plotting in the government, affairs would sometimes turn out for him as perfectly as if he had proceeded from the world's only source of wisdom. . . .[19]

The Emperor himself was not unaware that his diffidence represented a weakness. He once wrote to Marco d'Aviano that he could recognize proper courses of action but lacked the will to impose them.[20] This penitential mentality, with its concomitant, a fatalistic acceptance of God's will, was detrimental enough in peacetime. At moments of crisis it was even more harmful. Theistic stoicism may have helped to ensure a calm atmosphere, but it simultaneously prevented quick and forthright action.[21]

The Emperor's religiosity had other negative features as well. Like Louis, he was a bigot. To be sure, one must qualify the criticism. Firstly, to assume that he ought to have advocated religious liberty in the sense of an Enlightenment that was still decades away hardly seems reasonable. Secondly, the rational development of tolerance was precluded by environment, in particular by his training for an ecclesiastical future. His mentors likewise impressed upon him the special, politically-accented, almost Erastian traditions of Habsburg piety, which emphasized personal, Imperial participation in religious exercises, such as the worship of the Blessed Sacrament, the veneration of the Mother of God and the *Pietas Crucis*. In third place, one must concede that he did not personally countenance physical cruelty—although his subordinates might make a mockery of the famed *Clementia Austriaca*—and that he demonstrated some interest in Church reunion in the latter part of his reign.[22] On the other hand, he was perceptive and ought to have recognized that persecution of Protestants was politically unwise, indeed dangerous, and (as also applicable to the Jews) economically damaging. There was certainly more reason for him to be circumspect in domestic religious affairs than there was with Louis, who, after all, did not have powerful foreign enemies in his backyard.

Other virtues of Leopold that were sometimes transposed into faults were gratitude, kindness and generosity. He was apparently cheated blind by many persons who held important state charges. Even when the worst culprit, the treasurer, Count Georg von Sinzendorf, was finally apprehended, the ruler could not bear to punish him too harshly, and no real example was made.[23] Truly severe penalties were reserved only for outright conspiracy. It also seems inappropriate for the Emperor to have spent vast sums on court activities when he was so hard pressed to pay military expenses. Even in "restricted" form, amidst war-induced austerity, the Imperial progress consisted of sixty-nine coaches (a recent and costly French innovation), twenty-two heavy wagons, and 291 horses; another thirty-three coaches, twenty-two heavy wagons, and 203 horses were reserved for the children.[24] Although the prestige of a seventeenth century monarch seemed to require such outlays and while Habsburg splendor appeared picayune to Sèbeville, accustomed as he was to the luminous royalty of France, a more vigorous head of state might well have enforced genuine sacrifices. One cannot help but recall the often threadbare Frederick II of Prussia, incidentally no mean patron of learning and the arts. The French envoy also noted critically Leopold's devotion to his third spouse, who allegedly tried to advance the interests of her own, large, impecunious family. The experienced Parisian courtier remarked that the lady's charms hardly justified her great hold over her mate, a comment perhaps intended to amuse the more fastidious Louis XIV.[25]

This listing of both positive and negative features in the Habsburger's personality might, upon balance, seem equivalent to mediocrity. Yet there is one further, overriding factor in his favor. Despite all his procrastination and vacillation, Leopold I ultimately picked and upheld capable men, especially military figures. "And tho' Leopold was so little a soldier himself, that he scarce ever headed an Army, yet he was so successful in the choice of his generals, that by them he made greater Acquisitions, more humbled the Pride of the Ottoman Port [*sic*] than all his ancestors could do put together."[26] The final evaluation of a ruler should include a comparison of the condition of his country at the outset and at the end of his reign. In this respect the Emperor, who seems to grow into his job with the passing years, surpasses Louis. If fate had permitted the youthful Leopold to continue toward a priestly career, his own existence would probably have been more serene. Perhaps the rôle of abbot of some large, rich monastery like Melk would have suited him better. Nevertheless, as a sovereign he could have been far worse—and possibly a little better—for the highly-demanding age in which he lived.

THE PROBLEM OF MOTIVATION

One must ask, finally, a difficult and perhaps impossible question: for what was Leopold striving, or rather, what motives underlay his political actions? Once again religion was probably a prime factor. This may be seen in his (apparent) concept of the Imperial office. While the *Reich* had ceased to have much meaning for many seventeenth century Germans, it still made sense to its annointed leader. Many of the Emperor's utterances imply belief in a moral duty, imposed at the time of his coronation at St. Bartholomew's Church in Frankfurt (August 1, 1658). He had sworn a holy oath to preserve the existing legal order in both the secular and ecclesiastical realms.[27] Translated into practical terms, this pledge required resistance to Louis' forceful policies, which would of necessity alter conditions within the Empire. To be sure, it is unlikely that Leopold was stirred only by religious and ethical considerations. If one turns to the Eastern or Turkish theater, another pattern reveals itself. In this instance, the monarch was maintaining his own sovereign prerogatives (against the Hungarian magnates) and territorial interests (against the Ottomans), not those of his fellow German princes, and he proved to be every bit as determined in safeguarding Crown rights as he did in protecting others. Of course, the needs of the West long made it impossible for him to devote sufficient means to preserving his position in Hungary. The repulse of France took priority. In both instances, however, he sought to perpetuate the existing order, a stance which was simultaneously defensive and conservative.[28]

On the other hand, one must grant that the Emperor also exploited new opportunities as they arose throughout his reign. While he was not overtly expansionistic like Louis, he continued to press, after 1683, what had originally been an unwanted struggle, showing that he was prepared to grasp the unexpected fruits of his generals' successes. (Admittedly, these gains were of immediate benefit in fighting France). Although he may have rationalized the retention of Turkish lands as the recovery of property of the Crown of St. Stephen or as the liberation of Christian soil from infidel domination, his family had never before exercised jurisdiction over most of the region in question. He also pursued his claims to the Spanish throne. This effort was at least somewhat novel, for the traditions of the Austrian Habsburgs were more Central European than Mediterranean, while the precedent of Charles V's universal empire was basically chimerical. Clearly, a power vacuum will attract even a ruler whose predilections are modest.

B. Austria in Early Modern Times

Any attempt to set the stage for 1683 must also take into account a centuries-old process of state-building. The partly conscious, partly accidental assemblage of the great sixteenth-century Habsburg Empire, and its division (1556) into two separate but still formidable power complexes, one Austrian, one Spanish, is, however, a tale too well-known to require re-telling; and the subsequent fortunes of the Spanish branch of the family are also a matter of common record. Unfortunately, the same thing cannot be said about the internal development of the dynastic lands left by Charles V to his brother Ferdinand I and descendents—a subject of no small importance for world history.

THE GROWTH OF A BUREAUCRACY

The story actually begins before 1556 since Ferdinand had been functioning for decades as the effective ruler of the Central European possessions of the Archhouse. In this capacity he was, of course, only one of a large number of territorial princes although he stood out among his colleagues by virtue of the greater size of his domains and because of his sovereign rights over non-Germans. In keeping with the tendency of the age, he undertook to weld his disparate legacy into some kind of administrative unity. The task was, nonetheless, far from complete at the time of his death (1565), and for a while centrifugal forces made themselves felt. His three heirs partitioned the embryonic empire. The separation luckily turned out to be neither permanent, nor truly divisive (although its general outline remained as a part of the administrative framework of the latter seventeenth- and the eighteenth-centuries). The western lands—Upper Austria (Tyrol and Vorarlberg) and Further Austria (the Habsburg holdings in southwestern Germany)—were governed from Innsbruck, while the southern lands—Inner Austria (Styria, Carintria, Carniola, Istria, Trieste and Gorizia)—had Graz as their capital. These two territorial blocks, largely German, had some legal and bureaucratic similarity. Such, however, was not the case with the third region. It consisted, in the first place, of the ancient, original Austria along the two shores of the Danube, or, more specifically, the Archduchy Above and Below the Enns (Upper and Lower Austria in the stricter sense),[29] the capital of which was Vienna. It further encompassed the more recently-acquired, non-hereditary lands: Bohemia-Moravia with its northern Silesian adjuncts (taken together the richest portion of the whole monarchy) and Hungary-Croatia, both historically distinct, largely non-German kingdoms, difficult to assimilate administratively. So heterogeneous a polity could be knitted together only if given common state organs. Fortunately, the foundations that Ferdinand laid were strong, and it was possible for his successors to build upon them. This process is especially noteworthy because it was characterized by a curious kind of duality: while central institutions were ultimately useful only in the service of dynastic goals, they owe their origin and much of their growth to the overall Imperial duties of the Habsburgs.[30]

Because the names of the individual central agencies, in several instances the nuclei of modern ministries, frequently appear in the record of the struggle against the Turks, their nomenclature and individual functions are of relevance. The Imperial Aulic Council (*Reichshofrath*), which emerged in a clearly developed form in 1559, was the supreme judicial instance; after 1620, however, its radius of action became increasingly restricted to Imperial affairs. More important was its offshoot, the Imperial Chancellery (*Reichshofcanzlei*), the administrative organ for the Empire at large, headed by the Imperial Vice-Chancellor. (Control over this institution was long—and vainly—disputed by the Archbishop-Elector of Mainz, who held the office of Imperial Archchancellor.) The latter bureau, in turn, begot a subdivision for dynastic affairs, which in 1620, became autonomous as the Austrian Court Chancellery (*Hofcanzlei*). The line of demarcation between the two chancelleries remained somewhat blurred since the various emperors also used the Austrian one for foreign affairs (successfully) and for general Imperial business (unsuccessfully), apparently regarding it as a more manageable personal instrument. A particularly crucial arm of the government was the Court War Council (*Hofkriegsrath*). Although this body had serious flaws, as will later become apparent, it did constitute the highest military authority, and thus symbolized the great rôle which soldiers played in the formation of the modern Habsburg monarchy. Another influential administrative office was the Court Chamber (*Hofkammer*) or Treasury, which managed, or rather, mismanaged the insufficient revenues derived from the dynasty's private estates (patrimony), excise taxes, and the infrequent subsidies of the Imperial Diet. It had no jurisdiction over grants made by the local Estates. These latter funds, largely for military purposes, were jointly expended by the Court War Council and the Chancelleries.

Although the Habsburgs believed that they reigned through divine ordinance, they were either immune to delusions of autocracy or else too diffident to rule unaided. They sought advice from trusted and qualified persons whom they assembled in the Privy Council (*Geheimrath*), the immediate origins of which go back to 1527. Composed largely of nobles—although not originally the outstanding ones—this organ rapidly expanded in membership, and many appointments could only be regarded as honorific. Thus, in 1669, Leopold established the Privy Conference (*Geheimconferenz*). The head of both bodies was usually the chief court official, the Lord High Steward (*Oberhofmeister*). Under the chairmanship of Prince Wenzel Lobkowitz (1669–1674), a proto-prime minister, the Conference, like the Council before it, appeared as a kind of potential cabinet. However, it suffered the same fate as its predecessor, becoming too large and unwieldy. The basic reason for its failure, moreover, appears to have been the same: a dual dynastic-Imperial rôle.[31]

The relationship between the central government and its provincial representatives is best described as equivocal. In no case was the so-called "intermediate" administration a ready instrument of the monarch's will. Notwithstanding variation in terminology (*Statthalter, Landeshauptmann, Landmarschall, Oberstburggraf,* Palatine and Ban), each territory of the Crown possessed an Imperially-appointed governor. He was, however, answerable to both Vienna *and* the provincial estates and was assisted in his work by a college, appointed by the diet, usually for a limited time only. Moreover, practicants of certain occupations were subject to exceptional courts and thus removed from the governor's jurisdiction. In Vienna itself, apart from the *Hofcanzlei,* there were the Bohemian and Hungarian Chancelleries (the latter was not important) for the dispatch of provincial business. Government on the rural level was almost wholly dominated by the nobility as a result of its patrimonial prerogatives. Only in the formerly autonomous, economically static cities and towns was the central government in direct control.[32]

THE ESTATES

In Leopold's time, and perhaps for the entire remaining life of the monarchy, the crux of all governmental problems was the degree of power exercised by the traditional, individual components of the *Gesamtstaat,* the so-called "historico-political entities." By the very nature of its origin, by virtue of its multi-national character, the state was basically federal in structure. Yet the tendency of the seventeenth century was to exalt central authority as incorporated in the ruler, an ideal which Leopold, presumably prompted by his advisers, attempted to realize by fits and starts. The major obstacle to absolutism was the existence in each of his domains of a constitution (in the broad sense of the word), the tangible expression of which was the estates (*Stände*) or diets (*Landtage*). The latter theoretically represented the different social orders, in most cases the clergy, nobility and townsmen, and were organized in two, three, or four *curiae.* In practice these parliamentary bodies were under the control of the aristocracy, which often could think only in parochial terms.

Attempts to establish an estates-general (*Generallandtag*) came to nought. To be sure, the Leopoldine estates, in large measure tamed by the Counter-Reformation, were not a threat to dynastic sovereignty as they had once been. Bohemia, in particular, was docile, having been subjugated in the first stage of the Thirty Years War. There were also certain methods—the pressure of the pro-Imperial noble faction, and, occasionally, the subtle combining of force and persuasion—of facilitating the will of Vienna. Nevertheless, the diets retained considerable influence: the power of the purse (by their right to assess, collect and administer direct taxes), the privilege of participating in the organization of the army, and the exercise of broad police functions.[33] Thereby they were in a position to impede effectively any rapid and coordinated action by the central government. Events associated with the Turkish invasion of 1683 clearly demonstrate how damaging the estates' financial rights could still be. Despite his allegiance to new principles, Leopold neglected to undertake any reforms in this realm. Ironically, the only real effort he made to crush the old, late Mediaeval order of politics was in the one country where such action, before 1683, in any case, was least feasible: Hungary. Despite its central organs, its incipient absolutism, Austria under Leopold continued to be an agglomeration of the most varied territorial units, each traditionally autonomous, economically exclusive and differing in its judicial institutions—a whole made up of unsynchronized parts, the potentialities of which the common sovereign had not yet systematically exploited.[34] Substantial change was not to take place until the reigns of Maria Theresa and Joseph II. When it came, moreover, it was not an attempt to reform and broaden the estates (and thus to make them a useful arm of a federal system) but rather an emasculation in the interests of an historically illogical centralism.

ECONOMICS AND CULTURE

The financial and economic foundations of the Habsburg state, not surprisingly, paralleled its political superstructure. That is to say, while they were not entirely "modern" in the Western European sense, they were, on the other hand, no longer Mediaeval. While the ultimate source of government income remained the land and hence the labor of the peasant, the economy—which the Thirty Years War left relatively undamaged—was slowly being supplemented by the growth of industrialism and capitalism. In Styria and the Tyrol iron mining was becoming important, whereas the textile and glass enterprizes of Bohemia were already highly developed; Silesia was noted for linen manufacturing. The major problem of businessmen was markets; for not only was the location of indigenous industry unfavorable with respect to the main international trade routes, but Leopold's wars caused interruptions of normal arrangements. A striking feature of this still incipient industrialism was that it was not accompanied by social conflict as in France and England. The new entrepreneurs were often representatives of the old aristocratic order. They purchased or rented monopolies in trade and manufacture from the fiscally hard-pressed government, but they showed little inclination to change their previous patterns of life. Despite Vienna's temporary employment of the most talented German mercantilist theorists, there was no real effort at central planning of economic development, for which the long-term military involvement must once again be blamed.[35]

The cultural life of Leopoldine Austria has seldom been subject to sympathetic and thorough analysis. Despite the relative lack of originality, it is deserving of respect. Although the educational system, entirely in the hands of the Society of Jesus, was bent to fit the needs of a militant Catholicism, it should not be condemned out of hand. While it proved unreceptive to the grand scientific and philosophic speculation of contemporary Western Europe, it was at least socially undiscriminating and was very hospitable to drama, music, and the formative arts. Literature, while both rich and accomplished within the restricted practical framework of historical, socio-geographic, and descriptive economic writing, produced no genuinely inventive mind, although Abraham a Sancta Clara merits attention for his great technical-linguistic gifts and valuable revelations about the contemporary social and spiritual milieu. Austria's most eminent cultural achievements—as is perhaps apparent from the foregoing account of Leopold's own interests—lay in music, architecture, sculpture, and painting.[36]

C. Hungary and Transylvania

The Alpine provinces and the Kingdom of Bohemia were all securely under Habsburg control by the middle of the seventeenth century, but the adjacent, elective Kingdom of Saint Stephen stood in sharp contrast in almost every respect. Not only did Hungary lie outside the Empire, but, for the most part, the German ruling dynasty did not exercise effective sovereignty. During the sixteenth century (1527–1541) the Turks, under the gifted leadership of Suleiman the Magnificent (1520–1566), had seized the richest part of the country and had maintained their position ever since without serious difficulty. The country's nominal Kings held only a relatively small, crescent-shaped, marginally located region, roughly coterminous with present-day Slovakia ("Upper Hungary"), the Austrian province of Burgenland ("West Hungary"), and northern Croatia. The Principality of Transylvania, formerly an integral part of the Hungarian realm but a Turkish protectorate since 1547, existed as an autonomous political entity.

OTTOMAN RULED TERRITORY

The most cruel fate of all was reserved for Turkish Hungary, organized into five pashaliks or *eyalets* under the *Beylerbeyi* of Buda. Modern colonialism seems benevolent by contrast. According to Turkish theory, all land belonged to the Padishah; in practice, however, four-fifths was enfeoffed to his soldiers in order that the latter might be self-supporting. The great majority of Magyar nobles, whose status the Porte refused to recognize, fled to Habsburg Hungary or to Transylvania. Those who stayed, died out or sank to the level of the peasantry. The tillers of the soil themselves were subjected to newer, far more ruthless landlords. To be sure, as long as a man paid exorbitant dues, he was not molested bodily. Hungarian institutions—the Church, the commune—continued to exist, however precariously. The Turks had little interest in mixing with the local population and took no steps toward assimilation—although life in a foreign environment did not leave them entirely untouched culturally, socially, or eugenically.[37]

Often, especially in the far south (Banat of Timişoara) which was already decimated by the fighting of Suleiman's time, whole villages would desert their homes and head northward in a kind of internal migration, the burden of Turkish exploitation having become too great. The open character of the terrain left no place for shelter. Thus, while the relatively secure hills and valleys of the Carpathians became more densely inhabited, the Alföld became a semi-desert. Formerly fruitful pastures were transformed into desolate moors—the famous Puszta. Rivers, no longer artfully watched over by fishermen and ripuarian dwellers, overflowed their banks and inundated large areas that were once cultivated. Thereby much of the south became as impassable and impenetrable as in pre-Roman times. The swamps spawned disease, the redoubtable *morbus hungaricus,* which was carried by the few remaining country dwellers into the towns, thus causing further human losses. The Turkish lord, bereft of serfs, brought in less efficient Serb (Rascians, *Raitzen*) and Rumanian agriculturalists as replacements, a process in which military and political considerations of a *divide et impera* character also played a significant rôle. The Magyars never recouped their losses to any appreciable extent. The most fortunate natives under Turkish rule were the personnel of the Sultan's private estates (khases). Since their lot was easier—they paid taxes collectively rather than individually—, they managed to prosper amidst the general decline. The chief khas country, the central plain on either side of the Tisza, was a special case. Here people abandoned ancestral villages, laid waste by foraging parties from nearby Ottoman border garrisons, and congregated in unravaged, somewhat safer towns. Thus arose the unique "village-towns" of the Alföld (e.g., Debrecen). Permitted self-administration along traditional lines by practical-minded Istanbul, the peasant inhabitants remained a major source of Magyar ethnic strength. Their historical merit was to conserve the most productive portion of Turkish Hungary until that later day when their kinsmen on the other side of the frontier would return to reinforce them. To be sure, "urban" life flourished not only in the places just described. Certain localities such as Pecs and Eger, partly or wholly occupied and directly administered by Muslims, managed to achieve a degree of well-being.[38]

The Frontier

The Habsburg-Ottoman border region itself presented a rather singular set of circumstances, quite different from anything known in the rest of Europe. Although Vienna and Istanbul had been officially at peace since the Treaty of Zsitva-Török (1606) and although both governments desired the maintenance of friendly relations on the higher, international level, the limitrophic lands continued to be subject to disturbance and small-scale warfare of a rather unchivalrous nature. For more than half a century the vain task of regulating these local matters was left to the

Habsburg viceroy, the so-called Palatine *(nador)*, and to the *Beylerbeyi* of Buda. The reasons for the unsettled conditions included the lack of a legally clarified territorial demarcation and the fact that both parties claimed and exercised the right to levy taxes, governmental and manorial, upon people living on the opposite side of the boundaries. (The comitatal structure of occupied Hungary was preserved by the exiled nobility on Habsburg soil, and the peasantry of the former region, allegedly because of strong patriotic sentiment, was willing to pay dues to its old as well as its new masters). In addition, the Turkish bureaucracy, which was rather retrograde judged by Western standards of the time, actually found economic and moral value in permitting its troops to undertake raids against the erstwhile foe. The vicious, treacherous nature of the fighting had a deleterious effect upon the local population. It was not just a matter of looting, raping, and burning, but also of carrying off "hostages." The Turks held Hungarian slaves in high regard; indeed this predilection is another reason for the great damage they wrought in Hungary's demographic structure.[39]

Such assaults naturally evoked reprisals by the Habsburg border garrisons, made up of Germans and other non-indigenous mercenaries. Whether the warrior was Turk or Imperial, it was the politically passive Magyar peasant who, in the last analysis, paid the piper. Eventually, many Hungarians were themselves reduced to participation in the carnage and destruction. Men of sufficient means to equip themselves with arms and horses reverted more and more to the nomadic warrior pattern of their ninth-century ancestors, a development which served to strengthen the position of the gentry *vis-à-vis* both peasantry and magnates. Daring cattle-rustling expeditions deep into Ottoman territory became something of which a proud Magyar could properly boast. Itinerant Jewish traders, snatched up at village markets, brought fat ransoms. In the process new military tactics were developed: light cavalry, for example, reappeared. Another aspect of the situation was the establishment of a special, *limes*-type border defense system, which supplemented the regular troops and which helped, at least initially, to assure a degree of stability. The balance of power thus achieved with the Turks, who had reached the margins of their own expansive capability, was upset only as the result of the gradual development within Austria during the last part of the seventeenth century of a standing army more efficient than the Porte's (itself the pioneer of that form of military organization).[40]

The Turkish heritage in Hungary, then, was generally negative. The Ottomans, unlike their Arab co-religionists, left relatively little of cultural or intellectual value behind. The most that can be said of the Turkish occupation is that it afforded Protestantism a certain haven from the Counter-Reformation and that it eventually caused the Hungarian people to draw together in national self-consciousness. The Magyars, in contrast to some Balkan peoples, never willingly submitted to the Turks. The number of collaborators was not great; few Hungarian names were found on Turkish army rolls.[41] The legacy was one of embitterment.

THE HABSBURG LANDS

Perhaps the tragedy of Turkish-occupied Hungary would not have been as great if history could record that the Magyars found satisfaction and dignity in that portion of their homeland which remained directly under the Crown. Unfortunately, such is not the case. The Hungarian-Habsburg relationship was ill-starred from its very beginning in the disputed royal election of 1527 and in the tumultuously shifting events of Ferdinand I's reign (1527–1564). Ferdinand was the last of his line to reside within the Kingdom, and the absenteeism of his successors adversely affected cooperation between the monarchy and the Estates. To be sure, the general political tendency of Early Modern history—the final subjection of the former feudal aristocracy to central authority—would have made fruitful partnership unlikely even if the Infidel had been absent and even if the ruler had been a native, not a foreigner accepted reluctantly in the hope that he could provide from his other, non-Magyar domains the resources necessary to fend off the Turk.[42]

The removal of the administration to Bratislava, closer to Vienna, its modification and adaptation to the rest of the Habsburg patrimony (despite the existence of a mere personal union) were certainly measures in keeping with the reforming spirit emanating from Vienna, but at the same time they increased the estrangement of king and subject. The centralizing drive of the Habsburg government, latent in the sixteenth and conscious in the seventeenth centuries, was based upon a desire to consolidate power for the purpose of state security. The men who strove toward this end were completely unable to comprehend the concept of national autonomy, i.e., the psychological need of the Magyars for self-identity. Magyar writers complain with one voice that the Habsburgs never understood their people, by which is meant, presumably, their failure to recognize Hungary's particular national consciousness and pride in its own history and traditions. To the Hungarians, the issue naturally did not seem to be a struggle between royal power and feudal particularism but rather a battle for freedom from foreign domination. They believed, not entirely without reason, that the Habsburgs regarded Hungary more as an advanced post for the defense of Germany than as a realm in its own right.[43] The German government, for its part, saw only the arrogance and obstructionism of the antiquated estates. It was unable to perceive any distinction in this institution between Hungary and Lower Austria where it also existed.[44]

Of course, one would not be granting the Habsburgs their historical due if one were to assume that the estates—a body hardly representative of the whole Hungarian nation—were composed of particularly rational or amenable individuals. Apparently, many a great lord was not only chivalrous, dashing, and patriotic, but also fickle, unpredictable, and completely callous toward his peasant fellow countrymen. One seemingly unprejudiced observer of the latter seventeenth century wrote:

> The Hungarians make their laws energetically but do not hold to them. Every magnate could call himself a little king because he treats his subjects like slaves. The nobles, who disregard their own laws, paradoxically insist that their King observe them. They want him to be their protector but not their lord. They say openly that their freedom does not go well with the status of being a subject.[45]

While such claims are difficult to substantiate objectively, they are still worth noting, for many other foreigners and certain natives have also maintained that the Magyars are among the world's more ungovernable peoples.

If the Habsburgs are to be reproached, it surely should not be for their effort to establish centralized authority. Their errors did not lie so much in their goals—for they were hardly in a position to see that the inherent federal structure of their lands might be the answer to the nationalism of a later century—but in their lack of tactical insight. Not only did they rarely, if ever, throw any sops to Hungarian national pride, but they neglected to exploit the gap between the social classes, even though they possessed clear indications of the feasibility of such a policy. An even worse blunder—although not theirs alone since Louis XIV also made it—was the attempt to enforce religious uniformity. What makes this mistake particularly egregious is that they not only had evidence of the efficacy of other approaches—e.g., the subtle legal maneuvers, clever propaganda, and exploitation of socio-ethnic cleavages of Cardinal Peter Pázmány—but also that they repeated the error on several occasions. The brutal occupation of Transylvania under General George Basta (1603) and the subsequent collapse of the Habsburg position in that region should have permanently demonstrated the need for temporization.[46] Conceivably, the successes of Ferdinand II (1619–1637) in extirpating religious dissent and creating a malleable nobility in Bohemia blinded his successors, who failed to realize that they did not possess the same power base in a partitioned and exposed Hungary. In any event, the effort to eradicate Lutheranism and Calvinism was only intensified by Ferdinand III and Leopold I.

A Haven for Nationality

Although the Magyars in Turkish and Habsburg country might be discontented with their lot, there remained a third region, Transylvania or Siebenbürgen, where they could breathe an air more to their liking.

Admittedly, the "Land Beyond the Forest" was not theirs exclusively. Probably the most striking thing about it was its tangled religious, ethnic, and social structure. Within a clearly defined geographic framework lived Calvinist Magyar nobles, Lutheran German burghers, Roman Catholic Szeklers,[47] politically unrecognized Orthodox Rumanian peasants (for the most part of recent provenance), and even a few Unitarian Szeklers. Strangely enough, these groupings, each of which behaved more or less aloofly toward the other, accepted the leadership and initiative of Magyar princes during the sixteenth and seventeenth centuries and succeeded in developing a kind of state consciousness.

A further uniqueness of Transylvania was its relationship to the Sublime Porte. Although physical juxtaposition to both Habsburgs and Ottomans ensured a continuing *Eigenstaatlichkeit,* Siebenbürgen's ultimate *raison d'être* was the mere appearance of the Turks upon the Pannonian-Carpathian scene. The resultant legal and constitutional situation is difficult to analyze. While the Sultan enjoyed sovereignty, he always governed indirectly. The country was simultaneously a protectorate, a tributary, and a vassal. (The feudal status became most evident in 1683 when a Transylvanian army had to serve Kara Mustafa at Vienna). While Istanbul did recognize the right of the Estates to elect their own prince, the Ottoman government also appointed him on occasion. The Prince, who had to be an indigenous, Magyar Protestant (at least in theory), not only received the symbols of his office from the Porte but was directly subject to it. While he was treated with greater honor and dignity than most provincial Turkish potentates, he was in the last analysis no more than a territorial administrator. The Turks regulated his executive activities, in particular his foreign policy, and intervened directly in administration from time to time. The prince also paid taxes, personally led his troops into battle, imprisoned and extradited refugees from Turkey, and was required to keep Istanbul *au courant* and even to pray for the Sultan.[48]

On the other hand, it is obvious that a theoretical definition of state relationships is meaningful only insofar as it reflects actual historical circumstances. Certainly the latter varied considerably throughout the period of Transylvania's autonomy. During the Thirty Years War, when the Habsburgs were elsewhere engaged and the Ottomans sunk in domestic lethargy, it was possible for leaders such as Bethlen Gábor (1613–1629) and George Rákóczy I (1631–1648) to behave as if they were fully independent. By suppressing the magnates, restricting the rights of the burghers, and enhancing the position of the gentry, they were able to establish a semi-absolutist régime along the lines of the German territorial state—the chief difference being Transylvania's religious tolerance. Indeed, the princes even managed to play a rôle in the politics of contemporary Central and Western Europe. This phase of the state's history is significant not only as one aspect of Hungary's total political development but also for a cultural flowering that would scarcely have been possible otherwise. It does not matter that Transylvanian brilliance was quite transitory. It was sufficient that it existed, if only for the purpose of providing continuity to the idea of Hungary, of affording a center of orientation for Magyar national consciousness. Its meaning lay not in what it accomplished but in what it prevented. The concepts of the Holy Crown and of the indivisibility of the realm that it represented, deeply rooted as they were in the minds of Magyars everywhere, might have perished without Transylvania. The principality's rulers, apparently wishing to place no obstacle in the way of eventual reunification, never sought to assume the royal title. Bethlen Gábor, in whose hands the ancient symbol of kingship actually rested, rejected the suggestion that he set it upon his own head.[49]

D. Political Affairs 1648–1671

Transylvania's greatness ended in 1648 upon the death of the first George Rákóczy. This date, so pivotal in Western European affairs, is also important for the East as a whole. It signifies the commencement of major changes not only in Hungary and the Balkans but also in Poland and the Ukraine. The year which marked the accession of the second George Rákóczy constituted, namely, the beginning of a series of highly complex and rapidly shifting developments, which gradually resulted in the renewal of the old conflict between Christianity and Islam. Thereby the Habsburg monarchy became more deeply involved in Eastern affairs than ever before.

Hybris

The immediate cause of profound alterations in the region's political structure was the personality of the young Transylvanian prince. Raised in a religious atmosphere, lacking contact with the outside world, ignorant both of the politics of the Western nations and of the military arts, he embarked on a foreign policy far out of proportion to his country's resources. Imagining himself a crusader for Protestantism at a time when such sentiments were already *passé,* he commenced his career by interfering in the affairs of Moldavia and Wallachia. By 1655 he had extracted oaths of loyalty from the two voyvodes, and outwardly Transylvania seemed even more powerful than in the age of Bethlen Gábor. George II next directed his attention to Poland, which at the time was being threatened by Sweden, the Cossacks, Brandenburg, Russia, and its own dissident factions. Driven both by religion and by ambition for the Polish crown, disregarding the advice of the more prudent nobles and the express prohibition of Istanbul, he intervened with an army of 25,000 men in 1657. His sorry military leadership culminated in the capture of his army by the Tatars.

The result of the whole affair was to arouse the antipathy of the Porte (now being revived by Mehmed Köprülü). Deposed by the Sultan, fearful of so powerful a vassal, Rákóczy decided (January, 1658), after some hesitation, to fight, counting on his own vast domains in the Partium[50] as well as upon the Szeklers. Hoping for Habsburg support, he managed to regain the approval of the estates (which in the meantime had accepted a temporary replacement, Ferencz Rhédey). The Turks, however, reasserted their authority over the Moldavians and Wallachians, and Leopold could not make up his mind to help fullheartedly. Turks, Tatars, and Cossacks soon swarmed across the passes, pillaging and slaughtering on a vast scale. The country's fabled prosperity was now only a memory. One of Rákóczy's advisers, Akos Barcsay, then began negotiations with the enemy. Backed by the estates, he accepted the Turks' harsh conditions and was appointed prince (September 14, 1658). The hapless Rákóczy fought on. He won a few successes in 1659 but was mortally wounded in an engagement against the Pasha of Buda (May 22, 1660). The heads of 3000 of his followers, borne on pikes, were paraded through the streets of Istanbul. Once again, however, there was a shifting of sentiment in Transylvania. The fall of Oradea (Nagy Várad, Groβwardein), a critical strong point, cost Barcsay his popularity, and the nation rose behind Janos Kemény, Rákóczy's general, recently liberated by the Tatars. Elected prince on January 1, 1661, Kemény mistook encouraging words from the still hesitant Leopold for support. A second Turkish invasion drove the new ruler into royal Hungary, and the Porte, having demonstrated its sovereignty, sought, with some difficulty, for a suitable replacement. The choice finally fell upon a high noble, Michael Abafi, at that time a pious, scholarly, and retiring person (September 4, 1661).[51]

In the meantime, a reluctant, Francophobic Leopold found himself pressed by his Hungarian advisers and by Kemény to do something. Yielding, he sent his best general, the great military theorist, Count Raimondo Montecuccoli. It is difficult to judge succeeding events objectively because of the great divergence in view between Hungarian and Austro-German historians. To the former, the Imperial *Feldherr* was excessively cautious, Magyar-hating and unable to control his troops, who pillaged and terrorized the nation which they were supposed to be defending.[52] To the latter, Montecuccoli was a finely educated, scientific-minded, warmly human individual, who was shocked to find in Hungary an uncooperative and sometimes hostile population and a headstrong, factious nobility, hardly a secure material and political basis for a successful campaign, especially considering the untraversable nature of the countryside. Viewing the situation solely from a military viewpoint, unable to grasp its complicated historical roots, his opinion was that Vienna should bring domestic order and firm, central government to Hungary.[53] While it might be argued that Montecuccoli did indeed show some lack of initiative, since the audacious Eugene of Savoy managed to win great victories under not dissimilar conditions a few decades later, it is true that he had to think first of preserving his modest forces, which the government was unable to subsidize as it should have and which it could not replace.

THE TURKISH WAR OF 1663–1664

At all events Montecuccoli was unable to render Kemény any effective aid in the summer of 1661. Although the unfavorable reaction of Hungarian opinion caused Leopold to order more vigorous support, the Transylvanian was defeated (and killed) on January 22, 1662. Leopold, however, was not prepared to recognize Abafi, and since the Porte was unwilling to tolerate Imperial intervention and counted upon Hungarian discontent against Habsburg rule, a formal war now became a possibility. Although forewarned by its representative in Istanbul, Vienna failed to undertake extensive armament and apparently still hoped for peace. The reason for this policy was Leopold's reluctance to accept any help from Louis XIV or his German associates. The French king, Germany's would-be protector, had been forced to take an open stand because of a developing crusading mood in Central Europe. Desiring neither to support the Emperor openly nor to strengthen his army by financial subvention, not wanting to slight the potentially useful Porte, he cleverly proffered his assistance as a member of the anti-Imperial Rhenine League of princes. Leopold might well have achieved an understanding with the Turks, but the latter, apparently having lost patience with his procrastinating style of negotiation, declared war (April, 1663). A powerful Turkish army lumbered into royal Hungary, drove back the Imperial forces of 11–12,000 men, ravaged the land, seized the important fortress of Nové Zámky (Neuhäusel, Ersekújvár), and raided Moravia. Vienna itself, panic-stricken, might have been seized, had the Turks known that it was barren of defenders. Once again the inability of the Vienna government and the Hungarians to understand each other manifested itself.[54]

This time the contrast was illuminated by the personal clash of the Italian-born Montecuccoli and the Ban of Croatia, Nicholas Zrinyi (Zrinski), one of the most romantic figures in the history of his country. The great-grandson of a legendary hero, a poet of merit, Zrinyi was above all an Hungarian patriot—even if not himself a Magyar in the strict ethnic sense—, and a hater of the Turks. Although he was loyal to his Habsburg sovereign (unlike many of his fellow magnates), he was an advocate of Hungarian autonomy. Though a Catholic, he entertained good relations with his Protestant fellow countrymen and clearly saw the fallacies of forceful Counterreformatory measures.[55] His straightforwardness and nobility of character inspired confidence. As a general, he was accustomed to the speed and dash of border warfare and was a courageous, perhaps headstrong thruster. He wanted to lash out against the invader but was prevented from so doing by the coolly intellectual Montecuccoli, a prudent cunctator used to the battlefields of the *Reich*.[56] Infuriated by the latter's incomprehensible methods, he undertook, with Leopold's approval, a campaign of his own during the winter of 1663–64 and, despite initial successes, was driven back after the loss of his beloved, private fortress (Zrinyivár or Serinvar) and estates. Montecuccoli meanwhile obtained supreme command over a new, still-assembling pan-European army.[57]

The Turkish incursion into royal Hungary had aroused great concern in other Christian countries. It appeared as if the Grand Vezir, Ahmed Köprülü, would make good his threat to attack Vienna the next year with 100,000 men. The church bells rang out in warning across the Empire. Preachers and pamphleteers busied themselves with admonitions and encouragement. The Regensburg Diet, called already in 1662 and not to disperse before 1806, initially and begrudgingly approved a grant of fifty Roman months.[58] The personal presence of the Emperor was required to complete arrangements for the sending of a corps of 10,000 soldiers. The Electors of Mainz, Brandenburg, Saxony, and Bavaria had previously dispatched smaller contingents of their own. Almost desperate, Leopold also agreed to accept aid from the Rhine League, including 5400 crack French professionals under Count Jean de Coligny. Financial help came from Pope Alexander VII and from Spain. Of the 65,000-man-strong allied force, 25–26,000 finally (August 1, 1664) met some 100,000 Ottoman warriors at a ford of the Rába (Raab) River about ten miles upstream from the Cistercian monastery of Szentgotthárd.[59] Montecuccoli decided that the enemy had to be halted at this strategically-located crossroads between the Alps and the Pannonian Basin. The loss of the position would have opened both the routes to Graz and Vienna (via Sopron-Ödenburg). About 10,000 of the best Portal troops commenced the action early in the morning after crossing the river and broke through the German-Imperial center. The issue hung in the balance for eight hours, and it is just possible that a flank strike by the French regiments turned the tide. Although casualties were heavy on both sides, the 16,000 Turkish dead (many of whom drowned while retreating) included élite fighters. The Christians also took much booty, and the remainder of the Ottoman army showed no inclination to renew the attempt to traverse the Rába.[60]

THE TREATY OF VASVÁR

Only ten days later a twenty year truce was concluded at Vasvár (Eisenburg). The terms were inappropriate to the magnitude of the victory: it almost seemed as if the Turks had won the battle. Istanbul was permitted to keep all the territory, both Habsburg and Transylvanian, that it had seized since undertaking action against Rákóczy, including the strategic fortresses of Nové Zámky, Nógrád and Oradea. It was only a slight compensation for the Emperor that he was allowed to erect a new strongpoint (Leopoldov-Leopoldstadt, built 1665) for the protection of the Váh (Waag) River Valley and to retain the formerly Transylvanian comitats of Szatmár and Szabolcz in Eastern Hungary. Leopold further bound himself to recognize the Turkish satellite, Abafi, who had been the original reason for his going to war. He also obliged himself to send the Sultan a "present" of 100,000 thalers and later even footed the cost of Abafi's own tribute to Istanbul.[61] The European public was flabbergasted and the Hungarians were enraged. Superficially, at any rate, the House of Austria had made itself appear fatuous.

There were, nonetheless, weighty reasons for concluding peace. The Turkish forces—of whom only a third were engaged at Szentgotthárd—kept to the field. The arduously assembled allied army had been on the point of breaking up even before the battle, and there was little hope that the various powers would permit their forces to undertake an extended campaign in Hungary. Rains came, and the roads turned to mire. Vienna lacked the financial resources to support Montecuccoli on his own and was convinced of Magyar disloyalty, not without some justice. The French presence, small as it was, seemed embarrassing and was even thought dangerous. Above all, Leopold was concerned with events along the Rhine. Recognizing the impossibility of a two-front engagement, placed in the unenviable position of choosing between East and West, he elected to concentrate his attention on France. Although the Hungarians have never forgiven him, the Emperor was probably correct in his assessment of the situation.[62] Of course, associated with the Gallic menace was the question of the Spanish royal succession. Leopold was affianced to the half-sister of the physically degenerate, four-year old son of Phillip IV, while Louis XIV was espoused to her sister.[63] Since both he and Louis were also maternal grandsons of a Spanish monarch (Phillip III), the possibility of conflict was real. The interest in building the prestige of his dynasty, the traditions of a universal *imperium* going back to Charles V and beyond (whether unrealistic or not) exercised their pull upon Leopold.[64]

The only errors of the Emperor in the whole Vasvár affair were to have prematurely granted plenipotentiary authority to his representative in the Turkish camp, Simon Reniger, and to have permitted the latter to negotiate solely on his behalf without any representation of his associates, above all the proud Magyars.[65] One may ask whether a truly apt diplomat could not have obtained more advantageous terms, considering momentary military circumstances and outward appearances. In any case, even those Hungarians basically loyal to their German king were now alienated.

THE MAGNATES' CONSPIRACY

The next seven years of Hungarian history, comprising the so-called Wesselényi or Hungarian-Croatian Conspiracy, demonstrate that disenchantment with Habsburg rule was now shifting from tactics of passive opposition to outright resistance. The plot, replete with ludicrous and farcical elements, followed an extremely intricate course, almost impossible to summarize accurately and with justice to all parties. The affair began in 1663 even before the Treaty of Vasvár (formerly considered its sole cause) and, in fact, influenced the hasty conclusion of peace. The conspirators were not entirely independent historical actors but, in part, tools manipulated from Paris through the French representative to Vienna, the Marquis Bretel de Grémonville.[66] As might be expected, Louis XIV's interest depended upon the momentary exigencies of foreign policy. After Phillip IV's death in 1665 the French monarch was interested in keeping the intrigue alive as a potential weapon. Troubles at home might prevent Leopold from spoiling French designs on the Spanish Netherlands. In 1668, however, because of a momentary Austro-French rapprochement (First Partition Treaty), Grémonville became noticeably cooler toward the plotters.

The Hungarians involved represented some of the most important names and offices in the land: Zrinyi and, after his accidental death (1665), his brother and successor, Peter; the Palatine, Ferencz Wesselényi (d. 1667); the Prince Archbishop of Esztergom and Primate of Hungary, George Lippay (d. 1665); the *Judex Curiae,* Thomas Nádasdy, a personal favorite of Leopold; the Croatian magnate, Fran Frankopan and his German-hating wife; and Prince Ferencz Rákóczy I (son of George II), who was married in 1666 to the equally conspiratorial Helena Zrinyi (daughter of Peter), later the wife of Imre Thököly (whose father also participated). Even two Germans, the Styrian Count Erasmus Tattenbach, lover of Peter's wife, Katharina, and Count Karl von Thurn, Governor of Gradisca, were dragged in. The junto also established some contacts—largely fruitless—with other foreign powers and personages, including Johann Phillip von Schönborn (Archbishop Elector of Mainz and Archchancellor of the Empire), Michael Abafi, the Poles, Venice, and even the Porte. The goal seems to have been the reestablishment of a fully independent Kingdom of St. Stephen within its large, fifteenth-century boundaries (i.e., including Bohemia). It was rumored that the scheme included the physical elimination of Leopold, who allegedly had at least one narrow escape when a pious intrigante (Nádasdy's wife) suddenly began to suffer from moral scruples and declined to feed him a poisoned tart.[67]

Unfortunately for their sake the plotters could not coordinate their actions, were self-seeking, weak-willed, indecisive, and had no idea of internal security. Word leaked to Vienna from a number of sources, both direct and indirect. The government, headed after 1670 by Prince Wenzel Lobkowitz, deliberately bided its time. Indeed, Lobkowitz and his upcoming bourgeois subordinate, Dr. Paul Hocher, purposely and "perfidiously" led the conspirators on although a compromise with Hungarian national aspirations might have been effected. The Imperial ministers waited for the first overt action and then struck quickly and firmly. Zrinyi, Nádasdy, Frankopan, Tattenbach and von Thurn were arrested and given show trials. All save von Thurn (who spent the rest of his days imprisoned on Graz' famous Schloßberg) were sent to the block. The normally indulgent Emperor decided that he had to be "per forza" this time, adding, in a letter to a friend, that he hoped "to learn something about severed heads in the next mail."[68] He showed clemency only to Rákóczy, who had a strong advocate in the person of his Catholic mother, Sophia Bathory. Four of the trial judges (including Lobkowitz and General Kapliřs) were Czech, and there may have been an element of vindictiveness because the design for Turkish assistance called for a foray into Bohemia. Nevertheless, Lobkowitz was apparently moved mainly by belief in strong monarchical government and by the desire to protect his master's domains from a Turkish incursion (which most likely would have entailed the subjugation of the Croatians) . Most of the plotters did not realize that their plans for national liberation were premature precisely because of the Turkish danger. Moreover, their understanding of liberty was merely special privileges for the nobility. The realization of this ideal of government would have brought about conditions as chaotic as in the Polish Republic. Such a Hungary would probably have ended in a similar fashion. The conspirators held an essentially feudal view of monarchy, one that stressed mutual obligations between vassals and lords. The executed men can be regarded as martyrs only insofar as they were not fairly tried and punished; they certainly did not fall as champions of the cause of freedom in the modern sense.[69]

E. Absolutism Manqué 1671–1679

The break-up of the conspiracy might well have constituted the beginning of a new era in Hungary if the Viennese government had possessed greater political sagacity and the ability to judge power relationships correctly. Mildness and generosity in matters which did not relate directly to the Crown's sovereignty could possibly have brought about a general pacification of the country. A salutary example had been set, and many lesser participants and sympathizers who initially escaped punishment were inclined to remain aloof from further cabals. However, the presupposition for harmony was the maintenance of the Hungarian constitution and the continued enjoyment by the nobility of its autonomy and property. The government itself was now rich, for the confiscation of the wealth of the condemned men had put huge sums at its disposal. If the money had been disbursed wisely, not only would it have been possible to build up the perennially impoverished army, but influence and good will—which would have been useful in the coming years—could have been purchased in Transylvania. Above all, it was necessary to permit the Hungarian Protestants the exercise of their legally guaranteed rights and to avoid any kind of religious controversy.[70]

A Policy of Repression

Unfortunately for all concerned, the indignant Leopold failed to follow a course of moderation. Trials proceeded and further sequestrations took place, leaving the families and dependents of the convicted without means. Hatred was compounded. The wealth was distributed to local informers and court favorites, exactly as had been done with the property of the Czech nobility after the Battle of White Mountain (1620). People like Montecuccoli and Sinzendorf did well for themselves. Austrian administration, at least until the day of Eugene of Savoy (who forced through some reform), was marked by considerable slovenliness and laxity. Indulgent toward the dishonesty of the powerful, it was harsh in the treatment of the little fellow; tolerant of wastage for superficialities, it practiced economy with essentials.[71] In Hungary, unlike Bohemia, the result of all the inefficiency and peculation seems to have been a strengthening of the virus of treason; in fact incapable administration per se may have been a cause of rebellion.[72]

Another pernicious factor was the Emperor's bigotry. It appears likely that Leopold's Jesuit confidants related the instability of the Hungarians to their Protestantism. At the same time the largely Catholic magnates were prepared to sacrifice their Evangelical fellow countrymen of the Upper Hungarian "hill towns" in order to divert suspicion from themselves.[73] Perhaps even more decisive was the counsel of the elegant, secretly pro-French Lobkowitz and Hocher. The disgrace of the former (1674) and rise to power of the latter only exacerbated matters. For Hocher, as for many a seventeenth-century advocate of absolute monarchy, uniformity of religion and state authority seemed inseparable, a conclusion which he probably drew from his study of Roman law. The conspiracy provided an ideal opportunity to destroy Hungary's exceptional position. Leopold now expressed himself unequivocally in favor of a new, authoritarian approach.[74] Whatever qualms of conscience he experienced were quieted by the argument that the Magyars had forfeited their constitutional rights through rebellion. Hungary was to undergo Bohemianization.[75]

Hocher went to work vigorously. He left the offices of Palatine and Ban unoccupied, strengthened the hated foreign garrisons through subter-

(Vienna, National Library)

Court Chancellor Paul Hocher

Cardinal Leopold Kollonitsch

fuge,[76] and then tightened the screws with an arbitrary introduction of new taxes. Thereupon he turned to religious affairs, mistakenly identifying Catholicism with political loyalty. He persisted in his endeavors for several years despite the objections of more perspicacious clergymen such as Bishops Emmerich Sinelli and Francesco Buonvisi. The Magyar Catholic hierarchy, which, like its social and religious confrères of the great nobility, was actually autonomist in outlook and which deported itself as the advocate of Hungarian liberties, provided him support for the religious aspect of his program. Since it could not repress the Calvinist gentry of the northeastern Alföld comitats, it welcomed the idea of extirpating at least the German Lutheran middle class. The self-whitewashed secular magnates also found the moment opportune for completing the re-Catholicization of their peasants.[77] The government, for its part, was not astute enough to realize that the burghers, despite their Protestantism, were natural allies. It literally drove them into the arms of the Magyar gentry.[78]

In 1674 some 450 schoolmasters and ministers, mostly adherents of the Augsburg Confession, were cited before a Magyar tribunal in Bratislava. Although hardly more tolerant or less dogmatic than their Catholic tormentors, they seem to have been innocent of the more serious charges.[79] Those who refused to renounce their calling were harshly treated. Bishop Leopold Kollonitsch, a hero of the 1683 siege, finally packed off forty-one of the most obdurate to the galleys, and the incident rapidly became a European *cause célèbre*.[80] The effect upon Austria's Protestant allies in the Dutch War—who intervened without success, at least initially—was anything but salutary.[81] Hocher also found a pretext—an abortive attack in 1672 by Hungarian refugees (called *Bujdósok* or Exulants) operating from Transylvania—for implementing a plan to place the government of Hungary in the hands of a German stadholder, Johann Kaspar vom Ampringen, Grand Master of the Teutonic Knights. Despite the fact that he had been born in the Kingdom, was personally upright, and was assisted by Magyars, his régime seemed illegal to the nation and was resented by all Hungarians, regardless of religious affiliation, as a foreign, German usurpation. His indignant and jealous colleagues worked against him, and he was forced to bear the onus of the religious persecutions. His bureau, located in Bratislava and not properly coordinated with Vienna, was soon ignored and ultimately (1679) abolished. In the meantime actual business was conducted by the Hungarian Court Chancellery in Vienna.[82]

THE KUROCZOK RISING

The sudden Catholic-absolutist coercion—which had to be partly abandoned already by 1675[83]—exacerbated an armed resistance that had existed from the very start. Immediately after the failure of the conspiracy—which had produced a brief rising in largely Protestant northeastern Hungary as well as in Catholic Croatia—fighting remained limited to hit-and-run attacks upon the Imperial troops in the former area by robbers and other *déraciné* elements, rough and ready fellows like the Hajduks and the Betyars. The bands' numbers grew with the appearance of socially more responsible types, men enraged by governmental dragonades, overtaxed Protestant gentry, ministers, teachers, and peasants. The new recruits also included Magyar soldiers dismissed from fortress duty in favor of presumably more reliable foreign mercenaries. The aristocratic Exulants provided this mixed lot its leadership. The so-called *Kuroczok* or "Crusaders" (a term dating from 1673) were often beaten but could not be exterminated. In small skirmishes they were dangerous even to trained regulars. Their Catholic foes, the Imperial partisans and militia, were called *Labanczok*, an opprobrious term that originally signified a foot-soldier. The guerilla warfare conducted by the two factions knew no quarter. Horrible atrocities were committed by both sides, even by clergymen. Flaying and impalement were common forms of execution. The Imperial generals, it seems, hoped to master the situation by severity and terror, but they succeeded merely in turning their own names into symbols of unrestrained brutality and Habsburg oppression for yet unborn generations of Magyars.[84]

The struggle might not have lasted so long save for external factors. The Emperor, involved in the Dutch War, could only devote a fraction of his strength to the East, while his opponents enjoyed foreign encouragement and assistance, including the use of nearby havens. Transylvania continued to allow the refugee nobles to organize resistance. The Exulants or Malcontents, as they were also called, likewise benefited from implicit Turkish tolerance and later received active backing. They enjoyed, at least initially, the sympathy of John Sobieski, and from 1674 onward they entertained relations with the French. In 1677 a treaty was signed at Fogaras, providing for joint action by the rebels, the Transylvanians and the French. Communications were carried on via Poland, where the Marquis de Béthune, French ambassador and brother-in-law of the Queen, acted as coordinator. Although French support was, once again, to Louis' momentary needs, and although it was not essential to the rebellion and never corresponded in size to the promises made, French agents in Poland did recruit a small, largely Polish army, under the command of Colonel d'Allandy-Boham, which went into action in Upper Hungary in 1677.[85]

The next year started out badly for the Emperor. An attempt to conciliate the Magyars in Bratislava was marred by a tactless, public display of temper by Hocher.[86] During the summer, the Malcontents, under the new military leadership of Count Imre Thököly (1657–1705), temporarily seized the Hill Towns and made off with bullion from the local mines and mints. By the end of the year, however, the situation seemed to be brightening for Leopold. The approaching Treaty of Nijmegen would free his soldiers along the Rhine for duty in Hungary. Louis would no longer be willing to subsidize the rebels on as broad a scale as before. Sobieski had already begun to alter his pro-Magyar stand (which provided the French with an opportune excuse to withdraw).[87] The relationship between the Exulants and the Transylvanians was also deteriorating. Michael Teleki, the ambitious minister of the by now indolent and besotted Abafi, headed a local anti-Habsburg faction which at first had rendered substantial support. Teleki even commanded the rebel forces for a short time. However, he was a mediocre general, became jealous of the more gifted and popular Thököly (who soon replaced him) and generally could not get on with the "royal" Hungarians. The Transylvanian state, moreover, did not dare to intervene formally without the Porte's permission,[88] and there was even a faction secretly sympathetic to Austria.[89] The Turks, for their part, were favorably disposed toward the Malcontents, but they had become involved in a war with the Russians and the Cossacks after making peace with the Poles at Zhuravno in 1676. Istanbul did not wish to snub Vienna openly. These factors and a military reverse suffered in November of 1678 caused Thököly to accept an armistice with the Emperor and to initiate negotiations. The conference, held in Sopron, lasted into 1679. Although it was destined to fail, the establishment of contacts at least seemed to presage a détente.

Imre Thököly

Although the danger to the House of Austria was not yet acute, Thököly, the catalytic agent for its becoming so, was by now before the public eye. The rôle which the new leader filled can be placed in partial focus by taking into account the uniquely tragic situation of his fatherland. It is no wonder that contemporary Hungary, unlike Austria and Poland, could not produce a really genuine national hero. It is clear that such a figure must have at least some larger forces—social, economic, or political—working in his favor: strength of will alone is insufficient. Thököly suffered not only from crippling historical liabilities but also from serious personal weaknesses. Possibly his imperfect character makes him a symbol, even if somewhat exaggerated, for his own social class, devoted as it was both to its own well-being and to national honor.

The family from which the insurgent chieftain and later Turkish ally stemmed was of recent origin. His great-grandfather, who may have been Polish, had founded the family fortunes through a combination of successful horse-trading and distinguished military service, plus a smart marriage. Though Protestant, the clan's founder was loyal to the King-Emperor and was rewarded with a barony. The family seat was a huge estate in Késmarok (Käsmark) in the region of Spiš (Zips), Upper Hun-

Count Imre Thököly

gary.[90] The grandfather also wed for money and position. The father, Stephen, the first count, started out well but wrecked himself by involvement in the Magnates' Conspiracy. Upon his death while under siege by government troops, Imre fled, making his way under the most hazardous conditions, via Poland, into Transylvania. Fourteen years of age at the time, he grew up among fellow *émigrés* in an atmosphere of conspiracy and hatred for the House of Habsburg. His wealth and talents made him conspicuous. From 1678 onward the Kuroczok rising breathed a fresh spirit of daring and energy.[91]

There seems little doubt as to the initial vengeful motives of Hungary's young champion. However, the passage of time revealed that he had also inherited the acquisitive drives of his grandfather and greatgrandfather. His concern for his own interests, in the form of riches and titles, equalled or excelled his dedication to the cause of his fellow countrymen. The circumstances of his avarice do not suggest a policy of base means serving an exalted end as was the case with Sobieski. Hungarian historians have sought to make Thököly a hero and a martyr, but their arguments appear to be based more upon patriotic sentiment than upon fact.[92]

The rebel commander's policy was the well-known but exceptionally perilous game of playing both ends against the middle: he was planning, somehow, to use the Turks in order to free Hungary (or rather that part of it not already Turkish) from royal authority. It may well be that he was originally encouraged to undertake this project by Transylvania's example, although it seems that in remembering Bethlen he forgot the second Rákóczy. Again, although there were moments (arising from Leopold's two-front dilemma) in which the Magyar count could believe that he held the balance of power, neither his strategic situation nor his material assets were sufficient for the tasks he proposed to accomplish with them. His errors in judgment were apparent to contemporaries even before his cause was defeated.[93] Yet he remained blind to reality and thereby assured himself a death in exile and loneliness.

If Thököly made mistakes, it was not for lack of intelligence. He possessed a keen mind and could digest factual information very rapidly. He was a fertile inventor of alternative solutions and policies. A persuasive talker, he could allegedly sell anybody anything, perhaps another legacy from his horse-dealing ancestor.[94] His appearance was also advantageous. A broad forehead and squarish cheeks and jowls framed a pair of candid-looking eyes. Below his well-cut nose was a trim, downward-sloping mustache. These attributes must have been useful in arousing the impression of reliability. One may venture to suggest that the gap between the man's talents and achievements was in some measure the result of his greed, which probably narrowed his vision and prevented him from thinking in long-range terms. The quality of his education may also have been a factor. The stormy circumstances of his puberty and the intellectually flaccid company of Magyar nobles hardly provided a suitable climate for learning. Possibly, ignorance of the larger world helps to explain his failures as a leader.[95]

In 1679, however, Thököly's flaws were not yet apparent. For many of his fellow countrymen he was the man of the hour. He could draw upon the embitterment and hatred which the Emperor and his counsellors had created with their abortive absolutist experiment and religious persecution. For even though important Magyars had cooperated with Vienna, the German dynasty received all the blame. While Leopold retained the loyalty of a few Western Hungarian Catholic magnates, the confidence of the great majority of the nation's articulate elements, both Protestant and Catholic, was badly shaken. Some, Hungarians, repressing their feelings, were hesitant; others were biding their time; still others had come to believe that Turkish turbans and scimitars were preferable to Imperial helmets and pikes. Granted a change in the attitude of the Porte—which was still at war with Muscovy—, Thököly was in a seemingly excellent position to implement his plans and ambitions.

As the expatriate Magyar nobles connived in their Transylvanian lairs,[96] or while they led their followers on sudden raids across the Puzsta, to the north in Poland events were gradually taking a shape that would affect their own destinies in no small measure. These developments must be considered next.

CHAPTER TWO

The East and the Southeast

A. Poland in the Seventeenth Century

The easternmost part of Europe in the late sixteenth and seventeenth centuries might be compared to the bay of a great river, for events there have the character of an eddy in the mainstream of Occidental history. Although one must concede that at least the city of Warsaw, stood close to the West not only geographically but culturally, overall development in the region still seems anachronistic, in fact retrogressive. In the case of Poland the best example of this phenomenon is the evolution of a more or less atypical constitution. Instead of advancing toward strong central government, the Poles, despite kingship, turned about and transformed their country into an aristocratic Republic. As Western Europe moved toward Modernity, the Land of the Plain Dwellers was reverting to the late Middle Ages. Elsewhere noble particularism, loosely labeled "feudalism," succumbed to royal or princely authority, but along the Vistula a parochial mentality triumphed. The occasional rule of a personality such as Stephen Báthory or John Sobieski had no lasting effect.

INTERNAL CONDITIONS

The loose structure of the ethnically heterogeneous Polish state was simultaneously a cause and a manifestation of its increasing impotence. The nation's six million inhabitants were divided among four main territorial units: the Kingdom, the Grand Duchy of Lithuania (more closely associated with the others after 1569), Royal Prussia, and the almost entirely alienated Ducal or East Prussia. The kingly office was elective, the elections themselves a time of national crisis, massive bribery, factional strife, even of civil war. The *Sejm* or national diet represented only that tenth part of the population comprising the nobility or *szlachta* and was thus composed of petty country gentlemen and more prosperous manorial gentry, plus the great barons or magnates. Its power, absolute in fiscal matters, was really quasi-executive. Although—contrary to popular impression—the Polish constitution was not an unmitigated monstrosity, the conversion of the principle of unanimity, per se rational enough, into the infamous *liberum veto* proved crippling. Not only was the measure under consideration blocked but all previously passed laws were nullified and the session thereby ruptured. The king was permitted no effective standing army, no genuine finance ministry, and no professional bureaucracy. He was forced to live largely from his own domains and to pay public expenses from his private pocket. Thus, he enjoyed little more than a certain primacy, a superior dignity among the country's greatest lords.[1]

It follows that the economic and social substructure of Poland was equally retrograde. Apart from the Germans and their flourishing fellow Jewish townspeople, there was not much of a middle class unless the gentry be accounted such. The sole export commodities were grain, timber, and cattle, and they benefited only the landowners. There was no entrepreneurial system; forced manual labor, fixed services replaced circulating capital. The yoke of serfdom was gradually settled more firmly upon the peasants' necks. Between 1493 and 1521 a series of laws had put the rural proletariat under patrimonial jurisdiction, conditions being worst in Ruthenia. At the same time the communes came under the complete rule of the aristocracy. It almost appears as if the development of a commercial middle class was deliberately frustrated. In order to obtain foreign luxury products, the nobility promoted free trade instead of the mercantilism of Western European states, thereby seriously damaging local manufacture and business. In fact, even within Poland itself foreign merchants were given special advantages. The nobility exempted itself from duties and taxes of all kinds although it might contribute in time of war. It reserved for itself all military and ecclesiastical sinecures.[2]

In order to preserve these conditions the aristocrats further limited the powers of the crown. In preparing for the royal elections candidates had to strike private bargains that would later inhibit their freedom of action. This factor and the inability of kings, once elected, to play off the poorer gentry (itself too weak to have acted the rôle of the absent bourgeoisie) against the magnates favored decentralization. The dominance of the legislative branch was assured by provincial diets, which exercised sole control over wartime levies. Deputies to the national diet were also bound by the instructions of these bodies, which could reject or accept the decisions reported to them. A narrow local outlook thus came to supersede national interests. The Senate or Royal Council, made up of bishops and magnates, might force the king to follow its counsels and dispense justice as it saw fit. If he did not, it was released from its oath of fidelity. The same body kept the crown and royal insignia and instructed the provincial governors. By the law *Nihil Novi* (1505) the monarch could change nothing without the consent of the Senate and provincial deputies. The person of senators and diet members was inviolate. *Pacta conventa* or special pre-coronation agreements were another fetter. In 1573 Henry of Valois had to agree not to declare war or make peace without the Senate; not to order the *levée en masse* of the nobility without the Diet; to accept a council of sixteen senators; and to call the Diet every two years. If he did not hold to these commitments, his subjects would have the right to rebel.

Insufficiently aware of the gathering strength of her neighbors, from whom she was protected neither by natural borders nor by professional military forces in the new sense of the word, Poland was "dying from an excess of liberty."[3]

In culture, too, Poland was slipping away from the great heights of the fifteenth and early sixteenth centuries. (The only exception was art, in which a Gothic Renaissance was succeeded by the Baroque.) The year 1648, in particular, marked the beginning of a sharp decline in standards of intellectual attainment. Religious heterodoxy was replaced by an intolerant stress upon Roman Catholicism. The influence of the Church expanded greatly. Medieval asceticism reappeared, and Latin reassumed a predominant position, to the detriment of native literature. There was a deterioration in the quality of education, now under clerical control. There was less contact with the West than there had been formerly. Fewer of the great nobles went abroad for their "finishing." They restricted their activities to their estates, families, and fighting. So-called "Sarmatism," a supposed return to the simpler manner of existence of earlier generations, made itself felt both in fashions, as for example in oriental-type costume and décor, and in the daily mode of life. Among the nobility an ethnocentric attitude seems to have been common. Still, this new "Eastern" emphasis did not correspond to a fundamental reversal of spiritual direction. The underlying current of Polish history remained Western, and the nation continued to serve as a Catholic buffer between Orthodoxy and Islam on the one hand, and the rest of Europe on the other.[4]

THE DELUGE

This task imposed tremendous strains upon the Polish state. So great in fact were the pressures that the Republic was unable, in its imperfect and weakened form, to endure as an independent entity. Already during the latter part of the seventeenth century a political observer might have concluded that the nation lacked the vitality to carry out successfully the rôle that geography had thrust upon it. In all likelihood he would have first considered what happened in 1648. This year, probably the greatest hiatus in the country's history before the Third Partition (1795), is also the point at which there began a series of events that form the background of Polish intervention against the Turks in 1683.

The quarter century following 1648 was so replete with catastrophe that Polish historians have been able to find no other term than "Deluge" to characterize it. A respite came only in 1673 with a great military victory by John Sobieski followed by his election as king the next year. The source of Poland's "Time of Troubles" was in the southeast, in the Ruthenian-inhabited provinces, especially the districts occupied by the most vigorous representatives of that subject, Eastern Orthodox na-

tionality, the Zaporozhian Cossacks. Past Polish policy toward the free-
dom-loving but unruly and undisciplined frontiersmen had been very
ambivalent: conciliatory in wartime when military services were required
and stringent in peacetime when the economic interests of Polish and
Polonized landowners predominated. The decade prior to 1648 had witnessed especially severe repression and exploitation, with the restriction
of special rights and privileges to a very limited number of "registered"
Cossacks. The result of this approach was a revolt in the aforementioned
year by Bogdan Khmelnitskiy and his followers. It soon became apparent
that the insurrection was of considerable proportions, the rebels' strength
being all the greater because their grievances were not only socio-
economic but ethno-religious as well.[5]

It would be wearisome to pursue in detail rapidly shifting developments during the succeeding twenty-five years, but a few fundamental
features do require emphasis. Certainly the death of the relatively capable Władysaw IV at the outset of this period and the succession of the
mediocre, venery-prone John Casimir represents yet another of countless
examples of unhappy chance in human affairs. Still, the most critical
factor was the meddling of self-interested foreign powers—a foreshadow-
ing of the eighteenth-century partitions. The first to become involved
were the Tatars, invited by their quondam Cossack foemen. Next came
the Great Russians, whose interference may well have been determinative. If the Cossacks had been crushed by their former masters, their
society would have evolved in the same direction as Poland's. That is to
say, the more prosperous, partly Polonized members of the Zaporozhian
"sech" would eventually have become an economic interest group, an
aristocracy requiring the enserfment of its sometime warrior-
comrades—the same thing that took place among the descendents of the
Mediaeval Polish war bands. However this may be, Russia's intervention
in Poland's difficulties was followed by Sweden's (1655) and then (1657)
by Transylvania's. Also fishing in the troubled waters were ambitious
Polish traitors and Frederick William the Great Elector, who hoped to
detach East Prussia from its nominal Polish suzerainty. But then came an
unexpected outburst of patriotic ardor from the downtrodden peasantry,
aid from Austria and Denmark, and the death of the Swedish king,
Charles X. By sacrificing her remaining Baltic lands, Poland was able to
persuade Stockholm to withdraw its forces.[6]

The Treaty of Oliva (1660), which registered the peace with Sweden,
also permitted Louis XIV to establish himself as an arbiter in the North
and East. In the meantime Brandenburg was bought off with East Prussia
(1657) while Turkey undertook the chastisement of George II Rákóczy.
The conflict with Russia dragged on. Finally, in 1667 (Treaty of
Andrusovo), peace was again purchased with territorial concessions, this
time with a strip of White Russia. The only real military success of the

reign was John Sobieski's defeat of the Cossacks (now led by a new Hetman, Peter Doroshenko) and their Tatar allies at Podhajce (October 6, 1667). Unfortunately the end of foreign difficulties was not followed by domestic amelioration. The absolutist-minded, French-born Queen, Maria Ludowika of Gonzaga (inherited by John Casimir from his predecessor) sought to promote her fatherland's influence. She advocated, *inter alia,* the succession of a French candidate *vivente rege.* This project coincided with the hopes of some Poles for constitutional reform and a buttressing of the central government. The result was merely civil strife and, ultimately, a compromise which was of no value in strengthening the monarchy. The exhausted John Casimir finally abdicated (1668) and withdrew to France to seek peace in religious contemplation.[7]

Michael Korybut-Wiśnowiecki

The departure of the King exposed the nation to another interregnum and the vagaries of new convocation and election *Sejms.* The recently deceased (1667) Queen left behind not only a pro-French court party but also a legacy of resentment. Factional politics became increasingly bitter. The former court clique decided to work secretly for the election of the great Marshal Condé. The Gallophobes turned toward the Habsburgs, supporting Duke Charles of Lorraine, a dispossessed prince who had linked his fortunes to the house of Austria. John Casimir's brother-in-law, the Count Palatine of Neuburg, the *pro forma* French candidate (also backed by Brandenburg) was the third main contender. The gentry, however, frustrated the hopes of all three men. The lesser nobles apparently reckoned that their interests would suffer if the magnates, who were being bribed prodigiously by the foreign diplomats, should succeed in imposing one of their protégés. Possibly they were also moved by more elevated considerations of patriotism and national pride. In any event, they turned to an indigenous candidate, a supposed "Piast," and elected the impecunious, inexperienced and wretchedly incompetent Michael Korybut-Wiśnowiecki, whose only recommendation was the personal popularity of his late warrior-father. Elevated to the throne against the wishes of the great aristocrats, he sought support in Vienna where he had grown up and where his natural sympathies lay. Leopold, pleased to have an opportunity to exert his influence after all, confirmed the alliance with the gift of his daughter, Eleanora, for whose hand Charles had been hoping.[8]

If the simian-faced Michael had had any ability, he might have made a favorable start with the aid of the domestic elements which had elected him. The gentry at a later point proved willing to proceed against the King's highly-placed opposition. Before this juncture, however, foreign war again broke out, revealing the monarch's incapacity to one and all. The Grand Vezir, Ahmed Köprülü, aware of Poland's internal divisions and wishing to incorporate the Ukraine into the Ottoman Empire, seized the opportunity of new Polish difficulties with the Cossacks. The latter nation, whose vertiginous political gyrations in this period almost defy description, now decided to offer allegiance to the Porte. The object was to extricate the homeland from both Polish and Muscovite dominance—a policy that actually proved more popular in the Polish-dominated Western Ukraine than in the East. Sobieski, already Poland's greatest general, maneuvered brilliantly with inferior numbers. He failed, however, to receive sufficient reinforcement from his squabbling compatriots at home and was distrusted, not without reason, by his jealous sovereign. The Dnestr fortress of Kamenets Podol'skiy (Kamieniec), the major Polish stronghold in the East, fell on September 27, 1672, and Tatar "Tschambouls" (raiding parties) swept deeper into the realm, burning, looting, raping, and murdering. Sobieski once more outdid himself and at least managed to eliminate the vicious intruders.[9]

The pusillanimous King, more concerned with disconcerting his magnate enemies, thereupon signed the humiliating Treaty of Buchach (Buczacz), October 16, 1672. He gave up Podolia, recognized Turkish sovereignty in the Ukraine, and agreed to pay tribute. The Poles' first reaction was to plunge deeper into civil discord. Two opposing leagues arose, one pro- and the other anti-royal. The second was formed in self-defense by Sobieski, who, up to this time had wavered between the French faction, his own interests, and loyalty to a King he despised. But gradually the shame of Buchach made itself felt. The Senate refused to confirm the Treaty. A compromise between the two camps was effected by the papal nunzio, Buonvisi, and Eleanora. The generally discredited King was able to hold on to his crown for the few remaining months of his life. A strong Polish army gathered under Sobieski. The Turks, brought to battle at Khotin (Hotin, Chocim) on the middle Dnestr (10–11 November, 1673), sustained a great strategic and material defeat. Sobieski intended to press his advantage, but his army, already beginning to melt away before the victory, could no longer be restrained when the unexpected news of the King's death arrived two weeks later. The nation was once more cast into an interregnum.[10] As the date of the election *Sejm* neared, one thing was certain: whoever might be chosen, the hero of Khotin would bring a great deal of weight to bear.

B. John Sobieski

Of all the characters who appeared on the stage of 1683, none was a more sublime actor and none received a more enthusiastic applause from the European audience than the flamboyant, complex John III Sobieski (1629–1696), "by the grace of God King of Poland, Grand Duke of Lithuania, Russia, Prussia, Masovia, Samogitia, Livonia, Kiev, Volhynia, Podolia, Podlachia, Smolensk, Severia and Chernigov."[11] Beyond doubt

Venir, voir, secourir, remporter la victoire,
releuer de l'empire et le Trosne et la gloire,
proteger les Chretiens.Terrasser le Croissant,
rendre son effort impuissant,
Sa valeur confuse et trompeé,
cest pour vous O grand Roy louurage de deux mois;
et ce qui donne encor l'esclat a tant d'exploits,
cest que Dieu s'est seruy de vostre seule Epeé.

(Vienna, National Library)

King John Sobieski

the brightest figure in the last two, dismal centuries of the Republic's history, he is today for many Poles even more: an impeccable hero, the only man to whom the adjective "great" is automatically applied.

EARLY YEARS

The future King was the scion of a wealthy, distinguished Volhynian family residing in Olesko at the time of his birth. The fortunes of the landowning Sobieskis were irrevocably bound to the prosperity of their frontier homeland. During the age in question, Volhynia and the adjacent territories (Red Russia, Podolia, Little Russia and the Ukrainian steppe) were anything but a haven of peace and well-being. The involved relationships between Poles, Cossacks, Tatars, Turks and Great Russians assured any boy of noble origin, even in intervals of peace, early training in arms and the development of a sense of responsibility and duty. Sobieski's position was perhaps atypical insofar as he stemmed from a particularly stalwart breed. Also unusual, considering the troubled times, was his thorough education. His learned father, who carefully supervised his studies, arranged a grand tour, paying special attention to fortifications and military science. For the purpose of social and linguistic polish, the trip also included an extended stay in France. However, the death of the elder Sobieski and the deteriorating political situation at home forbade further dalliance with sophisticated society and belles lettres. In 1648 the son returned to Poland, almost immediately to be engulfed in the chaos that followed Khmelnitskiy's revolt. The young magnate's military talents were quickly revealed. With the passage of time he became, in turn, Crown Standard Bearer, Crown Field Hetman, and finally, as chief general of the Rzeczpospolita, Crown Grand Hetman. His greatest triumph (which brought Continental reknown) was of course Khotin.[12]

The preceding twenty-three years had been dedicated not only to Mars but to Eros. Sobieski himself frankly confessed his outright addiction to *veneris officium*. Yet his carnal appetites, initially gratified by camp courtesans and Ruthenian peasant maids, were complemented by a spiritual sensitivity and a tenderness of heart that ultimately enabled him to master indolence and debauchery and to become an ideal, faithful (conceivably too faithful) spouse. A very beautiful Frenchwoman, Maria Kazimiera de la Grange d'Arquien ("a white and rose complexion, black eyes, aquiline nose, small, red mouth"),[13] who had come to Poland as a four year old child in Maria Ludowika's entourage captured the general's heart. The romance was fraught with great practical difficulties. The lady was already married to another—a brutish but very rich fellow magnate. The death of the latter in 1665 allowed the secret lovers to be joined in wedlock. The marriage, despite its great tempestuousness, lasted a lifetime. The wife was regarded by many as ambitious, avaricious, conniving, and small-minded, unworthy of Sobieski. There is little doubt that she lacked the stature of her husband or that from time to time she made his life wretched. She wheedled and lamented in letters when he was away and made scenes when he was at home. Yet for a man as strong as he to have loved with such enduring fidelity implies that she also had qualities that lifted her above the ordinary. A woman who could inspire the lines:

> Si mon âge n'est pas celui de l'ardeur, mon coeur et mon âme sont aussi jeunes qu'autrefois. . . .[14]

must have had more than sensual allure. The most recent biographer of the pair stresses her piety, quick intelligence, kindness, naive tranquillity, courage, and powerful will, not to mention her own genuine, if less profound love.[15] Of greater historical significance is the fact that both "Jachniczek" and his "Marysieńka" shared the same goals in life, his for more elevated reasons and hers for baser ones (the material interests of her own family).

PERSONALITY TRAITS

Apart from carping, shallow assessments (not only by German historians, as might be expected, but also by certain Poles), the twentieth century has produced two theories to explain Sobieski's actions. The first stresses the King's Catholic faith to the exclusion of other factors.[16] The second considers the patriotic side of his nature and finds his behavior at least partly determined by a wish to assure the nation permanent security.[17] One manifestation of this were his efforts—which antedate the events of 1683—to organize an international coalition against Islam. Another was his attempt to provide the Republic with stronger institutions of central government (in particular his campaign to have his son elected his successor *vivente rege*). Thus viewed, the Polish sovereign was not so much a religiously motivated Crusader, despite his undoubtedly genuine Catholicism, as a clear-sighted advocate of the best interests of his fatherland.

Aside from the anti-Islamic traditions of his family and his own actions, the most convincing proof of Sobieski's national orientation is his correspondence with his wife during the 1683 campaign. These vivid letters, which also reveal other aspects of his character, contain a passage in which the King unequivocally states that he has come to Leopold's aid because the undertaking is beneficial to Poland:

> *D'abord* (Italics mine), il est de nôtre interêt de combattre un ennemi qui nous attaquerait en Pologne s'il n'était pas occupé ici. . . .[18]

Whatever his motives, nature provided Sobieski the proper attributes for the rôle of warrior-hero. Spiritually vital, sharp-witted and decisive, he was a tremendously vigorous, rather out-sized man with a well-made figure. Although his voracious appetite and his hankering for strong drink distended his stomach and filled out his oval face in later years, corpulence only made him more majestic. His complexion was fresh and ruddy, his eyes blue, and, like so many people in East Central Europe, he had a prominent, aquiline nose.[19] A fine mouth with excellent teeth set off his face and tonsured head. His gaze, vivid and fiery, according to the French engineer Dupont who was long his intimate, was difficult to withstand.[20] He clothed himself in the luxurious, then-fashionable costume of the Eastern steppes and generally laid great stress upon stylish dress. In reporting his meeting with Lorraine and the Elector of Saxony he makes invidious remarks about their garb, and at other points he depicts his own in self-admiring detail.[21] Indeed, he had a foible for all articles of richness and described booty with great pride and precision in the epistles to Marysieńka. Of course it might be argued that this was not so much greed, covetous though he was, as the sensuous pleasure of a Baroque prince in some newly acquired object of artistic merit.

Other failings were his pursuit of fame, his vainglory, and his stinginess. He carefully explains to his wife that he is racing ahead of his troops, toward Vienna, because he fears that the Turks may flee at the mere news of his approach and that the Germans will reap the honors of combat.[22] He was not only a consummate, actor but also his own best publicity agent. He instructs his mate to pass his letters on to the newspapers.[23] (That his self advertisement bore fruit is apparent in the fact that some persons still regard him as the sole savior of Vienna and even of Western civilization.) To be sure, there were two sides to the coin of his parsimony. Dalérac, one of the Queen's domestics, records how astonished everyone was that the King laid out his own treasure in order to equip the Vienna expedition.[24] Like many another French observer in Warsaw, the writer simply could not see that the cupidity of the Sobieskis was more than personal acquisitiveness, a means rather than an end. A man attempting to direct the affairs of a nation that denied him adequate revenue might easily succumb to avarice and miserliness.

Rapacity was thus a child of necessity and a virtuous flaw. The King's religiosity, however, was a kind of flawed virtue. While Sobieski had scholarly inclinations, his faith could hardly be compared with that of contemporary theological sophisticates like Bishop Bossuet (or even with the Emperor's). It has been described as impetuously enthusiastic and materialistically superstitious.[25] It had the pristine quality of shrines and pilgrimages. Częstochowa's miraculous icon of the Black Virgin, which still serves as the symbol of Poland's unique amalgam of patriotism and piety, is indicative. To be sure, John III showed not even a trace of Leopold's bigotry. The Polish monarch was prepared to accommodate Jews (who greatly admired him), Protestants, and Pravoslavs and seems to have felt little prejudice or animosity toward any people or race.[26] He was doubtlessly capable of deep sympathy for others: hardened soldier though he was, he could experience pity for the suffering of the guiltless victims of war.

The King's religious attitude implies a certain paradoxicality of character, which was apparent in other ways as well. Despite his mental and corporeal vitality, he was sometimes slothful and indolent. Altruism and egotism went hand in hand. His kindheartedness stood in contrast to an often obtuse insensitivity to the feelings of others. His passions could be matched by indifference. His spirituality was mated with sensuality. His sense of honor and intense pride in his word were paired with a remarkable suppleness and deviousness in politics.[27]

The catalogue of the hero's sometimes puzzling personal qualities is not complete if one fails to mention his patronage of the arts, letters, and science. The time required for the development of his military talents (the greatness of which was admitted by no less an authority than Clausewitz) and statesmanly brilliance did not prevent the nature-loving, artistically inclined monarch from earning a reputation as a friend of learning. He also possessed literary and oratorical gifts. His linguistic attainments were astonishing: he could speak and read French, German, and Italian, plus a little Spanish, Dutch and English. He likewise knew Latin, Greek, Rumanian, Russian, Turkish, and Tatar.[28]

THE RISE TO POWER

During the tumultuous years of Wiśnowiecki's reign Sobieski probably found it difficult to devote many hours to study and reflection. The King's death then threw him into a maelstrom, at the end of which himself ascended his country's unstable throne (May 21, 1674). It is not clear what John III's own policy and attitude were prior to his election. Scholarly opinion is divided over the question of whether he and his wife slyly planned their campaign or whether he was somewhat hesitantly swept along by the tide of mounting enthusiasm for his person.[29] It is certain that there were two camps among the magnates: 1.) the so-called Austrian faction (backed domestically by the Great Poles and the Lithuanians), previously concealed behind the gentry; and 2.) the French party, represented internally by the rich aristocrats of the Ruthenian southeast. Each grouping also had its own female champion, one the widowed Eleanora and the other the eager Maria Kazimiera. Although there were at least a dozen candidates, including Condé and the sixteen year old son of the Count Palatine of Neuburg (the French favorites), it soon became obvious that only two men had a real chance: Lorraine, again hopeful of both the crown and Eleanora's hand; and the Crown Grand Hetman. The French ambassador, Bishop Forbin-Janson of Marseille, dispatched by Louis XIV with a supply of gold to bribe the way clear for whichever French protégé had the best prospects, was a crucial figure in backstage bargaining. He was won over to Sobieski. There were a host of reasons for his shift: Maria Kazimiera's charms, the lure of a red hat, the realization that no other even partly acceptable candidate could win, and, above all, a secret promise to cease hostilities with Turkey (in order to free the Porte for action against the Emperor). An oral engagement to attack Brandenburg as a further diversion for the French side in the Dutch War seems also to have been made.[30]

The French King's money was used to counteract the pecuniary dispensations of the Austrian ambassador, Count Schaffgotsch. The victor of Khotin, also backed by the papal nunzio, Buonvisi, benefited from his newly-acquired popularity among the gentry. An impassioned speech by an old comrade-in-arms, Stanisław Jabłonowski, finally brought the necessary majority. French funds were then disbursed to assuage the feelings of the Lithuanians, whose Hetman, Michael Pac, hated Sobieski. The election was thereupon declared unanimous. Schaffgotsch yielded gracefully. The rejected Charles later (1678) received from the Emperor the consolation prize of Eleanora.[31]

C. International Relations 1674–1679

Sobieski's election, perhaps an even greater triumph for his mate than for himself, was due in large measure to the aureate influence of Forbin-Janson. The ambassador's decision to exceed his instructions and to use his weight in order to tip the balance in the general's favor was unquestionably in the best momentary interest of France. If the Bishop had chosen, instead, to withdraw from the race, there would have been one less star in his native country's diplomatic firmament during the next four years. The new King, whose cultural and personal sympathies had long been French anyway, was now bound to the Parisian court, and in the initial part of his reign he steered the ship of state generally in accordance with Louis XIV's wishes. This policy was misunderstood in his own lifetime and later on by short-sighted historians, who regarded him as an unprincipled, money-grubbing, Habsburg-hating satellite of the Gallic sun.[32] Overlooked was the fact that the internal circumstances of Poland and its delicate strategic situation gave a monarch no other choice but to rely on the financial and diplomatic backing of some strong, foreign potentate. If Sobieski wished to rule firmly, to bring domestic order and external security, and *eventually* to drive back the Infidel, he had to place himself on the auction block. Moreover, the buying and selling of political support was not at that time an uncommon phenomenon; the moral standards of private life are rarely applicable to international relations.

In the Wake of France

Tacking to the French wind was a very difficult feat of political navigation. The course ran "between Scylla and Charybdis." Sobieski's

(Vienna, National Library)

Prince Jerome Lubomirski

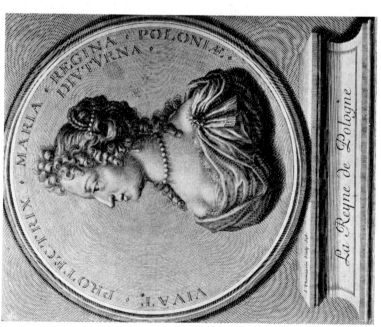

Queen Maria Kazimiera Sobieska

success must therefore be counted an important aspect of his greatness. The European situation of 1674, as viewed from France, required alliance with Sweden and hostility toward the Empire. Although anti-Hohenzollern action was not unpopular and while the personal, hereditary acquisition of East Prussia would have furthered the new ruler's dynastic hopes, the Swedes, traditional Polish enemies, were scarcely the most comfortable confederates. Enmity toward the Habsburgs, contrary to one of his two underlying aims, also raised the spectre of internal dissension in Poland. And, in order to pursue either policy, peace with Ottoman Turkey was necessary, something that would not sit well with those who had supported Sobieski precisely because of his victories in the anti-Muslim struggle. All these difficulties notwithstanding, the King managed to extract from Louis XIV cash subsidies and the domestic political backing of France's Polish clientage. Moreover, the mediation of the French diplomats, Forbin-Janson and Nointel (the ambassador in Istanbul) in arranging a truce with the Sultan also had one advantage: Poland needed a respite from warfare in Ruthenia in order to gather strength for the final reckoning.[33]

Whatever the momentary benefits, the pro-French policy could never have become a permanent guideline for Sobieski's reign. The great divergencies between the basic national interests of Poland and France and between the two rulers' political goals foredoomed it. The Polish king hoped ultimately to unite his fellow Europeans in a grand effort to rid Christendom of the Turkish menace once and for all. His crusading ideals corresponded to the purposes of Innocent XI, not to those of Louis XIV, who was primarily concerned with himself and with France. In Western Europe, moreover, the geographically distant Ottoman peril probably seemed somewhat unreal. Louis, unlike John III, could never identify the well-being of his country with that of all Europe. Thus, he remained entirely insensitive to the anti-Turkish suasions of the Curia. Sobieski's apparent belief that what was good for Poland was also good for Christians of other lands was, at the very least, not incompatible with the weal of the rest of the Continent. In fact, crusading fervor, moribund though it may have been by the latter seventeenth century, was by no means dead beyond recall. In short, not only did Polish national egoism fail to correlate with France's, but it was also in greater harmony with its surroundings. Another obstacle to any lasting Franco-Polish entente was the personal ambition of Maria Kazimiera, who counted upon raising the modest estate of her father and her family back in France. The rank and dignity-conscious Louis, who regarded the De la Grange Arquiens as upstarts, proved unwilling to grant substantial concessions, thus eventually earning the Queen's enmity.[34]

For the nonce, however, Sobieski sanctioned collaboration with France and was even prepared to commit himself on paper. The agreement signed at Jaworów on June 11, 1675, seemed to indicate that the Polish king had become Louis' puppet. In reality the treaty was a skillful diplomatic achievement for Warsaw. It foresaw the conclusion of peace between Poland and Turkey and thereafter a Polish assault against Brandenburg. France would provide monetary grants, which were to be doubled if the Poles should become involved in conflict with Vienna. It was this provision that interested the French most, but John III was canny enough to have it framed in such a way that he was not actually obliged to initiate hostilities. While he pledged himself to permit the French to recruit on Polish soil for the Hungarian rebels and to deny Vienna an analogous right, and while he agreed to aid the Malcontents, he was able to avoid promising a formal break with the Emperor. East Prussia was of course a different matter, not only because he felt that it had been stolen from Poland but because it could serve as a buttress to his own personal position.

THE WAVERING COMPASS

The Hohenzollern territory was in fact so great a temptation that the King directed his attention to it in the summer of 1676 even before beginning negotiations with the Turks. He was prevented from undertaking action only by a farcical combination of circumstances which related both to the ambitions of an illegitimate son begotten years ago in France and the extravagant personal plans of his wife and French in-laws. Relations with Louis became strained, and the East Prussian expedition was postponed. Then came the signing of a provisional armistice with the Turks at Zhuravno (Żórawno) on the Dnestr[35] (October 17, 1676). The two parties agreed to work out territorial details in Istanbul. Sobieski was free to devote himself to either of the areas mentioned in the Jaworów treaty. For a time he was inclined to assist the Magyars, at least to a limited extent. However, the activity of papal and Imperial diplomats among the *szlachta* cooled his ardor somewhat, and he avoided open support of the rebels. In early 1677 his tactics took an even more complex turn. While he approved the renewal of the 1657 alliance with Leopold he also permitted 4000 men under Prince Jerome Lubomirski to help the Malcontents. Part of his purpose was to dispose of the now superfluous and potentially dangerous Polish army at no expense to the government. Some veterans could be supported at France's expense in Hungary, and the others would gather, as a kind of free corps on the East Prussian border. While thus able to act militarily, the King could claim that the troops were only private forces, for whom he bore no personal responsibility.

In the summer of 1677 Sobieski showed renewed interest in the Baltic theater, and the Great Elector faced the danger of having to fight simultaneously on several fronts. Fortunately for Berlin, domestic troubles frustrated John III's intentions. Béthune, the new French ambassador and spouse of Marysieńka's sister, tried to restrain him. Paris not only preferred an Hungarian diversion, but its emissary secretly coveted the crown of St. Stephen.[36] The King hesitated because French backing was uncertain and his potential confederates, the Swedes, were failing militarily. In the meantime, Hohenzollern and Habsburg diplomats approached influential Poles and spread word of Béthune's plans. They succeeded in causing such turmoil that the East Prussian adventure was also affected. In any case, the Queen, who could not suffer her aspiring in-law, was becoming increasingly irritated over Louis' failure to do anything for her father. She now hearkened to the Austrian envoy, Zierowski, who implied that Vienna could better provide for her family's fortunes.[37]

Nevertheless, the decisive factor in the Baltic undertaking was bad news from Istanbul. Turkish unwillingness to grant concessions in the Dnestr region and the increasingly threatening attitude of the new Grand Vezir, Kara Mustafa, forced Sobieski to give it up. The obvious failure of the whole gambit was a blow to his prestige, from which he did not entirely recover until the time of the Vienna expedition. His internal enemies, the Great Polish magnates and the Pac family, were encouraged. Luckily, the Great Elector was circumspect rather than vindictive. Friendly overtures now came from Berlin and from Vienna as well. John III had no choice but to accept. In the meantime the Senate ratified the Turkish treaty (April 16, 1678), by which the Republic gave up Podolia and most of the Ukraine. So onerous a peace could only be temporary. By this time, moreover, a deep cleft divided the Poles from their Gallic ally, which had failed to make the Porte amenable to Polish interests.

A gradual process of realignment now commenced, facilitated by the papal nunzii, Buonvisi (transferred by this time to Vienna) and his replacement, Martelli. The first indication of an altered course was Sobieski's halting of recruitment for the Malcontents. Paris naturally became annoyed. A new era of "mutual pin pricks" then began. The personal frustrations of the Queen were again important. A symbol of the shift was that Leopold became the godfather of John III's second son, Alexander. Still, the trend was not yet permanent. Cross currents existed. The Hohenzollerns had no reason to support absolute monarchy in Warsaw, and the King had to reckon with the enmity of the so-called "Faction of the Three Eleanors" (Leopold's step-mother, half-sister and wife) in Vienna. It was only natural that the Dowager Empress and her ambitious daughter, now the Duke of Lorraine's spouse, should ally with the Emperor's mate from the House of Pfalz-Neuburg.[38] Another element was the approaching end of the Dutch War. Although Leopold did not share in the peace signed at Nijmegen on August 10, he could not be expected to continue war alone for long and, in fact, soon undertook negotiations of his own.[39] There was also a chance that the Great Elector might revert to a pro-French policy. Under these circumstances it would have been foolish for Sobieski to have slammed the French door shut. He could have been left completely without friends. His wife, however, yielding to her emotions, was driving toward a break. She failed to realize that Zierowski's hints of an archduchess for her elder son, Jakób, who she hoped would succeed Sobieski, plus the Hungarian *détente,* were an insufficient basis for alliance. Both Austria and Brandenburg maintained contact with anti-Sobieski factions inside the country, and if the King were to snub Louis or the Swedes, he would still have to contend with the domestic clients of the former powers. It is not hard to understand why he plotted a zigzag chart.

John III managed to retain French support throughout the critical *Sejm* at Grodno in the winter of 1678–79. He was also able, by diplomacy, to prevent Berlin and Vienna from aiding his domestic foes, who were conspiring to depose him in favor of Lorraine. Fundamentally, Frederick William preferred the King over the chaotic nobles,[40] and the Emperor turned a deaf ear to his female entourage. Nevertheless, Sobieski found himself in a delicate situation, and the peril of losing the throne was great. Had he followed Béthune's advice to act against the Austrian party, he might have fallen. In November and December, after intercepting Swedish correspondence with the Poles, the Great Elector suddenly became unfriendly. His recent successes against the Swedes and his rapprochement with Louis XIV made him a dangerous opponent. All Polish interest in East Prussia vanished. If Leopold, pushed by the Holy See, had not actively restrained his Polish adherents, John III would probably have been driven against the wall.

Surprisingly the diet session was fruitful in other ways. Especially significant was the confirmation of the fifteen year armistice with Muscovy, a decision which implied renewal of the war against the Porte. The goal of a Pan European crusade, which the King had never completely lost from view throughout the years of his association with France, now came more clearly into focus. The cessation of hostilities between France and the Empire (February 5, 1679) seemed to improve prospects.[41] Sobieski, like Innocent XI, was thinking in terms of a fully united Occident.

MUSCOVY AND THE UKRAINE

Although the assumption that Russia then belonged to the Western world might be debatable, John III's reasons for including it are not difficult to divine, considering the circumstances of his time. His neighbor was, after all, a Christian nation, to which Poland had been more or less allied for over a decade. To be sure, the Tsars' physical resources and political weight were still minimal. The first Romanov ruler, Michael (1613–1645), whose reign followed the debilitating Time of Troubles, lived long without achieving anything worthy of recall, while the government of his son, Alexis (1645–1676), has never been considered brilliant. Even Peter the Great's victories and reforms did not make Russia a great power. The latter seventeenth century was a period of gradual recovery of central authority and despotism, accompanied by the growth of serfdom and an increasingly serious technological lag.

The only relevant aspect of Russia's development at this time is her relations with Poland, the Cossacks, the Crimean Tatars, and the Turks. For the first two-thirds of the century Moscow had been concerned, firstly, with fending off the Poles and, later on, with recovering from them its ancient Kievan heritage, located on the middle reaches of the southward-flowing rivers. Until these goals had been attained, the tsars could hardly have been interested in a war with the Porte. The desire for peace with Istanbul was enhanced by the danger of the Tatars, Turkish satellites, whose incursions into the Russian land must have seemed like a divinely-ordained plague. Ivan the Terrible's concern with the east and south had only been ephemeral, and the interest of his immediate successors had remained limited to a surreptitious support of the Don Cossacks. Turko-Russian relations centered mainly around mutual complaints over raids by each other's wild liege men and some discussion of the possibility of making common cause against Poland. Only with the revolt of the oppressed Polish or Zaporozhian Cossacks (1648) did the basis for alignments in the region begin to shift. After some vacillation, Moscow finally accepted the homage of the Cossacks (1654) and thus switched from a defensive to an aggressive policy with respect to Poland. The decision also meant for Moscow the increased enmity of the Tatars, whose continual swinging back and forth among the powers seems to have been motivated by the desire to preserve a local balance of power and thus to ensure their own predatory manner of existence. In any case, grounds for a Russian conflict with the Turkish overlords of the Tatars were now at hand.[42]

In the meantime the long Russo-Polish War dragged on. The fealty of the Cossacks proved to be illusory, and the struggle became more and more burdensome. With time a Baltic-oriented, anti-Swedish faction, headed by the urbane Ordyn-Nashchokin, became vocal in Alexis' council. The realization that Poland and Russia really had the same enemies (Sweden, the Tatars and the Turks) and that Poland itself no longer represented a major threat to Muscovy gradually sank in. Thus came about the Treaty of Andrusovo (1667), which not only brought peace and alliance but actually endured for some three decades. Its most important feature, as far as the politics of the next few years were concerned, was the temporary nature of Russia's retention of Kiev (although the division of the Ukraine was definitive). It was painful for Moscow that it would someday have to yield its most significant gain, and the tsarist government was prepared to make sacrifices in order to assure the city's permanent possession. This was the lever which Poland, in the face of growing danger from Turkey, could use to get Russian help. While, for internal reasons, neither Poland nor Russia gave each other substantial aid during each of the powers' succeeding, separate wars with the Ottoman Empire (Poland 1672–1676, Russia 1676–1681), both states remained closely linked in their interests and sympathies. However, Russia's war with Turkey, evoked in part by the latter's concern over the growth of new Christian strength so close to the Black Sea and in part by the former's inability to govern her portion of the Zaporozhian Cossacks, proved to be inconclusive. The only notable result was that the Cossacks came more under Muscovy's sway and the Tatars under the Ottoman Empire's. Russia's "New" Ukraine also grew in population: tsarist government, which signified freedom from landlord exploitation, appeared more attractive to refugees from Turkish and Polish territory. The Russians, on the other hand, were still too weak to subjugate the southern part of the steppe. This explains why it was impossible for them to assume an important rôle in the great anti-Turkish coalition that began to be built up in 1683. While Muscovy did eventually render some assistance to the common European effort, the benefit was no more than indirect.[43]

If the tsars were unable to combat the sultans effectively, a lack of physical strength was not the only reason. It would be incorrect to assume that the Ottoman state had already become an opponent incapable of meaningful resistance. A closer look at conditions in Turkey will not only help to explain the outcome of the conflict in the Ukraine; it will also be useful in comprehending the origins of the expedition against Vienna.

D. The Structure of the Ottoman Empire

General histories customarily depict the Ottoman Empire after Suleiman the Magnificent as moribund, with relatively little significance for Europe, and hence unworthy of comment beyond a cursory mention of the depravity of the Sultans, the decay of the Janissaries, and the nefarious influence of the Phanariote Greeks, the Armenians, and the Jews. Nevertheless, to the Western world the Sublime Porte was a terrifying reality, at least until 1683. It is, moreover, difficult to conceive of Turkey's degeneration in such simple, straightforward terms. Another mystifying question is why the Empire took so long to collapse entirely. In short, the normal conceptions of Ottoman decline are clichés; the actualities of the situation were doubtlessly more complex. Fortunately, during recent years specialists have been giving increasing attention to the problem and have produced some fresh (albeit still tentative) interpretations. On the other hand, there is as yet no general consensus, and it is necessary to consider at least several alternatives. In so doing, it will also be possible to bring out certain objective aspects of Ottoman government, society and economy—matters of fundamental relevance to understanding how Istanbul organized its assault upon Vienna in 1683.

THE THEORY OF PARASITISM

One approach to the disintegration of the Turkish state stresses social exploitation on an institutionalized basis. Essential to this view is a critique of the Sultan's status as an "absolute" monarch. The Padishah, like his occidental confréres, was, in fact, subject to certain limitations. The Sacred Law (Şeria), guarded by the *Ulema* or Muslim-born educated class, represented a kind of inviolable Islamic state constitution. Another check was the conservative mentality of the Turkish people. The only possible instrument for effecting major change was the administration or so-called "Ruling Institution" which included all officials and servants from the Grand Vezir down to the humblest Janissary. The sultan controlled the state not by virtue of his relatively slight legislative (decretal) power but by means of the Institution's unique structure. Its personnel was supplied by the male child tax (*devşirme*) on Christian subjects, by war prisoners, and by purchased or donated slaves. It constituted a well-trained, privileged but non-hereditary, professional civil service that operated on a merit basis of promotion. At least these were the conditions which characterized it in its period of greatest vigor and effectiveness. From the seventeenth century onward, however, the native-born Turks attempted with ever-increasing success to gain admission to the administration, with its special prerogatives of life. A sharp contrast and a rival for authority was provided by the so-called Muslim Institution. Composed of the *ulema*, it included not only the most important muftis, but also local teachers, preachers and scribes. This body was the major hurdle to any profound or arbitrary change.[44]

The chief executive organ of government was the *Divân* or Council of State, formed by departmental heads but also embracing three representatives of the Muslim Institution. Initially it was presided over by the sultan, who later abdicated his position to his chief minister, the grand vezir. By the seventeenth century the latter was the virtual head of state. He was assisted by his fellow councillors: the *kapudan paşa* (navy commander), the Janissary Ağa, the *nişâncı* (chancellor), the *defterdâr* (treasurer), *cavuş başı* (grand steward), the *reîs efendi* (chief scribe), and by two *beylerbeyi*, who were originally responsible for Europe and Asia respectively. At a later time the number of *beylerbeyi* was increased in order to furnish governors-general for the larger provincial groupings. Their functions were both military and civilian. Under them were the *sancakbeyi* (provincial rulers), *alay beyi* (for counties), and the *subaşı* (town commanders). All of these latter officials enjoyed the same authority on their own levels as did the *beylerbeyi*. In wartime they commanded the "feudal" levies of *sipâhî*, i.e., the cavalry warrior class of landholders (*tımârlı*), who were provided with "benefices" (*tımâr*, "fief") in return for their military services. All of the territorial administrators had their own divans, replicas of Istanbul's with representatives of each of the central agencies. In wartime the whole system was mobilized, and all officials, regardless of level, accompanied the sultan and vezir into the field.[45]

In assessing the causes for the decay of Ottoman power—so this theory continues—one must also consider the purely human aspect, i.e., the characters and actions of the individual sultans. Whatever the underlying reasons—ethnic deterioration or a merely fortuitous succession of incompetents—they simply abdicated their responsibilities. Even Suleiman himself ceased to attend divan meetings. His successors delegated their authority completely to deputies who rose to their positions through favoritism rather than meritorious service. Withdrawing to the harem, the rulers retained only the right to appoint the highest officials in the hierarchy. In doing so they were generally influenced by their womenfolk, slaves and courtiers. Vezirs rarely had the opportunity to hold office long enough to carry out reform and were themselves able to obtain their position only by sycophancy and bribery. The resultant need for inordinate amounts of money forced them and their colleagues to require presents from those below, and the burden was passed on and on, finally to be borne by the ignorant peasant and the land itself. In short, the ultimate result of the Padishah's withdrawal from public affairs was the crumbling of the once effective bureaucracy, rampant maladministration, and peculation.[46] The armed forces of course were also involved in this process.[47]

In view of all this one may wonder where power lay in the Ottoman state. If the sultan was subject to the whims of his seraglio environment, it could hardly be said that the eunuchs and concubines were themselves a driving and directing force, for they were just as isolated from everyday life as was their master. Only the courtiers, the representatives of the now much altered Ruling Institution, had contact with the outside, and it appears that it was they who made tools of the sultans and vezirs. Normally they cooperated with the rest of their class as well as with the Ulema, keeping the sultan as a screen. On occasion they would expel him, and in time of danger they would permit a strong vezir to take over, as with the Köprülüs. The Ruling Institution had its internal quarrels but managed to close ranks against outside enemies. United on economic grounds with the Muslim Institution and the Phanariote Greeks,[48] it acted as a sort of society for a parasitic tapping of all available sources of national wealth. The lower class Muhammedans were provided certain fiscal crumbs in return for their support of the existing system. In wartime the Anatolian peasant's religious fervor was exploited, and he was tricked into fighting the battles of the rich capital city, into filling the rôle of the now useless slave army.[49]

Finally, the institutionalized exploitation viewpoint suggests why the Ottoman Empire managed to stave off dismemberment for so long. Part of the answer lies in the false presumption that the practice of bribery was all-pervasive. The existence of reformist writings indicates that there were at least some upright, thoughtful, and capable bureaucrats. The probability of the development of a kind of natural equilibrium in the process of exploitation supplies a second, equally significant explanation of Turkey's extended death-rattle.[50]

THE THEORY OF CLASS CONFLICT

A more recent interpretation of Turkish history stresses the "triumph of the *devşirme* class." Its basis is the theory and practice of Ottoman government and the Empire's peculiar social structure. The argument commences by defining the sultan's sovereignty: namely, the right to dispose of all sources of wealth. The task of exploitation was entrusted to subordinates, who organized state and society into units known as "muqata'as" ("leasings") —the most fundamental feature of the Turkish polity until the early nineteenth century. The muqata'as, in turn, were of three different types. The first were the timars, the revenues of which were assigned *in toto* to tenants as compensation for military and administrative services. The second were the "iltizams" (tax farms), the fruits of which were only partly retained by the holders, the remaining portion being sent on to the treasury. The third were "emanets," mostly urban properties, the full proceeds of which went to the Porte. The administration of all muqata'as was entrusted solely to slaves (*kul, kullar*), who enjoyed the same status as their master, the Padishah, and who thus constituted the ruling class, Ottomans (*Osmanlılar*), in the most genuine sense of the word.[51]

To be an "Ottoman" three basic attributes were necessary: a.) the dedication of one's life to the Sultan's service; b.) adherence to Islam; and c.) knowledge of the "Ottoman Way," a complicated system of customs, behavior and language ("high" Turkish). All other members of society were "rayah," the subject class—including anybody, even a Muslim or a Turk himself, who lacked any one of the three necessary qualities. Whether one was an Ottoman or a rayah, one had distinctive privileges and functions. The former's rôle was to administer and defend the Empire; everything else, including the production of wealth, was the responsibility of the latter. Each branch of society had its own internal structure. The *Osmanlılar* were split into four classes (imperial-dynastic, military, administrative and religious) and executed their functions within the framework of timars and iltizams. Human raw material came from three sources: birth (75%), recruitment (20%) of both Muslim and non-Muslim rayah (the latter via the *devşirme*), foreign slaves and converts (5%). The rayah were distinguished on religious grounds and constituted self-contained, autonomous communities known as "millets," ideally suited for exploitation by the "Ottomans."

Of particular importance to the whole Turkish politico-social system—and hence an essential feature of the *devşirme* triumph theory—was one particular region: the Balkans. In the first stages of Ottoman growth the Sultans attracted various Turkoman nomads and unemployed urban workers from neighboring Turkish states in Anatolia to serve as warriors in the campaigns on the other side of the Straits. This phenomenon, the so-called "Gâzi" tradition of loyalty, helps to explain why the Turks clung to their European domains after the seventeenth century when the latter had lost most of their financial and military value. Of even greater significance was the fact that the Balkans became deeply identified with the timar system. When the Ottomans were first expanding, booty supplied most of the needs of the fisc. What was really required for the work of conquest and administration was manpower. Central administration was at best embryonic and inefficient. The timar system and the profit motive seemed the most efficient means of supplying soldiers and officials. By the latter fifteenth and the sixteenth centuries things were different. A more effective governmental apparatus existed; it was now easier to exercise control over muqata'as. The *timârli*, heavy, feudal-type cavalry, no longer monopolized the battlefield. Infantry and other professional arms branches were becoming more essential. What was needed now was cash in order to pay for specialized services. New provinces added in the Near East were established as iltizams.

Nevertheless, the Balkan timars remained the foundation of political power. The people who had subdued the region for the Porte now constituted the aristocracy of the Turkish state. The bulk of the conquered land was parcelled out to them since it seemed expedient to provide fiefs far from Anatolia. Still, the numerous benefices acquired by certain families represented an accumulation of strength equal to that of the Imperial family itself, so the sultans were forced to cast about for means to preserve their own position. At first they employed indigenous (Christian) Balkan magnates as vassals, as counterweights to the ethnic Turkish nobility. In time, certain of these grandees became fully absorbed (yet still Christian) members of the ruling class. Initially left undisturbed as tributaries, once assimilated they came to hold fifty to sixty per cent of the timars. Yet the system failed to provide full security, and, as early as the reign of Mehmed I (1413–1421), it became necessary to seek another solution.

Two methods were used. First, the vassals became full-fledged Muslims; while sometimes allowed to keep their ancestral Balkan patrimonies, they were offered timars in western Anatolia. The second—eventually more fateful—method was the recruitment by the *devşirme* of a new caste of servitors from the non-Muslim millets. This technique provided a numerically broader and more reliable basis of support than that of the newly naturalized families. In pursuing this policy Istanbul halted the previous misrule of the Christian peasantry by the pre-Ottoman manorial overlords. Thus the tiller of the soil and the Church remained intact. Only with the gradual, Arab-stimulated *Ulema* fanaticism of the early seventeenth century did coercive measures become common. Only then was the Muslim millet raised in status and the "rayah" concept associated increasingly with Christianity. However, the *devşirme* system had previously spread among the non-Muslim millet, the result of which was the development of a second power class within the state. While ancient, the child-tax was applied extensively only after 1453. The body of dependable Imperial servitors thus created attained ever greater financial and military strength in the form of salaries and (at first) timars in the western Anatolian and Arab provinces. The old ethnic Turkish aristocracy naturally became resentful and opposed further expansion in the Balkans. The whole period 1453–1566 was characterized by a struggle between the two camps.

The newcomers won. The requirements of sixteenth century warfare—which the Turks recognized first—were the decisive factor. In the Balkans this development had three manifestations. In a strictly military sense, success over the Habsburgs was assured. In a political sense, the *devşirme* class and the specialized, professional soldiery of the Porte pursued common interests. The old, martially obsolescent aristocracy was no longer determinative (although still numerically predominant, as in 1683). The result was that from the early seventeenth century the *devşirme* class was supreme. Finally, in an administrative-economic sense, the timar system itself ceased to be a means of support for defense and government. Along with the decay of armored cavalry came a population increase and coinage inflation, as a consequence of which agriculture became more profitable. Increasingly, timars were assigned not for services but as support for the Christian-descended ruling element. The latter gained control of both the Sultan and the Empire through its monopoly in the Imperial and military classes while the old aristocracy held out passively in the administrative and religious categories. The sultans, puppets of the *devşirme* faction, permitted the latter to set up a new kind of muqata'a, the so-called "malikâne," virtually private property. Most Balkan fiefs were transformed into malikâne, milked for the benefit of their possessors. Admission to the ruling class became contingent upon the ability to intrigue, the effect of which was a decline in honesty and efficiency. The triumph of the Balkan component of the ruling class via the *devşirme* system thus constituted the rock upon which the whole Empire foundered.

To be sure, efforts to right matters—albeit in vain—were by no means lacking. They continued, in fact, from the middle of the seventeenth century until shortly before World War One. The work was carried on by two ethnic Turkish groups, the Muslim rayah of Anatolia and representatives of the old aristocracy who had managed to maintain their positions in the ruling class. Of the three main types of reform, only the first is of chronological relevance. Best designated as "traditionalist," it was propagated during the reigns of Murad IV (1623–1640), the Köprülü vezirs, and Selim III (1789–1807). Its proponents held that all that the Empire required was a return to the principles and practices of yore. Certain minor military innovations (e.g., flintlock muskets and hand grenades) were adopted, but, essentially, weaponry, tactics and strategy stayed as they had been in the era of grandeur. Old social and institutional systems were to be restored. The *devşirme* system would be retained, yet the aristocracy would be renewed and strengthened. The Christian and non-Christian millets would be preserved although the favored status of Muslim subjects would remain unchanged. Timars would be assigned only for service. The plan, however, was foredoomed. Its advocates did not realize that Europe had meanwhile developed techniques of socio-economic organization far superior to anything that the Ottomans had known at the peak of their glory. Thus, even had they been successful in their immediate objectives, they still would have lagged behind the West. They also could not grasp the fact that European institutions and Ottoman social forms were incompatible. Lastly, they were unable to perceive the potentialities of Balkan nationalism, which undercut even the policy of scrupulously restoring the millet.

FURTHER ALTERNATIVES

However persuasive the "*devşirme* triumph" theory, it may also be possible to identify other decay-producing factors. Thus, for example, one might ask whether economic-geographic relationships were not significant. The shift of commercial activity in the fifteenth and sixteenth centuries to the Atlantic seaboard, the rise of the maritime nations, and the subsequent decline of Germany and Venice are historical commonplaces. Certainly the Ottoman Empire was also affected, at least to some extent, by this development, and, what was more, the trade that remained was entirely in the hands of the non-Muslim millets and was not based so much upon indigenous productivity as upon Istanbul's function as an entrepôt. The Turks themselves had no commercial capitalism. Economically, they were like a nineteenth century European "sphere of influence" in China. Consequently, the technological lag between their civilization and the West's became progressively greater, making them dependent upon a few, imported foreign experts and upon French, English, and Dutch traders for whatever weapons and other equipment, including many luxuries, they might require.[52] It might even be that their own spiritual life suffered as a result of economic subservience. It has already been noted that the Turks contributed practically nothing of scientific or intellectual value to subject peoples as the Arabs had once been able to do—although, obviously, this is not to say that they were barbarians.[53] Conceivably, economic advance might have led to political growth and to the creation of an up-to-date bureaucracy. Yet even if this had been possible, it might only have been a palliative. The Turkish Empire, like Austria, was a multi-national and, to an even greater extent, multi-confessional political entity, in which a sense of community might never have been able to arise. The economically viable and administratively healthy Habsburg realm was itself eventually ground to dust in the mill of nationalism.

A further possible cause of Turkey's stagnation may well have been the essentially military nature of the state. More than one historian, starting with the seventeenth-century observer, Rycault, has noted that the country was healthy as long as its armies were successfully engaged, as long as the possibility of foreign conquest and pillage still existed; that it entered upon the downward path only after it had reached the physical limits of expansion or, conversely, until it encountered powers which possessed sufficient internal strength to defend themselves vigorously. A prominent American scholar has recently emphasized this view, stressing, among other things, the fact that the Ottoman army's radius of action was restricted to 90–100 days march (i.e., 700–800 miles) from Istanbul—a point especially applicable to the two Turkish sieges of Vienna (1529, 1683), a city about 820 air miles from the Bosporus.[54]

The same author has likewise considered the problem of the Ottoman Empire's slow death and, more specifically, its mid-seventeenth-century resuscitation, in which certain religious-ethnic developments played a rôle. Islam at that time appears to have had unusual attraction for non-Muslims. The decline of the strict Sunni orthodoxy of the first half of the century and the toleration of heterodoxy facilitated the conversion of Christians, above all in Albania. The adherence of large numbers, eventually the majority, of Shiptars to the faith of Muhammad was particularly significant because of their unique traditions of the friendship oath (*bera*) and loyalty to one's master. Whatever the reasons for the massive change in religious allegiance—the weakness of the local ecclesiastical hierarchy, Eastern-Orthodox-Roman Catholic rivalry and socio-economic advantages—, its effects upon the Porte were extensive. Albanians came to be regarded as singularly trustworthy servitors among the Turks and were granted positions of crucial importance, including, among other things, a monopoly upon bodyguard services. In one way or another the Köprülü revival was dependent upon the influx of this new blood—although the extent of the renewal was limited since the ploughing peasant was not affected and since basic social cleavages persisted.[55]

Whatever the causal interrelationships may have been, the greatness of the Ottoman Empire undoubtedly ended with the death of Suleiman the Magnificent. In the late seventeenth century some Western observers were able to perceive this; others were not. It depended, in part, upon the particular region in which the observations were made. Most of those who had direct contact with the court and government sniffed the odor of incipient decomposition. It is, however, certain that the overwhelming majority of the Turks themselves had little or no conception of what was occurring. They deported themselves toward the rest of the world just as arrogantly as they had done in the previous century.[56] All that one need do to confirm this is to glance at Turkish political affairs in the period 1648–1679, a time during which the virile Köprülü dynasty of vezirs made its appearance.

E. Ottoman Politics 1648–1679

The mid-century revival of the Ottoman Empire was immediately occasioned by continuing reversals in the twenty-five year struggle with Venice, beginning in 1646, over the possession of Candia (Crete). Sultan İbrahim IV (1640–1648) was so unlucky in his military endeavors that the Janissaries revolted and installed his ten year old son as Mehmed IV (1648–1687). However, the change did not bring about stability since various factions contended for power.

Mehmed Köprülü and His Sultan

Finally, in 1656, the competing cliques recognized the need to cease squabbling for a time and, almost as an act of desperation, permitted a capable statesman, Mehmed Köprülü, to assume leadership. The new septuagenarian Vezir was a rough and ready type of lowly Albanian origin, a self-taught reader who had begun his career as the cook of a *defterdâr* and worked his way up. His unusual abilities made him a prime candidate for the highest administrative office, but he was unwilling to take over unless his own uncompromising conditions were met. Negotiating with the *Valide,* he demanded and obtained the replacement of the Janissary Ağa, automatic imperial confirmation of all his decisions, full control over appointments, a monopoly in his rôle as imperial adviser, and immunity from backbiting and villification.[57] Astonishingly vigorous and of unrelenting will, he proceeded to work with a sanguinary vengeance. Embezzling officials and judges, mutinous Janissaries and *Sipâhî,* disobedient governors were brought to heel, while too successful colleagues perished. Mehmed, actually more a regent than a vezir, realized the urgency of fiscal reform. Numerous confiscations and the near miraculous, albeit only temporary restriction of court expenditures helped him to attain this goal. The nation's borders and the Dardanelles were buttressed with new fortresses.[58] The insubordinate Christian satellite states of Moldavia and Wallachia were disciplined, although the operation had to be repeated by other, later vezirs.[59] The punishment of George Rákóczy's Transylvania will also be recalled.[60] Such was Mehmed's success that he was able to secure the succession of his son, Ahmed, before his death in 1661. The by-now-adult Sultan had come to worship his first minister and declared to the old man upon the latter's deathbed that he would willingly give ten years of his own life in order to gain him a reprieve. It was a tragedy for Turkey that its sovereign was unable to follow most of the Vezir's supposed last advice: viz., to pay no heed to the women of the harem, to keep the treasury filled even at the cost of oppressing his subjects, and to see that the army was always occupied.[61]

Mehmed IV's regret over the Grand Vezir's passing was hardly a manifestation of love and devotion. It is likely that the Sultan's reverence stemmed from the fact that Köprülü had relieved him from the job of governing the Empire, a task he could hardly have accomplished by himself. The dead man's administration had given the red-bearded, olive-skinned, intelligent but phlegmatic Padishah the liberty to indulge in those pastimes that had become almost automatically associated with his office since the long-gone days of the great Suleiman. It is said that the ruler's first amatory tastes were homosexual. However, his mother, a bright and politically-experienced woman, allegedly diverted his interests into more customary channels by providing him with select "Circassians," especially beautiful slave-concubines:[62]

> The Grand Seigneur maintains among his servitors 2000 female slaves, and . . . he frequently bends them to his will since he is much inclined to carnality. Besides the Sultana, he has four other women, called Hashis [*Kadin, "lady"*] who, by protocol, are allowed a court of their own and are supported in special, separate seraglios. . . . When he succumbs to lasciviousness and wishes to choose some woman for his distraction from among the Empress' or the *Valide's* ladies-in-waiting, he invites either the one or the other to come and pluck blossoms during the month of May, the flower season. He then observes and decides which lady pleases him best. Thereupon he commands the Kish Agha [*Kizlarağaşi*], the steward of the womenfolk, to procure him the same. But this is a task that is not easily accomplished. In order not to arouse any jealousy on the part of his spouse, toward whom he always shows some respect, he invites the favored person to some other merry place.[63]

Of course, the Harem was a very costly institution, the more so since favorite concubines, when promoted to *odalisques,* expected expensive gifts. Often such a mistress would quarrel with the Sultana, and then both parties had to be placated with sumptuous presents.[64]

Even more memorable than sexual debauchery, the harm of which was thought to be apparent in the Sultan's weak eyes and legs, was his mania for slaughtering animals. In Turkish his name bears the epithet "the Hunter."[65] Leopold was a rank amateur in comparison. Hammer, the great Western chronicler of Turkish history, mentions as a typical example a drive requiring the services of 30,000 men and the population of fifteen judicial districts, which resulted in the death of thirty persons, but which yielded only a negligible quantity of game.[66] No less vicious a flaw was the ruler's greed for cash. He stubbornly refused to make meaningful contributions to the campaign in Crete and hoarded his private reserves in the Seraglio.[67] Ahmed Köprülü quickly learned that the only way to keep his master pacified and manageable was to pour money into his coffers.[68]

AHMED KÖPRÜLÜ

The second Köprülü, while only a shade less able than his sire, had an entirely different personality. A carefully educated, cultured gentleman, an exemplary "Osmanli," he neither required the Draconian means of Mehmed, nor did his character incline to them. To be sure, he was every bit as upright and incorruptible as his father. He ruled by wits rather than by brawn, skillfully manipulating the individuals and parties confronting him. His greatest single problem seems to have been the management of an increasingly depraved master. Mehmed IV was soon treating his country's most indispensable servant like a despised swineherd, denouncing him to his face with the vilest Islamic insults, hurling epistolary threats after him when he was in the field, and denying him the favor of his own elevated presence for months on end. The Sultan's psychotic comportment, in such striking contrast to his adoration of the first Köprülü, forced Ahmed to provide an ever growing stream of costly gifts, male and female paramours, fresh victories, and newly-conquered provinces. He was driven to condone a series of executions ordained by the ruler in order that the latter might enrich himself.

Nevertheless, the Vezir's adroit fingers held the government in tight rein. The very weaknesses of the Padishah made him as dependent upon the younger Köprülü as he had been upon the elder. Though he might threaten the Vezir's life during inebriated orgies, he and his court flunkies were perceptive enough to realize that they could not survive without Ahmed. Moreover, the chief minister, whose own material demands were relatively modest, continued to direct the requisite subsidies into the Sultan's chests. The raising of money, also necessary for aggressive foreign enterprises, forced him to employ all his ingenuity. The coinage was debased. Gold and silver *objets d'art,* gifts extorted from foreign diplomats, were melted down. Confiscations multiplied. Recently appointed administrators were deposed in order to obtain the presents of new nominees. Customs revenues were pawned. Foreign vessels and goods as well as local building lots were expropriated. Patriarchs were shaken down, and the mutual hatred of Catholics and Orthodox (on Chios and in Jerusalem) was exploited financially.[69] In the long run much of the reform work of Mehmed was negated. Moreover, Ahmed's never robust health eventually suffered, and he too is said to have begun to pay his respects to wine and Polish brandy.[70]

As viewed from abroad, however, the Turkish state seemed imposing and fearful. Its pugnacity awakened an impression of great strength. Ahmed's vezirate both commenced and ended in the midst of war. Almost certainly the first minister could have followed no other policy. Not only did he need such adventures because of the Grand Seigneur but he also recognized the wisdom of his father's last advice. While the 1663–64 Hungarian War was somewhat frustrating, the long Cretan campaign was brought to a successful conclusion in 1669–1670. The Polish War of 1672–1676 was not overwhelmingly victorious but still bore satisfying fruits. Shortly before its end, however, Ahmed's overtaxed body finally yielded up its spirit. The second Köprülü had succeeded in presenting a formidable front to the world, but, as he himself lucidly saw,[71] his triumphs constituted the last major gains which the Empire was capable of making. Its armies, its obsolescent economy, and its overburdened fiscal structure had reached the limit of elasticity. Erstwhile enemies, the new King of Poland, the still potent oligarchs of Venice, even the Francophobic Leopold, might feel momentarily impelled to uphold the peace, but their forces had kept to the field. If the new Pope, Innocent XI, an ardent crusader, should ever be given the opportunity of bringing these men together, their combined resources would surpass Turkish powers of resistance.

FRANCE AND THE PORTE

One aspect of the period 1648–1679 which deserves special consideration is the relationship to France, for the Most Christian King promoted a diplomatic policy toward Turkey deliberately intended to provoke anti-Habsburg undertakings. To be sure, Louis XIV's goals in the Near East were not at once clear: they unfolded only gradually. At the very beginning of his personal rule (1661) he reaffirmed the policy of Mazarin who had been cool toward the Turks without actually breaking with them. However, relations soon deteriorated a step further and remained strained for almost a decade. This was a natural consequence of the French strategy of subtly penetrating into Germany and Poland, of attempting diplomatically to weaken and discredit the Habsburg position. Open friendship with the Infidel could hardly have been reconciled with the chivalrous image the King was attempting to project. Louis' help to Leopold during the 1664 campaign has already been noted.[72] These years saw a marked revival of crusading zeal in France itself. Church leaders such as Bossuet publicly urged assistance for the Venetian forces on Crete, stating that such aid was a Christian duty. The stream of French volunteers included veterans of Szentgotthárd.[73] The relationship to Turkey could hardly be cordial.

At the same time, however, there was an undercurrent, of which Colbert was the chief representative. His commercial plans included the Levant trade. He foresaw an outlet for French textiles in Turkey and regarded Istanbul as the gateway to other markets, to the Red Sea and the coffee of Arabia.[74] While these efforts took second place, they were not without influence, even in the 1660's. In addition, the new, stiff French attitude toward the Porte brought some unexpected benefit in the Turkish capital itself. A mission was sent to Paris to seek the reasons for Gallic hostility and to express a desire for amity. The French could now see that a policy of friendship based on appeasement should be dropped. The arrogance and greed of Turkish potentates which had long made the lives of foreign ambassadors miserable could be overcome only with similar weapons. The King's representatives now began to show more self-assurance while the Turks began to worry about French strength and their own misdeeds. Admiral Duquesne's Mediterranean squadron was a potent argument, and the smarter Turks, aware of their country's own naval weakness, could see the advantages of French good will while they were struggling against other enemies. The royal diplomats made a point of describing their nation's power and scaring Turkish ministers. The seemingly ridiculous quarrel over the sofa (1677) can only be understood in this light. Louis persistently demanded his rights in the matter, and although the squabble extended over a long time, he eventually won.[75] However, he felt his way cautiously, realizing how difficult it was, psychologically, for the Turks to grant concessions. He threatened but never pushed matters to the point of rupture, not wishing thereby to do his own enemies a favor.[76]

In 1669 a new French ambassador, Nointel, arrived in Istanbul. In view of the still existing frictions, the task facing him was anything but easy. Nevertheless, by 1673 he succeeded in hammering out a commercial pact by which France gained a great deal. This year emerged as a significant dividing line in the history of the relations between the two nations for other reasons as well. For the first time diplomatic intercourse really became intense. Both sides had just initiated large scale military operations, the Turks in Poland and the French along the Rhine. It was something like the age of Francis I and Charles V except that Gaul now had its Louis while Turkey lacked a Suleiman. Nointel was particularly concerned with Poland and Hungary, for his master desired to see the Turko-Polish conflict ended in order that France might incite the Ottomans to attack Leopold's exposed rear. The conspirators (now executed) had already attempted to interest the Turks in Magyar affairs, but at the time Ahmed was too busy in Crete. Although the Polish War forced him to limit the aid of his Transylvanian vassals to the Kuroczok, before his death he had begun to consider Nointel's suggestions of intervention. Louis, on the other hand, was unwilling to accept the Turkish precondition of a no-separate-peace agreement. The French monarch may not have desired to circumscribe his radius of action, and he was certainly wise enough not to put his name to a formal document of alliance with the enemy of the Cross. He evidently felt strong enough to end the Dutch War by himself.[77]

In the meantime, however, Ahmed's protégé and heir-apparent, Kara Mustafa, had begun to evince independent interest in the ambassador's scheme. Although the Russian War (1677–1681) and the unpleasant sofa incident stood in the way of Franco-Turkish coöperation and amity during the first years of his rule, the new Grand Vezir continued to harbor secret designs of aggression against Central Europe. Tension notwithstanding, Nointel persisted in his endeavor to stir up the Turks. The Austrian representative, Kinsberg, having learned of these efforts, informed Leopold, although neither man was apparently aware of the true extent of Kara Mustafa's interest.[78] The Viennese envoy strove to exacerbate the strained relations between Istanbul and Paris by spreading the reports of Béthune's ambitions in Hungary and did succeed in embarrassing the French. The Turks continued to give the Malcontents little more than sympathy. It was also to the Austrians' advantage that the Sultan was personally opposed to another anti-Habsburg venture. The Grand Vezir, forced to bide his time and wishing to lull suspicions, gave Leopold positive assurance of peaceful intentions. Louis, for his part, laid much less stress on Turkey during the last several years of Nointel's assignment. He was fairly successful in his Western military operations and lacked the money to subsidize the Turks even if they should agree to intervene without the guarantee of an alliance. In 1679 Nointel was recalled and replaced by Guilleragues, whose appointment turned out to be no less a change of persons than of system.[79]

F. Kara Mustafa

The most important development in the Ottoman Empire during the 1670's was Kara Mustafa's gradual rise to prominence, for if Imre Thököly was to become the Hungarian protagonist in the crisis of 1683, the new Grand Vezir was to carry out an analogous rôle along the Bosporus. The interests and ambitions of the Magyar magnate and the Sultan's chief executive pointed in the same direction and would eventually coincide. If the former's overtures to the Porte in 1679 brought no positive results, it was only because they were premature. The idea of coöperation and association for the purpose of depriving the Habsburger

(Vienna, Municipal Historical Museum; taken from tomb in Belgrade in 1688 by the Society of Jesus and presented to Cardinal Kollonitsch; authenticated by *Oberrat* Dr. Walter Hummelberger.)

The Skull of Kara Mustafa

of part or all of his dynastic patrimony was planted firmly in the heads of both the rebel captain and the Turkish potentate.

EARLY CAREER AND CHARACTER

The origins of the leader who was willing to risk an enterprise that had proved too much even for the Ottoman state of Suleiman's day are not clear, although they appear to have been modest in any case. According to Giambattista Donado, a Venetian *bailo* (ambassador) in Istanbul, he was the offspring of a fruit peddler from a humble village in Asia Minor.[80] Another account makes him the son of a respected *sipâhî* from Merzifun and gives his birth date as July 27, 1634.[81] The two stories also differ regarding the circumstances of his rise to power and influence, the one being as romantic as a tale from classical Arabic literature and the other prosaic and more probable sounding. Donado relates that the future Grand Vezir accepted, purely by chance, some menial job in the household of Mehmed Köprülü. Supposedly the rustic youth attracted notice by his willingness, adaptability, strength, perseverence, and decisiveness. Thus he eventually came to the personal attention of his employer, who gave him increasingly important tasks and furthered his career. The second version of his childhood depicts his father as an old acquaintance of Mehmed, who more or less adopted the boy and raised him alongside his own son, Ahmed. In either case, the education that Kara Mustafa received cannot have been very thorough since he did not learn to read and write until well into adulthood. His influence with the Padishah developed from an early recognition of the latter's venality. The ambitious courtling deliberately sacrificed his rather meager resources in order to buy the gifts necessary for insinuating his way into the Imperial good graces. Preferential treatment and promotion rapidly followed. When Ahmed succeeded his father, Kara Mustafa became Kaimakan, i.e., second in command. The services that he performed during the conquest of Kamenets capped his rise to favor with the Grand Seigneur.[82]

Outwardly, the heir-apparent made a very decent impression. He was described as handsome, dignified, affable, humane, and punctilious in the performance of religious obligations. All the Venetian ambassadors mention his dedication to work and his self-exposure in battle in order to inspire the troops. He seems to have been filled with the characteristic Turkish sense of kismet *(forza del destino)*, and he was not at all avid for popular acclaim. Inwardly, however, his character was as black as his name. Several *baili,* using similar terminology, stress the darkness of his thoughts *(cupo ne' suoi pensieri)*. His customary tactics were those of dissimulation and deceit, although on occasion he was prideful, cocksure, and arrogant. The slightest opposition might cause him to burst into uncontrolled rage. Possessing neither of the virtues for which his friend Ahmed was praised—selflessness and a sense of justice—, he shared both of his predecessor's faults: a weakness for brandy (since burned water was not prohibited by the *qurân*) and a phenomenal appetite for the pleasures of the harem.[83] He may also have been bisexual. Ambassador Morosini says: ". . . tracannata di notte tempo con alcuni de' più favoriti, allora sciogliendo appunto la briglia alle più dannate libidini, e frammischiando l'un con l'altro, con abbominevole sensualità."[84]

Such reports lead one to infer a disturbed personality. Another indication of mental illness might be the Grand Vezir's unreasoningly intense hatred of Christians. (He himself was reputed to be an atheist.) His prejudice manifested itself in extreme physical cruelty. In 1674, accompanied by the Cossack Hetman, Doroshenko, he conquered the Polish city of Human. The captured Christians were flayed alive, and their hides, stuffed like prize game, were sent off to the Sultan as trophies.[85] The siege of Vienna later provided further opportunity for this striking blood lust.

Morosini's view that he was born to be a scourge of the nations seemed completely justified. His fearful reputation spread in advance throughout Europe, and terrifying tales circulated about his intentions. "His heart can be said to be a forge in which designs of aggression and extermination are being hammered out." Kara Mustafa's inhumanity, however, was no more noteworthy than his corruptibility and avarice, which apparently were equalled only by the Padishah himself. The blackmailing methods employed by the late Ahmed not only continued but their frequency was redoubled.[86]

OBJECTIVES

Despite the unanimity of the character portraits sketched by the Venetians, the Grand Vezir remains something of a puzzle. He was apparently not a mere wastrel like Mehmed IV. The one thing which is entirely clear is his desperate need for money. The Venetian *bailo*, Civrano, is explicit in this regard. According to him, the Sultan's first minister, "aggitato dall' emulatione de suoi competitori," became covetous simply to remain in the good graces of Mehmed IV. Foreseeing his own ruin in the jealous indolence of the court, the semi-literate Anatolian upstart hit upon the idea of persuading the Grand Seigneur to undertake a second war in Hungary.[87] Civrano remarks elsewhere that Kara Mustafa spent two thirds of his time tending political fences.[88] The ineluctable military expeditions imposed further strains upon the government's fiscal resources. Imported cannon and the new flintlock muskets, the services of French and Italian engineers and specialists, foundries and factories at Istanbul could not be had on credit. The Grand Vezir likewise permitted himself a great degree of luxury, although Civrano tells us that the reason was basically political: namely, the necessity of representation. Other contemporary sources claim that Kara Mustafa strove to take Vienna intact, by means of a capitulation rather than by a general storm (in which the troops would have enjoyed the right of plunder), because he lusted after the treasures which he believed to be stored in the city.[89] It was further held that he intended to carve out a realm of his own in the West.[90] Be this as it may, there is reason to believe that he sought a victory against Austria at least in order to achieve personal autonomy.[91] In short, it is probable that he was less interested in riches for their own sake than in the exercise, maintenance, and extension of power.[92] To be sure, like his predecessor, he was also a victim of his degenerate master and the whole contemporary system of government.

As determined as Kara Mustafa was, there were others in Europe of commensurate will. To attain his ends he would have to pit his strength against tough-minded men in several quarters of the Continent. Sobieski was not the only human obstacle in the Grand Vezir's path; and the Poles were not the only nation aware of the threat of Turkish conquest. The leaders of Christendom in the Mediterranean world also had their guards up. In fact, the Latin peoples had been facing an aggressive Islam much longer than the plain dwellers. Their story, too, is part of the background to 1683.

CHAPTER THREE

Southern and Western Europe

A. The Mediterranean World

VENICE

Apart from Austria and Poland, the only other major power in Christendom's front line of defense against Islam was Venice—at least in those intervals when it was impossible to trade with the Porte. To be sure, it is questionable whether the term "major power" should still be applied to the Most Serene Republic. The forces which it could muster during the *Settecento* were far less formidable than in past ages, especially when compared with the rapidly growing, technologically progressing navies of Europe's western seaboard. The main reason for this lag was certainly the Venetian state's relatively dormant economy. A crisis was evident even at the beginning of the century. The great shift in the geographic orientation of world commerce is often cited as the cause of the decline, but it may be that the changed mental outlook of the nobility, surfeited with money-making activities, and of the burghers, also less venturesome, was equally important. In any case, the bare fact was that Venetian businessmen, faced by the mercantilistic policies of the big powers, increasingly vigorous competition in the Ottoman marketplace, and dwindling purchases from old customers in Central Europe, retreated more and more into the Adriatic, which they could still call their own politically and economically. (The remaining share of the Istanbul trade should not be discounted, however.) The Signoria was non-plussed and vacillated between liberal and protectionist tactics. The most critical development, apparent by the end of the century, was the victory of foreign manufactures, especially French, over indigenous products. Only too late did Venice's leaders realize that it had been a mistake to devote most of their attention to wholesaling rather than to industry. The error was compounded by a somewhat neglectful agrarian policy.[1]

While the economy malfunctioned, social life remained brilliant, in fact became even more lustrous. It was the age of the cavalier par excellence. The attraction of Venetian society kept the city a world capital where pleasure-seeking aristocrats and bourgeois from all of Europe convened, especially at Carnival time. Austrian generals, seeking recreation and distraction after the arduous summer campaigns in Hungary, betook themselves to the beckoning fleshpots of the Grand Canal.[2]

The city's styles and manners set the pace for much of the Continent, above all for the Imperial Court. One particular feature of Venice's fame was its womenhood, renowned both for charm and intellect. The men, especially the juveniles (reputedly the world's most impudent), were distinguished by combativeness, disorderliness, and even criminality. The addiction to duelling was endemic.[3] Of course, from time to time there was opportunity for converting the inclination to violence into deeds of heroism. The War of the Holy League (1684–1699) would once again witness the departure of the small, swift galliots and the cumbersome, artillery-laden galleasses to do battle in the Aegean, thus absorbing Turkish resources that might otherwise have been employed in the Pannonian Basin.

THE PAPACY

The only other power in politically splintered Italy which shared Venice's concern over the Turkish problem to any appreciable extent was the Papacy. However, since it was a monarchically-governed state, the degree of its involvement depended primarily upon the character and ideals of the incumbent pope, who might or might not be moved by the ancient vision of Urban II. Mostly, the rulers of the Church during the seventeenth century, especially after 1644, did not supply strong leadership, and nepotism was again rampant. Historians consider the period one of marked weakness. There are, nonetheless, several exceptions to the rule. The most important one occurred at the same moment that the Ottoman danger was again beginning to rise on the Eastern horizon.

Benedetto Odescalchi (1611–1689), otherwise known as Innocent XI, is in fact the only pope of the 1600's for whom greatness in any sense of the word can be claimed. His qualities were sufficiently admirable to win him approbation even from Protestants,[4] a distinction otherwise reserved for his twentieth century successors. He also stands out because of the contrast to another, better-known contemporary, Louis XIV. His pontificate is, indeed, marked principally by efforts to countervail the Sun King's maneuvers, both in the ecclesiastical affairs of France and in international politics.

Innocent's background as the offspring of a venerable landowning and banking family of Como with a long tradition of service to the Church predestined him to a priestly vocation. His faith was profoundly militant and imperialistic. According to one apocryphal but figuratively apt account, he began his adult life by travelling to Poland in order to share in the local anti-Turkish struggle.[5] His crusading attitude was not fashionable among all contemporaries. Louis XIV was later to remark: "Je ne vous dis rien sur les projets d'une guerre sainte; mais vous savez qu'ils sont cessé d'être à la mode depuis Saint Louis."[6]

Another more plausible version of the Pope's early life has him arriving in Rome in 1636, dagger and pistol in hand, ready to fight wherever the Curia might wish.[7] The Spanish cardinal, Cueva, who became the young man's patron, nevertheless persuaded him to study law, and he earned a doctorate at Naples. While there, he fell under the influence of two Capuchins (for which order he subsequently manifested special trust), and took Holy Orders. His skill in establishing highly-placed connections, his devotion to hard work, and his sincere piety enabled him to mount the hierarchical ladder rapidly. By 1645 he was a cardinal. Assigned to diocesan administration in Ferrara and Novara, he revealed other sides of his character: generosity toward the poor; zeal for the reform of clerical life and morals; and an unwarranted scrupulosity in making ecclesiastical appointments, the unfortunate result of which was overly-long vacancies.[8]

After 1656 he resided inconspicuously in Rome, attracting public attention only by charitable acts on the occasion of public disaster. In the Sacred College he served as Cardinal Protector of Poland, to which nation he also made pecuniary contributions from private resources. A neutral in Curial politicking between French and Spanish factions, he nevertheless condemned French encroachments upon Church prerogatives. His only concern was for the welfare of Christianity as a whole. His stand earned him Louis' personal veto in the conclave of 1669, but by 1676, the year of his elevation, the French sovereign had changed his mind,[9] presumably because a neutral appeared preferable to the four previous, pro-Spanish pontiffs. The new pope carried on the same personal existence as before. Even more retiring as the years passed, in part because of physical infirmity, he passed long hours at work and in prayer, isolated in his Spartanically-furnished quarters and parsimoniously garbed in the ill-fitting vestments of his predecessors:

> His very exterior, his tall spare figure and stern features reveal the ascetic. Numerous busts perpetuate his strongly marked features, the lofty forehead, the aquiline nose, the prominent chin. In conformity with custom he grew a beard and moustaches. His bearing and expression were always dignified and grave, even on joyous occasions; his mood was often melancholy.[10]

Deliberately confining himself, lacking the broadening experience of foreign travel, he could not realistically interpret international affairs or appraise men's characters. He was poorly-trained in theology; his intellectual attainments were primarily legal, useful principally in defending his strong convictions of the Church's rôle *vis-à-vis* the state. Since he was elected upon a reform platform, even the slightest degree of simony and nepotism was intolerable. His own nephew was put off with the barest pittance, and the poor man's name became a by-word among Romans for bad luck. A stickler for equitable administrative practices, Innocent detracted from his popularity by attempting to enforce sumptuary legisla-

(Vienna, National Library)

Father Marco d'Aviano

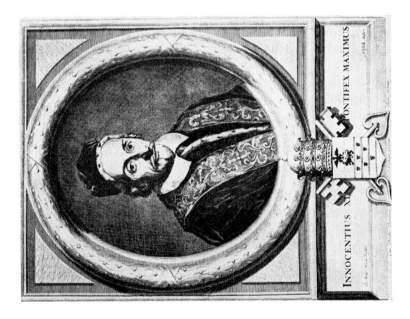

Pope Innocent XI

tion.[11] Apparently Roman society has always resisted efforts to restrain its *dolce vita.*

The Holy Father concentrated on curing evils in the exchequer. The abolition of nepotism was one aspect although every other conceivable means of saving money was also employed. The purpose was not merely to eliminate the chronic budgetary deficits that had brought the See of Peter to the edge of bankruptcy[12] but also to build up surpluses, to create a war chest for the project closest to Innocent's heart: namely, the reconciliation and unification of the major Christian powers for a new Crusade against Islam.[13] Superficially the Pope's goal may seem inappropriate to the diffuse *Zeitgeist* of the High Baroque;[14] it was more Gothic than Early Modern. Still, Innocent's ideals were shared by some of his contemporaries, both laity and clergy. The response of Europe to the events of 1683 in the following War of the Holy League demonstrates this. Surely the pontiff's ultimate success would have been inconceivable if he had not had the enthusiastic support of ecclesiastical colleagues. Among a score of prelates, *patres* and priests there are two names that merit mention.

Papal Helpers

Francesco Bunovisi (b. 1626), descended from a distinguished family of Lucca with traditions of churchly service like the Odescalchi, was perhaps the most persistent of the Pope's lieutenants in the field. A professional diplomat, he saw service in both France and Germany. His experience as nunzio at Cologne at the start of Dutch War (1672–1678) left him perturbed, for he had already recognized the possibilities of a united Christian undertaking against the Turks. From 1673–1675 he was stationed in Warsaw where he was again bothered by dissension among Christians but where he also established good relations with Sobieski. In 1675 Buonvisi was sent to Vienna, in which place his tireless devotion to the crusade was to bring him a small but significant measure of greatness—though this fact was scarcely recognized in his own day.[15]

The position of a great evangelist and wonder worker, unlike the secretive work of a diplomat, brings immediate attention. Father Marco d'Aviano (1631–1699), second only to Abraham à Sancta Clara as a master of the art of the pulpit, enjoyed such fame, albeit unwillingly. The man who was to function as a kind of papal unguent for the wounded feelings of Emperor Leopold and Sobieski was born near Pordenone in Friulia of a bourgeois family. Educated by the Jesuits, he too was stirred to action as a youth by the spectre of Islam. At seventeen he attempted to run off to Turkey to convert the heathen. He had to settle instead for membership in the Capuchin order, the ideals of which (poverty and eagerness to save souls) corresponded most closely to his own. Ordained in 1665, he accepted various administrative jobs, ostensibly with reluctance. While he professed a hot desire to convert the sinful and disbelieving, he also claimed to distrust the world and all its works. In later years he often spoke of his yearning for the solitary, contemplative life. His reputation as a preacher and a holy man grew rapidly in his homeland. He was brilliantly successful in popularizing abstruse dogma. He was thought to possess charismatic qualities and was subsequently able to preach in Italian to German-speaking congregations and still transfix his hearers. With his emaciated frame, pale face, sunken, burning eyes, beard, bushy eyebrows, tonsured pate, and prominent, jutting nose, he was the archetypical ascetic.[16]

There is considerable evidence of his success as a faith healer. By 1680 foreign princes were requesting that he visit their lands. Charles of Lorraine was soon his client. The Duke is said to have been cured of near-mortal illness by the Capuchin and his wife to have been enabled to conceive. Marco's visit to the hyper-religious Tyrolese became a triumph. He converted prominent Protestants, thus earning a harvest of denunciation from ministerial pamphleteers. By 1682, on the occasion of his second visit at court, he had become the Emperor's closest spiritual confidant.[17] The ascendency which the Italian padre held over Leopold's soul was exercised with responsibility, in the service of the Pope's goals and to the ultimate benefit of the House of Habsburg's own interests.

SPAIN AND ITS AMBASSADOR

The third Christian state of the Mediterranean that still possessed even a modicum of importance in international affairs was Spain. Moreover, while the traditional links between Madrid and Vienna were somewhat more tenuous than in previous decades, relations between the two branches of the Archhouse continued to be more or less intimate. Although the story of Hispanic decline is well-known, several aspects of the country's history in the latter seventeenth century require comment. The first, and certainly the most obvious feature was the problem of succession to the throne after the expected extinction of the indigenous Habsburg line. The disposal of the far-flung, still valuable Spanish domains affected, in one way or another, just about every political enterprise of the era. A closely related matter was the policy of the Spanish government, which did not view with equanimity the prospect of outsiders partitioning the Kingdom.

As a result of the impotence (figurative) of Charles II (1665–1700), the management of government lay almost entirely with the Council of State (*Consejo del Estado*), which exercised as much authority as did the Council of Ten in Venice. (While occasionally some *valido* (favorite) would gain credit, he would inevitably fall and power would again revert to the *Consejo*.) The King, while not unconscientious, was content to leave all business to his ministers and granted himself fewer prerogatives than many a later constitutional monarch was to enjoy. With respect to foreign affairs, Spanish agents abroad, while addressing their letters formally to His Catholic Majesty, in effect reported directly to the ruling body, which debated the subject under consideration and sent back, again in the sovereign's name, instructions in keeping with the opinion of the majority. At the time of the second Ottoman siege of Vienna the Council was once again entrusted with the affairs of the Realm. For more than two years after the death (1679) of the disappointing Don Juan José, the Duke of Medinaceli had been supreme. In 1682, however, the Duke found it necessary to yield his monopoly to other prominent courtlings although he did succeed in maintaining himself in the office of chief minister for another three years.

The main difficulty which the almost wholly incompetent councillors faced was financial. Unsuccessful efforts to improve economic conditions—there do appear to have been a few bright spots on the commercial horizon of the time—brought about a loss of prestige and effectiveness. Petty jealousies and intrigues worsened matters. It appears that, everything considered, the state reached its absolute fiscal nadir during this period. Only with Medinaceli's final disgrace and his replacement by the Conde de Oropesa, who pared expenditures and brought about certain reforms in the corrupt administration, was there some improvement. From all this it is quite apparent that the Spanish Habsburgs were in no position to render meaningful aid to their German cousins at the hour of Vienna's great trial.[18]

On the other hand, it would be erroneous to conclude that the Spanish rôle in the affairs of 1683 was negligible. The country's territorial interests in Western Europe—the preservation of sovereignty over Milan and the Southern Netherlands, the hope of recovering Franche Comté—caused the Council to press vigorous diplomatic efforts against Louis XIV, who seemed to represent a much greater threat to state security than the geographically remote Turks. An essential feature was to encourage Austria to make peace with the Magyar rebels and to do all that it could to renew the truce of Vasvár with the Porte. For this purpose, in March 1681, Madrid despatched to Vienna the best horse from its bureaucratic stable, Carlo Emmanuele d'Este, Marchese di Borgomanero (Don Carlos de Este, Marquès de Burgomayne) , Chevalier of the Order of the Golden Fleece, Royal War Councillor, Fieldmaster General of the Armies, former Governor and Captain General of Burgundy and Charlois, and, two years prior to his death, Grandee of the Realm. Borgomanero, (1622–1695) , to whose consummate abilities numerous contemporary accounts attest, was destined to acquire a strong voice in the Emperor's counsels and to function in a manner prejudicial to Leopold's immediate well-being. Conversely, the Marchese's warm sponsorship in August, 1683, of a penniless, young refugee—Eugene of Savoy—was to assure the Italo-Spanish nobleman a secure, if still little-known place in the history of an heroic era. Unfortunately, documentary evidence about the life of Spain's Viennese ambassador is too sparse for sketching a personality portrait.[19]

B. The France of Louis XIV

Perhaps the most enduring mental picture carried away by the student of history from the latter seventeenth century is that of the stately Sun King attended punctiliously by a host of courtiers at regular matutinal and nocturnal rites, the *lever* and the *coucher*. While the image is a little hackneyed, it retains some utility as a symbol. Certainly there are few judgments about history which remain as uncontested as the view that France was preponderant in Europe during the Age of Louis XIV. The most successful, and probably the finest general study published in France during recent years uses an analogous phrase as its title.[20] Of course the concept is by no means novel. The greater political authority and the cultural preeminence of France are so apparent from contemporary records that comparable terminology was used sixty and more years ago.[21] Although individual authors may choose somewhat variant chronological schemes or may express certain qualifications, the basic fact that France enjoyed more power than any other single nation and as much as all others combined—*nec pluribus impar*—can scarcely be doubted.

THE ROYAL ENIGMA

France's monarch was of course not only an abstract token of the nation's might. He incorporated the latter tangibly and exercised it willfully and purposefully. Thus he naturally became the main protagonist in the international affairs of his time. His figure has, moreover, particular pertinence for the siege of Vienna since there is evidence to indicate that he provided the final impulse that set the Turkish juggernaut rolling. Unfortunately, there is less scholarly accord over other aspects of Louis XIV's person and reign. His motivations, his foreign policy goals, his character, and his aptitude as a ruler all remain controversial.

Fatherless at six years of age, the King attained manhood under the patriarchal authority of Cardinal Mazarin. This secular-minded prelate proved a capable guardian of the nation's welfare under difficult circumstances. Nor did the Cardinal neglect the statesmanly education of his royal charge who learned from him, *inter alia*, the Italian style of politics, "habits of dissimulation" that were to characterize Louis until his death.[22] Whether the young sovereign really chafed excessively under the Churchman's benevolent "yoke," as St. Simon suggests, or not, by the time of Mazarin's death (1661) he had made up his mind to rule the country in fact as well as in theory. Never again did he suffer the existence of a first minister. Moreover, at the beginning of his reign the articulate segment of the population seems to have accepted willingly, perhaps even enthusiastically, the King's decision. It has been suggested that there was, for a decade at least, a correlation of sorts between the royal concept of government and the essential traits of the intellectual environment: harmony, balance, authority.[23]

What Louis was actually aiming for in his four wars and in countless other conspiratorial gambits in every part of Europe is difficult to know. Many observers of the day and later writers believed that he sought nothing less than the priceless crown of the Holy Roman Empire, the symbol of universal rule.[24] Other works emphasize the drive to the Rhine and the achievement of "natural" frontiers, a logical enough deduction under the given historical-geographic conditions, but a project nowhere directly attributable to the monarch himself. St. Simon simply speaks of his "weakness rather than . . . his taste for *la gloire.*"[25] In other words, the monarch's actions stemmed from a desire to achieve fame by realizing the potentialities of his person and station and his country's resources. This interpretation has its adherents even today.[26] Still other modern historians, while not rejecting St. Simon entirely, would likely emphasize, especially for the latter part of the reign, the King's specific goal of capturing the Spanish inheritance.

Well-proportioned, hardy of body, unaffected by inclement weather, a skilled horseman, dignified and commanding in appearance though not actually handsome, Louis provided the perfect stereotype for his royal office. Nevertheless, the awesome majesty of bearing that often caused courtiers to tremble inwardly before their audiences should not be equated with personal arrogance. Rather, his exquisite manners, his politeness, and his consideration for others' feelings regularly manifested themselves. The physical luxury and splendor with which he surrounded his person augmented his grandeur. This magnificence was dictated not only by his love of extravagance but also by domestic political factors. However, it is likely that its ultimate political effect was detrimental. Quite apart from its crushing cost, it may have dazzled the ruler himself, his insight already clouded by persistent sycophancy. The later isolation at Versailles possibly helped him to lose contact with everyday realities, thus impairing his judgment. Punctually-kept schedules and hard work were ineffective antidotes.

Still, it would be incorrect to view Louis as a floundering victim of his own vanity and pernicious flattery. If prone to error, he was honestly persuaded—his convictions fortified by the eloquent arguments of Bishop Bossuet—that God had given him the right to rule without any checks or controls save those of his own flexible conscience. While hardly a genius, he possessed an intelligence keen enough to protect himself from the delusion that he was a military leader.[27] Even at the apparent height of diplomatic success, in the few years between the Treaties of Nijmegen (1678–79) and the Revocation of the Edict of Nantes (1685), his self-will did not blind him to the need of advice from others. The diplomatic correspondence for that period indicates that his servants did not always bend the truth to ingratiate themselves; there is no evidence of a pervasive fear of speaking candidly. He was assisted by gifted and talented administrators of sometimes humble and generally modest origin, men who at least had the opportunity to express themselves freely even if their counsel went unheeded. He made mistakes, serious ones which eventually meant the ruin of the monarchy, but he was not a capricious or fatuous tyrant by any means. To call him an indefatigable, overly clever political manipulator, an immoderate and restless person whose position was too august to bind him to conventional rules of morality, would perhaps be more accurate.[28]

A FAVORABLE CONSTELLATION

The overriding prominence of France in European affairs at midcentury does not derive from any single set of conditions. It was, one might submit, the result of a concurrence of the instable, unclarified political situations that characterized the various larger geographic regions of the Old World with a series of fortunate circumstances inside Gaul itself. Astride the northernmost part of the continent was the outwardly mighty Sweden that Gustavus Adolphus had created. In the first part of the century this nation had succeeded for a glorious moment in escaping from its insignificant, peripheral status and had become a critical factor in the European heartland. Nevertheless, its resources, both human and material, were far too meager to support sustained intervention. Later, upon the voluntary retirement of the great king's eccentric daughter, Queen Christina (1654), the new, German-born ruler, Charles X, plunged Sweden into the First Northern War. This was essentially a struggle for dominance in the Baltic, since it involved all the powers on the inland sea: Poland, Russia, Denmark and Brandenburg. In this wise the energies of one whole section of Europe were diverted into a basically marginal issue. Although the conflict was concluded by 1660 (with the assistance of French mediators) and while the succeeding Swedish ruler, Charles XI (1660–1697), later redirected Swedish attention to the center of the continent, first against Louis XIV (1668) and then in alliance with him (1672), Swedish strength was proportionately less important than in the Thirty Years' War, and the Swedes were concerned with the more modest goal of Baltic hegemony.

Along Europe's western extremities there was also a relative isolation from the continent, at least for two decades. Both Britain and the Netherlands were troubled by domestic strife arising from the interrelated issues of religious controversy and conflict between middle class political aspirations and monarchical pretensions. England became involved in the struggle of Presbyterian, Congregationalist, and Episcopa-

lian while repulsing Stuart absolutism. The strong leadership of Oliver
Cromwell, lacking the foundation of national consensus, was more like an
interlude, while the succeeding reign of Charles II could scarcely be
regarded as a settlement. England was able to look beyond the Channel
only after 1688. The Netherlands, too, had experienced religious dissension (the quarrel of the Armenians and the Gomarists), the political
manifestation of which was the opposition of the capitalist bourgeoisie to
the noble and proletarian-backed House of Orange. The Dutch remained
apart until their very existence as a state was threatened by France.
Moreover, both they and the English were distracted by overseas interests
and mutual commercial rivalry. That France's predominance was due at
least in part to the Anglo-Dutch naval wars seems a fairly safe assumption.

If at the same time one recalls the trials of Eastern Europe, the internal
divisions of Germany and Italy, and the weakness of Spain, it becomes
apparent that the status of Europe after 1648 was uniquely favorable to
the French. To be sure, Louis' great strength did not result only from the
domestic or regional involvement of prospective adversaries. It was the
fruit, at least to an equal degree, of more than half a century of hard
efforts by a series of four unusually competent leaders all dedicated, in
one way or another, to building up the state apparatus and central
authority under the mantle of monarchy. It is a commonplace that the
vigor of the Sun King's France would have been inconceivable without
the patient activity of Henry IV, Sully, Richelieu and Mazarin. The
achievements of the last member of this gifted statesmanly dynasty nevertheless deserve to be emphasized as the capstone to the whole enterprise, as the final touch to developments which would permit the French
government to act in the field of foreign affairs with a forcefulness
unprecedented in European history. The work of buttressing the throne
was, in fact, not quite complete at the time of Richelieu's death (1642).
The princes of the blood and other aristocrats remained unconvinced of
the need for a strong royal direction of national affairs; the middle classes
also had to be brought to heel. The two Frondes provided Mazarin his
opportunity. By 1653, whether for good or evil, the triumph of absolutism over both incipient parliamentarianism and the remnants of a Mediaeval mentality was more or less assured.[29]

SOURCES OF STRENGTH

By the date of Mazarin's death (1661) France had attained its apogee,
a position it was to preserve until the end of the Dutch War (1679) and
possibly as late as 1685. Even thereafter, although unable to impose its
will upon all of Europe, it continued to withstand for another twenty-
nine years military and financial strains that would probably have rent
other countries asunder. There were, in short, sources of vitality—

material and human—underlying the political edifice. At first glance, however, the evidence would seem to suggest the contrary. Like the rest of Europe, France was predominantly rural. The status of the peasantry remained more or less at the subsistence level. Crops were dependent upon the vagaries of the weather. While there are no meteorological records for the seventeenth century, there are indications of considerable price oscillation and of a cessation of the great rise of 1450–1600.[30] Disease, malnutrition, near-starvation, and starvation were apparently all-too-common phenomena. "Misère" and early death were the lot of much of the population.[31] The picture, however, should not be overdone. France possesses, indisputably, the best soils of Europe (outside the Ukraine) and a normally dependable, ideal agricultural climate. If endemic poverty was the fate of the average Gallic peasant, it follows that his counterparts elsewhere must have been much worse off. Likewise, although the failure to improve farming methods beyond the advances of the Central Middle Ages had imposed certain limits to food production and hence to population growth, France, with its eighteen to twenty millions, had more human capital than any other Western land.

Although the backbone of the state was farming, the modern armies which first appeared in France at this time clearly required the economic services of a relatively ambitious middle class. While one may not yet speak of industry, entrepreneurs, artisans, and workers were sufficient in numbers and energy to supply the war ministers Le Tellier and Louvois with the requisite amounts of matériel. Employees may have been deliberately subjected to slave wage standards and may frequently have struck,[32] but they still turned out the finest military hardware in Europe. Businessmen may have chafed under government supervision, and they may not have labored with the ardor of Dutch burghers or the English, but neither did they spend all their time in indolent enjoyment of their *rentes*. Statism was not an unqualified failure. If mercantilist doctrines could afford no long-term answers and if Colbert fell short of his hopes, he was undoubtedly able to bring about a number of short-term gains.[33] Probably also Louis XIV's wars, generally held to have been an ultimate cause of the monarchy's collapse, initially quickened the pace of economic life.

Of course, the exploitation of physical resources and the continuity in political development presuppose a highly complex administrative superstructure. A discussion of the French bureaucracy, which was by no means faultless, would be superfluous. However, the fundamental fact of the greater efficacy of French administration requires emphasis when treating events in which the less advanced governments of Germany and eastern Europe are also involved. Similarly, while one must leave aside the technical and organizational details of the French army, it is essential to remain aware of its superiority. It should suffice to note that Le Tellier,

Louvois, and Vauban did not begin from scratch but worked from the foundations laid by the personal patronage of Louis XIII. Already in 1643 France maintained a standing force of 34,000 men,[34] a most respectable number for the day and age. By 1677 Louis had expanded it to 285,000.[35] Finally, mention must be made of Ludovican France's unquestioned cultural hegemony. Although science, literature, and the arts may seem irrelevant to politics, the achievements of French intellectuals were beacons guiding fellow Europeans to Paris. This phenomenon surely served as a psychological reinforcement of physical power.

C. Political Developments from 1648

For the century and a half prior to the Peace of Westphalia (1648) international relations were characterized by the enmity of the Austrian and French ruling houses. For the Valois and Bourbon kings this struggle was essentially defensive. The Habsburgs posed more of a threat to France than vice-versa. In the time of Richelieu and Mazarin the last attempt of the Austro-Spanish dynasty to achieve hegemony was frustrated. The outcome of the Thirty Years' War not only confirmed German princely particularism, but it also assured French security. Although the Franco-Spanish War continued until 1659, it was but an epilogue. The period after 1648 was also marked by Habsburg-Bourbon rivalry, but the rôles were now reversed.[36] The French rather than the Habsburgs became the disturbers of equilibrium. Of course French assertiveness did not immediately reveal itself; almost twenty years would have to pass before contemporaries became seriously alarmed. Habsburg leadership of the opposition did not really develop for a quarter century, and even then it was shared with the House of Orange. Nevertheless, the general outline is clear enough to provide a *Leitmotif* for European politics until the Treaties of Utrecht and Rastatt-Baden (1713–14).

The Last Years of Mazarin

At the very moment of success in international relations, at Münster and Osnabrück, Mazarin found himself forced to undertake a delicate and complicated defense of his domestic position. The two Frondes prevented him and his young master, Louis XIV, from garnering forthwith the fruits of the French meddling in the religious and civil strife of the Reich. Fortunately, Germany was so exhausted that France could afford some domestic turmoil of her own. Although the second Fronde was proved a more difficult affair than the first, the Cardinal was ultimately (1653) successful and free to attend to the unfinished Spanish war. The hostility of Cromwellian England toward Spain served his purposes. It found expression in the Franco-English Alliance of 1657, which in turn resulted in the crushing of Phillip IV's last hopes at the Battle of the Dunes, (June 14, 1658). Thus Mazarin vanquished the last obstacle to renewed French concern with the Holy Roman Empire.[37]

An occasion for intervention offered itself immediately, for 1658 was the year of negotiations for the election of the new emperor. Leopold had not been chosen King of the Romans during his father's lifetime since he was not originally expected to succeed the latter. Despite an interregnum of fifteen months, during which Mazarin did all in his power to keep the throne from the Habsburgs, Leopold was really in no great danger.[38] Nevertheless, his submission to an electoral capitulation, in which he had to promise not to aid his Spanish cousins, was doubtlessly a French triumph. A concomitant of the election was the League of the Rhine (August 15, 1658). While it was not the brainchild of the French and while its progenitor, Johann Philipp von Schönborn, Archbishop-Elector of Mainz, was not a tool of French expansionism,[39] it did serve to cover Mazarin's partial defeat by detracting from Leopold's prestige and hindering his actions. It also later provided Louis XIV a vehicle for French influence.[40] The French benefited further from the innate weakness of the Habsburgs' strategic military position. The Emperor, forced to choose between opposing either France or Turkey or running the risk of a two-front war, was faced with a dilemma that offered his Bourbon adversary a great opportunity for expansion to the north and east.

LOUIS XIV TAKES OVER

However, the French monarch was not yet in a position to press his advantage. The somewhat unexpected revival of the Ottoman Empire under Mehmed Köprülü and the first Turkish advance into Hungary (1663–64) were premature from his viewpoint.[41] No matter how much Louis XIV may have sympathized with the Infidel, for the moment he had to maintain his chivalrous image and send soldiers to help the Emperor. Nevertheless, he deemed it wise to excuse himself in private to the Turk.[42] Likewise, continuing anti-Turkish operations in the Mediterranean (relief of the Venetians at Candia and naval actions against the piratical North African "subjects" of the Porte) cannot particularly have suited Louis' purposes. At this time the only Ottoman-influenced gain was indirect: namely, the greater control imposed upon the Habsburgs by the now permanent Regensburg Diet (*immerwährender Reichstag*).[43]

The Peace of the Pyrénées (1659), was, in a sense, only a truce. While Spain's possession of the Southern Netherlands was reaffirmed, the French did not cease to covet the territory on their northern frontier, the object of their attentions ever since the reign of Phillip Augustus. Louis' marriage to the Infanta, Marie Thérèse, although theoretically the guarantee of Franco-Spanish reconciliation, was merely a covert means of keeping the Belgian door ajar as became apparent during the War of Devolution (1667–68). To be sure, the latter conflict did not evolve as foreseen. The sudden intervention of the Protestant Powers (Triple Alliance) gave the

French ruler an indication of the opposition that similar attempts at aggrandizement might encounter in the future. There were, moreover, faintly ominous signs from the supposedly docile Teutons. Already in 1664 French intervention against Erfurt, a disobedient, outlying (Saxon) territory of the Elector of Mainz, caused noticeable excitement. It was bad enough to have had to rely on French troops at Szentgotthárd. German national feeling was slowly becoming a fever, for which French gold was no longer an entirely effective remedy. Not only was the Rhine League moribund by 1667, but even the mere benevolence of France's supposed satellites proved more difficult to purchase than might have been expected.[44] The effect of the gradual abandonment of Mazarin's more subtle system of influence and pressure should have been apparent.

All the same, the Sun King had reason to feel satisfied. Not only was he permitted to retain a string of frontier cities, but the conquest of Franche Comté, while undone by the Treaty of Aix-la-Chapelle, was an entertaining and edifying demonstration of his army's capability. Furthermore, shortly before, Leopold had become reasonable in the matter of the Spanish heritage. Charles II surely could not survive long, much less beget offspring. Despite the tocsin-sounding of the German patriot, Franz von Lisola,[45] the First Partition Treaty was signed (January 19, 1668). For the sake of momentary expediency the Austrian Habsburgs loosened the ties with their traditional allies and truest friends.[46] Leopold, nevertheless, felt (allegedly) that his action was morally wrong and soon had to realize that it was a mistake as well.[47] A further sign of Louis' self-confidence after Aix-la-Chapelle was the occupation of Lorraine (1670), a territory that he had already attempted to assimilate by chicanery nine years before. Although the refugee Duke, the father of Leopold's general, received no outright help from his fellow Imperial princes, the incident contributed to growing German disillusionment with France.[48]

THE DUTCH WAR

At the moment, however, Louis' main preoccupation was preparing for the squaring of accounts with the contumacious Northern Netherlanders.[49] The dual background—personal rancor and Colbert's economic hostility—of the Dutch War is well-known. What needs to be stressed is the frailty of Louis' prearrangements, the diplomatic turn-about, and the awakening of permanent suspicion and alarm over the supposed goals of the French monarch. Not only did William of Orange, Prince Waldeck, and Leopold emerge as determined leaders of the opposition, but public opinion now became a factor even for the most vendible German prince.[50] Although the Treaties of Nijmegen brought Louis territorial accretions (at Spain's cost) and outward prestige and although his exhausted opponents would hesitate to oppose him again for some time, many Germans were now aware of his game. It was also clear that French armies were not invincible. Indeed, Louis had failed not only in his original goal of chastising the Dutch but also in annihilating or even impairing the military force of his enemies. Some historians hold that this was the point at which his decline actually began.

On the other hand, such reasoning may derive from too much hindsight. It does not necessarily follow that what happened thereafter had to happen. Variant courses of action were still open. If Louis was not really victorious, neither was he cast down in any sense of the word. What he did, how he acted in succeeding years would (in part) determine whether the Dutch War could be considered by a later age the beginning of defeat or of success. It is conceivable that he could have become the arbiter of Europe. It will be seen that he played his Turkish hand quite well (which compensated for the bungling of his Polish envoys). If Vienna had fallen, as indeed it nearly did, the King could have gathered in many valuable chips. In short, the scales balanced after 1679—certainly until 1683—, and they could have tipped in Louis' favor.

One reason why the position of the French monarch continued to be favorable after Nijmegen was the unchanged political and constitutional status of the Holy Roman Empire. The Dutch War had not swept away German *Kleinstaaterei*. Indeed, the latter is another major reason for French preponderance in the latter seventeenth century.

D. Germany After the Peace of Westphalia

Germany, like France, experienced a long period of domestic turbulence resulting from the sharp opposition of Catholicism and Protestantism and from the issue of central political authority versus territorial (provincial) particularism. But, unlike its Gallic neighbor, it had the misfortune to find no solution favorable to monarchical power and national unity, and at the same time it was plagued by self-interested foreign intervention, *per se* a major cause of its frustrations. The French enjoyed more than half a century of freedom from serious involvement in external affairs, during which they were able to work toward the final settlement of their internal problems—a clear time advantage over Germany. Thus, in 1661, they possessed a relatively healthy economy and a highly developed state apparatus while a divided Holy Roman Empire was only beginning to emerge from the chaos of fratricidal strife.

THE COST OF WAR

The Huguenot Wars of the latter sixteenth century doubtlessly blocked the progress of French civilization for a time, but one may well ask whether the destruction which they wrought can have equalled the ravages of Germany's Thirty Years' War. Not only were the social habits and the moral standards of the German people adversely effected, perhaps permanently, as Veit Valentin has suggested,[51] but the physical losses were of the most considerable proportions. The statement remains true despite the fact that there were great differences between regions in the extent of devastation and even after one has taken into account the deliberate exaggeration of contemporary sources. In many rural areas, especially those along the main routes of passage (above all a belt running across the Reich from northeast to southwest), the population was decimated and impoverished.[52] Moreover, the physically battered agrarian economy failed to benefit much from the coming of peace. High wartime prices collapsed, and the only important consumer market—the cities and the towns—shrank appreciably.[53]

Germany's urban inhabitants did not suffer as much as the peasantry, but they lacked both the capital and the energy to combat their own decline effectively. The golden age of the Fuggers and the Welsers was now only a memory. Not until 1670 did trade and commerce manage to attain even their pre-war level. Of course the war did not actually cause the business lag: it strengthened an already existing tendency, the result of worldwide economic and political shifts in favor of the maritime powers. Moreover, the slackening of business volume did not hinder the development of capitalism as a system. The demand for military supplies and weapons had stimulated both private enterprise and state-directed undertakings. Money was still available in some quantity although it had changed hands on a vast scale. Unfortunately, the debasement of coinage increased during the war, and as a result of the heavy burden of debt, total capital value is estimated to have depreciated from one to two thirds. The recovery of trade was further hindered by the spread of excise taxes and internal tariff barriers, especially river tolls. In addition, Sweden had a throttle hold on the Baltic coast while the relatively untouched cities of Bremen and Hamburg had to share prosperity with England and the Netherlands. The Dutch, astride the mouths of the Rhine, came to control shipping even on the upper stretches of the river. Foreign luxury goods flooded the land. And then still another pre-war trend now became more striking: the concentration of financial power in the hands of a few, highly successful manipulators, the so-called court-Jews or factors.[54] In his dependence upon the provision of supplies and cash by Samuel Oppenheimer, Leopold I was no exception among the rulers of his day.

If the war had a dampening effect upon commerce, it gave the *coup de grace* to the moribund guild system although the corpse continued to lie around, befouling the economic air, until the eighteenth century. Much more important from the end of the war onward were the so-called provincial guilds (*Landeszünfte*), actually less a craftsmen's organization than a control arm of the territorial prince. Production itself remained the monopoly of the skilled artisan, for true industry, from various causes, had yet to make its appearance. Rather, government often directly encouraged commercial entrepreneurs to bring artisans together in larger, handlabor workshops (i.e., manufacture in the literal sense) or to commission work at home on a piece basis (cottage industry). The luxury demands of court society and the clothing needs of armies and officialdom proved an important stimulant for this primarily textile-centered business activity. Transitionally industrial undertakings of this nature were, however, risky and often failed.[55]

Indeed, territorial mercantilism seems to have been a striking feature of latter seventeenth-century Germany, developing in concert with the sovereignty of the small prince. Put into practice before it was fully developed in theory, it was not as yet either a consistent or a complete doctrine. Its proponents were the bureaucrats. The latter, most likely socially parvenu lawyers of bourgeois, non-local origin (e.g., Hocher in Vienna), identified their own well-being with that of the prince and were his staunchest allies against the landed nobility. They have been called little Colberts and Cromwells.[56] Somewhat ironic is the fact that Austria, the state which employed mercantilism's three foremost advocates (Becher, Hörnigk and Schröder), failed to accept it in practice to any appreciable extent.[57]

Another feature of the territorial rulers' activity in the post-1648 period is the effect of their centralizing political and economic measures upon the nation's social structure. Insofar as the bourgeoisie was financially dependent upon the state's favor, that independence of outlook so characteristic of the same group in Great Britain and the Netherlands could not develop. The nobility, which had a psychological community of interest with the princes, submitted to the latter with a certain degree of ease and supported attempts to circumscribe the burghers' existence. For the peasantry also the latter seventeenth century was no time of social advance. In fact in the northeast, where it was not completely enserfed, the situation was worse than before the war. In short, the human atmosphere was one of increasing stratification of classes.[58]

SOCIETY AND CULTURE

While the Thirty Years' War was admittedly not the ultimate cause for the comparatively static condition of the German economy and society at mid-century, it was, beyond doubt, a powerful negative influence. Similar but less demonstrable is the interrelationship between the war and contemporary cultural life. It is difficult for the historian to investigate the subject because he cannot treat it with the customary tools of documentary inquiry but is required to make value judgments. Nevertheless, the intellectual sterility of the age, at least in contrast to the vitality of England and France, would not seem to be open to particular dispute. Barrenness, for example, is evident in the very language. Its corrupted status is apparent to anyone who has ever worked with contemporary records. Indeed, so permeated is the German tongue with Latinisms and

Gallicisms that the twentieth century scholar of English-speaking background has advantage over the native researcher. The dominance of foreign influence is even more obvious in the fact that French (in the case of the Habsburg Court, Italian) was preferred to the indigenous idiom, accompanying the popular victory of French *couture* and manners (*Alamodenwesen*). Native literary societies such as the *Fruchtbringende Gesellschaft* were prominent, but their reformatory endeavors were limited to poetry and had little effect upon prose.[59]

Of course, in cultural as in economic and social questions, the war cannot be made to bear the original responsibility for retardation. Not only was the vernacular language colored by the Humanist-trained, Latin-thinking officials of the princely chancelleries already before 1618, but it had not yet managed to overcome certain regional peculiarities.[60] It is conceivable that if national unity had been a reality in the sixteenth century as it was in the Western monarchies, the chances for the evolution of a standardized literary medium would have been better. What the war actually did, apart from creating social circumstances unfavorable to the intelligentsia, was to buttress and legalize national disunity, thus prolonging the existence of at least one major obstacle to a renewed blossoming of language, literature, and the arts.[61]

It might also be argued that the religious disunity of Germany was detrimental to the development of linguistic and cultural homogeneity. Be that as it may, the year 1648 was a milestone in the history of denominationalism. The lines between the three major confessions, previously fluid, were now sharply drawn, and their antagonisms, though removed from the realm of bodily violence, were frozen stiff for several centuries. The territorial prince proved to be the prime beneficiary of past dissension. The idea of Church unity did not die but was largely illusory because each sect regarded itself as its incorporation. The princes, for their part, were interested in the matter only on the level of their own local authority. The well-known irenic activity of Cardinal Rojas y Spinola was actually a chimera, not only for these reasons but because the Roman Church was basically prepared to concede little of what was important to most Protestants and because interest was restricted to a relatively small group of high church Lutherans.[62] Although the territorial religious uniformity foreseen in the Peace of Westphalia was never entirely realized, secular control tightened, and in the process secular goals and mentality naturally predominated, thus depriving the Churches of living spiritual foundations. Whatever was vital in Christianity, at least in its Evangelical form, came from outside the official, orthodox hierarchy. Pietism, with its emphasis upon an active, experienced faith, clearly constitutes an indictment of the inability of the established ecclesiastical bodies to provide expression for the religious drives of more sensitive souls. On the other hand, the most powerful intellects of the day were not to be found in the church circles but rather in the service of rational philosophy and mathematical-oriented natural science, at work laying the basis for the Enlightenment of the next century.[63]

THE IMPERIAL CONSTITUTION

Generally, the Thirty Years' War is remarked not as much for its negative effects upon economic, social, and cultural life as for its deleterious influence upon the nation's political cadre. It is frequently assumed that the Holy Roman Empire now became a meaningless relic.[64] There are good grounds for a more cautious estimate. To be sure, one indication of the *Reich*'s deterioration as a state is the amorphous condition of its borders. In northern Italy (Milan and Savoy) there were residual Imperial legal rights. Although the theoretical association of the Swiss Confederation and the United Netherlands ended in 1648, Alsace and Lorraine became clouded in a fog of conflicting sovereignty. The Spanish Netherlands technically remained incorporated but was ruled by a far-away monarch with a steadily loosening grip vis-à-vis an ever more expansive France. Denmark and Sweden possessed important footholds in the north while Brandenburg had recently extended itself beyond the bounds of the Empire by its acquisition of Prussia. Similarly, the House of Habsburg, as the holder of the Crown of St. Stephen, was located both within and outside the Reich.[65]

If there could be a question as to the location of the frontier, there was not the slightest doubt as to the reality of the Imperial office. To say that it was a hollow and meaningless honor would be to deny its undiminished attractiveness both to its incumbents and to other potential candidates. The Emperor remained the head of a government and the executive organ for any decisions the Diet might make. He was still the fount of justice. He bore the not entirely empty title of Protector of the Peace, Advocate of the Roman See, the Holy Father and the Church. The so-called reserved rights continued to be worth something. They included the issuance of patents of nobility, pardon, and legitimization; the exercise of supreme feudal investiture; the granting of privileges and dispensations; and the bestowal of exemptions from Imperial judicial jurisdiction. These prerogatives were mostly of financial value, sometimes controversial, and not clearly defined, but they were also flexible and hence cherished by the Imperial court. The crown obviously also conveyed great formal dignity: there was only one Emperor and for a long time only one "Majesty." Certain parties in the Empire also looked to the Habsburgs for guidance, at least to a degree: Catholics and the relatively impotent mass of small and medium-sized rulers. Standing firmly upon the ground of Westphalia, having renounced plans for the forceful implementation of central authority, Vienna strengthened its credit with a now reliable "Imperial" party. This was a situation which, if handled skillfully offered possibilities of exploitation.[66]

On the other hand, the Emperor was not a sovereign save in his own hereditary domains. The Peace agreements made it clear that the territorial princes exercised full rights within their own baliwicks. A phenomenon at least four centuries in the making was given the stamp of juridical validity. The Electoral College achieved great obstructionist power. An Imperial Estates Court, though less efficient and less popular than Vienna's, was established. The new Emperor Leopold was required to subscribe to an even more restrictive electoral capitulation. The Diet was perhaps the slowest moving body in the history of parliamentary institutions.[67]

Despite the value of the Imperial office there is no doubt that political initiative lay in the hands of the local rulers. Territorial absolutism was the main trend of the period. It was of course not an entirely new phenomenon. Nor was it solely characteristic of the larger political entities: it could also be found in medium and small-sized states. The technique of the princes was skillful. They extended their power stage by stage, generally by opposing the right of Imperial intervention, by improving the administrative apparatus, and by restricting the authority of the provincial estates. Indeed it is ironical that at the moment of the national estates' (the Diet's) triumph over centralizing tendencies, they assisted the princes in emasculating local representative bodies. While princely government did not succeed in making itself supreme everywhere, it did become generally dominant.[68]

Territorial absolutism cannot be explained solely as a mechanical political process. It was also related to a sense of duty on the part of the prince, the result of contemporary religious and intellectual forces. It might be justified either in the religious terms of a proneness to sin or in the philosophical terms of human subservience to passions, although in both cases it was the reflection of a definite concept of mankind. In the former context the idea of sovereignty by divine grace was important, and, despite the differing outlooks of the three confessions, the alliance between throne and altar became a major feature of the second half of the seventeenth century. In the latter context it was the unfolding of dogmas of natural law. Stimulated by the evolving contractual theory of government, German political theorists (Pufendorf, Thomasius and Wolff) strongly emphasized an ethical line, the doctrine of duty. Almost all of the leading representatives of princely absolutism had some acquaintance with the intellectual currents of the day, as had been the case with Richelieu, himself the model for Teutonic potentates.[69]

E. German States

Many German rulers were involved in one way or another in the Turkish wars of the latter seventeenth century, and the whole country was affected by French aggression, itself so closely linked to Eastern

European affairs. Hence the development of individual territorial entities has some interest.

Larger Units

The story of Brandenburg-Prussia has been told often. One need only recall that Frederick William the Great Elector (1640–1688) established the greatness of the House of Hohenzollern by implementing far-reaching economic, administrative and military reforms. Certainly he is the prime German example of the emerging absolutist prince.[70] He was, however, only a minor factor in the history of the southeast because of geographic remoteness and the concerns of his own dynasty. Neighboring, pro-Imperial Braunschweig-Lüneburg (later known as the Electorate of Hannover), had traditionally suffered from subdivision into appanages but was in the process of achieving territorial unity under a newly imposed primogeniture. Distant from the Turks and exposed to the French, it was not in a position to provide Leopold much aid. The Palatinate, reduced to its Rhenish segment after 1648 and restored to the line of the Winter King, experienced a few years of peaceful development but by the latter quarter of the century again found itself in turmoil. Devastated by Louis XIV's troops during the Dutch War, the land sought to insure itself with the French. The sister of the childless Elector was married to the Sun King's brother. However, the extinction of the Calvinist dynasty in 1685 and its replacement by the pro-Habsburg, zealously Catholic Pfalz-Neuburgs would naturally precipitate new troubles with France.[71]

The Electorate of Saxony, the traditional champion of the Evangelical cause, survived the great war with a somewhat tarnished reputation, for its collaboration with the Emperor and its stubbornly anti-Calvinist, pro-Lutheran attitude had caused much bitterness. Its government in the second half of the century was characterized by heedless exploitation of land and people, conducted jointly by court and nobility.[72] Its ruler was the meaty-faced, soldierly John George III (1647–1691). A well-tested veteran of the Dutch War, successor to the electoral throne in 1680, he was a characteristic German ruler, concerned above all with the maintenance of his sovereignty. Although an anti-Bourbon "Westerner" in outlook, he was nonetheless aware of the danger threatening his own domain from the East. Should Bohemia fall, Saxony would surely lie open. He was willing—for a substantial price to be sure—to lend his excellent little army and his own person for the relief of the Danubian capital. As an individual he does not seem to have been at all distinguished: Sobieski found him taciturn, unable to speak foreign languages, and devoid of any particular manners.[73]

Until 1685 the only secular Roman Catholic electorate was Bavaria. It resembled its north German Protestant competitor, Brandenburg, insofar as it was also well on the road to princely absolutism. Duke Maximilian vanquished his estates as early as 1612 and then lived through the war to see his strengthened, re-Catholicized land raised in rank. Bavaria's rise to prominence had come about in association with its Catholic neighbor, Austria. Indeed, these two major states of southern Germany were almost like brothers during the remaining years of their independent existence. Linked by a common dialect, they sometimes worked in fraternal harmony and were sometimes torn by rivalry. Perhaps no one symbolizes this better than Duke Maximilian's identically-named grandson, one of the heroes of the relief of Vienna and a leader in the War of the Holy League. Twenty-one years old in 1683 and already full of fight, Elector Max hastened to offer himself and his small, superbly trained army to Leopold. In 1685 he was rewarded with the hand of the latter's daughter, Maria Antonia, but his loyalty to the Emperor was by no means assured therewith. He later strove to obtain a part of the inheritance of Charles III of Spain and linked his fortunes to Louis XIV. He was a hotspur in the literal sense of the word. Unfortunately, other aspects of the martial art bored him to tears. He never bothered himself with the well-being of the troops, leaving all the work to his staff. When there was no further possibility of contact with the foe he hurried off to the sensual pleasures of Vienna and Munich. "In no matter can he take more pains than with a mistress or upon the hunt."[74] Nevertheless, he had a special utility during the relief of Vienna and in the following years' campaign against the Porte.[75]

The three ecclesiastical electorates of Mainz, Trier, and Cologne lay concentrated in the lower Rhineland, the so-called Priests' Alley (*Pfaffengasse*). Like the secular states and other great ecclesiastical enclaves, they followed the absolutist trends of the time, but the fact that their rulers were of necessity non-dynastic and their extreme exposure to French influence prevented them from becoming really strong. Among the other more prominent political entities of Germany, Hesse, Württemberg, Mecklenburg and Oldenburg deserve mention. The wealthy, prosperous Calvinist Landgraviate of Hesse-Kassel emerged in 1648 strengthened and under wise rule, while Lutheran Hesse-Darmstadt remained less noteworthy. Württemberg, Mecklenburg and Oldenburg constitute exceptions to contemporary political development, for in each of them the prince failed to overcome the estates. In the first-named the bourgeoisie remained preëminent, and in the latter two, especially Mecklenburg, the landed nobility was determinative.[76]

LEOPOLD'S ALLIES AND SERVANTS

Among the host of medium and small-sized territories relatively few stand out. Often they were characterized by war-hardened social habits, and their sovereigns continued to seek employment as mercenaries in the later conflicts of the century. Occasionally there were rulers of intellectual

(Vienna, National Library)

Prince George Frederick of Waldeck

Margrave Ludwig Wilhelm of Baden

attainment or aspiration. Others placed themselves in the service of greater princes. Among the latter are three men instrumental in the defeat of the Turks and the rise of the Habsburg Empire.

George Frederick, Count and later (1682) Prince Waldeck (1620–1692), was not actually an Austrian civil servant or soldier, but his later career was so closely tied to Leopold's fortunes that it is proper to consider him alongside those who were. Waldeck, a capable, determined, although scarcely brilliant soldier and statesman, first attracted public notice as the principle adviser of the Great Elector. At that time he manifested both a fiery disposition and great ingenuity in devising political schemes. As a Protestant, a lesser ruler and close relative of the House of Orange, he was adamantly anti-Imperial and anti-Habsburg. His frame of reference was still the Thirty Years' War. Hohenzollern policy in the Imperial Diet became sharply anti-Viennese. The new minister tried to convince his master to accept a plan for a Prussian-led, Protestant-dominated confederation of princes, which Mazarin was to subsidize. Dismissed from Frederick William's employ in 1658, Waldeck became a confidant of William of Orange. As time revealed where the real danger to princely "liberties" lay, the German, no less than his Dutch nephew, became a tenacious opponent of France. The Peace of Nijmegen did not cause him, old, choleric, and ailing though he was, to give up. In the face of the French annexation of Alsace he strove by ceaseless travelling to stimulate his sometimes pusillanimous fellow princes into forming a more united front. It was ironical that the forces of the Franconian and Swabian Circles, for the raising of which he was responsible, were to be first used against Turkish, rather than French aggression.[77]

The links between the House of Habsburg and the Upper Rhenine region were of great antiquity, and in the seventeenth century their interests were identical. It is not surprising that two representatives of the Margraviate of Baden were in Leopold's service. Margrave Hermann (1628–1691), President of the Court War Council, was, like his liege lord, Jesuit-trained and originally destined for a clerical career. Indeed he actually took Holy Orders and became a cathedral rector at Cologne. Released from his vows to compete in the Polish election of 1661, he remained a celibate until his death. After leaving Poland he became a soldier and gathered experience against the Turks in 1664 and against the French in the Dutch War. A big, strapping fellow, he was well suited physically for his new career.[78] A still rather obscure personality, untouched by historical research, the Margrave was regarded by many, especially by the Venetian ambassador and Buonvisi (who eventually engineered his downfall), as an incapable administrator, hardly a worthy successor to the late, great Montecuccoli (d. 1680). It has been said of Hermann that he was diffuse in action, yet rich in ideas.[79] He certainly must be given credit for realizing the weakness and obsolescence of

Vienna's fortifications and for having brought into Imperial service the brilliant military engineer, George Rimpler.[80] The Badener's greatest flaw was his deep antipathy toward the field commander, Charles of Lorraine, who had opposed his elevation to office.[81] The Emperor, initially beholden to his war minister, long hesitated to get rid of him: Hermann was automatically protected "per la qualità della sua nascità."[82]

Ludwig Wilhelm I, called "Türkenlouis" on account of his signal victories over Ottoman forces in the War of the Holy League, reigning Margrave, Lieutenant General and *Reichsfeldmarschall*, Knight of the Golden Fleece, proprietor of the Imperial and Royal Infantry Regiment No. 23, was born April 8, 1655, in Paris and died January 4, 1707, in Rastadt. His birth abroad was merely accidental, and he was brought up in Baden as a German by his father and grandfather, his French mother preferring the amenities of Parisian life. The young prince's military-oriented education stressed obedience to the Roman Pontiff, love for the German fatherland, and fidelity to the *Kaiser*.[83] Sent into the field against Louis XIV in 1674, he not only learned from Montecuccoli but demonstrated courage, independence, and presence of mind.[84] While all testimonies as to his intellect and capacity are laudatory, his personality enjoyed considerably less favor. He knew he was good. He threw money around and hence often lacked it. He did not find the advice of others palatable; and he did not care particularly what people said about him. "On the one hand he has all the good qualities required to command an army but on the other all the failings needed to counteract the wish to entrust one to him."[85] A specialist in the employment of infantry, he experienced more success against the Turks than he did against the French. Though he insisted upon the honors due rank, his rise was due primarily to his abilities.[86] The Duke of Lorraine was kindly disposed toward him, but his impatience and stormy nature caused him to criticize the slower-moving Charles and to side with his vindictive uncle. In any event he had never been an easily-controlled subordinate.

A PROBLEM OF DEFINITION

The territorial entities of the Empire that contribute most to the vexations of modern cartographers are the *Reichsritter* and the *Freistädte*. While they may lend color to school atlases, they added practically nothing to the political life of their time. The Imperial free knights, though in most respects the legal equals of their bigger brethren, were militarily impotent and economically weak; they dragged out an insignificant and sometimes wretched existence until 1803. The once distinguished free cities were now reduced in number, victims of princely expansionism. Only a few of the remaining odd fifty, such as Hamburg, Bremen, and Danzig in the north and Frankfurt, Nürnberg, and Augsburg in the south, maintained a measure of influence and stuffy, patrician well-being.[87] Brilliant futures lay in store mainly for the subjugated territorial cities such as Berlin, Leipzig, and, above all, Vienna, in numbers already a metropolis. Among Germany's minuscule states the only institution of significance—apart from Hamburg's vaguely democratic constitution—was the Imperial Circle, and it excluded the free knights. In the case of the Upper Rhine, Franconia, and Swabia, it showed certain signs of vitality during the Turkish and French wars.[88]

Under the circumstances one may fairly ask just how the *Reich* of Leopold I may be defined. Long before the witty observation of Voltaire, it was apparent that the Holy Roman Empire was a unique institution. Already in the seventeenth century Germans were trying to find a meaningful label for their fatherland. Proceeding from Aristotle's classifications, they sought to establish, in particular, whether it was an aristocracy or a monarchy. The effort was vain. The legal situation was so anomalous that it was not possible for the publicists of the day to develop any consensus. Sammuel von Pufendorf even went so far as to suggest that the Empire was "almost a monster." One thing was certain, in all events: it was still breathing.[89]

PART TWO

Prologue to War

The Siege and Relief of Vienna

A composite view (contemporary). "A" indicates
the burning *Schottenkloster*.

CHAPTER FOUR

The Disappointing Peace 1679–1681

A. Eastern Europe after Nijmegen

Even during a century in which warfare was more or less regarded as the natural state of human affairs,[1] there were brief moments when Mars rested. 1679 was that kind of year, at least outside the Ukraine. Frederick William the Great Elector was apparently the only European ruler left with any stomach for fighting. Certainly he was the last person to come to terms with France (at St. Germain on June 29). The Emperor, although reluctant and feeling frustrated, had already settled his differences with Louis XIV (at Nijmegen on February 5). While the advent of what the treaties labeled "perpetual peace"—a legal formality not taken literally—probably lifted some cares from the shoulders of Europe's sovereigns, there was little amelioration in the lot of the common man, above all in the Habsburg domains. Although the guns were silent and although the Emperor mustered out many soldiers, a trial of another sort, pestilence, now thrust itself with full force upon his people.

THE PLAGUE

Already during the previous year the disease had reached alarming proportions in Hungary, whence it now spread to Bohemia and Austria.[2] Vienna was caught completely unprepared despite the prompt warnings of an outstanding local doctor, Paul Sorbait. When the government did begin to take proper sanitary measures, all was haste and confusion. Bureaucratic *Schlamperei* had triumphed. The city was subjected to the worst scourge in its history, more terrible even than the Turkish siege four years later. With the advent of warm weather, the death toll skyrocketed. The horror can scarcely be depicted. Putrescent corpses lay about in the houses, on the streets, and out in the surrounding vineyards; the decimated municipal labor force simply could not keep pace in removing them. In order to escape their frightful surroundings some Viennese resorted to the proverbial "rioting, drunkenness, chambering and impurities," those sins which, paradoxically, the popular evangelist, Abraham à Sancta Clara, was later to cite as the original cause of all the suffering. Allegedly, "der liebe Augustin" was among the persons who sought solace in such fashion. Prostrated by alcohol, the happy-go-lucky folksinger and minstrel was taken for dead and tossed upon the charnel heap. Once sober, he managed to extract a little bagpipe from his belt and summon his astounded rescuers. More demonstrable and more edifying is the example of rich Prince Ferdinand von Schwarzenberg, who remained behind while most of the court fled. This brave peer, soon entitled "der Pestkönig," literally sullied his own hands, provided relief from personal funds, and succeeded in suppressing pillage by liberal application of the hangman's knot.[3]

Leopold himself, not for the last time, deserted the metropolis (August). Pious and well-meaning as usual, he offered prayers of intercession for his subjects, first from the hills above the city and then at Maria Zell, the lovely alpine shrine of the Blessed Virgin. Ampringen, the unhappy stadholder of Hungary, utilized the opportunity to relinquish his post in Bratislava. In fact, the general pace of the government—hardly known for celerity anyway—slackened. The social and economic effects of the epidemic were even more serious. Perhaps it is not going too far to say that the loss of taxable human resources was crippling, at least from the viewpoint of a really adequate military force. Two years later, in an interview with Borgomanero, the Emperor remarked that he had no money for augmenting his infantry because the deaths of so many persons had caused commerce to falter.[4] While the decrease in revenue may also have stemmed from a post-war business recession, not to mention the amounts siphoned off by Sinzendorf and his ilk, there is no reason to question Leopold's word. His greater than usual impecuniosity was doubtlessly another element in favor of France in the immediate post-Nijmegen period.[5]

THÖKÖLY IN LOVE

The conclusion of peace did bring the Emperor at least one advantage, albeit somewhat illusory. The Imperial government now believed that it held a stronger hand for negotiating in Sopron with the emissaries of Imre Thököly. Although the Nijmegen agreement included Transylvania, it made no mention of the Malcontents. Leopold thus asked the rebels to lay down their weapons as the prerequisite to a redress of grievances. To this the Magyar nobles could not agree. Equally important in the collapse of the parley was a more personal factor. Thököly was enamoured of a beautiful princess and needed legal approval to marry. Helena Zrinyi, widow of Ferenc Rákóczy, the pardoned conspirator of 1671, apparently shared her suitor's feelings. Her fully mature physical charms (she was 14 years older) were almost certainly enhanced by her wealth. In conjunction with her mother-in-law, Sophia Rákóczy, she was the administratrix of vast estates in eastern Upper Hungary, property held in trust until her children should come of age. Sophia, for her part, was a dedicted partisan of the Jesuits and the Counter Reformation, for which reason her late son had been forgiven his transgression.[6] As long as she lived and as long as Helena did not remarry, the immensely valuable patrimony remained an asset of the ruling dynasty. The prospective bride was, however, not only the widow of a rebel but also the daughter of one, that self-same Peter, whose head had fallen at Leopold's behest. And now the intermediaries of another rebellious vassal were asking not only permission for her remarriage but also assistance in gaining the mother-in-law's consent. Although the danger that such a union presented was obvious, a blunt refusal was out of the question. A rebuff would impair the negotiating mood, for it would deeply offend the groom, who, like his fellow magnates, possessed a highly-developed sense of honor in such matters. The solution was to establish preconditions that would be extremely difficult, if not impossible, for Thököly to accept: homage to Leopold and conversion to Catholicism. The rebels retired to their hideouts in order to organize new attacks, but as summer arrived, it became evident that, for a while at least, the major cause of death was going to be the plague and not the brutalities of guerilla warfare.[7]

BUONVISI'S MEAGER PROGRESS

However trying a year 1679 may have been for the head of the House of Austria, the signing of the instruments of peace did give cause for rejoicing in one other Viennese residence, that of the irrepressible nunzio. The cessation of hostilities was a ray of light after many months of disappointment and worry. A crusading zealot like his master, Buonvisi had witnessed nothing but misfortune since the commencement of his mission in 1676: the Polish-Turkish armistice, the futile attempt to impose absolutism in Hungary with its attendant *Kleinkrieg,* the estrangement between the ostensibly pro-French Sobieski and Leopold, not to mention the continuance of war in the West. Still, the era of waiting was not without profit. The papal representative had the opportunity to judge what was amiss and what needed to be righted. His conclusions were almost the same as his Venetian colleagues'. While praising the Emperor's virtues, he also recognized how detrimental the sovereign's faults were to the grand project of uniting the West against Islam. The nunzio likewise considered Leopold unlucky in the choice of his ministers, especially Lobkowitz and Hocher. The latter had led the country into a dangerous corner, had estranged natural allies, the Magyars and the Poles, and had irritated its real enemies, the Turks. Aware of the corrupt Austrian financial administration, Buonvisi saw that the anti-Hungarian feelings of some ministers were associated with personal interests. Forthright, even blunt in his conversations with the Emperor, he hoped that Leopold might be liberated from his nefarious environment and that his own good character might finally bear fruit. Only in the matter of religious concession was the Roman prelate restrained; he could not go so far as to press the interests of Protestant parsons.[8]

The conclusion of general peace seemed to offer Innocent XI a good chance to bring Austria and Poland together with Moscow and perhaps even with Paris, and the various nunzii received their instructions accordingly. For a short time, early in 1679, the Emperor appeared inclined to accept the papal arguments. Nevertheless, the monarch was dissuaded by his ministers, who, reasonably enough, were interested *only* if Louis would also participate. Buonvisi persisted and thus made himself an enemy of Hocher and his associates, who feared that they might lose influence. Every means was used to discredit the Churchman's advice and to besmirch his person. His only ally was Emerich Sinelli, Bishop of Vienna. The one success that the two were able to bring off that year was the dismissal of the peculating Sinzendorf, who had maintained himself only by bribing others and by satisfying every whim of the Court. The toppled treasurer was replaced by Christoph von Abele, well-meaning and honest but not energetic enough to cut the expenses of the Imperial entourage.[9]

SOBIESKI LOOKS SOUTH

Considering the wretched physical circumstances of 1679, Buonvisi can well have reckoned even this modest achievement a gain. The only advantage of the plague, aside from the quiescence of Hungary, was that the government had an excuse to discontinue discussions with the special Polish envoy, Prince Michal Radziwiłł. The matter nevertheless deserves emphasis as an indication of future developments. The almost simultaneous entreaties of the Lithuanian nobleman and the Italian archbishop constitute, namely, the first tangible sign of that conjunction of Polish and papal foreign policies which would prove to be the salvation of Vienna in the late summer of 1683.

There could hardly have been a more concrete symbol of Sobieski's *volte-face* in foreign affairs than the appearance of his messenger in Vienna. While the early winter of 1678–79 had been a period of political uncertainty, by the end of the Grodno Diet it was clear that John III was striking out along a new path, or, rather, returning to the highroad of his career, from which he had deviated only out of necessity. The tentative *rapprochement* with Austria, the confirmation of an unfavorable armistice with Moscow, the effort to appease a hostile Great Elector, without at the same time breaking ties with France, were all measures that furthered his altruistic goal: a united militant Christendom.[10]

The encouragement of nunzio Martelli and admonitions from the Holy Father himself were really unnecessary, either for the monarch or for numerous senators and deputies. Among the latter anti-Turkish sentiment was gradually coming to a boil. The only pacifists were one faction of Sobieski's own, pro-French party. It was ironical that the King now had to rely on the Polish partisans of Austria, previously his foes. In any case, it was the report (February 8) of Gniński, the Polish negotiator recently returned from Istanbul, that persuaded the Sejm to approve

Sobieski's new course. The ambassador, who had suffered both spiritual and physical humiliation, began his narration dramatically by asking: "Shall I speak or merely weep?". When he was finished, nobody could doubt that the Porte was unwilling to grant concessions in implementing the Zhuravno agreement. John III thereupon received authorization to build up the army and to seek a Pan European offensive league.[11]

Polish delegations soon departed for the most important capitals of the West: Radziwiłł to Vienna, Venice and Rome; Jan Morsztyn, the head of the French party, to the Sun King; Władysław Morsztyn to the States General and the Court of Saint James; Jerome Lubomirski to Italy and Portugal; and the Referendary of Lithuania, Brzotowski, to Moscow. The objective of the missions was threefold: 1.) to obtain an alliance with the Emperor; 2.) to get Leopold and Louis to coöperate; and 3.) to dispose of or smooth over differences with the Russians. Polish crusading fervor was premature at best. Foreign response fell far short of Warsaw's hopes.[12]

The pompous, arrogant, and incapable Radziwiłł, who already once had made an unfavorable impression in Vienna, was obviously unsuited to his task. Even if the Poles had sent a different personality,[13] the obstacles would have been insuperable. They included: the ever-present worry over French intentions; lingering mistrust of John III himself, still thought to be Louis XIV's tool and suspected of personal ambitions in Hungary; the lack of cash, the uncertainty of papal subventions, and the improbability of aid from the *Reich;* the slippery attitude of Muscovy, already secretly parleying with Istanbul; the excessive personal require-ments of the Sobieski clan, including an archduchess for Prince Jakób,[14] an Imperial princedom for the Queen's penurious father, and private financial privileges for the royal pair. The "Three Eleanors Faction" and the friends of Spain also worked to undermine the project. By the end of the year, however, as the result of negotiations conducted more subtly by others, the Austrians did announce their willingness to contract a *defen-sive* league.[15]

Morsztyn, a naturalized Frenchman, was sent to Paris in order to please Louis XIV personally, but this choice also turned out to be unwise. The legate showed little enthusiasm for his assignment.[16] The answer would have been evasive in any case because of France's different objectives in the Near East. Sobieski was still obviously suffering from illusions about his French confrère. The other ambassadors were able to report only slim results. From England and the Netherlands there came a vague promise of financial help but no real signs of ardor. Lubomirski received assur-ances of monetary aid, which, in Portugal's case, reflected genuine zeal.[17] The Russians pressed for the renewal of their Kiev rights but otherwise showed little eagerness. Radziwiłł was not even received in Venice, the plague being given as the reason.[18]

B. The Conflicting Aims of Rome and Paris

Nonetheless, in Rome the maladroit magnate could be certain of a favorable hearing. The Holy Father had also decided that 1679 was the proper moment to realize his dreams. The only question is whether credit for inventing the Pan European league plan should be given more to him than to John III. In particular, did the travels of the Polish envoys stem ultimately from Martelli (i.e., Innocent XI) or from the King?[19]

God Wills It!

However, even if one were to accord the Pope a larger share of honor than Sobieski, the concept surely did not spring from the Pontiff's head alone. Nor was it especially novel for the latter part of the seventeenth century. There was clearly latent popular support for a crusade, arising from a consciousness of the plight of those under the Turkish yoke or threatened by it. The Köprülü revival had found a reverberation in European public opinion. Although the extent of such feeling can be exaggerated, it was a force that might be stimulated and drawn upon, as the later response to the War of the Holy League would demonstrate. Its existence is apparent from the publicistic *Türkenschriften* and *Türkenpredigten*. Among the more prominent individual proponents of a joint attack upon the Porte was Leibnitz. Even before Innocent's reign, Clement X and XI had shown some interest in the idea.[20]

Innocent was likewise subject to the influence of two Capuchin monks, Frà Paolo da Lagni and Marco d'Aviano. Although the less well known of the pair, da Lagni was probably the figure of greater historical importance. Long a resident in the Ottoman metropolis, he was convinced that Turkey was an overripe fruit, about to drop from the vine. In 1678 he presented the Curia a series of four memorials on how an offensive might be effected. (Conceivably, the Pope himself suggested their composition, for he had been talking incessantly of a crusade for over a year already). The friar proposed a vast, strategic pincers movement, to be coördinated in advance. In Asia it would involve the Iranian Shah, who, according to Capuchin missionaries, was only waiting for the Christians to bury their quarrels and unite their forces. In Eastern Europe the attack would be carried out by Sobieski and the Tsar, who were to operate in the Ukraine; by Leopold, who would create a diversion in Hungary; and by Venice, which was to undertake a campaign in Dalmatia. Louis XIV's task would be a maritime venture against Palestine and Egypt, whereas Charles II of Spain was to send his ships and men to North Africa. The Papal State, Malta, Florence, and Genoa would occupy themselves with the Aegean theater. Paolo believed that the "King of Arabia" as well as the pashas of the region and of Egypt would also intervene since, allegedly, they were longing to throw off the insufferable regiment of the Grand Vezir.[21]

This plan, however ingenious, showed little comprehension of contemporary European politics. The Pope's own naiveté should be recalled. The Holy Father (who accepted the scheme fullheartedly) deceived himself regarding the extent of his own authority and his ability to implement so grand a design. He could not correctly evaluate the religious feelings of most of the secular rulers of the day. They were not all Sobieskis either personally or geopolitically. On the other hand, the project was not just a pipe dream. The masses gave some evidence of being receptive to it. An attack upon Turkey was also in Rome's self interest. Ottoman power represented a constant physical danger for the States of the Church. Its elimination would greatly increase the Pontiff's prestige, dramatize his claim to the headship of Christianity, and build up his material strength. To be sure, Innocent was probably also moved by a conviction that he would be doing a work pleasing to God. In any case, his mind once made up, the Vicar of Christ pursued his goals with remarkable faith, energy and endurance. Likewise, good fortune with subordinates (the nunzii in Paris, Vienna and Warsaw) tempered his own insensitivity to practical realities.[22]

The Pope's ambitions naturally conditioned his attitude toward the peace negotiations at Nijmegen. While the Curia could not consider its attempt at mediation successful, Innocent had good reason to be content with the outcome of the meetings.[23] He reckoned Christian armies would now be free for the effort against the Infidel and thus inaugurated the diplomatic steps heretofore described.

Although the benevolent Innocent never seems to have thought of Louis XIV as an enemy, there can be little doubt that the French ruler was his most obdurate Christian opponent. It is ironic that the Pope was forced to do battle with France (over both the Eastern Question and Gallicanism), for the quarrel was quite contrary to his inclinations and expectations, and it squandered energies that could have been expended in the fight against the Porte. The source of the conflict surely lay in the disparate *Weltanschauungen* of pontiff and sovereign. One must return to the Middle Ages, to Innocent IV and Frederick II, to find a parallel. The two differing concepts were also, one might argue, incipient manifestations of competing twentieth-century ideologies about the basic polity of Europe. The papal views implicitly stressed, as they have always done, that fundamental unity again recognized after the Second World War, while Louis' outlook prefigured the *sacro egoismo* of the nation-state which reached its culmination between 1939 and 1945.

The contrast between the viewpoints of Paris and Rome, previously obscured by the Dutch War, began to reveal itself during 1679. The Pope, in commencing his diplomatic campaign, evidently assumed that the Most Christian King could be made aware of the general weal, that he could be persuaded to keep peace with Leopold and perhaps even to contribute materially to the common enterprise. Nothing could have been less suited to the King's current aims.

FRENCH ADVANTAGES

The establishment of the Chambers of Reunion (October, 1679) definitely violated the spirit of Nijmegen, especially in view of the short intervening span of time. It has been remarked, in a reversal of the classical dictum of Clausewitz, that the Sun King was continuing war by peaceful means.[24] The struggle, in any event, was a defensive one, based, initially at least, upon trenchant strategic considerations. Louvois, concerned with perfecting the fortress system along France's eastern frontier and backed by Colbert de Croissy, had presented his master an eloquent case.[25] Unfortunately, the argumentation was of little public utility. Firstly, the legal reasoning behind the "reunions" was fallacious; the principle of desuetude rendered it meaningless. Secondly, other Europeans, especially Germans, were bound to regard the actions of the French courts as tyrannical usurpations, preludes to an eventual absorption of the whole Empire. The inherent suspicion of Louis' motives was most likely exacerbated from the very beginning by the *excès de zèle* demonstrated in particular by the Parlement of Metz. Paris, eager and impatient as it was, still deemed it necessary to recommend caution.[26]

One may well ask why the leaders of France undertook territorial aggrandizement, having so recently sought peace and being unwilling to push their claims so far as to provoke new war. The face of contemporary Germany provides the answer. On no other occasion had the various potentates of the Empire been so inclined to do the bidding of Paris. Although the servility of the German leaders can be exaggerated, there can be little question that French influence had reached great heights. The ecclesiastical lords, because of their exposed geographical location, had no choice but to keep on good terms with Louis. Their convictions were strengthened by the suasions of Wilhelm von Fürstenberg, Prince Bishop of Strasbourg, now first minister to the Elector of Cologne and for all practical purposes a French civil servant. The Palatinate, bordering directly on France, found itself in a position at least as delicate as that of its churchly neighbors. Charles, who became elector in 1680, could only hearken to the Sun King, while John George II of Saxony and Ferdinand Maria of Bavaria also showed little desire to sail a course not plotted toward the Seine.[27]

The most notable case of Gallophilism was Brandenburg, the foreign policy of which had undergone a complete transformation. Nineteenth century historians passed harsh judgment upon the Great Elector for turning to Louis, condemning the founder of the Prussian Monarchy as a cringing, greedy tool of French expansionism.[28] From the viewpoint of a state-building territorial prince, however, Frederick William was doing only what seemed necessary. Embittered at having to renounce his Swedish conquests in the Treaty of St. Germain and blaming his misfortune upon what he considered to be the desertion of his allies of the Dutch War, he decided to steer in the direction of France. The secret pact of October 25, 1679, was only the first of a series of three agreements. Presumably he hoped that his dynasty could move safely through the stormy international seas that appeared to lie ahead. At the same time his gaze remained fixed upon the Swedish-held shores of northern Germany. Probably he could already perceive the coming estrangement between Stockholm and Paris (which, in turn, would cause Denmark to switch from Leopold to Louis). While it is true that Louis ultimately profited more from the alliance than Frederick William did, the Great Elector was able to plunge his paws deeply into the tills of the French treasury, thus providing himself the means for strengthening his army and administration.[29]

Among the other powers of Germany only plague-stricken and financially exhausted Austria was of major importance. Spain was unable to offer effective resistance. In the Netherlands William of Orange had to cede his influence to the more pacific, commerce-minded, and, at this point, politically wiser bourgeoisie. In England Charles II, who had played an unsuccessful, double-dealing game during the last months of the Dutch War, was caught up in the popular hysteria evoked by the wretched Titus Oates and his spurious "Popish Plot." The Stuart monarch was then further embarrassed by the French ambassador, Paul Barillon, who obliquely disclosed the latest haggling over payment of subsidies to the English Crown. Soon Charles became embroiled with Parliament about excluding the Catholic Duke of York from the throne. The one faint sign of opposition to France was William's and Waldeck's efforts to establish a "Union of German Estates." The stadholder, requiring a German alliance as leverage at home, secretly set his uncle to work. At first (September, 1679) only relatively inconsequential states—a few, minuscule princedoms of the Upper Rhenine Circle—and, shortly thereafter, militarily more important Hesse-Cassel joined this league. While the initial purpose was more to keep the peace locally and to protect the little territories from the big ones than to oppose Louis XIV, the Union was fated to change its character and to achieve increased stature as the years passed.[30]

All in all Louis found 1679 well-suited to the pursual of his interests in Western and Central Europe. However, the French monarch looked not only to the Rhine. While it would be venturesome to suggest that by 1679 he had already conceived a definite plan to use Turkish aggression to facilitate his reunions, he apparently recognized the utility of good relations with the Porte. At least this may be inferred from his replacement of the old French ambassador in Istanbul, Nointel, with the more skillful Guilleragues (November 9). The new envoy's instructions were quite specific. They called for: 1.) expression of Louis' desire for friendship (without any manifestation of that humility customarily expected of foreign diplomats by the Turks) ; 2.) the promotion of trade; and 3.) just enough surreptitious support to Thököly to keep the Hungarian rebellion alive. Well received by the Ottoman government, Gulleragues soon learned of the Grand Seigneur's inclination to make peace with Russia and also came to suspect Kara Mustafa's interest in the presumably greener Hungarian pastures. The Turks, a folk who laid great stock in portents, had not failed to draw the proper conclusions from the fact that three Austrian representatives had died one right after the other within the course of a year and a half. There was, however, one major obstacle to an Austro-Turkish war: the tense relations between Istanbul and Warsaw. The French ambassador, given leeway by Louis because of the distance, forthwith undertook to dismantle this roadblock.[31]

C. International Affairs in 1680

A STANDOFF IN HUNGARY

At the moment Guilleragues was commencing to stir up trouble on Leopold's exposed eastern flank, the Vienna government was again endeavoring to achieve some kind of *modus vivendi* with its rebellious Hungarian subjects. The desire to have a free hand in Western Europe was fortified by concern over the effects of the plague and by a lesser victory won by Thököly in November of 1679. These considerations led to the signing of an armistice and to a new round of negotiations at Trnava (Tyrnau, Nagy-Szombat) beginning in late March. However, neither side was as yet prepared to yield anything meaningful. Thököly had no reason to give ground. He was stronger than before because he had succeeded in the meantime in gaining control over the dissident, Transylvanian-backed faction in his own camp. (The rebel chief had dumped Teleki's daughter for Helena.) By this time also the ambition to become a prince in his own right, after the style of George Rákóczy I and Bethlen Gabor, was apparently well-matured. The restoration of "constitutional" government, the interests of fellow magnates were probably no longer his major goals, if indeed they ever had been. Thus the summer of 1680 brought no respite to the sorely-tried people of Hungary. Once again the countryside was subjected to murder, rapine, looting, and burning. The fighting, however, was inconclusive, even if Thököly did manage to recover his home territory of Kéžmarok. At the same time the French usurpations of

German soil were becoming increasingly worrisome. By fall the Emperor decided to enter upon the path of concessions.[32]

The government was, in fact, intent upon a general pacification of the Kingdom. It was ready to renounce completely its abortive experiment in absolutism. The Malcontents were assured that a diet would be convoked the next spring in order to treat the nation's *gravamina*. Their leader was led to believe that under certain conditions Leopold might be inclined to approve his marriage. Sophia Rákóczy had recently died, leaving behind a will that cut off Helena entirely by granting the property solely to the children. (The Emperor was to function as legal guardian until the latter should attain their majority.) Since Thököly was aiming for the nullification of this arrangement, it was not difficult to obtain his assent to a truce, which was to run until June of 1681.[33]

STALEMATE IN WARSAW

While Vienna was striving to mend its badly tended Hungarian fences, it was also engaging in a diplomatic struggle to the north, in Warsaw. Although Sobieski was not trusted and was regarded as too demanding, although Austria had no use for an offensive league, good relations with Poland were useful. A defensive alliance would make the monarchy's position in Eastern Europe considerably more secure. The thought, however, was simpler than its realization. Louis XIV, despite his failure to understand John III and his goals, despite his underestimation of the price for Poland's support, continued to recognize that country's crucial importance and was not ready to submit by default. France needed a counterweight to Brandenburg and Sweden, and it also could not allow Warsaw to lessen Leopold's Hungarian difficulties by relieving Austria of the Turkish danger.

Thus, at the beginning of 1680, the immediate task of Béthune, was to sabotage Zierowski's mutual guarantee proposal. The King was inclined, *faute de mieux,* to accept a defensive tie. He submitted the whole matter to the Convocation (the standing committee of the Diet) on January 11. Zierowski and Martelli did all they could, but Béthune, gauche as he was, managed to block their efforts. It is not possible to reconstruct the debate, but it appears that the Frenchman's endeavors were supported by the magnates' fears of Sobieski's already articulated plans for strengthening the monarchy. Because the suggestion for the alliance seemed to reflect an initiative of the monarch, it was suspect as a devious means of perpetuating the Sobieski family upon the Polish throne (which, indirectly, it was). The nobles riposted by repeating the original demand for an offensive alliance, which they now knew to be impossible.[34]

Despite his success with the Convocation, Béthune's days in the land of the plain dwellers were limited. That he was a very poor diplomat is amply apparent. He had no understanding either of the Polish language or of basic conditions within the country. In his inordinate vanity he seems to have regarded Polish politics as a kind of Punch and Judy show with himself as the master puppeteer. Moreover, he was working for contradictory goals. On the one hand, he was attempting to further the interests of France, for which purpose he was supposed to promise Louis' backing for the succession of Sobieski's son, Prince Jakób (but did not). On the other hand, he was seeking to advance his own fortunes, viewing none other than himself as the proper replacement for John III, and for this reason he was busy among the great nobles undermining Prince Jakób's chances. It is clear that this entirely superficial man had no inkling of the underlying rationale of his sovereign's Eastern foreign policy. He believed, for example, that Franco-Polish cooperation against the Porte was possible. He was too obtuse even to take note of Louis' oft-expressed unwillingness to grant the personal wishes of the Polish queen and continued (inconsistently with respect to his own ambitions), to beg the Sun King for the desired favors.[35]

In April Louis, apparently surfeited with Béthune's antics, decided upon a change of envoys. Bishop Forbin-Janson, who had handled the Sobieskis so well before, and the Marquis de Vitry, French ambassador in Vienna, were chosen as the new representatives. (The Bishop came only for three months.) Because Béthune had been sending alarmist and tendentious reports, presumably in order to promote his own cause, the King especially desired accurate information. He wished to know whether John III had gone over entirely to Leopold. If he had, it would be necessary to promote an opposition party; if he had not, it would be necessary to lead him back to the path of virtue. Louis also desired the reëstablishment of contact, via Poland, with Transylvania (prohibited by Sobieski).[36]

In one respect, however, the new ambassadors were little better than their predecessor. Like him, they were entirely unable to grasp what Sobieski was striving for. They cherished the false impression that the Polish monarch was as corrupt as the magnates. Sobieski could be bought, it is true, but with a difference. He would sell himself only if the arrangement served his own principles.[37] The Austrians were more fortunate in their choice of a diplomatic representative for Warsaw. Zierowski, who had grown up along the frontiers of the Republic, was an ethnic Pole and was acquainted with the history and geography of the nation to which he was accredited. Moreover, administrative clumsiness and suspicion of Sobieski notwithstanding, the Viennese government had a more rational attitude toward Polish affairs than Paris.[38] And, most importantly, the interests of the Austrians and the Poles ran in convergent directions.

The Austrian suggestion for a defensive alliance having been rejected,

Zierowski reverted to the original Polish offensive league. He resurrected this plan in his report of March 21 and advised his government to expedite agreement by granting Sobieski's personal wishes: namely, an archduchess for Jakób, an Imperial princedom for Maria Kazimiera's mendicant father, and various cash bribes. Vienna's unusually prompt response was affirmative but with the preconditions of cooperations from Moscow and a non-aggression pact from Louis; the minister was also ordered only to *imply* the idea of a marriage. Negotiations, which began in April, were suspended during the summer in order that Sobieski could sound out the French king so that Zierowski could receive more precise instructions at home.[39] Leopold and his advisers gave the impression of taking Zierowski's project seriously. While it would be incorrect to infer a firm policy resolution, the Habsburg government was toying with the idea of cauterizing the festering Eastern sore. With some guarantee or even aid from France and with the help of its northern and eastern neighbors, Austria's resources might be equal to the task.

Forbin-Janson and Vitry arrived in September, and at first there was an aura of friendliness and good will. Soon, however, it became clear that no true meeting of minds or policies was possible. The new ambassadors brought no personal concessions for the Sobieski clan and no non-aggression guarantee. They had no money, as requested by John III, for use against the Turks, only a vague private declaration of assistance in the case of an attack. In short Louis was unwilling to fulfill any major Polish wish; he gave only empty promises. The French government was no longer prepared, as in the time of Mazarin and Lionne, to consider seriously the desires and needs of its allies. Louis seems to have expected big concessions in return for most insubstantial ones on his part. It is clear that such a policy could not hold Poland, especially when one takes into account the flattering attentions of Zierowski and the suasions of the Papacy (now represented by a new nunzio, Pallavicini). Even Béthune, in his final report, recognized the error of such an approach, foreseeing the ultimate Austro-Polish alliance of 1683. Despite Poland's permission for the restoration of communications with Transylvania, relations with France began to deteriorate. By the end of the year sentiment at Sobieski's Court was increasingly pro-Habsburg.[40]

THE CHAMBERS OF REUNION

By failing to show as much generosity toward John III as was necessary, the French king was running the risk of losing his Eastern European trump cards at a time when they were of great potential value in the game of international politics. In the meantime matters were coming to a head in the West. The great expansion in the activity of the Chambers of Reunion was beginning to create a crisis of major proportions. The deliberately partial French courts had set themselves to work with all due speed. The bar of Metz was busy absorbing Lorraine, Barrois, and Luxembourg while the judges sitting in Brisach and Besançon directed their efforts against Alsace and the Free Country, respectively. A fourth chamber functioned in Tournai (for Flanders, Hainault, and Namur). While Alsace suffered the most, important localities in the other provinces were also lost to the Empire. In several cases, the French rapidly undertook the construction of strategically important fortresses (Mont-Royal and Sarrelouis). Protests were not long in coming. Charles XI of Sweden, ruler of the one country which had remained loyal to France throughout the Dutch War, expressed himself in the most bitter terms concerning the seizure of the Duchy of Zweibrücken (Deux Ponts), the succession to which had been promised him. The Spaniards were incensed at being presented with *faits accomplis* in Luxembourg and Namur, for, according to a clause of the Nijmegen Treaty about possible disputes in the execution of provisions, they had been conferring with the French at Kortrijk (Courtrai) since December, 1679—a meeting deliberately stalled by the latter on technical grounds. German pamphleteers began to denounce Louis' actions as "pure and simple brigandage."[41] Their vehemence is easier to understand when one recalls that the French were extending their fingers right to the Rhine, well beyond what they ultimately retained by the Treaty of Rijswijk.[42]

The dispossessed and threatened Imperial vassals directed their complaints and laments to their nominal lord in Vienna. Many of them had doubtlessly regarded the Emperor as a potential tyrant not long before. Now he appeared to them as the only possible source of redress. It seems that Leopold knew his duty. If he did not, there were people to remind him. The Elector of Mainz remarked that Austria was no longer capable of protecting the Reich and that a new emperor must be sought.[43] It should also be remembered that the Habsburger was himself among those whose fiefs were being seized. In any case, the monarch now began to weigh possible means of assistance. He thought first of a meeting with the Great Elector, next to himself the most powerful prince of the *Reich*. At that moment the Emperor had no grounds to suspect that Frederick William had already begun to sail under Louis' flag. Fortunately, for the Empire's sake, there was also William of Orange. The essential element in his plans during 1680 was the slippery English King. During the previous two years, the latter had first taken an anti-Gallic line and then, unfazed by the recent French exposure of his duplicity, had renewed dickering with Paris for the money which he needed to free himself of legislative purse strings and thus to maintain the royal prerogative. William now sought to reconcile Charles with the Whig-dominated Fourth Parliament, which the harassed King had kept prorogued since its first session (October, 1679). The somewhat innocent Stadholder argued that alliances against France would serve notice that the Stuart ruler had really broken his ties to the hated, papist Bourbons. (The French sovereign had not yet revealed the Dover Treaty of 1670) . Eager to gain time by granting fictitious concessions to his domestic foes, Charles let his new, loyalist ministers, the "Chits," accept the Orangist suggestion to send plenipotentiaries to Madrid, Berlin, and Vienna. On June 10 (at Windsor) a treaty was signed with Spain. It guaranteed the convocation of Parliament and the preservation of the Nijmegen settlement.

However, the Great Elector naturally rejected London's advances and proceeded to undermine William's hopes further by sowing suspicion (justifiably) against Charles in Vienna. Leopold thereupon pursued his original intention of establishing close contact with Frederick William, but the latter evaded both the requested meeting and a commitment to support the establishment of an Imperial army by the Diet.[44] The Emperor nevertheless clung to the latter idea, which was also being promoted by the Estates of the Circles in southwestern Germany, and prepared to present it in appropriate form at Regensburg. As for the French monarch, the violent reaction of European public opinion ostensibly had some sobering effect. The *Reichstag* sent him an official letter of protest (albeit timorously and hesitantly) . To this the King replied on October 10, offering revision of the Chambers' decisions. On December 30 he wrote of temporarily suspending the annexation procedures. Dilatory tactics apparently seemed in order, not only because of the rearmament talk but because of momentary uncertainty about the reactions of Frederick William. The specter of a new revanche-driven, anti-French coalition seems to have hovered at the wake of the holiday season.[45]

AN UNHEEDED WARNING

Although the reunions had begun to encounter obstacles by the latter part of 1680, and although Poland was beginning to slip out of the French harness, the situation in the Ottoman Empire, while still somewhat unclear, gave promise of changes that could prove beneficial to Paris. At the beginning of 1680 a new Austrian envoy, the doughty Baron Kunitz, arrived in the Turkish capital. He carried a personal letter to the Sultan from Leopold and another epistle to Kara Mustafa from Montecuccoli (in charge of Balkan affairs in his capacity as President of the Court War Council) . The task of the freshly-appointed "resident" was the same as that of his late, unlucky predecessors: to prolong the twenty-year truce due to expire in 1684—an obvious indication of Vienna's nervousness and of the priority that it still gave to the West. Kunitz' interviews with the Grand Vezir were revealing or rather could have been if his superiors, preoccupied with the French menace, had been a little more perceptive. The Turkish minister was well informed about conditions in Europe; his questions touched again and again upon France and its relations with its neighbors. By August the Baron began to suspect that the Turks were thinking of attacking the Empire. The Venetian ambassador, Morosini, reported to the Senate upon his return home and voiced similar worries.[46]

Nevertheless, it cannot be said that 1680 provided any positive signs of what the future would bring in southeastern Europe. The Turks had not yet concluded peace with Muscovy. Relations with Poland continued to be unsatisfactory despite the mediation of Guilleragues. There was talk of armaments for a campaign against Austria and Abafi, who was no longer trusted. For the most part the French ambassador's activity was limited to counteracting anti-French rumors, started by his fellow diplomats. The situation remained fluid, but at the same time it must have given certain grounds for hope to Louis XIV.[47]

D. 1681: From East to West

It has been seen that already during the previous summer the Austrian government showed lively interest in the suggestions of its Warsaw ambassador. The temporary tactical retreat of Louis XIV in the matter of the Reunions quieted Austrian suspicions and helped to revive Zierowski's project, which was of course equally the plan of the papacy and its diplomatic representatives in Poland and Austria. The Emperor's ministers expressed pacific sentiments to France's Viennese envoy, Sébeville, and in January Hocher harangued the Frenchman on the virtues of a joint crusade—although the Austrians were apparently not thinking of any formal agreements with Paris or the states of the Empire. This line of thought was vigorously supported by Sinelli who had formed a strong, personal faction at court, consisting of Montecuccoli's successor, Hermann of Baden; Hocher's former secretary, Baron Abele; the Lord High Steward, Count Albert Sinzendorf; and the Commissioner General of War, Count Ferdinand Breuner.[48] The Habsburg cabinet was now ready to test Buonvisi's thesis that French bellicosity could be directed into less perilous channels, that it might even be made useful to Austria. While the newly-arrived Spanish ambassador, Borgomanero, remained dead-set against any Near Eastern adventure, affairs in the West had not yet deteriorated completely, and he was unable at first to convince either the dominant court faction or Leopold to drop the papal scheme. In a short time, however, his anti-French fulminations would appear entirely justified, and the opinion of the Hocher-Sinelli forces would shift in his favor.

CONCESSIONS IN HUNGARY

If the forces of Christendom were to be united against the Infidel or, conversely, if Vienna were to resist the French, it would first be necessary to pacify the Magyars. The abandonment of the absolutist regime was confirmed by the edict of February 28, which instructed the Hungarian Diet to convene at Sopron two months later. The government now

Serenissimus Princeps ac Dn. Dn. Hermannus.
Marchio Badensis et Hochbergensis etc —
S. C. M. Consily Aulæ Bellici Supremy Præses
et Campi Marschallus.

(Vienna, National Library)

Margrave Hermann of Baden

Reverendissimus ac
Domnus Dominus
Imperis Princeps Episcop
Cæs Mttis Consiliarius

Celsissimus Princeps
EMERICUS Sac Rom:
Imperii Princeps at Suc
Antistes de

Bishop Emmerich Sinelli

inaugurated a policy of moderate concessions. From the Hungarian view-point of course the King was only undertaking to restore a legal, constitu-tional order.

Due to an illness of the Queen the Diet did not meet until May 25, and it was apparently not without inner reservations that Leopold made his personal appearance: two companies of cuirassiers stood, horsed and equipped, before the city gates; and, more tactfully, a number of regi-ments remained out of sight, an hour's ride distant.[49] The predominantly Roman Catholic law-making body first restored the office of Palatine, to which honor Paul Esterházy was unanimously elevated. The monarch then granted a number of important political demands although he was unwilling to drop the cordially hated Kollonitsch, still President of the Hungarian Court Chamber (treasury). Such matters, however, took sec-ond place to the religious issues that were agitating the assembly. The government at first refused even to discuss the complaints of the Evangeli-cals and received support from the Catholic majority which would have suffered economic damage from recognition or extension of the rights of the other two confessions. The Protestants, supported outwardly by the absent Thököly, insisted on full toleration. There was an impasse until August, despite the efforts of Buonvisi (who soon thereafter earned a red hat), Sinelli, and others to smoothe the ruffled feathers of the non-Catholic minority. Finally, it began to dawn upon the Court that it would have to give way in this question, too.[50]

As was so frequently the case in the history of the Habsburg dynasty, domestic change was prompted by external pressure. Thököly had re-nounced his latest armistice on May 20 and did not participate in the Diet, presumably because it did not provide a good bargaining platform. In September he united his troops, albeit imperfectly and disharmo-niously, with those of the protean Abafi and Teleki as well as with the forces of the *Beylerbeyi* of Timişoara (Temešvar) and Oradea. Then came the French action against Strasbourg. Immediately upon receipt of the latter news Leopold began to backtrack in Hungary. It appears that his plan was to follow a middle path between the demands of the two sectarian camps. Nevertheless, the Evangelicals came off second-best. De-spite the grant of meaningful privileges, they were denied full rights and so remained embittered and unreconciled—a dangerous state of affairs in view of slowly-gathering but ominous clouds on the Eastern sky.[51]

Thököly, for his part, was unable to conduct a very successful cam-paign that fall. The 20–30,000 men of the disparate, mutually distrustful anti-Imperial armies made little progress against an opposing host one sixth their number. By December the rebel chief signed another armistice and once more obliged himself to negotiations with Vienna, ostensibly persuaded that he might gain by horse-trading what he had been unable to take by force. The Emperor's emissaries spoke of the government's wish to fulfill the "legitimate" desires of the Magyars, especially those of the Protestants, expressed the hope that their leader would return to the fold and induce others to do so also, and, finally, requested help in renewing the truce with the Porte. In return Leopold was willing to restore Thököly's confiscated inheritance and to grant his blessing for the marriage to Helena. The response of the refractory vassal was to up the ante. Setting a time limit of six weeks, he solicited a princedom for himself, genuine freedom for his co-religionists, the restitution both of his own and his adherents' estates, control over the Seven Comitats of eastern Upper Hungary that were once held by Rákóczy, and the title of "Lord of the Partium." In return he was prepared to assist Vienna by despatching a delegation to Istanbul (with the simultaneous purpose, as he claimed, of defending himself against the backbiting Abafi). It now seemed that Vienna would either have to pay the exorbitant price demanded or else settle matters militarily once and for all. However, the Austrian Court concluded that there was a third possibility: namely, to extend the armistice with Turkey by its own efforts and then lay down the law to the Malcontents.[52] In the meantime it decided to continue its dealings with the rebels: mediation, if attainable, would be worth the effort. The whole undertaking thus took on the character of an overly-ambitious *tour de force*.

RENEWED FRENCH AGGRESSION

The Magyars' own precarious game of political cards was possible primarily because of the developing crisis along the Rhine and the consequent shift of Habsburg court opinion westward, i.e., to the viewpoint of the voluble Borgomanero. Although the French ruler had begun to prevaricate in late 1680 and although he had agreed in February, 1681, to send deputies to confer with the Germans at Frankfurt, there seemed considerable cause for worry by late spring. Louis had made his pledge to stop the reunions effective only at the *start* of the conference, the opening of which he delayed on grounds of protocol (a favorite stalling device of the time). Presumably, his tactic was to give himself enough time to prepare sudden strokes against three strategic locations: Luxembourg, Strasbourg, and, in the northwestern Po Valley, Casale. The Emperor, in any case, somewhat naively sent his personal wonder-worker, Marco d'Aviano, to Paris to obtain a non-aggression guarantee. The famous holy man not only failed to get an interview; he was seized and deported before he could even pass through the gates of the French capital. Then in the latter part of July, Louis landed the first of his major blows: the seizure of the "dependencies" of the already annexed County of Chiny, i.e., the bulk of Luxembourg. Fortified, militarily crucial Luxembourg City and a few other villages still in Spanish hands were in imminent danger.[53]

Borgomanero, who had come to Austria April 2, now (July 31) turned the full force of his rhetoric upon the wavering Leopold, to judge by the report sent back to Madrid:

> Having represented this so evident peril to him with all the zeal of which I was possessed, His Majesty kept silent for a good time, not saying a word to me. And then, demonstrating an extraordinary sense of injury, he said that this was insufferable and that for his part he would do all that was possible for the defense of his House. [Leopold then seems to hesitate because of financial difficulties] . . . I endeavored to animate him, assuring him that as soon as His Imperial Majesty found himself well-armed and as soon as he was seen to oppose France resolutely, all would aid him, but that as long as he was observed in such a state, nobody would declare for him since he would be crushed. . . . I intend to cultivate all these matters at every possible moment in order that a suitable decision may be reached, knowing very well that all will be lost without attempting to oppose with force someone who acts only by it alone, trampling under divine and human laws. God protect the Holy Catholic and Royal Person of Your Majesty, of which Christianity has need.[54]

Whatever the immediate effect of this homily, the new French aggression gave the *coup de grâce* to the Buonvisi-Zierowski plan, already discredited by the fate of the Aviano mission and by Polish domestic developments. On August 13 the Court War Council concluded that dire reports sent by Kunitz were not reliable and that the pacific expressions of the Turkish government ought to be taken at face value. It was agreed that a special envoy, an *internuntius,* should be sent in the person of Count Albert Caprara in order to emphasize the desire for peace. The Austrian statesmen, while aware of French incitement at the Porte, were distant from the Turkish capital and thus not prone to pose the question that local observers pondered: had Kara Mustafa any secret ambitions of his own?[55] Fear of the Sun King blinded them, especially after the seizure of Strasbourg, which, despite forewarning, produced great distress.[56] (Casale was captured simultaneously). The confusion and worry became all the greater upon the partial blockade (November) and full investment (early December) of Luxembourg City, which Louis was now demanding as a substitute for his claims in Flanders.

Although Vienna's wishful and superficial thinking with regard to Turkey is thus understandable, the execution of the August plan (assuming for the moment even a remote chance of success with the Turks) was nevertheless faulty in the extreme. Too much time was allowed to lapse before it was put into effect. This was, of course, inevitable, for, as suggested, the government was following two basically contradictory policies. In order to improve its bargaining position it had postponed the departure of the *internuntius,* first while seeking to gain the allegiance of the Magyars at the Sopron Diet, and then while trying to win over

Thököly. Only after it again became obvious that the latter could not be had cheaply was the Italian nobleman ordered on his way (January 14, 1682), by which point the rebel leader, uncertain that Leopold would grant his demands, was sending his own mission to work simultaneously for and *against* the truce.[57]

As far as the Spanish ambassador was concerned, the events of the latter part of 1681 gave considerable cause for satisfaction. His warnings about France had proved correct, and opinion had swung in his favor. He was demonstrably pleased with the course Hungarian affairs were taking. On New Year's Day he wrote a sanguine letter to his sovereign. Although he noted the dissatisfaction of the Hungarian Protestants—who had refused to participate in the public hand-shaking ceremony with the Emperor at the end of the Diet—he was still convinced that the situation had improved.[58] His unjustified optimism, prompted to be sure by concern for the mortal danger to his own fatherland in the West, was to be a constant feature of Viennese politics during 1682 and 1683; and it goes a long way in explaining why Leopold persisted, even during and after the siege, in believing that Thököly could be "reduced to obedience."

Sobieski Again Stymied

It was not only because of French aggression in the West that the Malcontents were able to play such a large role in the affairs of the East; they also continued to receive cash subsidies from Louis XIV. The Polish Republic was an object of special attention for France during 1681. Warsaw provided a more convenient path into Leopold's troubled Hungarian backyard than the circuitous route via Istanbul.[59] In order to maintain Sobieski's good will the Sun King finally consented, although distastefully and condescendingly, to grant the Polish Queen's father the peerage which he had been seeking for so long. Forbin-Janson and Vitry were also amply supplied with gold with which to influence the new Diet. The bishop and his colleague thought themselves advantageously placed in the spring of 1681, not knowing that two of the great magnates whom they had bought, Jabłonowski and Lubomirski, were already in the pay of the Austrian ambassador. They likewise did not recognize how the cause of France was being damaged by their own personal clumsiness in dealing with the King and his clan. The frustrated ambition of the Sobieskis, their disappointed greed, mutual loyalty, wounded sense of honor, and, above all, the monarch's own interpretation of the true interests of the state made things easier for Zierowski and Pallavicini. The only card that the French and their Hohenzollern allies still held was the possibility of bribing some miserable wretch into casting his *liberum veto* and thus of breaking up the *Sejm*.[60]

The Diet had four assignments. The first was to vent a generally felt indignation toward the Great Elector who had suddenly married his son to the heiress of the Radziwiłł family in order to gain military leverage inside Lithuania. The second was conclusion of an offensive league with Moscow, a project which had to be dropped when it became apparent that the Russians' recent treaty with Turkey (at Radzin, February 11) was seriously intended. The third problem was the alliance with Austria, and it too was abortive, both because of the defection of the Muscovites and the failure of Louis to grant guarantees.[61] The only progress made in the direction of a Turkish war was a promise of 100,000 florins from the Papacy and a decision to establish a regular army of 54,000 men. The fourth question, albeit not in public, was Poland's relationship to the Malcontents. The King, who was rapidly loosing his sympathy for the rebels, was still unwilling to slight France openly. He had to keep himself covered, both domestically and internationally. The two French representatives were thus able to gain secret permission to send a French agent, Du Vernay Boucault, to the Transylvanians and rebels. Hungary continued to be a real problem for John III, for the continuing resentment and suspicions of the Austrians hindered the *rapprochement* which the monarch now desired. Even Zierowski was mistrustful. He had bribed his way into the Polish mails and had gotten hold of the correspondence of Absalon, the Malcontents' envoy to France and Poland. There he was able to read of Thököly's offer of the Crown of St. Stephen to Prince Jakób. Although Sobieski did not snap at this lure, he was attracted by it, and the memory of the incident continued, even after the eventual Austro-Polish Alliance (1683), to trouble relationships between the two nations.[62]

The Diet itself came to an end on May 22, for which Brandenburg more than France must be blamed. The Great Elector, erroneously advised that Sobieski was contemplating action against him while waiting for the Turkish war to mature, decided to deliver a stroke of his own first and instigated a *liberum veto*. The King was bitterly disappointed, for the individual laws necessary for carrying out the army decision thereby became void. He cried in despair: *"Vare, redde mihi legiones.* So I also say now to those who broke up the Sejm: give me back the army, give me back public security, give me back the glory which I could acquire and which waited for me. . . ."[63] The King might have been able to chastise Frederick William by independently plunging Poland into war with its northern neighbor. He might also have organized an absolutist *coup d'état.* But he was sufficiently wise not to take such risks. He continued to look to a crusade for the realization of his goal of a strong monarchy for Poland and was not yet prepared to break completely with France. He preferred to carry on his patient, cautious effort for an Austrian alliance. In short, he was ready to wait for the ripe moment.[64]

Forbin-Janson, for his part, was quite content. Leaving for France on July 29, he was convinced that he had reestablished French influence, even though he had failed to bind John III by an alliance. In his ignorance of Sobieski's character he was persuaded that a Polish link with the Emperor was impossible: the latter was not rich enough to satisfy Sobieski and his spouse. Moreover, the route to the rebels was open. Vitry could be left alone in good conscience. The latter's reports continued, one may assume, to tranquilize the Sun King, who was informed that Sobieski was thinking of nothing less than war.[65]

E. 1681: Diplomatic Alignments

While Louis may have been misled by the information that he received from Warsaw, his representative at the Diet in Regensburg, Verjus, left him in no doubt as to the growing opposition of Germany to the chambers of reunion. It was clearly necessary for France to prevent the Germans from becoming too excited: even if they lacked a Louvois, they were still formidable soldiers, as the previous war had demonstrated. Once already the King had found it tactically advisable to tread water.[66] The general European diplomatic situation, which had been so favorable to him in 1679, was gradually beginning to change. The rudiments of a new, anti-French alliance were at hand. Even though Stuart neutrality and the outbreak of general war in the East were to keep the new trend from developing broadly during the next few years, necessary foundations were being laid.

THE INCIPIENT COALITION

The first sign—admittedly feeble in its own context—of a militant reaction to French expansionism was an attempt to create a standing, peacetime national army, distinct from Leopold's own *Hausmacht* (troops customarily, although somewhat misleadingly called "Imperial"). On January 17 the Emperor formally requested the long-debated revision of the *Punctus Securitatis Publicae* or Imperial War Constitution (*Reichskriegsverfaßung*). This was a legal instrument, dating mainly from 1521 and 1555, that provided for a regular military force in wartime. By late summer the deputies finally approved a watered-down plan that called for a new, 40,000 man "simplum"; that is to say, they increased the amount of the soldier tax levied upon the individual estates. The number was actually rather meager, for Germany, a veritable mine of fighting men, could easily have supplied 100,000 professionals. The sum, however modest, was divided among the Circles. The latter, authorized to redistribute ("sub-repartition") the contributions locally, were charged with recruitment and organization. The new measure also provided for treasuries on both the national and the Circle level. These impractical, decentralized arrangements were necessitated by knotty financial problems and indirectly reflect the conflict of interests between the small and large estates. The latter, which came to be called "armierte

The Incipient Anti-French Coalition 1679–1683

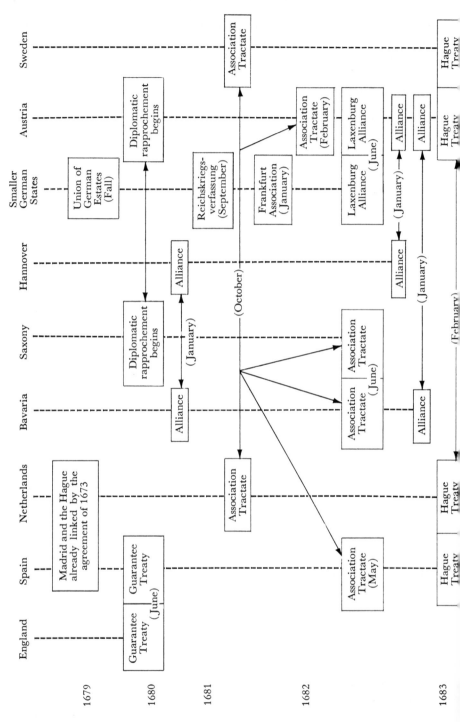

Stände" because of their own, autonomous armed forces, were either synonymous with the Circles (Spain with Burgundy and the Emperor with Austria) and hence not inclined to set up separate fighting bodies, or else they extended over several Circles, in which case they could scarcely be expected to parcel out their military units under a non-dynastic command. Brandenburg is the best example of such overlapping: it belonged to three Circles.[67] There was also continuing distrust of the Emperor as a potential tyrant, a point of view which the French sedulously encouraged.[68]

Only the smallest and most threatened principalities, located in the so-called "Forward Circles" of the Southwest, were to impart any life at all to the Imperial War Constitution. And they proceeded cautiously, more out of opposition to the "Armed Estates" and from resentment against the Emperor's policy of quartering his own troops and exacting contributions than from fear of the French. The measures which they eventually agreed upon provided for so fragmentized an organization that there was only a limited possibility of an effective military force. Obviously such a body could never become either an instrument of national policy or a matrix of national unity.[69] Nevertheless, the passing of the 1681 law was fortunate in at least one respect: it resulted in some increase in the number of soldiers available in the Franconian, Bavarian, and Swabian Circles and thus added strength to the army that relieved Vienna two years later.[70] Parenthetically, it was at this time also that the Electors of Saxony and Bavaria began building the first real standing armies that their principalities had known.

A more meaningful development was the extension of the Upper Rhenine Circle's Union of German Estates, for which Waldeck, stimulated by recent Dutch-Swedish amity, was largely responsible. Hesse-Darmstadt, Würzburg, and Bamberg joined the league during the fall, and by early 1682 the Franconian Circle and Fulda were also to bring themselves into what came to be called the Frankfurt Association.[71] An even more significant indication of the slowly-swelling anti-French tide was a shift in the sympathies of several of the more powerful princes. The most critical change was taking place in Munich, where skilled Austrian diplomacy (Nostic and Lobkowitz) was beginning to bear fruit. The romantic and cavalier Max Emmanuel, who had attained his majority in 1680, was upset over Louis' latest gambits. A meeting with Leopold in March served to encourage a pro-Imperial orientation. The Emperor, whose peregrinations were so frequently influenced by the location of holy places, decided to make a pilgrimage to the then fashionable shrine of Alt-Ötting which lay inside Bavaria. The Elector also came in order to pay homage. The Habsburger thoughtfully presented his vassal a pearled and bejeweled dagger. Thereupon the impressionable youth cried out: "I shall carry it only for Emperor and fatherland." It is improbable that anyone could have foreseen in what place and under what circumstances—the siege of Vienna—the vow would be fulfilled. Probably the prospect of a marital alliance also furthered *rapprochement*. Although at the very moment Max Emmanuel was negotiating for the hand of a lovely, but alas Protestant princess of Sachsen-Eisenach, there was still the possibility of espousing the archduchess, Maria Antonia. The thought of such a marriage probably opened up, even then, the alluring vista of the Spanish Succession. While plans for a political union did not ripen until the next year and while the nuptial question was left unsettled a little longer, by the end of 1681 the tide in Munich was beginning to flow in Vienna's direction. The didactic behavior of Louis' ambassador, evoked in part by the King's instructions, was of little service to the French cause.[72]

At about the same time the Emperor was also gaining fresh partisans in Saxony and Hannover. In Dresden John George III had recently taken up the reigns of government, and it rapidly became apparent that he was determined to reverse the pro-French stance of his predecessor. Even more resolute was Ernst August of Hannover, who was aiming for the reunification of his partitioned, ancient stem duchy. Although something of a dandy ("The First Gentleman of Europe"), the Brunswicker possessed great political skill and ultimately became the most successful Welf since Henry the Lion. This dynastic *Realpolitiker,* who was already calculating that his state's interests lay in a unified front with the Empire and the Emperor against France, was thunderstruck when he heard of the seizure of Strasbourg. Shortly thereafter, he proceeded not only to improve relations with Vienna but to develop and propose a strong alliance plan, which was of some influence in the formation of the Laxenburg pact of the next spring.[73]

Perhaps the most damaging desertion of all from the French camp was that of Sweden, which returned to its former tie with the Netherlands in the so-called "Association Tractate" (October 10), technically a "guarantee" to uphold the Nijmegen settlements. Charles XI had expressed distaste for Louis even before the latter had grabbed Zweibrücken, and no Swedish King could be happy about a Franco-Prussian *accommodement.* Even if Louis had not added insult to injury with the seizure of further personal property in the County of Chiny, it is likely that the northern monarch would have detached himself from the French. It was more difficult for William of Orange to swing the circumspect, Arminian oligarchs of Amsterdam toward possible hostilities. However, the French expansion in Luxembourg beyond the County of Chiny had aroused great indignation. It is evident from the correspondence of the Comte d'Avaux, Paris' representative in the Netherlands, that some of the most ardent Dutch republicans were disturbed: this was striking too close to home. In any event, the Stadholder enjoyed the backing of public opinion, the Calvinist masses being exercised over recent anti-Huguenot measures in France.[74]

Despite his frustrations of the previous year, William, backed by Waldeck, was continuing to press for the formation of a grand coalition in order to exert psychological pressure upon France.[75] Borgomanero was working along similar policy lines although, it seems, with a more bellicose attitude. The rôle of the Spanish diplomat, who had known the Prince of Orange since at least 1677, in helping to marshal the forces that later comprised the League of Augsburg is little recognized and deserves stress quite apart from the Eastern Question. Already in 1680, while he was still ambassador to the Court of St. James, he was apparently in league with William's project.[76] The Marchese's trip across Belgium and Germany and into Austria during the early spring of 1681 seems only to have increased his fears of France. In a report sent from Linz on April 10 he expressed concern over the construction of French fortresses in the "reunited" areas and took note of the dangerous, dilatory attitude of the Diet. With the sure instinct of an experienced courtier he began to work almost immediately with Sinelli, "hoy en dia Obispo de Viena y sin contradicción el que tiene la voluntad de Su Magd. Cessa."[77]

Thus it was only natural that in August, 1681, Borgomanero should coördinate his actions with a contemporaneous diplomatic mission of the Stadholder to London. The Dutchman, apparently little dismayed by Charles II's inability to assuage his last two Parliaments (the Fourth, the Oxford), was again striving to secure coöperation against Louis XIV. In view of the French aggression in Luxembourg it seemed reasonable to request implementation of England's guarantee treaty with Spain. (The King's insincere promises may have been of value to William in bringing about the Association Tractate). Borgomanero, who had negotiated the Anglo-Spanish pact, unfolded his oratorical skills before Leopold, who the year before had hesitated to join the proposed union of England, Spain, the United Provinces and the Baltic powers. In his memorial the Spanish ambassador submitted that the "restitution of the Most August House" and the Emperor's own power in the Reich depended entirely upon such an alliance, which, he noted, would preclude intrigues and a separate Protestant league.[78] At the time he thought that he had convinced the All-Highest, but he repored home that Charles' equivocations and the advice of certain Imperial ministers frustrated the enterprise. Of course, what neither the Marchese, nor anyone else aside from the French, can have known was that already in March the Stuart canary had once again ensconced himself in the gilded Bourbon cage.[79] Only on October 8, after

Strasbourg's fall, was Borgomanero able to persuade the Emperor to authorize Austria's minister in the Netherlands to co-sign the pending Dutch-Swedish agreement.[80]

Another factor inhibiting a grand alliance in 1681 was the continuing influence of France upon the remaining electorates. The defenseless Palatinate was at Louis' beck and call. Cologne was firmly in the hands of the Fürstenbergs while its neighbor, Mainz, dared not offend the Sun King. Trier was pro-Imperial at heart or at least told Borgomanero that it was; yet it did not feel that it was safe to speak out publicly.[81] The most important French satellite was Brandenburg, the support of which was firmly secured before the moves against Luxembourg and Strasbourg. The Great Elector, increasingly but mistakenly hopeful of Paris' aid in regaining Swedish Pomerania, signed his second treaty with Louis on January 11 and bound himself to support the reunions—preferably by suasion but with weapons if need be. Berlin thereupon became the command post for a French diplomatic offensive in Germany. Denmark, its eyes firmly rooted to the eastern shore of the Öre Sound, also reverted to the French camp.[82]

Ambassadorial activity became all the more intense after the successful *coups de main* against the Alsatian capital and Casale and the moves against Luxembourg City: Louis seemingly desired to take advantage of the numbing fright that his swift, efficient campaigning had evoked. He let one of his electoral mouthpieces do the talking. "In the event that the Empire should decide to renounce in perpetuity all that the Most Christian King had reunited to his crown before sending his ambassadors to Frankfurt [i.e., including the most recent seizures] we ought to be assured of a long and lasting peace." Louis would then generously guarantee the Reich's borders and he would send a host against the "common enemy," the Turk. Germany, however, would have to pledge itself not to intervene against France in any non-Imperial venture; in other words, not to oppose any French aggression in northern Italy or Spain proper, for which the King would be willing to neutralize the Southern Netherlands permanently. If this offer were declined—two months being given for a reply—"sixty thousand men would appear promptly with all the necessary equipment in order to make war. . . ."[83] Thus Germany was alternately proffered carrot and stick.

Another tack that the French took was to bid restoration of Freiburg im Breisgau to Leopold in return for the demolition of Philippsburg. Borgomanero reckoned that this proposal, which the Emperor could never accept for reasons of military security, was designed to make Vienna look bad in the eyes of the Empire, and he regarded (erroneously) the whole Frankfurt meeting as nothing but a device to lull the princes to sleep. The latter, as represented by deputies in Regensburg, still sat around waiting to see what the King of England, "el Paradero de esta

Dieta y el rumbo que tomara el Rey de Francia," would do.[84] Britain's ruler, however, had been exploiting the international situation for additional financial advantage. Under pressure since September from the Dutch and Austrian ambassadors, Coenrad van Beuningen and Count Franz von Thun, to join the Association Tractate, then harried by these two and their Spanish colleague, Don Pedro Ronquillo, to aid Luxembourg, he succeeded (late November) in extorting a raise from Paris. Yet his domestic situation became almost untenable after the harassment of the rock-bound fortress became a full scale investment. Charles, caught on the hook of the Whig opposition, now begged Barillon to ask Louis for some kind of relief. On Christmas Day the Stuart monarch sought to escape from his dilemma by offering France his services as an arbitrator.[85] Thus, as the new year arrived, Western and Central Europe remained in a status of flux.

ISTANBUL AT THE CROSSROADS

In the Ottoman Empire 1681 was also a time of uncertainty, although there were intriguing indications of a westward reorientation of aggressive energies. The Porte ended its long and fruitless conflict with Russia (the Radzin Treaty), thereby freeing itself from pressure on its eastern flank. The conclusion of this peace was obviously of great interest to Louis XIV and his ambassador. Guilleragues was also quick to report the Grand Vezir's growing interest in the Pannonian Basin and its appendices. For a time the envoy's letters foretold the deposition of the satellite Abafi, now even more than before a rival of Thököly and an object of Phanariote hatred as well. The French did not favor the project, reckoning that the Transylvanian would then make common cause with Leopold. They were doubtlessly pleased when the plan fell through, Kara Mustafa's approval notwithstanding. (Apparently, the slothful but sly Prince bought off the Sultan.)[86] However, Turkish military preparations continued, and the only possible foe, aside from Poland, was the Emperor. At the same time (May) Thököly broke his most recent armistice with Vienna. In order to encourage the Grand Seigneur to intervene, Guilleragues spread rumors of French fortress construction and troop concentrations in Alsace. Asked by the Turks whether his King was at peace with Leopold, he replied that this was momentarily the case but that his master was not accustomed to leave an army of 300,000 unemployed for long. Since the Porte greatly esteemed French prowess and even feared a Gallic attack, the insinuation of a joint front was bound to have a powerful effect. The French representative wrote that enthusiasm for war was at fever pitch: distinguished Turks assured him that an offensive would begin the next year and that Abafi would have to participate whether he liked it or not.[87]

This incitement of the Turks raises the question of what the French were aiming for. Contemporaries believed (followed by nineteenth century historians) that the Sun King, seeking the Imperial crown and universal domination, hoped to propel himself into Leopold's office by becoming the savior of a *Mitteleuropa* unable by itself to resist the mighty Turkish host.[88] In reality the goal was much more modest: namely, to obtain Imperial sanction for the judgments of the Chambers of Reunion. All that Louis required at Frankfurt and Regensburg was diversion of his opponents' armed forces to the East. Unlike the Habsburgs or other German princes, he was well aware of the dry rot in the Turkish body politic. Guilleragues made the point continually and in great detail. Under these circumstances it would have been nigh impossible for the King to conclude that the Ottoman army was capable of completely defeating the Teutons, and it therefore follows that the most that he could have expected was a diplomatic exploitation of the Emperor's two front dilemma.[89]

For the time being, however, the stratagem was cast into serious jeopardy. The bombardment of the Turkish port of Chios in August by the French admiral Duquesne in pursuit of Barbary corsairs seriously undermined Guillerague's position. The infuriated Turks seemed for a while to listen to the peace proposals of Kunitz and to look menacingly toward Poland. They also appeared to take note of the (superficially) better relations of Leopold with the Magyars that resulted from the Sopron Diet.[90] Although his personal situation was unpleasant, the French diplomat managed to keep his head. While refusing to humble himself, he tried to make a conciliatory impression. There the matter rested until the next spring when Louis would provide a skillful apology. The chief effect of the incident was that the Habsburg Court came, temporarily, to doubt the existence of a Franco-Turkish *entente,* to discredit even more Kunitz' warnings about Ottoman rearmament and intentions, and to reaffirm its decision to press negotiations with the Porte.[91]

CHAPTER FIVE

The Darkening Eastern Sky
1682–1683

A. 1682: A "Little" War

The decision of the Habsburg government to send Count Caprara to Istanbul did not meet with the approval of Kunitz. The faithful resident wrote home in January, indicating that in his opinion the Turks understood force only and that they would regard Vienna's peace overtures as a confession of weakness. His objections made little impression upon his superiors. The latter seem to have considered his reasoning primarily a manifestation of offended vanity, assuming that he resented being superceded by the *internuntius*.[1] Kunitz, a relatively humble sort, probably had little conception of the politicking that was going on at the Viennese Court—the ultimate reason why his advice was discounted. The fact of the matter was that for the moment the persistent Spanish marchese and his episcopal ally, Sinelli, enjoyed the Emperor's confidence.

"WESTERNERS" AND "EASTERNERS"

The Capuchin bishop, to whose views Leopold was so beholden, was of proletarian origin. According to the French ambassador, Sèbeville, who wrote with obviously malicious pleasure, the good father was born at Komárno or Győr, the offspring of a Savoyard chimneysweep and butcher. A child prodigy, he was educated by monks, who discovered in him a gifted, popular-style preacher. Lobkowitz, exploiting the Emperor's susceptibility to clerical promptings, allegedly slipped Sinelli into the august household as a chaplain in order to dispose of his rival, Count Auersperg. Sèbeville claims that the Capuchin was an intriguer himself and that he contributed to his own patron's downfall.[2] What is certain is that the padre's former association caused him no loss of influence. Named a Privy Councillor, he gradually came to function as a first minister without actually holding the title. Although appointed (1680) to the rich see of Vienna, he seems to have been devoid of selfish interest. Nor was he a fanatic proselytizer. Although he agreed with a policy of absolutist centralization, he opposed the unrealistically adamant Counterreformatory policies of the Hungarian Jesuits (albeit with success only when it was too late).[3] The Bishop's allies included, as previously, Hermann of Baden, who, as an Upper Rhenine Prince, was a natural enemy

133

GIOVANNI ADOLFO CONTE DI SVARTZENBERG SIGNOR DI HOENLANSPERGH, GIMBORN, MVRAV, WITTINGAW, FRAVENBERG &DEL CONS° SECRETO DI STATO DI S.M.TA CES°CAVALIER DEL TOSON D'ORO &

(*Vienna, National Library*)

Prince Johann Adolf von Schwarzenberg

Count Leopold Wilhelm von Königsegg

of France;[4] Count Albert von Sinzendorf (the Lord Steward) ; and Baron Christoph von Abele (the Treasurer). An apparently new adherent was Count Wilhelm von Königsegg (Vice Chancellor of the Empire).[5] The Spanish ambassador, the prelate, and their following represented what may be called the "Western," i.e., the belligerently anti-Ludovican standpoint. Hocher, now Court Chancellor, was a "Westerner," too, although in other matters an opponent of the Sinelli clique.[6]

The one member of the Imperial entourage who at this time was an "Easterner" was Prince Adolf von Schwarzenberg, President of the Imperial Aulic Council and founder of his illustrious family's greatness. Stately in demeanor, eloquent, and, surprisingly for old Austria, punctual, his character was nonetheless flawed in such a manner as to limit his political effectiveness. Addicted to overly-penetrating criticism, to excessive consideration of both the pros and cons of issues, he made a confusing, irresolute impression upon colleagues. This indecisiveness, however, did not extend to private financial concerns, nor of course to the paramount foreign policy issue of 1682.[7] Borgomanero considered him a French puppet, and it follows that Sèbeville regarded him sympathetically.[8] In any case, Schwarzenberg advocated acceptance of Louis' terms in order to fight Turkey, and thus in January he attempted to oppose ratification of the Association Tractate, arguing that the Dutch and the Swedes could not be counted upon and that arming would merely irritate the French.[9] The only support that he then enjoyed came from Buonvisi. While the passage of time and the ever more obvious revelation of the Turkish danger were to increase the number of "Easterners" in Vienna, the Prince himself was not destined to experience the complete victory of his ideas—which did not occur until a year after the great siege (Truce of Regensburg, 1684).[10] The Pope's representative was luckier in this respect.

The "Westerners" set great store in negotiations with *both* of Austria's Balkan adversaries. The Ottoman half of the peace offensive, already too long delayed, commenced January 14, 1682, with an Imperial farewell audience for Caprara and his host of Turkish-attired attendants. The mission received its final instructions, which were to offer "suma considerable para prorogar por otros diez años la tregua y para que no se assistencia a los reveldes."[11] Nevertheless, the absence of a sense of urgency, so obvious as to drive even the Spanish to desperation, kept the mission from overcoming practical obstacles to its departure, and it did not set off (by boat via the Danube) until February 3. Already in Budapest the signs of Turkish militancy were so apparent that the *internuntius* wrote home, requesting funds for individual bribery in Istanbul (which he seems to have received only at a later date, the treasury being exhausted by military disbursements).[12] As the embassy drifted farther downstream, outward appearances became even graver: it was amply clear that the Turks were making major military preparations.[13]

THÖKÖLY'S DOUBLE-DEALING

In the meantime, envoys of the supple Thököly had beaten Leopold to the punch in Istanbul. Their ostensible purpose was to persuade the Grand Seigneur to renew the truce. Fundamentally, of course, they were working for the personal interests of their own chieftain. Led before the Grand Vezir's sofa on January eighth, they requested that the Porte declare Thököly ruler of Hungary, promising that their master would pay a high tribute and would place the whole country under Turkish suzerainty within two years. The untiring Kunitz succeeded in learning of this interview as well as of the decision with which the rebel emissaries were sent home a month later: namely, a promise of help from the *Beylerbeyi* of Buda, the already appointed *Ser'asker* or commander-in-chief of the Turkish troops in Hungary. Thököly himself was sent a letter that implied the fulfillment of his request for a crown.[14] The resident advised his superiors that it was necessary forthwith to take strong military action against the Malcontents: he believed that this was the only means of impressing the Turks. However, Leopold hearkened not to the man on the spot but to his camarilla. Borgomanero, especially, persevered in soliciting a separate agreement with the Hungarians, notwithstanding his belief in the utility of a prior settlement with the Porte. By now it was probably not so much a question of contradictory as of *alternative* policies. The highly regarded Venetians had apprised Vienna of the Grand Vezir's bellicose intentions. (The Marchese forwarded a copy of the warning to Madrid.) If war was unavoidable after all, rebel help or, for that matter, just neutrality would be invaluable.[15]

In April, therefore, a new confrontation took place at Kapos, the Magyar headquarters. The Imperial representative was Baron Filippo Saponara, whom Spain's ambassador considered a reliable personal tool.[16] The choice was at least psychologically astute, for the Italian nobleman, an army officer who had dealt with Thököly the preceding fall, was ethnically and personally palatable to the Malcontents. However, the Emperor still could not bring himself to offer major concessions. He was unwilling to grant more than two comitats. As for marriage to Helena, once again he would go no further than to imply a favorable decision. Even the latter step was taken with hesitancy and in the recognition that the union was unpreventable in the last analysis. In return the Austrian government hoped that the bridegroom would abide by the laws of the Sopron Diet of the previous year and would continue to work in behalf of peace. The rebel leader, repressing any disappointment he may have felt, merely indicated a limited willingness to accept the latter of Vienna's requests.[17]

On April 25 Thököly proceeded in person to Buda where the *Beyler-beyi,* Koca (the "Venerable") Ìbrahim Arnaut Uzun (the "Tall") Pasha, resided. Received with all the honors due a head of state, the would-be Magyar monarch carried on two separate negotiations. The first related to his possible role as a mediator: the terms finally hammered out would not only have satisfied the Ottoman gold lust (a 500,000 florin annual tribute from Leopold) but would have accorded him the desired, Rákóczy-sized realm. The second series of discussions resulted in a fourteen article treaty, by which the Malcontents allied themselves to the Porte under the most favorable conditions imaginable. The agreement foresaw the establishment of a Thököly-ruled Hungary. All that the Magyars would have to pay was a fixed, annual sum of 40,000 thalers. Plans for joint military operations were also made.[18] It should be noted that Ìbrahim Pasha had been gathering a considerable force of soldiers from most of Balkan Turkey since the previous year, and it may well be that the summer of 1682 should be considered the actual start of that great Turkish war, which ended only with the Treaty of Zenta in 1699.[19]

Vienna, which obtained the first set of terms through Saponara, showed no signs of interest. It had hoped not to have to pay more than a lump sum of a million and to cede more than a handful of already disputed frontier villages. It had assumed that Thököly, whom the Turks were still supposedly planning to install in Transylvania, would not be so foolish as to put himself entirely into the Porte's hands.[20] And it continued to believe that approval for the Transylvanian project, plus the restitution of the confiscated Zrinyi family property to Helena's brother, Balthasar, would suffice to bring the rebel chieftain around. The young Prince was in fact dispatched to his new brother-in-law, (the marriage having taken place on June 15 at the fortress of Mukachevo in Saponara's presence). There can be no question of Leopold's enduring trust in the good faith of Thököly, "el qual continua en dar buenas esperanzas de quererse ajustar."[21]

On the other hand, by the first half of July the All Highest was beginning to indicate modest alarm over Istanbul's attitude. The news from Count Caprara was of a conflicting nature; a polite reception contrasted with the Grand Vezir's known warmongering. Fear at the Austrian Court increased to the point where the Emperor averred that he could see no way of forestalling the approaching storm except by paying a large personal bribe to Kara Mustafa, and for the immediate moment he contemplated sending 20,000 florins to Ìbrahim Pasha in order to assure continuance of negotiations in the Ottoman capital.[22] In the meantime the rebel leader received the Imperial rejection of the Buda proposals, and any doubts that he may have had about effectuating his Turkish alliance vanished, at least for the duration of the fighting season. By this juncture, moreover, Ìbrahim Pasha's military preparations were almost completed, a fact of which Vienna was by no means oblivious. The reprieved but still foot-dragging Abafi was sent firm orders to appear with his troops and to coöperate in the forthcoming campaign.[23]

THE REBEL PRINCIPALITY

The Malcontents were the first of the three uneasy allies to take to the field. On July 20 their forces snatched the citadel of Košice (Kaschau, Cassovia) from its garrison, the majority of which was enjoying more comfortable sleeping quarters in the town itself (which was simultaneously invested).[24] Thököly also found the occasion opportune to address a half-self-exculpating, half-threatening manifesto to his fellow countrymen; but despite hatred for the Germans, making common cause with the despised Turks was asking people to swallow hard. The *Beylerbeyi* was of course already en route. His forces made their appearance on August 11. (The reluctant Transylvanians did not arrive until after the town's fall.) [25] The dress rehearsal for 1683 was now fully underway.

The disquieting news of Turkish troop movements came to Vienna even before the union of the two enemy armies. By this point it was becoming apparent that making peace in one region, the East, in order to be sufficiently strong to risk war in the other, the West, was going to be harder than had been assumed. The Borgomanero-Sinelli faction was a trifle shaken in the face of the new facts. At the same time it still seemed impossible to wage hostilities on two fronts. Prince Schwarzenberg, "sus parciales y los Jesuitas," could now speak more insistently about a settlement with France. In fact, even as early as May the Spanish ambassador found it necessary to shout at his opponents.[26] About July 30 he had the opportunity to appear before the Emperor and to unleash all his formidable eloquence: he argued that Louis was the real foe because he was stirring up the Magyars and the Turks.[27] On August 11 the issue came before a great meeting of eighteen top Habsburg statesmen. Despite the ominous rumblings from Pannonia the conclusion was that the interests of the August House in the West continued to outweigh those in the East. Caprara should receive full power to proceed although there was to be no question of his begging for peace.[28] The Prince remained the only figure courageous enough to register dissent in an open vote.[29] Clearly Borgomanero and Sinelli were still in a position to exploit fear of the French. The news from Istanbul had to become absolutely unequivocal before Vienna would renounce all hope of averting attack; and even then the power of the partisans of Spain would remain so strong as to permit considering the dismal prospect of a double-barreled war.

As the summer advanced, the situation in Hungary became even darker. Two days after the Vienna conference Košice, its population mutinous, surrendered. Other Upper Hungarian cities also fell. Only in front of Fila'kovo (Fülek) was the Turco-Hungarian host stymied. The commandant, István Koháry, was a convinced royal partisan and resisted with leonine courage. He replied to a surrender demand by exposing his derrière in full view of the enemy and by impaling a pre-broiled Turkish captive. The taking of the city required a furious bombardment and a thrice-repeated assault. The citadel held out until the troops finally rebelled against their leader, who thereupon cursed Thököly to his face as a traitor. The victory was not cheap: it cost the besiegers 4000 dead.[30] Thököly, in any case, now claimed his reward. On September 17 Ibrahim Pasha published the Sultan's decree, naming the rebel "Prince of Central Hungary" (the Ottoman expression for the Partium). The new ruler received a costly robe, a sword, a scepter, and a golden hat from his Islamic patrons—which by Turkish custom was a symbol of vassalage. Horsetails and flags were also presented. In return Thököly had to pay only the 40,000 "black piaster" annual tribute previously agreed upon.[31]

The Malcontents next proceeded to organize outright a state of their own. A mint began to produce money with bullion from the Imperial mines captured in the western Slovakian hills. The coins bore the inscriptions "Emericus Comes Tekeli Princeps ac partium Regni Hungariae Dominus" and "Pro Deo, patria, & libertate."[32] A court with all attendant etiquette was established. A diet, at which twenty comitats were represented, was convoked. The Exulants returned to their families and repossessed their confiscated estates. Persecution of Protestants ceased and the Jesuits fell upon bad days. By October the bulk of Upper Hungary had slipped from Vienna's hands. Only by dint of great effort were the Imperial generals, Enio Caprara and Strassoldo, aided by the loyal Palatine, Paul Esterházy, able to hold the line of the Váh River.[33]

Borgomanero, writing to Madrid, drew consolation from the fact that the lost strong points were of such poor quality as to be at the mercy of whoever dominated the countryside and that the Turks had not placed a garrison of their own in Košice—which he interpreted to mean the absence of a formal state of war.[34] The campaign itself came to an end when most of the Turks, unused to fall fighting, went home to celebrate Ramadan. Thököly now lacked troops to continue holding the Slovakian hill towns and threatened General Caprara with destruction of the mines if he were not granted an armistice. Caprara consented, leaving the duration of the truce to the decision of the Emperor. Imperial forces reoccupied the mines but went no farther because of logistics. Rebel emissaries travelled to Vienna to discuss both the prolongation of the armistice and the possibility of a general settlement. Although their leader's credit with Leopold had finally begun to suffer, the Habsburg government was willing to talk, not only because of momentary military advantage but because of lingering hope of an *accommodement*.[35] In the meantime Caprara had written of almost unmistakable signs of an overall Turkish offensive the next summer, which made agreement seem even more essential.

Up to mid-1682 Vienna had been unwilling to cater much to Thököly's demands, for it had reckoned upon peace with the Porte. Indeed the Counter Reformation continued to rage unabated in West Hungary even into the fall.[36] Now, however, events led the Emperor to at least consider concessions that he had previously been unwilling to make. As a preliminary move Esterházy was instructed to offer amnesty to all who wished it. The next step was special treatment for the rebel envoys in Vienna, István Szirmay and Szigmunt Janoky. Leopold even permitted the two men, sabers at their sides, to enter his presence. Allegedly, the Magyars also exploited their stay within the city's walls for spying. Among their following was a Turkish engineer, and renegade Capuchin called "Ahmed Bey," who supposedly drew up plans of the Burg and Löbl Bastions and of the adjoining ravelin (that is, the sector later attacked). Meanwhile, a six-month truce was concluded. Thököly would get a three thousand florin monthly payment in return for evacuation of the Slovakian towns and renewed Magyar mediation at the Porte. Hermann of Baden, an outspoken advocate of conciliation, even favored granting him formal, life-long tenure over the territory which, in the armistice, Vienna had already tacitly recognized as his. Interestingly enough, there appears to have been little basic discord over this issue. Clearly, the "Prince and Lord of the Partium" could serve the purposes of either faction at the Court. Only the far-away Caprara, echoing the earlier warning of Kunitz, found the policy harmful.[37]

SOBIESKI BREAKS WITH PARIS

Thököly's undertakings during 1682 reflected not only his own drive for power and status. As in the past, the rebels received monetary encouragement from the Most Christian King. In fact, Louis' interest in the Magyar insurrection had increased as a result of the difficulties he was experiencing along Germany's western borders. It was unfortunate for the Sun King that the only practicable route for conveying France's offerings led through Poland: contact depended entirely upon the continuing approval of Sobieski. Moreover, it was the clumsy de Vitry who was charged with paying the money (both to du Vernay at the Polish-Hungarian frontier, and directly to the Malcontents). In any case, a promise of 100,000 thalers, made at the beginning of 1682 via this channel, influenced the rebel leader, for at the end of February Thököly told the Polish King that hostilities would commence after the spring thaw.[38]

Sobieski, who had sympathized with the Magyars in the past, kept his own counsel for the next several months. It is likely that he was once again mulling over the delicate problem of his relations with France. Apparently, he saw that the time was coming when he would have to choose once and for all between Vienna and Paris. Had the monarch been moved only by personal and family concerns, the condescending treatment of Louis would have assured a more rapid decision against France. Yet a complete break still had serious implications for Poland's international position, and Sobieski was unwilling to act too hastily. The ominous reports from Istanbul, the pressure of Austria's ambassador, Zierowski, and the household scenes of the mortally-offended Marysieńka failed to shake him. In April the King left to visit his Ukrainian estates, taking Zierowski with him and fending off the slightly suspicious de Vitry. The route that the ruler took is perhaps indicative of the direction of his thoughts, for he visited both his birth-place, with its relics of ancestral struggles against the Infidel, and the military installations that would have to brave the furor of any Turko-Tataric assault. He discussed the conditions of an alliance with Zierowski, read diplomatic reports from Moscow and weighed the various aspects of Poland's current situation. Then came the report of Thököly's treaty with the *Beylerbeyi*. This news appears to have tipped the scales for Vienna. Poland's vital interests forbade the presence of Turks both to the east and the south. All consideration of France's desires must now cease: the puppets of the Porte must no longer receive succor across Poland's frontiers.[39]

On June 12 de Vitry was informed of the King's decision to prohibit du Vernay's activities and to ally with the Emperor. The ambassador concluded that Sobieski's vanity had been hurt. It may be noted that while de Vitry had been in the country for over a year, he had not learned very much about its sovereign or its people. He spoke only French, was ignorant even of Latin (the official tongue of the *Sejm*), and conceived of politics solely as etiquette disputes, bribery, and universal adulation of his royal master. He was unable to perceive the changes taking place around him and, until late in the fall, continued to deny the existence of Austro-Polish agreements despite Versailles' dispatch of contrary information from other sources. He took comfort in the mistaken belief that, if necessary, he could mobilize the Polish partisans of France. He did not know that the nation's most powerful figures, men such as Wielopolski, Jabłonowski, and Jerome Lubomirski, had long since entered the Austrian camp. Leopold himself had won over the first-named with personal hospitality. A doubled pension had ensured the loyalty of the second. The third had been recruited to lead a private Polish auxiliary corps in the Austrian army. In the meantime Sobieski was neutralizing most of Louis' remaining adherents either by bribery (offices, dignities and cash) or by exploitation of personal friendship and patriotic-religious sentiment. Crusading fervor began to sweep the land, nurtured by the clergy and the nunzio, Pallavicini.[40] The latter carried on a heavy correspondence with Buonvisi, who supplied arguments to answer those still well-disposed toward the French.[41]

Each fresh bit of information from Hungary increased Polish unrest and militancy. The news of Turkish forces besieging Košice seems to have been the last straw as far as the King was concerned.[42] He now told Zierowski that he was ready to ally himself to Austria and that while he could not finish a treaty without the Diet, he was still prepared to pledge assistance. He had no doubt, he said, that his vassals would immediately concur since they knew that the loss of Hungary would indubitably bring about that of Poland.[43] During the spring the major obstacle to agreement had been Polish insistence upon offensive arrangements, a certain remnant of Gallophillism, and, as far as the Viennese Court was concerned, the predominance of the "Westerners." The summer's events and the increasingly pessimistic reports from Caprara put everything in a different light. Sobieski's initiative received an unusually prompt and favorable response. Even Borgomanero approved, although the idea of "applying brakes" against Brandenburg also entered into his calculations. He suggested to Madrid that agreement would be expedited if His Catholic Majesty would grant the Golden Fleece to Prince Jakób.[44]

The Austro-Polish discussions took place at Jaworów amidst greatest secrecy. The only outsider present was Pallavicini. By mid-September a draft treaty was ready for Vienna. Leopold quickly assented in principle and sent final approval at the end of October. The *Sejm*, however, was not due to meet until after New Year's, and in the meantime, preliminary diplomatic skirmishes commenced. The first struggle was over the continued presence of du Vernay. On October 6 a carefully prearranged *coup de théatre* took place at Jaworów. In the presence of the King, the grandees of the realm, de Vitry, and du Vernay, Zierowski stood up and read off a violent indictment of the activities of the last-named. The Austrian ambassador had all the proofs he needed, thanks to Sobieski's mail censorship. The King thereupon commanded the unfortunate Frenchman to leave the country while Zierowski arranged newspaper publication of the compromising letters and an account of the dramatic interview at the palace. Further evidence, a second royal order, and physical threats finally brought about du Vernay's removal to Gdańsk. With his departure there was no longer any reason for Franco-Polish amity. A final effort of de Vitry in December to purchase Sobieski's connivance failed. The King coolly rejected a 100,000 livre annual pension and stated that he could not be prevented from doing his duty. His counter-suggestion of Polish mediation between Austria and France—an idea that came from Vienna but which corresponded perfectly to the Polish ruler's concept of an all-European crusade—obviously had no chance of acceptance by a monarch whose actions served only the interests of the nation-state. Even before the receipt of de Vitry's report of the December interview, Louis had ordered his envoy to start organizing an anti-royal, noble faction.[45]

B. Louis Plays for Time

Warsaw was not the only capital city that witnessed internal meddling by Louis' ambassadors in order to facilitate French designs upon the Empire's western provinces. In other places, however, the tactics of the King and his representatives were not as gauche as in Poland. Relations with London provide a somewhat better example of Ludovican diplomacy. Paris' relatively greater attentiveness to happenings along the Thames is all the more understandable since the Court of St. James could easily have provided the spark for an anti-French explosion.

A REPRIEVE FOR LUXEMBOURG CITY

As shown previously, relations with France constituted Charles II's most vexing domestic problem. The first several months of 1682 brought the would-be autocrat little relief. Louis, who overestimated his own diplomatic strength at the beginning of the year, refused to accept Charles' despairing suggestion of December 25, 1681. The Sun King would permit no more than a memorial on French claims in the Spanish Netherlands and continued to insist upon annexation of Luxembourg City. The patience of the Ronquillo and van Beuningen was now at an end: they demanded that the British monarch keep his oral promise of the last fall to resist Louis upon the latter's use of military force. When Charles refused to convoke Parliament—which would have been tantamount to a declaration of war against France—, the Spanish formally demanded the fulfillment of treaty obligations in both London and Amsterdam. At this point (March), however, the clouds upon the Carolian horizon began to disappear. Firstly, the unwillingness of the Amsterdam burgher party to risk war broke the unified front in London. Van Beuningen adhered to his fellow oligarchs' viewpoint and now supported Charles' position—which was also that of Brandenburg (recently linked to France by a third secret treaty). It was argued that the Emperor and the Spanish King should accept Louis' demand at Frankfurt: i.e., the recognition of the reunions in return for a firm French guarantee as to the future. The exiled Duke of York's return also strengthened the pro-French party.[46]

Then, just at the moment when the indignation of the English public over Luxembourg City had reached its peak, Louis bethought himself and announced that he was withdrawing his troops. He now agreed to permit English arbitration, explaining that in the face of the growing Ottoman threat, he did not wish to harm Christianity. The reasons for this turn-about are not entirely clear. However, it is probable that the Sun King now gave greater heed to hostile opinion in England and to the possibility of a new anti-French coalition. In the meantime, William of Orange, despite the opposition of the Amsterdammers, had succeeded in getting the States General to agree to conditional fulfillment of the Dutch obligation to Spain: i.e., to send troops to help garrison the "Barrier" fortresses. All bluster notwithstanding, the Gallic ruler was unwilling to go to war so soon after Nijmegen. Perhaps he was also counting upon a Turkish attack more than before, for it was around this time that he dispatched his apology for the Chios incident. Lastly, adverse public reaction at home to what seemed to be *open* abetting of Ottoman militancy (i.e., France's own aggressiveness) may have influenced his decision.[47]

However this may be, the French monarch now decided to make *doubly* sure that there would be no danger of losing Charles' expensively purchased loyalty. The publication (June, 1682) of the secret Treaty of Dover (1670), the first of Charles' pecuniary contracts with Paris, may well have been calculated to create an uproar in England and thus to obviate Parliament's being called.[48] At the same time Louis sought to derive underhanded diplomatic advantage from Charles' arbitration offer. His Viennese ambassador, Sèbeville, began to spread the rumor that the Spanish and French had privately compromised and that "el Rey de Inglaterra está con toda esta maquina en el pecho." The ostensible purpose of this play was to weaken the none too firm confidence of the two branches of the House of Austria in one another, and, to a degree, the French succeeded.[49]

THE WALDECKIAN RECESS

Although the Most Christian King was able to prevent the addition of the English keystone to the alliance arch that William of Orange was seeking to build, he could not frustrate the gradual joining of other pieces. In February, with the exchange of ratifications, the Association Tractate between Sweden and the States General became effective. The Emperor adhered almost at once, and Spain followed suit in May after some equivocation.[50] Of greater importance was the Laxenburg Alliance or Waldeckian Recess (June 10, 1682). In view of the strength of the peace party in Holland, Orange and Waldeck apparently feared that France might succeed, in the case of immediate rupture, in detaching the States General from the Empire. It therefore seemed militarily advisable to pull together the lesser, anti-French potentates of Germany: with help from Austria and from several of the larger Imperial states it might be possible to defend the line of the Rhine. Leopold reacted so favorably to the suggestion that he offered Waldeck the rank of field marshal and command over the central unit of the prospective allied army. In fact, after conclusion of the agreement, he elevated the Protestant Count to the dignity of princedom.[51]

At the moment the Emperor had about 67,000 men under arms. He was willing to commit 26,000 of them to cover the Swabian Circle. 25,000 would remain in Hungary, it being supposed that this number would suffice "if the Turk does not make war against us with all his forces." The remaining 16,000 were to be lodged in Hungary as a strategic reserve. This disposition was purely defensive, an arrangement for waiting to see where and when there would be war. It was hoped that the force destined for Swabia could get winter quarters locally—thus relieving Austria of at least a portion of the crushing burden of rearmament—and would supply some moral fortitude to the Regensburg Diet. Bavaria was supposed to station its army opposite Strasbourg in order to join the Imperials in case of need. In this way the defense of the Rhine as far as Phillippsburg would be ensured. The Circles of Franconia and the Upper Rhine were assigned the middle sector, the region between Phillippsburg and Koblenz. The third, northern segment was to be the responsibility of Hannover and Saxony.[52] However, these two states did not formally sign the agreement. Their coöperation was merely foreseen. Indeed, apart from the Turkish threat, this was the major flaw of the whole plan: Francophilic Denmark and Brandenburg would effectively checkmate their pro-Imperial neighbors. Moreover, at the moment Vienna was not even certain that it would have the money to dispatch its 26,000 man contingent.[53]

Nevertheless, the Laxenburg Alliance was not without value. It was of immediate propagandistic benefit to the indefatigable Waldeck. In his memoirs the Prince relates how upon his return to Regensburg he found all the "patriots" depressed. The Bishop of Eichstadt was a good example: Verjus, the French plenipotentiary, had threatened the plundering of all his lands if he did not vote with those who favored France. When Waldeck revealed the good news, the "well-intentioned" party recovered its courage.[54] Parenthetically, France's opponents were themselves not uncognizant of the tactics of psychological warfare. It was during 1682 that Philipp Wilhelm von Hörnigk, later (1684) the author of the famed *Österreich über Alles wenn es nur will*, published three pamphlets purportedly treating of the Carolingian "kingdoms" of Austrasia, Germania, and Lotharingia. Writing under the pseudonym "Francopolita," the pro-Imperial publicist vigorously disputed the arguments of the French reunion chamber lawyers and called upon all fellow Germans to recognize the dangers arising from Gallic encroachment in the west. He did not hesitate to advocate continuance of the struggle against France even if there should also be war in the East.[55]

MAX EMMANUEL AND MARIA ANTONIA

Another positive aspect of the Waldeckian Recess was that it clearly revealed Munich's sentiments. Austro-Bavarian relations had become very close by this time, not the least reason for which was Max Emmanuel's growing interest in Maria Antonia. To be sure, the path of marital negotiations was by no means smooth. Although the thought of uniting Wittelsbach and Habsburg went all the way back to the early 1670's, it had become apparent by the end of the decade that the Archduchess' physical attributes were not her primary asset. Not only was the sportive Elector rather squeamish in such matters, but, as indicated, he had fallen in love with a Protestant princess from Eisenach. By August of 1681, however, it was obvious that this *affaire de coeur* was doomed, and the idea of a Viennese tie took on new lustre.[56] What complicates the tale at this juncture is that the Elector simultaneously entertained marriage conversations with Hannover and several other houses. In the early spring of 1682 and again in February, 1683, a clerical agent of the Duke of Brunswick-Lüneburg, arrived on the banks of the Isar.[57] The good *Abbé* Diné seems to have been acting especially for the Duke's spouse, the ambitious Sophie Charlotte, who apparently wished to make the best match possible for her charming little "Figuelotte."[58] While the only certain thing about this *entre-acte* is that nothing came of it, several intriguing letters of Borgomanero suggest that Bavaria's purpose in receiving the Hannoverian envoy may have been to gain leverage in Vienna or, for that matter, to have a second candidate to fall back upon.

In April, Max Emmanuel sent a personal representative, Count Preysing, to Austria to view the Emperor's daughter, "skillfully to obtain her picture and also, without making any commitment, to sound out the feelings of some people at the Court concerning the matter." In all likelihood, the Elector suffered disappointment, for his emissary was unable to elicit a positive response. Presumably the Austrian government was not yet willing to broach discussion of the sensitive problem of the girl's Spanish inheritance rights—the sole cause of her attractiveness. The whole affair, already distressing because of Leopold's desire not to offend the Elector, became doubly embarrassing when the minister of Hannover, also a prospective ally, requested Borgomanero to ask the Emperor to intervene with Max Emmanuel in Figuelotte's favor. The Spanish ambassador managed to equivocate, as did Leopold, although Prince Schwarzenberg's remark to Preysing that the Emperor would rather give the Archduchess to the humblest knight of his realm than to the Bavarian was upsetting.[59] Nonetheless, good fortune continued to smile upon the House of Habsburg. Max Emmanuel was eager to clash with the Turk—certainly more so than he was with the French. Discussion of a bilateral pact thus progressed as the months passed. The negotiations were furthered by the influence of Countess Kaunitz, the mature, voluptuous wife of Vienna's elderly ambassador in Munich. "La Dame est la Maistresse, et le Mary est le Maistre," said the French ambassador.[60]

The "Westerners" Hold Firm

However diverse the means which the Emperor, the Spanish, William of Orange, and Waldeck employed in the formation of anti-French alliances, the common purpose was, in the first instance, to strengthen the resolve of the pro-Imperial faction at the conference table in Frankfurt. It will be recalled that Louis' representatives had been demanding formal recognition of the Crown's rights to all territory "reunited" up to August of 1681. The French claims, of course, also encompassed the more recently usurped Strasbourg and Casale. In fact, the Alsatian metropolis was the single most important issue of the long, tedious and sometimes ridiculous discussions. As Brunswick's delegate laconically remarked: "Straßburg scheinet die Braut zu sein, worumb man tanzet."[61]

To be sure, Spain's interests were also at stake. Borgomanero's correspondence for the year is filled with references to the meeting. Madrid's envoy was in fact so concerned over what was transpiring in Germany that he maintained direct contact with Strattmann, the Imperial emissary. That the Spaniard was kept well-informed is apparent, for example, in his report of April 9. In relating the happy news of the rejection of French demands, he informed the *Consejo del Estado* that Austria had received support from Bavaria, Saxony, Brunswick, and Bamberg; while Cologne, Mainz, and the inwardly reluctant Palatinate had followed the French cue. The ambassador added that France was now working to transfer the conference to Regensburg where, presumably, it could exploit the fears of the less powerful states and where Brandenburg could also bring weight to bear. He likewise noted that Trier was secretly admitting Imperial troops to one of its strongpoints.[62] One must respect Borgomanero's achievement of buttressing Spain's position in Germany all the more because, apart from his own energy and talents, he had no resources with which to work. Money, the most obvious missing ingredient,[63] would have been a useful tool. One need only recollect Zierowski and France's diplomats. Castile's representative repeatedly implored his government to make a financial contribution to the common cause and complained that his exertions were seriously hampered by its failure to do so. There is no evidence of any aid at all being sent until the very approach of the Turks. In fact, the Viennese Embassy staff frequently had to go without pay.[64]

Another obstacle to concerting the policies of the two branches of the August House was their continuing lack of mutual trust. It will be remembered that in 1669 Austria had agreed with France to partition the Spanish Empire upon Charles II's demise, the first serious breach in the venerable principle of Habsburg unity. Then there were the even fresher memories of the anti-Viennese leadership of the late Don Juan. It is understandable that there was fear of a double-cross or sell-out. The intervention offer of the English Charles supplied fresh fuel to smouldering suspicions, for while the Spanish were not interested in *arbitration,* for a time they toyed with the idea of accepting *mediation.* Sèbeville continued to spread stories of a secret Franco-Spanish *entente* throughout the late spring and summer. This intrigue, combined with the ever more discouraging news from Hungary, made Borgomanero's task increasingly difficult. He worried all the more when Leopold, for some reason, slipped out of his immediate sight, as was the case for much of the dark month of August. The Spanish diplomat wrote home that during his absence the Emperor might weaken his stand over Germany.[65] However, on August 28 the Marchese once again obtained a hearing from the All Highest. The audience showed that while the monarch was upset by events in the East, he was still determined to hold out in the West: "que lo que mas cuydado le dava era el temer que estos muydos desanimassen al Imperio y a sus Aliados, y que viniessen a ceder a las pretensiones de la Francia. . . ."[66] In order to erase any lurking doubts that the Emperor might still entertain, Borgomanero submitted (September 12) a memorial which admittedly read "un poco fuerte."[67] By November, moreover, the ambassador succeeded in dispelling Austrian notions of separate peace negotiations and in the process secured a unity pledge from the Viennese Court, upon which his own, equally skeptical government had insisted.[68]

In the meantime, however, a new set of difficulties had arisen. On October 3 the French presented the dissolving Frankfurt Conference with an ultimatum for Regensburg: unless Louis' conditions were met by the end of November, the Empire would have to face the consequences. The French carefully avoided specifying what these would be, and the ultimatum was in fact to be extended several times. Yet the arrival of the news in Vienna caused consternation among certain ministers and momentarily strengthened the position of Schwarzenberg and the "Easterners." Borgomanero, Sinelli, and Königsegg were sick in bed at the time,—which fact the Prince allegedly strove to exploit. Reacting promptly, the Spanish ambassador drew up a fresh memorial for Leopold, who had again been absent for some time. Königsegg handed the document to the sovereign just as he was about to enter the state conference room. Read to the assemblage at the Vice Chancellor's suggestion before Schwarzenberg was able to deliver his own prepared statement, strongly supported by the Burgrave of Bohemia (Count Martinic, a member of Leopold's so-called "Old Guard"), and defended vigorously by Sinzendorf, "it had precisely the effect intended." "Nobody dared say a word."[69]

This triumph notwithstanding, the impassioned struggle between the "Easterners" and the "Westerners" was by no means over. It lasted on into the holiday season, which, incidentally, seems to have been celebrated with almost normal insouciance.[70] On New Year's Eve Spain's tireless ambassador composed a long summary of the current state of affairs. Conceding that war with Turkey now seemed inevitable, he reported that Schwarzenberg had succeeded in gaining a majority of the Imperial ministers for the policy of yielding to France in order to be able to concentrate resources against the Ottoman Empire. Allegedly, the Prince was telling Leopold that the projected army increase, now set to reach 80,000 men, was financially impossible and that even if such a force could be mustered, it could not be maintained. All alliances, both existing and prospective, were shaky. Everyone was trying to squeeze subsidies from the Emperor, who ought never to make such payments, particularly at a time when he had to face a frontal assault from the "Enemy of the Christian Name." Money should rightfully be the concern of His Catholic Majesty and of the Dutch. Schwarzenberg is also said to have gotten the Empress Dowager to admonish her foster son, although Leopold's own wife, "instruido por el Duque de Neoburg," spoke out for the opposite camp.[71]

Borgomanero's backers consisted of the same old clique, plus Martinic. Chancellor Hocher, on the other hand, could no longer be counted upon. Already in October the Ambassador had described him as a typical, narrow-minded scholar, now an old man, broken in health, full of fears and irresolution.[72] Despite its loss of support, however, the cabal remained as vocal, and influential, as ever. It openly advocated the long-dreaded, two-front war. It would keep 60,000 of the 80,000 soldiers in Hungary and would rely upon the Poles to absorb a goodly portion of the initial Ottoman onslaught. It asserted that the 12,000 Bavarians, the 20,000 Circle troops, the Dutch and the Hannoverians could defend the Rhine, while the Swedes and Saxons could checkmate the Brandenburgers and Danes; one should not even despair of Spain and England.[73] Although the specious quality of this reasoning was apparent to the majority of the advisers, Borgomanero's oratory continued to feed Leopold's deep-seated Gallophobia. The final, hard decision to renounce a militant stand in the West was to be deferred for eighteen months.

C. Unfurling the Sultan's Horsetails

The Emperor's preferences notwithstanding, the Austrian government had to shift most of its attention away from the Rhenine frontier. 1683, after all, did become the "Year of the Turk." Moreover, it was Istanbul, not Vienna, where the decision between an eastern and a western war was really made. While the two factions in the Hofburg were vigorously contending for the Imperial ear, the events that would shape the future were taking place along the Golden Horn.

THE FRENCH CATALYST

A great difficulty of analyzing major historical occurrences is to determine which of numerous causes was actually crucial. The question of Ottoman antecedents to the second siege of Vienna is no exception. Four elements—inherent Turkish belligerency, the person of the Grand Vezir, the Hungarian rebellion, and the policy of Louis XIV—stand out.[74] Yet there can only be relative certainty that it was the last of these which triggered the ordeal of Austria's capital.

It has been shown earlier how the Porte found continuous employment of its armed forces the only practical means of ensuring internal stability. One need only add that the Turks themselves sometimes reminded Westerners that Islamic scripture commanded Allah's people to wield the sword unceasingly.[75] On the other hand, there are good reasons for ascribing Istanbul's new aggression to the influence of Kara Mustafa. Both the sharp-eyed Venetians and Caprara regarded him as the chief villain. Civrano's emphasis upon the Grand Vezir's need for cash may be borne in mind.[76] With the great riches he believed heaped up in Vienna, the "Golden Apple" of the Turk's imagination,[77] he could either continue bribing the Sultan or set himself up as an autonomous potentate out of the latter's treacherous reach.[78] Perhaps also his authority as commander-in-chief would provide a convenient way to eliminate personal enemies.[79]

Demetrius Cantemir thought that the main factor was the Magyar insurrection. Speaking of the Russo-Turkish conflict, the Hospodar asserted: "But all this [physical exhaustion] could not have diverted the Othman Court from prosecuting their first design, if new commotions in Hungary had not induced them to turn their arms that way, where they thought the war might be carried on with less difficulty, and more advantage." The Malcontents' embassy of January, 1682, in which the offer of "forty thousand rix-dollars" a year was made, seemed particularly critical.[80] Still, for this interpretation to have been correct, renunciation of the existing armistice with Austria would have to have been approved either at the time of the mission's arrival or when the news of Thököly's fall successes reached the Bosporus. Information of Turkish provenance indicates that the final Ottoman deliberation took place only on August 6, a date that corresponds with the arrival of unequivocal encouragement from Paris.

The Rumanian prince, however, is probably correct in maintaining that the issue was not resolved without a struggle. As in Vienna, the fight was won by a minority. On the one side stood the Grand Vezir, initially at least without even the support of the Padishah. All of the *Ulema* and the Sultan Valide opposed a new military venture. They maintained that it was unjust to start a war with a prince who gave no cause for complaint, who had indeed observed all conditions of the existing truce. The Janissaries also objected.[81] With the forces of both the Muslim and the Ruling Institutions thus united, Kara Mustafa could scarcely expect to obtain the Sultan's consent. The would-be conqueror therefore resorted to subterfuge. He purportedly showed the ruler forged, militant-sounding letters from Ibrahim Pasha, who was in reality an advocate of peace.[82] The

Grand Vezir also seems to have secretly enticed the Janissary Ağa and other officers and thus to have instigated a demonstration of enlisted men in favor of war. Finally, he was able to persuade Mehmed IV that peace should be prolonged only if the Austrians would give up Győr and neighboring strongpoints—terms that were staggeringly harsh.[83] The next task was to win over the other still unconvinced, highly-placed personalities. Cantemir goes on to assert that the Sultan and his conspiring minister worked jointly for this goal and again emphasizes the force of the argument that one ought to strike while the Hungarian iron was still hot.[84]

This struggle of opinions appears to have taken place during the first seven months of 1682. It is unlikely that the Sultan, who was away for as much as two months at a time in pursuit of venery and wild game, changed his own mind much before the exorbitant Turkish demands were presented to the Austrians (June 23). The French meanwhile had been watching developments intently. In February Louis expressed his regrets over the Chios incident while Guilleragues incited Abafi against the Emperor and endeavored to bring the Transylvanian together with the rulers of Moldavia and Wallachia. The French ambassador also combatted tales that Kunitz was spreading of an Austro-Polish alliance. In April and May Franco-Turkish difficulties arose over a report that the Dauphin would be chosen King of the Romans and over the appearance of Admiral Duquesne's fleet in the Dardanelles to demand an apology for the treatment accorded Guilleragues at the time of the Chios incident. The Sun King instructed his representative to deny the election rumor energetically and called off the navy. At the same time Louis warned against exposing any proofs of efforts to encourage the Turks. Despite the growing warmth of his relations with the Ottoman government, Guilleragues seems to have been concerned by early summer with the slowness of the decision process. Despite evidence of rearmament, he saw no signs of a move northward, and he noted the disagreement between the war and anti-war factions. It also seemed obvious that there could be no major undertaking until the next spring. Thus at the beginning of August he used his May instructions to make the crucial declaration that under no conditions would Louis give the Emperor any help, but that his sovereign would assist the Poles if the Turks should attack them.[85]

With the various domestic and foreign obstacles out of the way, Kara Mustafa probably felt quite secure when, on August 6, he entered a grand meeting of all vezirs, high religious dignitaries and other state officials. The council quickly voted to unlimber the Turkish war machine. The first outward manifestation of change was the planting of horse-tails (*tuğ*) on a small mound in front of the Paradise Gates of the Istanbul Seraglio. Although this action did not constitute a declaration of war but signified, rather, any impending departure of the Sultan from the capital, its overtones seemed ominous to Western observers. Unknown to the latter, at least initially, the Porte also began to issue a stream of orders for mobilizing the armed forces,[86] a process already partly underway for some time at the command of the Grand Vezir.

A further problem about the decision to renew hostilities is whether from the very outset the Turks agreed among themselves that Vienna should be the goal of operations. The Venetian, Contarini, reported that the Grand Vezir had spoken of besieging the city during his argumentation before the Divan. The Austrians were overconfident, the walls were bare of artillery, and the gates guarded only by incompetent militia. The Porte possessed bases nearby that would serve as excellent springboards.[87] One of the two major Ottoman informants provides a more likely identification of the objective.[88] Following Kara Mustafa's earlier agreement with the Sultan, the plan was simply to seize Győr and adjacent localities, and Mehmed IV remained oblivious of his prime minister's intention to attack the Austrian capital until the latter could no longer be halted. A related issue is whether the Grand Vezir acted primarily on his own initiative. According to the same Turkish source, his *reis efendi*, Laz Mustafa, recognizing the master's ambition, suggested and promoted the project and thus should be regarded as the guilty party.[89] Caprara and Kunitz laid the blame squarely on Thököly *personally*, a problem to be considered shortly. It is likewise possible that Western scoundrels living in Turkey were responsible for making Vienna the target of the expedition.[90] In any case, the Austrians were to remain uncertain to the last minute where the Turks were heading.

THE CAPRARA MISSION

Finally, there are certain aspects of the Caprara Mission that merit additional attention. The main question concerns Vienna's tactics in attempting to persuade Istanbul to extend the armistice. The matter is of interest because the major student of diplomacy at the Porte has suggested that the Austrians tried to purchase peace at any price.[91] While it is true that Leopold had *authorized* Caprara to offer substantial sums[92] and while the special embassy's expenses, which included gratuities for Ottoman officials, were heavy, there is no evidence that such a bid was ever made. In fact, in his report of June 17, the Count stressed that a bribe would be futile. Moreover, he was demonstrably without communication or supplementary subsidies from home until late in the fall, when he finally received 15,000 ducats.[93]

Another striking feature is that the Habsburg government apparently thought that it could gain its objectives without granting any territorial concessions. This seems obvious from the report sent after the bargaining session of June 23. (The Austrians arrived on April 14, but did not formally present their credentials until June 4.) Interrogated by the Turks, the *internuntius* stated that he did not hold a plenipotentiary commission. He was only charged to renew the truce on the existing terms and would have to refer any new suggestions to Vienna. His Muslim counterparts thereupon proceeded to demand Győr, Leopoldov, Gúta, and a long list of villages and *portes* near Nové Zámky. To be sure, it would be unjust to reproach the Austrian emissary with being naive about peace. As early as May 11, he wrote that the only way to preserve the truce was to make Istanbul favorable, *concrete* proposals over frontier adjustments while vigorously prosecuting the anti-rebel campaign. Then, as a result of the June 23 meeting, he became convinced that the Turks, who seemed continually to be upping the cost of agreement, were not sincere and that therefore he ought to be recalled.[94]

The second conference, on August 6, was much like the first save that the impression of Ottoman hypocrisy was even stronger. Caprara did not fail to notice the ill-boding horse-tails—although he remained unaware of the decision of the Turkish state council. By September 25, having heard a rumor that the Grand Seigneur would depart for Székesfehérvár (Stuhlweißenburg), the Austrian envoy was certain of war and urged Leopold to take immediate defense precautions. The Count's October messages were absolutely unequivocal. On the 19th of that month he was forced to follow the Turkish government to Adrianople, and there, on December 23, he met with its negotiators for a third and final session, upon which occasion the Ottomans posed yet another requirement: the recognition of the Porte's new satellite, Thököly. Since this new condition far exceeded any claim for the payment of annual tribute—something Leopold had explicitly instructed him to reject in recently-arrived instructions—, Caprara now considered his Mission concluded and requested his dismissal from the Sultan's Court. The Turks nonetheless detained him. They claimed that they wished to negotiate further, a statement which was probably not entirely untrue, at least as far as Mehmed IV was concerned.[95]

However, in looking back, it appears that the chances for a settlement had never been very good. Caprara recognized that a single, large bribery payment would be useless. Even if he had had permission to sign over a few border domains, he could scarcely have come near the Turkish price, which was probably set so high on purpose. Presumably the Grand Vezir realized that the Austrians could never give up fortresses like Győr which constituted their last strategic defense line. Most likely, the only chance the Mission ever had was at the moment of its arrival. Had it been made up of genuine connoisseurs of the Osmanli world instead of men, however brave and dutiful, who do not seem to have grasped all the complexities of the situation, conceivably it could have exploited local differences of opinion and factional divisions.

D. The "Year of the Turk" Begins

It seems fairly clear that the Turks more or less made up their minds to wage war upon Austria in August of 1682. There is, however, no such relative historical surety in the case of the slippery Imre Thököly, who continued to treat with the Emperor to the very beginning of the siege of Vienna. The basis of the 1683 negotiations was the old rebel offer of mediation. The Austrian government's reaction to this proposal, made again when the fall (1682) armistice was ratified, reflected awareness of Thököly's dependence upon Istanbul: a query went off to Ambassador Caprara as to whether the Turks were behind it or whether it originated with the rebels.[96] Still, the idea so dear to the "Westerners," was not entirely discounted: the Emperor not only permitted his Hungarian adherents to attend a diet called by the Malcontent leader at Košice on January 12 but also sent a personal delegate to continue discussions.[97]

Last Minute Parleying

In the meantime, Baron Saponara came back to Vienna with Thököly's latest suggestions. The cost of assistance remained high: 1.) annual payment of 400,000 thalers to the Ottomans without the money being called a tribute; 2.) non-interference in Transylvania; 3.) creation of a principality for Thököly in eastern Upper Hungary (the Seven Comitats), which, although theoretically under Leopold's sovereignty, would enjoy the protection of the Turks, who would then reduce Transylvania into a pashalik. The Magyar chieftain added that if "la Porta no viene en este ajuste y el Sr. Emperador le diesse los condados, que gocaren en Boscay y en Ragocy por su vida, que vendría al seno de Su Magd. Cessa. con todo su partido, y serviría contra los Turcos." Above all, however, it would be necessary for Leopold to maintain in force the diploma he swore when he was crowned King of Hungary.[98]

The Habsburg Court immediately took counsel, but since Ottoman assent seemed improbable and Thököly so dependent upon it, the proposals were not given great credit. Nevertheless, they were not rejected out of hand, for the Austrians wished to await the effect that their rearmament and the pending Polish alliance would have. The rebels might thereby be frightened into obedience.[99] Another reason for continuing contacts with Košice was the influence of Hermann. The Badener took it upon himself to answer the objections of the skeptics, arguing that since a two-front war and peace with France were both impossible, there should be no reluctance in accepting the mediation that Thököly had meanwhile publicly announced to his Diet. His viewpoint prevailed, and negotiations continued. Polish ratification of the alliance (March 31) seemed to expedite matters, for Zierowski, conscious of Sobieski's desire to reconcile the Magyars with their lawful sovereign, could now bring Warsaw's influence to bear. Vienna was prepared to accept Polish intervention, for it now saw no other way to achieve a settlement.[100]

Backed by John III's threat to attack the Malcontents if they did not hearken to reason, Saponara once again travelled to rebel headquarters. At the beginning of May, the Baron sent his secretary back to the Hofburg with the result of the latest conversations. Leopold, knowing that the wheels of his cumbersome government would revolve slowly, requested Borgomanero to write the Magyar leader, "pues siempre ha querido el Teuquel, que yo tuviese mano en este tratado," and to impress upon him the importance of Polish intervention so that "no se desesperse . . . por el retardo, y no se entregue al Turco."[101] To be sure, by now the idea was no longer rebel mediation but rather direct military assistance. The price, understandably, was more outrageous than ever. Thököly demanded the rank "Prince of the Empire," control over *thirteen* comitats (all Upper Hungary), recognition of the already usurped title of "Lord of the Partium," and immunity from the authority of the Palatine and *Judex Curiae*. Like Prince Jakób, he coveted the Golden Fleece. As insurance against defeat in fighting the Turks, he requested an estate in Germany. He also insisted upon amnesty and restitution of goods for all concerned, absolute secrecy of discussion, and the use of both the Poles and the Spanish as go-betweens.[102]

Only after the rebel chieftain announced (about June 21) that he would take up arms again at the expiration of the truce a month later, did Vienna despatch its answer. Although Leopold indicated that he would concede the title, he was not ready to hand over Upper Hungary without considerable bargaining. He instructed Saponara to proceed in piecemeal fashion. If Thököly's demands remained excessive, the Baron was to stall for time and try divisive tactics. The Fleece was impossible since recipients had to be Catholics, but there was a prospect of the Danish Order of the Elephant (via the Dutch Admiral de Ruyter). The German estate would be difficult to obtain, but there might be something in Spain. Amnesty, restitution, and secrecy were approved, but the dignity of the Archhouse could not be compromised through Spanish participation in mediation. By the time Saponara received his orders, it was too late. The armistice, which Thököly had respected only in a relative sense, was running out, and the rebel forces were commencing their lukewarm coöperation with the Turkish host. Although Saponara surrendered the town of Saros Patak voluntarily in the hope of conciliation and although he attempted to arrange neutrality for the area of Satumare (capital of Szatmár) and Ecsed, by the beginning of July that there was clearly no hope of the insurgents coming over actively to Leopold's side. By then Thököly's manifestoes, which openly proclaimed alliance with the advancing Turks, had spread throughout Royal Hungary.[103]

QUESTIONS OF INTERPRETATION

The rebel chieftain's actions during the years preceding the siege of Vienna were, to say the least, devious. The traditional outlook is that he was all along committed to siding with the Turks, that he was only waiting for them to come to Hungary in force and, hence, that his dealings with Leopold were only a means of deception. With particular reference to 1683, he allegedly sought to gain time before the arrival of the Ottomans because of fear of an Austro-Polish army corps stationed along the Váh River.[104] Generally, but not necessarily, this view incorporates the belief that Thököly strove, both by letter and in person, to convince the Grand Vezir that an attack on Vienna was feasible. Supposedly, the insurgents' chief went so far as to forward the plans of Vienna's fortifications.[105] However, such a standpoint presents a number of difficulties. Firstly, the data derive entirely from Western sources, from Donado Caprara and Kunitz. These men can have been deliberately misled by their Turkish informants in order to perpetuate the alienation of Austrians and Hungarians. Secondly, Thököly may have deduced that simulated coöperation with the Porte (whether against Vienna or in Hungary alone) would frighten Leopold into making truly substantial concessions or, concomitantly, that it was expedient to have two alternatives. Thirdly, Thököly himself vehemently denied responsibility for urging Kara Mustafa to go to Vienna.[106] Finally, the "Prince of the Partium" advised the Emperor to move against the Turkish fortresses of Nové Zámky and Esztergom in order to draw off the Grand Vezir.[107] Fighting in Upper Hungary could have led either to expansion of the rebel domain with Turkish assistance or to alliance with the Emperor after obtaining favorable conditions. Conversely, the suggestion could have been a trick to weaken the Austrian military position farther south (which would have helped open up the route to Vienna via Sopron and Wiener Neustadt). There is evidence which suggests that Kara Mustafa promised his Calvinist ally control over the Austrian capital once it was captured. Since the information available is somewhat contradictory *in toto,* it is hard to avoid the impression that the head of the Malcontents was much given to taking out insurance on all sides simultaneously.[108]

Another question is whether the Imperial government's more lenient approach since the fall of 1682 was mistaken. Was Leopold making a major error in listening to Hermann and Borgomanero, as earlier writers have maintained? Probably not. In the first place, the reversal of course was more apparent than real. Vienna actually did not offer much. Had the Emperor made a more attractive bid, had he not taken so long to decide, the Hungarians might have switched camps, even at the last moment. On the other hand—and in the second place—, the failure of the Habsburg court to be more accommodating was by no means tragic.

Thököly turned out to be of as little practical help to the Turks as he probably would have been to the Austrians. Presumably, the reasons for refusing to buy Magyar loyalty included prestige factors and the binding nature of any agreement that might have been made. Balking at the cost was equally justified by the inferior quality of the object for sale. Finally, if there were any reason at all to think Leopold a Machiavellian type or any evidence of this in the reports of Spain's sly ambassador (there is not), one might even suggest that the whole affair was an elaborate device to keep Thököly on the fence.

One may also ask whether the Emperor should not have forsworn negotiations that made him appear somewhat fatuous to his contemporaries, especially the caustic Venetians. While Hermann's evaluation of Thököly was a bit myopic and the idea of mediation tenuous, it is only just to point out that Austria could not have followed Caprara's advice to castigate the rebels without the requisite military force. There were simply not enough troops to pacify Upper Hungary *and* to cover the hereditary provinces. (The job might have been done in 1681 or 1682 but only by acceding to French demands.) Thus, although nothing was gained from discussions with the rebels, little was lost save face.

THE AUSTRO-POLISH ALLIANCE

The continuance of contacts between Vienna and Kapos seemed justified partly because of a dramatic turn of events along the Vistula. At the beginning of the year it was by no means certain that Leopold and Sobieski would succeed in joining hands. Agreement required the approval of the *Sejm,* the notorious burial-ground of the hopes of Poland's kings. De Vitry, ordered by his master to coöperate with the minister of Brandenburg in frustrating the treaty, set about creating an anti-Sobieski party. However, John III was not just an ordinary Polish king, and thus an anti-royal majority was not the obstacle that it might have been. Moreover, for the coming parliamentary struggle, Poland's sovereign possessed an unusually well-sharpened tool of contemporary diplomacy: postal counter-espionage. Both the Poles and the Austrians could read de Vitry's reports before they reached Paris. The former organized an efficient system of "stage-coach robberies" and enjoyed the services of the most talented code-breaker of the day; the latter, in keeping with what became a long tradition of letter snooping, were no less successful in discovering what the unsuspecting de Vitry had written. Another of Sobieski's trumps was dexterous manipulation of public opinion before the Diet started (January 27). Aware of strong opposition among the magnates, especially in Great Poland, he had his propaganda stress the danger to the Republic posed by a Turkish satellite state on the nation's southern borders. A further advantage was the special Austrian envoy, Count Karl Waldstein, an unusually competent diplomat, a man unlikely to stumble on the tortuous terrain of a *Sejm*. Also, the adroit Zierowski remained on the job in Warsaw.[109]

The first tactical step was to purchase the gratitude of a number of more influential magnates with lucrative Diet honors. While not all remained loyal, de Vitry was deprived of the support of at least some of the people upon whom he was counting. Other nobles, who might have opposed the King, held back for fear that the Frenchman might publicize their acceptance of gratuities. While bribe-taking was a national sport, it was technically illegal, and to be branded a traitor under the momentary circumstances would have been most perilous. Louis XIV's only remaining adherent was Jan Morsztyn, the Crown Grand Treasurer, who had already transferred his private assets to France. An intellectual, emotional, and material Gallophile, he labored vainly to find a hireling who would cast a *liberum veto* (to have done so personally in such a super-heated patriotic atmosphere would have meant risking assassination). However, the Sun King's partisans did succeed in arranging a "secret" supper meeting between himself, de Vitry, and two eminent figures of the Diet—the supposedly secure Austrophile, Jabłonowski, and the Lithuanian, Kazimierz Sapieha. The Poles agreed to support France, in return for which, *at some future time*, Jabłonowski would receive Louis' backing for succession to the Polish throne. This machination and the fact that the negotiations of the Diet committee with the Austrians were lagging caused Sobieski to prepare another spectacle like Jaworów. He had all the materials necessary for flawless staging. There were several private confrontations first, in one of which Jabłonowski and Sapieha were tearfully reconciled to their forgiving liege lord. The *pièce de résistance*, a "furiosissima tempesta," to use Nunzio Pallavicini's words, was presented in the *Sejm* on March 16. The deputies, excited by a well-timed release of diplomatic reports about the Porte's gigantic rearmament, were read incriminating excerpts from Morsztyn's intercepted correspondence. Five days of uproar ensued. Accused of high treason, Louis' Sarmatian bondsman seemed destined for the hangman's noose. However, fate—judiciously encouraged by Sobieski—was kinder. The ruined magnate resigned his office, begged piteously for mercy, swore not to exercise his veto, and promised to equip a military unit out of his own pocket for service against the Turks. He thus secured tacit permission to retire to France, which was probably what he had long been striving for anyway. With Morsztyn out of the way, the great aristocrats' resistance to the alliance was broken: a threat by Sobieski to convoke the war-happy, almost uncontrollable *szlachta* sufficed to erase any remnants of magnate opposition.[110]

Only two obstacles remained. The first was the opposition of Brandenburg, which disappeared as soon as it became apparent that the French were defeated. The Great Elector's Polish partisans thereupon flocked to

Sobieski, their resistance already weakened by liberal disbursements from Waldstein's treasure chest. The other difficulty was familial. The Queen discovered that hopes of obtaining Maria Antonia's hand for Jakób were illusory. The King, however, had never really been taken in by the Habsburg deception and was not disposed to argue the point at so critical a juncture. The final negotiations were hard enough anyway. There had been much dissension over Austria's payment of subsidies, for Waldstein was not authorized to promise money. When the problem was solved, thanks to Pallavicini's intervention, the statesmen could proceed to the equally tricky questions of an old Austrian claim to influence the Polish succession and Poland's demand that the Emperor swear an oath to uphold the treaty. The Austrians finally gave way on the first point, also agreeing to cancel a long-standing Polish debt of two million florins. Both the Nunzio and Borgomanero, in Vienna, helped overcome the second hindrance. Leopold's dignity was preserved and Sobieski's mistrust assuaged by an agreement for mutual oaths to be deposited into the hands of a papal plenipotentiary in Rome. Thus, it became possible to sign the pact on April 1—superstition, however, requiring that the document be dated as of the previous day.[111]

The alliance was both defensive and offensive in character but the latter only for the duration of the war already underway and valid only against the Infidel. The Emperor pledged himself to provide 60,000 troops whereas the Poles were to arm 40,000 men. If either Vienna or Kraków were besieged, the partner whose capital was not directly threatened was to hurry to the help of the other. Military operations were to be conducted according to a common plan. Tentatively, the Emperor was to undertake diversions in Hungary and the Poles to advance in Podolia and the Ukraine. Conquered regions were to revert to the previous legal holder. There was to be no separate peace, and other states were to be permitted to accede to the league. Whichever monarch was present in the field with the army was to take over united command—which to the Poles seemed to imply Sobieski, in contrast to the Emperor, an experienced warrior. The price Leopold had to pay for all this was 1,200,000 Polish florins (200,000 Reich thalers or 300,000 Rhenine florins), plus the ecclesiastical tithes of the Habsburg provinces in Italy.[112]

With the conclusion of the treaty the position of de Vitry became untenable. In fact the hapless French envoy became physically endangered. It was suggested publicly that he be castrated in order that he might not beget freaks similar to himself. John III, however, was content merely to request the diplomat's recall. The stiff, final audience with Sobieski took place on May 9, and therewith official relations between France and Poland were broken, not to be renewed for a decade.[113] The ambassador, who had deliberately snubbed Maria Kazimiera by refusing to make a farewell call, still had to endure a drunken midnight demonstration in front of his residence. Some Lithuanian magnates, desirous of defending the Queen's dignity and punctuating their remarks with pistol shots, screamed a host of insults to the "infamous traitor." The Marquis left the country in a huff because Sobieski's Grand Marshal, sent to apologize in the King's name, would not actually censure the perpetrators of the imbroglio.[114]

THE CALL FOR A CRUSADE

While the successful consummation of the Austro-Polish alliance appears to have been due largely to John III's careful planning, considerable credit also accrues to the Church in the person of Pallavicini.[115] The actions of the Nunzio, on the other hand, were not merely the accomplishments of a single individual or even of two persons (remembering Buonvisi in Vienna). They reflect, rather, the overall efforts of the Holy See to organize a league of Christian powers. By the spring of 1683 Innocent XI can have had little doubt that the great moment was at hand, albeit under circumstances far more critical than originally envisioned. A veritable stream of epistles gushed forth from the Papal Chancery. The Holy Father requested support from Tuscany, Savoy, Venice, and the Shah of Persia, who, it was hoped, would coöperate with the Russians in attacking the Turkish rear.[116] The Pontiff also appealed to Roman Catholic hierarchs throughout Europe. The response from this quarter was rather disappointing, which is both a comment upon the limitations of Curial power at the time and, in the case of the Rhenine archbishops, a measure of the influence of the French King. Still, Innocent's pleas were by no means ineffective, especially as to money, which was crucial in view of the decrepit state of the Austrian Treasury. Portugal gave 100,000 thalers. The clergy of Spain scraped together 200,000 florins—derived at least in part from the "superficial" gold and silver ornaments of the nation's sanctuaries. The Italian states, presumably more sensitive to the danger because of geographical proximity, opened their coffers generously. Grand Duke Cosimo of Tuscany sent 100,000 lb. of powder and 100,000 florins (to Poland); Genoa, 300,000 thalers; Lucca, 20,000 florins; the Duke of Massa, 1000 gold doubloons; Savoy, 50,000 ducats; and the Prince of Castiglione 30,000 florins.[117] The papacy dug deeply into its own reserves, more or less accumulated for such a purpose anyway. Innocent is said to have transmitted as much as 400,000 florins to Vienna, 500,000 to Warsaw and 300,000 to Munich. He even rented his gardens to obtain additional cash. The cardinals gave their share: some are said to have melted down their table services.[118] The Pope likewise consented to a 1% capital tax on all Church property in Austria, which was supposed to bring in 500,000 florins.[119]

As necessary as subsidies were, the Pope would have been even more pleased by adherence to the Austro-Polish accord. The time, however, was not yet ripe. The international situation remained precarious. Louis XIV was an insuperable obstacle to any general *détente*—a fact which the Vicar of Christ was still unable or unwilling to concede. While the Pontiff had found it necessary already before 1683 to express regrets over the conflict with the Empire, he continued to place high hopes in the Most Christian King, depicting the possibility of thrones in the East for cadet Bourbon princes. There was even a chance of gaining an Imperial crown by liberating the City of Constantine. In early 1683 Innocent vainly attempted to mediate between Louis and Leopold, implying that the latter ought to make some concessions. The Holy Father's enduring faith in Louis revealed itself again in April with the arrival in Paris of a new nunzio, Ranuzzi. The orders were to obtain French aid against the advancing Turkish hordes or, failing that, to calm the West's troubled political waters so that Leopold might concentrate his forces in the East. The Pope's self-deception is all the more striking when one recalls that Paris and Rome were currently at bitter odds over the Gallican Question.[120]

Still, one can go too far in impugning Innocent's political judgment. The momentary status of Christendom appeared desperate. When Ranuzzi left Rome, the Pope had not yet heard of the conclusion of the Austro-Polish alliance. Leopold had been begging insistently for help. Moreover, Louis had passed on assurances of pacific intentions during the crisis. He had been willing to help nineteen years previously and, so, why not again? The Pontiff trusted the French King personally and ascribed the monarch's attitude to the bad advice of his advisers. By dispatching a new representative the Pope showed that his sense of duty had overcome whatever feelings of resentment or personal pride he may have harbored. Unfortunately, this magnanimity of spirit was completely wasted. Ranuzzi was not even received until August, by which time the French army was poised to strike, if necessary—but northward, into Belgium, not eastward in the service of the common European cause.[121]

France Checkmated

Clearly, Louis' reason for ignoring papal appeals was his concern for the Reunions. Leopold, however, remained adamant on the matter, at least in public at Regensburg. The continuance of this unrelenting stance was due in part to the conclusion of several new alliances—which were, in turn, the fruit of a carefully-planned, concerted drive throughout Central Europe to obtain effective support in the face of the threatening two-front war. The first agreement, with Hannover, was signed January 14. Its purpose was to build up a pro-Imperial army (Leopold to foot the bill) on the Lower Rhine and thus forestall the French in that region.[122] The second Austrian diplomatic success of the year was a mutual defense pact with Bavaria (January 26). Although the clauses dealing with Western

Europe were relatively mild, probably weaker than Vienna wished, Max Emmanuel was now at least tentatively on the Imperial side.[123] In return for an annual payment of 400,000 florins, the Austrians were assured the services of 5000 Bavarian infantrymen and 3000 cavalrymen in the coming struggle with the Turks. In the case of an armed clash with France, the Emperor was to come to Bavaria's help with a force of 15,000. The Elector's subsequent visit to Austria (May–June) firmly cemented relations. The young sovereign, pleased with the entertainments of his discerning host and subjected to a barrage of argumentation from the voluble Borgomanero, commenced making anti-French noises and soon consented to join the Association Tractate. The favorable impression that Max Emmanuel made may have helped to soften Leopold on the marriage issue—although Borgomanero fails to record any conversations on the topic at this juncture.[124]

The third of Vienna's 1683 alliances was the Hague Treaty of February 6, which reaffirmed and extended the commitments of the Association Tractate. Luckily for Louis, the practical value of this contract was vitiated by the pacific predilections of the Amsterdam oligarchy. Without the Netherlands, any rolling-back of the French was unthinkable. Moreover, Paris created an effective counter-alliance at Soest (February 17). The ostensible purpose of this union between Münster, Denmark, Brandenburg, and Cologne was the peaceful (i.e., pro-French) settlement of the Empire's dispute with France. In practice it also tended to isolate Brunswick-Lüneburg.[125]

Nevertheless, in Regensburg the French delegates continued to experience nothing but frustration. While their proposals enjoyed the support of five of the eight electors, the Colleges of Princes and Cities remained firmly opposed. Austria, moreover, insisted that any settlement at all must be "general," including both Spain (the Southern Netherlands) and the "Imperial fiefs" of Italy (Spanish Milan). It resisted the French demand for two different accords—a tactic presumably designed to divide and weaken foreign support for Spain. Louis, not wanting war, and perhaps concerned with adverse French and European public opinion, again found it necessary to bide his time.[126] The moment when he could act with impunity was not yet at hand; the Turkish cannons would have to be trained upon St. Stephen's Cathedral first. Perhaps another reason for the Sun King's patience—apart from reliance upon the Turkish onslaught—was knowledge of the behind-the-scenes squabble in Vienna between the "Easterners" and the "Westerners." In the latter part of April and early May it appeared for a time as if Prince Schwarzenberg had scored a point. In the physical absence of the Sinelli clique and in view of Madrid's failure to send monetary assistance, the Imperial government drafted a legal empowerment for negotiation with France at Regensburg. The document made no mention of Austria's allies or the

Burgundian Circle and thus represented a surrender to the French policy of separate peace treaties.[127] It raised a horrible spectre for Spain: a German settlement would mean the loss of Dutch aid for Flanders and Luxembourg since an isolated William of Orange could not continue to oppose Amsterdam's appeasement tendencies.

Whether the new Austrian move reflected an attempt to blackmail the *Consejo del Estado,* some subterranean intrigue, or even a momentary vacillation on Leopold's part cannot be determined with certainty.[128] Borgomanero, in any event, set to work furiously and bombarded the Emperor with another of his wordy memorials.[129] The Spanish government, hanging with bated breath upon the arrival of the Latin American treasure fleet, talked of diverting funds that were to be sent to Brandenburg in payment of debts from the last war and by the end of the year did succeed in dispatching to Leopold 555,000 florins.[130] By the beginning of June Borgomanero seems to have gained the upper hand again. After a day of excited arguments, Schwarzenberg dropped dead of a stroke.[131] Shortly thereafter the Spanish ambassador got the letter of authorization altered to his liking and persuaded Leopold to agree to submit to him for prior approval all future documents destined for Regensburg.[132] This victory, however, was one of Borgomanero's last. Although the Emperor was not to reverse course definitely until June of 1684, the siege of Vienna would set irrevocable changes into motion. By the fall of 1683 the scenery on the international stage would start to revolve and by winter the protagonists would be declaiming their lines before a radically different backdrop.

CHAPTER SIX

The Opposing Armies

A. The Imperial Military Establishment

A prominent American military historian has written that warfare may be analyzed from three different but interrelated viewpoints: (1) the political, emphasizing the social, economic, and diplomatic aims and resources of the powers in question; (2) the technological; and (3) the institutional, administrative, and organizational.[1] Previous chapters have examined the background to 1683 especially under the last part of the first heading. The other two facets are also worthy of attention.

After the Treaties of Westphalia three paths lay open for the development of military science and institutions within the Holy Roman Empire. The first was territorial, that is, in conjunction with the growing sovereignty of the princely state. The second was *ständisch*, that is, linked to the actions of the Estates at Regensburg. The third was imperial-absolutistic, that is, associated with the expansion of the Emperor's authority. All three of these routes were pursued, albeit with greatly varying emphasis and although only the first was ultimately to lead to success. The reason the armies of the princes prevailed was that the objective of the latter—the exercise of effective stately power—depended, above all, upon the development of a completely reliable instrument of force. The services rendered by lesser lords under feudal law and the publication of a general ban were scarcely practicable solutions. Nor was the temporary establishment of a regular, wartime army a much more satisfactory approach: it could degenerate into the ill-disciplined, self-seeking mercenary rabble which in part characterized the Thirty Years' War. Only a permanent, salaried body of troops, set up not merely *ad hoc* but maintained even after the conclusion of peace—in short, a modern, standing army, constantly at the beck and call of its creator—filled the needs of the times. Naturally, the precondition for this new *miles perpetuus* was steady pay, and it cannot be said that the standing army was fully meaningful until the territorial ruler had succeeded in liberating himself from approval of funds by the provincial estates.[2] Although several post-1648 acts of the *Reichstag* facilitated this task, the process was by no means complete everywhere by 1683, as Leopold's frustrating experiences with the Lower Austrian Estates were to show. Nevertheless, the establishment of trustworthy armed forces made considerable progress in the three and a half decades after Westphalia. While it is exceedingly difficult to assign definitive dates for the origin of any standing army, it does appear as if the process of formation took place earlier in Prussia and Austria than elsewhere in the *Reich*—which is only logical in view of the more mature political-institutional status of those countries.[3]

ADMINISTRATION

As far as Austria and the Imperial army in the strictly dynastic sense are concerned, the main nerve center of military operations was the much maligned and misunderstood Court War Council (*Hofkriegsrath*), the nucleus of the later War Ministry. This organ, often criticized on the mistaken basis of its being a high command, was also significant as the directing agency for all Habsburg affairs in the Balkans. While hemmed in its activity by financial dependency upon the Court Chamber (Treasury) and often ineffective, the Council shared responsibility with field commanders. The *Hofkriegsrath* issued only rather general guidelines to the *Feldherren,* but the latter would attempt to follow such advice religiously when they themselves were lacking in ideas.[4]

While the origins of the Council go back to the early sixteenth century, it really developed only with the rise of the Turkish menace, and did not become truly distinct until 1556. It served: (1) as the highest military administrative office; (2) as the staff and chancellery of the Imperial high command; and (3) as the personal military cabinet of the Emperor, who was, of course, the constitutional commander-in-chief. The heads of the field armies received their instructions directly from the monarch who was advised beforehand by the Council. The latter, for its part, could provide the generals only with as many troops as the Court Chamber was able to finance. Matters of pay and supply were the concern of the General War Commissariat, which fulfilled a somewhat confusing mediating rôle between Council and Chamber, illustrated by the accompanying chart. The major flaw of the *Hofkriegsrath,* as seen by Eugene of Savoy, was that it was made up of jealous persons and/or arm-chair strategists. The fault, in short, was the body's personal composition, not the institution *per se.* Further difficulties were the clumsy overall structure of the government, the appointment of civilians, and an overload of work and responsibility. Its slowness of function should not be judged by contemporary standards, however; seventeenth-century communications should be taken into account. Its attention to details, moreover, is a characteristic of any behind-the-lines organization, while the defensive nature of the wars Austria was compelled to wage often forced the Council to begin from scratch. The burden of two-front fighting ought not to be forgotten either. In the last analysis, the problem was that of the position of any field commander. The complete solution lies only in concentrating all power in his hands alone, something which occurs rarely anywhere, and a phenomenon which Austria has never known.[5]

Austrian Military Administration in the Latter Seventeenth Century

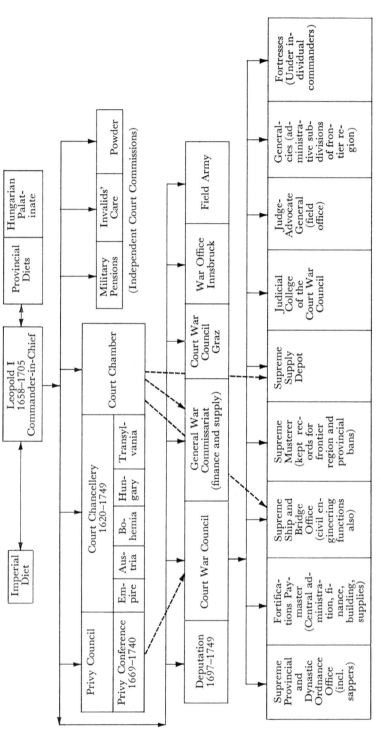

NOTE: broken line indicates additional overlapping relationship. Adapted from: 1. Regele, *op. cit.*, p. 11–12.   2. Feldzüge, *passim.*

Whatever the flaws of the *Hofkriegsrath,* the fighting forces which it helped to direct normally gave good account of themselves in battle, particularly when engaged against the Turk, the so-called "Hereditary Enemy." While the Austrians certainly did not possess any monopoly on courage, the gradual changes that had taken place in the structure, equipment, and tactics of the Habsburg military machine, beginning with reforms undertaken by the great innovator, Maximilian I (1459–1519), gave it an advantage over its technically less progressive Ottoman foe. Hence, the evolution of the Imperial Army's three major service branches—foot, horse and artillery—in the two centuries that preceded 1683 is worth studying.

THE INFANTRY

Threatened by the sturdy, commercially-marketed Swiss *Landsknechte,* Maximilian organized similar corps of troops for his own country, thus laying the foundations for all future growth. These soldiers, however, served only for the duration of hostilities and fought under the command of an autonomous, entrepreneurial colonel, with whom the sovereign signed special capitulations. By the end of the century the term *Landsknecht* fell from usage in favor of "German" and "Walloon" *Fußvolk* or simply *Knechte.* By this time also the word "regiment" had come to mean not just the "rule" of the colonel but rather a single, uniformly-led body of men. The Thirty Years' War brought about even more significant alterations, especially under the leadership of Wallenstein. Both he and the Emperor replaced the colonels as the army's overall organizers and recruiters. The colonels, although retaining considerable prerogatives, were now in the same position *vis-à-vis* the generals as the captains had once been to them. The most crucial change was that the commander-in-chief now held the right of disposal over a regiment. Henceforward the latter followed only one will, was organized, equipped, and led according to somewhat more consistent standards. The standing army was well in the process of becoming a reality.[6]

This development seems to have reached its culmination under Montecuccoli, who, without getting all that he wanted, effected noteworthy reforms. Among other things, the "Cunctator" established the (tactical) battalion and reduced the size of the regiment. The latter, divided into ten companies, now counted 2040 men, although the understrength units of 1683 were to average somewhat less. The total number of regiments during this period varied greatly depending upon whether the state was at war or not. Montecuccoli likewise directed his attention to weaponry. His most significant innovation was to lower the proportion of pikemen to musketeers, the new company consisting of forty-eight of the former, eighty-eight of the latter, and eight shieldmen. (Curiously enough, the Italian soldier-intellectual continued to regard pike as the queen of battle). Montecuccoli also introduced, for his own regiment, an experimental musket, half matchlock, half flintlock.[7] The true flintlock did not begin to be regularly manufactured until 1686 and did not become standard until 1699. Thus the majority of the troops at the time of the siege still carried the old, albeit much improved matchlock musket (model 1657). This nineteen-to-twenty mm. weapon shot a thirty-five gm. ball, weighed 12.32 lb., was 5'4.5" long, had a wooden ramrod and could be fired accurately up to 300 paces.[8] Rifles were also known in 1683, but only the Emperor's private gamekeepers (*Jäger*) used them. Some eighty to ninety of these Alpine stalwarts were present in Vienna and soon taught the besiegers that a hundred yards was not always a safe demarcation line.[9] At least some Austrian troops had bayonets at this time, although in the primitive and clumsy form of barrel-plugs.[10] The socket type which had become known three years before,[11] was not introduced even on a partial basis until 1689 (fourteen years earlier than in France). Another innovation, at least with respect to general issue, was the paper cartridge, containing both powder and ball. It facilitated more rapid firing. Instead of pouring directly from a horn, the infantryman bit open the bottom of a partitioned casing, placed its contents in the pan and then used the other half, with the ball, for the bore.[12]

The advent of the bayonet foreshadowed the final abolition of the pikeman and his twelve to eighteen foot pole with its iron grip and snake-tongue tip. However, engravings of the Battle of the Kahlenberg show that these weapons were still in use; in fact, they did not disappear entirely until 1689. Non-commissioned officers used a half-pike, one or two feet shorter, also known as a halberd or partisan. Commissioned personnel hefted an officer's partisan or spontoon, a four and a half foot staff with a broad, iron tip. The colonel's model sported a golden tassel while those belonging to the lesser ranks were variegated. The infantry also carried short swords (before the bayonet), daggers and components of the "Spanish Riders," light *chevaux de frise,* which they threw up for protection in the open field in a way similar to today's barbed wire. The troops also had one to three lb. cast-iron grenades, although the grenadiers did not yet constitute special units.[13]

The foot soldier's garments in 1683 were not really uniform. Although attempts had been made to institute standardized garb, the financial strain of frequent wars caused continual postponement. Thus, at Vienna, there were probably both old, Thirty Years' War elements and new, eighteenth-century features. Generally speaking, the outer vestment was a flared, knee-length overcoat with wide cuffs, lapels, and pewter or brass buttons. The narrow collar framed a white kerchief. Underneath was a tight-sleeved camisole, stretching to the hips. Further apparel items were linen-lined, calf's leather knickers with knee-high stockings or tight cloth pants with leggings, Muscovy-hide shoes, and a rough cloth or leather knapsack. The wide, floppy brim of the felt hat was only later pulled up and made rigid by a string. The old leather bandoleer with wooden capsules and hooks for other musket paraphernalia was now largely replaced by a cartridge pouch affixed to a broad belt. At the same time the idea of at least some regimental uniforming progressed, the cuffs and lapels providing space for individual colors and the hat for insignia. As for color, red had always been a favorite of the Imperials, especially since green was dropped (1661) because of its use by the Hereditary Enemy. Red fabrics, however, were too costly and too little weather-resistant for the mass of the troops, who preferred, especially for the much used overcoat, wolf's grey or pearl grey (later the uniform color). Needless to say, the officer's attire, left to his own fancy save for a yellow-black sash, was considerably more luxurious, and the general, apart from the modest Duke Charles of Lorraine, was an elegant apparition indeed, decked out in the finest brocades and silks and covered by a copious, carefully-crisped *allonge* wig upon which there sat a brightly feathered hat.[14]

THE CAVALRY

While the simple private of peasant origin, who had to gather up his locks in pigtails, gaped in wonder at the splendid accoutrements of his commissioned superiors, so also did the partly bourgeois infantry officers look up in envy to stylish colleagues of the cavalry. Rare was the burgher who could succeed (or wanted to) in breaking the nobility's monopoly over leadership of the horsed troops, especially the ultra-prestigious cuirassiers, whose traditions derived ultimately from the knights of the Middle Ages. There was, however, no unbroken line of development from Mediaeval times. As with the infantry, credit must go to the circumspect Maximilian I. Wishing to free himself from unreliable feudal-style mounted service rendered by a decreasingly warlike aristocracy, the Emperor established a corps of "Kyrisser" for those noblemen in whom the martial spirit did survive. One heavily-armored, sword-and-lance-bearing knight was permitted a suite of six men: a light, mounted sharpshooter; two servitors, also furnished with lances; a partly-armored, halberd-carrying esquire; a groom; and a lightly-armed page. This integrated fighting unit constituted the seed, from which there sprang, during the course of the sixteenth century, the three basic types of mounted warriors that also characterized the succeeding hundred years: heavy cavalry, marksmen or horsed arquebusiers, and light cavalry.[15]

With the passage of time the "Kyrisser" became an "armed German reiter" and finally, in 1596, a cuirassier, having in the meantime lost most of his companions and having laid aside his lance. Fitted out with a saber and a wheelock pistol but keeping most of his armor, he rode into the Thirty Years' War. In the meantime his scantily-armored marksman-comrade, equipped with a hackbut (arquebus), had begun to form a separate unit of light cavalry, although, in 1586, with the addition of some armor and two pistols he once again became a "light heavyweight." The Great War was to work considerable changes. The mounted arquebusier vanished, his place being taken (1623) by a horsed, carbine-toting infantryman, the dragoon (from a dragon-shaped embellishment on his gun). The latter's steed could transport him speedily to that portion of the battlefield where his firepower was needed on the ground; he later learned to shoot from the saddle as well. Another innovation of the age was the use of "Croats" of "Hussars" ("Pollacks" on occasion). These irregular, unarmored fighters from the realm of St. Stephen moved with such swiftness that their value for scouting and raiding overcame the liability of a lack of discipline and holding power.[16]

After Westphalia the need of further emendations became apparent, and Montecuccoli once again set to work. The Imperial field marshal— this rank itself being of cavalry origin—clearly defined the tactical meaning of the word "squadron." The latter now comprised two companies, whereas the five squadron regiment counted 800–1000 riders. Montecuccoli also thinned the line of battle, establishing the principle of only three ranks of sixteen-hand horses for use against the Turk and two against the "regular" foe. The latter part of the century also saw the laying-off of much of the cuirassier's armor although he remained *the* heavy trooper. In most instances all that he wore were blackened, bullet-tested breast and back plates, a ridged helmet, and perhaps gauntlets. If he was an officer, his cuirass was finely engraved or inlaid. However, the brilliant uniforms for which the cavalry, especially the Hussars (who did not become a distinctly Magyar unit until 1685), became famous, did not begin to make their appearance until the end of the century. In 1683 only the dragoons wore standardized garb. The main weapons of the cuirassier were the *Pallasch* (a broad, double-edged blade with a basket grip), a carbine, and a brace of long-nosed pistols. The dragoons wielded an arc handled sword and, eventually, the bayonet flintlock.[17]

THE ARTILLERY

The appeal of the cavalry was clearly linked both to social status and to a dashing rôle on the battlefield. While, on the one hand, such service did not necessarily bar exercise of the intellect, on the other, anybody with a probing, technologically-oriented mind, above all a non-aristocrat, would have preferred to join the artillery. The latter, moreover, was the youngest of the three military arms, at least from the vantagepoint of the Middle Ages. Its initial growth was associated with the taking of fortified towns, which, in turn, directed their greater wealth and human skills to defense by the same means. The cities gradually gained such preeminence that the territorial rulers were forced to ask for their help in wartime. Thus, two kinds of ordnance developed in Austria: the Dynastic or *Haus*

Artillery and the Provincial or *Land* Artillery, owned by the estates but paid for principally by the municipalities.[18]

However, urban resistance to outside service and the cumbersome nature of mobilization led Maximilian to stress his own ordnance, thus also making himself the founder of Austria's third weapons branch. The *Kaiser* attempted to bring more order into the chaos of types and calibers, encouraged the immigration of cannon artisans, and established a central ordnance administration, which included manufacture. Nonetheless, municipal gunnery continued to exist, and although its importance gradually diminished, the pieces stored and maintained in the Vienna City Arsenal played no small part in the 1683 siege.[19] What Maximilian did not do was to set up a permanently active artillery or to distinguish in any way between mobile field artillery and the hard-to-transfer siege guns. Cannon were simply hauled from the dépôts when needed. The only indication of future organizational change was adoption, of the term Field Ordnance Master (*Feldzeugmeister*) as a general's rank. By 1650, however, the Field Artillery had separated from the *Hausartillerie*. The Thirty Years' War had also resulted in further reduction and simplification of gun categories, in lightening of the pieces and in more flexible tactics, for the Austrians were not slow to copy Gustavus Adolphus. Another change was that the highly-skilled, privileged, and generously remunerated civilian artillerist, often a Bohemian, became more of a soldier, although the dichotomy of his status remained a problem for commanders. Until well into the eighteenth century, the guilds were especially successful in maintaining their prerogatives in the manufacture of the artistically embellished cannon.[20]

In Austria, in contrast to France, the immediate post-Westphalia period witnessed something of a decline or at least a slow-down in the development of ordnance. The quality of the continuously refounded guns deteriorated, and there was a dearth of good ordnance-masters on duty in the arsenals. Still, Montecuccoli's tome on artillery deserves mention: it gave the finishing touch to conceptual and organizational clarity. After his death the names of Christoph Börner and Peter Miethen, the latter remembered for publishing a technical study, stand out. Both men were present in 1683; both rose from the ranks.[21]

The accompanying charts indicate the dimensions of Habsburg artillery. The first shows more or less long-barrelled, straight trajectory weapons, used for field or siege purposes. The ranges given are only those of real accuracy. If elevated more, the guns could shoot five to six times as far. Although the science of ballistics had advanced, aiming was still crude. All that was necessary was a sight, a quadrant, and a quoin for raising or lowering the barrel. The arsenals also stocked howitzers (not shown), chambered pieces firing a medium arc trajectory. They were good for shooting fireworks and for dropping hail, explosive shells, and

The Classification of Habsburg Artillery in 1683[22]

I

GUNS

Type of Gun	Caliber in Weight (Nürnberg pounds)		Caliber in Diameter (mms and inches)			Caliber as Length Times Width	Length (Feet & Inches)	Average Weight (U.S. pounds)		Effective Range (Yards)
	Bore	Ball	Bore	Ball	Full			Charge	Barrel	
1. Full carthoun; full cannon	54	48	198 / 7.78	194 / 7.62	325 / 13.17	17	11'1¼"	24.2	11,000	1152
2. Three quarters carthoun; double culverin; *culebrina*	40	36	176 / 6.92	170 / 6.68	323 / 12.69	19	10'11"	18.7	9240	1344
3. Demicarthoun; demicannon; double field culverin	27	24	156 / 6.13	150 / 5.90	315 / 12.38	21	10'9"	15.4	6160	896
4. Full field culverin; dragon; *Mediaculebrina*	21	18	144 / 5.66	135 / 5.31	392 / 15.41	29	13'8"	9.9	6600	1280
5. Quarter carthoun; field culverin	14	12	124 / 4.87	119 / 4.68	274 / 10.77	23	9'4"	6.6	3300	1024
6. Field demiculverin; saker	10.5	9	112 / 4.40	107 / 4.21	375 / 14.74	35	12'10"	5.5	3740	890
7. Falcon (*Falke*), "full & good"; quarter culverin; pelican	7	6	105 / 4.13	95 / 3.73	248 / 9.75	26	9'11"	4.4	2860	768
8. Reduced falcon (*Falkaune*)	7	6	105 / 4.13	95 / 3.73	162 / 6.37	17	5'10"	2.2	1980	640
9. Regimental piece, "full and good"	3.5	3	85 / 3.34	70 / 2.75	189 / 7.43	27	7'6"	2.2	1540	640
10. Reduced regimental piece	3.5	3	85 / 3.34	70 / 2.75	105 / 4.13	15	4'2"	.088	770	512
11. Falconet (*smeriglio*)		1	28 / 2.08	50	175	35	6'3¾"	.066	660	320
12. Serpentine		½	28 / 1.1	26 / 1.62	101 / 3.97	39	3'6"	.022	264	192

II
MORTARS[22]

Name	Caliber in Weight (Nürnberg lb.)		Caliber in diameter of bore		Caliber in diameter of stone shot	
	Bore	Ball	Mm	Inches	Mm	Inches
Pöller	345	300	590	23.19	560	22.01
Pöller	232	200	515	20.24	480	18.86
Pöller	120	100	410	16.11	375	14.74
Pöller	72	60	335	13.17	308	12.10
Mörser	35	30	280	11	250	9.83
Mörser	16	12	200	7.86	180	7.07

(Range: see footnote 22)

stones into beleaguered cities. The wagon-borne mortars listed in the second chart were also well-suited to siege work.[22] All of these tools of war were horribly expensive. In 1620, for example, a full carthoun cost 500 florins. The great cash outlays resulted both from the initial purchase and, then, from the complex shaping process of the various metals used (bronze, cast and wrought iron, copper, and lead, the choice being determined by the size and purpose of the gun). Powder, while not as difficult to handle as in the days when it had to be mixed on the battlefield, was still a problem. Special buckets and paper cartridges facilitated matters. Powder was also the essential raw material for Austria's sappers, who were few in numbers and low in skills—an unfortunate state of affairs since mining and countermining were more likely than artillery to seal the fate of a fortress.[23]

A good arsenal also had to carry a multiplicity of projectiles. While the long field guns fired only iron balls (including bar and chainshot), round stones (in decreasing measure), and cartouche (grape, canister), the chambered pieces required not only the former but also explosive shells and incendiary and illumination missiles of the most varied types. The "bombs" (shells), much improved since the sixteenth century, were surprisingly sophisticated. The cannon-makers also constructed hand grenades. The latter were entrusted to particularly tall and hardy pikesmen and musketeers but remained so unpredictable that they sometimes were shot from muskets or tiny, hand-portable mortars. The incendiaries, like the shells, were devilishly ingenious. One type was booby-trapped with so-called "Murder Strokes" (*Mordschläge*) to assure that it would not be doused upon landing. It contained small sections of pipe, packed with powder and lead balls, that would go off in the face of anyone approaching. In the same category were illumination projectiles, important for night action during sieges. Likewise essential in trying to pry open a fortress-city was the petard, the forerunner, in a sense, of the modern sapper's plastic explosive. A further device was a two-wheeled cart, loaded with incendiaries, balls, "Murder Strokes," and hand grenades, that was sent rolling downhill toward the enemy (*Sturmblock-, balken* or *faβ*). The artillerist's outfit was incomplete unless it included "Fire Lances" or "Fire Pipes," tubes that discharged a series of musket balls.[24]

Even though seventeenth-century cannon had a limited firing speed (thirty shots daily for a full carthoun, 100 for a small regimental piece), the amount of ammunition, plus other equipment, staggers the imagination. The result was a baggage train of enormous proportions. Horse requirements were prodigious. A single half carthoun, barrel, carriage and supply wagons, might require thirty-eight stout animals. The latter were supplied by the government or the Estates, or were bought on the spot. Other supplies, sometimes even the guns, came both from the state and from private entrepreneurs like the fabled Oppenheimer.[25]

Support, Recruitment, Training

While the blast of cannonry, the élan of cavalry, and the tenacity of infantry constituted the major barriers against an aggressive Islam, these forces—Austria's regular army—did not bear sole responsibility for national defense. Another establishment of great significance in frustrating Turkey was the Croatian Military Frontier. This unique institution, reminiscent of the Roman *limes,* has recently been the subject of a fine monograph by an American historian.[26] All that one need say of the *Militärgrenze* with reference to 1683 is that under General Herberstein, its Slavic peasant-soldiers succeeded in holding the relatively quiet southern flank. Far less efficacious, however, as a means of resistance was the Mediaeval-descended general ban (*Aufgebot*). The calling-up of large masses of the population was done only in times of national emergency, and the percentage of men drafted depended upon precisely how great the peril was calculated to be. Led by the local estates, the burghers and peasants were supposed to appear with their own weapons and to set up road blocks and build warning fires. The advent of the standing army made the ban far less important.[27] Despite the fact that it now came under professional command, it was clumsy, unruly, and practically impotent, as the happenings of 1683 within Lower Austria were to demonstrate.

The only civil defense units that had any real meaning were the burgher militias and the Hungarian insurrection. Vienna's home guardsmen were organized on a ward basis and, in 1683, by guild and profession as well. The city likewise maintained its own arsenal, packed with a large assortment of weapons, many obsolescent. Of greatest value was the municipal artillery, which counted fifty pieces, including eight howitzers, and a company of master-gunners.[28] The citizen-warriors, however, do not appear to have been well-trained or easily utilizable, and their reputation as heroes of the siege is largely unfounded.[29] The insurrection (from *insurgere,* "to mount") differed from the Austrian militia particularly by virtue of its aristocratic character. The *banderia* were normally a more useful, more martial, if not especially well-disciplined military tool, and from their service as the Portal Militia they had some real experience of war. Unfortunately for Leopold, political conditions in Thököly's Hungary rendered them almost worthless.[30]

If the quality of these corps left something to be desired, improvement was no less needed in logistics and recruitment. Not only did Leopold meet blindly irrealistic opposition when he asked the estates—provincial both in geography and in mentality—to grant him funds for the proposed new, 80,000 man army.[31] He was also unable to get a full return, in regiments, from the cash that he finally did manage to obtain. Because of their continuing prerogatives, officers often became rich men. According to the Venetian Morosini, a colonelcy was worth a marquisate and a generalcy an Italian duchy.[32] Opportunities for embezzlement included recruitment money, soldiers' "pay" (supposedly intended for reimbursing civilians required to supply quarters and meals), the keeping of campaign stores (especially perishables), and funds for the purchase of equipment and clothing. Officers' charges and promotions were saleable, which was no help to a soldier's morale. The government sought to improve conditions by passing out more food and fodder directly. It compensated itself by keeping one half of the pay and giving the other half directly to the soldier. In 1681 a new bookkeeping system, based upon accounting principles, was introduced. Fraud seems to have continued nevertheless.[33]

Recruiters preferred solid, hearty peasant louts, preferably Germans, over less tractable city slickers. They took men between eighteen and forty-six but were supposed to spare yeomen's sons. There were three different approaches: "voluntary," "cunning" and "forceful." While the rustic may have been easy to hook, he was harder to hold. The conditions of military life were extremely rugged. Food and pay were bad and frequently non-existent. Medical aid, even if available, was painfully primitive (only field apothecaries and barber-surgeons). Discipline was brutal, with overtones of perversity—perhaps in part because of the proprietary colonel's judicial rights. On the other hand, the behavior toward civilians, even in friendly lands, of the often deprived and needy soldier seemed to demand stringent measures. Desertion, easy because of loose local government, did not carry the death penalty. Understandably a common phenomenon, it resulted in the loss of one's ears and nose. Capital punishment, practised only in wartime, was meted out for refusal to obey, physical resistance, and flight in the face of the enemy. Shooting was the right of the "honorable" malfeasant, hanging the cost of "dishonorable" infractions (including common civil crimes). Indeed in all disciplinary matters an attempt was made to play upon feelings of pride and duty. The officers also showed psychological insight by emphasizing flags, symbols, ceremonies, customs, and even superstitions.[34] Music, too, was used to stimulate troop morale. After the ensign raised his flagstaff as the down-beat for the drums, tambourines, fifes, shawms, and bagpipes, the racket became so intense that the marching troops dropped back thirty paces. Trumpets served to infuse the cavalry with ardor.[35]

B. Tactics and Leadership

All the features of the Austrian army heretofore described do not represent anything especially remarkable. Apart from its greater size, the Habsburg host was apparently similar in most respects to the fighting forces of other Central European territorial states, especially Bavaria, Saxony, Hannover and Prussia, lands that already had standing armies or were in the process of creating them.[36] With tactics, however, the story is a little different. Austrian generals, faced with the problem of fighting on two fronts, had to devise solutions appropriate to the nature of the terrain and the enemy in question, and this sometimes meant divergency from concepts and practices characteristic of the West.

A New Rôle for Foot

The infantry—since the late Middle Ages the dominant element in battle—profited from the lessons of the Thirty Years' War. The huge, unwieldy, oblong Spanish tercio (2,500 men), which emphasized pike over musketry, was a thing of the past. Maurice of Nassau had first developed the principle of smaller, shallower, more flexible squares (800–1000 men), based upon thorough drill and increased firepower. The technique was improved by Gustavus Adolphus, who used a variety of ingenious weapons combinations, the most famous being a 1,200 man wedge composed of pike, and musket blocks of roughly 100–200.[37] Monte-cuccoli's battalions, numbering but 1,280 men, were similar. Drawn up in two lines of battle (three or even more if the ground required it), the individual units had nuclei of 480 pike, eighty wide and six deep and were flanked by files of musketeers. The Italian general recommended that they be capped in front by one rank of shield-bearers and one of musketeers, but he did not regard this arrangement as binding in all cases. The musketeers might stand in a number of positions: as "sleeves" only, at the flanks of the pike; half at the head of the latter, half at their sides; all at the rear with the pikemen kneeling to permit a clear firing field; mixed with the pike; or behind the intervals of pike squares (for sudden sallies). Moreover, what could be done with the big-sized battalion could also be done on a smaller scale, e.g., the company, if occasion demanded. Likewise, the square was not immutable; it could evolve into a tenaille, quoin, croissant, or porcupine formation. As for shooting, after the first ranks—the foremost kneeling—had discharged, the men wheeled to the rear of their respective files in order to allow others to fire in turn. In this way they could provide a continuous barrage. If attacked by reiters—to whom they were rather vulnerable—, they had the protection of their comrades' steel-tipped poles.[38]

However, as indicated, the number of these stout shafts was decreasing, the consequence mainly of the growing lightness and faster firing rate of muskets. The famous, old "push of pike" became ever more difficult and finally impossible. Although the hedgehog seemed for a while to retain its defensive value, it became out-of-date with the advent of the bayonet. The fact that the Turks had invented the sport of deftly cleaving wooden pike stems seems to have hastened the adoption of the new type of blade. To be sure, it, too, played only a secondary rôle in view of improved musketry. Clearly, the invention of better longarms was also the chief reason for the growing flatness of the squares (which finally turned into the three-man deep linear formations of the eighteenth century). The resultant lengthening of front automatically led to abandonment of frontal attacks and to preference for flanking movements. An accompanying phenomenon was the greater use of natural or artificially-erected shelters in the terrain for loose, stubbornly-conducted firefights in or around inhabited places—by which means the enemy could be kept at a distance and the decision sought through a massive wing stroke. (It seems clear that while the Eastern steppes favored the continuation of the hallowed traditions of mounted combat, their open expanses, as contrasted to the more heterogenous countryside of the Empire, were well-adapted to the thinner and more extended lines of rigidly disciplined foot). Nevertheless, the schematic *ordre de bataille,* with its several parallel lines, now more widely spaced because of longer firing ranges, had not yet yielded to the tighter, individually-briefed tactical units that would characterize the next century. The Kahlenberg engagement as well as the encounters of the Holy League War still saw use of the traditional arrangement. In short, the late 1600's witnessed an intermingling both of old and new weapons and of old and new tactics.[39]

HORSE AND CANNON ON THE PUSZTA

While infantry techniques were changing, so also were the cavalry's, in fact so much so as to give the horsed troops a new lease on life in major clashes between armies. Although the wheelock-equipped reiter, executing his caracole, had replaced the expensive and increasingly hard-to-obtain lancer, pistol barrages alone brought no more success in cracking open a really sturdy, pike-protected square. When Sweden's great king, drawing upon the experience of the Huguenot Wars, ordained the vigorous application of the saber after an initial pistol discharge, he introduced shock tactics that permitted the cavalry—when properly coördinated with longer range weapon units—to swing the tide of a battle. To Gustavus Adolphus must also go the credit for revolutionizing artillery tactics. His integration of highly mobile light guns—the regimental pieces—with infantry greatly strengthened offensive firepower. Drawn by one or two horses or even man-pulled, stationed directly before the squares and charged with cartouche, the little guns, advancing in step with the whole line of battle, had a devastating shotgun effect. The heaviest pieces (over fifty lb.), unable to smash the new, improved fortresses, had fallen out of favor already during the Netherlands Independence War; the field guns then used had become less massive. The remaining, still relatively heavy cannons were thereupon indiscriminately massed for greater effect; they continued to be hard to maneuver, service, and supply—and vulnerable to capture during a swiftly-moving encounter. Lightened even further during the Thirty Years' War, they were carried around as the "field artillery" proper, separate from the regimental pieces, for use in the army's van. By the last quarter of the century modest technical progress, facilitating mobility and rapidity of fire, effected a renewal of their rôle. Heavier guns were to be sent up to the crest of the Vienna Woods in 1683, while, under Louis of Baden and Eugene, the massing of mixed, increasingly large caliber batteries became common.[40]

One tactical trick practised upon the Turks was to hide lighter guns behind the infantry front, which would suddenly open up, exposing the unsuspecting foe to a withering barrage. On the march across the plains, the less-quickly unlimbered heavy guns were kept protected in the center. In the event of a lightning attack, the wagons formed a circle around them in the manner of the Wild West. The progress of an Austrian army across Hungary was in general a precarious undertaking that compelled the officers to enforce the rules and regulations ruthlessly.[41]

In the same context one might note that men waging war in the East showed an inhumanity that contrasted sharply with the gentlemanly behavior of the highly-trained, expensive-to-maintain professional armies of the West, which spent their time trying to outmaneuver each other. There were few courtesies and formalities between opponents in Hungary. A soldier who shot at an officer meant to kill. The civilian's lot remained unenviable. There were revolting atrocities. Combat seems to have had an ideological aspect long absent among Christian nations. The "Hereditary Enemy" appears to have been regarded as unworthy of mercy. Of course, as will be shown later, the Turks' own religious attitude and laxer discipline encouraged brutalization of combat. In a way one is reminded of the vicious circle of horrors that distinguished the fighting between the Yugoslav Partisans and the Germans during the Second World War.

CHARLES OF LORRAINE

However harsh the deportment of Habsburg soldiers, the Emperor did possess in his field commander, Duke Charles V of Lorraine and Bar, a decent and just human being. History has borne witness to the generalissimo's qualities by paying him more attention than his colleagues such as the jealous (but not ungifted) Hermann. On the other hand, it is true that the noble Lorrainer received relatively little attention during his own lifetime and was forced to take a modest place in the shadow of the more extroverted Sobieski. The flood of encomiastic writing that followed the lifting of the siege wove laurel wreathes exclusively for the Polish sovereign. Only after the Duke's death did his worth come to be appreciated by most leaders of the time, and only then did his fame unfold among the European public.[42]

Charles' childhood and youth were decidedly inauspicious. Born April 3, 1643, he was the son of Duke Nicholas Francis, brother of the reigning Duke Charles IV, and became heir to the Duchy in 1658 upon the death of his elder brother. Charles IV, however, had been absent from his French-occupied homeland for almost three decades; only in 1659, by the Peace of the Pyrénées, was he able to return, under humiliating conditions of virtual French vassalage. In 1662, in a moment of weakness, he even declared Louis XIV his heir. Charles V, who was born in Vienna and apparently inculcated from an early date with a strong sense of dynastic rights, now stepped forward as the sole defender of an autonomous future for his country. After early childhood in Austria, he had resided at the French court, where he was the object of several abortive marital projects. These experiences were presumably painful, for the evidence suggests that he was much enamored of the ladies in question. Charles now reserved his rights in defiance of Louis, fled from France, and finally (1663) settled down at the court of his godfather, Leopold.[43] Regaining his inheritance was to be the main objective of his life. In an age of pervasive French influence over the Rhine region, however, his efforts soon became a mere struggle to be recognized ceremonially as Duke by his fellow German princes.

At the time of his arrival in Vienna it appeared that his stay would only be temporary. Yet is proved to be the beginning of a career that linked his name forever with the House of Habsburg. The next year, as a regimental commander, he fought with distinction in the Battle of Szentgotthárd. His unit remained in service after the Peace of Vasvár (1665), and Charles caught chickenpox while in winter quarters. His face was left disfigured, which fortified an already marked reserve in social intercourse. In 1668–1669 he lost the Polish election to Wiśniowiecki. The reversal was all the more bitter because of his beloved Eleanora's marriage to the

CAROLUS V. DEI GRATIA
LOTHARINGIÆ. BARRI Etc. DUX.

(*Vienna, National Library*)

Charles V, Duke of Lorraine and Bar

new king. The year 1670 brought yet another blow. The erratic Charles IV suddenly attempted to reassert control, whereupon French troops took over the Duchy outright. Four years later the second effort to gain the Polish crown also miscarried. In the meantime the Dutch War (1672–1679) had broken out, the *Reich* becoming involved in 1674. Charles now had an opportunity to work out his frustrations physically and at the same time to fight to win back his homeland. He acquitted himself well, and imbibed military knowledge from Montecuccoli in the process. Then, in 1678, he was finally able to wed the now widowed Eleanora. The union was not only a matter of the heart but politically expedient: the bride's mother, the Dowager Empress, became the Duke's protector. This was a matter of no small consequence since Leopold and Charles, perhaps because of certain personality resemblances (melancholia in particular), never became close. Lorraine's ceremonial position was now assured. He and Eleanora made Innsbruck their residence, for the Duke was the newly appointed Stadholder of the Tyrol. The Treaty of Nijmegen had made it impossible for him to return home: the conditions imposed by the French were too onerous to accept. He had every reason to be a "Westerner." Only in 1682, under the influence of Marco d'Aviano, did he begin to alter his viewpoint.

The Innsbruck period was the happiest in Charles' life. His relation to his wife and children was particularly close. It was at this time too that he established his association with d'Aviano. Lorraine was a deeply religious man as the mutual correspondence shows. The Capuchin's ministrations during Charles' nearly fatal illness (June 1682) may be recalled, for they give the monk yet another claim to a crucial rôle in history. By this time the Duke was also commander of the Imperial army, as lieutenant general. He thus inherited one of Montecuccoli's two offices, the other, the War Ministry, going to Hermann.[44]

Despite certain physical flaws that developed with the passage of time—his pockmarked face, a leg broken in a fall from a collapsing bridge at the siege of Philippsburg (1676), increasing corpulence—Charles remained a dignified and imposing figure. He was tall and well-formed, and had an aristocratic air about him. His darkening red hair, admired by Sobieski, was later covered up by a fashionable wig. Yet Lorraine was anything but a dandy. He was simple in his habits and showed not a touch of class arrogance. Indeed, it is impossible to find any witness who mentions an unattractive personal trait. He was envied by some but never apparently disliked. John III, who had been his rival, found him a grand fellow.[45] An accomplished horseman and of unquestioned physical courage, the Duke was, nevertheless, a friend of belles lettres and a bibliophile. His linguistic attainments were respectable: perfect German, French, Italian and some Latin. "Il parloit peu, mais il parloit bien et à propos."[46] Toward strangers his manner was grave and serious, but with intimates he was affable. He laid great stress on rationality and disliked pettiness.[47] He enjoyed arguing in a closed circle but liked to sustain a thesis not so much to convince as to exercise the minds of his associates and to become acquainted with their mentalities and characters.[48] Lorraine's character definitely struck a responsive chord in the ranks. The troops under him seemed to have been marked by unusually good morale, in which connection the cruelty of discipline should be recalled.[49]

Despite these virtues, no one has ever maintained that the Duke was the greatest captain of his age, this honor being reserved for Eugene and perhaps Marlborough. Villars mentions Charles' faults. The Frenchman found him too slow. He was occasionally unable to seize the advantage in a rapidly changing military situation unless stirred by vigorous subordinates. He did not always attend to orderly troop movements. He might show lack of concern for march arrangements, food supplies, baggage security, stationing of pickets, and other details. His gifts, thought Villars, were more tactical than strategic.[50] Of course it must be remembered that he labored under liabilities of which Eugene was able to rid himself: circumscribed powers of decision because of a command shared with Hermann, unsubordinated fellow generals, and governmental financial debility. Probably Charles' talents could have found fuller expression if the Emperor had been able to steel himself to remove the Margrave earlier than 1687. In any event, Lorraine managed to attain eminence in the face of adversity, and accomplished enough in the campaigning of 1683 alone to assure himself a secure, albeit modest place in the ranks of Europe's outstanding military leaders.

C. The Poles

Despite organizational weaknesses, the army that the Duke led was fairly homogeneous and relatively pliable. It is questionable whether he could have attained fame if fortune, instead of permitting him to remain in Austrian service, had let him become ruler of Poland-Lithuania. For the fighting forces of the other dual monarchy were unique in many significant respects. Their structure, ethnic composition, and mentality—partly Western and partly Eastern—were so diversified that in all likelihood only a man with the special qualities of Sobieski could have done anything with them.

Command and Muster

Although the King was head of state in both parts of the country, each had its own separate military body, its own generals, staff, and financing. However, internal organization, tactics, and equipment were the same, and the King was overall commander-in-chief, with the duty of personal leadership.[51] The next highest officer was the Crown Grand Hetman (*Hetman wielki Koronny*), who exercised extensive authority over both the troops and the territory they occupied. Below him was the Crown Field Hetman (*Hetman Polny*), who was responsible for intelligence and security. The great power that these men enjoyed was symbolized by a special marshal's baton, the *buława*, a hollow, pear-shaped object, affixed to a three-foot stock, gilded and set with jewels. It contained a dagger that could be withdrawn and used if needed. Another badge of high rank was the *bunczuk*, "a Great Lance, adorned at the end either with Feathers, or Knots of Ribbons, or some other sort of Plume, under a Great Ball of some rich Stuff." It was carried in front of the king or the hetmans by a special rider. Also indicative of authority were horse-tails, taken over from the Turks and Tatars.[52]

The troops themselves were raised from a score of sources, clearly a major reason for the lack of cohesion. The cornerstone was the Standing Army, a rather small organization considering the size of the land. In 1683 it counted only 11,000 men. In wartime it was supplemented by the General Ban, (*Pospolite Ruszenie*) composed primarily of the nobility. The latter were not required to serve outside the nation's borders, unless remunerated. If money was not forthcoming, which was usually the case, the Ban was entitled to go home. The third reservoir of manpower was the Volunteers. The country had a law, according to which nobody could hold public or ecclesiastical office unless he had rendered military service. Many young aristocrats therefore served of their own free will and without compensation. Others hoped to become rich through booty. The magnates, as opposed to the gentry, had private armies, well trained and often as numerous as the regular units. In the event of national emergency, a great aristocrat would lead his warriors against the fatherland's enemies, often without pay. A fourth way to raise fighting men was by conscription or levy. Good infantry was lacking, and therefore the right of the peasantry to bear arms, previously abrogated, was partly restored. Of every twelve peasants, one received, at the state's expense, saber, musket, and ax and joined the ranks as a foot soldier. A fifth method was recruitment; most of the troops used at Vienna were gathered in this fashion, thanks to papal subsidies and money from the private royal treasure chest. A sixth approach was hiring mercenaries outside the realm. Such forces generally remained under foreign command. A seventh means was to mobilize vassals, above all the hard-riding Zaporozhian Cossacks, men greatly cherished by Sobieski for their reconnoitering and pursuit value. Lastly, the Poles sometimes relied upon allies, such as the wild Tatar hordes, nominally subject to the Turks. (The Tatars serving on the Christian side in 1683 appear to have stood under Lithuanian suzerainty).[53]

THE NATIONAL ARMY

The host thus brought together fell into two main divisions, the National Army (*Autorament Polski*) and the Foreign Army (*Autorament Cudzoziemski*). Organized separately, they marched and camped apart, supporting each other only in battle. The former, made up almost entirely of nobility, included heavy, medium, and light horse. The heavy detachments, or hussars, came from the great aristocracy, although the esquires (*pocztowi*) who followed each knight (the "comrade," *towarzysz*), might be from the gentry. The "comrade" had to provide, both for himself and his followers, horses, weapons, equipment, clothing, food, and fodder. He also had to take along his own men to care for the animals, baggage, and supplies. Coachmen and servants exceeded the warriors in number, but the first-named fought upon occasion. The hussar was doubtlessly the most magnificent cavalryman in the Western world. He was still heavily armored. His helmet included pieces covering the cheeks and the back of the neck; a ridge extended downward to protect the nose. Some reiters were seen in brigandine. Their chests, backs, arms, and thighs were encased in beautifully engraved, glittering steel. Boots were of heavy leather. Since the Turks utilized essentially the same battle dress, the Poles attached to their bodies a Saint Andrew's cross or a representation of the Blessed Virgin. Affixed to their shoulders was a panther's skin, and sprouting from the rear cuirass was a pair of eagle's wings. The extraordinarily strong and handsome horses were also armored. The costly bridle equipment was adorned with feathers and tassels and included foot-warmer stirrups. The mounts obviously had to be powerful, for the weaponry they supported was formidable. A knight disposed of a curved saber, a straight one, two pistols in holsters, two others in the stirrups, a battlehammer on the saddlehorn, and a nineteen foot long *kopia* or lance. The latter, from which a pennon fluttered, had a wooden shaft; its base fitted into a shoe on the saddle. Polish partisans claim that this cavalry was far superior to that of the West. Certainly the weight of its rapidly delivered attack, carried out to the sound of kettle drums and trumpets, was tremendous. However, it was possible to shoot the horses from under the knights, who then lay helplessly on the ground in their armor. Sobieski was forced to devise a new tactical order in order to remedy this deficiency, and in the course of the War of the Holy League it was thought best to deprive the cocky and ill-disciplined cavaliers of their lances once and for all.

The next category of horse, also the aristocrats' monopoly, was the *pancerny*. The less extensive armor included complete head protection, a mailed shirt, lower arm pieces, and a shield of steel or a pipe covered with embroidery. Weapons were short lances, falchions, daggers (handžars), poleaxes, pistols, and musketoons or bows and arrows (in variant combination). While good in battle, greater mobility suited these troopers, especially for reconnaissance, pursuit of the beaten enemy, and guard duty. In appearance they were said to resemble satyrs on account of the long mustaches that decorated the small, non-covered portion of their faces. The light cavalry (*kwarciany*) consisted of poor Polish gentry and non-nobles, Germans, Cossacks, Moldavians, Wallachians, and Tatars. Outfitted with short lances, sabers, perhaps a pistol or two, but little armor, they brought their own horses and wagons, supposedly with six months' supplies. Their ill-disciplined, ragged, scavenging servants attended the impedimenta separately, as a part of the general army train. Their military use was restricted to scouting, advanced skirmishing, quick flank and rear jabs, and pursuit.[54]

THE FOREIGN ARMY

Serving in the *Autorament Cudzoziemski* were the Crown Guard (horse, plus a few Janissaries and Hajduks), infantry, dragoons, and artillery. The foot were made up of Poles, Germans, Wallachians, and, as irregulars for vanguard duty, Cossacks, Hajduks, and Lithuanian Tatars. Appearance, equipment, and discipline varied greatly, in part according to national origin:

> One was not able to observe the infantry quite so precisely because many of them marched at night rather than during the day on account of the great heat. Yet as far as one could observe, the majority of them were fresh-looking, well-equipped folk with sabers, matchlock muskets or long flintlocks and pikes. Their music instruments were round drums and flutes. They kept good order. On the other hand, there were also many who seemed to be untested, worn-out and poorly equipped. Besides sabers they had either matchlocks, flintlocks or small pikes, while quite a few had only maces, handžars or poleaxes. They marched only with drums or flutes, even silently. They kept bad order or none at all. Many looked more like gypsies than soldiers. The most wretched creatures that one could observe were the Tatars. . . . They are a wild, raw and barbaric people and seem to be bad soldiers. In place of a flag they have horses' tails on a long pole. They have no weapons apart from handžars and poleaxes and no music at all. Their officers, however, had the fanciest weapons, and their insigne was a spear like those carried by pig-gelders. . . . They are very revolting in their eating habits. Their favorite tid-bit is horse meat or foal's flesh, which they toss on the fire and which, not even half-cooked, they stuff, unsalted, into their mouths, so that the blood runs down their chins.[55]

The eating habits of the Polish soldiers were not impressive either. While passing through Moravia on the way to Vienna, they gobbled up vegetables and fruit, raw or half-ripe, ruining gardens and vineyards. Nor was their tact particularly noteworthy. They told their hosts that the latter were not sufficiently thankful to God for the bounteous land vouchsafed them and "reproached us for not being willing either to fight or to offer our lives, as they, foreigners, were doing voluntarily for us, to save so noble a fatherland. . . ." The writer did, on the other hand, specifically mention the exquisite manners of the nobility, who paid for what they took, and added that the "excesses were not committed by the stout-hearted soldiers and virtuous fellows but by tramps and common rabble" (presumably including the incorrigible baggage attendants). It is also dubious whether the Wallachians, game poachers recruited because of fine marksmanship, showed much respect for their Austrian allies' property. The dragoons, frequently commanded by Germans, staffed with German enlisted men, clothed and organized in the German fashion, looked smart as they marched by. The artillery, also composed in part of hired foreigners, was protected by a special infantry detachment. The bronze guns were very light and mobile: one, two, and three pounders. Six pounders had proved too clumsy in the many forested regions of Poland. Other technical services were poor: the Poles were said to understand nothing of making sieges. Logistics were equally bad, a major obstacle to a prompt and effective deployment of the army.[56]

ORGANIZATION, TACTICS AND FINANCE

The tactical-administrative structure of the Polish forces, apart from the dragoons, bore little resemblance to the West. The standard cavalry unit was a *chorągiew,* a troop consisting of fifty to seventy hussars in the first line of battle and perhaps eighty to one hundred *pancerny* in the second and third lines. The basic infantry corps was a *pulk* of about 400 men, in turn subdivided into "legions" of varying size. This was somewhat less than a battalion: i.e., half of a Western-style regiment. Tactics, too, were quite different. On the march, the Polish army moved either too slowly in terms of its objectives or too quickly as far as the well-being of the ill-supplied infantry was concerned. When the Poles camped in the open field, they formed a rectangle. The side facing the enemy contained the infantry and the artillery, with the dragoons on their wings. On the other two sides of the square was the light cavalry. The hussars and the dignitaries held the rear. In battle the spirit was decidedly offensive. The idea was to strike a crushing blow as soon as possible since lack of activity for the often unpaid troops would result in a crippling rate of desertion. Despite the lack of discipline and sometimes mediocre equipment, the individual soldier generally was brave, his motto being to "load and shoot dead." He practically never sought cover. The Poles initiated a battle by attempting to disconcert the enemy with all kinds of maneuvers by small units. One trick was to simulate flight in order to lure the enemy into pursuit for the purpose of ambush. The cavalry made its charge in a carré, trusting in its steamroller effect. The foot followed as the second wave, their job being to mop up the battlefield and bring in the captives. If the enemy could not be lured out of his positions, the artillery was ordered to soften him up with a preparatory bombardment.[57]

As for remuneration, the freely-serving nobility and volunteers, once outside the nation's borders, received their pay according to the quality of their equipment. The Diet, or in 1683 the Pope and the Emperor, provided certain sums for mercenaries and for recruits, but the grants were only for one year at a time and always insufficient. Arrears were constant. The standing army, the artillery, and the fortresses were supported from the King's own resources, which is at least a partial explanation for Sobieski's miserliness and cupidity.[58] It is clear that the prospect of loot was much more important to the Poles than to Western soldiery. This attitude, which also reflects Poland's long association with the Eastern steppes, combined with the stormy, intractable character of the nobility, made the Polish army a less reliable machine for waging war on a systematic, intellectual basis. The defeat of the Turks in 1683, to which Sarmatian presence and valor contributed significantly, could have amounted to annihilation rather than mere humiliation, if, among other things, John III had commanded a properly disciplined and well-integrated body of fighters.

D. The Turks

TYPOLOGY

While heterogeneity was the most striking characteristic of Sobieski's forces, the King was the only general of 1683 who had to cope with the special problems raised by commanding troops vastly different in organization, training, and quality. Kara Mustafa encountered the same difficulties. The ethnically kaleidoscopic Ottoman host included five major categories. First came the standing army, the *kapu kulu* ("servants of the Porte"), made up of soldiers who were regularly paid from the public treasury. Practically speaking, it was composed of five crack corps: the *topcu* (gunners); the *lâğuncı* or *lâğimcı* (sappers and miners); the *cebecî* (armorers and munition carriers); the *sipâhî* ("horsemen"), a body of cavalry that should not be confused with identically named feudatories; and, finally, the partly degenerate, still pugnacious Janissaries.[59] In wartime all others—"civilian" servants of the Porte as well as provincial government officials (the next classification)—were mobilized, so that, in effect the whole state became one great military machine—a phenomenon deriving from the primaeval martial customs of the Ottoman people.[60]

The second grouping encompassed unsalaried feudatories, the *topraklı* ("landed ones") or *tımârlı*. It furnished heavy cavalry, the territorial *sipâhî*, including some poorer, (originally) cuirassed warriors (the *cebeli*), who were also obligated to dismounted service as trench laborers and artillery hands. The third aggregation was formed by troops of the border province governors. These irregularly-paid fighters, the *serhadd*

kulu, were volunteers who flocked to the colors at moments of particular urgency. Their heavy cavalry, called *gönüllü* ("volunteers"), were feudal aspirants of especial boldness. Their light horse were known as *beşli.* The *deli* ("mad ones") were daredevil mounted rangers. The infantry was made up of select garrison troops (*azab*); a scorned peasant militia of dragoons (*seymen*), sometimes including Christians; pioneers (*müselem*); and others. The fourth subdivision, not always distinct from the third, was the *yerli kulu,* the "local troops" of government administrators. Theoretically levelled with the Porte's authorization, they served, in some cases, as instruments of autonomous power. They assisted the various branches of the *serhadd kulu* with *tüfekci* (fusiliers), *icâreli* (border fort gunners) and even *lâğuncı.* There were also regularly maintained *gönülü* and *deli.* The fifth type of soldier available to Istanbul were auxiliaries from tributary nations. However, the Crimean Tatars, Wallachians, Moldavians, and Magyar rebels were a motley assemblage that frequently could not be trusted under fire.[61]

THE JANISSARIES

The glue that bound all these jumbled components together was the Janissaries. Baptized the "new troops" (*yeniçeri*) when they were created in the fourteenth century, they long took their human raw material from the *devşirme,* from prisoners of war, and from among the offspring of their own retired comrades. By the latter seventeenth century, however, the child tax—supported by the traditionalist reformers and opposed by the old aristocracy and Turkish rayah—was falling into desuetude (abolished 1685), and ethnic Turks were entering the ranks in large numbers. By the time of the siege of Vienna, because of a combination of reasons, the Janissaries had ceased to heed many of their fourteen fundamental commandments.[62] Nevertheless, the corps, or *ocak,* retained its traditional threefold subdivision into *cemâat, bölük,* and *seğbân.* Each of these had somewhat differing prerogatives and functions, practical and ceremonial, and each was composed of an unequal number of "ortas." The latter, the

---

(*facing page*)
Types of Turkish Soldiery

1. Janissary	2. Territorial *sipâhî*
3. *Deli*	4. *Gönüllü*

rom *Der Türckische Schauplatz* (*Türckischer Estaats- und Kriegsbericht*), Hamburg, 685. (Vienna, National Library). The drawings stem from the hand of the late sixteenth entury Danish artist, Melchior Lork. Except for the adoption of more modern fire-rms, the next hundred years presumably saw little change in the equipment of the radition-bound Ottoman army, and it is unlikely that the troops of 1683 had much ifferent accoutrements from their predecessors, sketched as living models by Lork. See rik Fischer, *Melchior Lork: Drawings from the Evelyn Collection at Stonor Park, Eng-nd, and from the Department of Prints and Drawings of the Royal Museum of Fine rts, Copenhagen,* Copenhagen, 1962.

name of which should not be confounded with the *oda* ("chamber"), a self-contained barracks unit, nominally counted 500 men, but was generally much smaller. Commanding all 196 ortas was the Janissary Ağa, assisted by six other high staff officers and some lesser functionaries.[63] The ortas were controlled by "colonels," *çorbacı*, i.e., "soup carriers," whose symbolic rôle was to bring pilaf from the kitchen. Below them were "captains" (*odabaşı*), "lieutenants" (*vekilharç*), and several minor officers. There were no "non-coms" in the European sense.[64]

One important aspect of command was to make sure that the military band (*mehterhane*) kept playing during an attack, since without music the troops might falter. The Austrians found the Turkish instruments sufficiently stimulating for adoption by their own army. The standards which the Janissaries carried into battle were a half-green, half-yellow, forked flag (*bayrak*) and a soup kettle. Replacements for casualties and pensioned veterans (the *oturak,* whose status later became a sinecure) first received thorough training as *acemi oğlan* or "unexperienced boys." The school's most distinguished pupils became eligible for personal service with the Sultan in the Seraglio, as *içoğlan* or "boys of the interior." Janissary pay varied considerably. Food—mutton, bread, rice and butter—was provided gratis by the state, which levied special taxes in kind upon certain provinces. The amounts were more than adequate, and the Turkish soldier had the reputation of being both muscular and well-nourished. The toughest troops were probably the men who volunteered for hazardous wartime missions, particularly assaults against fortified points. Called *serdengeçti* ("those who have given up their heads"), they were organized into special companies and received supplementary pay. Soldiers from all other army branches might join them, as at Vienna in 1683. A number of miscellaneous smaller units were likewise linked to the *ocak*. Of these, the most noteworthy were the choushes (*çavuş*). They served as adjutants and liaison officers but appear to have evolved more or less into courtlings.[65]

The garb of the Janissary was anything but uniform. Although red was the dominant color, there were notable differences according to rank and function. To the Turks, the shape and color of hats, feathers, coats, dresses, belts, and shoes—not to mention banners or the number of one's horse-tails—were marks distinguishing station and dignity. Moreover, other Turkish troops, both regulars and irregulars, sought to emulate the Janissaries. The *sipâhî*, for example, were attired in practically the same manner. The one real difference was headgear. All non-Janissaries wore either fezzes or turbans, while the "new troops," at least normally, were recognizable by their high bonnets, equipped with backward-flowing, felt flaps. The latter originated, according to legend, from the sleeve of a patron-dervish who had extended his hand in blessing. The hats were decorated, moreover, with a spoon, like the kettle a symbol of the ancient nomadic fellowship of the common meal. Officers' models displayed plumes, worn by the men only on festive occasions. More luxurious, fur-fringed caftans were also a prerogative of higher rank. In battle, steel casques, mail, or armor were customary. Weapons were varied: matchlocks, flintlocks, bows, crossbows, arrows, sabers, handžars, and one or two pistols, stuck in the belt.[66]

THE SIPÂHÎ

Also élite and even more privileged were the Istanbul *sipâhî,* drawn from the ranks of the richer nobility and from the *içoğlan.* The word itself can easily lead to confusion. Not only is it synonymous with the feudal cavalry, but it also has both broader and narrower applications among the *kapu kulu.* Its wider meaning was all six subdivisions of the Porte's paid, professional horsemen. In a more restricted sense it referred only to the first branch of the latter, composed of light, unarmored, dragoon-type warriors. The second of the standing units, the *silâhdar,* made up of heavy reiters, served together with the first as the Imperial or Grand Vezirial Bodyguard. The third and fourth squadrons were known as the *ulûfeci* ("mercenaries" at least nominally) and the fifth and sixth as *gurabâ* ("foreigners," since they may originally have been Persians and Arabs). Both the *sipâhî*—narrow sense—and the *silâhdar* had their own ağas. The former appears to have been the cavalry's over-all commander. The clothing of these troopers, if anything, was even more diverse than the Janissaries'. Equipment too, was mixed, including not only the saber but also a long thin lance with a triple cutting edge tip and a pennon, pistols, and carbines. Sometimes short-range defensive weapons and a reserve saber were carried. Of course, the type or combination of weapons used by the various corps reflected in part their differing tactical functions.[67]

The rôle of heavy cavalry was more or less monopolized by the *toprakli.* Feudatories insofar as they enjoyed usufruct of landed property in return for military service, they were by no means as unmanageable (at least initially and during reform periods) as their Western predecessors. Firstly, the term of their field obligation was unlimited. Secondly, there was no sub-infeudation. Lastly, the Porte's provincial slave-administrators, the *beylerbeyi* and the *sancakbeyi,* depended entirely upon the capital, since their own *tımâr,* which represented both their remuneration and a large portion of all feudal holdings, were non-hereditary. The *toprakli* were divided into three classes on the basis of yearly income. The richer ones not only had to appear as mounted warriors but also to provide a number of *cebeli* proportionate to their wealth. The poorest ones appeared simply as *cebeli.* Organized into "regiments" under "colonels," they constituted tactically larger units than the Portal *sipâhî.* There were great differences between the Euro-

pean and Asiatic timariots. The former were like the Polish hussars and
pancerny while the latter were lighter and carried bows and arrows along
with lances and sabers. High command lay with the provincial governors,
who appointed special officers to mobilize and, sometimes, to lead the
troops. In the Balkans there were even some Christian *toprakh,* non-
assimilated remnants of the indigenous landowning element. Indeed, in
Bulgaria, the whole Orthodox population was divided into classes for
military service. The thorough logistical preparations of the 1683 campaign saw their mobilization. Finally, in many instances the line of
division between the timariots and other classes of Turkish soldiery was
fluid: Janissaries and other regulars (plus the Sultan and his kin) could
hold a *tımâr,* while feudatories looking forward to succeeding their
fathers or to obtaining richer benefices would join the *serhadd kulu* in
the hope of winning battlefield distinction and the reward of a fief.[68]

WEAPONRY

The numerous disparities of the Turkish army naturally contributed to
the wide variety of weapons used. The diversity, however, was not so
great as to preclude generalization. Ottoman muskets—flintlocks already
in 1683—had the reputation of being first-rate, well-made, and sturdy.
Longer and heavier than the European models, they shot smaller balls
and had to be fired from some kind of support—although forks were not
used. Since there were no bandoleers or powder horns, the rate of fire was
slower. On the other hand, the fine quality steel permitted a heavy load of
excellent Turkish powder, thus affording longer, more accurate range.
The artillery left a great deal to be desired, notwithstanding its earlier
distinction (e.g., in the capture of Constantinople) and high standards of
metal working. By 1683 the guns which the Turks cast themselves were
inferior to those they bought from the West or took on the battlefield.
Turkish artillerymen wisely preferred the foreigners' products. The thick,
cylindrical shape of the locally-made models facilitated aiming but complicated handling. The carriages were equally awkward. The great weight
of some pieces, the lack of standardized calibers, and the unsystematic
storing and transport of the plentiful but frequently defective ammunition also prevented effective utilization. Likewise, as Vienna showed, the
number of guns carried was frequently insufficient. One peculiarity was
the camel artillery, more mobile than cannon borne by the lumbering
oxen and buffaloes of the monstrous supply trains. Turkish fortress mines
(developed during the siege of Candia) were held in fearful respect, but
successes with this tool of warfare were not due to superior theoretical
knowledge or to greater practical skill but simply to huge numbers of
workers, fantastic energy, and the use of enormous quantities of
powder.[69]

Another notable feature of the Porte's arms were artistic and esthetic

(*Vienna, Army Historical Museum*)

A Turkish Flintlock Musket, c. 1683

qualities. Like all Asiatic peoples the Ottomans went to war with an inconceivable show of splendor. Whatever the reasons (perhaps the religious, "Holy War" mentality), Turkish weapons were the most richly decorated of all Islam. They are also a major source for the art history of the Ottoman Empire. Distinct from, yet influenced by the Arab-Moorish and Persian traditions, the most characteristic feature of Turkish art was decorative articulation of surfaces. There was a great love for arabesques and for floral patterns such as the rose, the hyacinth, the carnation, and, above all, the tulip. Geometric and calligraphic design was also important, not to mention East Asiatic elements such as dragons and cloud bands. All these things were synthesized and harmonized in a compromise between the abstract and the representational. Techniques were also quite manifold. There were many types of weaving, knitting, and leather-working as well as all methods of metal finishing: cupellation, engraving, chiseling, and, particularly, damascening. Another skill was the inlaying of silver upon black enamel.[70]

Not only muskets, sabers, and knives, but also flags, horse-tails, and tents provided opportunity for artistic expression. Particularly impressive were the silken pavillions, with their artificial gardens, fountains, baths, rugs, divans and other pretiosa. The headgear of the Janissaries likewise reflect the mind of the craftsman, as do their handy, round shields, woven from reeds, and the coats of mail sometimes used. On talisman shirts were embroidered verses from the *Qurân,* to ward off both enemy bullets and the evil eye. The cavalryman's magnificent equipment and attire were legendary: the brilliantly decorated horses, the velvet-bedecked shabracks, the brocaded blankets and satin pillows, the saddles and bridles, glowing with gold and jewels. Special mention must be made of archery, in which the Turks' attainments were unexcelled. The bows, which took years to make, shot hollow, steep-tipped arrows with great accuracy for several hundred yards, even piercing armor. Equally remarkable were the elegantly-curved, holster-shaped quivers, constructed of gold-studded, colored leather or covered with velvet and brocade. The symbolic, honorary act of presenting caftans in the name of the Sultan was another occasion for the display of luxury. Even more highly prized gifts were golden, bejeweled, and enameled *objets d'art.* Before the siege of a fortress the Sultan sent the Grand Vezir a special damascened saber and dagger. Battleaxes, javelins, and maces received equally loving treatment.[71]

BEHAVIOR, MORALE, LEADERSHIP

There is more than a touch of irony in the fact that Ottoman arms, deservedly the object of admiration when seen lying within the museum cases of the twentieth century, were *not* intended for ceremonial purposes but for dispatching fellow members of the human race. The lovely blades and daintily-finished barrels not only attest to the sensitivity of the artisans who made them, thus revealing mankind's creative impulse: they also call to mind the horrors of the battlefield. Thereby the question arises whether the Turks deserved the reputation for barbarism which they managed to acquire among their European contemporaries. Of Ottoman indiscipline—apart from the still well-knit Janissaries—, there can be little question. Turkish officers found it rather more difficult to restrain their troops than did their Western counterparts, dedicated to drilling recruits into mechanical obedience. Surely it would be hazardous to suggest that one people was intrinsically more violent than another. Not only are there frequent examples of Austrians getting out of hand, but there are also numerous cases of Muslims having shown kindness to prisoners. Nevertheless, the great emphasis which Christian sources place upon wanton acts of murder, plus the proud notation of such slaughter in the Ottoman version of the events of 1683, probably justifies the conclusion that the looser control over enlisted men, combined with a religious fanaticism so strong as to cause the Turks to overlook Islam's very teachings on the subject of mercy, resulted in a markedly lesser respect for the value of life.[72]

If the Ottoman soldier was often inhumane, he was also vigorous and courageous. His reputation for valor remained intact even in the eighteenth century, at least with respect to the lower ranks. (A decided decline in the quality of higher commanders was apparent.) The Turk's plentiful rations, his physical strength, and his thorough training have already been mentioned. His supposedly "clean" way of life (no alcohol, simple fare), his expectation of reward or punishment, prompt receipt of pay, material rapacity, belief in kismet, and use of mild narcotic stimulants before combat are alleged to have provided additional foundations for his stamina and bravery.[73]

In any case, the Porte was no longer able to derive full benefit from the high personal caliber of its troops. To understand why this is so, one must consider not only the increasing self-interest of the dominant elements within the military but also, and perhaps primarily, the unique, by 1683 largely outmoded techniques, according to which the Ottomans organized and conducted a campaign. The general ban of all Muslims capable of bearing arms was normally announced by means of a *hatti şerif* (sacred rescript) and by unfurling the *sancaki şerif* (Holy Flag of the Prophet).

It was also only appropriate to implant horse-tails at this point to indicate that the Sultan himself would take to the field. Simultaneously feudatories and others received orders to congregate on the plain at Edirne-Adrianople (as well as at points upon the intended line of march), to which place the Padishah then repaired with great ceremony. Since most of the fighting men were feudal lords and servitors torn from their normal agricultural pursuits and forced to maintain themselves at their own expense—as was also true of the auxiliaries—, long-lasting operations were impossible. Furthermore, even though logistical preparations were painstaking, they were insufficient to satisfy the needs of the gigantic baggage train, to which the luxury-minded Turks were addicted. Thus, the Ottomans had to return, in part, to the customs of their nomadic forebears, who waited until the grass of the meadows and the fruits of the field ripened and who moved from pasture to pasture (an approach not unknown to the better supplied Austrian armies either). Likewise, the Porte strove to end a campaign as soon as nature's sources of supply began to dry up. With the approach of winter, the feudatories and tributaries returned home, while the standing army mounted a guard of sorts over the frontier. The same thing was then done the next spring. Hence, the Austrians came to expect their foes to move into the field only with the advancing season, to unleash a relatively sudden, very hard blow, and to retire at the end of September. Winter campaigns were entirely unknown to the Turks. Operations so dependent upon considerations of supply and season might seem to be circumscribed to the point of futility. Yet the offensive spirit that permeated the whole army, the wave of fear that swept over populations lying in its path, and the huge advantage of numbers that it almost always enjoyed continued to assure it the initiative—a major element of success—and to make it a force which the Austrians, their technological advantages notwithstanding, regarded with considerable respect.[74]

If the Ottoman leadership had not been so deficient, it is conceivable that the army's virtues would have at least balanced its defects. However, the fact is that as soon as its generals faced a determined foe they lost the initial benefit of their greater weight and more powerful momentum. The typical procedure, after rendezvousing, was to move into a covered position that lay as close as possible to the enemy. There, counsel was taken over what to do next. Command (so absolute, on the top echelon, as to be envied by Montecuccoli) was now handed over to the Grand Vezir, who paid with his life if he failed. While Kara Mustafa did not hesitate under these circumstances, those who came after him, conscious perhaps of his unfortunate example, frequently vacillated, gave up their original operational objectives and showed uncertainty when the opposing host could not be impressed with sheer magnitude.[75]

TACTICS

The Turks were handicapped not only in organization, technology, strategy and leadership: their tactics were also much inferior to the West's. The standard position in battle was the customary oriental half-moon or oval arrangement, the object of which was to envelope the adversary by a pincer movement of the cavalry wings. This formation, covering more ground, also allowed the Muslims to exploit their superiority in men. (Some troops remained in reserve for sudden flank and rear attacks) . The warriors did not advance in strictly ordered battalions but as large, irregular bands. Real maneuver was out of the question. If the ranks lost momentum, if they got themselves into the kind of difficulty from which Western units might escape by rapid shifting-about, they became helpless. They lacked the cement of tight organization, which alone makes it possible for a thinking commander to snatch salvation, or victory, from defeat. Examples of ordered retreat in Ottoman military history are rare. Normally, Istanbul's armies dissolved into wild flight after the moment of decision. While the Turkish soldier carried out his assault impetuously and impatiently, he had no staying power, either by tactical training or instinct. He also had no pike behind which he could seek shelter. The only time he held out stubbornly was when he was bottled up in a strongpoint, and even then the mediocre quality of indigenously-built fortifications hampered him. Before the latter half of the War of the Holy League he did not bother to secure his camp or field position with temporary obstacles—a crucial omission for 1683. Another liability in was the vast number of pioneers and other non-combatants.[76]

The core of the Porte's line of battle remained the Janissaries. As indicated, they showed no evidence of diminution in courage from earlier times. After they had fired off their muskets, they seized curved sabers and charged, howling and screaming in order to keep up their own spirits and to paralyze their opponents. Their greater skill in wielding a blade was at least one advantage over their Habsburg antagonists. Obviously, it took tremendous composure to stand firm when confronted by such a mob. If the first assault failed, the succeeding ones decreased in intensity. In fact, sometimes the first attack might be followed by a *détente* that would precipitate a flight as unregulated as the advance had been. Still, there are instances of Janissaries keeping up the offensive well beyond the triple storming sanctioned by the *Qurân*. The cavalry, the Ottomans' national specialty and main weapon, was—obsolescence notwithstanding—no less offensive-minded than the infantry. Superb mounts and a fine native riding style had long assured the Turks superiority in this arm and had made them the terror of other nations. Breaking out of their camp or position in long columns, they threw themselves forward in lightning fashion, without any order, upon one or both wings of the foe, attempting to exhaust him by quickly repeated attacks or to lure him out of his strong point into a trap by means of simulated retreats. Continual movement, constant aggressiveness, was the real forte of the Ottoman horse. The adroitness of the animals, the skill and daring of the men on their backs seemed almost unlimited. The reiters showed particular tenacity in guerilla warfare and real perfection in reconnaissance. They were even more dangerous in cut-up terrain than in open country. On the other hand, they could not withstand powerful infantry or artillery fire, if properly combined with cavalry. Moreover, the aforementioned qualities of excellence were found primarily in the Istanbul *Sipâhî*. The non-regular feudatories were less well-trained.[77]

The auxiliaries of tributary states were not suited for use on the regular battlefield, yet they were not without military value. The Moldavians and Wallachians were used for building bridges, clearing brush and forests, improving roads, digging trenches, supplying forage and other needs, and, above all, for border guarding and scouting—which meant a saving of Turkish manpower.[78] The Crimean Tatars, who did not carry out the same tasks as their Lithuanian relatives in Sobieski's army, deserve special mention:

> [They are] a crazy-looking people, more like wild men than human beings both with respect to their clothing and their food. . . . They are much afraid of muskets, and, when there is resistance, will not risk their own lives . . . They only go to war because of looting. Their weapons are arrows and sabers. They have horses of good wind, which can go a whole day without fodder and which can swim rivers easily. They serve for raiding and burning and provide the Turkish camp with many things.[79]

The campaign upon which Kara Mustafa was about to embark would provide them sufficient opportunity to exercise their talents.

PART THREE

Vienna a Turcis Obsesa,
. . . a Christianis Eliberata

The Relief of Vienna
Gray monochrome drawing by anonymous, late seventeenth-
century artist.

CHAPTER SEVEN

The Turks Advance

A. The March to Győr

MOBILIZATION

Once the conglomerate Ottoman host was massed together, it constituted the largest single war machine of Central and Eastern Europe. Clearly, however, the mobilization of this colossus called for extensive central planning and direction—a job undertaken with vigor once the decision to wage war with Austria was made (August 6, 1682). In order to assure prompt execution of the general ban, inspectors were sent to Anatolia and Rumelia. *Timârlı* in all parts of the Empire were told to meet the coming spring at Belgrade. Men and materials were dispatched to repair roads and bridges and to carry out new construction, as required, along the projected route of march. Scouts rode forth to collect information on the status of the enemy. Border garrisons went on the alert and, when necessary, improved their forts. The fleet sailed into the Aegean in order to secure the coastline from any unexpected assault. The outfitting of the regular army in Istanbul was accelerated as much as possible. Troops not yet fully equipped learned that they would receive what was lacking after the preliminary move to the traditional assembly point at Edirne.[1]

Preparations for departure from the capital began on September 24 when the Sultan's tent was erected in the Cyrpycı Meadow. The Janissaries mustered there October 6, and the Padishah appeared four days later with a great suite. The harem followed on the 12th, and on the same day, amidst much pomp and circumstance, the Imperial cortege set off for Edirne. Since the "Hunter" indulged in the pleasures of the chase along the way, he did not reach his destination until December 7. The army, which left Istanbul on October 19 under the Grand Vezir, had arrived some time earlier. The next four months were spent in the Thracian metropolis—but not idly. A Muscovite envoy came and renewed the existing peace with Turkey. Transylvanian representatives were entertained at banquets. New military and civilian appointments were made; functionaries were shifted about as seemed advisable. Rearmament was completed. The Austrian *internuntius*, Caprara, was also present. Once more the Turks offered peace in return for the cession of Győr, presumably at the insistence of a still somewhat reluctant Mehmed IV. The reply was negative, and thus the *tuğ* were planted in front of the palace, facing toward Hungary. It was decided that the Sultan should accompany the army as far as Belgrade where Kara Mustafa would assume command. On March 15 the sovereign's tent was again set up in an open field, and the troops began to leave their barracks to gather around it. On the 20th the *topçu* and the *cebeci,* who had wintered in Istanbul, presented themselves. On the 30th the Janissaries decamped, followed two days later by the Grand Seigneur and the bulk of the army.[2]

Caprara and his companions somehow managed to peek at the procession as it filed by, observing what they saw with all the spellbound attention of a protocol-conscious age. While they were impressed with the magnificent attire of their enemies—they considered the tiger skins and sable pelts especially worthy of mention—, they also found occasion for amusement when they espied the hunting dogs. The animals were not only covered with "golden brocades and other costly cloths . . . but their paws and tails were dyed red and yellow, the way women color their hair and nails." For the Sultan's personal conveyance there was a "big, gilded coach with small mattresses and silken pillows, drawn by eight grey-white steeds, as well as a sedan chair, likewise gilded and borne by four asses." The equipage also included a pageboy, "of the most pleasant visage," to rub the master's feet when it was cold or to fan him when it was hot. The Harem likewise continued as part of the Imperial entourage, which caused some murmurs among the troops since taking women upon campaigns was contrary to custom. Then, also, there was an omen that did not seem to bode well: a sudden wind squall arose, tearing off the Padishah's turban and dashing it to the ground.[3]

FROM EDIRNE TO BELGRADE

Caprara and his following were required to travel northwestward along with the army. However, before they left, they managed to get some of their number released for return by the sea route, and thus it was possible to smuggle further warnings home. The *internuntius* likewise made use of a secret courier, who travelled a round-about way over Moldavia in order to admonish the Poles. It must be admitted that the ambassador was personally courageous. The discovery of the hidden message might well have resulted in his death. The Austro-Italian diplomat and his colleagues also continued to carry out their invaluable function as historical witnesses. The Mission's secretary, Giovanni Benaglia, kept notes and recorded adventures as the Sultan's cohorts slogged ahead. (The vivid account was later published, becoming a best seller). The army represented almost as great a menace to Turkey's own subjects as it would to the foe. Villages along the route—the ancient Roman military highway still roughly maintained by Istanbul—had to provide supplies such as straw, hay, tent poles, and oats for the whole army. Guards prevented the inhabitants from leaving until the Padishah had gone by. People were then free to burn their own homes and flee into the hills in order to escape the cruel attentions of the Asiatic forces in the rear. In front of the long columns was a large flock of sheep, some of which were slaughtered each evening at the blast of a horn in order to provide the next day's meat. From time to time, along each side of the road, there appeared two small mounds of earth, indications of the proper direction. When a halt was made, the Janissary *mehterci* began to play. The enlisted men sang the verses of the satirical ditties that they seemed to prefer. If someone had dropped behind during the previous march, he was received by this merry company with scorn and derision and accompanied to his tent under a hail of blows. The Janissaries were particularly proud of being able to sustain the rigors of the journey and demonstrated little indulgence for laggardly comrades. Each evening also included more solemn moments when the soldiers recited prayers in unison, invoking Allah's blessing upon their debased sovereign.[4]

The intention of the Turks was to reach Belgrade by forced marches, camping only at night and with little time for rest. However, heavy rains, bad roads, and over-exertion caused a slow-down. By April 8 the army had gotten only as far as Plovdiv, and the men were complaining loudly. A three-day halt was decreed while the train was sent on ahead. At Sofia, reached April 17, it was necessary to take off another two days, while at Niš, entered on April 24, a further twenty-four hours were lost. The rains still hindered progress. Finally, on May 3, Belgrade came within sight. The Sultan commanded a triumphal entry into the "White City." The next day the troops began to traverse the Sava to Zemun over a bridge composed of fifty pontoons. At the same time a portion of the artillery and munitions was forwarded by boat to Buda. The shipment included nineteen medium field culverins and forty larger siege cannons—only a small fraction of what would be needed.[5] Since Belgrade was even more important than Edirne as a place of rendezvous, each day saw the arrival of new and different units. Among the nationalities and races eventually represented were Turks, Arabs, Berbers, Bedouins, Greeks, Armenians, Kurds, Caucasians, Indo-Aryans, Negroes, Shiptars, Macedonians, Serbs, Bulgars, Bosniaks, Rumanians, Magyars, Szeklers, Tatars, and renegades from the West. On May 13 the Sultan named Kara Mustafa *Ser'asker* (commander-in-chief) and, with great ceremony, handed over the *sancaki şerif*. Apparently also it was around this time that a grand review and muster took place: "And so the Grand Seignor being placed in a high Scaffold erected for that purpose, all the soldiers in their several Ranks and Degrees, according to their Countries and Nations, passed in their several Orders before him."[6]

The size of the Ottoman host, both at this time and later on, cannot be determined with real accuracy. One seventeenth-century chronicler avers that there was a grand total of "180,000 actual fighting men besides Miners, Pioniers [*sic*], Sutlers, Gunners, Attendents [*sic*] on the Train of Artillery, and Servants belonging to the Tents, with a vast Number of Rascals and Rabble following the Camp, which may very well be calculated to mount to 40,000 more."[7] A direct observer, the Austrian resident, Kunitz, who includes all categories of troops but not civilians, lists a total of 180,000 soldiers, of which 120,000 appeared before Vienna.[8] Another Western eyewitness, a trained officer held captive like Kunitz directly behind the siege works, corroborates the second figure. He speaks of "120,000 combattenti" (presumably including technical troops) as well as "100,000 o di servitori, o di mercanti o d'artefici" and explains that the Vezir made the number look larger by artful distribution.[9] Other sources are not of much help, as they refer only to the Zemun parade which took place before the rendezvous was actually finished. Benaglia, the secretary of Caprara's mission, notes merely that the sum of all warriors marshalled for the Sultan's inspection was just under 40,000.[10] The Ottoman Court Master of Ceremonies states simply that some 7–8000 Janissaries were there, organized into fifty-eight ortas of varying strength, some as large as 150 men, others counting only forty to fifty.[11] Although it appears that later additions brought the Janissaries to 20,000, while the Tatars may be fairly calculated at 20,000 and the Rumanians at 10,000,[12] there is no way of estimating, even roughly, the aggregate of newly-arriving *kapu kulu* and feudal contingents, and the number of the Magyar forces is somewhat unclear.[13] Thus one can only accept, tentatively, the statements of the two incarcerated Westerners.[14]

It was also during the stay of the Turkish army near Belgrade that the conscientious Caprara made his last efforts to renew the truce. Learning by courier of the conclusion of the Austro-Polish alliance, he sought vainly to dissuade the Ottomans from their undertaking. In his report of May 13 the *internuntius* stated that he had not yet been able to pinpoint the Grand Vezir's objective (although he had seriously considered rumors about an attack upon the Austrian capital in earlier communications). He noted merely that the decision would be made later, which was in fact correct. As long as the Sultan was still around, the *Ser'asker* presumably could not reveal his plan to lead the army to Vienna. Finally, on May 19, the Habsburg emissary was able to transmit a letter from Margrave Hermann. The War Minister requested release of the ambassador and, with great dignity, expressed continuing hopes for a settlement. There was no immediate response from Kara Mustafa. Even now he did not declare war formally. For him personally the advantage of all the negotiations since August of the preceding year was probably no more than deception of the foe. Years before Montecuccoli had emphasized the Porte's predilection for this tactic.[15]

FROM BELGRADE TO SZÉKESFEHÉRVÁR

On May 20 the Janissaries broke camp and headed northward. Four days later the Grand Vezir followed with the rest of the army. The Sultan and his court remained behind in the more comfortable accommodations of Belgrade. Halting for two days in Mitrovica, the army reached Osijek (Esseg) June 2. Rains were still plaguing its progress. Now another time-consuming obstacle intervened. Although under construction for six months, the long, pier-supported bridge over the Drava was incomplete. A further twelve-day wait was necessary. (This delay probably cost Kara Mustafa the prize for which he was aiming.) During the enforced halt, cannons, other fire-arms, munitions, and supplies were shifted from river barges to wagons, and field rations were distributed to the troops. Tardy contingents continued to dribble in. Hermann now got his answer, a bombastic declaration in which Vienna was accused of responsibility for the outbreak of hostilities. Caprara was not immediately released, as international practice would have required, but was sent off to Buda, presumably for security reasons. Kunitz had to stay behind, probably because the Turks intended to use him later as a peace intermediary. This was a mistake, for the resourceful resident was secretly able to provide his superiors valuable intelligence information during the siege.[16]

Imre Thököly also put in an appearance at Osijek and had several long conferences with the Grand Vezir. What was said during these meetings is open to question. Since it is probable that the *Ser'asker* had already made up his mind to attack Vienna, Thököly may have been told that he could have Vienna as a fief and that he could be crowned in Bratislava (both ideas allegedly stemming from Laz Mustafa).[17] It would then follow that Kara Mustafa informed the Magyar leader of his plans *before* revealing them to his fellow Muslims. Whether Thököly, on his own, encouraged the Grand Vezir to attack Vienna is unclear.[18] For the nonce, however, the rebel chieftain was proclaimed "King of Hungary" (or "of the Kuroczok").[19] About the same time the disquieting news arrived that the Austrians had laid siege to Nové Zámky. Old İbrahim Pasha was despatched from Buda with a relief force, but since the enemy quickly broke off the engagement, the Turkish detachment turned back at Esztergom (Gran) and joined the main army. Thököly left Osijek on June 14. The Porte's forces, arrayed in battle marching order, departed for Székesfehérvár twenty-four hours later. The reluctant Voivode of Wallachia, Şerban Cantacuzeno, and his troops, who had arrived the previous day, followed. The host did not reach its destination until June 25. The two-hundred-mile journey was taxing. This time, however, it was a case of too little water: the Austrians had sent (Magyar?) detachments to contaminate the wells. During a two-day pause in the rock-bound city above Lake

Balaton the Tatars rode in on their swift ponies. Most were incorporated into the now 28,000-man-strong vanguard. The remainder, under the personal command of the Khan, Murad Girey, were organized as an independent advance corps to carry out the traditional shock function of rapine, murder, theft, and arson.[20]

THE DECISION TO ATTACK VIENNA

However, the Ottoman steamroller could not advance farther until its course had been charted definitively. A great council of war therefore took place in Kara Mustafa's sumptuous tent. The Grand Vezir declared that while the intention was to capture Győr and Komárno (*sic*) it would be even better to conquer a whole country, and so he intended to march upon Vienna. Would those present give their opinion? Repeating his question three times and receiving no answer, the *Ser'asker* addressed himself directly to the *Beylerbeyi* of Damascus, who replied: "It is for thee to command and for us to serve." All the others thereupon assented and, as a sign of confirmation, recited in unison the *Fâtiha,* the opening sura of the *Qurân.* The only person who dared contradict, even indirectly, a commander-in-chief holding absolute power of life and death was the sly, cautious Khan, who invoked strategic reasons for postponing the operation until the following year. Kara Mustafa had avoided inviting Ibrahim Pasha, who was opposed to his plans. When the governor of Turkish Hungary did object in a private interview, the Grand Vezir responded that he was an "old fool" and, in order to prevent meddling, commanded him to remain behind at Győr and guard the bridges. A general warning then went out: anyone presuming to interfere would suffer capital punishment.[21]

Having intimidated his associates, Kara Mustafa was free to proceed to the Austrian capital. The most direct route led westnorthwestward, via Sopron and Wiener Neustadt. It has been suggested that this was, in fact, the *Ser'asker's* original choice but that he now altered his design in favor of heading northnorthwestward to Győr. Purportedly, the foe's movements presented him an irresistible opportunity to cut off Charles of Lorraine from Vienna or even to smash the Austrian field army altogether.[22] It has also been argued that he wished to pay at least some heed to his colleagues' unspoken, yet obvious opposition by first attending to the initial purpose of the expedition.[23] A more likely explanation of the "detour" to the Habsburg river strongpoint is that even the Grand Vezir could not venture to disobey the Padishah's instructions so flagrantly. Moreover, an attempt to seize or at least thoroughly reconnoiter the place was desirable, for it was necessary to ensure rearward communications. Finally, Kara Mustafa had shown outward respect for the Ottoman tradition of joint decision in picking a campaign objective, and he had, after all, obtained the nominal acquiescence of his subordinates and the agreement *in principle* of the Khan. His plenipotentiary authority would suffice for determining the proper means and date of the attack upon Vienna.[24]

Thus, the Turkish army, reinforced by a few more Levantine troops and finally complete, moved out of Székesfehérvár on June 28 and crossed the "border." Since his forces were entering the enemy's presence, the Grand Vezir ordered even stricter security measures. Behind the much extended vanguard came the *yerli kulu.* The center was divided into three columns: on the right, the timariots from Anatolia; on the left, the Rumelians; and in between the Janissaries, *cebeci,* and *topçu.* The huge, ungainly train followed and was succeeded in turn by the rear guard. On July 1 the Ottoman juggernaut hove in sight of Győr's bastions. Austrian field guns opened fire at a number of points. The first action in the struggle for Vienna had begun.[25]

B. The Imperials Take to the Field

PREPARATIONS FOR WAR

There can be little question that the position of the Austrian regiments at Győr was perilous. Some writers impute this unhappy state of affairs to the Duke of Lorraine's preliminary military movements. The blame, however, probably lies elsewhere and may be ascribed to more fundamental factors. The chief difficulty was that Austrian preparations for war were insufficient. Only in early December of 1682 did the Emperor become convinced that hostilities were imminent and that the army needed to be strengthened beyond the increases already carried out during the previous two years. Credit for what *was* done, both before and after December, must go mainly to Hermann, who, to be sure, was more concerned about Western Europe and Louis XIV than about Turkey and Kara Mustafa. In any event, it was decided that the army should now consist of 80,000 men, including twenty-three infantry regiments, seven dragoons, seventeen cuirassiers and three and one-half Polish mercenary cavalry (the Lubomirski Corps). In order to reach this figure, patents for eight new regiments were issued in January, February, and March. Simultaneously, arrangements were made for enlarging the Hungarian and Croatian militia (not accounted part of the total). Since twenty regiments had been set up in 1682, most units were new. On the other hand, many of the men did not lack experience, and the expansion was not overly difficult. The reason is that the existing forces were a cadre. When Austria's military establishment was reduced at the end of the Dutch War, non-coms and officers of disbanded regiments were attached to those kept in service.[26]

The latent economic resources of the state would surely have sufficed for the much larger army that the situation called for. However, what immediately counted was cash in hand, and this was a commodity in very short supply. Even 80,000 men, per se a tremendous increase over the mere 30,000 troops of the 1679–1681 period, imposed a terrible strain on the country's liquid assets. Vienna was, in fact, financially crippled. Its credit among lenders was nil, for it still carried a heavy debt—even the interest was unpaid—from the Thirty Years' War. Some of its established sources of income were pawned. The coinage was debased. There was extensive corruption in the civil (e.g., the Sinzendorf case) as well as in the military administration. The effects of the plague upon commerce were not yet overcome. Finally, and worst of all, the provincial diets, although politically emasculated, were frequently able to frustrate, in one way or another, the Court's annual requests for special appropriations, the only means of balancing the ledger sheet. Nevertheless, Leopold had no choice but to resort to the estates in the moment of danger.

The reception accorded the Imperial pleas by the Lower Austrian Diet provided a good example of the infinite difficulties of this approach to governmental financing. The latter body finally agreed on March 31, 1683, after much haggling and tergiversation, to grant 650,000 florins, 226,000 less than the amount requested, which does not appear, this time at least, to have been deliberately inflated. Of the sum approved, the estates were ready to pay at once only 120,000, plus a loan of 100,000, deductible from the overall figure. They would provide the remainder only in 1684 and only after subtracting whatever costs the province might have to bear from military operations in the meantime. Vienna's role in the deliberations, it should be noted, was no more praiseworthy than that of the dominant clerical and noble elements. The response of the Upper Austrian and Styrian Estates was equally disappointing and unrealistic. It seems clear that there was no sense of community or recognition of interdependence. All that mattered were the narrow material interests of the tiny, privileged elements of Austria's social structure. What they could not squeeze from their already hard-pressed tenants, they were unwilling to cover from their own pockets. The practical result was a general budgetary deficit of 3,370,000 florins. The government attempted to fill the gap with a one percent capital levy upon ecclesiastical property but was only partly successful because some of the clergy refused to pay, and Rome's influence could not be brought to bear immediately. Without the direct contributions of the Curia and other friendly foreign powers the House of Habsburg would almost certainly have been doomed.[27]

Foreign help notwithstanding, the Emperor was unable to get all the money he needed. The natural consequence was that the pace of rearmament began to slacken. It is highly doubtful whether the government ever really obtained the total number (76,568) of regulars it reckoned it did have. Many regiments remained understrength for lack of recruitment money (*Werbegeld*). Others could not take to the field in time for the initial actions. As previously noted, even 80,000 men were not enough, since, aside from setting up a strong operational force, it was necessary both to maintain a few troops in the Rhineland as a symbol of unrelenting opposition to Louis XIV and to garrison the fortresses and smaller posts in the Hungarian theater. The story in other respects is only slightly better. Although there appears to have been plenty of material for bridges and for rivercraft, the engineers were able to make several fortresses (Győr, Vienna) ready with only hours to spare. Miners and sappers were recruited from Tyrol, but the siege was to show that both their numbers and their skills could have been greater. The measures taken by the Lower Austrian Estates for preparing places of refuge, lighting warning fires, blocking routes and passages, and stationing peasant militia were not very effective. The brightest side of the picture was ammunition and food: there is no genuine evidence of shortages.[28]

A NEW KIND OF STRATEGY

While the numerical and material insufficiencies of the Emperor's forces were considerable, it cannot be said that there was a dearth of ideas. Hermann and his fellow councillors already decided early in 1683 to divide the available regiments into three groups. Two of these were relatively small "flying" corps, destined to hold the most critical sectors in the northern and southern regions of a front stretching all the way from the Beskids to the Adriatic. The first, hopefully 8,000 men under Count Johann Schultz, plus 2,700 Poles under Lubomirski (in case of need), was to stand along the upper Váh and cover Moravia and Silesia. It would be flanked on the lower Váh by 5,000 Hungarians under Palatine Esterházy. The second, 4,600 regulars under Count Herberstein of the Karlovac Generalate (Croatian Military Frontier) would post itself along the Mur and the Drava (Muraköz) in order to guard Croatia and Styria. Its right flank would be held by a levy of 5,000 Croats and border troops under the Ban, and to its left, from Körmend to Győr along the course of the Rába, there would be 6,000 Hungarians under Counts Batthyányi, father and son. The third group, the main field army, was to be stationed in the center for use wherever necessary in countering the major Turkish blow. According to the war minister's calculations, it would consist of 14,400 foot and 28,600 horse.[29]

Hermann had not, however, developed any campaign scheme. This was probably because he was an advocate of a somewhat novel strategic viewpoint, tied to position warfare. Already in 1681 he had brought to Austria the brilliant Saxon military engineer, Georg Rimpler, who might have become a German Vauban if his employers had not been so impecunious and if he himself had not been killed during the siege of Vienna. Rimpler, like his French colleague, designed complicated systems of broken-up but interlocking forts to replace the old sixteenth century bastioned trace. He held that the enemy should be enticed into attacking powerful fortresses where he would batter himself bloody. The works themselves should be so strong as to permit defense with very modest means; men should not be withdrawn from mobile units. Fortress and army should second one another in defense. The next phase, after the enemy was exhausted by a vain siege, would see the offensive advance of the field troops. This new concept seemed to apply especially well to the approaching conflict with the Porte. Already during the summer of 1683 Rimpler strongly recommended renovation of the bulwarks at Győr, Komárno, Bratislava, Leopoldov, and Trenčin. By November he decided to regard Győr as the focal point of resistance. In December the Court War Council approved the proposed work, plus the repair and modernization of Vienna's walls and the establishment of better defenses for Wiener Neustadt, the Morava (March) and Leitha Rivers, and Inner Austria. Apparently, in addition to the first line of defense represented by the already described troop dispositions, there was to be a second inside Austria proper—which would help to seal off the Alpine valleys and force the Turks upon Győr. Construction commenced early in 1683, but, as previously indicated, seems to have gone slowly because of the lack of money and materials. It does not appear that much, if anything, was done on the second line.[30]

Although there is presently no evidence that either Hermann or Rimpler thought deeply about the broader geographic aspects of strategy, it is likely that the peculiar aquatic network of the Little Alföld provided a basis for their planning. The Váh—not only an ideal natural line of resistance but also the location of Trenčin and Leopoldov—stands at a sharp right angle to the Danube. The latter river itself possesses two meandering, lateral channels. The lovely, productive, but in part swampy area between the northern Malý Dunaj and the main stream is known as the Velký Ostrov Žitný or "Big Wheat Island" (Grosse Schüttinsel, Csallóköz). Its far eastern tip shelters Komárno. The low-lying, fertile terrain between the central artery and the southern Mosoni Duna is called the Szigetköz or "Interriparian Island" (Kleine Schüttinsel, Maly Ostrov Žitný). It contained no major strongpoint in 1683, but just opposite its southeastern shore lies Győr. West of Győr, flowing into the Mosoni Duna, one encounters the Rábca (Raabnitz) and the Leitha (Laita), the latter springing from the Alpine foothills of Lower Austria. Directly south of Győr and the Mosoni Duna is a third Danube tributary, the Rába. In earlier days it was an essential feature of the Rábaköz or Raabau, the Rába "Island" (literally the Rába *interfluvial* area), a vast tract of marshy land, encircled and in part dissected by waterways. Although its shape was somewhat altered by nineteenth century regulation, canalization, and reclamation projects, the "Island" is still cartographically recognizable. In the east and south it is marked off by the forested left bank of the Rába, which forms an irregular convex loop before reaching its confluence with the Mosoni Duna on the western side of Győr. The northern and western boundaries consist of the intertwined courses of three rivulets: namely, the western branch of the Rába; the Rábca, which arises from the center of the "Island"; and the Alpine-born Répce. (Austro-Germans make no distinction between the latter two, which they regard jointly as the Raabnitz.)

The most crucial fact about the region is that the point of the three smaller streams' tangency lies within the scientifically-perplexing drainage basin of Lake Neusiedl. The resultant broad belt of swamp, the Hanság, stretched formerly all the way from the Lake to the main Rába just below Győr. The narrow strip of dry ground between the southernmost Danube and the Hanság still serves as the chief land route between Austria, Győr, and central Hungary. While, in the seventeenth century, the Rabaköz could be traversed by crossing bridges and by journeying through its relatively solid, southern segment, it still represented a formidable obstacle to any large-scale military movement, especially if its eastern passageways were fortified or blocked as a part of a larger, potamically based defense complex such as that apparently envisioned by the Austrian war minister and his head engineer.[31]

From these fundamental geographic facts it is possible to reconstruct tentatively Hermann's and Rimpler's reasoning. Were the Turks to undertake an invasion of the northern part of Lower Austria, Moravia and Silesia, they would have to hurl themselves against the line of the Váh, whereby their only advantage would be the proximity of the Ottoman fortress of Nové Zámky on the Nitra, another right-angle Danube tributary, some twenty miles farther east. Should they decide to attack Vienna, they would have to deliver a frontal assault against the narrow, central corridor with its big fortress and supporting streams—which of course was what the war minister and his associate presumably wished to see them do. Conceivably, they might try to pass farther south and move toward Vienna via Kapuvár, Sopron, and Wiener Neustadt, but then they would have to overcome the great hindrance of the Rábaköz. In theory these calculations were doubtlessly quite sound. In practice they would prove to be less so. Not only were there insufficient resources to carry them out, but, as will also become evident, they were compromised by another, conflicting set of ideas and by the unreliability of the Magyar contingents, to which crucial supplementary roles had been assigned.

The weakest spot in the whole Hungarian defense line was the Rábaköz. The story of what happened there is fairly clear, thanks to accounts written on various occasions by the famous Italian engineer and geographer, Luigi Ferdinando Marsigli, who was given the job of supervising local operations. Marsigli travelled to Austria as a volunteer in the late summer of 1682, obtained the protection of Borgomanero among others and served his apprenticeship with the Imperial forces at Győr during the winter. While he was there, he talked with one of the Batthyányi and learned about the Rábaköz. His curiosity aroused, he visited the place and drew a map. When Hermann and Rimpler arrived in Győr on a spring inspection tour, Marsigli's sketch was the only one available. He himself was invited to participate in the conferences. Shortly thereafter he travelled back to Vienna and was commissioned by Hermann to reconnoiter the region in question once more and to make a new map and report.[32]

A Clash of Viewpoints

In the meantime—early April—Charles of Lorraine had been called to the capital from his stadholdership in Innsbruck, despite Hermann's opposition, to assume command of the field army. The first complication now quickly became apparent. Charles, who held more conventional professional views than Hermann and Rimpler, seems to have thought mainly in terms of maneuvering battalions, regiments, and corps over larger expanses of open land, and his reactions to the situation were thus radically different. Worried about reports concerning the huge size of the Turkish army and its alleged goal of either Győr or Vienna, Lorraine, according to his secretary, was "not convinced that the arrangements made so far were adequate." He proposed that several regiments still in the *Reich* be summoned home, the Emperor's allies be asked to supply cavalry reinforcements, and the peasantry be armed. After the conclusion of the Polish alliance he suggested that Sobieski be requested to move toward Hungary rather than the Ukraine since it was too late in the season for organizing a major siege in the latter place and since mere raiding was of no real diversionary value. While anxious to move the army into the field *as soon as possible* in order to take *offensive* advantage of the two month interval before the expected advent of the Turks, he did foresee (allegedly) that the bad hygienic, alimentary and forage conditions of the Puszta would weaken the troops. He therefore demanded more than the 32,000 men ultimately allotted his center corps, which, he said, was too small both to staff the fortresses and operate as a field force.

Settlement of the matters at issue was left for conferences to be held in connection with the general rendezvous of the main army at Kittsee (just opposite Bratislava in present-day northern Burgenland), an undertaking already postponed once because of the late spring and the marching distances involved. By May 6 most of the regiments in question had arrived, and it was possible to hold a great review with much ceremony and protocol. The Primate of Hungary celebrated an outdoor Mass, to the musical accompaniment of the Leopold's famous—and expensive—100 voice male choir. The troops received both a blessing and a special Papal indulgence. All this took place in the presence of the Imperial clan, the diplomatic corps, and a host of characteristically curious Viennese, who had swarmed out to gape at the spectacle. Marsigli was also present in the first row. The equipment and appearance of the 20,848 infantry and 11,158 dragoons and cuirassiers (plus 3,000 of Esterházy's militiamen) were impressive, but the small numbers appear to have had an adverse effect upon many Hungarians who were undecided whether to go over to Thököly or to stay on the side of the King-Emperor.[33]

On the next day discussions began.[34] Hermann's opposition notwithstanding, the generals recommended that Leopold authorize an assault against Esztergom with the proviso that it be executed without unduly straining the troops and before the arrival of any Turkish relief force. Nové Zámky was the second choice. The main argument of Charles and his supporters for mounting an operation at this juncture was that the Emperor could best uphold the "reputation de ses armes" by putting a force into the field well before the foe did so. A second point was that an Austrian offensive would increase Turkish dissatisfaction with the Grand Vezir while inaction would have just the opposite effect. Such an expedition would supposedly also cause Poland to move more rapidly and would prevent the friendly states of the Empire from abandoning Leopold, a distinct possibility if he sat around doing nothing. It was likewise suggested that the seizure of a Turkish fortress would cause the Ottomans to occupy themselves with its recapture. Even if the Austrians could not hold the place, they could still destroy it before retiring and could profit from its stores.[35] A cognate line of reasoning, apparently advanced at the same time, was that the Turks could be diverted into Upper Hungary. This thought, apparently put into the Austrians' heads by Thököly for his own obscure purposes,[36] probably rested on the assumption that a Turkish drive north of the Danube would also serve to accelerate Polish aid. Finally, it is possible that Esterházy's pleas to do something that would buttress the morale of the loyal Magyars had some influence.

As for defensive action, the meeting merely confirmed the Váh-Győr-Rába plan. This decision and the careful phrasing of the offensive recommendation indicate an attempt at compromise between Charles' and Hermann's widely differing concepts. The war minister, however, remained adamantly opposed to any forward movement at all and attempted with near success to convince the Emperor to accept his view. Nevertheless, in a second conference on the ninth Leopold gave Charles the right to proceed, permitting him to choose either of the two Turkish fortresses according to circumstances. In addition the Duke was specifically enjoined to assure the security of Győr and Komárno and to forestall any attempted "ravages des pays héréditaires"—a constantly reappearing theme in the instructions of the conscientious Habsburger. Thököly was not to be molested, since the truce with him was still in effect. The army was to leave private property untouched in order not to impair further the Magyars' wavering loyalties.[37]

OPERATIONS COMMENCE

The gingerly attitude toward the Hungarians also revealed itself in connection with the Rábaköz, which, according to Marsigli, received special attention at Kittsee. Allegedly, Leopold and his paladins, aware that the army was already overburdened by its main rôle and recognizing more fully that the Turks *might* attempt a lunge across the Island toward Vienna, weighed measures for buttressing that portion of the overall line. However, upon the advice of Batthyányi and Count Drasković, the other important local magnate, it was decided to rely primarily upon the Magyars after all. *No* Germans, except fortification workers, would be sent unless the main Turkish army appeared. The two aristocrats begged Leopold to let "their nation express its firm devotion." The dispatch of German units would only aggravate matters, would result in the destruction of property and in discord among the Magyars themselves. Lorraine, perhaps piqued over Marsigli's closeness to Hermann, first snubbed the scholarly Italian but then decided to utilize him all the same for carrying out the necessary construction work.

Marsigli thus proceeded to Kapuvár where he attended the deliberations of the representatives of the three comitats of Western Hungary. The deputies approved the raising of 10,000 labor troops and 7,000 warriors. The Duke's agent helped distribute the new forces and then directed his attention to building redoubts at the eastern ends of five bridges, two (Keszo, Arpas) across the main Rába to the Island and three (Sarvár, Körmend, and Szentgotthárd) in the area farther upstream, for which he was also responsible. Forty-two other crossings were provided with lesser works: trenches, *chevaux de frise* in the river bed, and palisading on the banks. The job supposedly took only ten days. When it was done, it afforded a line of defense which really-determined soldiery could have held. However, the task of guarding the posts had to be entrusted solely to Magyar hussars. The younger Batthyányi stationed himself in front of the Rába, just behind the parallel-flowing Marcal. Marsigli also wanted to arm the labor troops but could not get Batthyányi to cooperate with Drasković, a personal rival, in doing so. Nevertheless, the two men were in correspondence, and Marsigli became increasingly suspicious, particularly of Drasković, who spoke openly of old grievances against the Habsburg Court.[38]

In the meantime Lorraine advanced from Kittsee with the field army. It soon became evident, however, that effective leadership was going to be extremely difficult, if not impossible. Already, before the troops' departure, Charles and Hermann had had a personal tiff. The War Minister had issued a command which was not only couched improperly but which called for the transfer of Dünewald, a strong Ducal supporter. Knowledge of the squabble, which also involved Bishop Sinelli, spread among the generals, who chose sides. Only Dünewald, Starhemberg, and Caprara stood by their chief. All the others, led by Rabatta, adhered to the Margrave and even ostracized Lorraine at dinnertime. The latter soon came to believe, probably correctly, in an intrigue designed to deprive him of officers whom he desired. By May 19 there was also indication that most of the generals, influenced by letters from Vienna, were changing their minds about campaign goals and aiming for a new council of war. By the twenty-sixth Charles—who brushed aside oblique apologies from Hermann—was complaining bitterly of logistical insufficiencies and toying with the idea of quitting. His chagrin was all the greater because of suspicion that the ubiquitous Borgomanero was assisting his adversary back in Vienna.

About the same time there came a message from the Imperial Chancellery, in which Leopold suggested that it would be wiser to attack Nové Zámky after all. The Duke now had no choice but to convoke his generals (May 27), all of whom were "of a different sentiment" from Kittsee. Even Starhemberg appears to have been swayed by a note from his pro-Hermann father. The majority rejected any offensive at all for fear of exhausting the troops. Even those who were still willing to go ahead, Gondola and fiery Ludwig Wilhelm, favored Nové Zámky. All that Lorraine could do was to forward the results of the meeting to Vienna and, in the conviction that Leopold still wanted action, continue preparations. He himself set out to reconnoiter Esztergom personally. At first the project seemed feasible, and the army began to move forward. But then reports arrived from Styria that the Grand Vezir was already underway in force. Afraid of being cut off in a distant, exposed location, aware of his subordinates' reluctance, the Duke turned his regiments around. Thereupon (May 31) he received the Emperor's reply to the recent conference. The All Highest stated that while there were good reasons for hesitating, he had to protect his reputation. Hence, some sort of enterprise, either a siege or a field battle, was necessary before the advent of the main Turkish corps. This missive and news that the information about Kara Mustafa was incorrect prompted Charles to reconsider. After a discussion with Starhemberg and Caprara, he resolved upon the Slovakian fortress. Heavy artillery and other items were requested from Vienna and the men ordered to break camp.[39]

Rapid progress attended the first three days of effort at Nové Zámky, and Lorraine was much encouraged. Then on June 7 things started to go awry. The first blow was a communication from Leopold, who now questioned the whole undertaking, stressing the need of preserving the army and covering the homeland. There was no mention of the extra cannon. Apparently Hermann and the Sinelli clique had persuaded the monarch to reverse himself. The nonplussed Duke answered that he would set up the guns he had with him but otherwise hold back until the receipt of further instructions. The next morning brought additional annoyance: the six disposable demi-cannon were shifted by an indirect route and became stuck in the mud; another six pieces and mortars at Komárno suffered the same fate. Charles suspected deliberate obstruction by Leslie since it was customary to examine road conditions beforehand; Rimpler's absence, on grounds of "illness," also aroused mistrust. The by-now-shaken Duke began to waver and talked matters over with his secretary, Le Bègue, who wanted to wait until the return of the courier sent to Leopold. Despite the contrary factors, which added up to a lack of support from all concerned, Charles was determined to stay as late as 2:00 p.m. Then Leslie, Starhemberg, and Caprara arrived to deliver their opinions, which were apparently negative. Lorraine also learned that the fascines, spread atop the mud, were sinking and that the Magyar rebels and the Tatars were on the move. It seemed questionable from private letters to the generals that the Emperor would give his blessing. Charles had no course but to withdraw his forces to Komárno. By June 9 he was in the depths of depression. He was especially upset because of the effect that his seemingly senseless maneuvers would have upon his personal reputation, the maintenance of which was so important for the eventual recovery of his duchy.[40] Le Bègue advised him to retire to either Győr or Bratislava and play sick until he could get control of the army on his own terms. The secretary also suggested preserving Leopold's hand-written letters for the Duke's own justification. This was done, for the material lies today in the Viennese *Haus-, Hof- und Staatsarchiv*. Lorraine was so irritated that he remarked that it would be better to accept Louis XIV's mercy. On the other hand, he could not agree with Le Bègue's assertion that he ought to have remained at Innsbruck and, in his frustration, even cast aspersions on the latter's loyalty.[41]

By June 12 the distraught Charles had calmed down somewhat. The arrival of his good friend Taaffe helped to soothe him. Nevertheless, both he and Le Bègue were convinced that a great opportunity had been lost. They pointed out that Nové Zámky was garrisoned by only 1,200 Janissaries and 700 horse. It was no consolation to learn that Leopold would have permitted the operation to continue, for the conditions which he had set were too stringent. In any case, Lorraine now had to think only of the defensive. At Komárno he was in a position from which he could survey the Turks' approach and oppose them either north or south of the Danube, as the situation might require. For a time he thought that the foe intended to sweep westward into Styria. But from intelligence data received on the twentieth he deduced, correctly, that the Grand Vezir was moving toward Győr. So the Duke also headed for the place, arriving two days later. By this time his army included only 12,500 infantry and 9,500 cavalry. Although three more regiments had joined him meanwhile, he had lost many men to disease and he had to detach two regiments to reinforce Schultz (who was facing the rebels while awaiting Lubomirsky's Poles) and one to strengthen Komárno and Gúta.[42]

C. The Withdrawal from Hungary

RETREAT FROM THE RÁBA

Charles' most urgent task at Győr was to complete the renovations prescribed by Rimpler. For the moment at least he was following the engineer's thinking, at least in a general way, for his plan was to hold the town with the aid of the field army. He had three choices of position: to camp on the Szigetköz, behind the Rábca, or between the Rábca and the Rába. He hesitated for a while because he knew that it would be difficult to defend a river line without risking a dangerous, uncertain engagement (which was contrary to his instructions). However, while the Court had ordered him to take no chances, he was also supposed to oppose the enemy's possible advance against the hereditary lands. Since the first two locations would have left open the narrow passage to Austria proper, he took the third, hooking his left wing to the lower edge of the fortress and his right to the swampy terrain farther south. In the meantime Marsigli, who had been called to Nové Zámky, had returned to the Rábaköz with orders to perfect defenses there. At first all seemed well. However, the Italian volunteer soon began to smell "treachery." With the Turkish advance, he had to order demolition of the Rába bridges and start work on a new crossing over the swamp to Győr. A personally supervised effort to remove the span at Keszo failed because of the refusal of the Magyars to cooperate, but at Arpas it proved possible to set up some cannon (June 22). Here also Marsigli called for help both from Lorraine and Batthyányi. A second message to the Duke, sent two days later, made mention of three unguarded fords leading into the swamp area. Even more serious was news that proclamations from Thököly had begun to circulate and that revolt was clearly in the air.[43]

The attitude of the Magyars of western Hungary is not difficult to understand. Not only did the long and turbulent history of their relations with a foreign king, hardly predispose them to loyalty, but they were no more than average mortals with a natural desire to save their own lives and property and to be on the winning side. Their confidence was first shaken when they saw the meager size of the Imperial forces at Kittsee. Then came the withdrawal from Nové Zámky, which both perplexed and disgusted them. Already at that point many persons left their *banderia* for home.[44] Moreover, the government had provided no pay, supplies, or moral support (whether unavoidably or deliberately one cannot say). At the same time Thököly began to circulate declarations among the population, justifying his alliance with the Turks in the name of national liberty and threatening all who opposed him with fire and destruction. Appended to his manifestoes was a similar statement from Kara Mustafa.[45] One locality after another came to terms with Turco-rebel forces, including eventually even Bruck an der Leitha in Lower Austria.[46] On June 30 Esterházy, a beneficiary of property confiscations after the Wesselényi Conspiracy and hence a man with good cause to remain faithful to Vienna, despairingly sent off a delegation to Leopold. The Palatine entrusted the mission with a dramatic, personally-penned appeal in which he expressed disappointment with Lorraine's operations and the behavior of the German troops toward the Magyar population. "Nobody here at my side is prepared any longer to serve Your Majesty. . . . I stand all alone, bereft of assistance in the face of the enemy's open jaws." The Hungarian dignitary also reproached the Emperor for his secret dealings with the deceitful Thököly and stated that unless immediate help were forthcoming, the very last man would depart. Leopold was obviously powerless. The only point in the letter he could do anything about was the suggestion to rescue the crown of St. Stephen from Bratislava. Esterházy had to disband his own shrunken *banderium* and ride up the Danube into exile, leaving his rich estates to the mercy of the enemy.[47] Marsigli meanwhile had become a classical example of a man in a forlorn post. His sole support was a party of 120 Imperial dragoons recently dispatched by the Duke. While this small force successfully repulsed a Turco-Tataric attack at Bondonhély on St. Peter's Day (June 29), to its right everything was collapsing. Veszprém, Tata, and Pápa were already in Ottoman hands. Batthyányi had withdrawn from his position behind the Marcal. Although he conferred with Charles' representative on July 1 and 2, the talks were apparently only a sham: Turco-Tataric contingents were already sweeping through the firmer, southern Rábaköz, having swum the Rába or having crossed its undefended bridges and fords.[48] Marsigli was still able to organize a successful stand of his own at the southeastern extremity of the Hanság. However, the lateral bridge over the swamp that he had ordered built apparently remained unfinished, for he was unaware of what was transpiring at Győr. Thus he was eventually cut off from retreat and taken captive (much to the benefit of history since he became one of the two Western observers inside the Ottoman camp). The last Magyars he saw told him that he could inform his comrades that no longer would Germans be quartered in Hungary, which now owed obedience to a new master.[49]

In front of Győr preliminary skirmishes had begun already on June 30. The next day the main Turkish force appeared. Its monstrous size was literally breath-taking:

La mattina di quel giorno, a due hore di Sole, compara alla nostra vista, tutta in battaglia, l'Armata Turchesca, ch'ampa di là dal Fiume Rab,

longo le sue rive, sot'il tiro de Cesarei cannoni, comprendo pianti e
monti di Padiglioni, mostrandosi in verità un nuovo Essercito di Xerxes:
mentre occupava la loro linea de battaglia più di due leghe di Paese di
Torrente ed un fondo incomprehensibile, non arrivendo gli occhi a
vedere il fino del campo in latitudine e longhezza.[50]

The Turks began almost immediately to sound the river bottom. The
opening Austrian bombardment was designed to dissuade them from
continuing. Toward noon they detached a large cavalry corps (the vanguard actually), which was seen to move upstream toward the southern
Rábaköz. The several regiments that Charles had stationed directly adjacent to the swamp in order to guard the "neighboring passages" (presumably the three fords mentioned earlier by Marsigli) found their position
untenable and withdrew. In the interval the rest of the Ottoman army
began to build batteries in preparation for forcing a crossing. By 6:00
p.m. the whole horizon to the south and west of the Austrians was lit up
by fires. Allegedly the Duke was not surprised at the rapid dispersal of the
enemy horse since he himself had insufficient cavalry to cover the huge
spaces involved.

Just reminded by the Court to protect the *Erblande,* recalling previous
orders not to risk anything and facing overwhelming odds with an exposed right flank, Charles resolved to retire the same night. Three infantry regiments were sent into Győr as reinforcements. The remaining foot
and the artillery, under Leslie and Starhemberg, were ordered to the
Szigetköz with the idea of sustaining Győr, should it prove to be the main
target of Turkish interest. The cavalry would ride to Mosonmagyaróvár
(Wieselburg-Ungarisch-Altenburg) to head off what, hopefully, were still
simple "incursions". If, on the other hand, the enemy objective did turn
out to be Vienna, the infantry and the artillery, sheltered on the north
side of the Danube, could rejoin the cavalry via the bridges at Bratislava
or Vienna. Since it was known that the huge Turkish armada could only
move slowly, there was little worry about being overtaken.[51]

THE PETRONELL SKIRMISH

The withdrawal from Győr was executed quickly, in full order and
without *perceptible* panic. On July 2 Lorraine drove off a lesser, harass-
ing attack of the Tatars near Mosonmagyaróvár. He was still inclined to
believe that the enemy was only raiding in the area between the northern
end of Lake Neusiedl and the Danube, and was really going to concentrate upon the nearby fortress. Therefore, on the third, he moved only a
few miles up the road to Deutsch-Jahrndorf, where he halted for two
days. His intention was to cover the course of the Leitha, which bisects
the pan-flat terrain between the lake and the bigger stream into which it
empties a little farther on. To the south of the Leitha everything was in
flames. The Duke, hoping to combat marauders there and to the west in
Lower Austria, detached a small number of troopers. On July 5 and 6 he

retired only a slight distance, staying at Berg just inside the Lower Austrian frontier. On the seventh, while preparing to approach the Leitha again in search of better water, he was warned that a big Turkish force (actually only the vanguard) was moving into Mosonmagyaróvár, and at the same time he saw a cloud of dust on the plain below. His first conclusion was that the foe was indeed heading for Vienna in full strength or at least trying to cut him off. This impression was supported by an alarm brought in by several tattered survivors, fellow Lorrainers, of an observation corps left behind in the Hungarian town. Charles therefore ordered the baggage and, shortly afterward, the main body of cavalry to move up the Danube to Fischamend in Lower Austria. Unfortunately, the men were now openly shaken by the advance of what they thought were vastly superior enemy forces. It also seemed wise to send a courier, Count Auersperg, to warn Leopold. Next, instructions were dispatched to Count Leslie, whom the Duke had wanted to depose the previous day for leaving the Szigetköz (without, as it then seemed, adequate reason). The march of the infantry and the artillery was to be accelerated, first to Bratislava and then to Vienna. Starhemberg was to leave posthaste in order to resume direct command in the metropolis. However, the first messengers who rode out fell into rebel hands. Only the vain, dauntless Lt. Col. Tobias von Hasslingen succeeded in slipping through to the other Imperial corps, which had been without word from Lorraine for six days. The result of the delay was that the foot soldiers and gunners were forced to exhaust themselves in marching more rapidly than would otherwise have been necessary.[52]

Riding forward himself as far as Petronell (near the ruins of the old Roman city of Carnuntum), Lorraine observed fires to his left in the direction of Wiener Neustadt and saw that the foe was also aiming for Fischamend. Shortly thereafter a pack of Tatars fell upon the baggage. Elements of the main body rushed to the defense and repulsed the attack easily. At the same time, however, a second group of Tatars, stiffened with Turks, hurled themselves furiously upon the Austrian rear. The latter, demoralized by what it thought to be the retreat of the baggage and the main body, was thrown into dust-beclouded confusion and routed. The Duke had to intervene personally to rally the folding regiments. With exemplary composure he addressed himself to one fleeing squadron, saying, "Quoy, Messieurs, vous abandonnez l'honneur des armes de l'Empereur, avez-vous peur de ces canailles? Je veux les battre avec vous et les chasser." His valor and example turned the tide. The light enemy horse—perhaps 6,000 men to Charles' 9,500—faded away. Pursuit in force did not take place. The Austrian cuirassiers were too heavily mounted to engage in a chase, and it was feared that the foe might be a part of the main Turkish army. The Duke was also anxious to reach Vienna as rapidly as possible. However, when he considered how relatively effortless his recovery had been, he developed new doubts about the Grand Vezir's intentions. Only after Győr confirmed the departure of the whole Ottoman host did he become absolutely certain of his position.[53]

THE "FIRST HUNGARIAN CAMPAIGN" IN RETROSPECT

With the arrival of Austrian troops in Vienna the initial field fighting was over, and one may resurrect the question of the Duke's overall generalship. The facts seem to justify a relatively mild judgment. The difficulties which Lorraine faced have an air of insurmountability. It would hardly be just to hold him responsible for the state's financial decrepitude and the concomitant of a military machine too weak to perform the tasks demanded of it. Likewise, there was nothing that Charles could have done about the thoroughly spoiled relationship with the Magyars, which caused the loss of the Rábaköz and hence the exposure of an alternate route to the hereditary lands, which, again, he was especially enjoined to protect.[54] The only criticism that might be levelled against the Duke is that he was wrong in advocating offensive action prior to the arrival of the main Turkish forces. And yet even here it is apparent, whatever the merits of the conflicting strategic viewpoints, that Leopold's failure to establish a clear-cut, harmonious command structure was the critical element. The Emperor could either have forced Lorraine to accept Hermann's concepts or vice-versa. In the former case, the army—which could hardly have avoided evacuating Hungary ultimately —at least would have been able to conserve all its original strength. In the latter event, a prompt, efficient strike, carried out with the full co-operation of the *Hofkriegsrath,* might have succeeded and the advantages that Charles foresaw in his original argumentation harvested. Finally, the frequent and inconsistent Imperial directives were a major hindrance to the conduct of operations.

Another aspect of the campaign, the Petronell clash, deserves special comment, for it has significance quite apart from its strictly military character. Firstly, the "Chevalier de Savoie" (Louis Julius of Savoy), commander of a brand-new dragoon regiment and an elder brother of Prince Eugene, was mortally injured when thrown beneath his horse. (The Austrians suffered several hundred dead.) The news of his demise was the immediate reason for Eugene's leaving the French court, where he had grown up, and joining the Imperial service as a volunteer—a decision, the historical implication of which hardly needs emphasizing.[55] Secondly, some terrified valets who fled from the baggage train and a few fugitive cavaliers brought reports of a great Austrian reverse to Vienna. This misinformation, received at 2:00 p.m., was the chief cause of Leopold's decision to flee. The rumors and the quickly-passed word of the Imperial exodus had a disastrous effect upon public morale. Then too, there was the paralyzing and partly-justified fear of enemy raiders. Lower Austria could be seen bursting into flames. The Tatars, who had also cut in south of Lake Neusiedl via Sopron, were sweeping right into the mountain valleys. Stories of their activities—the slaughter of old people, enslavement in chain gangs, multiple rapings—lost no force in retelling. The unhappy Austrian cuirassiers could do little to help.[56] The three light Croatian regiments might have been of some use, but they were serving with Schultz' corps north of the Danube. The result was that Vienna fell into a panic, which seriously impeded efforts to organize its still-imperfect defenses.

THE OTTOMAN ADVANCE TO VIENNA

As Charles slowly withdrew from Western Hungary—plagued both by bands of predators and by uncertainty as to Kara Mustafa's intentions—, the main enemy force continued for a short time to occupy the position it had taken on July 1. While the failure of the Austrians to give battle before Győr may have surprised the Grand Vezir, he can scarcely have been discouraged: his mere presence had caused the accursed Giaours to flee, leaving the road to the Danubian metropolis unobstructed. On the other hand, the rest of the Turkish generals were hardly reconciled to the impending operation. While there appears to have been no further council of war,[57] much less outright opposition, several dignitaries indicated reluctance about leaving behind an important place like Győr. The Vezir replied that it would not be easy to take the fortress and that the time lost would be used by the enemy to strengthen the defenses of Vienna. (Kara Mustafa was presumably aware of the unhappy state of affairs upstream). Although it is not clear whether the point was raised specifically, it seems that another objection was logistical. Austrian artillery controlled the Danube water route, while the land passage could be cut off were the Poles to appear suddenly from the north. An army besieging Vienna could find itself without supplies. The Turkish commander was surely acute enough to recognize these problems and probably regarded the security measures he did take adequate response to any criticism. Twenty-two Austrian posts—stockades and the like—were seized and destroyed, while 1,500 men were thrown into Veszprém, Tata, and Pápa. İbrahim Pasha was told not only to guard the bridges but to blockade the approaches to Győr, for which purposes he was assigned a mixed force of some 21,000 men, plus two field culverins and twenty siege cannon. Another 22,000 odd troops, including Thököly's partisans, were placed under the command of the *Beylerbeyi* of Eger (Erlau) and instructed to capture Nitra and Bratislava.[58] Needless to say, these detachments seriously reduced the strength of the army destined for Vienna—a loss of manpower that may well have been decisive.

However firm the decision to proceed, its execution was not and could not be instantaneous. It was physically impossible for so large a force simply to break camp and, without further ado, embark upon one of the greatest siege operations of modern times. The Rába and Rábca Rivers had to be spanned by structures strong enough to support not only hordes of warriors but also heavily laden munition and victual wagons and big siege cannons. Supplies and guns, not yet present in sufficient quantity, had to be brought up from Buda. *Çavuşi* and couriers were sent scurrying.[59] Finally, a letter was dispatched to the presumably uninformed Sultan, revealing the change of plans and asking for all possible assistance. The ruler is said to have been dumbfounded:

> But the goal was the fortresses of Győr and Komárno! There was no talk of Vienna. The Pasha [the Grand Vezir] has committed a serious impropriety in seizing upon this idea. Very well and good, may Ever Magnificent Allah grant him success! Nevertheless, if he had said this before, We should not have given Our consent.[60]

There can be little doubt that the Rába was Kara Mustafa's Rubicon. If the audacious gamble failed, the *Ser'asker's* own life would surely be in jeopardy. His foes at court would not neglect to exploit any defeat he might suffer.

On July 7 the bulk of the army crossed the Rába and, two days later, the Rábca as well. While it was slowly getting underway, the vanguard proceeded to seize Mosonmagyaróvár (July 8). The detachment left behind by Charles departed so hastily that it was unable to destroy a large dépôt of food stores. The enemy carried off as much as he could and put the torch to what remained. On July 10 Kara Mustafa himself rode in to inspect the ruins. On July 11 the center corps marched up the road for another five hours (the customary daily stint at this point) and reached the Austro-Hungarian frontier near Gattendorf (Gata). About nine miles to the north of the evening encampment, on the Danube Water Gap just west of Bratislava, lay the Mediaeval castle and town of Hainburg. Although this strategically located strongpoint had resisted Tatar attacks for over a week, it was unable to withstand storming by a Turkish task force under Kara Mehmed Pasha and Deli Bekir Pasha. The few regulars and municipal officials had fled and the Turks were forced to limit vengeance to those burghers who had dared to offer resistance. By evening severed heads were rolling in the dust at the Grand Vezir's feet, the bearers of the grisly trophies being rewarded with the customary honorary caftans and cash gifts. Hainburg itself was destroyed although apparently not to the extent claimed in the official Turkish record of the action. On the twelfth the Ottoman multitudes surged into the hamlet of Wildungsmauer. After his noontime prayers Kara Mustafa accepted some more Hainburg heads and then went back to inspect the scene of triumph in person. By mid-day of the thirteenth the main units arrived in Schwechat, about seven and a half miles southeast of Vienna's bastions. The morning's journey had led past Fischamend where the Turks discovered a large supply of various kinds of lumber, millstones and finely ground flour—all of which was destroyed.[61] It hardly bears remarking how short-sighted this kind of behavior was. By failing to exploit such finds the invaders only increased the burden which their own caravans would later have to carry. The lovely little Imperial villa of Ebersdorf was also set on fire.

After a brief rest at Schwechat the *Ser'asker* remounted his prize charger and, accompanied by 10,000 cavalrymen, proceeded to survey the environs of the Vienna fortress in order to decide once and for all where the approach trenches should be built. Imperial dragoons came out to meet the Turks. A skirmish ensued, the results of which both sides regarded as a victory. Meanwhile, the Grand Vezir, in what may have been a psychologically astute gesture of patriotism, betook himself to the Neugebäude, a favorite *Lustschloß* of Leopold (located on the spot where the crematorium of the Central Cemetery stands today). The Turks were as much impressed with the glories of early Baroque architecture as they were with the richness and beauty of the country through which they had passed. The villa's gilded roofs, glinting in the summer sun, its marble-encrusted pillars and walls, the geometric gardens and floral rarities, the ripening fruit orchards, and, above all, the Emperor's private menagerie elicited great wonder. According to tradition, the costly edifice rested upon the very ground where Suleiman the Magnificent had pitched his tents during the first Turkish siege in 1529. Indeed it was said to have been laid out partly in keeping with plan of the old Ottoman encampment. The would-be conquerors of 1683, overcome by admiration and in pious recollection of their country's greatest hero, for once withheld sledge hammers and firebrands. In fact, Kara Mustafa even posted a guard to ensure preservation of the delightful country retreat.[62]

D. Antemurale Christianitatis

CONDITIONS OF LIFE

While the Ottoman chief's feet may have touched soil hallowed by his illustrious predecessor, his eyes were focused upon an urban profile much higher than what Suleiman had once seen. The reason for the change was simply Vienna's growing population and a consequent demand for new housing. As no open land remained within the constricting fortifications (roughly three and three quarters miles in circumference), the only recourse was to add extra stories to existing buildings. The street plan stayed more or less the same. However, tighter utilization of space did not alleviate the pressure, and overcrowding was a common phenomenon. A complicating factor was an influx of aristocrats who were attracted to town by the increasing brilliance of court activities. Since nobles were

Vienna in 1680

Viewed from the west, facing the Scottish Gate and Palace Gate. The suburbs of Rossau, Währingergassen, Alsergassen, and St. Ulrich are visible in the foreground. To the left is the Danube Arm and Leopoldstadt. In the center is St. Stephen's Cathedral.

freed from taxes and from the onerous obligation of quartering Imperial functionaries (including servants and purveyors), both burdens fell increasingly upon the burghers' shoulders. The only even faintly democratic social phenomenon was that bluebloods and commoners frequently inhabited the same dwelling, the former occupying, of course, the more desirable lower floors.[63]

The houses, which now had as many as five or six stories, made the only partly paved streets even darker and did nothing to improve sanitary conditions. The Viennese were accustomed to dumping cattle entrails, garbage, and animal cadavers into the gutters. Another source of pollution was the slop water of cabbage curers and herring merchants. Ordinances forbidding these practices and others equally noxious bear witness to the vain efforts of officialdom to promote public health. The byways were not particularly safe in another way either. At night complete darkness reigned, there being no municipal lighting until 1688. Each man carried his own lantern, and there was public illumination only during festivals. The buildings themselves were solid enough. The use of brick, mortar, and stone preserved the city from the frequent holocausts that plagued a city like Moscow in the seventeenth century. On the other hand, the splendor of the eighteenth and nineteenth centuries was yet to be. There were few public monuments. The Leopoldine Tract of the Hofburg was dignified, yet hardly imposing, and the predecessor of the present-day plague monument was made only of wood. Churches, however, were a different matter. St. Stephen's tower, "der Steffl," and other ecclesiastical structures were the dominant elements of the skyline.[64]

There was of course more to Vienna than the "Innere Stadt," the area today encompassed by the Ring Boulevard. Suburbs had existed already in the Late Middle Ages. Wrecked during the first Turkish siege, their restoration and expansion were erratic. There was a tendency for houses to creep onto the glacis. This threatened the proper functioning of the defense works, and from time to time orders went out for dismantlement. Divided more or less into four separate groupings, the outlying habitations were interspersed with palaces, gardens, orchards, and fields. One of the most beautiful features of this architectural garland was the Imperial Neue Favorita (the later Theresianum). Located on the island formed by the Danube Arm and the branches of the main stream, the somewhat disreputable Second District of today, was another palace, the Alte Favorita (Augarten). Nearby was the Leopoldstadt (Unter Werd), the suburb inhabited by the Jews until their expulsion in 1670–71. Otherwise the area was forested, the Prater of modern times serving as another Imperial hunting preserve.[65]

Some of the people who inhabited the Austrian capital in 1683 seem to have conformed to the still widely-accepted, perhaps not inaccurate *fin de siècle* stereotypes invented by the great Arthur Schnitzler. There is evidence to suggest that even then large numbers of Viennese were inclined to frivolity, self-indulgent living, and outward display—for which qualities the Court presented an example. Even the Church, despite condemnations of secularism in the sermons of preachers like the facile-tongued Abraham à Sancta Clara, bore some responsibility. The rich liturgies of the Counter Reformation can hardly have predisposed men to simplicity of taste. The many religious parades can only have encouraged the penchant for spectacles and the tendency to gratify curiosity. In an age of superstition, witch trials, torture, and cruel punishments, there was more than adequate opportunity for another classical trait of the Viennese character—not minding one's own business. Rough manners, the carrying of daggers and the like (firearms being prohibited), brawls between students and guildsmen, and duelling were customary. As in the case of sanitation, the city fathers tried to impose limitations. Among other things, they extended their efforts to strictly personal behavior, clothing, and eating habits. The many sumptuary regulations also reflect the arrogant class consciousness of a nobility determined to monopolize, for prestige reasons, ownership of society's fanciest material goods. To be sure, the frequent reissuance of such legislation was an admission of the futility of dictating taste and mores. (Even Leopold himself could not forbear violating the anti-card-playing ordinance, which applied to everybody.) All in all, it appears that many Viennese were not made of the stern stuff necessary for enduring the rigors of a prolonged siege.[66]

The government of Vienna was oligarchic, being concentrated in the hands of the patricians and house owners. There was a clear distinction between run-of-the-mill inhabitants and burghers, the property-owning, tax-paying minority. The administrative apparatus consisted of so-called Internal and External City Councils, (the latter largely advisory), both headed by the burgomaster, in 1683 the courageous and dependable Andreas von Liebenberg. Justice, which was slow, was the province of the City Judge and his 12 assistants, a self-electing body (save for the judge). The functions of officialdom were manifold, including tax and toll collection, market regulation, diet representation, public morality, sanitation, fire-fighting, town-crying, citizenship registration, naturalization, and supervision of the hospital, schools (however poor), and municipal arsenal. There was also a police force of sorts: thirteen constables.[67]

Religious, social, cultural, and economic conditions left much to be desired. The monopoly of Roman Catholicism was absolute. The Jews had been expelled, and, as the Turks approached, the few remaining Protestants (apparently immigrant German apprentices) were being deported.[68] The most ubiquitous of the many religious orders were the Jesuits. The few schools were clerical-dominated. The University had but 136 students although it could boast of a professor of oriental languages and Dr. Paul Sorbait. The scientific collections of the Court were closed to the people. There was only one public library. The most noteworthy field of learning was theology; the level of popular preaching was also high. The estate of law on the other hand was low. The formative arts, save for music and the popular theater, were retarded although the extent of the lag ought not to be exaggerated. (The physical destruction wrought by the siege served as a tremendous fillip.) While the municipal hospital was a large institution, its services did not fill the town's needs, even when supplemented by private charity such as the Merciful Brothers. The apothecaries and barber-surgeons were regarded as mercenary. As for economic activities, wholesaling seemed to rest principally with foreigners although retailing was the prerogative of natives. Among the more important manufacturing ventures was fancy drygoods. Court demand was the chief stimulus as, indeed, it was for the economy in general. There were no genuine factories, however, and no markets for export. In fact, one of the basic flaws of the trade structure was the demand for expensive, stylish French imports. Crafts, save for persons under Court appointment (*Hofbefreite*), were the monopoly of burgher-guildsmen, who were naturally reluctant to see others admitted to citizenship. These declining organizations squabbled both among themselves and with the *Hofbefreiten*. There were many unemployed, at least before the plague; beggars abounded. On the outskirts of the capital the main enterprise was viticulture, of greater overall significance than at present. The space occupied by the vineyards was also more extensive.[69] Beer was the monopoly of the Municipal Hospital and of Königsegg, who owned a brewery in Gumpendorf. Food was supplied by various tradesmen and markets, the cattle being driven from Hungary. The government, moved in part by mercantilistic considerations, sought to regulate prices, restrict the role of middlemen, and maintain acceptable quality standards.[70]

THE FORTIFICATIONS

Commerce, culture, and social life flourish only when men are assured of physical security, a truism not so apparent to the average denizen of the sprawling twentieth-century city which no wall or contiguous defense system can possibly surround. However, in the pre-industrial age there was a daily reminder of the questionable character of personal safety: every locality of any importance had a circumvallation. It is also likely that the people never felt entirely free of danger because—then as now—the changing nature of military technology required continual revamping of the existing means of defense. Vienna found itself in this situation most obviously right after its narrow escape from Suleiman. There was no doubt about its inability to resist a second siege, if undertaken with a larger quantity and broader range of equipment, especially artillery. It was clear that the "Bulwark and Forewall of Christianity" had to be fortified as strongly as possible.[71]

ELEMENTS OF FORTIFICATION

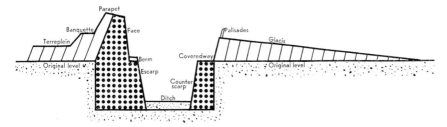

The first problem was whether the new works should be erected around the old Mediaeval core or around the recently devastated suburbs. The number of men needed to man a line including the whole metropolitan area and the expense of construction indicated that only the first alternative was really practical. Thus it was decided to adapt and modify the old, tower-and-wall system of the Middle Ages in keeping with the new, Italian "manner" of the bastioned trace and to solve money problems by carrying out the plan in successive stages. At the outset there was much enthusiasm for the project, and a number of stately orillon (spade-shaped) bastions, 400–600 paces in width, arose relatively quickly. Yet as the danger from the East seemed to decrease and as the memory of the sufferings of 1529 paled, zeal lessened. The flow of financial contributions from other parts of Germany began to dry up.[72] The tempo of activity slowed, and there were long periods when work ceased altogether. It is understandable that some 130 years passed before the original design was fully executed. It is also not surprising that the piece-meal building process gave rise to many a flaw. A critical study undertaken in 1674 pinpointed what was wrong. The trace was irregular: some bastions were too big, some were too small for efficient utilization. Some were too high, some were too low, some too wide, some too narrow. The intervening wall was weak in places and in danger of collapse. The ditch water (from the Ottakringer Creek which poured into the moat, plus a diversion from the Wienfluss) needed regulation in order to protect subterranean arches. One bastion, the "Preacher," was objectionable because it was covered with stone, instead of brick, which would mean deadly flying splinters during a bombardment. The fortification sector on the Danube Arm was weak. There were no outworks, and the bastions were tiny, a situation all the more perilous since the partly-silted stream could be forded at low water. Another disadvantage was the proximity of the deeply-cut bed of the Wienfluss, which, if dry, could afford protection to attackers. The glacis was uneven in width. As indicated, the government had not been resolute in preventing house construction. This oversight would permit the Turkish sappers to push forward their approaches with greater than normal ease.[73]

A number of independent witnesses corroborated the engineering deficiencies of Vienna's walls. One of them, who made his observations just after the end of the second siege, wrote:

> This fatal Experience hath since occasioned them to remove the Suburbs at a greater Distance. . . . As to the Fortifications, some of them are strong and others weak. There are twelve Royal Bastions, faced with Brick, with Cavaliers, Ravelins, Half-Moons, and fine Gates, all fac'd with Bricks, as the Bastions, and adorn'd with Wreathes of hewn Stone. The Ditch is large and deep, part of it dry and part full of Water. The Counterscarp is very sorry, ill pallisaded, nor did I see anything that deserved to be called a Covert-Way, or any detached Works beyond it.[74]

An Italian officer who served in the city during the siege stated that "les fortifications de cette place ayant été construites dans les temps differens sont défectueuses presque partout y avoient été longtemps négligées."[75]

The Turks were well informed about Vienna's defenses. It will be recalled that the renegade Capuchin, Ahmed Bey, (allegedly) studied in person the fortress that he would later be called upon to help capture. He apparently concluded that while the river front could be breached with great ease, the possibility of a sudden rise in the water level made an attack at that point inadvisable. He therefore chose the landward sector that he deemed weakest. Whether he based his judgment upon the fact that the moat was relatively dry or upon the inherent feebleness of construction, he decided that the area between the Palace (*Burg*) and Löbl Bastions (*Basteien*), which comprises the present-day *Burgtheater, Volksgarten,* and *Heldenplatz,* was most suitable.[76] Austrian officers later affirmed the wisdom of his selection. While the *Burgbastei* (first erected in 1541 and later remodelled) was more or less satisfactory, the *Löblbastei* (built 1544–1547 and also later renovated) was definitely unsound. It was not only far too small, making a retrenchment on its top impossible, but its faulty design prevented it from functioning efficiently. Troop movement in its neck was choked by superimposition of an overly large cavalier: only a few soldiers could pass back and forth or hold an enfilading post there at the same time. It was also located at too great a distance from the *Burgbastei*. Its muskets and cannon, even culverins, were able to reach the latter bastion only when set up down below on a supplementary *flanque basse*.[77]

Between the Palace and Löbl Bastions lay the Court Ravelin, which, along with similar structures at other appropriate spots in the trace, had been added to the original plan in order to account for advances in fortifications made since the first half of the sixteenth century. Unfortunately, it was so awkwardly located that it could not receive adequate fire-cover from the *Löblbastei*. Furthermore, its berm (a ledge running along its two outer facades) was so broad that the soldiers stationed above were unable to fire directly to the base of the bulwark, something that proved to be extremely harmful once the Turks had succeeded in lodging themselves in the moat and working their way up to the ravelin. Another serious deficiency was that, apart from a cunette, there was no protection against mines.[78] Likewise disadvantageous was the fact that there was little space between the ramparts (the broad backing of the courtine) and the city houses. The Leopoldine wing of the Hofburg was, for example, absolutely flush to the terreplein, which served as a promenade for the Imperial apartments. This meant that there was room for only one retrenchment. Otherwise it would be necessary to rely on makeshift street barricades.[79] Probably the most fundamental defect of Vienna's defenses was that they had become obsolescent as a result of new developments in the art of fortification during the last quarter of the seventeenth century. One need only recall the highly sophisticated, geometrical complex of self-sufficient, interlocking forts that Vauban was then creating at Strasbourg. Vienna's walls did not provide good cover for men and guns since there were no proper casements, loopholes, or traverses.[80]

Still, it cannot be said that the Court War Council was insensitive to peril. If it had been, it would not have paid for the services of Rimpler, who knew precisely what remedies were indicated. Supported by other gifted military engineers—his fellow Saxon, Daniel Suttinger; a former Turkish captive, Elias Kuhn; the Italian, Leander Anguissola—Rimpler suggested a number of practical measures, some of which represented real innovations. First, and most basically, he urged that the glacis be widened by removal of the encroaching houses. At the same time the moat should be cleaned of débris and silt and deepened. A second essential was improvement of the covered way. Adequate palisading, i.e., sharpened stakes behind and between which the troops of the first line of resistance were to be sheltered, was indispensable.[81] It would also be necessary to prepare log and earthen traverses for lateral defense. The reëntering salients should have caponières (half-sunken, pillbox-like blockhouses), the usefulness of which Rimpler stressed very heavily. Made of poles, boards, thatchwork, covered with beams and earth, they too facilitated lateral resistance and simultaneously protected the defenders from grenades, stone projectiles, and musketry.[82] Next, the chief engineer called for supplementary works in the moat itself. The most fundamental device was a covered passage from the ravelins to the courtine; it would enable the defenders to communicate safely and to enfilade the moat. Traverses, a faussebraye,[83] and additional caponières, built in a "v"-shaped fashion so as to flank both ravelins and bastions, would also be needed. All these structures were in effect independent forts, extremely dangerous obstacles which would cost the enemy much blood. Their effect would be to constrict his approach to a narrow path, thereby exposing him to continual close-quarter fire.[84]

Apparently another of Rimpler's enfilading techniques was the afore-mentioned *flanque basse* (also erected on the far side of the Löbl and on both sides of the adjacent Mölk Bastion). Its usefulness, however, proved limited: the 200 troops that it contained had no place to fall back upon. A fifth, particularly expedient idea was to strengthen the Burg Ravelin with two retrenchments behind the parapets. Each would have three banquettes so that it would be possible to station soldiers in files four deep and thus assure uninterrupted volleys. A further object of attention was the main wall and the bastions and ravelins not subject to assault. For these locations artillery embrasures and shutters (on the Löbl cava-lier), plus further traverses, would have to be built. Finally, there was the possibility, once the Turks had broken into the moat, of having to erect traverses behind the courtine and, even farther back, street barricades, for which lumber, grating, and chains would be needed.[85] A large quantity of other supplies were likewise necessary, indeed essential to any siege. They included fascines, gabions, sandbags, and wool-filled sacks—used for artil-lery emplacements, breastworks, and barriers thrown up on a stopgap basis in breaches. *Cheveaux de Frise,* caltrops, nail-studded boards, and other temporary field obstacles would also be required. The gun beds would have to be laid out so as to ensure proper angles of fire. The cannon themselves, normally stored in the arsenals, would have to be hooked to carriages and trundled into position. The great gates of the city would have to be bricked up solidly and the wooden bridges across the moat removed.

Supplies and Artillery

A discussion of Rimpler's advice naturally leads one to ask when the work was done. The question is of importance because a number of nineteenth-century historians imply that Leopold and his government failed to do as much for Vienna as they could have—a point of view sometimes too vigorously rebutted.[86] The truth of the matter seems to be that while the Austrian Court undertook some steps during the late fall of 1682,[87] work proceeded at so slow a pace that the city was not in a state of defensive readiness when the Duke of Lorraine rode in fresh from the Petronell engagement. Contemporary witnesses leave no doubt about this. Embrasures were lacking on the courtine and other bulwarks. There were no fascines or gabions for the gun emplacements. ". . . Notre contrescarpe n'étoit point du tout en état, ny ayant ny parapets ny palissades plantées."[88] (Of course Rimpler could not have carried out *all* his ideas until he knew for sure which part of the walls the Turks were going to attack.) There appear to have been four reasons for the neglect: 1.) concentration of attention upon the Hungarian fortresses; 2.) inabil-ity to believe that the Turks would besiege the capital city; 3.) failure of the Lower Austrian Estates to provide enough *robot* workers; and 4.) the absence of Starhemberg, who does seem to have appreciated the true extent of the danger.[89]

While it is fairly certain that the work was far from finished by July 8 and while the Turks could have overrun the city *then* if the weather gods and their own logistic problems had not retarded the advance, there can be no question of any failure to stockpile construction materials, food-stuffs, fodder, munitions, and arms. During the fall of 1682 the government had placed orders for lumber and bridge-building supplies. The Imperial Forests and neighboring tracts eventually provided whatever wood the Lower Austrian Estates were unable or unwilling to send. In November of 1682 the population of Vienna started to lay in provisions, and in December a commission was checking on householders individually. At the same time there was a burst of activity in both the Imperial and Municipal Arsenals. Toward the end of March, 1683, a contract was signed with the Quicksilver and Copper Administrator, Mittermayr von Waffenberg, for 3,650 hundredweight of powder—which arrived in the city during the latter part of June. Other entrepreneurs, including the famous Sammuel Oppenheimer, also received orders. The Archdiocese of Salzburg, albeit under pressure, contributed 300 hwt. of powder. An adequate reserve of oats and flour was obtained. The City of Vienna, worried about the low stock of munitions in its own arsenal, wrote to Steyr (October, 1682) for ball and chain, which appear to have been delivered during April. Other shipments continued to arrive in the city until it was entirely cut off. The only item in really short supply was hand grenades. On the other hand, it must be admitted that the presence of ample stores in Vienna was due at least partly to the fact that the place was an advance dépôt for the field army and not just to concern about an attack.[90]

The inventory of material dispensed by the Municipal arsenal during the course of the siege gives some idea of the amounts as well as types of equipment on hand. The list includes: 612 double-hakes (old-style two-man muskets) with bandoleers, 2,972 matchlocks, fifty-six flintlocks with cartridge pouches, 25,511 "murder strokes," 1,000 assault hooks, 460 cuirasses with casquets, 4,626 halberds and other similar weapons, 1,212 pike stems and vaulting poles, forty-eight pike tips, 521 hand fire extinguishers, 460 leather fire buckets, 382 hwt. of arquebus and matchlock powder, five hwt. of disced powder, fifteen hwt. of artillery powder and "all sorts" of fuses, 310 lb. of refined saltpeter, 664 hwt. of pitch, 262 slow matches, 63,000 pitch wreathes, 569 pitch tubs, 146 wagonloads of pitch-dipped shingles for nighttime illumination of the moat, seventeen sections of heavy rope, forty-six fifty-pound fire barrels (explosive bodies for defending breaches), 1,016 "battery nails" (foot obstacles), ten pitch pans, thirty-eight powder flasks, 312 howitzer bungs, 1,026 caltrops, 136 small measures of coal, and 319 hwt. of lead (which was made into

165,300 double-hake balls, 258,300 musket balls and 5,250 wire balls).
The two large Imperial Arsenals distributed even greater quantities of
military hardware, *inter alia:* 212 double-hakes, 9,337 matchlocks, 456
carbines, 104 pairs of pistols, plus a vast amount of numerous varieties of
shot and shell. They also produced certain equipment not issued by the
Municipal Arsenal, such as spiked helmets, cavalry lances, morning stars
(holy water sprinklers) and rivermen's spears (*Nassadistenspiesse*), all of
which were of great value in the hand-to-hand fighting on the breaches.
Another indication that Vienna did not want for defensive matériel is the
fact that it eventually turned some 317 artillery pieces against its besiegers. The Imperial Arsenals provided twenty full carthouns, four three-
quarter carthouns, four double culverins, one thirty-pounder, twenty-
three half carthouns, one short twenty-four pounder, six whole culverins,
thirty-five quarter carthouns or culverins, two demiculverins, twenty falcons, eight double falconets, two six pounders, ten four pounders, twenty-two long field culverins, fifty-seven regimental pieces, two three-pound
Grindel-Prince Robert pieces, twelve howitzers, nine big mortars and
twenty-five medium and small mortars. The Municipal Arsenal contributed another fifty pieces and almost 13,000 projectiles.[91]

Among all the death-dealing tools of a siege it might seem, that for
either side cannon would have been most fundamental. However, this
was not quite the case. In fact, it is essential to recognize that in the
seesaw battle between fortifications and artillery during the seventeenth
century, the former generally retained superiority. Only toward the very
end of the period did the guns begin to win out. On the other hand,
nobody would have assaulted a fortified city without possessing large
caliber ordnance. Starving out a garrison took too long. A surprise stroke
or *coup de main* was rarely possible. Thus it was still necessary to extend
saps or approaches, bring up heavy siege pieces, and blast out breaches.
The defenders obviously also needed similar weapons to keep the attackers at bay. The continuing importance of cannonry is illustrated by the
fact that every army maintained a great variety of types (notwithstanding
the standardization achievements of the previous century). Emplacement
of guns remained a major task. The attackers had to mount them both at
the head of their trenches on the glacis and, if they knew what they were
doing (as the Turks did not in 1683), along a rear-facing contravallation,
adapted to the terrain. Proper stationing required much skill and experience. The batteries had to be protected by solid walls of earth, and the
aforementioned absorbtive devices. Platforms, consisting of solid planks,
and a covered trench for sheltering powder and balls had to be built.
Caissons were still unknown. Level ground or a properly-situated height
had to be found, except for mortars, which were set up in depressions.[92]

At Vienna, in any event, the efforts expended in mounting artillery
would not be commensurate with the results. A more arduous, but also

more efficacious siege technique was mining. It would be the chief means upon which Kara Mustafa would rely in attempting to pry open the city walls. Scarcely a day was to pass without industrious Turkish moles having discharged several such "infernal machines." Another sign of artillery's relegation to second place in 1683 is that the besiegers seem to have inflicted relatively little damage apart from the immediate area of attack. There were at least four different reasons for this: the solidity of Vienna's stone and brick buildings; the inferior quality of Turkish munitions; the fact that the Turkish guns, the number of which was about the same as the Austrians', were of too small caliber for a cannonade of crushing proportions; and lastly, the possibility that Kara Mustafa restrained even the cannon he did have because of his supposed desire to take the city and its riches intact. As for the defense, the relatively large number of pieces would not mean a particularly heavy counter bombardment: the daily average would be but two projectiles per gun. The most important actions would take place at close quarters in the moat, upon the Court Ravelin and the two bastions, and underground. To be sure, the guns stationed in the attacked sector would be fired more frequently than those on more distant, uninvolved bastions. Moreover, a knowledgeable Austrian participant stated that artillery was very useful in preventing the enemy from establishing his batteries on the counterscarp.[93] In other words, while artillery's rôle should not be overstressed, it remained a factor—and could possibly have been of greater influence—in the outcome of the siege.

OTHER DEFENSIVE ASSETS

Another siege preparation was mobilization of Vienna's own municipal military establishment. Already on September 6, 1682, the minister of Hesse-Darmstadt reported home: ". . . heut hat man angefangen die bürgerschafft im Arsenal zu exercieren."[94] Utilization of local forces was by no means an innovation of the latter seventeenth century. As far back as 1444 the city had been divided into four defense sectors (the Stuben, Kärntner, Widmer, and Schotten Wards). However, only in the sixteenth century were indigenous resources organized on a regular basis. The first of several civil defense institutions was the Burgher Militia (*Bürgerwehren*). Theoretically, every citizen was obliged at moments of alarm, fire, or other emergency to appear at a pre-determined rendezvous with the necessary tools or weapons, procured at his own expense. Weapons for the population at large were kept in storage at the Civil Arsenal. (During the period 1619–1627 the people were disarmed because of an attempt to assassinate Ferdinand II.) The main military rôle of the citizen soldiers was as infantry although there were a few cavalry units for festive purposes. The city also maintained a company of 100 master gunners.[95]

The eight companies of the Burgher Militia (1815 men) should not be confused with a number of *ad hoc* volunteer contingents set up during the course of the siege: the six, so-called "Free Companies" (unemployed apprentices of innkeepers, bakers, butchers, brewers, cobblers, etc.), the three student companies, the self-equipped merchants' company, and the court servants' and caterers' company. A small number of nobles, unwilling to follow the fleeing majority of their confrères, also joined the ranks. Lastly, there were the crack-shot, Imperial gamekeepers of Baron von Kielmannsegg.[96]

Another local military corps was the City Guard (*Stadtguardia*). In the beginning it had been a purely municipal body, designed to relieve the citizenry at large from guard duty outside the gates and on the walls. Its function was then expanded to include keeping the peace inside Vienna. Finally, it was subjected to the regular military discipline of Imperial officers, and it thus fell under the supervision of the Court War Council. By the end of the sixteenth century it was the permanent Imperial garrison in the capital and a professional unit of soldiery. Its origin was largely forgotten although the city continued to pay the bulk of its expenses. In 1680 the Guard—ravaged by the plague and in poor condition—came under Starhemberg's aegis. Its new commander decreed more regular training and better pay and soon whipped it into shape. Then also there was the minuscule police force (*Rumorwache*). It was established by the Lower Austrian government and the City Council in 1646 as an administrative organ. It enabled the officials to dispense with military assistance in making arrests and executing sentences. It also patrolled the streets day and night, called the hours, and gave fire alarms. To be sure, it was not especially successful in keeping order among the city's swarms of beggars, ruffians, gamblers, and confidence men.[97]

The arsenals must also be listed among Vienna's various defense institutions. The Civil Arsenal, first set up in 1547, stood approximately where the Main Post Office is presently located. In 1562 it was moved to the square, Am Hof, opposite Carlone's early Baroque Church of the Nine Choirs of Angels. It still exists today, encased in eighteenth-century dress and used by the Fire Department. The city also owned powder mills and a gun foundry. The first of the Imperial Arsenals goes back to the time of Maximilian I, the father of the Austrian army. Known as the *neue Zeughaus*, it became the *Arsenal*, properly speaking, when the *Obere Zeughaus* was erected next door in 1588. Both structures were situated north of the famous *Schottenkirche*, on the hill that slopes down to the Danube Arm. The former, also called the *Untere Zeughaus*, served as a repair shop, weapons factory, and base for the Danube Flotilla (more a supply and transport force than a battle squadron) via a canal from the Danube Arm. In 1683 this artificial waterway had been sanded up for several decades, and its clearance was one of Rimpler's recommendations.

There was also a third arsenal in the Seilerstätte, but it was used only for making and repairing weapons.[98]

Despite its interest to the connoisseur of Viennensia, the story of civil defense (except for the Guard and the arsenals) is not overly significant. The point demands emphasis because of the much cherished legend that the place owed its salvation to the heroic resistance of the townspeople. A recent examination of the death protocols has revealed that no more than thirty-nine of some 4,900 local fighters fell in action, while only fifteen other residents died violent deaths. By far the greatest number of losses was due to disease, but even here the figure (553) is only one-third of what was previously supposed. Probably no more than one percent of the total population lost life and limb—not much for a two months' siege. There are other signs that civilian behavior was not, on the whole, very courageous. The local chronicler, Dr. Nicolaus Hocke, mentions a number of incidents, including direct reprimands to militia units and hunts for deserters and draft-dodgers, that permit one to infer unexemplary conduct. Afterward, the Emperor had no praise for the inhabitants, merely the admonition that their sufferings were the result of their sins. Starhemberg issued only one certificate of bravery, plus a few commendatory words to several burgher companies. His low estimate of the military value of the militiamen is apparent from the fact that they were assigned only to guard duty, street patrol, and posts not under direct attack. There can be no question that Vienna was saved mainly because of the skill and valor of the regular troops who were thrown in at the very last minute. Their extremely high casualty rate attests to their rôle. All that may be said of the civilians is that their services elsewhere permitted concentrating the professionals on the front under assault. Apart from a few cattle-rustling expeditions by devil-may-care students—of scant tactical significance—and the temporary recruitment of some 550 men to fill gaps in the regulars' ranks, there is nothing worthy of mention.[99] The brave and dedicated service of the magistracy is, however, another matter, to be treated elsewhere.

STARHEMBERG

When considering the capital's defense resources, one cannot neglect the personality of the commander. Ernst Rüdiger, Count and Lord of Starhemberg (1638–1701), a hardened master-sergeant in the garb of a field marshal, was unlike his superior, the Duke of Lorraine, in every respect save moral and physical fortitude. Destined to immortality in Habsburg's age-long roll of honor, the city's redeemer came of a family which had given military help locally as far back as the thirteenth century. Childhood and youth were spent on an ancestral estate in Lower Austria where the Jesuits provided an apparently not very thorough

Ernest de Rüdigeri Cheuallier Comte de Staremberg Con[er] de sa Majeste Imperialle en ses Con[eils] son mareschal de Camp gnial, et son gouuerneur de la ville de vienne, il est impossible de comprendre dans ce petit Espace les admirables actions de ce grand homme, qui a soutenu auec vne valleur extraord[re] l'effort de l'armee des Turcs deuant la ville de vienne Capital te de l'Empire d'Allemagne, ce grand ouurage ne pouuoit estre conduit que par le genereux Staremberg, aussy sa Majeste Imperialle le choisit entre tous ses officiers pour commander en chef dans cette ville, se reposant sur la fidelite et l'experience de ce digne Comte, qui s'est aquitte de son employ auec tout le merite d'vn Capitaine acheué, et a resisté pendant 2. mois de Siege et tranchees ouuertes a ce formidable ennemy du nom Chretien, ce qui a donne lieu a sa Majeste Imp[le] de demander et receuoir le secours du Serenissime Roy de Pologne Jean Sobieski, dont le seul nom faict trembler les Turcs, et de faict sy tost que ce monarque belliqueux se presenta a la teste de l'armee Chretienne, pour forcer ces infidelles dans leurs lignes, et que le bruict de son approche fut repandu dans leur Camp, il ne fut pas possible a mustapha leur grand Vizir de les rasseurer de les pouuante ou ils estoient, ny de les retenir, et ces trouppes commenceant a defiler d'elles mesme pour chercher leur salut dans la fuite, ce gnal Turc se vid contrainct de leuer le Siege le dimanche 12. 7bre 1683. Paris chez J.Hainzelman graveur, sur le petit pont a l'escharpe blanche. auec Priuil. du Roy. 1685.

(Vienna, National Library)

Count Rüdiger von Starhemberg

education (The hero's spelling of the German language was completely erratic while his only non-professional interests in later life were hunting and card-playing.), though presumably a grand tour afforded at least some sophistication. In early manhood Starhemberg served in both civil and military capacities. Only after the Battle of Szentgotthárd, in which he fought under Montecuccoli, did he commence a soldier's career permanently. A full colonel and regimental commander by 1669, he saw action the next year in rebellious Hungary, where, for a time and through trickery, he was a captive of Helena's first spouse, Ferenc Rákóczy I. Next came service in the Dutch War. Wounded several times and present at the siege of Philippsburg under Lorraine—with whom his relations were generally quite good—the Count entered the senior ranks of Austria's army when appointed commandant of Vienna (1680). His post-1683 career was something of an anti-climax. Although he took part in subsequent campaigns and eventually became war minister, fate and his enemies denied him further glory. His greatest achievement in later years was to have recognized the brilliance of Eugene of Savoy and to have placed the latter in supreme command of the Hungarian theater of operations (1697).[100]

Starhemberg does not appear to have had as engaging a personality as Charles. The impression his letters provide corroborates the somewhat reserved judgment of individuals who had the opportunity to observe him first hand.[101] There seems little question that his frankness in expressing opinions was too blunt for certain of his associates. His truculence in maintaining them was combined, it would seem, with a self-satisfied attitude if later events proved him right. Rinck remarked that the good general possessed "more heat than head."[102] His management of the *Hofkriegsrath* also left much to be desired, at least according to the Venetian ambassador:

> It is true that while he gave proof of great, personal valor when in combat, he is only so-so in the direction of military affairs. He appears unable to bear the great burdens encountered in the disposition of such far-ranging matters. His talent is of a more limited nature. His indefinite distractions are hardly in keeping with the daily urgency of a heavy load of business.[103]

On the other hand, it is evident that, for history, the man's virtues far outweighed his faults. His physical appearance was a prime advantage. To judge by contemporary engravings, he possessed deep, searching eyes, a pensive forehead, that large aquiline nose so admired in the Habsburg domains, and a small mouth. Of even greater practical value was his courage: he seldom hesitated to expose himself to the hail of enemy bullets. Another asset was an understanding of the principles of leadership, the most vivid expression of which was insistence upon rigid discipline. Starhemberg was, however, no mere martinet. He possessed a deep sense of justice and showed sincere concern for the personal well-being of both soldiers and civilians. His more intimate private relationships reflected much human warmth. Epistles to his cousin, Gundacker, bear witness to a faithful and long-lasting friendship, and he also enjoyed uncustomary marital felicity.[104] Still, the most important thing seems to have been a vigorous, aggressive approach to tactics. The Count was, above all, a thruster, an enthusiastic proponent of the sally or the sortie when a garrison found itself locked up in a fortress by the foe. While it is true that a besieged commander had to be more sparing of human capital than an attacker, maintaining uninterrupted troop morale was essential when relief was not impossibly remote. He was, in short, the right man for the job.

CHAPTER EIGHT

The Siege

A. The Organization of Resistance

The appearance of the Turkish behemoth upon the plains of Hungary does not seem to have evoked much anxiety among Austrian ruling circles initially. During the latter part of June effete Court cavaliers were still of fairly good cheer, putting all their faith in the "beautifully polished soldiers."[1] However, the news of Charles' withdrawal from Győr did arouse concern. Not only were the capital's defense works incomplete, but, at the beginning of July, the garrison consisted only of the City Guard and half a regiment of foot—less than 2000 men. The government, unhappy about the Duke's separation of the infantry and artillery from the cavalry, demanded (July 2) reunification of the three service arms so that Vienna would have full cover on its landward side. On the same day the orders went out to transfer the Hungarian royal insignia from Bratislava. Since Erdődy and his colleague Count Zichy (the official keepers) refused to permit removal of the regalia without a written promise from Leopold regarding later restoration, the matter was not settled until July 5. The Emperor, for his part, remained placid. The hunt in Perchtoldsdorf, which took place on the third and the sixth, was indicative. His stepmother, the Empress-Dowager, was not so imperturbable and fled from the outlying Neue Favorita into the less exposed Hofburg. While plans for departure of the whole Imperial family were under discussion, Leopold remained adamant about staying, not only because of his alleged desire to keep the population calm but also due to his wife's pregnancy.[2]

TERROR AND ABANDONMENT

There can be little question that Vienna's collective psychological temperature had begun to rise. Reports of Tatar incursions were multiplying while some refugees were already knocking at the city gates. On July 5 the common people expressed their frustration and fears, ironically, by smashing Bishop Sinelli's windows. The incident was one of numerous manifestations of disapproval of recent policies in dealing with the Magyars. As noted initially, the masses held the Church responsible for conditions in Hungary and, therefore, the intervention of the Porte. As the peril grew more obvious, the lot of the individual priest or brother, especially the Jesuit, became increasingly difficult. Verbal abuse,

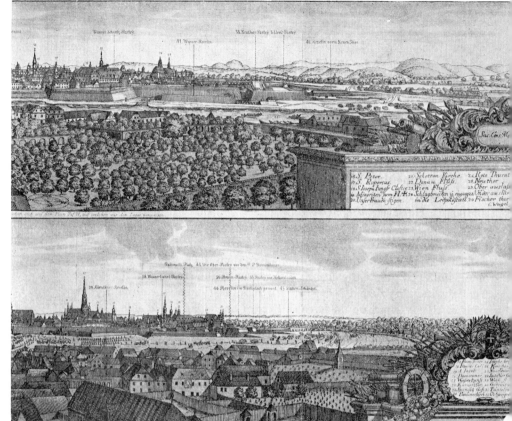

(Vienna, Municipal Historical Museum)

Vienna in 1683

As seen from the north (above) and south (below). (Daniel Suttinger.) The foreground of the top view shows the Taborstrasse and the Augarten in Leopoldstadt. The background of the bottom view shows the heights of the Wienerwald (Leopoldsberg, Kahlenberg, etc.).

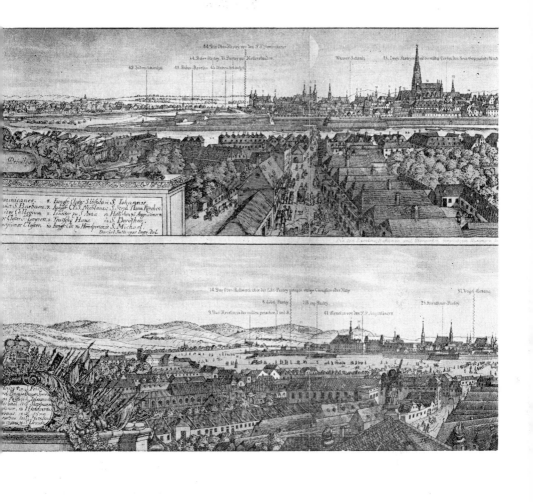

body blows, and actual danger to life soon caused many a cleric, above all in the countryside, to clothe himself in mufti.[3]

The pace of events now made the Imperial ministers bestir themselves more than was their wont. On July fifth a number of edicts were published. Older monks and nuns had to leave the capital while the young and strong were to stay. For security reasons, all Frenchmen and other errant aliens were told to leave. The first steps toward improvement of hospital facilities were taken. Landlords—accustomed to ignoring a regulation requiring registration of strangers—were directed to make weekly lists of roomers in order to provide some control over newly-arrived persons. The peasantry was to block off passageways through the Vienna Woods. The rapidly-building emergency also required that attention be given to financial resources. A conference of July 6 devoted itself to the possibility of borrowing funds left in Vienna by several wealthy refugee prelates from Hungary.[4] The next day, however, the ministers were forced to suspend deliberations for the time-being. The arrival of the news from the Duke of Lorraine that the whole Turkish army was thought to be advancing into the hereditary lands and, shortly thereafter, the misleading reports of the Petronell engagement made it appear that the Emperor was in danger of being trapped. It was decided that both the sovereign and the greater part of the government should leave forthwith for safer quarters in Linz—a move doubtlessly correct as *raison d'état* but deleterious in its immediate psychological effects. It was further resolved to establish a kind of regency council, the Secret College of Deputies, to carry on in the ministers' place. Conveniently, precedents existed for such an institution. Similar arrangements had been made during the plague of 1679 as well as on earlier occasions. Before going, the Emperor also signed orders for the return home of the regiments still stationed in the Reich and commanded Schulz to retire from the Váh. Finally, Leopold scribbled hasty appeals to the princes of the Empire. He wrote Waldeck, somewhat sanguinely, that because "the whole might of Turkey is pressing upon me and this good city in so formidable a manner, I find myself constrained to retire from here for a few hours."[5] The absence was destined to last sixty-nine days.

In the meantime packing commenced in the Hofburg. Some officials began to flee without even awaiting further notice. Knowledge of this activity rapidly spread among the jittery population. People had heard that the army had been completely defeated, and that there was no hope of getting the foot soldiers back to the south shore of the Danube in time to fend off the immanently approaching Turks. Now, so it was said, the whole Court and bureaucracy were in the process of deserting Vienna, leaving everybody else to the tender care of the Infidel.[6] The result was a general panic, "una notable confusione," and a mad rush to escape:

> Whatever boats, carts, wagons and horses were available, whatever there was in the way of servants, hired-hands and other tramps—a rabble

normally not even considered—, not to mention all kinds of worn-out, useless horses and rigs, in fact even little ragamuffins, whatever carriage and baggage mares could be dragged up for a tenfold payment—all this was rented and contracted for. A shame it was that so many hundred strong, well-nourished and tested arms-bearing lackeys, whom the city could have used, were seen going and that in their place only weak and wretched persons (refugees) were admitted. With this running and scampering and packing of things the time from afternoon to nightfall was passed. For lack of proper vehicles, respectable, proper matrons and mothers with adult sons and daughters threw themselves upon open, normally despised peasant wagons. They fled their houses, court-yards and beautifully tapestried rooms, leaving wine in the cellars and rugs on the floors. In short, they deserted everything they could not tie together and take with them. Many women, whose husbands previously could find no horse fancy enough to satisfy their luxurious tastes, were now happy if they could have their carriages drawn by spotted, sway-backed, one-eyed old nags, suitable only for a manure cart. Thereupon they stupidly overloaded them with maids and baggage so that many vehicles lost their wheels, broke down and were left standing on the road. They then stood by helplessly, not knowing what to do to alleviate their misery. On top of all this, they were in momentary danger of attack and robbery either by the Turks or by our own soldiers.[7]

About 60,000 people, including most of the economic élite, appear to have fled. In recording the exodus of socialites another chronicler was moved to remark: "And so this beautiful residence-city was deprived for some time of its elegant laurel-wreathe."[8] On the other hand, an equal number of persons, suburban and rural refugees (the former upon invitation of the City Council), flocked in. The newcomers were, generally speaking, a problem, although certainly no worse than the faint-hearted, self-seeking well-to-do whom they replaced. They would not only uselessly consume painfully accumulated food reserves but posed a threat to the maintenance of order. The cramming of so many individuals into so tight a space could cause the "vacillating common rabble to forget its sense of duty and obedience in a moment of tumult and commotion and evoke a general insurrection."[9] Thus, to a degree, the unreliability of the population during the siege may be ascribed to non-native elements. Neverthe-less, one eyewitness, an aristocratic Savoyard officer, claimed that the peasants who had taken shelter in the city were more public-spirited and dependable than the indigenous Viennese. He also noted that the only noble volunteers were cavaliers of French nationality (whom the expulsion order apparently exempted).[10]

THE RESTORATION OF ORDER

With Leopold's own departure at 8:00 p.m. the confusion reached its zenith. The yammering and lamenting of those left behind lasted into the wee hours of the night: "Ach, ich arme Frau! Ach, mein armes Kind! Ach, mein Mann! Ach, mein Hausrath! Ach, ach. . . ."[11] The general misery was heightened by the sight of fires rising over Schwechat and

Fischamend, thought to be caused by the foe but in reality due to careless Imperial stragglers. Fortunately, there were still a few cool-headed, courageous individuals around. The mayor and his fellow councillors held to their posts and undertook to speed completion of the defenses. Margrave Hermann and a part of the Court War Council were also present. After gaining a clearer picture of what had transpired near Petronell, they recognized that there was still a period of grace. At three in the morning of July 8 they called Burgomaster Liebenberg and two colleagues to their quarters and announced that the Emperor had transferred supreme power to Starhemberg and had named Count Kašpar Zdenko Kapliřs, an elderly Czech noble and experienced soldier, head of the Secret College of Deputies. The latter body was to be responsible for civilian affairs only. For the details of army administration the Emperor had established a second office, the so-called "hinterlassene Hofkriegsrath." Composed of the remaining portion of the war ministry and vested with full autonomy, this organ, too, was placed in Kapliřs' hands, as Hermann was supposed to follow Leopold to Linz. The Count's dual rôle had the effect of facilitating coördination. However, both bureaus were clearly subordinate to Starhemberg. The Emperor seems to have realized the necessity of avoiding conflicting competences at a moment of such peril. Kapliřs, personally, was not happy about his assignments and at first refused to stay in Vienna. Ordered back to the capital from Krems, he asked, in writing, to be relieved, objecting that he was too old and run-down physically. When Leopold rejected the request, he took hold of himself and carried out his tasks with skill and devotion. But the rigors of the siege appear to have permanently undermined his already uncertain health.[12]

The mayor can have gotten but little sleep during the night in question, for the City Council met again at 8:00 a.m. The town fathers, continuing efforts to accelerate defensive measures, ordered firewood and lumber lying outside the Neuthor brought inside the walls. House owners had to store water in their attics. Disposal of ox-hides, useful for making bags and buckets, was prohibited. Mobilization of the militia commenced. In the meantime the appearance of the Duke of Lorraine and his cavalry had put an end to public hysteria. Passing through St. Marx and along the Rennweg, the troopers paraded down the Kärntnerstraße to the sound of drums and trumpets and crossed over the Danube Arm to the Leopoldstadt and the Tabor Meadow. The Duke's first concern was to finish construction atop Vienna's bulwarks, which, up to this point, had been pursued only by the few soldiers already present and a small number of other workers. His sense of urgency must have been all the greater, for it was at this point that he received confirmation of the Grand Vezir's advance—news that he kept to himself for the immediate moment. At 3:00 p.m. the City Council convened for yet another session. Its most important decision was to draft civilian labor. Under pain of death, 500 men from two wards were to appear the next morning, shovels in hand, for service on the ramparts. Several hours later Starhemberg himself dashed in, having ridden ahead of the infantry, the bulk of which was still four days' march away. He, too, was taken aback by the condition of the fortifications. In all likelihood he conferred intently with the Duke, who slept that night within the gates in order to reassure the population.[13]

At 4:00 a.m. of the ninth the good burghers, attired in rough clothes, began to throw up parapets and plant palisades. Liebenberg himself set the example by dumping several wheel-barrels full of dirt. The clergy, secular and regular, also came and rolled up its sleeves like everyone else. The churchmen, explicitly granted permission by Sinelli, began to practice marksmanship too. Cavalry units took up position on the glacis to protect the sweating civilians from marauding Tatars. Later in the morning the City Council resumed attempts to mobilize Vienna's civilian resources, this time with Starhemberg's name to back it up. On the next day it became generally known that the Turks were really on the way. The effect was no longer panic but an increase in energy and determination. The Viennese now succeeded in completing gun emplacements on at least the *Kärntnerbastei*. Toward evening came the encouraging news that seven companies of Scherffenberg's infantry regiment, about a thousand men, the most forward unit of Leslie's command, were approaching the city. Leslie also forwarded the information that Austrian saboteurs had managed to blow up Turkish magazines at Esztergom. Likewise welcome was a report from Col. Count Donat Heissler, whose unit had chopped a party of Tatars to pieces near Lake Neusiedl.[14] The same day also saw removal of the most precious part of the Imperial library, the last of Leopold's valuables to be transferred. Already in safety, although almost captured en route by the Tatars, were the dynastic archives. The Hungarian regalia had gone into exile with the monarch and were kept in an iron chest in his private chambers. The richest portion of the Austrian state treasure had left Vienna already on the sixth and ended up eventually in Innsbruck. However, the hastiness of the government's departure made it impossible to carry away all the pretiosa in the Hofburg: silver plate, costly furnishings, and *objets d'art* remained behind.[15]

FINANCES AND STRATEGY

One rescue problem Leopold did not have to worry about was transfer of cash: his coffers were almost empty anyway. Starhemberg was informed on July 10 that the Court had left only 30,000 fl. in the city, money already allotted to construction and the field army's everyday expenses. The Count replied that one could not overlook the troops' wages for June—not yet paid—and for the period of the siege if one expected them to defend Vienna "well and vigorously." 40,000 fl. monthly would be required for this purpose. A report of deliberations was sent to the government, which in the meantime was negotiating a financial agreement with Archbishop George Szechényi of Győr and Kalocsa. The Magyar prelate finally declared he would lend 61,000 fl. deposited in Vienna, albeit at five percent interest. Since the city was cut off before this news could be forwarded, the Secret College was forced to go ahead and appropriate the funds on its own authority. The sum was obviously only a fraction of what was needed, as were the 50,000 fl.—and 1000 buckets of wine—already voluntarily turned over by the "King of the Plague," Prince Ferdinand Schwarzenberg. Much richer was the hoard of George Szeleptseny, Archbishop of Esztergom and Primate of Hungary. The total value of cash and plate, which was melted down and coined, was 493,000 fl. The circumstances under which these resources were obtained gave rise to much embitterment and complaint once the siege was over. The confiscation operation was carried out (July 20) by the controversial Kollonitsch (the only high-ranking ecclesiastic to remain behind in the beleaguered city) and was preceded by a confused tumult at Szeleptseny's house. The former cleric not only seized his absent colleague's cash and mintable assets but chalices, liturgical crosses, and bejeweled monstrances—an action that apparently reflected personal animosity. While the sacral objects were eventually restored, Szeleptseny never seems to have been compensated for his monetary losses. Thus the regular payment of the soldiers during the siege—an occurrence so unusual per se as to merit special mention by several of the chroniclers—was made possible only by robbery. Szechényi asserted that his counterpart had become wealthy by extortion in the first place and that it was only just that the loot be spent in the struggle against the heathen persecutors of the Hungarian nation.[16]

Another event of July 10 showed that the authorities were still not in full control. A decision to give the public the remaining stores of firewood, lumber, and earthenware stacked on the Danube landing stage outside the Neuthor (present Deutschmeisterplatz) resulted in a turnout of rabble that promptly proceeded to loot neighboring Rossau. Doubtlessly the municipal commandant was glad to see Scherffenberg's men tramp into the city the next morning, succeeded later in the day by half of Starhemberg's own regiment. Unfortunately, the soldiers were too exhausted by their forced marches to participate in readying the fortifications. Work was, nevertheless, progressing. Emplacements were finished on several bastions and guns were mounted on two others. The eleventh also witnessed an important council of war at the Duke's field headquarters in the Tabor Meadow. The question was how to defend Vienna with the help of the army, in particular what to do with the cavalry after posting the infantry in the city. Charles, who initially wanted to keep at least a few foot, had to decide whether to try to maintain the capital's communications with the outside world by hanging on to the Prater Island in the face of the Turkish assault. The Duke then consulted in the city with Kapliřs and Rimpler. It was finally agreed that, after having strengthened the fortress with as many men and supplies as possible, the Duke should retire beyond the Big Danube and do all that he could to prepare the place's quick relief. The idea of retaining the Island was discarded for a number of reasons. The Danube Arm was at low water, fordable almost everywhere and in some places so shallow as to permit simultaneous crossing of whole squadrons. The Austrians would have been exposed to Turkish artillery fire. Even worse, guns placed in Nussdorf could destroy the bridges (which commenced on the far side of St. Brigid's Meadow), thus cutting off outside communication and depriving the horses of access to forage, already exhausted on the Island. The swampy, channelled, and forested terrain was unsuited to cavalry operations, and there would be no infantry available after garrisoning Vienna. Finally, the rebels were advancing toward Bratislava and Lower Austria north of the river and could pin Charles down on the Island.[17]

FIERY PRELIMINARIES

Monday, July 12, while without untoward incident, was no less crucial than the preceding days. The City Council worked to improve the administrative side of civil defense. A big shipment of powder arrived from Krems. A commissioner was sent out to the Marchfeld to gather grain from the peasants (although this measure appears to have been taken too late to have any practical result). The Duke secured his line of retreat by sending five regiments across the bridges and placing the other seven at strategic spots on the island. The field artillery arrived, although the two batallions of infantry who accompanied it were so worn out that 200 wagons had to be sent to bring them in. The bulk of the foot was still delayed because the peasantry had destroyed the bridges—whether as a precautionary step against the Turks or from sheer malice is hard to say. Another critical council of war was also held. An especially delicate problem was what to do about the suburbs. Already in the spring and again during the past week dismantling had occurred, but there was opposition on the part of those whose property was affected. Now the issue was whether the army would be justified in setting fire to what remained, indeed to all of the faubourgs, in order to deprive the Turks of shelter and so hinder construction of approaches. In some instances the houses were only 200 paces away. After a thorough discussion Lorraine and Starhemberg took the responsibility of approving the work of destruction, which got underway the same night. By this time the burghers themselves were willing to cooperate and helped lay the torch to their own dwellings. "By nightfall all Vienna was illuminated by the flames of the burning suburbs, set on fire by both the Turks and our own people.

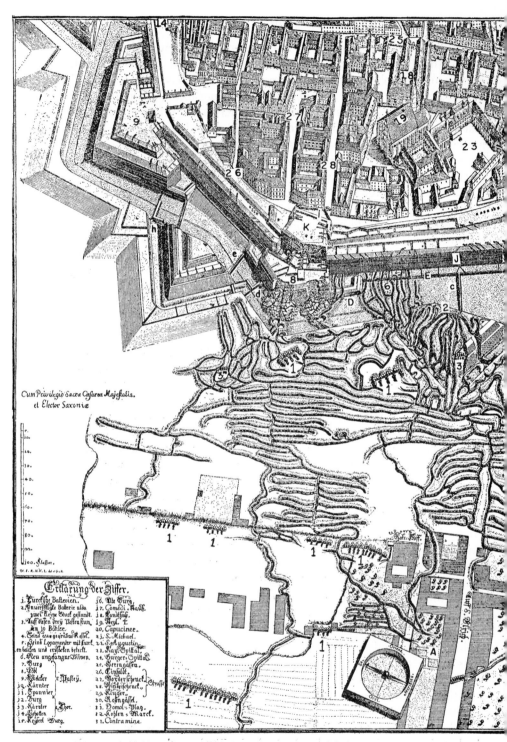

The Siege Works, as Drawn by Daniel Suttinger
(see key on following page)

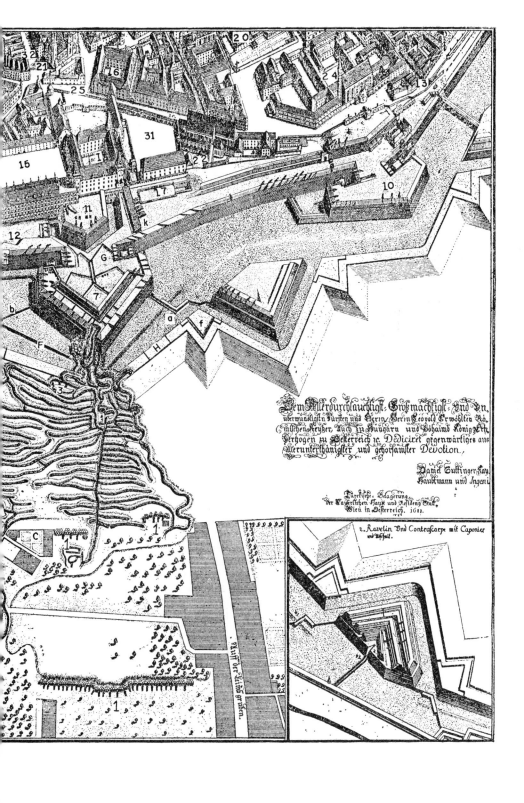

Dem Allerdurchlauchtigst, Großmächtigst, Und ðn,
übermundiglistn Fürsten und Herrn, Herrn Leopold Erwöhltn Rö.
mischenkeyßer, Auch zu Hungarn und Böhaimb König ðc.
Herzogen zu Oesterreich ꝛc. Dedicirt gegenwärtiges aus
Allerunterthänigster und gehorsamster Devotion.,

Daniel Suttinger, Kay.
Hauptmann und Ingeni

Fürstliche Belagerung
der Kayserlichen Haupt und Residenz Stat,
Wien in Oesterreich. 1683.

2. Ravelin Und Contrascarpe mit Caponier
und Abfall.

The Siege Works as Drawn by Daniel Suttinger

(preceding page)

1. Turkish batteries
2. Uncompleted battery, location of two small cannon.
3. Thirty mortars (ten in each location)
4. Excavated depressions (for bunkers)
5. Command-post bunkers
6. Newly begun mines
7. Palace (Burg) Bastion
8. Löbl Bastion
9. Mölk Bastion
10. Carinthian (Kärntner) Bastion
11. The "Spaniard" ("Cat")
12. Palace Gate (Burgtor)
13. Carinthian (Kärntner) Gate
14. Scottish (Schotten) Gate
15. Imperial Palace (Hofburg)
16. Old Palace
17. Comedy House (foundations)
18. Lower Austrian Capitol
19. Imperial (Minorite) Church
20. Capuchin Church
21. St. Michael's Church and Square (Michaelerplatz)
22. St. Augustine's Church
23. Imperial Hospital
24. Municipal Hospital
25. Herrengasse
26. Teinfaltgasse
27. Vorderschenkenstrasse (present Schenkengasse)
28. Hinterschenkenstrasse (present Bankgasse)
29. Klugerstrasse (not enumerated, near No. 19)
30. Rosengasse (not enumerated, between 26 and 27
31. Domol Square (present Josefsplatz)
32. Cauliflower Market (Kohlmarkt)
33. Countermine (not enumerated)

a. Caponière
b. Trench
c. Covered passageway
d. Caponière
e. Caponière
f. Reëntering salient
g. Reëntering salient
h. Caponière
i. Street barriers
j. Unenumerated
k. Lumber stacks

Inset:
Ravelin and counterscarp with
caponière and traverses (note triple banquettes)

Supplementary Key:
A. Trautson Garden: the Grand Vezir had a smaller tent and a bunker here.
B. Canal built by Turks to divert spring water from approaches.
C. Reikowitz Garden
D. Flanque basse
E. Faussebraye
F. Cunette
G. Demi-Gorge
H. Traverses
I. Schweizer Hof
J. Courtine
K. Cavalier

Many beautiful palaces, superb homes, fine gardens, many monasteries and churches, with a huge quantity of goods that could not be salvaged in time, were reduced to ashes."[18] Unfortunately, the sacrifice was largely in vain. Fire might ravage the interiors of buildings, but it could hardly demolish structures made of brick, mortar and stone. The Ottoman troops could later scarcely believe their eyes. They insisted that never in the history of their Empire had trenches and dug-outs been commenced inside a suburb amidst delightful arbors, gardens, and fountains. There was room for the whole army, and the soldiers could ride their horses right into the entrances of the approaches.[19]

The council of war also took up the problem of the Tatars, who by the twelfth had swept past the weak barricades in the Vienna Woods and were swarming across the Tulln Plain. Should the raiders seize the bridge at Krems, they could extend their operations to the north side of the river. Moreover, the Austrians had to retain a southern bridgehead in order to start relief operations once the field army was strengthened by the Poles and contingents from Germany. Since the Duke could not be sure that he would be able to keep even a toehold on the Prater Island, Krems was all the more important. He therefore sent off a regiment of Croats, another of dragoons, and a few squadrons of cuirassiers under Dünewald. The detachment arrived just in time to drive off a party of the enemy and to prevent removal of the bridge by the Lower Austrian Government. A secondary benefit was at least some relief for the suffering rural population.[20]

The burning of the faubourgs continued on the thirteenth. The operation, executed by infantry, was supervised and guarded by Ludwig Wilhelm of Baden with other Croats and dragoons. About 10:00 a.m. a troop of Turks appeared in St. Ulrich (Burggasse and VIIth District of today) and threw themselves murderously upon inhabitants who had not yet fled. The sight of the enemy dragging off and cutting down old men, women, and children—the Turkish war diary claims the killing of over 800 Giaours and the capture of many more—was too much for the Margrave. He ordered his men to charge directly through the flames. After killing perhaps a hundred foe, the small Imperial force had to withdraw. Meanwhile sparks from burning houses in Rossau blew over and ignited stores still lying on the landing stage. The fire, fanned by the wind, threatened to spring over the walls and attack the nearby arsenal and powder towers. Starhemberg and some of his officers ran out to supervise salvation of the lumber while Liebenberg, the City Chamberlain, and a number of citizens rushed up with pumps and water buckets to douse the palisades and simultaneously bricked up the windows and apertures of the towers. The fire was contained, but as nothing could be done about its cause, the peril of a great explosion—which would have torn the city wide open for the entry of the Turks—was still very much present as the events of the succeeding day were to show.[21]

B. The First Month
July 14: A Decisive Day

On the evening of the thirteenth the remainder of Leslie's fatigued infantry finally arrived outside town. The next morning the Duke ordered the soldiers into the city, retaining eight batallions in the Tabor Meadow in order to hold his position long enough to slip into Vienna at least a portion of an ammunition shipment expected from Linz by evening. The supplies arrived on schedule and, under the direction of the tireless von Hasslingen, were carried over the burning Danube Arm drawbridge into the arsenal. Thereupon the Duke yielded the rest of his foot and Dupigny's regiment of heavy cavalry. The garrison now consisted of seventy-two companies of infantry from ten different regiments, the cuirassiers, the City Guard and a few odds and ends, making a total of about 12,000 regulars. However, because of sickness, accidents and casualties, the units were not at full strength, and it appears that 10,000 would be a more accurate estimate. Of these, more than half would fall, be wounded, or be laid up with dysentery before the end of the siege. There is no way of telling precisely where the troops were posted upon entering the capital, but evidently a thousand were placed near or upon the Löbl and Palace Bastions, the attacked front. Another group, slightly larger, was spread over the remaining bulwarks and the rest kept in reserve, to be brought up as needed during individual assaults. Sleeping quarters were in the few casemates and in barracks erected in the moat (the unattacked part). The 4900 civilian fighters—only gradually mobilized and never this numerous at any one time—were distributed, as indicated, among the non-attacked fronts and used mainly for keeping their fellow inhabitants in line. As for command, Starhemberg was unequivocally in charge. After him came the two eldest colonels, Counts Daun and Serényi, as assistant commanders; Counts de Souches and Scherffenberg, as brigadiers; then Baron van der Beck, the Prince of Württemberg, Count Heister, and Baron Dupigny (commander of the cavalry regiment). Next in line were the Marchese di Obizzi, commanding the City Guard, and the artillery colonel, Christoph von Börner. Rimpler functioned as chief engineer. As the generals were inclined to be jealous, determining the order of seniority was a matter of greatest importance. Leopold acted wisely in addressing himself to the problem beforehand.[22]

The entry of the exhausted, partly sick and wounded infantry into Vienna meant that the Secret College of Deputies had to concern itself at once with medical care. The incapacitated men could not be allowed to lie around helplessly in the streets, for both humanitarian and practical reasons. It was decided to assign each regiment to a different monastery and to make the practicants of religion responsible for care and treatment, under supervision of the city's doctors and barber-surgeons. However, the regular clergy, with the exception of the Merciful Brothers (professional nurses), proved somewhat remiss in fulfilling its duties. The churchmen were unwilling to take the soldiers into their rooms, and let them lie on the bare ground and the floors of passageways until the Deputies could supply crude straw matresses. The College eventually found it necessary to reprimand a number of the convents. The local apothecaries provided medicines but, like other merchants, soon began to demand exorbitant prices for their wares.[23]

Hardly had the people of Vienna begun to breathe easier because of the infantry's arrival than they were overcome with a new terror. Early in the afternoon another fire broke out, this time in a barnyard and shed at the rear of the Schottenkloster. In a short time the whole monastery was affected, and the blaze began to spread to the wooden eves of the neighboring house and to shutters on the walls of the powder-packed Imperial arsenal on the other side. Liebenberg, both city chamberlains, Serényi, and Captain Guidobald Starhemberg (cousin of the commandant and later a famed associate of Eugene of Savoy) ran to the scene with a recently organized fire brigade and a number of militia. The panic was all the greater because nobody could find the man who kept the keys to the arsenal gate, which therefore had to be smashed open. The Turks, moreover, seemed to be shooting deliberately toward the conflagration, endangering the lives of those who were trying to fight it. Starhemberg, nevertheless, plunged into the arsenal, drenched the immediately threatened barrels with water and, dagger in hand, forced the conscripted firemen to brick up the windows. Outside, Liebenberg supervised dismantlement of a burning stair case. In the meantime, the wind shifted, drawing the flames over to the Auersperg, Traun and Pálffy palaces. Although the embers were not extinguished for several days, the situation was under control and the city saved from what would most certainly have been complete catastrophe.[24]

The fire's origin could not be pinpointed. Proximity to the still smouldering suburbs suggested the possibility of flying sparks. Or a stableboy may have been careless with combustibles. The overwrought Viennese accepted neither explanation. Laying the blame at the feet of a supposed fifth column sent in by Thököly, they vented their rage on whatever suspicious-looking characters they could get hold of. A local prankster, known as "Baron Zwifl," had shot into the flames with his pistol, whereupon he was seized by the mob and struck dead. The body was dragged to St. Peter's Cemetery and skinned. A teenage male transvestite, also thought to be a saboteur, was torn to pieces. Persons in Magyar or Croatian garb or speaking a foreign tongue were subjected to threats and insults. A minor Imperial official who had the misfortune to be found with some fireworks in his wagon barely escaped with his life. The incidents, however brutal, were not entirely irrational. Incendiarism was a common tool of warfare at the time. The authorities themselves did not discount it, for they immediately increased security measures. The violence is also of interest because it reveals the continuing instability of the populace at large. The strict-minded Starhemberg and the city officials had to exert themselves considerably to regain control. It was also decided on the same day to order house owners to remove their shingle roofs, and on the next to shift some of the powder to the deep cellars of monasteries and private houses.[25]

Lorraine was apparently still near the city at the time of the fire, for he withdrew the cavalry from the island only during the night. He left with little confidence in Vienna's ability to hold out. The city's defenses were after all still incomplete. Indeed, one reason why he finally gave up the very last of his infantry was "les ouvrages à faire dans la place." While the palisading appears to have been finished, it was only due to an extraordinary, last-minute spurt of energy that the Turks could be met with artillery resistance as they began to dig their trenches. "On this day, we would not have shown the slightest readiness on the bastions—there not being over ten pieces up there, not a single gabion, nor battery, nor traverse—but for the order of His Excellency, General von Starhemberg. Because of his great efforts, which were universally admired, everything was directed most rapidly into the defense works, and the enemy was met with an equal cannonade."[26] Another source states that the mounting of guns and cutting of embrasures was concluded only on the following day, and even then some emplacements and carriages were lacking. The missing gabions were first replaced with earth-filled barrels, but as the Turks began to pick off these objects, which burst with a shrapnel-like effect, they were replaced with sand bags. Börner, a Mecklenburg nobleman, proved highly competent in mastering the problems of his craft.[27] Although the chroniclers do not mention him specifically, one may be fairly sure that Rimpler, too, was very busy. Now that he could tell for sure where the Turks were going to attack, he could commence work on those traverses and caponières, which, to his own way of thinking, should have been present everywhere in the fortress even during peacetime.

THE TURKISH WORKS

While the defenders labored desperately to perfect various devices for strengthening Vienna's bulwarks, the Turks were starting to erect their camp. It stretched out in the form of a great crescent, commencing near St. Marx opposite the lower tip of the Prater Island and continuing through Simmering, the Laa Forest, Inzersdorf (just below the Wiener Berg with its famous landmark, the Spinnerin am Kreuz), Schönbrunn,

Hundsturm, Gumpendorf, Penzing, Breitensee, Hernals, and Währing down to the Danube Arm at Oberdöbling. The line ran roughly along the present-day Gürtel and so encompassed today's X, XI, XII, XV, XVI, XVII, XVIII and XIXth Districts. It represented a complete encirclement, apart from certain gaps in the clusters of irregularly-pitched tents, of the city on its landward side. Extending the net to the water side required only the occupation of the Island. The sight was simultaneously dreadful and beautiful. "It is impossible to conceive what a breadth of terrain they occupied [actually about fifteen miles]. In the middle of their camp [in the meadow "auf der Schmelz"] arose the pavillion of the Grand Vezir, which looked like a magnificent palace surrounded by several country-houses, the tents being of different colors, all of which made for a very agreeable diversity."[28]

In the afternoon the Grand Vezir left his luxurious quarters and rode into St. Ulrich (VIIth District). There he dismounted in order to regulate details concerning the approaches and artillery. The main question was sector assignments. He himself took the center, facing the Palace Ravelin, along with the Janissary Ağa, the *Kulkâhyaşı* (Janissary first deputy commander), the *Beylerbeyi* of Rumelia, with his (unhorsed) portal and provincial forces (including *topraklı*) and twenty ortas. Five culverins (eight to twenty-four pounders) and twenty smaller field guns were also assigned posts here. The right, pointing toward the *Burgbastei*, was given to the *Beylerbeyi* of Diyabekir and the *Beylerbeyi* of Aleppo and their men, supplemented by the *Beylerbeyi* of Anatolia with artillery and the *Zagarcibaşı* (fourth highest Janissary staff officer), with twenty ortas, five culverins, and twenty smaller pieces. The left, *vis-à-vis* the *Löblbastei*, fell to the troops of the *Beylerbeyi* of Jenö (Timişoara) and the *Beylerbeyi* of Sivas. They were reinforced by the *Samsuncubaşı* (next highest Janissary general), twenty ortas, 500 technical troops, and the same number of artillery. (The *Zagarcibaşı* and the *Samsuncubşı* each had an orta of his own.) The third sector was buttressed a week later by units from the province of Karaman.[29] The *sipâhî* and *silâhdar*, mounted *topraklı, serhadd,* and *yerli kulu* remained in the camp. While it is not possible to say exactly how large the actual assault force was, it probably represented a minority, however substantial (perhaps 15–20,000), of the less than 90,000 Turkish combatants estimated to have been present at Vienna.[30] The bulk of the troops were needed to seal off the rest of the fortress, to act as reserves, to guard the rear, and to carry out missions in the countryside together with the Tatars. The reluctant Moldavians and Wallachians were stationed the next day off to the left of Oberdöbling.

Kara Mustafa also took the occasion of his visit in St. Ulrich to send an ultimatum into the besieged city. In keeping with Muhammadan tradition, the Giaours were asked either to convert to Islam, render tribute (in

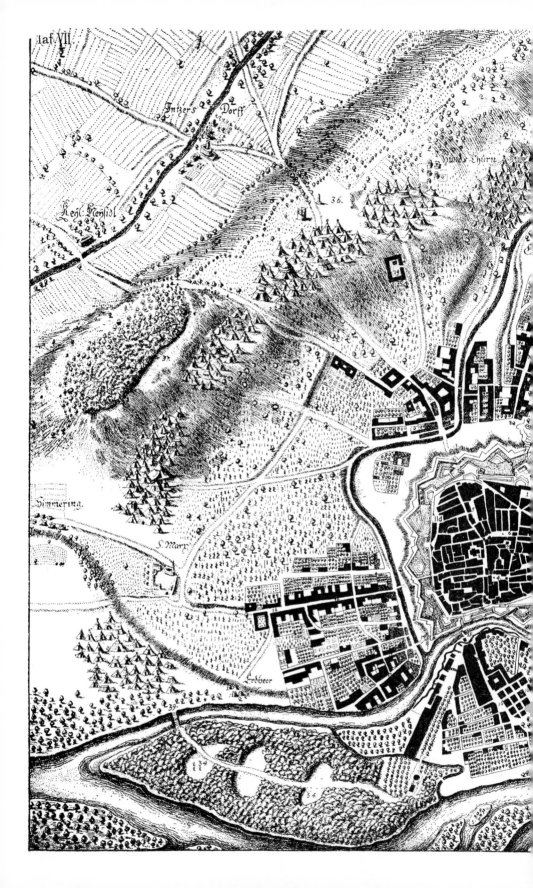

Taf. VII.

Intzers Dorff

Hunds Thurn

Kehl: Kohsidl

36.

Simmering.

S. Marx

Erdbeer

39

34

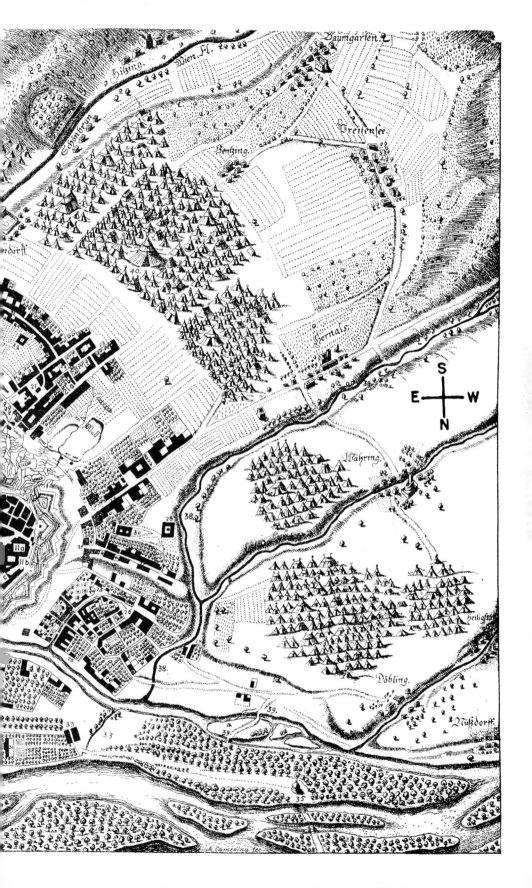

The Turkish Encampment During the Siege
(after Daniel Suttinger)
(*preceding page*)

1. The Imperial Palace (Hofburg)
2. St. Stephen's Cathedral
3. Square "am Hof"
4. Highmarket (Hoher Markt)
5. Newmarket (Neuer Markt)
6. The Graben (limit of original Roman *castrum*)
7. St. Peter's Church
8. "Stock im Eisen" (locksmiths' monument)
9. Palace Gate (Burgtor)
10. Carinthian Gate (Kärntnertor)
11. Scottish Gate (Schottentor)
    11a. Scots' Monastery (Schottenkloster)
    11b. Upper Arsenal (Oberes Zeughaus) ; Municipal Arsenal across street to left
    11c. "New" Arsenal ("Neues" Zeughaus) ; moat water to this point, docking facilities
    11d. Seilerstätte Arsenal (water to here but no ingress from Danube Arm).
12. Stuben Gate
13. Newgate (Neutor)
14. Red Tower Gate (Rothenturmtor)
15. Drawbridge over the Danube Arm (destroyed)
16. Leopoldstadt
17. Bei den Weissgerbern
18. Landstrassen
19. Auf der Wien
20. Laimgruben
21. St. Ulrich
22. Neubau
23. Neustift (*not* Wienerwald village)
24. Alsergassen
25. Währingergassen
26. Rossau
27. Spiergebiegel (now location of Liechtenstein Palace)
28. Hospital
29. Catholic Cemetery
30. Protestant Cemetery
31. Neue Favorita Palace ("Favorita auf der Wieden")
32. Zoological Garden
33. Tabor
34. Prater (Hunting Preserve)
35. St. Brigid's Meadow (Brigittenau)
36. Wienerberg and "Spinnerin am Kreuz"
37. Laa Forest (Laaerhölzl)
38. Alserbach
39. Turkish Bridges
40. Grand Vezir's Pavillion

Note: Heiligenstadt and Nussdorf are incorrectly located.

return for security of life and property), or leave matters to the sword.[31] Starhemberg did not deign to reply. Thereupon the Grand Vezir ordered cannon wheeled into position and commencement of firing. As the batteries, especially of heavier guns, could not be mounted instantaneously, it is likely that the first day's bombardment came only from a few light regimental pieces.[32] The Turkish army's artillery park, consisting of only nineteen culverins and 120 of the smaller guns, was of course inadequate, both in number and in caliber, for sustaining an operation of such magnitude. There appear to have been no genuine siege cannon at all.[33]

At the same time the Turks also began hacking out their approaches and parallels and building their dug-outs—tasks pursued uninterruptedly throughout the night. The trenches of the center sprang from the garden of the old Trautson Palace (not the present structure of the same name) in the block formed by today's Lerchenfelderstrasse, Neustiftgasse, Myrtengasse, and Neubaugasse. Here too a fancy bunker was erected for Kara Mustafa. The works of the right wing started just to the left of Laimgruben (Mariahilferstrasse) in the area behind the present Messepalast. Up on the hill behind the latter, in the so-called "Croatendörfl" (vicinity of the Renaissance Theater), construction of a massed battery was completed within twenty-four hours. The left flank commenced above the Mala Spina House or "rother Hof," several blocks to the rear of the modern Palais Auersperg. Each sector had at least two approaches, and all were linked farther up on the glacis by the same parallels. The trenches were usually about six feet wide and deep enough so that a man could stand comfortably, protected from musket fire. Later, as fire from Vienna became more intense, they were covered for long stretches with boards, beams, sandbags and earth which provided protection against hand grenades and shells. Dug-outs were distributed at suitable forward intervals for the commanders. The soldiers serving in what was a well-designed siege system could feel fairly secure on all sides. Toward the city there were strong bulwarks; on their sides the Janissaries manned deeply excavated vertical lines; and in their rear (although lacking a circumvallation) was the camp with the cavalry. The construction, despite stony ground in at least a few places, progressed rapidly. Begun at about 300 paces from the covered way, the trenches had only sixty to seventy more to go by the evening of the fifteenth.[34]

The work, however, did not progress without numerous casualties. It was at this time that Kielmannsegg's gamekeepers, posted upon the Burg Bastion, proved their worth:

> Many people observed how the Baron himself aimed his cocked gun from a distance of 450 paces at a Turk whose head was covered with a stately turban. This fellow, who, as we later discovered, was an engineer, had jumped out of the trenches onto the glacis, where he was parading back and forth, holding a cane in one hand and insolently

twisting his mustache with the other. At the crack of the Baron's rifle he fell dead as did another who sprang out to help him. The remaining Turks were forced to leave the two bodies lying until the deep of the night.[35]

The other *Jäger* demonstrated a marksmanship no less astounding than their chief's, if one may believe the chronicler. The Turks also began to suffer casualties from sorties. The first was made during the night of July 15–16. As the initial impression of the Austrian soldiers concerning the vigor and numbers of the enemy was not yet effaced, a number of the men in the party held back. However, the few who followed the officers and volunteers chased the Turks out of their forward trenches and retired without loss. The action served at least to restore the garrison's self-confidence. The only misfortune of the day was minor: Starhemberg was wounded by flying brick splinters and had to take to bed for a few days. Kapliř assumed command temporarily.[36]

In the meantime the Duke, camped on the far side on the Danube, received news of the impending arrival of another powder shipment and decided to re-establish communication with the city. He therefore ordered rebuilding of the already dismantled, somewhat smaller first and second spans of the four unit system. (There were at that time three islets between the Prater Island and the opposite shore.) However, Kara Mustafa had already made up his mind to cut off Vienna completely, and so on the morning of the sixteenth a large force of Turks, especially cavalry, led by the *Beylerbeyi* of Adana and the *Sancakbeyi* of Nicopolis, Hamîd, Saruhan, and the *Serçeşme* (c-in-c) of the *Seymen,* charged across the Danube Arm at both the upper and lower ends of the Island. They were supported by Egyptians, the *Sancakbeyi* of Köstendil, and 200 sappers, who were ordered to build trenches facing the city. The Ottomans encountered three dragoon regiments, led by Schultz (who had arrived on the eleventh). The outnumbered Austrians and Lubomirski's Poles were driven to the far (northeastern) side of the island and onto the first bridge where they blasted the Turks with grape at point-blank. The Muslims attacked ferociously but were stopped with the loss of several flags and a number of higher officers. The Austrians, who could not help admiring their foes' courage, burned the two "little bridges" behind them. After the battle was over, the Turks turned their attention to the Leopoldstadt, which was soon a mass of flames. The city historian writes, rather reproachfully: "Many hundred thousands of guldens worth of furniture, other effects, wood, hay and straw of the burghers and inhabitants—who had transferred little or nothing into the city because they had felt assured that the island would be held—burnt up."[37] The Emperor, whose other country villas were already laid waste, suffered as well, for the Augarten (Alte Favorita) likewise fell into the hands of the Ottomans. (The Grand Vezir came to view it the next day and was greatly impressed by its birds and fruit trees.) The Turks immediately rushed in reinforcements, Bosnians opposite Vienna, a big contingent under the *Beylerbeyi* of Damascus in St. Brigid's Meadow, and thirty small field guns. The Moldavians and Wallachians threw up bridges across the Danube Arm, not only for communication but to prevent the descent of boats. The Viennese, who had disassembled their own drawbridge over the Arm and had blocked up the Rothenturm Gate, were now locked in tightly, and it proved difficult for the Duke to get messages back and forth.[38]

Austrian Countermeasures

By the sixteenth the city's situation was no longer a matter for jesting either literally or figuratively. Workers began to knock down Imperial *Theatralingenieur* Ludovico Burnacini's grandiose, 5000-seat, Baroque "Comedy House," in which a few years previously Leopold had permitted the Viennese public to witness, gratis, performances of Cesti's elaborately staged opera, "Il Pomo d'Oro." Made of wood and located right on the Burg Courtine, the building would have been a major fire hazard. Its timbers were utilized for various military purposes. Another humorless event was the erection of three gallows, a clear hint of the fate Starhemberg reserved for the traitorous and careless. Equally ominous was the excavation of a large hole near the Freyung for the cadavers of fallen soldiers. The number of dead was bound to increase, especially with continuance of sallies (another successful, raid being made the same night). In the Turkish camp, too, the stench of decomposing flesh was beginning to spread. Enraged over the murder of a Turk by a captive Christian laborer, the Grand Vezir ordered the slaughter of 150 prisoners. On the two succeeding days over a thousand more were beheaded. It was on the sixteenth also that the treacherous massacre of Perchtoldsdorf took place.[39]

Presumably, not all of the Muslims' captives were put to the sword. Many hands were needed for cutting the approaches, a task being executed with great efficiency and dispatch. So encouraged was the Grand Vezir with the progress of construction that he entered the trenches himself on the eighteenth, declaring that he would remain there (and in his bunker) until, with Allah's help, the city was taken. As his troops and the chained, cane-prodded slaves dug their way closer to the counterscarp, they began to raise the level of their works, which permitted them to fire down into the covered way, forcing the Austrians to huddle closely behind the parapet. While this technique, unknown in conflicts between Christian princes, prevented the besiegers from making sallies, it did assure success in the effort to lodge troops in the two glacis salients. Once they were ensconced in the latter positions, the Turks could start mining operations under the counterscarp, which they had to capture before they could cross the moat and attack the ravelin, bastions, and curtain-wall. The Ottoman forces especially pressed their assault on the two lateral ends of the chosen terrain in order to direct a barrage into the rear of the covered way. The Austrians countered these efforts by carving out trenches on the broad inner tips of the latter, by strengthening the most threatened points with palisades, and by erecting traverses. Posts, armed with sharp sickles, and other types of personnel obstacles—presumably caltrops and nail-studded boards—were set up out in front. The former device proved to be so effective that the Turks—allegedly—protested that its use contravened accepted standards of military practice.[40]

Starhemberg, foreseeing that he would be forced to yield the counterscarp sooner or later, also commenced erection of secondary defences in the ditch: cunette, caponières, faussebraye, and a hard-to-place "espèce de 3me deffence à droit et à gauche du Lebel." At the same time he started the first of the previously described retrenchments atop the ravelin.[41] For all these undertakings it was of course necessary to continue drawing upon civilian levies.[42] Meanwhile, the defense of the covered way was being conducted with great stubbornness. Although the Austrians were successful in holding out there longer than was usual, "cela n'est point arrivé sans qu'il nous en aye coûté fort cher, car nous y avons perdu beaucoup d'officiers de distinction et grand nombre de soldats."[43] On July 19, for example, Guido von Starhemberg undertook another sortie into the Turkish approaches. Since the enemy trenches were deep and were faced by high piles of loose dirt, it was difficult for the men to get out again. Casualties were heavy, most of the hundred men involved being lost. It was decided to desist, at least temporarily, from such actions, and the further advance of the foe was opposed primarily with artillery. The Turks replied with musketry and hand grenades. The latter weapon became increasingly important for both sides as time passed. The Austrians, who expended almost their entire store of 80,000 grenades by the end of the siege, were forced to manufacture an ersatz type of infantry missile. Kielmannsegg, who also appears to have been a kind of technical handiman, produced and demonstrated a baked plaster grenade although there is no evidence of its having been manufactured in quantity. The Baron also supervised the making of gunpowder, case shot, and *cheveaux de frise*. The grenadiers themselves were led by an Englishman, of whom Viennese records know nothing save the name: Edy Lacy (sic).[44]

THE EMBATTLED RAVELIN

By July 23 the Turks had pushed ahead their trenches sufficiently for the *lağuncı* to explode their first two mines. The heavy losses which the assault troops had already borne, especially because of mortar-fired shrapnel, appear to have resulted in increased reliance upon subterranean means of attack. Although the Ottomans may not have killed as many Giaours as they seem to have thought they did, they were successful in establishing themselves in the craters that now interrupted the line of the counterscarp. Two days later a somewhat more powerful mine was set off in the sector facing the Löbl Bastion. It failed, however, to produce the desired effect, for it blew up only a few Austrians and no more than a small portion of the palisading. The *serdengeçti,* who stormed out immediately after the blast, fell into an Austrian trap when they advanced too far and were met with a sudden hail of crossfire. Only during the night were the Turks able to fortify the breach. The Austrian losses, while not numerous, were serious, for Guido von Starhemberg was seriously hurt and Rimpler suffered mortal wounds. The bitterness with which the defenders were now fighting was revealed when they began impaling their fallen enemies' severed heads in full view of the Turkish trenches. The Muslims on the other hand were commencing to show signs of discouragement, which Kara Mustafa apparently sought to counter by personally animating the commanders of individual combat units.[45]

Conditions in the enemy camp were not unknown to Starhemberg and his men and most likely served to inspire them even more than the relative success of their own resistance. Kunitz managed to smuggle two messages into the fortress, one on the 22nd and another on the 25th, by means of his valet, Jakob Heider. Unfortunately, the daring courier was caught on his way back the second time. Although he quick-wittedly threw away Starhemberg's reply—the correspondence was written *en clair* since Kunitz possessed no cipher—, he was locked up as a suspicious character, and the besieged were temporarily deprived of a valuable source of intelligence. The Turks also caught another estafette who had reached the city by swimming the Danube (August 7) and who was returning to the Duke of Lorraine. Since the letter he carried was coded, the Turks could not grasp its contents. On the 26th they shot it back into Vienna by means of an arrow, appending a new surrender demand and the statement that they knew that the city was in a bad state anyway. The terrified captive had provided false information, which the Grand Vezir also seized upon to enhearten his own fighting men. Starhemberg again granted no reply apart from a fourneau (small mine), the effect of which was limited.[46]

During the two succeeding days the Turks attempted to perfect their works in the face of an incessant cartouche, mortar, musket, and hand grenade barrage. The good morale of the garrison was shaken only on the 29th when the enemy exploded two mines simultaneously. The initial confusion was considerable, for not only were numerous officers and soldiers interred or blown to pieces, but a long section of palisading was overturned, the parapet behind it wrecked, and a huge hole, reaching to the middle of the moat, gouged. A number of high officers ran to the scene, and after some initial hesitation it was decided to occupy and fortify the gap (with wool-bags and fascines) to prevent the foe from penetrating into the moat. Two hundred men jumped over the neighboring traverse and maintained themselves, initially without cover, only six feet from the enemy trenches. Inexplicably, the Turks failed to launch an assault, limiting their efforts to a hot musket and grenade barrage. Thus the Austrians were able to throw up breastworks within two hours and, later, to fill the craters. By now the opposing sides were in such close proximity that more direct weapons such as rocks and halberds were being used. Upon occasion the soldiers found themselves engaged in individual tugs-of-war and hair-pulling in the spaces between the palisades. By this time moreover, the strain of the engagement was beginning to tell seriously on the Turks. The Grand Vezir, who bravely stationed himself even farther forward in the trenches, found it necessary, to replace his heavy casualties by calling for new *serdengeçti* from among the élite *sipâhî* and *silâhdar*. He also began rebuking and/or deposing commanding officers whom he considered negligent. Common soldiers who had behaved meritoriously were given gold pieces.[47]

On July 30th another Turkish mine ripped off the tip of the covered way *vis-à-vis* the Palace Bastion, and after a grueling, see-saw fight, the Austrians found the position too costly to hold. The next day Starhemberg was also compelled to remove his artillery from the exposed and hence, badly shot-up cavalier of the Löbl Bastion. He placed the guns under cover in the interior of the structure and created a make-shift casemate by piercing its walls from place to place. Simultaneously, he partly dismantled the bastion's parapet and thereby improved the firing field of the cavalier, which later rendered good service. During the first several days of August, mining and countermining continued as the Austrians stubbornly held on to the thoroughly churned-up counterscarp. In the meantime, however, the Turks had begun the construction of stair-equipped shafts, by which they could descend safely into the moat. On August 3 they unleashed a particularly vigorous attack and were able to entrench themselves at the edge of the ditch facing the ravelin. On the next day the Austrians had to yield the adjacent portion of the counterscarp. On the fifth they suffered yet a further reverse. Encouraged unduly, it seems by several modest successes, a team of more-or-less amateur miners that Starhemberg had thrown together from various human resources present in the city became careless and inadvertently blew up an Austrian-held sector. Then, on the sixth, the Turks undertook to push their lines across the moat to the ravelin. The defenders succeeded in frustrating the foe temporarily after a bloody, shifting engagement, which Starhemberg led personally with a hundred picked men from his own regiment. However, Count Leslie (brother of the infantry general) and another staff officer fell, thereby adding to the already high losses of command personnel. Throughout its whole history the tradition of officers serving in the most advanced positions had both advantages and disadvantages for the Imperial Army.[48]

On August 7 the besiegers exploded a mine under the moat, the purpose of which was to raise a mound of earth beside the counterscarp. This would enable the *topçu* to direct their pieces at the exits of the caponières, whose crossfire in the ravelin moat was so damaging. Such an emplacement would also help to cover the *lağuncı* who were pushing a tunnel to the tip of the ravelin. When a mine inside the gallery was set off two days later, it tore off fourteen ells of wallwork. The Austrians dashed into the breach and fought off the enemy in the open. The dead piled up six high in one place, yet the rear ranks did not fail to come forward and deliver their volleys. The gap was finally sealed, and for a time at least the Turks were kept off the ravelin. The same day, however, the attackers also detonated a huge charge under the covered way facing the *Burgbastei* and thereby managed to achieve a third toehold in the ditch, a second having been gained on the left flank already on the night of August 6–7. During the two succeeding days the Austrians sought to disturb the enemy works with sorties, but the results were meager.

Then, on the twelfth, the greatest calamity to date occurred. Despite forewarning from counterminers and seemingly adequate precautions, the defenders were thrown badly off balance by the simultaneous explosion of two mines, so powerful as to rock not only the ravelin but to cause the whole city to tremble. The dirt excavated by the blast provided a ramp across the moat broad enough for fifty charging men. The ravelin's retrenchment was also filled and its tip completely shattered. Hardly had the dust settled, when eight horsetails could be seen advancing. The Imperials quickly threw up *chevaux de frise,* then palisades, wool, and sandbags. After a two-hour carnage in which every possible weapon was employed, the Turks were halted. While the latter had lost at least several hundred men and could not maintain their most forward position on the ravelin, they had indeed succeeded in attaching themselves to it. The garrison, which by this time had suffered over 1200 casualties, was in serious trouble, as was evident from a coded message of Kapliř's smuggled out to Leopold. Nevertheless, Starhemberg, by now bed-ridden with dysentery, remained determined to hold the ravelin. He ordered construction of a second retrenchment parallel to the first while at the same time giving up the inner angle of the counterscarp to the right. With these actions the first month as well as the first stage of the siege of Vienna were concluded. The next task of the Ottoman army would be to drive the Austrians off the ravelin, seize the moat behind it and plant mines under the bastions and curtain wall, the city's last major bulwark.[49]

C. Starhemberg's Vienna

MARTIAL LAW

The transformation that the Austrian capital underwent in the period between the hysteria and confusion of early July and the stern determination of mid-August is, to say the least, striking. The sources imply that it was due largely to the vigorous leadership and stringent discipline of Starhemberg. Recorded incidents give a vivid picture of how the city commandant dealt with persons whose actions he regarded as detrimental to security.

The first indication of his standpoint came already on July 23 when the town criers announced that henceforward climbing over the palisades would be considered a capital crime. The decree seems to have been evoked by the establishment of an impromptu market, just outside the *Schottentor,* in which Viennese women were trading the Turks bread for fresh vegetables. The next manifestation of military severity was the execution (July 28) of a mutinous cavalryman, whose corpse was left hanging all day. The militia, which came increasingly to exercise Starhemberg's patience, was sharply rebuked on July 30. The public drummers were sent out to proclaim that in the future participants in unauthorized sorties, dangerous *per se* and of little profit to the beleaguered town, would meet the firing squad. Starhemberg obviously was not amused by the previous day's cattle-rustling foray. During August at least three more soldiers were gunned or beheaded. Two Viennese boys, one fifteen, the other supposedly only ten, were convicted of having spied for the enemy and sent to the block. On other occasions the commander's sense of justice was a trifle more lenient, yet still distinctly macabre. In one case two military malefactors were ordered to toss a coin for the privilege of being shot. In a second instance a lieutenant, thought to have been remiss in his duty, was permitted to choose between the rope and saving his honor with a sally into the enemy trenches. The officer took the latter option and fell, along with most of his twenty-odd companions. It might be argued that this was an expensive way of setting an example, all the more so because the numbers of the garrison had been sharply reduced by the date in question (September 2). However, as already shown, the whole framework of seventeenth-century warfare made such measures appear indispensable. As for the burgher-soldiers, there is no record that punishments were actually inflicted: perhaps the commandant feared that the municipal authorities might take umbrage. Nevertheless, it proved necessary to keep issuing (through the City Council) threats of the death penalty for various delinquencies.[50]

CIVIL ADMINISTRATION

Starhemberg's discrete use of established channels in matters not pertaining directly to the regular troops is not only important in indicating the quality of his leadership; but it also shows that he was *dependent* upon the support of civilian officials, who served with devotion and competence. The foremost non-military body, the intermediary between the commandant and the City Council, was the Secret College of Deputies. Initially, its task was to issue ordinances relating to food and munitions and to conduct correspondence outside the besieged city. After August 4 it directed its efforts exclusively to internal affairs. The deputies approved Bishop Kollonitsch's seizure of the Hungarian archepiscopal treasury. They also helped the prelate in efforts to improve medical facilities. They levied a tax in kind upon wine—of which there was no lack in Vienna—and published a series of hospital regulations. The College likewise legalized dragooning of replacements for both the professional units and the militia. It drafted refugees for labor service, and kept order among the soldiery quartered in civilian housing.[51]

The chief executive instrument was, of course, the local magistracy and the burgomaster. It is a pity that not much is known about the life of Andreas von Liebenberg, for he too, in a modest way, was a hero of the siege. Unlike Starhemberg, his body was unequal to his will. Afflicted with dropsy, he was bed-ridden by August 7. Even before that time, in deference to his debility, council meetings took place at his house in the square "am Hof."[52] After contracting dysentery he was finished. His death on the night of September 9–10 did not permit him to witness the city's salvation:

> Today, after a five-week illness, Lord Mayor von Liebenberg, strengthened by the Holy Sacraments, passed away peacefully to his heavenly reward. His death was greatly regretted. . . . Not only did he exert himself most faithfully and laudably during the horrible contagion of 1679 when he was city judge, but he also industriously and successfully presided over the common welfare and other municipal matters. He likewise served in all civic offices before becoming burgomaster and was well-informed in everything. Almighty God grant his soul eternal bliss![53]

The other members of the Internal City Council demonstrated a behavior scarcely less exemplary. A particularly deserving figure was the First Chamberlain, Daniel Fokhy, who handled the difficult job of fire-fighting. Also outstanding was one of the city's professional civil servants, the Syndic Dr. Nicholas Hocke, an energetic and capable Saxon, who not only managed to fulfill manifold secretarial duties but kept a diary, which is a prime source for the history of the siege. Other councilmen cared for such problems as price-control and the distribution of munitions and bread. Their collective courage is illustrated by the fact that seven of them (forty three percent), exhausted by what they had gone through, died before the end of the year.[54]

Representatives of other municipal bodies likewise distinguished themselves, as, e.g., Simon Schuester, the City Judge and Starhemberg's successor. The members of the External City Council served in a number of ways, many as commanders of the admittedly rather ineffective militia. An especially important salaried official was Georg Altschaffer, the Subchamberlain, whose account book is a lively record of the city administration's labors. This man, it seems, supervised the carpenters, brick and stone masons, day laborers; published decrees; had wooden roofs torn down; secured refuse removal (as far as possible); organized the conveyance of shot from the arsenals; closed the city gates; extended chain barriers across streets; transferred building materials to the bastions; supplied wood for palisades and *chevaux de frise* (by breaking up winepresses); and, finally, despite shortage of space, found places for desperately-needed mass graves. Seven other External Councillors acted as Good Samaritans by collecting free-will offerings for the benefit of a large number of paupers who were lying sick and unattended in the streets. The objects of this charity nevertheless proved to be rather recalcitrant. When a money-lender named Zeislmayr made it his job to pick them up for delivery to the hospitals, they resisted, yielding only to force. To be sure, their opposition is understandable. Despite Kollonitsch and his two commissioners, who did most of the actual administrative work, the emergency facilities were simply inadequate for the numbers of patients involved. The poor performance of most of the religious orders was thus a matter of serious consequence.[55]

Problems and a Myth

The cause of hospital overcrowding was an epidemic of amoebic dysentery, which, in the last analysis, broke out simply because people were packed hermetically into the narrow circumference of Vienna's walls. The refugees had difficulty in obeying the city's sanitary regulations—i.e., in following habits to which they were unaccustomed. (The trying conditions of life were also detrimental to health.) Then came the troops, for whom no proper hygenic arrangements had been made. Which of the two groups brought in the disease is not clear. In any event there was no mass contagion at the start, and the incidence of illness began to increase only toward the end of July. In view of the jammed housing it is only a wonder that it did not happen sooner. Meticulous cleanliness, particularly removal of *all* offal and excrement, would have been necessary. As previously noted, even the Viennese had little understanding of the 1679 ordinance that forbade indiscriminate littering of garbage and animal remains. While formerly at least some refuse could be carried outside the town and dumped, it now had to be buried in pits (of which there were few). Filth thus piled up. Passers-by could not avoid treading on the faeces of the street derelicts and tracking infectious material into the houses. Insects, flies especially, spread the bacilli even further, the process being favored by the great summer heat.[56]

The report of the municipal commission that studied the matter is of interest as it reveals the not-entirely-uninformed state of contemporary scientific knowledge:

> The following are the causes of the current epidemic: 1.) improperly baked, black army bread; 2.) salted foods, such as salted and smoked meat, to which people are not inured, and the already prohibited herring which is enjoyed especially by the poor, who then drink water or sour wine, wherefrom result the fermentation and spoiling of the viscera; 3.) unaged, newly brewed beer, which is drunk just as soon as it has cooled off; 4.) the great uncleanliness. . . . [one aspect of which is the derelicts] whose blood seeps out, giving off a stench that is absorbed by those who walk by, [not to mention] the soldiers and market people who throw the blood of slaughtered cattle into the gutters, causing a great odor and illnesses; lastly, the great fear, worry and depression of the people, who are not used to being shut in.[57]

Obviously, both high and low were susceptible. Starhemberg himself was laid up for some time. However, dysentery has a relatively low mortality rate—one death for every eight cases—, and so no credence can be given to reports of its having carried off thousands of Viennese at this time.[58] The main danger of the disease was physical incapacitation of sorely-needed soldiers.

The work of the medical doctors represented the only cultural or scientific activity going on in Vienna aside from divine services, which recommenced after the initial confusion. Manufacturing and commerce, lamed in the beginning, also revived within a short time. Apparently most artisans remained behind, which was fortunate as the services of many, such as carpenters, masons, and cobblers (who made new shoes for the footworn infantry), were essential. The most important tradesmen were the food retailers: bakers, butchers, and various kinds of specialized grocers. Their poor performance as militiamen might possibly be explained by the fact that they had to do double duty. However, even in their regular vocations they did not evince much public spirit. Although it is apparent that scarcity of a commodity will inevitably bring about rising prices, the extent of the merchants' gouging exceeded the patience of the authorities. The bakers seem to have been the most culpable, and they adulterated their product as well. The City Council seemingly had little success in its endeavor to control inflation. In desperation it instructed the clergy to condemn from the pulpit the "accursed usury."[59]

The same issue raises the question of the sufficiency of food supplies in the surrounded city. The sources at no time make mention of starvation, and one may safely infer that the only serious problem was a shortage of perishables. The growing lack of meat is well reflected in the various diaries of the siege. As the store of beef and fowl dwindled, some people turned to horses and mules. Another alternative, at first something of a joke but later much in demand, was cats:[60]

> Whoever delighted in French delicacies could purchase, for one gulden apiece, from the women sitting around in the High Market and St. Peter's Plaza so-called "roof rabbits." Interlarded with smoked bacon, broiled and devoured along with a bottle of French muscatel, they tasted quite good. The result was that this kind of wild game was secure from hunting and pursuit neither inside houses nor atop them.[61]

Although the investment of Vienna choked off normal victualing channels and forced the citizenry to resort to rather unusual forms of nourishment, the blockade was not quite so tight as to sever all contact with the friendly, outside world. Starhemberg was able to get letters back and forth, thanks to the heroism of a number of couriers, several of whom spoke Turkish and disguised themselves in Ottoman garb. The topic is of special interest because one of the messengers, Georg Kolschitzky (Kolczycki), a man of uncertain nationality (either Polish or Rascian), is the central character of another dearly-held Viennese legend, according to which coffee was introduced to the city as a consequence of the siege. The fact of the matter is that Kolschitzky, who only made one round-trip and who was more a self-promoting huckster than anything else, deserves only modest praise and had nothing to do with the advent of the Near Eastern beverage, which is documented in Vienna as early as 1663. He was not even the town's first *Kaffeehaus* operator, the institution in question dating from well after the immediate post-siege period. He merely had the right, as a reward for his services, to boil coffee for public consumption on the street. In all fairness the other couriers—an unknown cuirassier, the aforementioned Jakob Heider, an infantry lieutenant called Gregorowitz, a certain Stephen Seradly, and a Rascian named Michaelowitz (Mihailović)—deserve to share his fame. Michaelowitz, it should be noted, was no less self-centered than Kolschitzky. Manifesting a characteristic Viennese predilection for titles, he signed himself ever after as "zeitwehrend Belagerung der Stadt Wien zweimal ausgegangener Kundschafftder."[62] Whatever their personal flaws, the couriers played an essential rôle in saving Vienna, for reports from outside, telling of victories elsewhere or of preparations for the city's relief, kept hope alive; as, for example, on August 22, when "alle Innwohner der Stadt/ Geist und Weltlich/ hoch- und nidern Standts sehr aufgemuntert/ und respirirend gemacht wurden."[63]

D. The Second Month of the Siege

THE TRIUMPH OF SAVAGERY

The measures which Starhemberg took to strengthen the ravelin after the great Turkish assault of August 12 were no more than palliatives. The loss of the structure was only a matter of time once the besiegers had succeeded in affixing themselves to its face. Thus it was necessary to accelerate completion of improvements on the next line of defense, in particular the Palace Bastion. At the rear of the latter bulwark was a remnant of the Mediaeval wall called the "Spaniard." A tower-like work fronted by a ditch, it had to be readied for action while the bastion itself required a palisaded retrenchment and obstacle pit. Accordingly, civilian services were once more commandeered. The laborers also erected a network of log traverses in the space between the retrenchment and the ditch of the "Spaniard." Because of the inherent flaws of design, nothing could be done to reinforce the Löbl Bastion, apart from building traverses and scooping out a fosse below the cavalier. Countermining proved to be of no value since the passageways were located under the (main) moat and not under the bastion.[64]

While the defenders were bracing themselves, the Turks were busy planting a new mine under the counterscarp opposite the Palace Bastion. Exploded on the fourteenth, it forced the Austrians to give up the last portion of the covered way in the sector under direct assault. The dislodged soldiers fell back to a caponière located at the beginning of the adjacent, non-attacked portion of the counterscarp. On the next day the attackers also managed to entrench themselves in the ditch facing the Löbl Bastion. They threw up a crescent-shaped barricade big enough for 200 men and then pushed forward as far as the cunette. Serényi and Scherffenberg, the local Austrian commanders, decided at once upon a counteroffensive. Two separate sallies were carried out, the result of which was the burning and wrecking of enemy works. Favored by the wind, the fire also swept onto the counterscarp where it destroyed a supply of wool bags, gabions and lumber. The Janissaries did not return to the area for fully twelve days. The action was of great significance in the salvation of the city.[65]

The victory of the fifteenth was of benefit to morale also, for by now suffering had become intense. Not only were the Austrian troops forced to tighten their belts to conserve food, but the effect of living in cramped quarters was likewise beginning to be felt. The units stationed in the moat, lacking all freedom of movement, were worst off, for they had to live amidst their own waste. In addition, the soldiers were unable to properly inter their deceased comrades: the intense August heat quickly produced an almost insupportable stench. The continual enemy bombardment was also a terrible trial. While the Ottoman guns were too few and too small for breaching, they were well served. Mortar-tossed stones proved particularly harmful. Also lethal were swarms of well-aimed arrows. The fact that these missiles could be sold to Viennese merchants encouraged the infantry to expose themselves needlessly. Despite all the torments, and thanks to the rigid discipline, the men manifested no open discontent.[66] Their attitude is perhaps best summed up by words of their chief in a letter to the Duke of Lorraine, dated August 18–19: ". . . nous avons jusques à cette heure disputé le terrain aux ennemis, pas à pas, et . . . ils n'ont pas gagné un poulce de terre, qu'ils n'y ayent laissé de leur poil . . . ; . . . je ne rendray la place qu'avec la derniére goutte de mon sang." Speaking of an expected Turkish mine, Starhemberg added that: "je leur en feray encor sauter un à la sainté de vostre Altesse." Interestingly the garrison's commander was at that moment prostrated by dysentery and able to perform his duties only by having himself carried around in a stretcher from post to post.[67]

The prime concern was still the ravelin, under which the Turks detonated another mine on the seventeenth in order to widen the space for their saps. The Ottoman troops, a hair's breadth away, began to heave the dirt from their excavations into the Austrian positions, forcing the defenders to invent a wooden instrument, "lequel étoit fait en manière que plusieurs soldats poussant en même tems renversoient toute la terre du côté des ennemis." On the eighteenth a party of twenty dismounted cuirassiers and an equal number of foot undertook a new sortie, one unfortunate result of which was the mortal wounding of Colonel Dupigny. This redoubtable old warhorse, half-crippled by a wound dating from the Dutch War, fell behind his retreating companions and was attempting to surmount the cunette when the main artery of his leg was ripped open by a bullet. In the succeeding days still other mines ploughed up the moat, both in the area fronting the Palace Bastion—where the Turks needed loose soil for easier entrenchment—and under the ravelin, which was now an "amas de terre informe pleine de sang et de corps morts." Sometimes the struggle was conducted underground, as on the twenty-fourth when the miners of each side bumped into each other beneath the ravelin. On the surface the defenders began throwing boiling water and pitch, kept ready in heated kettles. The bitterness of the fighting had increased to the point where the Austrians were not satisfied with mere head-impaling; they now resorted to flaying their captives alive.[68]

By the last week of August both sets of adversaries were beginning to show signs of exhaustion. Conditions in the Turkish camp were scarcely better than in Vienna. The Austrian authorities at least recognized the necessity of proper hygiene. Kara Mustafa did not, and consequently disease began to add to the huge number of battle casualties. On several occasions rain turned the Ottoman approaches into an impassable quagmire. By the twenty-fifth the Janissaries were becoming unruly, grumbling that Holy Writ obliged them to remain no longer than forty days at a siege. In order to keep up their spirits the Grand Vezir planted rumors about Leopold's death; the defeat of the Imperial field army; and starvation, disease, and mutiny within the fortress. He likewise called upon the oratorical skills of the preacher Vani Efendi. The troops in the rear also gave trouble. Some Armenian bakers had to be punished for selling bread to the Viennese, and the *tımârlı* were castigated for failures in the preparation of munitions. A number of lesser troop commanders at the front were dismissed and placed under arrest. The difficulty of maintaining discipline was enhanced by a shortage of food and by price-gouging, the Turkish army caterers being no less avaricious than Vienna's tradesmen. The foolishness of the wanton destruction earlier in the campaign now became evident. The men were kept from starving only by the belated arrival of supply caravans from Hungary and by the contributions levied upon subjected towns such as Sopron. The scarcity of provisions and, presumably, feelings of frustration led to the outright slaughter of at least several thousand Christian captives, who had been herded together into the garden of the Neue Favorita. Doubtlessly there was some distinction made in the choice of victims, for the Turkish harems could always use new recruits. There is evidence that the lot of the more pulchritudinous female prisoners was anything but unpleasant: many of them declared that they wished to remain with their gallant captors.[69]

The high death rate among the Turks may have induced Kara Mustafa to consider for a moment the possibility of negotiations. Receipt of information concerning the rendezvous of the Christian relief army may also have been a factor. Unquestionably, the changing situation led him to summon reinforcements. İbrahim Pasha was commanded to come from Győr with the bulk of his detachment. Thököly, too, was ordered to appear, but, playing it safely as always, chose to remain in Upper Hungary. The Wallachians, who had been present at Vienna all along, also took out insurance with the Austrians. (To be sure, these Orthodox Christians had found their work for the Grand Vezir distasteful from the very start.) It was Şerban Cantacuzeno who facilitated Kunitz' continued contact with Starhemberg after the arrest of Heider. The Rumanian Prince likewise suggested that the Austrians fire upon his men, misaiming deliberately. Then he would have a good excuse to withdraw. Finally, he left standing in the Schönbrunn forest a seventeen foot wooden cross with a Latin inscription, from which his real sentiments could be inferred.[70]

Meanwhile the situation within the fortress was becoming critical as is apparent from a letter written by Starhemberg on August 27. Charles, its addressee, could not have been more clearly admonished: "mais, Monseigneur, il est temps de nous secourir, nous perdons beaucoup de monde, et beaucoup d'Officiers, plus par le flux de sang que par le feu des ennemis. . . ."[71] In order to lend emphasis to the appeal Kielmannsegg fired rockets from the tower of St. Stephen's Cathedral. Unfortunately, this display with its all too evident meaning was also visible to the Turks. It seems that knowledge of the enemy's distress not only uplifted their sagging morale but spurred them on to new and greater effort. Certainly, the pace of the Ottoman attack did not slacken, for between the twenty-fifth and the thirty-first of August six more mines, mostly under the ravelin, were set off. The attackers also succeeded in appropriating the tip of the bulwark which now looked more like an ant hill than anything else. When Starhemberg—who was ultimately forced to take to bed for several days—was able to get up again (September 1) and surveyed what had transpired during his convalescence, he was appalled to find the besiegers nestled directly under the bastions. Although his associates were strongly opposed to additional sallies, he concluded that it was necessary to make a last effort to expel them from the ditch. They argued that recent failures and the relative impregnability of the enemy works had made the troops lose all taste for such undertakings. The heavy losses suffered by the 400 men sent out the same day demonstrated that this time the rejected counsel was correct. A further setback was suffered during the night as the *lağunci* managed to press forward their galleries to the face of the Löbl Bastion, which they immediately proceeded to undermine (a development which led to the fatal disciplining, mentioned earlier, of the lieutenant held to be responsible). The garrison's predicament was by now so desperate that Starhemberg and Kapliř's deemed it necessary to dispatch one more courier to the Emperor in what amounted to a final appeal for succor. Both officers stressed that the danger was all the more acute since no sectors could be established atop the constricted bastion.[72]

The second day of the new month brought yet another reverse. The Austrian miners unexpectedly met their Ottoman counterparts and, seized by fright, deserted their post. Since the persons in charge were the most fear-stricken of all, Starhemberg's pleas—the men were apparently mostly civilians—brought no result. Taking into account the foe's proximity to the bastions and the imminent danger of breaches, the commandant decided to abandon the ravelin. (Ironically this blood-drenched, now shapeless pile of earth, labeled the "bear cage" by the Imperials and the "magic hill" by the Turks, was to become the site of Johann Strauss' open air waltz concerts some two hundred years later.) It was also necessary for the defenders to evacuate the caponière on the counterscarp and another on the ravelin's right flank.[73] The final defeat notwithstanding, it is clear that the long defense of the outer bulwarks was an achievement that finds few parallels in the annals of military history.

Furthermore, the validity of the deceased Rimpler's ideas for practical improvement of fortification systems was demonstrated.

On September 4, the fate of the city hung in the balance, and the burghers appear to have known it. The Turks, smelling success, exerted themselves as never before. At 2:00 p.m. a monstrous charge was loosed beneath the Palace Bastion. As soon as the dust settled, the first of an estimated 4000 Muslims stormed upward, preceded by their horse-tail standards. The Austrians sprang into the open at the breach, some thirty feet wide, and formed an infantry square, one rank firing and retiring to be succeeded by the next. The action lasted more than two hours. Since the gap was steep, the defenders were able to drive their opponents back behind big chunks of wall lying at the bastion's base, from whence the unprotected musketeers were subjected to a veritable deluge of balls, bombs, stones, and arrows. Starhemberg and other high officers, scorning death, personally directed operations. The battle might well have ended in victory for Kara Mustafa had not it begun at the precise moment of the guard change and if the late Dupigny's cavaliers had not been stationed in the immediate vicinity. The fighting finally stopped when the Austrians brought up Kielmannsegg's wheel-mounted *chevaux de frise* and a quantity of sandbags. The losses were great on both sides: the Turks fell in uncounted droves; the Imperials suffered some 200 dead, twelve of whom were the victims of a single shell. The men stood so closely packed that the bodies of the slain were kept from dropping to the ground.[74] The ghastliness of the encounter, indeed of war in general, is revealed in the eloquent words of a participant:

> While I was holding a soldier by his scarf, his head was knocked off by a cannon ball. Blood and brains were splattered onto my nose and right into my mouth, which was open because of the day's great heat. . . . This incident caused me great suffering afterward, above all, violent heart palpitations and vomiting.[75]

Although the Austrian troops had manifested exemplary courage in the action, they were rapidly approaching the limits of their endurance. While they did not all have to be on guard at the same time, the never-ending alarms permitted no real sleep. There were signs of incipient demoralization. There is also evidence that elements of the civilian population were contemplating surrender. Starhemberg thus continued to launch help-beseeching rockets into the night skies.[76]

On the morrow of the fifth all the Austrian soldiers still on their feet—no more than two-fifths of the original garrison—were distributed among sixty-four permanent defense posts. There were now no reserves apart from the ill-trained, untrustworthy militia. The *serdengeçti* once again stormed into the breach on the Court Bastion. In spite of an incessant, point-blank barrage of caseshot, crossfire from the Löbl Bastion, and musketry from the courtine, they succeeded in entrenching themselves. Once more their skill and bravery evoked the admiration of the Habsburg officers. The heavy losses of the previous day only seemed to animate the Porte's warriors. However, as long as the other bastion threatened the Ottoman left, the hope of breaking through at the *Burgbastei* was vain. Thus, on September 6, precisely at noon, the attackers set off two mines under the latter bulwark. As the brickwork was well-cemented, the explosion had a murderous, shrapnel-like effect. The whole tip and the left face of the antequated defense work were demolished. The Austrians within the casemate were crushed or suffocated by débris. The Janissaries and cavalry volunteers immediately charged up the breach. They were met with a withering salvo and were hit simultaneously in the rear by fire from the remaining caponières. The hot, late summer sun once again magnified the sufferings of the combatants. The Austrians, standing unshielded in thick ranks at the gap, were picked off in large numbers by unerringly-aimed arrows and cannon-balls. The assault force, which was also badly cut up, might have succeeded on its second attempt, had not the well-prepared defenders quickly brought up portable obstacles in the meantime. A large chunk of the blasted wall also served to impede the attackers' progress. That same night, as well as on the seventh, the defenders saw answering rockets from atop the Kahlenberg, to which the Duke of Lorraine had sent out a special advance party. Thus informed of the impending arrival of the Austro-Polish-German field army, the exhausted garrison was able to pull itself together to withstand another Turkish mine and assault of equal or even greater violence on the eighth.[77]

However, it is highly questionable whether the fortress could have fended off a fourth major attack.[78] Fortunately for the Viennese, Kara Mustafa, also aware of the approach of the multinational Christian host, now decided to leave the trenches for his tent-castle in order to direct his main efforts to securing the rear. Still, the defenders were hardly able to sit back on their haunches and placidly await rescue. The *topçu* kept up a regular bombardment, and the untiring *lağuncı* continued to burrow forward. The task of the latter had been much facilitated by the capture (September 10) of the feebly-defended faussebraye. Shafts could now be driven directly under the courtine—where huge powder charges were being placed at the very moment of the Battle of the Kahlenberg. Mining beneath the two battered bastions also continued unabatedly. It is evident that if the relief army had delayed its arrival even a day, Vienna's last line of defense would have been breached and the way left open for penetration by the still substantial Janissary units that the Grand Vezir left behind when he turned to face Charles and Sobieski. Starhemberg thus braced himself for the final blow. Barricades were set up and chains stretched across the streets. Burgher houses were converted into strong-points. It was obvious that the intention was to fight, foot by foot, to the very finish. "Nous nous préparions à la triste consolation de périr les armes à la main, l'esclavage nous paroissant plus rude que la mort même."[79]

On the morning of September 11 the bone-weary troops atop the walls espied a great commotion within the enemy camp. Every one could see that the moment of truth was but hours away. For the officers, who had never really believed in the possibility of relief, the exhilaration must have been overpowering.[80] Moreover, despite all the horrors and priva-tions of the past two months, there were still a few men, at least among the militia, who were able to view the immanent outcome of the city's ordeal with remarkable levity:

> Even though it was late at night, the Royal Bohemian Court Caterer Raitz, a good comrade serving in my unit, had a couple of bottles of prime St. George brought up from his cellar. I came in from guard duty, and we sat down at the oval table in our room (in the Leopoldine Tract of the Hofburg). We were about to drink a farewell toast to this renowned siege, to welcome its happy conclusion, to salute the health of the commanding general, and I had just raised the glass to my lips, when a Janissary fired at me with his musket. The bullet broke the stem of the glass and splashed the wine into the faces of the whole com-pany . . . We deduced that the enemy positions were at about the same level as the windows of the palace . . . and that they could observe our every action. . . . We therefore overturned our table, squatted on the floor in the Turkish manner, leaned our backs against the sandbags with which the room was equipped for our protection and finished off the wine in complete security.[81]

E. Fighting in the Countryside

While most of the Turkish invaders were occupied with the siege, a number of lesser detachments, especially the highly mobile Tatars, rav-aged a vast territory bounded in the east by Lake Neusiedl, in the south by the higher elevations of the Alps and in the north by the Danube. Road blocks in the (intermediate) Vienna Woods were not effective. Kara Mustafa's raiders simply circumvented the few undermanned barri-cades and were able to fan out over much of the Tulln Plain and beyond to the upper course of the Ybbs, which thus constituted the western extremity of the Ottoman incursions. Within this vast area, rapine, murder, looting, burning, and mastiff-conducted slave hunts became the order of the day. Although the Muslims were for the most part only lightly equipped—the Tatars lacked even firearms—, the population, virtually paralyzed by fear, offered little resistance, preferring precipitate flight or meek submission.[82]

OTTOMAN ATROCITIES

Perhaps the most striking single incident of horror was the massacre at Perchtoldsdorf, the town that otherwise serves as a symbol of the Emperor's unpreparedness for war. This locality, today an organic part of Greater Vienna,[83] has preserved much of the mien of the Leopoldine Era. Still partly girded by a high-standing, Mediaeval wall, it also possesses a somewhat stronger defensive complex, consisting of a stone-block church, a donjon-like bell tower (*Wehrturm*), and the remnant of a castle. These bulwarks, although hopelessly obsolete by the standards of even the sixteenth century, seemed to offer the inhabitants and a few refugees from outside some prospect of successful resistance. However, circumstances soon convinced the defenders that their efforts were foredoomed, and they accepted the surrender conditions of the enemy. As the citizen-soldiers filed out of their ecclesiastical retreat, they sent forward a garlanded, young virgin with loose, flowing hair, a living symbol of Perchtoldsdorf's hitherto inviolate history. From her hands the besiegers received the municipal keys, cradled upon a pillow. Thereupon the already disarmed burghers were forced to line up, ostensibly for a head count.

Suddenly, at a signal from the "Pasha," as the Austrians called him, the Islamic warriors fell upon their captives with drawn sabers. Perhaps three hundred men, the flower of the male population, were slaughtered. Two rivulets of blood flowed downhill to form a pool in the yard of the adjacent rectory. At least several hundred other persons were butchered nearby. Torches were tossed into the church and tower, which remained crowded with women and children. Heaps of corpses continued to lie around until November, according to the account of a traveller who recognized the body of his friend, the late market-bailiff, still clad in gay, green boots.[84] Frankly admitting that the parleying had only been a ruse for his compatriots, the Ottoman Court Master of Ceremonies remarked: "This, too, is proof of the favor of Allah, who hath so confused the senses of the Giaours that they are no longer capable of acting clear-headedly in such a situation."[85] The story of Perchtoldsdorf, while particularly vivid, is by no means exceptional. There are other well-documented reports of Ottoman barbarity. Kara Mustafa's grisly trophies from Hainburg on the Danube come to mind again.[86] Mosonmagaróvár and countless other villages suffered similar agonies. Large segments of the horizon were marked by rising columns of smoke to judge by contemporary maps.[87]

CENTERS OF RESISTANCE

Destruction, however, was not universal. Three larger centers of habitation, Bruck an der Leitha, Sopron, and Eisenstadt, preferred, sagaciously, to sacrifice a portion of their honor by throwing themselves upon the mercy of Thököly's partisans, whose never-too-reliable word did prove more trustworthy than that of Ottoman predators. The price of immunity was the contribution of extensive stores of victuals to the Turks at Vienna, including fancy fowl for the Grand Vezir's table. There were, moreover, a few noteworthy instances of opposition among all the panic-evoked paralysis. Wiener Neustadt, which was sufficiently fortunate to possess both a strong, if outmoded wall and, more significantly, a portion of Castell's dragoons (left behind by Lorraine), contemptuously rejected the Tatar surrender demand and repelled the enemy easily.[88] Although the majority of local prelates and secular lords appear to have abandoned their subordinates and tenants, a few, stouter-hearted potentates did remain behind to organize armed resistance.

Of more than local significance was the salvation of Klosterneuburg, a fortified town and Augustinian monastery situated some five and a half miles upstream from Vienna at the head of the two valleys that dissect the northernmost part of the Wiener Wald. The abbot having fled, a simple lay brother, assisted by one priest and the steward, rallied the inhabitants of the place, women and children as well as men, and fought off three separate Turkish attacks. To be sure, the victories were facilitated by some professional help from the Austrian army, which was stationed directly on the other side of the river. It appears that the Duke, with the relief battle already in mind, wished to hold, if possible, an advance post of such great strategic importance.[89] Fortunately for the Habsburg cause, the Turkish assaults do not seem to have been particularly violent, the later claims of the defenders notwithstanding. Another instance of monastic martial vigor was the decisive reaction of Gregor Müller, Abbot of Melk (d. 1700), whose Benedictine convent, perched on a cliff towering over the Danube at the entrance to the legendary Wachau (Nibelungengau) could not have been better situated for purposes of self-protection.[90] A rather more impressive achievement was the defense of the town and cloister of Lilienfeld by its abbot, Matthäus Kohlweiss (1620–1695), who thrice beat off the foe and even managed to conduct several successful sorties. The Cistercian father ordered that the naked corpses of Turks and Tatars "bagged" by his men be distributed along the country roads as a warning to other marauders. His steadfastness was all the more useful as the abbey sat astride the pass leading to the treasure-strewn shrine of Maria Zell and other parts of northern Styria, which were thus spared the horrors of war.[91] Similarly resolute was the behavior of the Ausustinian Canons at Herzogenburg (between St. Pölten and the Danube).[92] These feats all stood in sharp contrast to the performance of Lilienfeld's mother house, Heiligenkreuz (beyond Mödling and Baden), which was the scene of frantic disorganization and which ultimately suffered great human and material losses.[93]

A few provincial nobles also perceived that the Turko-Tataric skirmishers were really not too formidable, that sufficient *sang-froid* and a few well-aimed shots would keep them at arm's length. The Sinzendorf and Pàlffy estates, on the road from Vienna to St. Pölten, where the burghers also held out, defied the raiders.[94] On the opposite eastern side of the Vienna Woods, in the so-called "Viertel unter dem Wienerwald," a number of old, Mediaeval fortresses, several still existant, did likewise. South of Wiener Neustadt, the castle of Pitten, lying on a high rock over a tributary of the Leitha River, granted asylum to refugees and drove off the attackers from the steppes just as it had done far back in the Babenberger era.[95] About nine miles to the northwest of Wiener Neustadt, on a promontory above the Piesting (a branch of the Danube), stood a second strongpoint, the now ruined *Stammburg* or ancestral keep of the Starhembergs. It afforded shelter to even larger flocks of rustics.[96]

The most impressive sanctuary was surely Burg Forchtenstein, like Pitten a barrier to incursions from the Alföld since time immemorial. Magnificently preserved even today, this formerly impregnable fastness occupies a spectacular site high on the western slope of the Rosaliengebirge, the Alpine spur that forms the border between Lower Austria and Burgenland. It is flanked by powerful, "modern" bastions erected thirty years after the Esterházys' acquisition of ownership (1622). Its appearance in 1683 was so formidable that the Ottoman hordes did not dare to launch an assault. It was the only place in Western Hungary to remain in Imperial hands.[97] (Far less happy however, was the destiny of Burg Merkenstein at Gainfarn near Baden where the attackers gained entry by using a little-known hill path leading to an open rear window.[98]) Farther south on the then Hungarian border, the fortified city of Fürstenfeld, the traditional bulwark blocking access to Graz and the interior of Styria, repulsed Thököly's bands and their local Magyar adherents with the aid of regular soldiers from General Herberstein's southern command. The situation here was not quite so critical because of the distance from the main theater of action and because Batthyányi and Drasković, who had submitted to the rebels only from opportunism, were tacitly in league with the town fathers.[99]

Accountability and Cost

The chaotic conditions in the wide arc of countryside around Vienna must be ascribed to the lack of effective leadership by the privileged elements of society and their representatives, the Lower Austrian Estates and the defense committee of Count Traun. While it would be untrue to assert that officialdom, especially the provincial bureaucracy, did nothing, there seems to have been a general inability to recognize the immanence of war, despite warnings from Vienna.[100] Indeed, the major provincial effort, the aid given to the gathering relief forces, took place mainly in July and August.[101] It was made, moreover, in the area north of the

Danube, in the two so-called "Districts above and Below the Manhartsberg," as opposed to the two shattered Wienerwald sections.

Another aspect of the general breakdown was the rebellious attitude of the peasant draftees, who engaged in an only slightly disguised form of highway robbery. Refugees were held up at road blocks and forced to hand over their last groschen as "tolls." The clergy, subject to both verbal and physical abuse, fared even worse. As noted earlier, this seemingly egotistical and unpatriotic behavior was an expression of outrage over the results of Vienna's policy toward the Magyars.[102] Also, there was bitterness over the failures and desertion of the indigenous social hierarchy. For years the rural proletarians had been required to pay the special "Türkensteuer." Now they were left unwarned because of the failure of the signal fire (*Kreudefeuer*) system; unprotected as a consequence of the inadequacy or unprepared state of most of the officially designated refuges (*Fluchtörter*) ; and unled due to the flight of "their lordships." Probably also, at least in certain parishes where Crypto-Lutheranism lingered on, long suppressed hatred of the Roman Church expressed itself. To be sure, there is nothing strange or surprising about the sudden surfacing of latent socio-psychological factors in a time of unusual political stress. Further manifestations of the same phenomenon were an apparent Gypsy persecution during the spring and, in Prague, some sort of anti-Semitic tumult, which necessitated the dispatch of a company of Piccolomini's foot, badly needed in Vienna itself.[103]

A precise calculation of material and human losses is surely impossible. Destruction, of course, varied in degree from area to area. Northern Burgenland, the environs of Lake Neusiedl, was almost completely laid waste. The centuries-old pioneering enterprise of Heiligenkreuz, which held great estates here, was ruined. Esterházy paid dearly for his loyalty (whatever the reasons) : Thököly's partisans performed an especially thorough job of wrecking his properties. (The Palatine doubtlessly felt entirely justified when he later recouped his losses at the expense of the Sopron Protestants who had helped loot the precious contents of his palatial Eisenstadt residence.) Southern Burgenland, for the reasons previously indicated, was not badly hit.[104] Estimates of damage and casualties in Lower Austria are contradictory. One contemporary report lists the kidnapping of 6,000 old men, 11,215 womenfolk, 14,692 maidens up to twenty-six years of age, and 5,603 minors.[105] A document of 1689 spoke of an overall loss of 500,000 persons.[106] A modern writer suggests 30,000 dead and 70,000 captured.[107] The prisoners were generally irrecoverable. Many were worked to death or slaughtered in connection with the siege operations.[108] Of those carried off to Buda and, eventually Istanbul, the majority apparently never returned, although many Turks strove to capitalize on their slaves by having the latter write home to request ransom. The sociological effects of dislocation were extensive: co-habitation and re-marriage without assurance of the demise of prior spouses, who did sometimes come back.[109]

The economic effect of depopulation, exacerbated by the earlier as well as by a later plague outbreak, was enormous. The already decimated labor force was further reduced by government drafts for repair of Vienna's fortifications and other military construction. There were, for example, few able-bodied hands to restore once-lucrative vineyards. Inflation was an obvious consequence. Vienna endeavored to alleviate conditions by temporarily lifting internal duties and by lowering the annual tax contribution asked of the States. It also proved necessary to import new settlers from neighboring provinces and from the *Reich*. Perchtoldsdorf, for example, was repopulated with Styrians. It may well be, as claimed, that Lower Austria did not finally recover from its wounds until the middle of the eighteenth century.[110]

Finally, one may ask to what extent, if any, Ottoman military operations in the provinces influenced the outcome of the siege. While it appears that Kara Mustafa failed to exercise much control over the hard-to-trace movements of the irregulars, the evidence does not permit one to conclude that wanton destruction of usable supplies was universal or that the roving horsemen completely neglected their foraging assignment. The success of the Tatars in supplying the slave labor required for the siege works deserves to be noted. Likewise, the shock of their vicious assaults was valuable in ensuring undisturbed communications.

CHAPTER NINE

Kara Mustafa's Defeat

A. The Lower Austrian Campaign

Probably nothing that happened during July and August of 1683 is as memorable as the desperate, hand-to-hand struggle waged along Vienna's defense perimeter. Yet the story of those fateful months would only be fragmentary without relating the actions that occurred in the northern part of Lower Austria and in the adjacent area of western Hungary. The battles which took place there are not only almost as dramatic as the fighting beneath the Löbl and Palace Bastions but are directly relevant to Kara Mustafa's defeat. The Duke of Lorraine's little cavalry army, while exiled to the far shore of the Danube and unable to oppose the siege independently, was still free to maneuver strategically. Firstly, it could impose limits upon the pillage and despoliation of Leopold's domains. Geography already presented one major barrier—the fluvial bisection of Lower Austria—to the swift Muslim raiders. The availability of troopers both to guard the river's banks and to block off the region's eastern border along the tributary Morava enhanced the benefits afforded by nature. Secondly, by securing the septentrional portion of the province, the Duke preserved, near the Austrian capital, a safe operational base for the various Christian armies which were supposed to come to his aid.

Actions During July

After permanently withdrawing from the untenable Prater Island on July 16,[1] the Habsburg regiments took up position next to the village of Jedlesee, just above the fortified mainland end of the partly burned-down bridge system. It is not easy to locate the latter point on modern maps, but it was apparently near the terminus of the present Floridsdorfer Brücke. (This spot also adjoins the upper tip of the "Alte Donau," the dammed-off easternmost channel of 1683, which with its famous Gänsehäufel presently serves as a colorful focus of Viennese aquatic recreation.) Here, for a space of ten days, the exhausted horses and men of Charles' command gradually recovered their physical powers while the Duke plunged into a fury of planning activity. The first concern of the Austrian generalissimo was to "incommode" the enemy as much as he could. One of his initial moves was the transfer of Count Dünewald's three regiments up the river to Krems.[2] Another was to instruct Count Herberstein to harass the Turks in his theater. Similar orders went out to the garrisons of Győr and Komárno, and to Castell's dragoons in Wiener Neustadt. It was at this time, too, that the Duke decided to buttress the defenses of Klosterneuburg. A further measure was recall of two of the three-and-a-half infantry regiments thrown into Győr at the beginning of the month. As this fortress was no longer seriously threatened, and in view of the projected relief operation, it seemed wise to employ superfluous troops with the field army. It also appeared advisable to shift the heavier field artillery, under Leslie, to Krems to await arrival of the troops either on their way from the *Reich* or being organized there.

In addition to these tactical *démarches,* Lorraine weighed the question of how long Vienna could hold out. There were many unfavorable factors, among them the addiction of the citizenry to a "soft and comfortable mode of existence," and his conclusions were not overly optimistic. In order to persuade the government to press even harder for assistance from Germany and Poland, Count Taaffe was despatched (July 16) to the Court, which by then had taken refuge at Passau on the Bavarian border. Two days later Barol Welsberg hurried off to Innsbruck to fetch several Imperial regiments still stationed in the Forelands. Finally, Charles took supplementary steps, mostly independent of Passau, to encourage the speed-up of allied help.[3]

On July 26 a report arrived in Jedlesee stating that Thököly had massed his rag-tag army near Trnava (Tyrnau, Nagy-Szombat) in easternmost Slovakia and was heading toward Bratislava. This turn of events can hardly have surprised the Duke, for the recent recall of General Schultz and his Polish adjunct, Lubomirski, from the Váh River line had deprived the region of any mobile Austrian striking force. Bratislava, Győr, Komárno, Leopoldov, Nitra, Gúta, Levice, Sered, and far-away Satu Mare possessed loyal garrisons,[4] but most of them were too small and weak even for limited sorties. Only on the Muraköz and in Croatia— Herberstein's distant, southern portion of the original tripartite Austrian front—were the Imperials still in control. The enemy troops advancing upon Bratislava were a mixed force of some 6,000 Turks, under the command of Kör Hüseyin Pasha, the one-eyed *Beylerbeyi* of Eger, and perhaps 15,000 Magyars.[5] Charles, unsure of the Imperial governor in the threatened city, sent a detachment of 500 men to reinforce the citadel and followed the next day with the bulk of his army, roughly 10,000 troopers. Two regiments remained behind to guard the now completely destroyed Vienna bridges.[6]

While underway, Lorraine learned of the disastrous repulse of his vanguard and of the ravishment of the surrounding countryside. On July 28, after he had reached the Morava, he received further distressing news: Thököly had obtained the homage of the largely Protestant townsmen, formerly the object of Bishop Kollonitsch's attentions, and was about to bombard the fortress. Even more ominous was the message that a bridge was being built to the south shore of the Danube. Should this effort succeed, the Turco-rebel force could be greatly strengthened by the addition of units from the main Ottoman host. Not only would northern Lower Austria be subject to the same fate as its southern half, but the Austrian field army might have to retreat beyond Krems. The enemy could further improve communications by restoring the Vienna bridges and could cut off or delay the advance of Sobieski and the main Polish army. It seemed clear that the fate of the whole relief effort hung in the balance. On the other hand, to advance farther was to risk destruction of the army and thus total defeat in the war. The majority of the generals were opposed to going on. The Duke, encouraged by the dashing Ludwig Wilhelm and, apparently, Lubomirski, decided to proceed.[7]

In the meantime, however, Thököly seemed to be losing his nerve. He had already experienced some difficulty in controlling his own men, who had run amok in the streets of Bratislava. When, on the evening of the 28th, he discovered that the Austrians were coming through the narrow defile in the hills to the northwest of the city, he withdrew most of his forces to the plain on the northeast. On the morning of the 29th, Imperial dragoons, led by the Margrave, quickly recaptured the town and wrecked all bridge matériel. Baden then advised the Duke that the enemy forces, drawn up in line of battle on the plain, seemed weak and worth attacking. Charles had come to the same conclusion. For a moment it seemed as if there might be a major encounter. But as the Austrian squadrons swept forward, the Magyars faded back. Contact remained very limited. Only the Turks showed stomach for fighting and clashed sharply on the left with Lubomirski's equally bellicose mercenaries. The Poles, aided by a few of the more lightly mounted Austrians, also chased the Magyars all the way back to the Váh. Lorraine and the more cumbersome cuirassier regiments were unable to keep up the pace and in any event had no cause for pursuit. For the nonce, at any rate, the massing of the relief forces could continue without disturbance. The 600 enemy dead, the 1200–1500 wagons taken as booty, not to mention the Pasha's own tent (in which the high-spirited Lubomirski facetiously held court) constituted a satisfying bonus. The Duke's only remaining chore was to scold the vacillating burghers and increase the garrison of the citadel. He could then retire safely as far as the Morava, some fifteen miles away, and there await further developments.[8]

There can be little question that the Imperial victory was facilitated by Thököly's pusillanimity. He had wanted to retreat altogether the moment he learned of the Habsburg advance and had stayed in the area solely because Kör Hüseyin Pasha had insisted upon making a stand. The reasons for this striking diffidence are not clear. Perhaps the rebel leader really did believe, as he claimed, that the Imperials enjoyed overwhelming numerical superiority, although in reality the opposite was true.

Perhaps also he was conscious of the difficulty his amateur troops would have in facing well-trained professionals on an open field. It is further arguable that he did not wish to contend quite so forcefully with Leopold's army until the outcome at Vienna was clear. It is difficult to imagine that so confirmed a double-dealer was as yet willing to place all his eggs in the Turkish basket. One thing, however, is certain: the *Beylerbeyi* was thoroughly disgusted with his Calvinist associate, and the two contingents reunited only at the express command of the Grand Vezir.[9]

PLANS FOR AIDING VIENNA

Despite the discord in the Turco-Magyar camp, there was still the chance of a second lateral thrust into northern Lower Austria. The Imperial army, encamped at Marchegg, about nine miles above the Morava's confluence with the Danube, could not have returned to its former position near Jedlesee with any peace of mind. Moreover, the Duke's actions were circumscribed by the receipt (August 1) of instructions from the Court. The Emperor, although unaware of the situation in Bratislava on the day (July 24) the orders were drawn up, was much perturbed about the prospect of additional damage to the hereditary lands. In order to assure the "conservation" of his domains, he commanded Charles to re-occupy the line of the Váh.[10] Actually, however, the threat of attack from Slovakia was not the major issue of the moment. Considerably more important were two interrelated questions: a.) what route should be followed back to Vienna once the expected foreign assistance had arrived? and b.) would it be possible to postpone the relief action until all reinforcements had become available?

Discussion of these matters had been underway ever since the decision to evacuate the Prater Island (July 11). With respect to the route itself, certain subordinate generals favored recrossing the Danube downstream at Bratislava in order to interdict Kara Mustafa's communications with Hungary. Thereby the Grand Vezir would be forced to retreat automatically, while the Austrians could avoid the uncertainties of a pitched battle. Charles objected to the idea because the level nature of the terrain would permit the foe to deploy his great cavalry strength. Since he himself expected to dispose eventually of large numbers of infantry, he preferred closed to open country. Also, inasmuch as the troops from the other Christian states would be tardy in arriving, it would be unwise to lose even more time by marching so far down the river and by constructing a bridge—at which juncture, moreover, the army would be vulnerable to surprise attack. Instead, the Duke favored, right from the beginning, a transfer to the south shore *upstream* from Vienna. With the Krems bridge secure, the allied forces could gather quickly and easily on the Tulln Plain and deliver their assault through the dense, mountainous, but not impenetrable Wienerwald.[11] Thus, when Count Taaffe left for Passau on July 16, he was not only bidden to press for an acceleration of relief preparations but was given two other assignments as well: to propagate Lorraine's strategy; and to suggest that the advance be made without awaiting the advent of all the various contingents *if* it should seem that some of them were going to be unduly late and *if* the condition of Vienna should become desperate.[12]

On July 20 the Duke's own war council definitively accepted the Wienerwald plan and immediately forwarded its recommendations to the Court.[13] Conceivably, the arrival on the same day of Lubomirski, an intimate of Sobieski, influenced the conferees, for the Polish monarch had himself followed strikingly similar schemes upon a number of occasions.[14] Two days later Lorraine sent off yet another emissary, Military Field Secretary Rostinger, whose job was again to urge haste in the completion of preparations, to reëmphasize the desirability of the Vienna Woods passage, and to suggest that 50,000 Germans might suffice to save the city.[15] The message was addressed directly to Leopold, probably because Charles was worried about the dilatory ways of Hermann of Baden.[16]

However, even before the missive reached its destination, Count Taaffe was on his way back with the aforementioned instructions. The Imperial letter clearly implied approval of the general geographic orientation of Charles' plan. Lorraine was also specifically enjoined to protect the bridge at Stein-Mautern (suburbs of Krems). Thereby Bavarian cavalry, which was already at the frontier, would be able to reach the Tulln Plain where, assisted by Dünewald's three regiments, it could prepare for the eventual advance by dispersing the remaining Tatars. The Electoral infantry would temporarily bivouac on the north side of the river near Krems. Charles was likewise told to collect as many boats as possible for transporting troops and supplies and for pontoon-bridge construction. Apparently this last order had something to do with an earlier request that the Duke himself had made.[17] It referred, in any event, to a second crossing which would be needed for the main Polish army and which was actually built a month later at the town of Tulln.[18] The Emperor then went on to stress the necessity of *not* attempting the relief action until all components of the international relief force had been assembled. If the enterprise were executed with insufficient numbers and should fail, the results would be disastrous, wrote Leopold, a man not prone to err on the side of daring. The monarch also raised the possibility of traversing the Wienerwald not directly behind Vienna, i.e., in the vicinity of Klosterneuburg, but rather farther south toward the Styrian frontier. By debouching near Wiener Neustadt—toward which the Croatians of Herberstein's command would proceed in the meantime—the Christians could trap and annihilate the Turks. This suggestion, unfeasible because it would take longer to realize, emanated from Hermann.[19]

Pessimistic about the rapid progress of their allies, poorly informed about what was occurring in Vienna and dubious about the city's prospects of continuing resistance for very long, the Duke and his staff do not appear to have been happy about the response from the Court. Making immediate use of the right of objection Leopold had accorded them, they commissioned Count Pálffy (August 2) to travel to Passau to present their views afresh. The new envoy carried the proposal that if the receipt of more precise news from Starhemberg should show that the fortress were genuinely endangered, "in case" it should appear that the Poles would not arrive "promptly," and, finally, assuming the addition of some 25,000 foot to the cavalry (15,000 men) already at hand, the relief operation might be undertaken without further ado. The question of the route, whether directly behind Vienna or via Wiener Neustadt, was left open temporarily.[20] According to Charles' secretary, Pálffy also carried, perhaps only orally, a slightly different suggestion. If, by August 25, 40,000–50,000 men could be accumulated—Imperials, Bavarians, and the earliest Polish units—, the allies might advance to the crest of the Vienna Woods and there entrench themselves. While waiting to attain their full strength, they could draw off and exhaust a portion of the besiegers, of whose previous great losses and bad morale Charles was quite aware, thanks to Kunitz and intercepted correspondence. The city's defenders would thus gain new courage. Should immediate relief prove entirely unavoidable, the Christian host would be in a position to undertake the offensive.[21]

MOVEMENTS IN AUGUST

The closely related questions of routing and timing were, to be sure, not the only problems that vexed the Austrian field commander during the month of August. Barely two days after Pálffy's precipitate departure for Passau the small detachment guarding the Vienna bridgehead called for help: Turkish units on the Prater Island were trying to reach the far side of the Danube. The enemy had already managed to seize control of one of the islets with boats confiscated from the local peasantry. Simultaneously, Charles received a second, apparently unrelated dispatch which indicated that still another party of Turks had passed over to the north bank near Bratislava, using vessels sent down from the Váh by Thököly. Supposedly, this group was advancing upon Großenzersdorf, the location of an important Austrian supply magazine. Charles immediately left Marchegg with four of his regiments and ordered the remaining troopers to follow in due course. After discovering that the second report was unfounded, the Duke pushed on to the Vienna bridgehead where through a cannonade, he dislodged the Turks from their insular position.

The main beneficiary of the whole contretemps was Thököly, who used the occasion of the Duke's withdrawal to demand payment of tribute from Moravia.[22] Lorraine at once (August 6) retraced his steps, returning to the Morava at Angern, a few miles to the north of his previous encampment. No sooner had he arrived than he learned that a force of rebels had actually entered into the Czech province a short distance upstream and was looting and burning the countryside. He sent forward some 800 of Lubomirski's swift-riding Poles, who fell upon the numerically superior but quite drunken Magyars, inflicting heavy losses and recovering prisoners and booty. However, similar, smaller-scale incursions continued. The only solution to the problem was to warn Thököly that unless the raiding ceased, the Imperial garrison at Satu Mare would be instructed to ravish his own personal estates. The tactic worked. The rebel chieftain even let Charles know, indirectly, that he himself had not sanctioned the attacks upon Moravian soil.[23]

In the meantime Pálffy had arrived in Passau. It must soon have become apparent that the government did not share the Duke's doubts about Vienna's ability to hold out for an extended period. Whether this was due to the Court's customary phlegm or to a sounder evaluation of the sparse intelligence available about conditions in the capital is hard to say. In any event, Leopold made no immediate reply. Back at Angern, however, Lorraine managed (August 15) to obtain somewhat more accurate information from Vienna. Although the news was by no means catastrophic, it seemed serious enough to Charles to warrant a fresh series of efforts to stimulate the organization of the relief. Once again he sent messengers scurrying in all directions, especially to the auxiliary commanders, who were urged to increase the tempo of their march.[24] The Duke also informed Passau that he would leave the Morava for Wolkersdorf, fifteen miles farther west, on the 20th in order, for the immediate moment, to cover bridge-building operations at Tulln.[25] On August 16 he sent two regiments forward to establish themselves at the latter place and to make engineering surveys.[26] The next day Lorraine's confidant, Taaffe, wrote his brother, the Earl of Carlingford, that he and his colleagues were determined to succor Vienna by the end of the month when all the expected forces would be at hand; if Sobieski should delay too long or if Vienna became too "pressed," it would be necessary to proceed without the Poles.[27]

On August 19, however, a letter, dated August 11, arrived from John III: it showed that the Poles were finally underway. This communication apparently served to persuade the Duke that it was now time for him to proceed *directly* to Tulln. He seems to have decided that it was safe to retire since the first of the advancing Poles could assume the burden of protecting northern Lower Austria. He informed the Court of his intentions, indicating that he would march up to Krems, cross the bridge there, and move downstream in order to build the bridge for Sobieski from the southern bank of the Danube. Arriving in Wolkersdorf on the 20th,

Charles received new dispatches, grave in content but reassuring in tone, from Starhemberg and Kapliřs. They were sent on to Passau. On the morning of the 21st came another encouraging letter, dated August 16, from Poland's ruler.[28] The Imperial army itself pressed on to Stockerau, a favorable point at which to begin an inspection of the swampy, multi-channeled course of the river, known then and now as the "Danube Meadows" *(Donauauen)*.[29] On the succeeding day Charles ordered the troops sent ahead on the sixteenth to occupy Tulln. The Plain itself seemed fairly safe. The foe had taken no action to expell Dünewald, and the remaining 6,000 Tatars had vanished at the sight of Baron Hannibal von Degenfeld's Bavarians on August 17. It also appeared unlikely that the Turks would risk engaging a larger cavalry corps on the far side of the Danube. On the 23rd Lorraine personally reconnoitered the marshes, found them "suitable for his design," and instructed his men both to bring up pontoon boats and to begin building roads to the main stream down through the willowy thickets and lesser water courses. In view of the great difficulties that were to be encountered in constructing a route through such a region during the next several weeks, it was well that the Duke took the matter in hand at an early date. Nevertheless, in withdrawing from his previous position before the gap between him and the Poles was reduced, Lorraine had miscalculated, as was to become evident upon the morning of the 24th.[30]

During the intervening period the Emperor was apparently becoming even more worried about the actions of his field commander. As previously noted, the Court simply did not view the situation with the same degree of concern. In fact, it placed a rather optimistic interpretation upon the Viennese reports forwarded to it by the Duke on the 15th.[31] Not until several days later did it send its answer to the questions broached by Pálffy at the beginning of the month. On August 23 Charles finally learned that he was not to budge until every single reinforcement was present.[32] (He did, however, receive conditional permission to use the Wienerwald route about this time.)[33] Even the second set of letters from Starhemberg and Kapliřs failed to make much of an impression upon Passau. On the 24th the Emperor told Prince Waldeck that he was going to forbid the Duke to cross at Krems and make him wait on the north side for the Poles: apparently Leopold continued to suspect Lorraine of intending to relieve Vienna without Sobieski. Waldeck's memoirs reveal what was the probable cause of the ruler's mistrust (apart from Charles' own original and tentative suggestions): personal enemies, who were insinuating that Lorraine wished to have all the glory for hmself.

It is improbable that the Duke would have gone ahead independently even without the express prohibition of his liege lord. From the nineteenth onward it was apparent that Sobieski's forces were definitely underway. Moreover, until September 1 Starhemberg issued nothing like a despairing appeal. Whether Charles would have disobeyed the Emperor had the conditions underlying the earlier proposals actually come about is a question that is both intriguing and impossible to answer. Likewise one can only speculate what the result of the Battle of Kahlenberg would have been, had the Poles been absent and had the Christians been forced to spread out their men more thinly.[35] Charles may well have been overanxious—and certainly sounded so, perhaps with calculation—, but it does not follow that his overall military judgment was beclouded or faulty.[36] In any event the early relief plan was not to be put to the test. Sobieski bestirred himself vigorously, and Starhemberg's tenacity provided a period of grace. Lorraine was thus able to fight the final engagement under very comfortable numerical circumstances.

THE BATTLE OF THE BISAMBERG

The Duke was, however, destined to fight another battle before advancing into the Vienna Woods. On August 24, as he was about to proceed to Tulln according to his plan of August 19, he learned of fresh peril from the direction of Upper Hungary. Ordering Leslie to take over the bridge operation, he swung in his tracks. This time the opponent was not the reluctant knight, Thököly, but rather his more bellicose Turkish adjunct, Kör Hüseyin Pasha. The Turkish general, after the débâcle at Bratislava on July 25, had written to the Grand Vezir for reinforcements, claiming that he was boxed in by Charles and another, allegedly huge but actually small and weak, Imperial force at Komárno. He also informed the *Ser'asker* of the Austrian intention to cross the Danube in the Krems area and stressed the immanent advent of the "accursed" Sobieski. Kara Mustafa, who scornfully minimized the warnings, replied that he would send five to ten thousand Tatars and that with their assistance the Pasha should proceed to Vienna via the north side of the river, ferry his men over to the Prater and rejoin the main army. Upon receiving at least some of the promised Tatars and anticipating the Austrians' withdrawal to the Krems Basin,[37] the Ottoman field commander struck northward for some sixty miles along the course of the Váh. He then veered sharply to the west, cutting directly through the White Carpathians, a land that had never before heard the tread of Turkish feet. After scourging the central region of the Morava, he headed southward under the assumption that Thököly would march directly up the shore of the Danube to meet him opposite Vienna. By noon of the twenty-fifth the Turks were encamped near the old Austrian bridgehead. The rebel leader was of course nowhere in sight.[38]

In the meantime (the morning of August 24), Charles had ridden off from Stockerau with some 13,000 horsemen, including Lubomirski's corps. The Duke, who afterward regarded the enemy move as an effort to divert his attention from Tulln, thought at the moment that his junction with the Poles was being threatened.[39] By 2:00 p.m. he found himself atop the Bisamberg, a prominence just across the river from Klosterneuburg. The location provided an excellent view of the plain opposite Vienna. In the distance Lorraine could see the villages near the bridgehead burning brightly from fires set by the Tatars. The outlines of the ensuing battle, apparently waged on the lower eastern slope of the Bisamberg between Langenzersdorf and Stammersdorf, are not entirely clear, but it seems that the Turks and Tatars, whom the Austrians estimated at 12,000 men,[40] attacked with only a portion of their full strength. The Turks, taking the left, fought with leonine courage. They succeeded in turning two Habsburg squadrons and in penetrating to Lorraine's second line. However, they were quickly enveloped, while the Tatars, who attempted to outflank the Imperials on the right, were roughly handled and forced to fall back upon the main body.

The Austrians then pushed forward cautiously. Panic seized the Ottoman ranks. One part of the army fled in the direction of the Morava. The other made for the burned-out bridges. Hotly pursued by bloodthirsty Poles and Croats, the Muslims deserted their mounts, arms and equipment, threw themselves into the Danube and attempted to swim to the islands with the aid of the stumpy remnants of the bridge piers. Many drowned. Others were slaughtered or seized before they could jump into the water. Kör Hüseyin Pasha, bled white by wounds, was among those whom the current sucked away. The Duke, who had exposed himself in his customary manner, could be well satisfied with the results of the sudden and unwelcome excursus: 1000–1200 enemy dead and captured, including "prisoniers de distinction"; twenty-five standards and even more highly prized timbals and tambours.[41]

Charles, understandably concerned about the possibility of a third enemy advance, retired only as far as Korneuburg. For a short time he planned to employ the advance elements of the approaching, main Polish army in order to cleanse eastern Lower Austria once and for all, but the news that the rebels had withdrawn in the direction of Tyrnava and the increasingly rapid progress of Sobieski himself caused the Duke to drop the scheme. The only further action in the area took place in the islands next to the Prater. Kara Mustafa, in an alleged second attempt to divert the attentions of the gradually swelling relief army, set the Moldavians and Wallachians to rebuilding the bridges. A contingent of troops, dispatched to the first island in boats by Lorraine, set up fieldpieces and persuaded the demonstrably unenthusiastic Rumanians to "desist from their enterprise." The piers, which had been exposed by a dropping water level, were smeared with pitch and ignited (August 31).[42]

B. The Organization of the Relief

THE GOVERNMENT IN EXILE

While the Duke was assuring Imperial control over the strategically critical northern portion of Lower Austria, the Habsburg Court was also contributing its moiety to the salvation of Vienna, the anti-Lorraine cabal notwithstanding. To be sure, it took the government some time to recover from the panic and confusion that marked its exodus from the capital on July 7. Ten days passed before it could really begin to address itself wholeheartedly to the administrative and diplomatic exigencies of the moment. During this period it was in almost continual flight. Upon arriving at Krems on July 8, the Emperor and his suite, fearing a sudden lunge by the Tatars, transferred to relatively safer water conveyances. After a day of troubled rest at Melk, they beat their way upstream to Linz (July 13). However, the news that the Tatars had pierced the blockaded Wienerwald and the suspicion that the young Count Zrinyi, son of the executed conspirator, would betray the Emperor's person, led to further flight in the early morning hours of the fifteenth.[43]

The odyssey finally concluded in episcopally-ruled Passau at 2:00 p.m. on July 17. The little hillside city, so suddenly transformed into the capital of the dynasty and the Empire, had probably never seen such hustle and bustle. Its inns and other places of accommodation were so jammed that some of the courtiers, bureaucrats, and foreign diplomats (and their flunkeys) were compelled to seek quarters in neighboring towns. Church bells rang out as intercessory prayers were offered; sacerdotal processions wended their way through the crowded streets. The Emperor, presumably wishing to exploit all possible sources of assistance, was a frequent attendant at such observances. Traffic on the Danube exceeded its normal proportions as men, animals, provisions, and equipment flowed through from the *Reich*. All this activity was subject to central planning and direction, at least insofar as the government of the day was capable of such functions. The various agencies appear to have begun their work forthwith. The very afternoon of his arrival Leopold was presented with a written program that specified the measures to be taken in both the diplomatic and logistical fields. However, the memorandum failed to make any mention of what was doubtlessly the Court's most urgent momentary concern: money.

Demands for cash were coming from every possible source: from prospective or actual allies, from diplomatic missions abroad (for their own maintenance), from suppliers of war matériel, and from units in the field. Even staunch friends expected compensation, as, for example, the Prince Bishop of Würzburg, who had been demanding payment of 4000 measures of grain since March. The Treasury was so hard-pressed that it could not even remunerate the army generals, who felt constrained to send a special delegate in an attempt to obtain their back wages. The monarchy's financial credit had sunk so low that no more funds could be raised on the open market. There were even threats of action over the collection of past debts. The Archbishop of Salzburg flatly rejected an appeal for a loan, written personally by Leopold. If the Papacy and its indefatigable agent, Cardinal Buonvisi, had not sprung into the financial breach, both with direct subsidies and with aid in the effort to shake down Salzburg and other wealthy prelacies (e.g., Prague, Olomouc, Wroclaw-Breslau), it is hard to imagine how the relief operation could ever have been initiated. When Buonvisi handed the Emperor a Papal exchange letter on August 16, the harassed sovereign broke into tears. There were not even 10,000 florins in his coffers at the time.[44]

If the financial support from Rome relieved Leopold of his most urgent immediate care, another source of encouragement was doubtlessly the appearance of several hundred noble and princely volunteers from the length and breadth of Europe. Among them was Eugene of Savoy, whom the far-sighted Borgomanero presented to the Emperor, presumably on August 14. On the other hand, the advent of chivalric young, bluebloods did not necessarily reflect devotion to the dynasty itself—the prestige of which had clearly suffered. Leopold almost certainly was aware of the adverse psychological effect created by his "desertion" of Vienna. Apparently, he also felt deeply humiliated. In writing to his spiritual confidant, Marco d'Aviano, he unburdened himself: "O my Father, who could have thought that it would come to this with me? Yet I will still always say: *Justus es, Domine, et recta judicia tua.*" Almost certainly the Emperor knew of the attitude of men like Prince Waldeck who told Count Harrach quite bluntly that the sovereign ought to have spent at least some time, sword in hand, at the head of his field forces. There is evidence that the masses harbored similar sentiments.

While it would be inaccurate to accuse Leopold of cowardice, it does appear that he was guilty of excessive familial solicitude. Harrach replied to Waldeck that it was necessary to consider the condition of the highly pregnant Empress, who could not bear to be separated from her spouse, and the well-being of the children. Surely, a ruler of heroic stature or even a monarch with a more lively sense of propriety would soon have found occasion for some gesture of militancy, if only a visit to the Duke's headquarters. Such qualities, of course, were not among the Emperor's virtues. Although certain advisers eventually persuaded him that he ought to involve himself more directly, the recognition came too late. Another head of state, who better understood the art of public relations, was destined to pre-empt the Viennese scene. Nevertheless, the flight itself, even if decided upon too late and executed maladroitly, was justified. Had Leopold allowed himself to be shut up in Vienna, the government would most likely have been immobilized and the organization of the relief would have become nearly impossible.[45]

Help from the *Reich* Germans

Perhaps the most efficient branch of the often unwieldy and creaking Austrian government was the diplomatic service. Here, the Emperor had as much good luck—or rather showed as much good judgment—as he did when he chose his generals. The first success achieved by a foreign mission was in Munich. On August 6, after much haggling, the venerable ambassador, Kaunitz, signed a treaty providing for implementation of the existing Habsburg-Wittelsbach alliance. While strategic interests were a major consideration for the Bavarians, equally important, perhaps even decisive, was the martial enthusiasm of their ruler, Max Emmanuel. His army, small and new but very well drilled and equipped, including at least some bayonets and flintlocks, provided the Austrians five infantry regiments with 1,200 men apiece (6,000), four of cavalry with 600 apiece (2,400) and one of dragoons (600). The overall total of 11,300 was reached by incorporation of a thousand Salzburgers, a battalion of Pfalzneuburgers, the Bavarian Circle regiment under Baron von Rummel, and five Imperial companies.

However, the young prince did not supply these forces without insisting firmly upon his sovereign rights. He reserved command to himself or, in his stead, Degenfeld. His soldiery would be subordinate only to the Imperial Field Marshal General or whoever should hold supreme allied command in his place. Otherwise Max Emmanuel was more generous than the rest of Austria's allies: his corps would pay its own food costs although the Emperor undertook to provide artillery. Eight of the regiments were underway even before the signing of the treaty: they tramped through Passau at the end of July and, as indicated, passed downstream to Krems. Degenfeld, a rather difficult character, balked at Lorraine's order to submit to Leslie's control and advance to the Tulln Plain. Although the Bavarian general was technically correct, his master nevertheless told him to obey Charles. The Electoral troops were joyfully received by the Austrian populace as the first outsiders to come to its rescue.[46]

The second contingent from the Empire represented the Franconian and Swabian Circles. It was under the leadership of Waldeck who had hurried off from Holland at the news of the Turkish advance in order to help Austria's emissary, Baron Schlitz von Görz, induce the local estates to round up and dispatch their men. The deputies needed much suasion: already in April they had protested the removal of two cuirassier regiments from Bohemia, and Leopold had found it necessary to remind them that he would have to quench the fire in his own house before saving his neighbor's. It was, in any case, ironical that Waldeck's Laxenburg Alliance, which had been directed primarily against Louis XIV, first came into play in the East. The Franconians, 6,000 foot and 2,000 horse, reached Passau on August 21 and Linz nine days later. They were followed in short order by the Württemberg Regiment (infantry apparently) of the Swabian Circle. Other Swabians were also supposed to come but did not put in an appearance until the end of October at the very end of the season's fighting. The delay was due to the uncertain relations with France. The recall of one full and two half Imperial regiments, which also traversed Passau in July and August, rendered the upper Rhine almost defenseless. The only remaining Habsburg unit was at Philippsburg, a citadel the security of which had worried Vienna ever since spring.[47] The Swabians therefore stationed the bulk of their troops nearby.

The unclear intentions of Louis XIV also complicated Leopold's efforts to obtain military help from the Electorate of Saxony. Not only did John George III (provisionally allied with Leopold since June 7) need to worry about the actions of France. He also had to consider possible moves by its Nordic clients, Denmark and Brandenburg. During the spring these two powers, abetted by French diplomats, had revived a plot of the previous year to despoil pro-Imperial Sweden of its German holdings. Left in the lurch by the Sun King at the last moment, they were now maneuvering shiftily, in competition with Brunswick-Lüneburg, for the lesser prizes of Lübeck, Hamburg, Bremen, Sachsen-Lauenburg and Mecklenburg-Schwerin (which better suited French purposes).[48] The Saxon ruler, also allied with the Welfs, could not be certain what Brandenburg would do next. Would it concentrate upon aiding Passau, or would it exploit the international situation for local advantage? An exchange of letters with Frederick William in the latter part of July did not clarify matters.

John George, however, had promised as early as July 13 to come to Austria's aid. A battle-hardened soldier himself, he seems to have recognized that the Turkish invasion posed a danger to his domains too. On July 21 the Duke of Sachsen-Lauenburg, who was serving with the Imperials, arrived with a personal appeal from Lorraine, an old comrade-in-arms of the Elector. The emissary also spoke, without authorization, of highly favorable terms. John George replied positively to Charles on July 22, and the next day the Dresden chancery began to issue mobilization decrees. However, the Great Elector's equivocal responses about participation in the relief effort and the absence as yet of a formal, detailed agreement with Leopold provoked a further round of doubt. Reassuring letters from Count Johann Philipp Lamberg, Austrian minister to Berlin (now a kind of roving ambassador), and notification of Imperial ratification of the alliance finally caused the Wettiner (August 1) to join his rendezvousing troops in an encampment outside the capital. To be sure,

(Vienna, National Library)

Elector Maximilian II Emmanuel of Bavaria

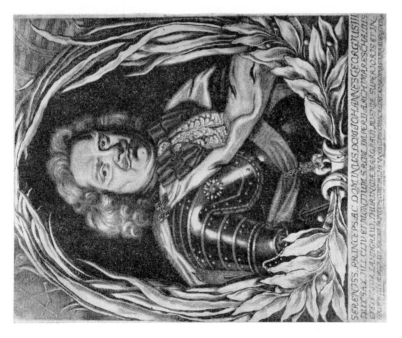

Elector John George III of Saxony

the exact conditions of Saxony's assistance were not yet spelled out. Above all, the Elector had to consider the cost of the expedition. He had already experienced some difficulty in getting his estates committee to sanction appropriations for the *future* expenses of the new, standing army. He had failed entirely to obtain hard cash for meeting its *momentary* needs. It was only natural for him to conclude that the Emperor ought to foot the bill. A further factor was probably suspicion that Frederick William was driving a hard bargain for Hohenzollern help. Imperial subsidies would serve the basic international interests of the Saxon state and neatly solve an irritating domestic issue. Hiring-out of one's army was of course a practice destined to become increasingly popular not only in the coming War of the Holy League but during the succeeding century as well.[49]

The demands of the Saxon Court, pressed by three separate agents sent to Leopold while the troops were being mustered and on the march seemed outrageous. They included maintenance costs, supreme command for John George over *all* German territorial contingents, winter quarters (a major worry of military administrations of the day), replacement of expended ammunition, a favorable decision in an old legal dispute over a strip of border land in the Erzgebirge (important to Saxony for mining purposes), and security measures in Moravia and Silesia to protect Saxony's rear. The Habsburger's response could only be negative. The result was that the Elector's advance through Bohemia became a casual promenade. Twice, as unfavorable reports arrived from Passau, he stopped and dawdled: once at Teplice and once at Prague. On the first occasion, after sending an ultimatum, he was induced to move on by Lamberg, who had rushed down from Berlin. On the second, having received no reply, he marched ahead of his own accord but threatened, probably insincerely, to halt after two days.

The situation was made all the more difficult by the fact that the Saxon soldiers, refused supplies by the Bohemian estates, had to take from the local population what they needed. John George himself strove vainly to raise money from home, one difficulty being that many Saxons were indignant over Austria's treatment of Magyar Protestants. Finally, messages arrived from the Emperor, indicating that he would yield on what was, after all, the heart of the matter: food, fodder and forage, which would be supplied on credit. Ammunition would be replaced without charge. As for pretensions to supreme command, Leopold labored under the illusion that his own appearance would automatically resolve all rivalries.[50] The other points were glossed over or ignored. The Elector, surely also influenced by Lorraine's repeated pleas, now crossed into Lower Austria. He led his 7,000 all-musketeer foot, 2,000 horse, and superb field artillery as far as Maissau, just inside the "Quarter below the Manhartsberg." While the army camped in driving rain, John George hurried off to confer with the commanders of the other contingents.[51]

If the unsettled state of affairs along the lower Elbe helped to make Austria's parleys with Saxony difficult, it had an even unhappier effect upon the posture of the Emperor's other north German ally, the Duke of Brunswick-Lüneburg. Ernst August, who might have provided as many as 18,000 men under other circumstances, could not possibly transfer his army to the far-off Danube and had to content himself with dispatching a battalion of reiters, perhaps 600 men. As an additional sign of his good will, he sent two of his sons, including the then twenty-three-year-old, future English King, George I.[52] Almost certainly the two Saxon princes were envied by their Hohenzollern counterpart, the shy, sickly Frederick, who would gladly have travelled the same southward route but could not talk his father, the Great Elector, into assisting Leopold.

Indeed, Berlin, the only real failure of Austrian diplomacy during the summer of 1683, was the scene of an impassioned, shifting diplomatic tug-of-war. In June and early July, the pro-Imperial faction, which also included Frederick William's personal confidant, Prince George of Anhalt-Dessau, and the former's best general, the Austrian-born Derfflinger, appeared to be ahead, in part because of France's failure to join in the Danish-Hohenzollern plot that might have given the Brandenburger his much-covered Swedish Pomerania. Upon receiving the news of the Emperor's flight from Vienna, the Great Elector declared his willingness to help if a precise agreement could be worked out; shortly thereafter he ordered the mobilization of his troops. However, the French party and Louis XIV's ambassador, the Comte de Rébenac, exerted themselves strenuously, and by late July the ailing and crotchety sovereign was increasingly hesitant. In his mind, the opposing arguments probably seemed to strike a balance. To assist Leopold was the manly, soldierly, and German thing to do; and, conceivably, the Turks endangered Brandenburg too. On the other hand, the promptly-transmitted French subsidies were essential, and it was questionable whether the Emperor could provide equal financial or territorial benefits. Leopold could scarcely compel his Swedish friends to renounce Pomerania: the most that could possibly be had from him was a favorable settlement of Brandenburg's long-standing claim upon the Jägerndorf section of Silesia.[53]

In the last analysis, Frederick William seems to have made his decision dependent upon the results of negotiations which Anhalt, dispatched to Passau, was conducting. The remonstrations of the tireless Lamberg were now seen to have been of little avail. The Austrian government, informed of Brandenburg's financial and territorial requirements, was appalled. However, it had little difficulty in prevailing upon the fundamentally pro-Habsburg envoy to give in. The treaty, signed August 12, even contained a clause that tied the Great Elector to Leopold in resisting the

French over the reunions. Anhalt had exceeded, indeed virtually discarded his instructions, and it is hardly surprising that his patron refused to ratify the document.[54] It was a *dénouement* quite in keeping with the basic character of the Great Elector's reign. While Passau thought it worthwhile to continue discussions, it was now obvious that no Hohenzollern troops could arrive in time to reinforce Lorraine. Leopold's disappointment must have been all the more intense, for it appears that he had definitely counted upon some 12,000 Brandenburgers and, above all, the doughty Derfflinger.[55]

POLAND MOBILIZES

If the Emperor was somewhat naive in placing so much faith in Frederick William, he was, on the other hand, justified in trusting John Sobieski. After all, the Polish king was contractually obligated to come to the relief of Vienna. His troops, or at least a goodly portion of them, were already mobilized, thanks in part to Habsburg subsidies. The Poles, of course, had not waited for the Turks to appear at the gates of Austria's capital in order to take to the field. The *Sejm* that ratified the alliance with Leopold laid the legal foundations for Polish rearmament on April 17. In a *scriptum ad archivum* the deputies not only strove to vindicate their prospective breach of the existing peace treaty with the Porte. They also authorized a threefold increase of the 12,000 man standing army and a doubling of Lithuania's 6,000 troops. The King, for his part, reckoned that he could muster some 4,000 of his beloved Cossacks. Thus the Republic would dispose of a force of 52,000 men, 12,000 more than were required by the alliance. The next step was to settle upon a definite campaign plan, for which purpose a war council met at Warsaw on April 30. The conferees resolved that Poland should launch an offensive against Turkish-held Podolia (Kamenets) and the Turkish sector of the Ukraine, which was no more than what was foreseen in the alliance agreement. Only 4,000 cavalry would be made available to the Imperials in Hungary.[56] This decision merits special attention because of Sobieski's oft-cited criticism of Leopold for having failed to heed Polish warnings that the Grand Vezir would attack Vienna.[57] Had John III really believed such reports himself, it is unlikely that he would have arranged to marshal his own forces in the far distant southeast.

In May the Poles pursued their mobilization efforts further by putting the southeastern frontier on defensive alert and by fortifying Kraków. The security of the latter place was also improved by blockading the nearby Żywiec (Saybutsch) Pass in the Beskids, which controlled egress from Upper Hungary. Arrangements were made with the Austrian ambassador Zierowski for an Imperial regiment to assume temporary guard over the place. In the meantime recruiting was well underway. On May 19 Pallavicini reported to Rome that 36,700 men were already under arms. The relatively rapid organization of so large a force was possible partly because Poland possessed a vast reservoir of aristocratic cavaliers. (Ironically, the King would have preferred a greater number of foot. He did not wish to be dependent upon Leopold for infantry and had modified the Diet's original scheme as to the relative size of the various components of the army.) Another reason for the fairly swift military expansion was the fact that the standing army, made up of troops retained after the last peace with the Sultan (1677), was a cadre of officers and non-coms. These units, stationed near the Podolian frontier, were brought up to full strength. A third advantage was the general enthusiasm of the public for a new war against an old enemy: the nation had come to regard the terms of the existing peace treaty with Turkey as unduly onerous. By May 25 the crown Grand Hetman, Stanisław Jabłonowski, and the Field Hetman, Nicholas Sieniawski, had left Warsaw for the designated theater of operations. John III, however, tarried in Warsaw. He did not intend to proceed eastward until the end of July, which was the seasonable time to open a campaign in that part of Europe. In the meantime he would look after additional mobilization and logistical requirements.[58]

While a large number of men could be mustered rather quickly in the various parts of the realm, concentrating them in one region and assuring their material support was altogether another matter. The vast distances involved and the more or less underdeveloped status of the national economy made it impossible for the Poles to *consummate* their mobilization as readily as Leopold's other allies could. The geographical propinquity of the more densely settled and technologically advanced German territorial states assured the prompter arrival of the latters' contingents. Another obstacle to attaining the full strength authorized by the *Sejm* was financial. The original momentum of Poland's military preparations seems to have been due mainly to the prospect of Imperial subsidies, which were transferred during May and June via Prague and Breslau, the capitals of the conveniently wealthy provinces of Bohemia and Silesia. Of almost equal importance were the 300,000 fl. sent from Rome by the end of June. However, these sums, for all their significance, constituted only a fraction, perhaps no more than one tenth of the total expense of rearmament. Since the state's revenue officers had little success in their initial efforts to collect the imposts voted by the Diet, Sobieski found it expedient to dip into his own private coffers, an action which surprised certain less-penetrating observers of the Polish scene. A further problem was that the aristocratic cavalrymen, although enlisted with the promise of wages, were responsible for their own fitting-out. Finally, the peasants, also expected to pay for equipping themselves, were entirely without means, the result of which was that the King failed to raise as many infantrymen as he originally planned upon.[59] Both kinds of difficulties, geographic-economic and fiscal, became all too obvious when the news of the siege of Vienna compelled John III not only to shift his campaign westward but also to draw his troops together in a compact and efficient striking force suitable for immediate emergency engagement.[60]

Troubles already began to appear during the latter part of June, for by then Sobieski deemed it advisable to address a circular letter to his generals and palatines urging greater speed. At the same time it was becoming clear that the initial campaign plan was in jeopardy. As early as the middle of the month it was rumored that the King would move from his palace of Wilanów near Warsaw to Kraków, in order to survey carefully "il Tratto del Reyno, che confina coll' Ungheria." Orders were also sent to Sieniawski to retire from his advanced post near Trembovlya to the vicinity of Lvov, these moves apparently caused by a story to the effect that Thököly, reinforced by a body of Turks, intended to drive across the still weakly-held Beskids and lay waste to southwestern Poland. Another factor in the weakening of the original strategy was the Pope's refusal to release Curial subsidies until at least some of the Cossaks were committed to action in Hungary. Talks with Muscovy concerning joint action against the Turks and Tatars were also making only slow progress.[61] That John III was reluctant to shift his emphasis westward is a fairly safe assumption: his country's major political interest was, after all, Podolia. By July 4, however, it was apparent that action in that region was no longer feasible. Under instructions from Leopold, Zierowski and Pallavicini went to the ruler and requested 7,000 men for the Váh: the imminent expiration of the truce with Thököly meant that Schultz and Lubomirski would need help in guarding the approaches to Moravia and Silesia. The Emperor also asked for assistance in arranging new talks with the rebels. Sobieski agreed to recall Sieniawski and to establish a sort of strategic reserve near Kraków.[62] He also accepted the other proposal, presumably with greater alacrity: apart from some vague sympathy which he felt for the Magyars, an Imperial *rapprochement* with them would be advantageous to his own land on both a long and short term basis.[63]

SOBIESKI'S MARCH

In the meantime the Austrian position in Hungary had begun to collapse. On July 5 the Habsburg Court sent Count Philipp von Thurn (Conte della Torre) to Poland to plead for the dispatch of as many troops as circumstances would permit. After a ten-day, 375-mile journey and a further day's wait, the new emissary was granted an audience at Wilanów, accompanied by Waldstein and Pallavicini (July 15). The King now agreed to let Sieniawski advance to the Danube; if Vienna were besieged, he would come himself. Within a day more bad news arrived: the ambassador and the nunzio appeared again to report the Emperor's flight and to request immediate fulfillment of the royal promise to go in person.[64] The Polish leader wrote Leopold that he would leave forthwith. Marching orders also went out to most of the troops still in the southeast. Pallavicini was doubtlessly relieved. He had been pressing the monarch to proceed to Kraków for at least a month, but the parleys with Muscovy and the after effects of the Queen's recent accouchement had interfered. On July 18 Sobieski, his elder son (Prince Jakób), and the clinging-vine Marsieńka took to the road. Since geography prevented a rapid rendezvous of the various troop units, haste was unnecessary. There was time to make a detour to Częstochowa in order to seek the help of the Black Virgin. There was also opportunity, while en route, to mull over military plans. A letter of July 19 to the Great Elector, which called attention to a small, vestigial East Prussian, feudal obligation, reflected concern for drawing troops from every possible source.[65]

A longer epistle in redundant Baroque Latin, written July 22 in reply to the Duke of Lorraine's announcement of the beginning of the siege, shows that the Polish sovereign was studying not only the strategy but also the tactics of the projected relief operation. This document, the lost antecedent of which was apparently very brief, is of unique significance. It proves that John III (who was rather piqued for not having heard from the Duke earlier and for not having received more substantial information) was coming *independently* to the same conclusions as Charles about the best route for approaching the besieged city. The King emphasized proper selection and use of the Danube bridges, whether at Vienna, at Krems, or in between. He specifically rejected crossing at Bratislava. He was, moreover, anxious to learn about the terrain near and above Vienna and repeatedly implored Lorraine to provide precise details. The letter also demonstrated awareness of the continuing danger of a flank attack from Upper Hungary, for Sobieski enquired about measures along the Morava and reported that a Polish vanguard had left for the lower Beskid region (Bielsko). Finally, Poland's ruler was having second thoughts about Sieniawski. He asked whether the Field Hetman should be sent on ahead. If any Sarmatian was going to gather glory, it would have to be John III: a throne so shaky required a full monopoly on military prestige. Had the Duke been less sensitive and perceptive, the salvation of Vienna might well have been impaired. His answers to the July 22 missive and to later, sometimes rather peremptory notes, are masterpieces of modesty and tact. Among other things, the Duke flattered the elective monarch with the use, in Latin, of the title "Your Majesty" rather than "Your Serenity"—a legal concession the Emperor could not bring himself to make.[66]

On July 29 Sobieski entered Kraków. Four days later Sieniawski also appeared. Jabłonowski arrived on August 8. How many troops were present by then is unclear but surely not enough to proceed farther at once. It seems that men were coming in daily from different parts of the country by drops and driblets.[67] Regrouping an army first scheduled for mobilization some 300 miles to the southeast was not easy. On August 6 the King, having learned from Lorraine of the Bratislava victory, sent his congratulations. He added that he was exercising all diligence to speed the expedition's departure, that within a few days his armies would advance beyond Kraków; he himself would follow shortly after St. Lawrence's Day (August 10) in order that "primus diebus Septembris actualiter Nostra Caesareis iungamus arma."[68] St. Lawrence was a special recipient of royal veneration. On the day in question, a vast throng, comprising all social orders, filled the cathedral. Pallavicini preached a fiery sermon, celebrated a Solemn High Mass, pronounced a public indulgence, imparted the papal blessing in *articulo mortis,* and blessed the army. The tearful Queen observed the scene from her hidden loft. John III then descended to the building's crypt and, displaying his characteristic flair for the dramatic, picked a spot for his own grave amidst the tombs of predecessors.

On the next day came Lorraine's reply to the letter of July 22: it included maps, a request for the fast dispatch of Sieniawski, and an appeal for great haste. The answer, sent forthwith, stated that Sieniawski had already advanced as far as Bielsko and would move on to the Olomouc area where he would rest his horses while waiting for the separately marching main portion of the army: should the Duke really need him, he could be ordered ahead. The other part of the army under Jabłonowski was leaving Kraków the same day for Silesia. The Polish sovereign himself would follow around the Feast of the Assumption (August 15). Unfortunately, it would be necessary to leave behind a large part of the army, especially some thousand Cossacks and all the Lithuanians. Hopefully, some troops would come later, but it was clear that a substantial number would have to stay in Poland, in particular to guard Volhynia and Ruthenia against a surprise Tatar attack.[69] There is no sure way of telling exactly how large the Vienna-bound force was then or later, but in no case did it reach the 40,000-man figure specified by the alliance. When it left Kraków, it was described by Pallavicini as probably consisting of 13,000 good, experienced horse, and 2,000 Hussars—but only "qualche migliaia" of foot, who would travel in carts from Silesia onward in order to save time and strength.[70] While there are some indications that further troops joined on the march, it appears unlikely that there were many more than 18,000 men when Sobieski reached the Danube.[71]

Originally, the Polish army was supposed to have taken three separate routes to Austria, probably in order to ease pressure upon the countryside through which it would pass. It is not clear why it ultimately formed only two columns, one of which, led by Sieniawski, moved along the northern edge of the Beskids (the Cieszyn or Teschen region), while the other, commanded by the King, travelled to Upper Silesia and across the Jeksenik Range of the Sudetes. Possibly, the reason was again the political necessity of absolute royal control. On the other hand, a third, even more circuitous line of march might have entailed too much delay. In any case, John III left Kraków on August 15 and, with his spouse and the whole Court still in tow, wended his way leisurely to the Silesian border. Greater speed would probably not have served much purpose anyway: the monarch calculated, correctly, that the news that he was underway would stimulate further units into appearing. At Tarnowskie Góry, upon Imperial soil, the overweight but still saddle-worthy Sobieski halted for a full day (August 21) ; then on the next morning took leave of his wife—who became regent in his absence—and began to ride at a brisker tempo. In the meantime two further letters had arrived from the Duke. The first, dated August 7, asked once again that Sieniawski be sent ahead of the main Polish corps. The second, dated August 15, included the recent communications from Vienna, and begged the King himself to hurry on ahead with the first troops available. At the same time Lorraine despatched Count Caraffa to reinforce his pleas. John III replied on August 22 that after supervising the start of his army's march another day he would advance in person "cum selecta et expedita militiae manu." He made no mention of Sieniawski. Nor did it prove possible to leave the army for another three days. Even the arrival (August 24) of the Duke's letter of the 19th, which announced the departure of the Austrians for Krems, had no immediate effect.[72]

Only on the 25th, after receipt of news that Lubomirski and Charles had been pressing Sieniawski directly, did the ruler race ahead of the main body, attended by only twenty standards of light horse, some 3,000 men. He wrote his wife that day that he feared that the Duke and Sieniawski, whom he now expressly ordered to halt, might carelessly precipitate matters. He added, candidly but illogically, that he was worried that he might be deprived of glory, should the Turks flee at the news of the mere advent of the first Polish units. Adulation was another matter: the King would soon have more of it than he could bear. He had been fêted, wined, and dined already at Gliwice (August 22) and Raciborz (August 24) ; more of the same awaited him at Opava (Troppau) on August 25 and, in particular, at Olomouc on August 26. By the 27th he was complaining he was sick of the continual harangues, parades, ceremonies, and the need to dress up "like a bridegroom." The Emperor's welcoming envoy, Count Christoph von Schaffgotsch, had also annoyed him by presuming to give advice. Furthermore, although the sovereign and his personal following were treated as guests, the troops were not. Food was expensive by Polish standards, and the population was reluctant to sell, most likely because the Austrian government had ordered the acceptance of light-weight Polish coins.[73]

Around noon of the 29th the Poles reached Brno, and having been

regaled *à la Française* by the local governor, Kolowrath, proceeded in the
afternoon to the outlying village of Modric. They were now entering the
southern part of Moravia, a rich agricultural land, the bounty of which
greatly impressed both the monarch and his troopers. Many of the common soldiers (especially the bedraggled infantry) who passed through a
few days later fell ravenously upon the ripening crops.[74] Without opportunity to purchase food or lacking money for it, they had no choice but to
rob. Sobieski, for his part, seems to have been momentarily less concerned
with victualing his men than with increasing their numbers. Where, he
wrote home to Marysieńka, were the Cossacks, bought so dearly, and the
Lithuanians? The next day (August 30), as the Sarmatian reiters approached the Lower Austrian frontier near Drnholec, it became clear that
the long odyssey from Wilanów was nearing its climax. A short side trip
to the east brought the King and his son to Mikulov (Nikolsburg) where
they viewed the sights and conferred with Sieniawski who had loyally
followed the order not to join Lorraine. The Field Hetman and his royal
master discussed arrangements for linking up their forces the next day.
There was much else to talk about, because, although the correspondence
with Charles had become much more frequent during the previous
week,[75] John III still felt uninformed and uncertain about his army's next
moves. At 2:00 p.m. on the 31st, Lorraine, who had rushed forward upon
Sobieski's request (August 29) for a conference, took the latter somewhat
by surprise on the open road just to the north of the Lower Austrian
town of Oberhollabrunn. Personal rapport was almost instantly achieved
although the style-conscious King did not fail to take critical note of the
Duke's sartorial inelegance. The relationship was firmly cemented in an
evening of alcohol-permeated bonhomie. The tact of self-effacing Charles
was beginning to pay off.[76]

C. The Advance into the Wienerwald

THE STETTELDORF CONFERENCE

The circumstances of the Oberhollabrunn meeting hardly favored serious discussion of military matters. In addition to the general state of
inebriation, no other allied potentate was present with the exception of
Prince Waldeck who put in the briefest of appearances. A full-fledged
council of war, which would dispose of all outstanding issues, especially
command responsibility and strategy, was indispensable. In the interval
several lesser conferences took place, the best-documented of which was
between Charles and Waldeck. The Duke and the Empire's Field Marshal General found their "sentiments to be in conformity." With Saxony
in mind, they agreed that the leader of each individual contingent ought
to guide his own troops in battle. Much squabbling could thus be
avoided. However, this problem and the related question of protocol

could not be settled quite so easily, as became apparent the next day at the chateau of Stetteldorf (near Stockerau and the Danube Meadows), the scene of the main council-of-war. The initial item of business was who should have the honor of speaking first, the Imperial generals or the Polish hetmans? Likewise Lorraine, sensitive about his own status as a sovereign ruler, was unwilling to yield to the Electors of Bavaria and Saxony. Fortunately, the former failed to appear, and the latter arrived only rather late. Sobieski, who was more interested in observing whether his partners' dress was stylish or not, proposed having the representatives of each national or territorial group consult separately and then refer their conclusions to him for final examination and approval. Waldeck, who could scarcely conceal his impatience over procedural "vanities," could not see any point in wasting time in so many separate conferences and said that he and Degenfeld would join the Imperials while the Poles talked among themselves.[77]

Since the Polish ruler and (later) John George more or less accepted the results of the Austro-Franconian-Bavarian parley, the notes Waldeck took of its deliberations are of prime historical significance. It was agreed that the only feasible route for the relief army was directly over the Wienerwald.[78] If the Emperor did not come in person, supreme command would remain with the King, but each chief would lead his own troops. All the armies would approach the Danube bridges on Sunday, September 5, where they would find sufficient forage and could be provided with bread. They would cross over on Monday or, at the latest, Tuesday. The Imperials and the Poles would traverse the river at Tulln. The Saxons would pass at Krems in order to unite with the Bavarian and Circle troops who were already on the other side at the Traisen near the latter's confluence with the Danube. Despite the apparent inactivity of the foe, it would be necessary to provide for security during the crossing. The Saxons would be covered by the forces on the Traisen. The Poles would precede the Imperials in order to link up with the Bavaro-Franconians; the Duke would follow in turn. Eight days' rations of bread and oats would be dispensed from barges at Tulln. The bridge and the magazine at Tulln would be protected by the town on one side and by a palisaded work on the other. Soldiers and burghers would defend the Krems installations. Supplies would follow the army's further march down the river. As for tactics, it was decided for the time-being only that the infantry would bear the brunt of the attack, backed by some cavalry; the cavalry wings would have some infantry cover; and the rear would be ensured by a reserve. Northern Lower Austria would be shielded by a corps of 2,000 horse joined to the Poles still on their way; the Lithuanians, still far distant, would guard the frontiers of Silesia. Should the Turks penetrate the Wienerwald farther south and seek to strike the Christian rear, they would encounter the reserve. As soon as the relief action was executed, the allied armies should be used to pursue the enemy and to attack Nové Zámky.[79]

It should be emphasized that Lorraine, Waldeck, and Degenfeld did not recommend a specific *ordre de bataille*. Records of the Stetteldorf meeting show only that three different proposals for aligning the troops were under consideration. The biggest problem was whether the allies should, in fact, adhere strictly to the principle of each chief leading his own men. From the viewpoint of sovereign dignity, this approach was still desirable. On the other hand, the Bavarian, Saxon, Franconian and even some of the Polish units were newly-organized and untried in combat: on military grounds one ought to mix them with the now veteran Imperial regiments. Common sense finally carried the day. The conferees concluded not only that their forces should be regarded as one body in setting up the *ordre de bataille* but that the question of their segregation or mingling should depend upon the character of the terrain and upon considerations of operational effectiveness. All of the infantry would likewise constitute one body. Some expedient would be found for settling the matter of special commands for the Electors. Most importantly, it was decided that the whole army would rendezvous at Tulln on September 7. It would then take three to four days to cross the plain and the Vienna Woods and so reach the city.[80]

Aside from the initial clash over precedence the allied war council seems to have been held in an atmosphere of relative cordiality. One of the reasons for harmony probably was that there could be no real argument over who, of those present, ought to be commander-in-chief. As far as the Austrian generals were concerned, John III was legally entitled to the job: the treaty with Poland specified that whichever sovereign should happen to be in the camp would be in charge. The German territorial rulers, while traditionally unwilling to yield priority of rank to foreign kings, did have to face the fact that there was no one who had as much experience in battle against the Turks as Sobieski. Nevertheless, one cloud still hovered threateningly over the Stetteldorf horizon: namely, the possibility that the Emperor might also take to the field. Should Leopold, indisputably the first monarch of Christendom in questions of protocol, appear, the Polish king would have to take second place. That such a prospect failed to gladden John III's heart is hardly surprising. Already once (with respect to Sieniawski) he had revealed how critical it was for him to maintain royal prestige. His first reaction—before August 30—to the suggestion that Leopold might come was the remark that he himself would have no objections but that he would not be able to explain it to the people back home.[81] His reluctance is all the more understandable when one considers that the Austrians had begged him to come, the logical inference of which was that he should have command of the united armies.[82]

In Passau the ministers themselves had not been of one mind in the matter. Some advised the Emperor that he ought not to go since Sobieski would be offended at having to renounce the "gloria de esta tan considerable operación." Buonvisi especially opposed the idea.[83] Nevertheless, by August 16 the Austrian ruler decided that the maintenance of decorum required his attendance in the field. He would leave for Linz as soon as possible, then proceed to Krems and there govern himself according to circumstances. The King, however, could retain control of military affairs since he was "un tan bueno General." Doubtlessly, the determinative factor was the influence of Sinelli, Sinzendorf, and Borgomanero. The Spanish ambassador reported to the *Consejo del Estado*:

> I replied to [His Majesty] that I had already told the Bishop of Vienna and the Lord Steward that he should and could not remain away from the army because of his personal dignity; that it would look very bad in the world at large if, while a king and two electors came in person to defend his domains, the Imperial crown, and, indeed, the whole of Christendom, he would stay here; that his presence was also useful in overcoming the disunity caused by the meeting of so many high chiefs.[84]

To be sure, the cabal found a ready hearing. The Imperial letter to Marco d'Aviano may be recalled, and there are also documents in the Spanish archives which imply Leopold's painful awareness of the degrading side-effects of the flight from Vienna. Thus, on August 25 the Court made its way to Linz. However, the Emperor was by no means resolute. Already the next day he asked Waldeck whether the plan of proceeding to the army was wise. While the Prince believed that such a move would have been appropriate earlier, he apparently recognized that the situation had since changed and therefore gave a guarded reply. Then came the first direct news of Sobieski's reaction. These rebuffs ought to have settled the question once and for all but did not. At least three different persons were commissioned to press the issue. They included: Hermann, who went off to Stetteldorf; Schaffgotsch, the Imperial emissary with the Poles; and Aviano, who was on his way to the army as special Papal legate. The Emperor apparently also expected Lorraine to put in a good word and even went so far as to write the King personally.[85] Then, on September 7, a message was sent forward stating that Leopold would depart the next day. The response to all these gambits was negative. Hermann neglected to report. Schaffgotsch's pleas were rejected twice, once by the Vice-Chancellor Gniński and once by the King, who used the excuse that Leopold would be running the risk of a Tatar attack. Aviano did not lift a finger and avoided mentioning the question in his letters.[86]

In the meantime the barge containing the Imperial party floated downstream as far as Dürnstein where it lay at anchor below the romantic ruins of the castle where another Leopold, a Babenberger, had once held Richard the Lionhearted captive. This feint fooled no one, least of all

John III. On September 10 the Emperor received the most unequivocal advice yet. General Rabata and Count Lamberg arrived and announced that everybody was against Leopold's coming. The King, the Duke, all the generals had stated bluntly that his presence would be more burdensome than useful. Memories of his unfortunate involvement in the First Hungarian Campaign may also have played a rôle. The Emperor and his suite hurriedly conferred and concluded they had no choice but to stay in their awkward, momentary location until they learned of the Turks' withdrawal. Then they would move on to Vienna and celebrate a *Te Deum* in St. Stephen's. In the meantime no one else would be permitted to enter the liberated city.[87] The last two days of exile were passed with increasing impatience: Leopold's correspondence with Aviano shows that he hoped to the very last for a reprieve. Only on the eve of the Battle of the Kahlenberg did the priest reply—obliquely—to the Imperial entreaties: the unresolved problem of the proper ceremonial in a meeting with Sobieski could cause disturbance, were Leopold to appear. As things stood, all was running smoothly—for which circumstance the padre was himself to some degree responsible.[88] Thus, in the interests of Vienna's salvation, the Austrian ruler sacrificed his pride and swallowed the last bitter dregs from 1683's cup of humiliation.

THE ALLIES SET FORTH

While the Emperor and his courtiers were fretfully pondering the question of participating in the relief action, the allied armies were effecting their rendezvous at Tulln and commencing the arduous march up into the Wienerwald. The passage of the Saxons at Krems appears to have been relatively secure and easy. The crossing of the Poles and Austrians at Tulln was, however, considerably more complicated and dangerous. To be sure, the omnipresent von Hasslingen, put in charge of construction by Leslie, had outdone himself in extracting lumber from the Lower Austrian Estates and in obtaining hardware at Steyr as a substitute for material which had been ordered from the Netherlands earlier but which had failed to arrive, allegedly because of French machinations. The irrepressible junior officer had also succeeded, with the aid of a crew of 600 peasants and 1,000 musketeers, in hacking out the road through the Donauauen, commissioned by Lorraine on the twenty-third. The presence of Bridge Captain Peter Rulant and several other technicians, whom Starhemberg had foresightedly recalled from Philippsburg in April, and the prior efforts of the Court Chamber were likewise essential to the progress of work. Nature, on the other hand, failed to cooperate. Continual rains raised the level of the Danube. The greater volume of water coursing through the lesser branches of the river seems to have hampered the use of fords and to have necessitated the building of an additional span (making a total of three). There were not enough boatmen and beams for the last part of the job, the completion of which was delayed, much to the annoyance of certain Poles. The powerful, rising current continually ripped pontoons loose. The new, low-lying road became muddy and required patching.[89]

Nevertheless, by September 6, Sobieski was ready to risk the transfer. He himself rode over to the opposite shore first, had his tent pitched and observed the undertaking in the company of a group of allied princes and generals. The sun finally broke through the clouds, dried up the puddles, if not the subsoil, and cast its rays upon the highly-polished armor of the Polish cavalry. The sharp contrast between the lavishly equipped and garbed troopers and the slovenly infantry that succeeded them was surely a source of embarrassment for the King. He covered his feelings, however, by quipping to his foreign colleagues that the men marching past should be watched closely: they were the cream of his foot units and had vowed to clothe themselves only in the rich raiment of the beaten enemy. The difficult maneuver was completed the next day without incident. The only problem was that it did not possible to bring over more than a fraction of the heavy supply wagons, upon which the Polish soldiers were dependent because of Tatar ravishment of the Tulln Plain and the Wienerwald.[90]

Despite recurring rain, the Duke of Lorraine followed immediately with the Imperial army, having detached three mounted regiments and two foot battalions to join 3,000 Poles in covering the Moravian frontier. At the same time (September 7) Col. Heissler and 600 horse were dispatched to the crest of the Kahlenberg to light a fire and so inform Vienna of its impending relief. By the eighth the whole army was united and encamped outside Tulln. While the troops were issued rations, the generals again deliberated. Once more there appears to have been a wrangle over command responsibilities, for the settlement of which Charles was (allegedly) responsible. The *ordre de bataille* finally approved provided that the Austro-Germans would form three wings, left, center, and right, while the Poles would take the extreme right. The left, led by the Duke, would consist of Imperial cavalry and infantry, mixed with Saxons; John George, who had first wanted command of the whole wing, contented himself with directing his own men. The center, under Waldeck, was to be made up of Bavarian and Franconian foot; Max Emmanuel agreed to accompany his troops in a volunteer capacity only. The left fell to the Duke of Sachsen-Lauenburg and a mixed body of Bavarian, Franconian, and Imperial horse. The extreme right, from the viewpoint of etiquette the most desirable location, went to Sobieski, whose mostly mounted forces required a greater breadth of terrain. The position was also the most dangerous as it was exposed to possible flank attack by Turko-Tataric cavalry. Soon after these measures were taken, Baron Mercy rode off in the direction of Mauerbach, a town in the vertically-extending valley to the right of the projected Polish sector, in order to reconnoiter movements in the Turkish camp.[91]

On the ninth, at daybreak, the Austro-Germans broke camp, traversed the Tulln Plain for some six miles and halted at the northwestern rim of the Vienna Woods between St. Andrä and Königstetten, preparatory to entering the mountains and seizing all stations necessary for further advance. Sobieski, who had agreed to the march at Charles' insistence, remained behind for reasons which are not entirely clear but which probably include both truculence over the Emperor's possible advent and concern over the continuing absence of sufficient supply wagons.[92] Intelligence from Vienna and Baron Mercy's report caused the Duke to write the King, again urging him to depart. John III, who was clearly flattered by the deferential treatment accorded him as commander-in-chief by Lorraine and all the other princes, generals, and aristocrats, assented immediately, for by evening the Poles lay in the burned-out region between Königstetten and Tulbing. The various leaders then conferred and decided upon the routes to be taken by their respective forces through the Wienerwald the next day.

The line of rendezvous lay behind the last major range of peaks opposite Vienna, that is to say, in the valley of the Weidling, which runs horizontally out of the hills and into the Danube at Klosterneuburg. Charles himself scouted the biways and posts lying ahead the same night and sent forward a substantial advance guard of infantry and dragoons. On the tenth the main allied units, guided by well-oriented Imperial huntsmen, ventured into the rugged terrain between themselves and the besieged city. Charles, with the Austrians and the Saxon infantry, took the two northernmost passages, one directly along the river via Greiffenstein and Höflein and the other through the valley of Gugging and Kierling. The cavalry of the left wing followed. Both roads were fairly level although blocked by felled trees (presumably the barricades of early July) that had to be removed. Waldeck and Lauenburg led their commands into the Hagenbach Ravine above St. Andrä where they split into two columns, the foot driving their way across the Kierling (Klosterneuburg) Forest into the Rotgraben, the horse proceeding directly into the upper Weidling Valley. Imperial headquarters were established in the town of Weidling, just west of Klosterneuburg, the retention of which now proved to be most advantageous. The day's travel was extremely arduous. The lanes and trails often seemed almost unusable. The result was that the artillery lagged far behind. The Poles had encountered the hardest going of all: they literally clambered their way in several columns up past Mount Tulbing, stubbornly dragging their fieldpieces with them. The path beyond, leading over rocks, through narrow gorges and thick forests, was hardly any better. Empty stomachs made matters even worse: the horses at least could feed on leaves, while the Austro-Germans ob-

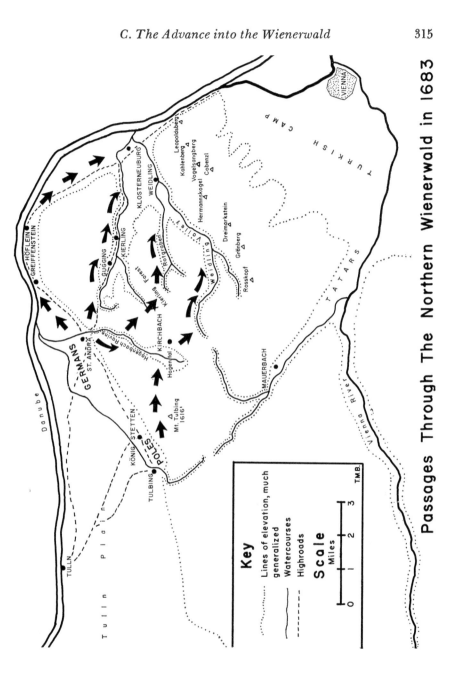

Passages Through The Northern Wienerwald in 1683

tained some supplies via the river. By sundown the exhausted cavalry and infantry had gotten only as far as Kirchbach in the upper Hagental, barely two miles from the morning's camp: the cannoneers continued to labor throughout the night.[93]

THE SEIZURE OF THE CREST

Sobieski himself hurried off the same evening in the direction of Weidling to confer with his colleagues.[94] The first object of discussion was the heights today known as the Leopoldsberg and the Kahlenberg. A particularly critical point was the wrecked Camaldulensian Monastery of St. Joseph, atop the Kahlenberg.[95] Should Kara Mustafa decide to reinforce weak observation detachments already there, the allies would find themselves in serious trouble. The King and his associates agreed that Imperial troops should secure the position. When this was accomplished, the full allied force of about 65,000[96] men could climb from the valley and occupy the ridge between the two summits mentioned and others farther to the southwest (Vogelsangberg, Cobenzl, Hermannskogel, Dreimarkstein, Gränberg, Rosskopf), which would make a front of approximately six miles. Charles thereupon rode off into the night, which he spent reconnoitering the various ascents and preparing an attack upon fortified St. Leopold's Chapel (Leopoldsberg), a necessary preliminary to the capture of the monastery.

By dawn sixty musketeers and the Marchese Parella's band of Italian volunteers (*avvanturieri*), including probably Eugene of Savoy, had overcome the small Ottoman unit in the place. The commandos then appropriated St. Joseph's and were quickly reinforced with Saxon foot. By 11:00 a.m. the main body of the army, the Austro-Germans at any rate, were on the scene. In the meantime, Charles had returned to the valley. After hearing Mass, he met Sobieski and, from the heights to the north of Weidling, explained to the King how the soldiers would advance up the Kahlenberg. Strengthened spiritually by Marco d'Aviano's apostolic blessing, the Christian host set forth in three columns. Once they had reached the crest, the men encamped in three lines (four or more in some places according to the terrain) in approximate accordance with the previously established *ordre de bataille*. Rough entrenchments were thrown up and *chevaux de frise* mounted. Apart from six small regimental pieces, the artillery was still lacking. It arrived only during the course of the night, the steep, muddy tracks requiring the use of double and triple teams. The twelve pounders had to be left behind altogether.[97]

To be sure, the occupation of the heights above Vienna was anything but a precise and coördinated operation. The Poles, retarded and exhausted the previous day, arrived in the valley rendezvous only during the afternoon of the eleventh, a windy, cloudy day, and did not make their way upward until shortly before nightfall. In fact, the artillery and

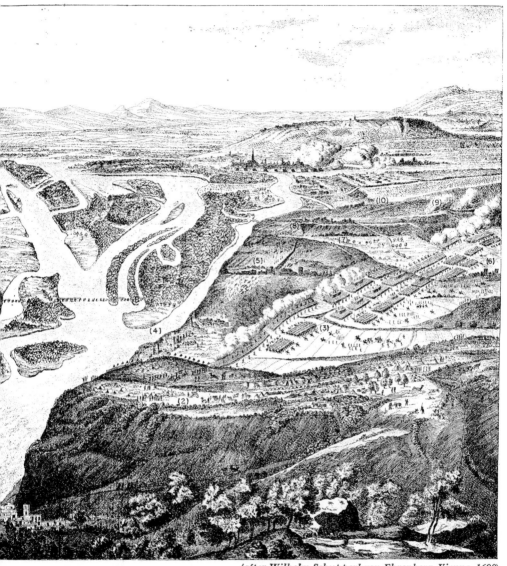

(after Wilhelm Schupperl von Ehrenberg, Vienna, 1690)

The Austro-German Advance

The Struggle for Nussdorf and Heiligenstadt as seen from atop the Leopoldsberg.

1. Kahlenbergerdörfl
2. Nussberg
3. Muckental and Schreiberbach
4. Nussdorf
5. Heiligenstadt
6. Grinzing
7. Unterdöbling
8. Oberdöbling
9. Türkenschanz
10. Turkish camp, northern sector

some of the infantry did not stumble in until after dark and were unable to begin their ascent until early the next morning. Sobieski, whose twenty-six-hour absence from his own troops had caused concern, finally returned and supervised the climb. The cavalry headed for the Hermannskogel where it made confused contact with the Austro-German right. Dragoons moved over to the next peak, the Dreimarkstein, and blocked off intermediate passages leading up from the Viennese suburb of Sievering. The prominences further to the right do not seem to have been taken over at all on the eleventh.

After he had gotten his forces underway, the King, accompanied by his French engineer, Dupont, set off for Charles' new command post in the ruins of the monastery. John III, already briefed by Dupont, expressed astonishment over the terrain which he saw lying beneath him in the light of dusk. The area between the Kahlenberg, its sister elevations, and Vienna was not a plain, as the map given him earlier by the Austrians seemed to indicate. It was made up, rather, of a further chain of mountains, some lower, some just as high, and one even higher than the point where he stood (Nussberg, Krapfenwaldl, Pfaffenberg, Neuberg, Hackenberg, Michaelerberg, Schafberg, Gallitzenberg, Heuberg). Moreover, these unexpected obstacles were succeeded by yet another set of barriers—a series of occasionally very steep creek ravines which curved easterly toward the Danube (Waldbach, Schäblergraben, Schreiberbach, Steinbergerbach, Reisenbergerbach, Nesselbach, Erbsenbach, Krottenbach, Döblingerbach, Währingerbach, Alserbach). To cap everything, the loamy soil of the region supported countless vineyards, which were dissected by hedgerows, stone embankments, and sunken lanes. Dupont appears to have made a scene before the assembled allied generals by attempting to convince Sobieski of the unsuitability of such country for the relief action. John III concluded that while the enterprise ought to be continued, it would not be a formal, full-scale battle but rather a sequence of individual skirmishes, which would take at least several days. He simultaneously requested and received four battalions of German foot, troops that he was to find considerably more manageable than his own bedraggled infantry. The meeting, however, ended on a somewhat inconclusive note: since most of the artillery was still not present, it was agreed to reserve final tactical decisions for further talks the next morning.[98]

Its uncertain outcome notwithstanding, the evening's discussion cannot have lacked a sense of urgency. Enemy forces, which the Grand Vezir meanwhile had transferred from positions closer to Vienna into the rough terrain directly below the heights, had already drawn fire from the six small pieces atop the Kahlenberg. The foe was not only visible but also within earshot: the hustle and bustle of moving arms and equipment and cries of "Allah" kept many a Christian warrior awake during the night.

All the same, as Sobieski noted in a letter written to his wife just before dawn, it was surprising that the allies had been able to get as far as they had without encountering serious opposition from the Ottoman host.[99] The story of developments within the Turkish camp during the first days of September is thus of more than casual interest.

TURKISH PREPARATIONS

For all his insouciance about the area to his rear, Kara Mustafa was by no means oblivious to allied movements. For a while he apparently had hopes, despite Kör Hüseyin Pasha's defeat and death, of mounting a new offensive on the north side of the river in order to prevent the junction of the relief armies. By September 4, however, it was obvious that he himself would need reinforcements. The interrogation of a Christian taken prisoner by the Tatars provided a greatly exaggerated estimate of the size of the allied force and led the Turkish generalissimo to send for İbrahim Pasha and some 13,500 men from the units investing Győr. Four days later an Egyptian detachment caught an Austrian courier on his way to Starhemberg. The message borne by the soldier and the questioning of another captive the next day revealed that the foe had crossed the Danube. A troop of horse set off to determine the Christians' routes of approach from Tulln.

In the evening the vezirs, *beylerbeyi,* and two Janissary generals left the forward trenches and entered Kara Mustafa's bunker for a conference. For the moment the only decision was that the Grand Vezir should retire to his tent pavillion "auf der Schmelz." On the morning of the ninth a second, more conclusive, hour-long consultation took place. In the presence of Abaza Sari Hüseyin Pasha *(Beylerbeyi* of Damascus), Kara Mehmed Pasha *(Beylerbeyi* of Diyabekir), the *Beylerbeyi* of Sivas, the *Beylerbeyi* of Aleppo, the *sipâhî* and *silâhdar* agas, and the heads of the *cebecî* and the *topçu,* it was resolved to leave the "men" (i.e., the Janissaries, the *serdengeçti, topçu, lâǧuncı,* dismounted *topraklı,* and *azab*) in the trenches and to send all the pashas with their mounted troops (i.e., *topraklı* not serving in the approaches, *deli, gönüllü,* and *seymen*) to oppose the enemy. (The *seymen,* however, were not commanded by the provincial administrators but by a specially appointed officer, the *serçeşme.*) Were the relief force defeated, the fall of the fortress would be assured.[100] The Turkish sources say that the vote was unanimous, but there may be some truth in Cantemir's assertion of opposition by the lesser generals especially İbrahim Pasha. The old *Beylerbeyi* of Buda, who had arrived only the day before from Győr with the bulk of his corps (including *topraklı,* Janissaries, *cebeci,* the *ulûfeci,* and the *gurêba*), was excluded, probably deliberately, from participation in the council but appears to have expressed his opinion anyway. Allegedly, he recommended what was the only rational—but already too tardy—course of action: to leave no more than a small observation corps in the siege works, march up into the Wienerwald and fortify it.[101]

Abaza Sari Hüseyin Pasha left the meeting at once and led the troops of his own and several other provinces to the line Weinhaus-Ottakring-Baumgarten, a position immediately adjacent to the original main camp (Penzing-Breitensee-Hernals) and the Grand Vezir's pavillion. On the far left, behind Mariabrunn and in the vicinity of Hütteldorf, the Tatars were already stationed. This disposition of forces was designed to cover the Alsbach Valley (Dornbach, Neuwaldegg) and its flanking hills (Michaelerberg, Schafberg, Heuberg, Gallitzenberg), one route of issuance from the Wienerwald. In the meantime Kara Mustafa and the rest of the conferees reconnoitered the other defiles and foothills. Shortly thereafter further contingents, several of which included *toprakli* taken directly from the approaches September 8, rode out to establish a solid right wing. They pitched their red, white, and green tents on the ridge overlooking the deep ravine of the Döblingerbach and the Krottenbach. Overall command of this flank fell to İbrahim Pasha.[102] Its 5,400-man-strong van was entrusted to Kara Mehmed Pasha, who moved to the foot of the Kahlenberg behind Nussdorf and the Nussberg. Sixty regimental pieces and two columbrines were taken from the siege works and planted in three places, two of which were presumably hastily-fortified Nussdorf and the location still called the Türkenschanz (between Gersthof and the Krottenbach). There was, however, no regular circumavallation either here or on the left. Marsigli, who observed the Turks' activities at first hand, was amazed at the Grand Vezir's negligence. Any tactician worth his salt knew that a good encampment, especially at a siege, was itself an *ordre de bataille*.[103]

Apparently Kara Mustafa himself soon had doubts about the stability of his new front, for that same day he decided to buttress it by withdrawing further dismounted *toprakli* from the left sector of the trenches. On the tenth he also pulled out the Rumelians and, from the Prater works, the Bosnians. Vienna's exhausted defenders observed these movements as well as the earlier breakup of the cavalry camps on the far side of the city (St. Marx, Laaerhölzl, Wiener Berg, and Hundsturm) and found grounds for feeling encouraged. The same day the Ottoman chief personally inspected his rearranged lines. Perhaps he took some comfort in noting the vineyard hedgerows and embankments which would hinder the foe's advance and provide sheltered firing positions for his own men. Late in the afternoon came news of the Christians' entry into the Vienna Woods. The Grand Vezir now placed his private Janissary corps (the *solak*), his red-jacketed Albanian bodyguard ("Arnauts"), his court suite, and the *sipâhî* and *silâhdar* on battle alert. It was also deemed advisable to transfer the Janissary Ağa and a detachment of his men from the forward approaches to guard duty at the rearward exits. On the morning of the eleventh there seemed reason to relax for a while, but the enemy's advance up the opposite side of the Kahlenberg caused Kara Mustafa to shift the Ağa's Janissaries and some of his own troops to the Türkenschanz behind Kara Mehmed Pasha and alongside İbrahim Pasha. The generalissimo himself spent the night, his last at Vienna, in his pavillion.[104]

The untrustworthy auxiliaries from the two Danubian principalities having formed just opposite the Prater Island, the Ottoman host was now as ready for battle as it ever could be. There is no way of establishing its exact size. Its numbers most likely equalled the Christian army (without counting the Rumanians or the *kapu, serhadd,* and *yerli kulu* remaining in the approaches).[105] Its condition is less a matter of speculation. The Tatars were no more reliable than the Moldavians and Wallachians. Unsuitable for use against disciplined cavalry anyway, the Crimean reiters were mainly interested in preserving their loot. Their Khan, allegedly offended by the arrogant behavior of the Grand Vezir, may have deliberately contemplated treachery. The Turks themselves, while loyal, were in poor shape. The reports of the enemy's advance sent a wave of fear sweeping through their ranks. Already weakened by the rigors of the siege and shaken by news of the Bisamberg catastrophe, they dared not venture out to forage during the three days they were awaiting the Christians. Their starved horses were hardly capable of battle service. The men were resentful of Kara Mustafa, who had levied a tax on their booty. Marsigli believed that they could have been brought to build retrenchments, had it not been for this; and that the Tatars, who had refused outright to pay, might also have been so employed, if they had not been so annoyed over the attempted extortion. Yet another unfortunate morale factor was the behavior of the merchants and camp rabble, who, smelling defeat, began to pack up and depart while there was still time. Possibly also the strength of some Ottoman soldiers was dissipated by indulgence in wine, to which they were unaccustomed and which was present plentifully in the cellars of suburban houses. The Turkish historian, the Silâhdar, held that imbibing led to the equally debilitating sins of whoring and sodomy.[106]

D. The Battle of the Kahlenberg

A Fortuitous Beginning

To what extent, if at all, the Christian leaders were aware of the adverse, psychological condition of the enemy army cannot be determined. Its immediate, awe-inspiring presence may well have served to dispel any suspicions they may possibly have had. Lorraine, who had reconnoitered the terrain at the foot of the monastery late in the afternoon of the eleventh, was himself bothered by the Ottoman advance so close to his position. Even before the evening conference with his colleagues he ordered Leslie to begin placing infantry at the exit from the woods down along the semicircular base of the Kahlenberg. The plan was to have the troops construct an artillery battery in order to assure the projected debouchment of the left wing.[107] At about 5:00 a.m. of the twelfth, before the men were finished, warriors of Kara Mehmed Pasha's vanguard pushed forward and interrupted the work. The Turks opened fire from behind a nearby embankment and, at a greater distance, a palisade-like fence that normally served to protect the vines from the depredations of the Wienerwald's wild game, which the vintners and peasants were not permitted to harm. The Austrian commander, the Comte de Fontaine, quickly arrayed his two battalions. Reinforcements, led by the Duc Eugène de Croy, appeared swiftly, and the united force extended itself laterally, thereby establishing a regular front. To the left, opposite the Nussberg, the line was held by Imperials, and, to the right, in the Wildgrube, facing the narrow Muckental and the Krapfenwaldl (the hill just behind Grinzing), by the Saxons. The movement was executed so vigorously that the Muslims deemed it advisable to abandon the first embankment and to retire to a second. The encounter was, however, by no means bloodless: among the Christian wounded was Croy and among the dead, his brother Thomas, a company commander.[108]

With this spontaneous action the Battle of the Kahlenberg may be said to have formally commenced. The Duke, continuing to observe developments closely from his vantage point in the ruined monastery, noted that the whole Turkish right was now beginning to advance from its encampment behind the Krottenbach. (Indeed, the Grand Vezir himself—who had moved up to the Türkenschanz with the rest of his suite, the preacher Vani Efendi, the *sipâhî,* and the *silâhdar*—supervised the action from underneath a sun canopy set up within range of the Giaurs' guns.) Charles thus concluded that it was time to throw in the bulk of the left wing. Shortly thereafter Waldeck and Sachsen-Lauenburg also received orders to descend from the thickly-wooded Dreimarkstein, Hermannskogel, Cobenzl, and Vogelsangberg. Lorraine simultaneously sent a messenger to Sobieski to inform him of his decisions. Knowing that the King was coming over to St. Joseph's for the morning conference anyway, he then apparently thought that it would be wiser to meet him en route and explain matters in person. It is not clear whether a second, full-blown council-of-war took place, but, allegedly, the commander-in-chief expressed agreement with the measures already taken, whereupon he proceeded to prepare himself spiritually for battle by attending a Mass celebrated in the burned chapel by Aviano.[109]

The events of the preceding hours are significant not only as the overture to the relief of Vienna. They also have interest because they lie at the heart of a nationalistically-accented conflict between twentieth century Austro-German and Polish historians. Was John III the real, not just the honorary commander-in-chief? Did he exercise general tactical control over the battle, and was he thus personally responsible for the victory? François Dalérac, like Dupont a Frenchman in Polish service, states in his memoirs that the King dominated the scene, giving orders and keeping himself informed through a courier system set up by the Duke.[110] Modern Polish and Polish-oriented writers naturally accept this view.[111] Indeed, one goes even further and asserts that the King devised a comprehensive scheme *beforehand.* Apparently seizing upon a passage in the letter composed by the monarch during the wee morning hours, the author deduces that Sobieski ordered an attack by the Austro-German left wing in order to divert the enemy while he himself was preparing a decisive surprise assault on the Polish far-right.[112] Austro-German scholars, however, are generally wont to consider Poland's ruler a merely nominal chief and to regard Lorraine's left thrust as the key to the battle's outcome. If they wished, they, too might claim the prior existence of a plan to defeat the Turks, for the Duke's secretary asserts that "Charles' design in the enterprise of the morrow was to adhere closely to the Danube's shore and to attack the enemy camp on the right."[113]

Regarding the first problem, one may reasonably doubt that Sobieski was physically able to exercise tight command, whether for the purpose of implementing preconceived ideas or merely in order to exploit momentary opportunities. The great extent of the front, its difficult terrain, and, messengers notwithstanding, the inevitable slowness of communications must have posed almost insuperable barriers to central control. As for the existence of a master scheme, it is highly questionable whether either leader was so prescient as to foresee every eventuality. Surely there was much about the further course of the engagement which, like its beginning, was haphazard. The sober-minded Waldeck, a relatively impartial participant, comments in his memoirs that the generals employed their troops as events unfolded, re-inforcing each other whenever necessary. Neither time nor location permitted otherwise.[114] To be sure, a left-flank maneuver proved to be the ultimate determinative factor. Thus, even if there are other, equally weighty reasons for the Christian victory,[115] it is not altogether irrelevant to ask which general, the Duke or the King, deserves credit for *planning* an offensive on that wing (i.e., before the enemy himself precipitated matters). The logic of the situation clearly favors Charles. It was he who really knew the area and he who scouted the grounds prior to the Comte de Fontaine's advance. The Austrian forces were in the closest physical proximity to Vienna and their commander was evidently more anxious about relieving it than was the Polish ruler. A left thrust was simply the quickest way to reach its gates. Thus Sobieski, in writing to his wife, was probably only reflecting Lorraine's arguments presented tentatively during the inconclusive evening conference. Of course, the former may have perceived, independently, some advantage for his own, later assault.

PHASE ONE: THE AUSTRO-GERMAN LEFT

In view of these considerations, the Duke's secretary is probably correct in claiming that his master did not attend Aviano's Mass but hurried off to the head of the Austro-Saxon troops, who had meanwhile swarmed off the Kahlenberg. The Christian advance was surely an impressive sight: to the Turks it seemed "as if a flood of black pitch was flowing down the hill, smothering and incinerating everything that lay in its way." A large red flag with a white cross fluttered from on high. Both spectacles were visible from Vienna's walls and gave new heart to the defenders. Lorraine, for his part, was concerned with creating a unified front and thus at once secured his extreme left by instructing Count Caprara to take Heissler's dragoons and a Saxon regiment to the foot of the Leopoldsberg. At 8:00 a.m. Heissler received orders to attack. The Turks opposite him on the rise between the Schäblerbergraben and the Waldbach were firing up the ravine into the rear of the infantry, which was also commanded to advance, the two movements being initiated simultaneously. The foot soldiers met some resistance but soon drove the enemy behind yet another embankment. At about this point the artillery, the lighter pieces at any rate, arrived. Additional infantrymen also descended, making it possible to strengthen and extend the front further. Herman of Baden, seeing his nephew Louis endangered in a forward position, arrived on the scene personally with help and aided in breaking through the palisade fence.[116]

On the left the dismounted dragoons took their objective but advanced beyond it too rapidly. Forced to drop back to their first goal, they suffered some losses. Among the dead was Baron Kasimir von Königsegg, the commander of one of Lubomirski's regiments (a later reinforcement), whose skull was cleft by a scimitar despite the protective horseshoe in his hat. Kara Mehmed Pasha's men, now bolstered on the left by some of the Grand Vezir's own warriors and by the *serçeşme's seymen,* quickly decapitated the fallen Christians and also managed to pick up a few prisoners and abandoned standards. Nonetheless, the original line of allied foot pressed forward all the while, maintaining an uninterrupted musketry barrage, now mingled with caseshot. The Turks were forced to drop back again and the Austrians occupied an embankment "stretching almost all the way from the Danube to a point *vis-à-vis* the monastery," i.e., the rim of the Nussberg (Eichelhofweg). However, the new front was by no means secure. On its right flank, at the Krapfenwaldl, a gap had opened up, caused by a sharp, leftward swerve on the part of several Saxon battalions which had first stood in the Wildgrube but which had been ordered to join in the effort to dislodge the Turkish units from the slope of the Nussberg. Waldeck's center had failed to move up far enough either on account of terrain difficulties or because it was being held back deliberately as a tactical reserve. A subordinate Franconian officer refused to budge without the express command of the Prince, and if the chief of the Hannoverian battalion had not sprung into the breach independently —laying down his own life—the situation might have become critical. The hole was completely plugged only upon the incorporation of the second and third lines of battle.[117]

By now it was 10:00 a.m. Charles halted the advance units while the remainder of the left wing—the Imperial second and third lines—filled the ground just taken. Artillery was also implanted atop the Nussberg in order to facilitate the next advance. The Duke, apparently bearing the Saxons' experience in mind, ordered Waldeck and Sachsen-Lauenburg to continue their march until they were parallel to the left wing. The two generals also stretched out to the right in order to be able to link hands with the Poles who were expected to issue from the defiles behind Neustift and Neuwaldegg-Dornbach. After making these dispositions, doubtlessly with Sobieski's blessing, Lorraine rode off to the head of the left wing in order to take personal charge of the march of the German soldiery. He was joined by the Elector of Saxony, both men thereafter remaining more or less together under frequent exposure to point-blank enemy fire. The King, for his part, soon left St. Joseph's Chapel in order to hasten the movement of his own, necessarily tardy army.[118]

The pause on the left was but of brief duration. The Grand Vezir and İbrahim Pasha, apparently recognizing that the loss of the Nussberg was a serious threat to their right flank, mounted a counter-attack against the whole Austro-Saxon line. Repulsed the first time and driven back onto the flatter terrain between the Schreiberbach and the Nesselbach (Grinzingerstraße), the Muslims made one more effort. The Imperial foot began to waver, and it proved necessary to throw in not only the dragoons but the cuirassiers, who up to that point had not seen action. John George, fighting on the far left (next to the river) with his cavalry bodyguard, became involved in the melee. Wounded in the cheek by an arrow, he cut down a Syrian lancer who was about to deliver the final blow. The Turkish assault faltered upon the appearance of Saxon reserves who struck hard at the enemy's left flank. The Germans at once pursued their advantage and launched a double drive, the Saxons debouching from the lower Muckental in the direction of Heiligenstadt and the Nesselbach and the Austrians down the Schreiberbach into Nussdorf.

The resistance in the latter place was "rather considerable:" the foe had fortified houses and cellars and had taken cover in ditches behind fences and ruined walls. It fell first, however, and the Duke, who continued to worry about maintaining contact between the various parts of the army which were bobbing up and down in the rough countryside, ordered another halt so that the rest of the battle line could attain the same parallel. The Saxons, who had been forced to fall halfway back to the Krapfenwaldl in their first attempt against Heiligenstadt, now apparently regrouped and by exerting all their strength were able not only to recover the lost ground but to seize a Turkish retrenchment hastily erected along the steep bank of the Nesselbach. For a while it seemed that fighting would continue in the same general area, that there would be a struggle for control of the next and last Ottoman position there: the encampment on the ridge overlooking the Döblingerbach-Krottenbach Ravine (route of the present-day suburban railway). However, around 1:00 p.m.—the time can only be estimated[119]—the focus of the battle began to change. The Poles now began their descent from the Wienerwald peaks. The Duke once more stopped his forces, probably in order to give the by-now-short-winded troops a chance to regain their breath and certainly to observe the course of action on the extreme right. The equally exhausted foe also rested. Waldeck and Sachsen-Lauenburg meanwhile appear to have met relatively little opposition as they pushed down into Grinzing, the Grinzinger Allee, Sievering, and Neustift. Despite the firm defense of Nussdorf and Heiligenstadt the Turks' overall performance had been mediocre, especially when one considers how the terrain favored them. Such, in any event, was the opinion of Taaffe.[120]

Phase Two: The Polish Right

The delayed appearance of the Poles is not difficult to understand. While the Austro-Germans were defiling from the Kahlenberg and Leopoldsberg just after dawn, their allies were, in part, still climbing to the crest of the Vienna Woods from the Weidling Valley. The diary of the Po-

---

(facing page)

**The Battle of the Kahlenberg:
Collapse of the Turkish Flanks**
(According to Leander Anguissola)

A. Kahlenberg	M. Jabłonowski's Wing
B. Leopoldsberg	N. Austro-German Artillery
C. (Above) Imperial Troops	O. Turkish Artillery at the *Türken-*
C. (Below) Waldeck's Wing	*schanz*
D. Sachsen-Lauenburg's Wing	P. Turkish Camp
E. Sieniawski's Wing	Q. Neugebäude
F. Sobieski's Wing	R. Schwechat
G. Saxon Troops	S. St. Marx
H. Rumanians	T. Danube Bridges (burnt-out)
I. Turkish Artillery	V. Fleeing Turks
J. Vienna	X. Vienna River (*Wienfluss*)
L. Abaza Sari Hüseyin Pasha	

Note: in contradiction to the sources, the Turkish flanks are shown here as collapsing simultaneously.

VIENNA
da Turchi assediata e da Chri.ⁿⁱ liberata

Leandro Anguissola fecit

Dom.^{co} Rossetti sculp.

lish artillery commander, Martin Kątski, presents a vivid picture of the difficulties encountered. The passageways were "painful," the wooded terrain clogged with men. With great effort the fieldpieces were brought up, but the heaviest of the cannon had to be left behind. Finally (by about 1:00 p.m.), the troops stood between the Dreimarkstein (occupied the previous evening), the Gränberg, and the Rosskopf. The left (Dreimarkstein) was commanded by Sieniawski. The center (Gränberg) was reserved for the King. The right (Rosskopf) was led by Jabłonowski; on its side were stationed dragoons to thwart any surprise attack by the Tatars. The men were arranged in five lines of battle, with the infantry, consisting of eight brigades of several pułks each plus the four German battalions, out in front. The successful ordering of the army was due in large measure to the appearance of the King in the course of the morning. Sobieski had apparently not tarried long with the left wing. After Aviano's Mass he returned to the valley, ate breakfast under a canopy, and then, wishing to spare his steed the combined weight of his huge body and heavy armor, walked back to his own flank, supported by two servants. The first problem facing the King after having drawn up his forces along the heights was to advance across the series of lesser elevations and the Alsbach Valley which lay in front of him. Only after reaching the "plain" before Vienna—the area just to the rear of the Turkish camp and the siege works—would he be able to exploit the full strength of his primarily mounted troops.

The hilly terrain, while apparently not as heavily wooded as today, was difficult to traverse, for it was covered with thorny underbrush, grapevines, ditches, and hedgerows. Moreover, individual *gönüllü* valiantly threw themselves upon the advancing lines of pike, spurring their mounts forward even after they themselves were impaled. Abaza Sari Hüseyin Pasha was apparently resisting as best he could with the relatively limited forces at his disposal. The Poles, nevertheless, pushed on steadily, preceded by a continuous barrage of caseshot from Katski's twenty-eight guns. The rest of the cannon fired from behind the ranks, first from the Gränberg and then from the next elevations. Sobieski himself seems to have taken the lead. By about 2:00 p.m. the Michaelerberg was reached. The royal army's left was now visible to the other allied troops. A mighty cheer rose from the throats of the German soldiery. For a moment, however, the junction of the Christian forces was less than perfect. A thousand-odd "Janissaries" had crept into secure positions among the vineyards behind Pötzleinsdorf. Several of Sachsen-Lauenburg's units suffered heavily in the attempt to dislodge the foe, and the area could be cleared only with the aid of cuirassier reinforcements (3:00 p.m.). The Polish drive then continued. The valley was swept clean, and the Schafberg was seized after a rather costly assault. Meanwhile Jabłonowski took good care of the right. Having conquered the Heuberg, he next fended off—easily—the only blow which the Tatars even attempted to deliver that day. The attack, near Mariabrunn, was led by Hadshi Girey Sultan, the Khan's cousin and successor three weeks later.[121]

The Poles were thus able to begin deploying themselves in a more orderly fashion at the mouth of the valley and on the more level land beyond the Schafberg (4:00 p.m.). To be sure, the Turks were also starting to build a more contiguous and solid front. The Grand Vezir, presumably aware of the danger of being outflanked in the vicinity of the Vienna River and thereby of being cut off from all retreat, now withdrew the bulk of İbrahim Pasha's men from the right and joined them to the left in front of the old, main camp. The new Ottoman line of battle was so thick that not all of the warriors could participate in the ensuing struggle. The first clash on the new terrain appears to have been a skirmish on Sieniawski's wing. In keeping with custom, Sobieski sent out a *chorągiew* of Crown Hussars, so-called *eliery* (*enfants perdus*), under Zygmunt Zbierzchowski in order to reconnoiter the ground. The little troop—150-odd horse—crashed through the first and second enemy lines but was quickly forced to retreat, losing a third of its number. The second Polish onslaught was also a failure, evidently because it was launched before the line of battle was entirely formed. The bloodthirsty, probably over-eager Sieniawski—whether with or without Sobieski's encouragement is not quite clear—sent out (from the Michaelerwald) Felix Potocki, Voivode of Kraków, and his hussar *chorągiew,* supposedly to deflect an impending Ottoman blow. Stanisław Potocki, nephew of Felix and Starost of Halicz, attached himself voluntarily with his *pancerny* and took the lead. The assault was vigorous but undermanned. The Starost fell, the top of his head sliced off like an apple. Further units—hussars, *pancerny,* dragoons and light reiters—had to be thrown in. The Turks, it would appear, had succeeded at least partly in luring the Poles into a trap, pretending to retreat and drawing their opponents into the heart of the army. Other Polish lords, including Andrzéj Modrzewski, the Crown Grand Treasurer, dropped lifelessly from their steeds. The Ottoman commander now thought the moment right to counter-attack and threw forces against the Polish right whither the attacking cavalry had escaped, taking shelter behind the four battalions of German infantry posted on the slope of the Heuberg. Sobieski also requested relief from Sachsen-Lauenburg: special help was given by Schultz' and Styrum's dragoons, led and supported by Rabata's cuirassiers—an encounter in which Count Trautmannsdorf, colonel of the first-named regiment, was killed. Struck on their right flank, the pursuing Turks fell back.[122]

Apparently this was also the point at which Abaza Sari Hüseyin Pasha, recognizing that the supreme moment was at hand, caused a sixteen-by-twenty foot flag to be unfurled next to his red tent in the middle of the front. The Poles thought, erroneously, that this was the Standard of the

Prophet, which served to admonish Muslim soldiers to fight to the last drop of blood. Greatly animated, Sobieski strove to bring into action forthwith the two or three cannon in his immediate vicinity (i.e., on the Schafberg). The fire cannot have been very accurate, for the ordnance had been shoved forward on rollers, carriages having been found too clumsy to handle under the circumstances. Ammunition was short, too. The King offered fifty crowns for each discharge. Dupont, lacking wadding, stuffed his wig, gloves, cravat and newspapers taken from his copious pockets down the barrels. At about the same time Jabłonowski completed his work on the far right by gaining control of the Gallitzenberg. Now all the heights were in Polish hands, and the task of establishing an even, unbroken front on open terrain could be finished.[123]

PHASE THREE: THE DECISION

While the fury of the Turkish lunge was being absorbed by the German foot and horse on John III's wing, Lorraine was also striving to relieve the pressure. He commanded his men, who had already been straining on the leash for some time, to approach the Turkish camp on the high bluff of the Krottenbach-Döblingerbach. The enemy forces, weakened by the dispatch of so many men to face the Poles, formed in line of battle and turned some artillery against the Austro-Saxons in order to defend what was actually the strongest natural position of the whole front. The *dénouement* of the battle was now at hand. It was apparently at this juncture that Charles asked his Saxon colleagues whether one ought to be satisfied with the progress so far that day or whether, at the least, another war council should be called before proceeding further. The Saxon general Goltz is said to have replied that it would be better to go on fighting. God was already pointing the way to victory, and it was necessary to strike while the iron was still hot. He himself was an old man and was looking forward to comfortable quarters in Vienna that night. The Duke, supposedly much pleased with the advice, responded loudly, "Allons marchons!" The musketry barrage of the Christian squares had a withering effect upon the thin Turkish front, which collapsed entirely about 5:00 p.m. The Franconians and Bavarians began simultaneously to assault the Türkenschanz, the actual location of the Holy Banner. Lorraine, seeing the chance to strike the nearest flank of the main Ottoman force, which had girded itself to withstand Sobieski, had all his men swing sharply to the right instead of marching directly to Vienna along the Danube arm. The way led through the northern section of the great arc of Ottoman tents, but the troops managed to suppress the temptation to loot and kept perfect order.[124]

On the right, probably at the precise moment of Goltz' remarks and Charles' answer, Sobieski, too, decided to make an end of matters before nightfall. According to the Polish sources his original intention was to

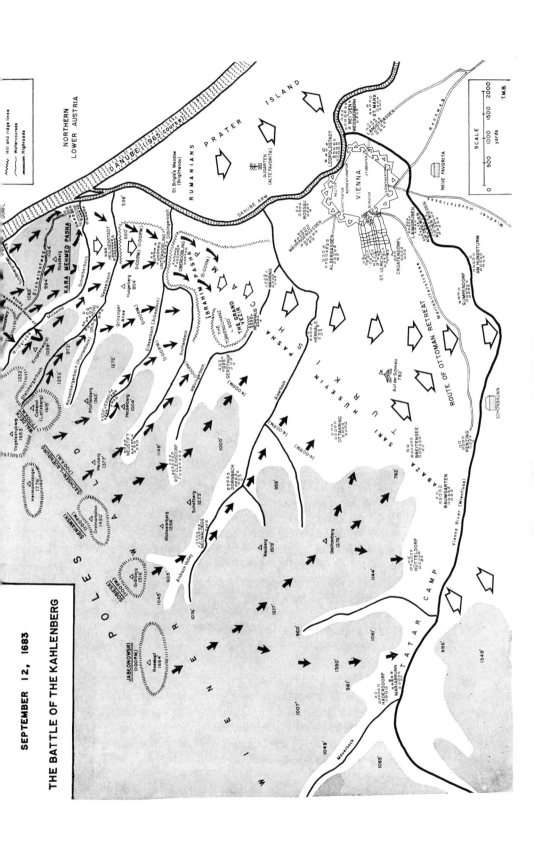

SEPTEMBER 12, 1683

THE BATTLE OF THE KAHLENBERG

content himself with the capture of the forehills and to reserve the final stroke for the morrow. The factors which caused him to change his mind were, it seems, the eagerness of Sieniawski and the men of his command, the equally aggressive spirit of the Germans, and certain signs that the foe "was commencing to be troubled." The reconstituted royal line of battle thus began to move forward in an action that proved to be the last glorious chapter in the annals of Sarmatian chivalry. To the cry of the day's password, "Jezus Maria ratuj," the Poles lowered their nineteen-foot, pennon-tipped lances as the wind uplifted the eagles' wings on their backs and the tiger and leopard pelts affixed to their shoulders. The polished and gleaming armor plates and helmets, visible from afar, caused the Germans on the far left to pause briefly and gaze in wonder. Organized in Sobieski's own, special chessboard formation—hussar blocks in the front line with saber and carbine-equipped *pancerny* stationed in the intervals a hundred paces behind—, the heavy reiters of Sieniawski's left wing and the royal-led center were buttressed farther back by dragoons and *kwarciany*, and flanked to the northeast by Sachsen-Lauenburg's regiments and to the southwest by Jabłonowski's corps. In the lead, astride a handsome dun, was John III himself, decked out in luxurious, semi-oriental garb. Upon his head rested a kalpak, its feather held fast by a priceless jewel-clasp; covering the body armor were a dark blue, silken żupan; clutched in the monarch's hand was the fearsome buława. Next to the King was fourteen year old Prince Jakób, unarmored and carrying only a curved saber, with a dagger tucked under his saddle after the Polish manner. Close by were a herald and a hussar, bearing, respectively, the crown escutcheon and the *bunczuk*. The magnates of the realm, attired in similarly splendid fashion, were not far behind.

The magnificent, and hence very weighty, array of cavaliers was able to pick up speed only very slowly. Before reaching the open space just to the left of the Turkish camp in the Baumgarten-Ottakring-Weinhaus area—into which the Ottoman horse had advanced—it had to pass through further vineyards and other terrain obstacles. Once in the clear, the King and the forward units crossed swords with Turkish skirmishers, who were supported by artillery fire from the edge of the tents. Sobieski then ordered the *chorągiew* of young Prince Alexander—the boy himself was not on the scene—to charge toward the middle of the camp. There was an audible shattering of lances, and Polish casualties were severe. The Turks, however, recoiled under the shock of the assault, their will to resist already sapped by İbrahim Pasha's desertion and Lorraine's thrust in their direction. (Prince Jakób notes in his diary that this lunge occurred while the Poles were *still* at the base of the slope, "auf der Schmelz," upon which the tents stood; in other words, amidst the viticultural stumbling blocks.) The sovereign was able to follow and capture the guns. The beaten Ottoman troops did not immediately flee but rather joined their own left wing opposite Jabłonowski, against whom the combined force launched a last-gasp counterattack. The Grand Hetman parried the blow with great skill and sealed his nation's triumph by pressing directly into the foe's habitations. The Muslim front now completely disintegrated, the men rushing pell-mell toward the Vienna River and safety.[125] The action had taken place so smoothly that most of the Poles in the rear ranks lost all opportunity to blood their weapons.[126]

Meanwhile, in the Ottoman center, the Grand Vezir—who had remained aloof from the earlier fighting—noted that the Flag of the Prophet was endangered. He therefore mounted his horse and—flanked by his whole personal following, Vani Efendi, the *sipâhî,* and the *silâhdar*—intervened directly. Although both flanks were dissolving, the *Ser'asker* held firm for a few additional minutes. To be sure, Waldeck's Franconian-Bavarian foot were attacking the Türkenschanz doggedly: "The army of Islam was drenched by a rain of cannon and musket balls." The risk of being cut off and annihilated, it seems, then caused the men at Kara Mustafa's side to turn and run. Most dashed back behind the collapsing left sector in order to reach the old main camp in the hope of saving their lives and property. The generalissimo himself and his closest associates withdrew directly to the former's pavillion with the Holy Banner in tow. An order now went out for the troops in the trenches —who had continued to bombard Vienna vigorously throughout the day—to retire. Apparently also, the Turkish commander still possessed sufficient presence of mind to call for the destruction of equipment and the slaughter of captives, although it was already too late for either measure to be implemented effectively.

When the enemy, in this instance Jabłonowski, reached the Executioner's tent, the Grand Vezir made one last reckless but gallant attempt to resist, rushing ahead, lance in hand, to rejoin the fray. His private secretary, numerous agas and pages, and all his Arnautic body-guard fell, and he himself could be prevailed upon to leave only by the argument that his loss would mean the total destruction of the army. Seizing the Prophet's Standard and his private treasure—but nothing else—, he fled through the rear exit of the pavillion, most likely just before 6:00 p.m., in order to lead the general retreat back to Győr. The King, led by a surrendered page, was allegedly the first to enter his quarters. Worried over the possibility that the Turks might return, as they had at Khotin, Sobieski forbade all but the lightest pursuit and ordered his men to stay on guard all the night with a strict prohibition against plundering. Lorraine's forces, which do not seem to have advanced beyond the new northern part of the camp, had meanwhile established contact with Starhemberg at the Schottentor. The honor of formally relieving the city fell to Ludwig Wilhelm and a corps of mostly dragoon units, which marched up to the gate to the "happy tune of kettle-drums and trumpets." This force and detachments of the weary, shrunken garrison then undertook to clean out the approaches. There was some fighting, but the great majority of besiegers had followed Kara Mustafa's orders in time. At the very most only 600 Muslims were cut down in the final action beneath the battered bastions. The last shots were fired at about 10:00 p.m. Vienna was saved, and the allies could now afford the luxury of falling out among themselves.[127]

Epilogue

A. The Aftermath

When the firing finally petered out, the Christian host found itself spread out all the way from Oberdöbling to east of Baumgarten, a somewhat awkward position that it was to occupy for approximately the next thirty-six hours. On the far left, in the newer section of the enemy camp, stood the Austro-German regiments. Throughout the night they kept up their guard in strict adherence to the instructions of the commander-in-chief. Way off to the right, on the far bank of the Vienna River, lay Jabłonowski's wing. Here, too, Sobieski's orders were precisely followed. On the south side of Vienna, several Polish squadrons, dispatched to observe the fleeing enemy, managed to strike down numerous Ottoman stragglers but failed to accomplish anything else because of darkness, their own unfamiliarity with the terrain, and the worn-out condition of their chargers.[1]

The Spoils of War

The King, together with his own center and Sieniawski's left, halted directly in the center of the main Turkish camp. The monarch himself, exhausted, without food or drink since breakfast, finally dismounted and lay down to rest, cradling his head against a saddle tossed onto dusty ground beside an old tree trunk. His men, surely no less tired than their master, did not pause even for a brief wink. The incredible riches, heaped up in the multi-colored tents all around them, were more beckoning than sleep. Within a short time discipline and order broke down. Torches were lighted to facilitate the feverish search for pillage. Whether by accident or by some prankster's design, sparks were showered into a powder magazine. However, the monstrous blast that resulted destroyed only a portion of the total supply, so huge that it was valued at more than a million florins.[2]

Undeterred by the explosion, the royal army doggedly pursued the job of looting, which in accordance with the traditions of the steppe, it doubtlessly regarded as a natural right. By morning it had siphoned off the cream of an unusually diverse plunder. Only then were its Teutonically-drilled—but surely no less avaricious—comrades of the left wing allowed to rummage for whatever perquisites remained. John III, whose nap can hardly have lasted beyond the roar in the powder dump, obtained the lion's share himself (a not unfitting metaphor). Led into the Grand Vezirial pavillion by Kara Mustafa's own servants, the ruler became, in his own words, his late opponent's "heir." There were all sorts of "very pretty and very, very rich gallantries and a mass of other things such as I have never seen." Several arrow quivers, studded with rubies and sapphires, were alone worth several thousand ducats. "You will not be able to say, my Dear," so he wrote to Marysiénka, "what Tatar women are wont to tell their husbands when they come home empty-handed: 'thou art no warrior, for thou returnest without booty.'" One of the most gratifying prizes was the *Ser'asker's* own steed, with all its bejeweled trappings. In addition, there was a pile of golden sabers and much other artfully worked weaponry. Although Sobieski was too cautious to mention the fact in the uncoded letter to his spouse, the war chest as well as the private funds of the Grand Vezir also fell into his hands. Of little monetary importance but of immense prestige value were Kara Mustafa's horsetails and the erroneously identified "standard of the Prophet." An ultimately rather troublesome acquisition was the Ottoman campaign archives, which contained the correspondence with Thököly.[3] The pavillion itself was by no means the least of trophies. It was made of absolutely superb materials: gold brocade set with precious stones, Chinese silk, and scarlet tassles. Among its many chambers were various dining halls and lounges. "In addition, there were courtyards and corridors, baths and gardens with fountains and other evidence of opulent Barbarian ostentation." In the Ottoman generalissimo's own inner sanctum was a veritable Oriental wonderland: an unusual soapwort plant, tame rabbits, a parrot (which escaped the Poles' clutching fingers), and various breeds of cats. Luxurious garments, expensive pelts, silver tableware, and admirably incised bridles and harnesses lay scattered about.[4]

Throughout the rest of the camp were copious amounts of war matériel, foodstuffs, and various quotidian articles. Indeed, the goods were so overly abundant that the Poles, already gorged with unique and priceless items, either did not deign or were simply unable to extend their monopoly to what was left. In addition to the powder, there was iron, lead, copper, tin, grease and oil, turpentine, pitch, saltpeter, nails, horseshoes, sheepskins, linen, ropes, tools, workshops, carts, and wagons. The munitions also included handgrenades, fuses, powderhorns, and all sorts of shot and shell. Among the weapons were muskets, scythes, halberds, and, of special significance, the complete artillery park, which counted over 300 pieces. Siege paraphernalia were likewise seized: mining equipment, sandbags, sacks, and the raw wool for stuffing them. The stores of victuals, many of them apparently only recently arrived from Hungary, were prodigious. The chroniclers mention grain, flour, bread, butter, lard, rice, coffee, sugar, honey, cooking oil, and kitchenware, as well as camels, buffaloes, mules, oxen, and sheep.[5]

The Austro-German troops and the Imperial-Municipal arsenals were not the only harvesters of the more prosaic spoil. On September 13 the hungry although by no means starving Viennese proletariat was also given license to scavenge. The mob at once poured forth from the city, clambering over the defense works since the gates were still blocked up. Overcome with curiosity and cupidity, it descended into the labyrinth of trenches and swarmed over the tents to the rear. The supplies which this rabble made off with at once put an end to the price inflation within the city. In the meantime the Poles, Bavarians, and other auxiliaries had broken into the cellars of burned out suburban houses, where they discovered still intact casks of "heuriger" wine. Once inebriated, they smashed the remaining barrels, much to the detriment of the refugee burghers, who might have used the capital which the wine represented for repair and reconstruction.[6] In their haste and greed both the troops and the canaille of Vienna not only ignored the ubiquitous stench of putrifying corpses and the attendant buzzing of flies, but also still-living victims of Turkish brutality which the camp likewise contained. Generally unable to carry off their Christian captives, many Turks massacred the former on the spot, both men and women without distinction. For the most part, however, children were spared and left to fend for themselves in the chaos of retreat. Finally, the ferociously anti-Protestant, but otherwise humane and kindly Cardinal Kollonitsch took upon himself the task of sending out wagons to collect an estimated 450 derelict minors. They were found cringing among the human and animal cadavers. Indeed, some babies were still nursing at the nipples of their butchered mothers. The good prelate made it his duty to restore the youngsters, wherever possible, to their parents or friends. For some of the orphans, he found foster homes with "pious Christians," and others he raised himself with alms specially gathered for the purpose.[7]

Slaughter, to be sure, was not the exclusive prerogative of the Turks, for the Imperials turned out to be no more lenient than their foes. The first Ottoman prisoners to experience the victors' brand of cruelty were twenty-three *lâǧunci* (including five renegades), who emerged from their holes unaware of the fate of their own army. Upon begging quarter they were told to defuse their mines. The Austrians, apparently recalling their own deficiencies in the same military branch, then asked who were the chief masters of the art among the forces of the Porte. The *lâǧunci* responded that they themselves were. Certain of their captors:

> were of the opinion they should have their lives, being men of Parts and capable to render good Service to the Emperor. But 'tis too well known that the Turks seldom prove sincere Converts to the Christian Religion, to the great damage of the Christians, to whom they might prove exceeding prejudicial on like occasion. This Opinion prevailing, they were instantly cut off. . . .[8]

Greater severity was reserved for some three thousand Ottoman sick and wounded. Most of these had been prostrated as the result of their diet, "more especially by eating of Horse Flesh which, being of a very uncommon digestion, caused an ill habit, which immediately turned into a White Flux with Grapes and soon after degenerated into Dyssenterie or Bloody Flux." Without awaiting any orders from Starhemberg the brutalized garrison troops burned them alive, "for the Purification of the Air (denying them the Honor of Dying by their Sword) ." The savagery of the act was not much lessened by the fact that the ringleaders were punished afterward.[9] The remaining prisoners were assigned the job of disposing of the corpses, which were buried, incinerated, or cast into the Danube. The number of bodies was so staggering that the Turkish slaves were unable to cope with them alone, and Vienna's magistrates found it necessary to pay good wages to local laborers to complete the grisly task. The total number of Infidel dead will never be known for certain. Perhaps 40,000 perished in the course of the siege, and the Battle of the Kahlenberg is estimated to have taken 10,000–20,000 more lives. Of fallen Christians—who received some sort of consecrated burial—there was also a plenitude. In addition to the 5,000 not-fully-interred dead of the garrison (plus 2,000 sick and wounded, many of whom failed to survive), there were the victims of the relief action, perhaps 1,500 altogether, including not a few persons of quality, both Poles and Germans.[10]

Sobieski's Viennese Triumph

The consequence of developments during the night of September 12–13 was that the Christian forces were in no position to pursue the totally demoralized enemy the next morning and thus fully to exploit their victory—surely not an uncommon phenomenon in the annals of the operations of allied armies. To be sure, there were those, among them the Duke of Lorraine, who felt that a singular opportunity was being wasted. Charles had not only ordered his own army to be ready to march at daybreak but personally sought out Sobieski to discuss the details of the proposed advance. The King showed "little resolution" in the face of the Duke's insistence and ignored even the suggestion to send the cavalry alone or merely a large detachment thereof. Since the monarch could scarcely reject Charles' subsequent plea to dispatch the Imperials alone, he promised, in an apparent play for time, to leave himself in the afternoon. The Austro-German officers were puzzled, for they reckoned that it was much to John III's interest to see the Ottoman host entirely destroyed. Some believed that the Polish sovereign did not wish to hazard the glory he had already garnered in a second encounter—surely a serious misreading of his character. Others thought that it was the prospect of further booty and the pressure of his own men that held him back. One probably impartial observer noted that, Sobieski's many merits notwithstanding, "je le soupçonne. . . . d'avoir trop d'attachement pour le bien." Still others were willing to accept the King's own word that he wanted to see Vienna and to let his fatigued troops have one day of rest after five of extreme exertion (which of course would not prevent them from continuing to pick over the enemy camp). It was also argued that the monarch thought it futile to follow the swiftly fleeing enemy cavalry, above all at the risk of ruining the Christian army in a countryside deprived of food and forage—a viewpoint disproved by the events of the fourteenth.[11]

What is certain is that John III allowed his vanity (and need for domestic political prestige) to get the better of him before the day was out. After failing to agree about the advance, he and the Duke proceeded to inspect the Turkish siege works in the company of the two Electors and Vienna's commandant. Thereupon the King made known his desire to visit the city. Starhemberg, while probably not informed of the Emperor's wish to be the first to make an entry, realized the impropriety of the request. Despite embarrassed excuses, the Polish ruler persisted, and there was no choice but to yield gracefully. The tour that followed turned out to be an impromptu, Roman-style victory parade. Sobieski ordered the Grand Vezir's steed, horsetails and the gold-brocaded "Prophet's flag" to be included in the procession that wended its way to the Jesuit Church in the square "am Hof" where the Burgher Militia formed the honor guard.[12] The adulation of the populace further stimulated his ego, already inflated with the praise of fellow generals: "The Common People in my going to and from the Churches, payed their veneration even to my very garments, and made their Cry's and Acclamations reach the Sky, of *Long Live the King* of Poland. . . ."[13]

A brief visit at least to the portal of St. Stephen's Cathedral (which was filled with sick and wounded) was succeeded by Mass in the famous Loretto Chapel of the Augustinian Church. Then, at the end of the service, in keeping with Polish custom, Sobieski suddenly began to intone the *Te Deum,* in the chanting of which he was promptly joined by his fellow countrymen and the monks. The surprised Austrian officers present were silent, and, to judge by his evening letter to Marysiénka, it began to dawn upon John III, albeit vaguely, that they were offended at his stealing Leopold's thunder. On the surface, the remainder of the day passed amicably enough. Starhemberg gave a convivial banquet at his own house, the festivities being marred only by the omnipresent odor of rotting corpses and the necessarily limited range of viands. Underneath, however, allied relations were rapidly deteriorating. The Poles' seizure of the best booty was bad enough, but the probably unintended, nevertheless grievous affront to the Emperor's already tattered dignity was simply too much. The tactful, self-effacing Lorraine (and his troopers), who waited in the saddle all afternoon for Sobieski to return and keep his word, also had cause to be irritated.[14] Within the next several days the atmosphere of cordiality was to vanish completely and friction to mount almost to the point of physical conflict (a situation to which the contentious Viennese plebs was also to make its contribution). The ill-feeling was intensified by the continuing failure to pursue the Turks. Ironically, however, now that the possible opportunity of September 13 was gone, it was the Austrians who were in no hurry to get moving again and the Poles who were annoyed.

For the immediate moment Sobieski's mood remained ecstatic. Upon leaving the party at Starhemberg's he took up night quarters within the Grand Vezirial pavillion. It was here that he composed the aforementioned letter to his wife, which, by his own instructions, was released to the press (the "gazettes"), translated, and spread throughout the length and the breadth of the West. The publicity effort, however, was not limited solely to Kraków. A special emissary, the royal secretary Talenti, departed for Rome the next day, carrying the captured "standard of Mahomet" and an epistle prefaced by the pompous phrase, "Venimus, vidimus, Deus vicit." Letters were also dispatched to other Christian sovereigns. The Simancas Archives contain a florid personal message to Charles II. The fact that even in the twentieth century the King of Poland has been regarded as the knight in shining armor, the sole author of Vienna's miraculous escape appears to be the result of his flair for creating an "image."[15]

In any case, the reaction of Europe to the news of the Ottoman disaster was an outburst of unrestrained jubilation. The lifting of a fear which had hung heavily for at least a year—and which probably had even deeper psychological roots in the immemorial nature of threats from the East—occasioned thanksgiving celebrations all the way from St. Peter's Basilica to the Protestant temples of the northern and western seaboards. Journalists, publicists, diarists, popular poets, and playwrights, too, were now moved to spew forth a mass of broadsheets, brochures, and booklets, material which continues to the present day to delight the collector of Viennesia. Among the flood of publications, the outpourings of satirists were prominent. One ditty in particular seems to have been successful in evoking guffaws from the burghers of the Baroque Age. Entitled "The Most Celebrated and Well Constructed Turkish Bath" it belabored in twenty-nine stanzas the idea of the steam and sweat of Kara Mustafa's sojourn before the walls of the Austrian capital.[16]

Doubtlessly the Grand Vezir and his men had inhaled vapors in front of Vienna, but it could hardly be said that the effects were salutary. Indeed, the Christians marvelled that the Turks could have withstood the odor of their own filth for so long. Lorraine, who was of no mind to match this kind of endurance, had his men pull back from the camp as early as the evening of the thirteenth. The next morning the whole allied army evacuated the infected area in favor of stations on the southeastern side of the city. The Austro-Germans marched to the vicinity of the unscathed Imperial country villa, the Neugebäude, and the Poles proceeded on to Schwechat.[17]

In the meantime the Emperor himself was finally able to make his appearance. Disembarking at Nussdorf, he was received by Starhemberg and the two Electors and conducted to the Ottoman camp and siege works for an inspection. The sight of the riddled Leopoldine Tract of the Hofburg allegedly caused him to break out in tears. The august company then entered into town by the freshly-opened Stubentor where the waiting magistracy made the appropriate signs of welcome and obeisance. The Burgher Militia, in dress uniform, formed a cordon as the Imperial party passed through the Wollzeile to St. Stephen's, where Cardinal Kollonitsch celebrated Solemn High Mass and a three-fold choral Te Deum. The ruler and his entourage thereupon betook themselves to the Renaissance arcades of the "Archducal Castle" (now Stallburg, the home of the Spanish Riding School), the only habitable portion of the whole Imperial Palace, for audiences and a festive supper. At this point the laconic Waldeck arrived to pay his respects but became "indisposed"—the polite phrase for a bout of dysentery—while waiting in the antechamber. Lorraine also strode in, anxious to discuss arrangements for supporting the army in a region stripped bare of forage, but was put off until later in the evening.[18] It was, indeed, a critical moment for the further management of the campaign, and Leopold does not appear to have handled matters as well as he might have. A case in point was his failure to assuage John George of Saxony, who had a variety of reasons for feeling offended. Although the Emperor allegedly listened benevolently to the Elector's dinnertable lecture on the proper treatment of Hungarian Protestants and meddling Catholic ecclesiastics, the German prince remained indignant and stalked off abruptly for Dresden early the next morning. This was a pity, for the fine little Saxon army would have been an invaluable asset in the fall fighting in Hungary.[19]

THE SCHWECHAT INTERVIEW

At about the same time the Polish Vice Chancellor Gniński also showed up, bearing an Ottoman standard as a gift for Leopold. Sobieski and his army, their saddlebags and wagons jammed with plunder, were now ready to renew the advance, and the King apparently had been fretting all day about the Austrians dallying behind. The Emperor, basically a man of good sense, seems to have overcome any resentment he may have harbored over Sobieski's behavior on the thirteenth and to have concluded that he should thank the Polish monarch and his troops in person. This tactful resolve was probably, to a large extent, the fruit of Cardinal Buonvisi's earlier efforts to smoothe relations between the allies. Already at Linz the crusade-preaching Papal emissary had sought to counter the influence of the Western-oriented ministers and Borgomanero, whose attitude toward the Poles in matters of ceremony and prestige was stiff and uncompromising. To be sure, even in Vienna, there was backing and filling over the question of the "right hand" (right side), which the Austrians were unwilling to concede the Poles in front of the two Electors. Moreover, John III's gauche conduct can hardly have disposed Leopold to be even more accommodating and to accept the Nunzio's advice to yield the position of honor. On the other hand, Habsburg stubbornness reflected more than the arrogance of the most conceited court of a protocol-dominated age. The presence of two territorial rulers, ambitious men who already possessed every attribute of sovereignty save outward acknowledgement, represented a genuine, not a superficial dilemma. Despite the Peace of Westphalia, Vienna's aspirations within the *Reich* had not vanished—and would not until the last shot was fired at the Battle of Königgrätz. In any case, it was finally decided late in the evening to dispatch an envoy to Polish headquarters with an invitation for a meeting and with authority to negotiate on etiquette. The emissary, Count Schaffgotsch, returned early in the morning with a solution which Sobieski himself had devised: the two rulers would simply come together face-to-face on horseback.[20]

The famous Schwechat Interview (September 15) has long been the subject of nationalistically-impassioned historical debate. The factual aspects are relatively clear. The Emperor addressed the King graciously in Latin and received an equally engaging reply. When introduced to Jakób, however, he did not shake hands or raise his hat and conducted himself in similar fashion before the assembled Polish soldiers and nobles. Leopold's intentions are a somewhat different matter. Polish writers and their partisans have long argued that he was a prideful ingrate, who deliberately slighted his valiant allies, which was, to be sure, just another example of the reprehensible habits of his family.[21] The most interesting and best-documented Polish viewpoint is that Leopold wished to disabuse John III of any notions the latter may have had about obtaining the hand of the Archduchess Maria Antonia for his son. The basis for this interpretation is a secret addendum to the Austro-Polish agreement of March 31 in which Vienna promised to support the Prince's election to his father's office and, possibly, the establishment of a hereditary dynasty. In the past, moreover, Habsburg diplomats had held out the vague but tantalizing prospect of a marriage alliance and now, as a consequence of Poland's help, the calculating Marysieńka had come to take such a development for granted. At her instigation Sobieski had gone so far, shortly before the lifting of the siege, as to send a representative to broach the matter with the Austrian Court. (The latter's reaction was apparently a formally polite but frosty rejection.) Meanwhile the Queen had proceeded a step farther. On the basis of a message from an obviously deluded Lubomirski, she was entertaining the idea of Jakób being elected King of Hungary with the support of Thököly and Leopold, a fantasy of which the Imperial Government simultaneously gained knowledge. Thus, at Schwechat, Leopold, although desiring to maintain proprieties, could not refrain from acting frigidly when Jakób was suddenly presented to him.[22]

Unquestionably, both the King and his troops were mortally offended. Moreover, from that moment on it seemed to John III that he and his army were being deliberately mishandled. In a letter written to Marysieńka on the seventeenth the ruler listed a whole series of insults and injustices. He himself was being ostracized. His men were being treated like lepers. The wounded and sick lay on dung heaps in the open air; arrangements could not be made for their transportation to Bratislava even at royal expense. The dead were refused burial in respectable graves inside Vienna and were assigned to ruined suburban cemeteries half-filled with pagan corpses. There were no supplies for the Poles despite the treaty obligation. Some soldiers were being physically assaulted, even robbed. One detachment, which was guarding captured cannons prior to division among the allies, was set upon and relieved of its clothing and horses. (The incident appears to have been the work of the Viennese scavengers, who had already evoked the ire of the City Council for having appropriated not only government-confiscated Turkish equipment but Imperial and Municipal goods as well.) Poles trying to gain entry to Vienna were driven off at gun point.[23] While several of these complaints were probably unjustified and the product of the hypersensitive monarch's imagination, it is unlikely that they were entirely fictitious. What is striking is that the Polish sovereign, with that peculiar obtuseness of persons who are themselves testy, could not see that his own demeanor on the thirteenth, the booty-hogging and the lax discipline of his followers, had resulted in wide-spread resentment and enmity.

It is improbable that the full truth of the Schwechat affair will ever be discovered. The evidence is both circumstantial and conflicting. The strictures of Spanish etiquette may have prevented Leopold from acting as cordially as the more spontaneous Poles expected. Jakób himself thought that the Habsburger either could not see clearly because of a long peruke or had to hold on tightly to the reins of his fiery steed. If the Emperor's behavior did in fact constitute a kind of spontaneous rebuke to Marysieńka's effrontery, the Austrian cannot have attached much importance to it at the moment. He is said to have doffed his hat to the very last of the Polish units he reviewed after being told that the first Sarmatians he had ridden past were offended at his failure to do so. A letter to Marco d'Aviano written shortly thereafter shows that the All Highest did not regard the meeting as unusual in any respect.[24] Later, upon being informed that he had wounded his royal colleague's self-esteem, he followed

Lorraine's advice and sent the King and his son rich presents to make amends.

Nevertheless, the incident was by no means inconsequential. Above all, it appears to have increased disarray and dissension in the Polish ranks. Among the nobility were men who were Sobieski's domestic political foes, latent Francophiles basically opposed to the Austrian course. People such as Jabłonowski, unhappy over the prestige which the monarch had won, were agitating for an immediate return. Others—perhaps not inimical to the ruler personally but conscious of the unique situation, in which a Polish host had advanced beyond the frontiers of the realm to fight for a foreign sovereign—were sincerely convinced of the ingratitude of the Austrians. In addition, the physical suffering of the army was mounting hourly. Although there were sufficient *munitions de bouche,* good water was in short supply, and dysentery was beginning to approach near epidemic proportions. Horses were dropping left and right for lack of fodder. Gradually, some groups began to leave for home on their own. Although the army was not quite at the point of disintegration, its strength was being depleted, and its outlook boded ill for the forthcoming fighting in Hungary. Why, under these circumstances, John III himself did not yield to the general clamor to depart does, however, seem fairly clear. He still clung to the ideal of an international effort to banish the sign of the Crescent from Europe for all time.[25]

DISSOLVING UNITY

Sobieski's foul mood during the two days after the Schwechat interview resulted not merely from Leopold's alleged snubbing of Jakób and other inter-allied friction but also from a conviction that the failure to get underway was a shameful squandering of a splendid opportunity. It might no longer be possible to pounce upon the shattered Ottoman army as it withdrew from Lower Austria but one could proceed to Hungary and engage the foe in the Rába region before he really had time to recover from the chaos of retreat. The Duke of Lorraine shared these sentiments wholeheartedly and became disgusted when long hours were wasted in taking counsel at Vienna on the sixteenth and the seventeenth. By the very nature of things, however, the delay was probably unavoidable. Swift, cohesive action could not be expected of an army composed of troops from a congeries of states that were unwilling to accept the single will of a genuine supreme command. The Elector of Saxony had already made his exit. The sick Waldeck, who had discussed matters with Lorraine as early as the morning of the fifteenth, objected to continuing operations on both military and political grounds. (Concern for the most recent aggression of Louis XIV was clearly the overriding consideration.) The Margrave of Bayreuth, the second-ranking Franconian general, was even more adamant. The Prince had himself transported to Klosterneuburg for "better air" and eventually informed the Austrians that he required new instructions from the Bishops of Würzburg and Bamberg and from his Circle associates before deciding about participation. The only concession he granted was to assign a corps of Swabians sent to help in the relief of Vienna but still underway in late September.[26]

A further hindrance to prompt renewal of the campaign was the youthful Elector of Bavaria. No longer willing to play a subordinate role, Max Emmanuel insisted upon a command of his own. He wanted to besiege Nové Zámky while the Imperials engaged the Turks elsewhere —failing which he would return to Munich. In order to get his way, he obtained the intervention of Borgomanero, Sinzendorf, and Strattmann. Lorraine, however, firmly opposed further weakening of an already much depleted army, stating that he would find some way to assuage the Elector's ego. The threat should not be taken seriously, and he himself would resign if Leopold gave in. There also appears to have been some difference of opinion over the objective in Hungary. The Duke, whose major concern was to exploit the remainder of the fighting season, weighed the suggested alternatives. One might attack either Nové Zámky (apparently the majority preference), Esztergom, or Buda. In all events, the recapture of Upper Hungary was essential because of the pressing need for winter quarters. For any of these moves strong forces would be necessary since the Turk, although repulsed, was not beaten and the rebels, too, were still in the field. It would not be wise to decide beforehand what to do. One ought to wait and see where the enemy stopped and what measures he was taking to secure his posts. It was only necessary that the army march to Hungary as quickly as possible "with all dispositions necessary to act according to those of the foe."[27]

The Emperor, although not yet ready to make peace with France for the sake of a Papal-sponsored crusade, nevertheless accepted the Duke's conditions late on the eighteenth. Sobieski, all the more irritated with the Austrians for not having consulted him, had impatiently broken camp the previous day. The Austrians now followed, and on the nineteenth he agreed to advance jointly without prior definition of the target—despite his personal preference of heading straight for Buda. Max Emmanuel contented himself with a compromise suggestion according to which he would lead all the troops from the Empire (the position of the Franconians still being unclear) under the overall command of the King. However, the *Reich* Germans lagged far behind, and it remained questionable to what extent they would support the Poles and Austrians. By the twentieth only the latter were linked, and even they were forced to cool their heels at Kittsee just opposite Bratislava. The pontoon bridge, which would permit them to cross over the main Danube to the forage-rich, strategically more suitable Velký Ostrov Zitný, had not yet arrived from Tulln. The withdrawal of the Saxons who needed to use the bridge where it was, the dispersal of unremunerated rivermen, and high water combined to delay its transfer and reconstruction until the twenty-fifth, to the mutual annoyance of John III and Charles. Thus, divided in spirit and numerically weakened, the allies had once again taken to the field.[28]

B. The Fall Campaign

THE OTTOMAN RETREAT

The Giaours' failure to mount a quick pursuit—whether on the thirteenth because of Sobieski, or in the succeeding four days because of other factors—was clearly a gift from Allah. In the Grand Dragoman's opinion the Ottoman army would have suffered a far worse fate if the Christians had not paused at Vienna. To be sure, the opportunity for such a victory (which would probably have accelerated by several years the relatively arduous reconquest of Hungary in the forthcoming War of the Holy League) was fleeting and, most likely, was lost already during the Poles' one-day halt rather than in the following period of inaction. What is certain is that the Grand Vezir himself, with a large portion of the army, managed to withdraw to beyond the Rába in just under a day and a half, İbrahim Pasha and the Tatars having preceded him by a full twenty-four hours. In short, by whirlwind flight the Turks had assured their own safety, at least temporarily. They now enjoyed all the defensive advantages of a position based upon the unusual potamic relationships of the region in question.[29]

The retreat and subsequent developments within the beaten Ottoman army are relatively well-documented. The most interesting account stems from Marsigli, who was goaded along in fetters by his Turkish captor. The always-observant Italian nobleman, ransomed the following spring, reported his experiences to Leopold in great detail by letter. The abandonment of the Viennese camp, started by merchants and other hangers-on even before defeat in battle (which probably damaged further the already shaken morale of the front line troops) was an incredible pell-mell. Horses and men stumbled over tent ropes, hitching-posts, feed troughs and water-filled ditches in the effort to reach the far side of the city as quickly as possible. Kara Mustafa restored some semblance of order, at least for a brief time, after his men had traversed the Vienna River and gathered atop the Wienerberg. However, the march to the Leitha and then to the Rába was disciplined only in a relative sense. The Grand Vezir, seen (by a gleeful Marsigli) hunched over his stallion and bandaged on one eye, lost his way for a time. Broken-down wagons and horses littered the roadside. For the troops there was not even a crumb of bread and for the animals scarcely a blade of grass. Stragglers were chopped down by Sobieski's detachment prior to dawn of the thirteenth and by other small Polish scouting parties during the next several days.

Only one night's rest (September 13–14) was permitted. Kara Mustafa himself, alleges Marsigli, was already weighing the means by which he might escape Grand Seigneurial retribution. Scapegoats were not lacking in the persons of İbrahim Pasha and Murad Girey. No sooner had the *Ser'asker* reached safety on the far shore of the Rába than he began a series of summary executions by ordering the strangulation of the *Beyler-beyi* of Buda. Perhaps he also hoped thereby to prevent knowledge of his own mistakes from penetrating to his master. The slaughter was so extensive—ultimately embracing several pashas and fifty other subal-terns—that when intelligence of what was happening reached Austrian ears Count Taaffe was moved to write his brother: "This will be a ready way to make an end of their army, if he kill thus on one side, and we on the other."[30]

The Grand Vezir also despatched the faithful Vani Efendi and the *Telhîşî* (Court Messenger), İsmail Aga, posthaste to the Padishah in Belgrade, probably with a personal letter. Both men enjoyed Mehmed IV's favor and were successful, initially, in their job of convincing the Sultan that what had occurred was not Kara Mustafa's fault but was due rather to the negligence of his subordinates. The sovereign sent off appropriate gifts as a sign of his enduring confidence and apparently granted the *Ser'asker's* request for command in the next season's cam-paign as well as authority to raise fresh troops to that end. The ruler himself, whose immediate reaction was evidently an attack of physical weakness followed by rage at Christians in general, utilized the opportu-nity to replenish his coffers and confiscated the fortunes of some seventy fallen pashas.

In the meantime his chief minister had begun efforts to salvage the army. It was hardly possible to remain along the Rába. There was no artillery, the men were forced to sleep in the open for lack of tents, and the food for which everyone had hoped was not available: the magazines of Buda were already exhausted and nothing more could be sent forward. The few victual wagons remaining were turned over to the Janissaries. The other troops were forced to live on herbs, fruit, and boiled barley and wheat. This diet, along with polluted Rába water, broke the already-shaken health of many. A Christian attack, a sortie apparently from the fortress of Győr, resulted in turmoil, and Kara Mustafa was able to prevent a complete rout only by commanding élite units to cut down the fugitives.[31]

Thus after only two days' rest, the Ottoman host once more took to the trail. Within another four days it completed the journey to strongly-fortified Buda. The march had to be rapid, although the army was weakened thereby, because of a lack of water. Drought had caused even the marshes of the Rábaköz to dry up. Another factor was continuing harassment from Győr and its sister fortress of Komárno. Equally perilous was the changing attitude of the local Magyars. Count Batthyányi set the example for side-switching by suddenly massacring most of the 1,500-man Ottoman unit attached to his militia. The indigenous garrison of Pápa also rebelled and slaughtered 700 Turks in its vicinity. Despite the physical protection it afforded, Buda was not much solace either. Disease spread rapidly, affecting among others the commander's own sons, many *Beylerbeyi*, and the Grand Dragoman, who nearly died. Quarters were unavailable except for the chief officers who received new tents from Belgrade. The by-now-unruly men had to keep on sleeping under the open sky. Increasingly inclement weather, still unresolved supply problems, and failure to receive pay caused many soldiers, especially *Seymen* and *Deli*, to attempt unauthorized departures for home. The numerous executions did little to restore morale.

The *Ser'asker*, fearing complete chaos, ordered counter-measures in the camp and reinforced the guard posts at the Osijek bridge, the deserters' most likely goal. However, even some of the more reliable Turks ridiculed their leader's commands, and, driven by terror of the Christian forces, thousands of semi-starved men headed toward the Drava, crossing the river by boat in several places above the bridge. The effect of this movement was to undermine the Grand Vezir's other efforts. Although the Sultan had pardoned him for failing to accomplish what even Suleiman the Magnificent could not achieve, further failure could have disastrous personal consequences. Above all, it was necessary to assure retention of the Danubian strongpoint of Esztergom and the fortified bridgehead of Parkan (Štúrovo since World War II) on the far bank, which together secured the line of communication to the no-less-crucial Nové Zámky. In pursuit of these goals, Kara Mustafa dismissed Murad Girey, and sent the Tatars under a new khan, Hadshi Girey, across the Danube at Pest in order to join the evasive Thököly, now lurking in the region of Levice. The untrustworthy Rumanians and Transylvanians— Abafi was providing intelligence to Sobieski—were simply dismissed. Perhaps 20,000 men were (ultimately) scraped together for strengthening Esztergom, Parkan, and Nové Zámky. Kara Mehmed Pasha, newly promoted to the late Ibrahim Pasha's office, was put in charge of the operation. Apparently the Grand Vezir hoped that he could count upon the young, vigorous, and battle-tested *Beylerbeyi* to overcome the poor morale of the troops. Thus the stage was set for the so-called fall campaign.[32]

THE FIRST BATTLE OF PARKAN

The Turkish generalissimo's efforts to shore up the Porte's border defense system were doubtlessly accelerated by information from scouts that the enemy was once again underway. To be sure, the allied army, while finally able to traverse the Danube below Bratislava (September 27), could not immediately resume the offensive. The advance was evidently impeded by a combination of causes. The Austrian command structure was shaken when several high-ranking generals, including Sachsen-Lauenburg, suffered fits of jealousy over the rewarding and promotion of the relatively junior Starhemberg. The infantry, led by the latter and incorporating the still-fit troops of the Vienna garrison, had not yet caught up. The intentions of the Franconians remained uncertain, and it was even unclear whether Max Emmanuel, who had retired to Brno because he, too, was "indisposed," would make good his promise to continue fighting. The Duke, fearing that the absence of the *Reich* Germans would preclude meaningful action, dispatched Ludwig Wilhelm to conciliate the Elector.

In the meantime, however, fall was rapidly closing in, and additional delay would spoil any chance of success. Thus, without waiting, Lorraine and Sobieski proceeded to the environs of Komárno, with the Poles well forward as previously. The maneuver was completed by October 2, and the two commanders at once began to confer, both with their own generals and with each other. The Austrians, who continued to favor a siege (either of Nové Zámky or Buda at this point) suspected their allies of being mainly interested in winter quarters. Since the politically discordant Sarmatians were now suffering terribly from dysentery and the "morbus hungaricus," there were doubtlessly some grounds for irresolution. On the other hand, the King, like the Duke, knew of the confusion and poor morale on the Ottoman side. Thus an aggressive move still appeared feasible. It was only necessary to choose wisely among possible objectives. Powerful Nové Zámky was not very tempting: John III recalled the dismal example of a royal predecessor (Wencelas-Václav II, 1399–1405), who squandered the fruits of an earlier victory by becoming involved in a siege at too late a date. A direct lunge at Buda seemed out of the question because of the forage problem. The return of the Margrave, who reported that the Bavarian infantry, at least, would be available, did not alter matters. The one remaining possibility, so it seemed to the Polish monarch, was to march toward the Hron (in the Levice-Parkan region) and then, depending upon the "countenance of the enemy" push on to Pest. Possibly, however, the pontoon bridge could be shifted downstream to a point above Parkan. If prospects appeared promising, the army could transfer to the lower shore of the main Danube and move upon Esztergom, a plan quite different from what was originally envisaged. The Austrians, who again (October 4) took counsel among themselves, concluded that Sobieski was right about Nové Zámky: the season was late, the terrain swampy, and the garrison strong, with possible relief nearby.[33] Therefore they accepted the Polish ruler's suggestion, and early on the sixth, galvanized by news from scouts that Kara Mehmed Pasha's Turks had arrived at Esztergom and were passing over the bridge to Parkan, the allied regiments once more set off eastward.[34]

During the day's march, news came that the ever-cautious Thököly had left Levice, and it was thought that his goal was either the Slovak hill towns or Košice. Although the rebel leader was actually under orders to rendezvous with Kara Mehmed Pasha at Parkan, the Duke feared renewed incursions into Moravia. Consequently, he organized a special mixed brigade under Count Caraffa to operate around Trenčín—a decision which proved to be the first step in recovering Upper Hungary. In the meantime the Poles pushed on at the head of the main army, burning and looting, activities hardly consonant with the objective of securing well-supplied winter quarters. In the evening Sobieski, Lorraine, and their generals conferred over possible moves on the seventh. The King wished to strike out immediately against the Ottoman forces at Parkan, for he worried that the foe might refuse to give battle by suddenly retreating into the fort (which consisted merely of palisading and an earthen wall). The Duke wanted to hold back until Starhemberg's infantry and artillery could catch up. He felt that it would be unwise to approach a reinforced position, backed by a considerable body of troops, without proper means of assault. The Turks, if kept uncertain of the allies' intentions, were not likely to retire. The majority agreed with Charles, and John III acquiesced.

During the night, however, the King changed his mind and decided to break camp the next morning independently. He apparently reckoned that the Austrians would be compelled to follow willy-nilly. Why he was so bent on retaining the initiative for himself was unclear to contemporaries. Some held that he coveted the glory of having the Poles seize Parkan alone. Others, remembering Vienna, believed that his purpose was to monopolize the booty. In a letter to his wife the ruler explained that the idea was to have the vanguard snatch some Danube barks for use by his handful of Cossacks, and halt, until he came, some fifteen miles above the Ottoman bridge. Above all, however, scouts would have to investigate the environs of the town. If the Turks were seen to be returning to Esztergom and dismantling their span behind them, then the Poles might occupy Parkan. If, on the other hand, the enemy appeared set on defending the place, the royal host would camp where the advance units had stopped and would wait for the Imperial foot and artillery.[35]

When Lorraine learned what his colleague-in-arms was about to do, he was so indignant that he was tempted "to let him go it alone." Nonetheless, the Duke had his men saddle up immediately. At the same time he told Dünewald to gallop forward and attempt to dissuade the impetuous monarch. Sobieski's reply was that the Turks on the north shore were reported to be small in number—which was probably true at the time—and that there was no obstacle to continuing. Charles had little choice but to order the Imperials to follow. It was scarcely an auspicious beginning. Another unfavorable factor was the Poles' sloppy order of march. The van—led by the Castellan of Sandomir, Stefan Bidziński, and made up of dragoons, *pancerny,* and the Cossacks—proceeded with unlighted matches or, in some cases, none at all. Behind it came John III with a corps of hussars. Some troopers became enmeshed with the baggage; none were arrayed in battle formation. Altogether there were about 5,000 reiters. Far to the rear were the royal foot and artillery. An even larger number of Sarmatians lingered in the last camp, more concerned, as the King himself lamented, with guarding herds of cattle and other plunder. The country through which the army was passing should also have evoked greater care. Although relatively level, the area was nevertheless marked by slight rises and fairly broad intervening dips. This was especially true of the northwestern outskirts of Parkan (itself situated on flats just south of the confluence of the Danube and the Hron). Several hillocks ran parallel to the main river (southwesterly) and a couple more to the left of its tributary (northwesterly). Bidziński's contingent approached Parkan from the west along a road in the plain between the two ridge lines. It could see the town directly ahead but not the opposite side of the northwestern elevation, i.e., the bottom land farther up the Hron.[36]

The foremost Poles, who allegedly ignored Sobieski's admonition to reconnoiter, happened upon a party of perhaps 500 Turks at some distance from the fort and gave chase right to the bridge (at the King's own orders, so the Austrians claimed). Hearing the firing from farther back, Jabłonowski rushed up and commanded the dragoons to dismount. Suddenly, Kara Mehmed Pasha and the main portion of his 4–5000 man élite cavalry emerged from nearby bushes. The Ottoman warriors—*toprakli* from Rumelia, Buda, Karaman, and Sivas—had apparently just slipped over from Esztergom *in force* and had been hiding behind the rises to the Poles' left (alongside the Hron). As the Polish ruler himself later admitted in a letter to Charles II of Spain, the *Beylerbeyi* had succeeded in perpetrating an old *ruse de guerre.* Although in the confusion and disorder of the moment some Polish officers had refused to carry out the Grand Hetman's instructions, a goodly number of dragoons were now on the ground and could not be saved in the event of sudden withdrawal. Even worse, they were unable to fire because of the match problem. Jabłonowski, in any case, set up a makeshift battle line and only then sent word to John III. As the latter hurried forward with his still-unprepared hussars, the Ottoman horse smashed the thin opposing front, the Cossacks being the first to break. The mobile members of the Polish van now fled, and their dismounted, defenseless comrades were decapitated by the foe. The troopers fell back pell-mell upon the advancing King, who strove desperately to organize a new front. Jabłonowski was given the right, the Palatine of Lubin (Marcin Zamoyski) the center, and the Palatine of Kraków (Felix Potocki) the

left. The harried monarch then dispatched a courier to Lorraine and
the Polish foot.

However, the intervening distance was too great for help to arrive in
time. The Turks attacked *en masse* on the right, and although the Grand
Hetman beat them off twice, they crashed through on their third try.
Zamoyski's center, which might have given aid, unaccountably failed to
intervene. With one flank turned, the other two wings also collapsed in
spite of Sobieski's desperate efforts and even though the enemy were not
facing them. Discipline, never a forte of the Poles, now broke down
entirely. Hussars threw away their lances and cornets their standards and
timbals. The mad dash to the rear took place over freshly ploughed
terrain, and many fugitives were unhorsed, thus falling into the murderous hands of the pursuers. Among those killed was Władysław Denhoff,
Palatine of Pomerelia. The foe, including "Bosniaks" (Bulgars probably) whose language the Poles could vaguely understand, screamed insults and jeers as they pressed ahead. The King, battered and bruised by
his own men in the crush of retreat, was left with only eight companions
and twice narrowly missed death. On the first occasion he was saved by a
German reiter. The soldier instantly shot a Turk whose saber was but
inches from the sovereign's throat. Seconds later the rescuer himself fell,
and a squire drove off another Turk who was likewise perilously close. By
this time the corpulent Sobieski, fortunately borne by an unusually
strong stallion, was slumping from exhaustion and had to be propped up
in his saddle by the cavaliers at his side. Already thought dead by his
compatriots, he finally reached safety and was relieved to learn that
Prince Jakób, whom he had sent ahead earlier, was also secure. Embar-
rassingly, credit for the boy's salvation had to be given to Jabłonowski.[37]

The wild flight continued for some eight miles back to the Polish foot
and artillery. The Imperials appeared at about the same moment. Although they were emerging from a defile across a swamp and could not be
deployed at full strength, their weight proved decisive. The Duke took
the risk—for which he was later criticized—of ordering the forward units
to draw up in order to shield the routed Sarmatians. The Turks showed
no disposition to dispute the field with the formidable appearing cuirassiers, through whose intervals the King's army passed. Although preserved
from probable destruction, the royal forces had suffered grievous losses,
including perhaps a thousand dead. That night many a severed Polish
head, stuck on the discarded lances and standards, adorned the walls of
Parkan. The mood among the survivors, who encamped on damp ground
near the Danube, was a mixture of despair, shame, and rage. Austrian
officers came over to express condolences. It was suspected that they were
secretly gleeful although Lorraine's regrets were regarded as sincere. The
general fatigue notwithstanding, there was lively discussion. Many Poles,
especially the anti-Sobieski faction, were strengthened in their wish to go

home. Others wanted to delay further action until the advent of the Bavarian infantry. The proud, irascible John III, who self-righteously asserted that God was chastising his countrymen for their sins against the local population, apparently also felt great personal humiliation. Determined to make amends for his obvious lapse of military judgment, he advocated an immediate offensive. His resolution was shared by Charles, who had meanwhile successfully accelerated the march of Starhemberg's command. The Duke unleashed a powerful battery of arguments against the faint-hearted. After pointing out, *inter alia,* that the Turkish force was obviously quite small, he was able to make the King's standpoint prevail (October 8) . Nevertheless, it was held desirable that the Germans take the lead. The Poles were also no longer inclined to insist upon the more "honorable" right side, and Lorraine was unequivocally in command.[38]

THE SECOND BATTLE OF PARKAN

In the meantime, Kara Mehmed Pasha was savoring the delights of revenge. He at once packed off trophies to his master in Buda. For Kara Mustafa the juncture of affairs was now critical. There was clearly a chance of repairing the damage of the previous campaign and thus of completely restoring his credit with the Padishah. Thus the Grand Vezir responded favorably to his subordinate's request for reinforcements. A major portion of the dwindling Ottoman reserve, perhaps 8–9,000 élite troopers under the command the *Beylerbeyi* of Silistria, quickly covered the forty miles from Hungary's capital to Esztergom and crossed the river to Parkan during the night of the eighth. (Thököly and the Tatars were also prodded into moving but, characteristically, hung back idly outside firing range.) The united army huddled behind the northwestern hillocks where Kara Mehmed Pasha had lurked on the seventh. On the morning of the ninth it climbed to the crests, posting itself on the opposite slopes in one deep front with a three-tiered strategic reserve. The left wing was linked to the landward side of the fort, and the right to higher, wooded terrain farther to the northwest, whence Thököly was (erroneously) expected to emerge. The host was composed entirely of cavalry, apart from some 1,200 Janissaries stationed on the outskirts of Parkan. With the Hron River and its swamp to the rear and with the fragile (pontoon) bridge on the Danubian side of Parkan, the Turkish commander had selected a position that offered only the most tenuous routes of escape. It was not that he lacked adequate warning. His own council-of-war had advised evacuation of the fort, burning the bridge and a defense on the opposite shore, supported by the craggy parapets of Esztergom. However, the lure of victory in the field and a reversal of Ottoman fortunes proved too strong. It was a recklessness matched only by Sobieski's behavior two days before.[39]

As the Turkish commander marshalled his forces, the Christians likewise girded themselves. One hour before dawn the Austrian bugles
sounded the signal to harness up, and by the time the sun rose the
Imperials were riding out in three lines of battle. The 9,000 cavalry were
divided between Ludwig Wilhelm (to whom the additional 1,500 horse
of Lubomirski's auxiliary corps were attached) on the right and Dünewald on the left. The center naturally fell to Starhemberg with his
artillery and 7,600 foot. There were no intervals, since Charles feared a
repetition of the Ottoman maneuver in the Bisamberg encounter.[40] The
Poles were split up between both wings, with Jabłonowski in charge on
the far left and the King on the far right, facing Parkan rather than the
shorter Ottoman front. The royal infantry was divided, but the Grand
Hetman took the cannon. There is no clear indication of Sarmatian
strength, but 12,000 men is a fair estimate. In any case, the 12–13,000
Turks were outnumbered by at least two to one. Nevertheless, John III
hesitated, thinking the foe to be greater than they actually were and
having heard a rumor that the Tatars and even the Grand Vezir had
arrived. Lorraine quickly assuaged him by pointing to the uniquely
favorable terrain, and the King thereupon cried out, "Allons, au nom de
Dieu!"[41]

The Turks' hopes lay in launching a sudden, overpowering stroke that
would allow them "to make as cheap a business of it" as on the seventh. It
was equally logical to direct the thrust at the already softened-up Poles.
Since Parkan stood in front of Sobieski, Kara Mehmet could only assail
the allied left. As the two armies closed to within three cannon shots'
distance—the Muslims howling at the top of their lungs with Christian
tambourines, kettle-drums, and trumpets adding to the ear-splitting
din—, the Ottoman chief seemed to be heading toward the Duke's middle. Then, suddenly, some 2,000 beautifully-equipped *toprakl* broke off
from the right to hit Jabłonowski. The Grand Hetman, seconded by
chevaux-de-frise-protected infantry and artillery, sustained the first charge
with his hussars but called for support from rearward reiters. Lorraine,
who sped to the scene forthwith, discovered that the Polish reserves were
reluctant to answer the plea and so lent the support of Austrian dragoons
and cuirassiers. The attackers now reeled back in great disorder and with
heavy loss. The Ottoman center, which first pretended to assault Starhemberg, thereupon swung sharply to the right to try its luck in turn upon
the Poles, carefully avoiding Dünewald's intervening cavalry. In doing
this, it exposed its flank to the latter, an opportunity that Charles
promptly seized. It was the beginning of the end. The combined Austro-
Polish horse pushed back the demoralized Turks, both to Parkan's walls
and the marshes of the Hron. Halleweil's cuirassiers wedged themselves
in between, and the ensuing carnage amidst the reeds and muck was
frightful, although only a mild sample of what was to come.[42]

As the corps of Jabłonowski and Dünewald delivered their smashing blows, so also did Starhemberg, Baden, and Sobieski drive back the enemy on their side, and thus the whole Turkish front was crumpled. However, Parkan itself remained in Ottoman hands, and the Duke now issued the command to storm it. The Poles attacked on the right (south) with two regiments, falling upon Janissaries who lay in gardens just outside the palisading. Some German infantry and dragoons were ordered to carry out another assault a little to the left (west). As they were preparing to do so, the Margrave reported to Lorraine that the Danube bridge had broken apart under the weight of a jammed up throng of survivors from the earlier encounter and that all was in confusion within the town and along the shore (east). Charles now redoubled his efforts. Baden was told to take another three dragoon regiments for a drive against the fort on the extreme left (north). The place fell almost effortlessly, the troops entering by the gates and across uprooted sections of palisading without losing a man. The Austrians simultaneously brought up five cannon with canister shot and turned abruptly south along the beach. The fleeing Turks, who resembled a bunched up flock of sheep being forced across a ford, also took heavy fire from the Polish right.

What followed shook even battle-hardened Christian veterans such as Taaffe. While some of the enemy jostled each other on the ruptured bridge, others cowered on the bank. A few asked and received quarter, at least from the Austrians. As the combined artillery and musket barrage intensified, a large number of the foe plunged into the waters, either directly astride horses, clinging to saddle horns, or grasping loose, floating planks. Some stripped off their garments and attempted vainly to swim against the strong current. For an hour and a half the ghastly spectacle continued. The Danube, choked with bodies and clothing, gradually began to redden. Corpses drifted up in a pile against a tangle of ropes and beams in the breach of the bridge, forming a link over which a few of the living were still able to cross. It was ultimately calculated that around 9,000 of the enemy, including Hızır Pasha and Sişman ("The Fat") Mehmed Pasha, *Beylerbeyi* of Karaman, perished in one way or another. Perhaps 1,500 men were captured, among them Mustafa Pasha and Halil Pasha, *Beylerbeyi* of Sivas, who surrendered personally to Jabłonowski. Only 8–900, led by the valiant but headstrong Kara Mehmed Pasha, got to Esztergom before the overloaded span snapped.[43] The remainder appear to have slipped through the Hron swamp and to have made their way to Nógrád and Pest. The loot, consisting mainly of weapons but also camels, a few tents, and some baggage, was substantial. Much was fished from the river, and the Poles recovered items lost on the seventh. The allied dead counted scarcely fifty men. The captured fort was garrisoned with 400 Germans and the two Polish regiments, but the Duke soon had to pull out his men because of friction over booty. In short order, the Sarmatians, joined by marauding compatriots from other units who slaughtered already-pardoned prisoners, set the whole town afire. Whether the blaze started by accident or by design—the discovery of the impaled heads from the fiasco of the seventh evoked great wrath—was unclear, but judicious observers of every nationality were disgusted at the wanton destruction of badly needed victuals and the loss of a still valuable strongpoint.[44]

The destruction of Parkan notwithstanding, the events of October 9 represented a major strategic victory. The Turks could no longer hope to recover their fortunes in 1683. The remaining elements of the once imposing Ottoman armada rapidly scattered to winter quarters in the various corners of the Empire. Kara Mustafa himself left Buda for Belgrade on October 16. The seriously wounded Kara Mehmed Pasha stayed behind in his capacity as *Beylerbeyi* and was entrusted with guarding the now-badly-threatened northern frontier until the next spring. Although (presumably) somewhat chastened by the most recent disaster, the Grand Vezir had by no means given up the struggle and was already busily forging plans for the next season's campaign. The terrible trials of his dissolving army—Hungarian fever, dysentery—and the spectacle of dead littered along the roadside did not deter him as he moved leisurely southward. As soon as he reached the White City (November 17) it became clear that he had lost none of his customary energy. Yet while he was throwing himself into a new round of organizational activity, his domestic political opponents had turned to undermining his already weakened position. All they needed was one more piece of bad news for the Sultan—who had meanwhile gone on to Sofia and Edirne.[45]

THE CAPTURE OF ESZTERGOM

Such tidings were, in fact, already underway. For the Duke of Lorraine, who could have been well satisfied with his earlier achievements, was not ready to quit even after the success at Parkan: there were still a few weeks of tolerable and hence militarily exploitable weather. The only problems were to concentrate available human and material resources and to persuade the increasingly reluctant Poles to endure a bit longer. The Christian forces had several alternatives. They might cross the Danube and besiege Esztergom, or march to Pest, or pursue Thököly and his partisans. The Duke preferred the first option. A personal reconnaissance which he undertook on the tenth seemed to show that as long as the fortress remained in Ottoman hands, supply boats could not safely move farther downstream. Just upstream from Esztergom were several islands which would greatly facilitate passage of the army. They also contained forage, and on the opposite bank of the southernmost channel was an old but utilizable retrenchment for covering the crossing. Győr, too, was not far away in case of need. Anticipating the assent of the other leaders, Charles at once sent orders to Komárno for transfer of the previously used pontoon bridge. Simultaneously Count Herberstein was instructed to conduct his Styrian regiments and Croatian militia toward Osijek in order to prevent any possible turn-about of Kara Mustafa. Construction of the Danube span began on the twelfth, and an effort was also made to restore Parkan. The same day 1200 Brandenburgers appeared on the scene as Ducal Prussian vassals of Sobieski. On the fourteenth 5,000 Bavarian infantry arrived. Whatever the goal should be, there was plenty of weight for attacking a fortified position.[46]

By the fifteenth the bridge was finished, and three days later enough supplies had been accumulated to overrule the objections of Lorraine's own generals. Polish approval of an operational decision thus became indispensable. Upon consulting the King and his colleagues, the Duke not only found agreement on an objective difficult but he could hardly get any cooperation at all. John III opposed Esztergom ostensibly because of a lack of forage but more probably because of fear that a time-consuming siege would impair securance of winter quarters. (Once more the Austrians unfairly suspected him of fearing to expose his reputation to new risk.) He likewise rejected an assault on Pest since heavy artillery could not be brought up promptly enough—a valid-enough argument. The third possibility was equally unpalatable. The monarch, who was still trying to mediate between Vienna and the *Kuroczok,* asserted that it would be "inopportune" to chase Thököly while one was still negotiating with him. Apparently, Sobieski was again concerned about his own quarters, which he now sought in rebel-held Habsburg territory instead of in Transylvania as originally intended. It would be better to obtain them with the Magyars' consent than to have to fight one's way through. At the same time the King hoped for an accord because it would help establish a united, crusading front the next year. Finally, however, he acquiesced to a reconnaissance, at least, of Esztergom, and on the nineteenth some 2,000 cavalry rode over to the far side of the river. The Turks thereupon burned several outlying villages and the palank on Mt. St. Thomas, an elevation on the southern, landward side of Esztergom. The destroyed fortification could have prolonged the resistance of the main strongpoint if the Ottoman troops had really been determined. This sign of the enemy's demoralization and news of Count Herberstein's departure provided Lorraine strong arguments in persuading Sobieski to sanction a full-fledged enterprise.[47]

Polish reluctance about besieging Esztergom is partially understandable. The fortress, a military post in Roman and Carolingian days (Med. Latin: Oster Ringum, Strigonium) and thereafter the chief castle of the Árpád dynasty, lay atop a massive, three-sided rock, the Danube face of which was a veritable escarpment. The walled town, Hungary's primatial see even under the Turks, nestled on the river's bank just below the latter point. The works, dating from the sixteenth century and not in the best state of repair (as was characteristic of the Turks), were located only on the two landward margins. They consisted of solid north and south towers, between which ran a thick rampart along a simple, pointed trace. A stone-paved ditch, planted with sharp stakes, completed the defenses. Although obsolete by Western European standards, the place could still offer formidable resistance, especially since impending bad weather did not give the assailants time for a really proper investment. Furthermore, the Turks customarily withstood assaults upon permanent positions with great obduracy—at least so it seemed before the fall of the outlying palank. The Grand Vezir himself, although destined to be let down by his unwilling subordinates, had made the preparations for holding the post before he left Buda. He despatched a large quantity of supplies as well as his very last human reserves—under the command of Arslan ("The Lion") Mehmed Pasha (*Beylerbeyi* of Nikopolis), Deli Bekir Pasha (*Beylerbeyi* of Aleppo), Süleyman Aga (*Samsuncubaşı*), and Mustafa Aga (*Zağarcibaşı*).[48]

To be sure, the physically weakened and dispirited Poles did not have to launch the attack themselves but stayed rather on the opposite side of the river, confining their support to a field artillery bombardment of Turkish water-drawers. (The rock was arid.) The main burden of the operation fell on the Germans' shoulders, and thus Bavarian and Imperial infantry crossed the Danube on October 20. The next day the Austrian cavalry and dragoons followed, which meant that the whole allied army, save for the Poles, was encamped only fifteen minutes from its destination. The Bavarians took up station on the north, the Imperials on the west and south. The Duke did not waste time building a contravallation but instead sent scouting units down the two roads leading from Buda (i.e., the river route along the great bend of the Danube and the more direct passage southeast of the Pilis Hills).

However, at this juncture the operation was momentarily cast into doubt. Within the Polish camp pressure upon Sobieski to go home or at least to enter winter quarters forthwith (as he himself was inclined to do) had reached a new peak. The Queen, too, having fallen into an anti-Austrian mood and once more susceptible to pro-French influence, was sending messages urging an immediate return. Driven into a corner, John III consented to withdraw. He evidently continued to oppose the demand that he lead the army back to Poland—the course advocated by his domestic foes. In order to hide his embarrassment, the King provided the Austrians a whole, new set of *military* reasons for stopping the attack. While Lorraine was able by now to proceed without the Poles he still believed that it was advisable to bend every effort to keep them. If they were allowed to seek their quarters in Upper Hungary without Austrian escort, they would wreak havoc upon the countryside. The news of their departure might induce Kara Mustafa to turn about, or it could enable Thököly to disrupt communications with Komárno. Only after vigorous and repeated representations, including ultimately a personal plea by the Duke, did Sobieski relent. To judge by the reply to Marysieńka, another factor was the sovereign's fundamental optimism about the chances for completely liberating Hungary—which would promote his plan for a crusade. However, it took a threat to attend the siege as "commander-in-chief" of the German troops alone to get his objecting paladins to remain.[49]

Finally, on the night of the twenty-second, some 3,000 foot moved up to Esztergom and opened approaches. The operation was supervised, under direct enemy fire, by Starhemberg, who was still so weak from his illness during the Vienna siege that he had to be shifted about in a calash. Twenty-four hours later, in the midst of a drenching rainstorm, work began on three regular siege batteries, one atop Mt. St. Thomas, another on a neighboring rise (Mt. St. Martin), and the last along the shore of the Danube. Shelling commenced on the twenty fourth, and the Turks at once fled from the town into the citadel. At the same moment German infantry managed to reach the ditch. The Bavarians forthwith laid a mine, an action doubtlessly quite satisfying to Max Emmanuel, who had recovered from his "indisposition" and arrived just in time to see the last important fight of the campaign. By the twenty-sixth the cannon were able to breach the wall in one place, and the Duke, in the King's name, summoned the garrison to surrender with an offer of the honors of war. After some hesitation—there were so many high ranking Ottoman officers inside—, further bombardment, and the placing of a second mine, the enemy accepted.

The Austrians thought that the relative ease of capture was due in part to the effect of explosive projectiles upon a fortress which had no subterranean passages. It was also apparent that the Battle of Parkan, the flight of the Grand Vezir, and the speed of the Christian sappers added to the defenders' poor morale. In any case, 4,000 Portal warriors, plus their families and the town's (Turkish) population, now filed out. The men were allowed to keep their arms and baggage but not the artillery and munitions, most of which had arrived just before the attack. Part of the group was conveyed to Buda in boats supplied by the Christians. The rest went by road. Death awaited three of the four commanders: Kara Mustafa promptly had them beheaded for cowardice. In order to honor the terms of capitulation fully—hostages were also exchanged—the Austrians had to use force against some marauding Sarmatians. As the Count of Provana remarked, the Poles simply did not have the same "gentlemanly" (i.e., Western European) code of military ethics. In any event, Lorraine once more had cause to be pleased. For 140 years, with but one brief interruption, the Othman banner had waved over Esztergom. It was the first place containing mosques that the Austrians had seized in eighty years. Not only was Charles able to take it without the serious loss of life that storming would have entailed, but the Austrians now possessed a strategic base that both choked off Nové Zámky and provided a spring-board for the recovery of Buda and the reconquest of all Turkish Hungary. The reoccupation in the meantime of Pápa, Tata, Veszprém, and Levice only enhanced the Habsburg advantage.[50]

THE HOMEWARD MARCH

After the dramatic happenings at Parkan and Esztergom the remainder of the campaign could only be an anti-climax—although not entirely without significance for future developments in both Austria and Poland. Once Charles had garrisoned the freshly captured fortress, he ordered the bulk of his forces to recross the Danube (October 30). Inevitably, the allied army began to disintegrate. The Bavarians marched off almost immediately. Some 3,000 Swabians, who arrived only on October 27 (and who constituted but a half of the force originally promised) also departed, Lorraine's pleas notwithstanding. The Poles, too, broke camp and started to move northwesterly along the course of the Ipel. For a few days the ever-sanguine Duke contemplated a joint strike against Nógrád and even Pest, which lay just to the south of this route. However, because of increasingly rainy weather and muddy roads, the project had to be dropped (October 3). Only operations of a relatively minor nature remained feasible.

Charles thus turned his attention to mopping-up the *Kuroczok* and to recovering various smaller localities in Upper Hungary lost to Thököly during recent years—an objective closely tied to the sensitive issue of Polish winter quarters and, consequently, to Sobieski's own relationship to the rebel chief. Discussion of the quartering problem, which had commenced as early as October 20, dragged on for two-and-a-half weeks. Initially, the Austrians had hoped to station all of their troops on Magyar soil in order to spare the sorely-tried Hereditary Lands. They were unhappy that the King had changed his mind about Transylvania and the comitats on the far side of the Tisza which they had been willing to concede in any case. Although John III's explanation about not wanting to pay good money to Abafi was plausible, it was harder to understand why the Polish monarch could not simply lead his men back home. There was speculation that he needed the permission of the *Sejm* to maintain the army outside of its normal cantonments along the Podolian frontier. At Vienna, moreover, his motives were still under suspicion. (Marysieńka's hare-brained scheme of obtaining the crown of Hungary for Prince Jákob continued to disturb relations with the Habsburgs until Pallavicini intervened to restore the Queen's perspective.) The real reason—a desire to keep units mobilized near the anticipated scene of the next year's fighting—was not, it seems, generally understood. In any event, the Duke gave in to the Poles. Although the alliance treaty did not bind him in the matter, he presumably did not wish to appear as an ingrate.[51]

The only remaining practical concerns were to assure a minimum of physical damage and to guarantee the restoration of Habsburg authority. Thus, while the King was granted the comitats of Saros, Abaujvár, and Zemplin, he was to be accompanied by five Imperial regiments, led by Dünewald and Scherffenberg, which would winter in the same general region. The chief military goal would be the recovery of Košice. The matter of a settlement with Thököly was discussed at the same time (October 4). Again Sobieski sought, vainly, to play the "honest broker." The rebels' conditions were as extravagant as ever, even though their bargaining power had sharply declined. The Duke listened politely to the presentation of the Polish Vice-Chancellor but was hardly disposed to offer meaningful concessions. Under such changed military circumstances it was a bit naive of Sobieski to expect the centralist-minded Viennese government to restore the traditional "liberties" of Hungary. Although the Polish ruler made one last effort in writing a few days later, the cause of conciliation was doomed. (He himself was destined to learn shortly how misdirected his own trust in Thököly's good faith was.) In any event, the King and Charles, who now had to part, did so on the best of terms. Their last night together, like the first, was charged with alcoholic conviviality, and Sobieski expressed his esteem for Lorraine by the gift of two richly caparisoned horses. It had been a thoroughly successful meeting of personalities—a rarity in an age of particularly jealous and self-centered military figures. The outcome spoke well for both men, but especially for the Austrian.[52]

The Imperial army, which had been moving slowly up the Hron, now proceeded to the vicinity of Levice, where twenty-eight of its regiments were assigned quarters in western Upper Hungary. Charles himself set off for the Hereditary Lands with the remaining units and finally arrived at Linz—whence the Court had repaired from pestilential Vienna—on December 3. Before leaving, however, the Duke received the Grand General of Lithuania, Kasimir Sapieha, who had just appeared in the area with a horde of 10,000 followers. Lorraine hoped that this contingent, which was supposed to catch up with the Poles and Dünewald, could still be employed usefully and made various suggestions to its commander, whom he supplied with maps and letters for Sobieski. Clearly, Lorraine was not cognizant of political conditions in the Republic. There are excellent grounds for suspecting that the Grand General, a secret adherent of Louis XIV and the Great Elector, had deliberately delayed the march of his troops in order not to assist the King.

Furthermore, the trail of arson, theft, and rapine which the Lithuanians left behind as they travelled from the Spiš district, via the upper Vah, to the Hron, exceeded the ravages of the Poles themselves and even of the Turks. Instructions to spare rebel property were ignored. Protestants were picked for special treatment by these fanatic Catholics. (To be sure, co-religionists along their previous path in Poland had also suffered.) There was no contact with the Turks. The choice of route assured as much. The Magyar population became so embittered that any even remote chance that Sobieski may have had for manipulating Thököly vanished. The insurgent chief himself publicly reaffirmed allegiance to the Porte upon rejection of his newest proposals and, after ordering his adherents to resist the Poles vigorously, took shelter in Turkish-occupied Debrecen. As the Austro-Polish task force, joined by Sapieha at Rimavska Sobota on November 17, pushed toward Košice, it found itself in increasingly hostile surroundings. There was an ambush behind every clump of bushes. Wounded who were left behind were slaughtered. Losses mounted rapidly, both from disease and combat. The last fragile bonds of discipline snapped. The army, in effect, was decimated. Its casualties from October 7 onward far exceeded earlier losses, and of the original numbers that left Poland, considerably less than one half returned. Among the last victims was Sieniawski, who passed away just inside the Polish frontier at Lubowla on December 15. The King, who had originally sympathized with the Magyars, now considered them worse than the Germans.[53]

The military benefits of the march toward eastern Upper Hungary were relatively modest. Although, at the start (November 10), Turkicized Szécsény, the ancestral seat of the noble family of the same name, was taken at the cost of pillage and massacre, and while several other nearby posts were staffed with Imperial garrisons, both Košice and Prešov (Eperies) proved too strong for assault. In Saros, stockaded Sabinov (Zeben) fell but only temporarily. The sole success in the remote east was Dünewald's capture of Levoča (Leutschau) in Spiš, Thököly's home stamping grounds, on December 11. The Austrian regiments were then dispersed for the winter in its environs. Sobieski, whose worst fears about quartering were now realized, also made arrangements for settling the fragments of his army in the same general area. However, no sooner had he himself crossed the Polish border—he was reunited with his wife at Stari Sącz on December 15—than his demoralized soldiery ran wild, causing considerable destruction and soon breaking up almost entirely. Only a few infantrymen remained in the region until the next summer.

Thus the King's hopes of keeping a force in being for the campaign of 1684 were frustrated. The army which had traversed such great distances in order to assist in the relief of Vienna was but a memory. The consequence of its horrible sufferings and excessive casualties was widespread domestic criticism of John III and new fuel for the ovens of his magnate opponents—the friends of the French and enemies of strong government. Polish historiography has long disputed the wisdom of the whole expedition, and one may still ask whether its *dénouement* justified the heavy costs. The most balanced judgment—valid, moreover, for the whole reign—is that in theory the royal policy of removing the Turkish danger and thereby of buttressing central authority served the nation's best interests but that the instruments in the monarch's hands—the almost hopelessly retrograde political institutions of Poland—were not commensurate with his talents and vision. His fate, although thirteen years away, was to die a disappointed and broken man.[54]

C. The Victory of the "Easterners"

THE DEATH OF KARA MUSTAFA

Long before his own end the King had the satisfaction of learning how Christendom's erstwhile scourge met his destiny. Although a dearth of first-hand evidence makes impossible a completely accurate reconstruction of the circumstances of Kara Mustafa's overthrow, available accounts do provide at least an approximate outline of what happened, and there is a detailed report of his execution. Clearly, the Grand Vezir was unable to slaughter *all* high-ranking witnesses to his mismanagement of the 1683 campaign: so massive an extermination would certainly have evoked the immediate suspicion of the Ottoman Court. Hence, the Turkish generalissimo is said to have bribed those persons whom he dared not kill. As the weeks passed, however, he began to fear that they would not hold their tongues, and he wrote to the Sultan in an effort to discredit them. The letter came at a time when the situation in the Padishah's entourage was beginning to change. On December 10 the French ambassador informed his royal master that the Turks were experiencing a real fright over developments in Hungary, that they feared that the Christians would capture Buda and even Belgrade. The Divan had decided that retreating Asiatic troops should not be stopped at the Bosporus bridge because of the risk of rebellion. The tight-fisted Ottoman sovereign had found it necessary to dip into his own funds in order to pay for new levies. The number of the *Ser'asker's* foes was steadily increasing. He would fall as the result of public hatred alone, should the Austrians take "several towns where there are mosques" or should he give up "his plan of avenging himself and of repairing the losses which he has caused." Simultaneously, Mehmed IV received more accurate accounts of the Viennese fiasco although, allegedly, the courtiers were still afraid to tell him of the true extent of damage to the army—something his chief subordinate had concealed. In any case, the friends of the most recently accused officers, who had gotten wind of the new intrigue, were in a position to counterattack.[55]

The moment of truth came quickly. By December 14 messengers had arrived with the reports of Esztergom's capitulation and, apparently, full details of the great loss of life at Parkan as well. The security of the whole northern frontier was unquestionably in jeopardy. Kara Mustafa's old enemies and rivals (including the *Kizlarağaşı*) also intervened and pointed to the earlier slayings in order to stress the enormity of his crimes. Guilleragues now wrote to Louis XIV that "desertion, terror, disorder and murmuring against the Vezir and even the Grand Seigneur are growing daily." If one may believe Rycault, the Janissaries were threatening mutiny and openly demanding the first minister's head. The ruler's intimates argued that the *Ser'asker* would have to be "deposed"—strangulation was taken for granted—even if innocent, since an orderly change in so troubled a situation was impossible. Finally, the Grand Vezir's "treachery and tricks" were painted in such vivid colors— another meeting of the Divan took place—that the reluctant Sultan was swayed into sacrificing him.[56]

Shortly before noon on December 25 the High Chamberlain and Court Marshal arrived at the palace in Belgrade with instructions to confiscate the Imperial Seal, the Holy Banner and the Key to the Kaaba—symbols of executive authority with which the main servant of the throne was customarily invested. The Portal emissaries were further empowered to "entrust his soul to the grace of the Ever Merciful Lord." Their victim, who was saying his mid-day prayers, accepted the respectfully delivered death sentence without demur. In a perfect manifestation of the Osmali sense of *kismet,* he completed his devotions, took off his fur mantle and turban and asked only for the removal of the rug, upon which he had been kneeling. He wanted his corpse to fall in the dust—a reflection of the Muslim belief that those who perish in battle enter Paradise at once. Then, with his own hands, he lifted his long beard and was quickly and efficiently throttled. The body was washed and dressed in a mortuary cloth. After recitation of the office for the dead the executioner skinned the head, which was stuffed and sent off to the Court. The other remains were interred in the yard of a nearby mosque. The *Ser'asker's* property, including considerable sums tucked away in Istanbul, was confiscated. Certain associates of the deceased also suffered. His thirty year old *defter-dâr,* Hasan Efendi, was executed in January. Mavrokordatos, beaten, despoiled, and carried back to the capital in chains, would doubtlessly have suffered the same fate without the intervention of the new Grand Vezir, Kara İbrahim Pasha, a protégé of Kara Mustafa and a major agent of his destruction. In short, nemesis had run its course. Perspicacious Turkish contemporaries found little cause for satisfaction, however. For all his errors of judgment, the late premier was probably the only man in the realm with sufficient energy and organizing ability to avert the impending peril from abroad. It is ironical that he was the sole remedy to the dire consequences of what he himself—at least as an immediate historical cause—had wrought.[57]

THE HOLY LEAGUE

The collapse of Turkish fortunes in September and October of 1683 was not only a major turning point in the history of the Porte but also had a far-reaching effect upon relations between the various European states. In fact, even before the lifting of the Viennese siege, the mere prospect of an Ottoman setback roiled Western political waters, which had been relatively quiescent for some seventeen months. It will be recalled that Louis XIV gave up his investment of Luxembourg City in March, 1682. From that point onward the Sun King sought to achieve his political goal, recognition of the reunions, through negotiations. He presumably hoped that Turkish pressure would eventually help him to succeed. In latter 1682 and early 1683 the French ruler patiently bided his time: when the deadlines he set the Empire for accepting his conditions expired, extensions were proclaimed.[58] In the Hague his ambassador, d'Avaux, persisted in efforts to get the Dutch to drop their support of Spain and to force Madrid to sign a separate agreement with France.

Then came the assault upon Vienna. Whether or not Louis banked upon the city's fall (a moot point), he can hardly have expected a Turkish drive deeper into Central Europe. All that he could rationally hope for was the achievement of his relatively limited territorial aims. Indeed, he even moderated his demands: his last offer, presented in Regensburg at the end of July, called for a thirty year truce on the basis of *uti possedis* rather than permanent cession. Leopold allowed the terminal date of August 31 to approach without giving an answer, and the Spaniards, who insisted upon a single, universal treaty, continued to ignore the March, 1682, French suggestion of English arbitration. Simultaneously Paris learned that Sobieski was proceeding to Austria's aid. In order to derive any benefit at all from the Habsburg predicament it was necessary for France to act quickly. On September 1, an army of 35,000 men under Marshal d'Humières entered Spanish Flanders and laid the countryside under contribution. When the Nunzio, Ranuzzi, complained to Colbert de Croissy, the latter replied blithely that his master's decision was only in the interest of peace and Christendom: the Spaniards, who frustrated the acceptance of French conditions at the Habsburg Court, were prejudicing the common good and had to be given a genuine fright.[59]

A report of the French aggression reached Linz September 10. Cardinal Buonvisi turned livid with rage—a reaction indicative of Continental opinion in general. The "Most Christian Turk"—as the King was now called—had done little to improve his public image. The bombardment of Algiers by Duquesne's fleet (a matter of little consequence to nominally sovereign Istanbul) and the persecution of the Huguenots could hardly be considered measures beneficial to Christendom at large. The Papal spokesman was all the more incensed because the chances for realizing Rome's—and Sobieski's—dream of a crusade seemed better than ever before. However, the new setback did not cause him to lose heart, for he and his diplomatic colleagues in other capitals now redoubled their efforts. At first, the Cardinal's own task appeared as difficult as ever. Although weakened by the march of events and smaller in numbers, the "Westerners" in Leopold's entourage remained vocal and could still raise strong arguments. Louis' latest outrage was *per se* a point in their favor. Then there was the irritation with Sobieski over the events of September 13 and the suspicion of his continuing relations with the Magyar rebels. The unwillingness of the Swabians and the Franconians to participate in the pursuit of the Turks (itself conditioned by French actions) was a further obstacle to the implementation of the Curia's wishes.

The Emperor hesitated. On the one hand, he authorized continuation of the campaign into Hungary instead of shifting troops to the Rhine. On the other, he allowed the faithful Kunitz to write a letter to Mavrokordatos in order to determine whether the Grand Vezir might be willing to make peace (September 24). Rome was informed of this strictly secret *démarche,* whereupon the Pontiff declared that he would cease payment of subsidies to Leopold. The Pope would not be a party to wars between Christian princes. The threat was unnecessary. There is no record of a reply from Kara Mustafa. At the same time, fate dealt Borgomanero a serious, perhaps crucial blow. By the time they had returned to Linz, most of the Imperial ministers were stricken with dysentery. No conferences were held for some time, but worst of all, death claimed Sinzendorf, "el principal que se opoñe a los que inclanavan a tratados particulares." The Ambassador sought to divert Imperial forces westward but found himself blocked by Buonvisi, who again exercised the power of the purse. All that the Spaniard could promise his masters in Madrid was that he might be successful with the Franconians and the Bavarians; he added in a separate note that he was working upon the sick Elector "debajo de mano."[60]

In the meantime the great victory of Parkan was won. It appears to have removed much remaining doubt about the advice of the "Easterners." On October 20 an Imperial conference, chaired by Hermann of Baden himself, concluded that even a new grand vezir would probably not want peace, that it was necessary to prepare for further war both militarily and diplomatically. These decisions, which initiated a fundamental change of course, were vigorously seconded by Buonvisi and Marco d'Aviano, who lingered at the Habsburg Court for some time. The Pope's representatives also sought to ameliorate relations with Poland, still troubled because Sobieski persisted in mediation efforts with

Thököly. Yet another voice favoring the East was the Venetian ambassador, Contarini, whose superiors, the Signoria, were now seriously considering a renewal of the struggle for control of the Aegean. International developments in November further strengthened the new tendency. While Louis XIV applied new pressure upon Spain by besieging and capturing Kortrijk and Diksmuide, he simultaneously softened his demands a little. The Comte d'Avaux, who was playing a tight game of cards against the Stadholder, announced on the fifth that his master would be content with Luxembourg City and its dependencies as an "equivalent" for French reunion claims upon Flanders (Alost and the "old town" of Ghent). Other "equivalents" could be Diksmuide, Kortrijk, and several border towns in Hainault (Ath, Beaumont, Bouvines, and Chimay) or else pieces of Catalonia or Navarre. The Empire could now have a twenty or a twenty-five year truce.[61]

It was wise of the French monarch to strike a comparatively reasonable pose. In the face of strong opposition from Amsterdam William had sent some 14,000 men to garrison the other "places fortes" of the Southern Netherlands, thus more than fulfilling the States' General treaty obligation to Spain (8,000 men). The Dutchman was striving mightily to get approval for a new levy of 16,000 troops—a step which almost surely would have led to outright war. A harder French line would have weakened the hand of d'Avaux and his indigenous allies and might have led to a victory of the Orangist party and hence to a strengthening of the nascent anti-French coalition abroad. More inordinate royal demands would likewise have evoked unfavorable reactions amongst other states independently. The King also had to bear in mind that recent efforts to stir up Brandenburg against the Netherlands' ally, Brunswick-Lüneburg, had failed and that while he had been able to achieve a sort of checkmating of forces in northern Germany, he could not exert any pressure from that quarter. Restraint, however, was a policy that would bear dividends almost immediately.[62]

The shift of emphasis at the Habsburg Court became increasingly evident as the weeks passed. Even Spain's ambassador, who was now contemplating a two-front war, was caught up in the crusading spirit. At the beginning of November he dropped his support of Thököly and told Contarini that the Emperor ought to crush the rebel leader as the prelude to pursuing the anti-Turkish struggle. The Marchese, who claimed to be speaking "da buon Italiano," also gave his blessing to the incipient union of Venice, Austria, Poland, and the Papacy. (To be sure, he had little choice in the matter, and it was judicious to yield gracefully.) The Duke of Lorraine, for his part, indicated even before coming to Linz (December 2) that he was enthusiastic about continuing the fight in the East—something which did upset Borgomanero, who held that Charles ought to be more concerned about the recovery of his hereditary domains. The

Emperor expressed great pleasure over a successful action by Croatian forces at Kanisza and then advanced a plan of his own for the destruction of the Osijek bridge. Under these circumstances it is not surprising that Waldeck was unable to secure Leopold's support for a really firm stand in the West. On November 18 the Imperial government agreed merely to hold a long-discussed congress with its allies in the Hague early the next year in order to devise a common policy toward France. Waldeck would function as the Emperor's representative. This decision was begging the issue and stalling for time, and it almost certainly weakened the Stadholder domestically. Thus, the ultimate result of Louis' caution was to bring about an interaction of cause and effect: William's inability to overcome the Amsterdammers buttressed the "easterners" in Linz while the Dutch deputies wavered without assurance of strong Austrian and other foreign backing.[63]

By the end of November Buonvisi was able to write Rome that there need be no further fear that Leopold's resolve would be shaken. Upon his arrival Lorraine immersed himself in the various military and political preparations necessary for the projected campaign of 1684. Additional promotions were granted to assuage the vanity of the officers who had been offended earlier. The restoration of Vienna's battered defenses was accelerated. Recruitment difficulties were worked out. Among other things a regiment was given to young Eugene of Savoy. Up to that point the penurious refugee from the French Court had been living at the expense of Borgomanero, who perceived future political advantage from maintaining a link to the geographically critical Alpine duchy, of whose ruling dynasty his guest was a scion. The Ambassador's foresight was commendable from the perspective of history. Momentarily, however, the gratitude of the future victor of Zenta and Blenheim could hardly be regarded as compensation for the Marchese's almost complete loss of influence with the Emperor. In late December 1683 and early 1684 it became increasingly obvious to Spain's representative that the Austrian government would eventually accept Louis' offer of a truce and that the best that his superiors could hope for was continuing resistance to the French demand for separate agreements.[64]

Meanwhile Linz proceeded to lay the diplomatic foundations necessary for carrying on the war in the East. At the beginning of December Count von Königsegg, Borgomanero's quondam ally,[65] approached Contarini and formally proposed a league between Austria, Poland, Spain, Venice, Tuscany, and Malta under the presidency of the Pope. At this point also Leopold's motives were clearly revealed. Buonvisi informed the Venetian ambassador that the sovereign desired revenge for the humiliations which he had suffered and believed that a final removal of the Ottoman threat, especially the reconquest of Hungary, would enable him to resist Louis XIV more effectively. It was also clear to what extent papal thinking had influenced the Emperor: his plans likewise called for efforts to secure the adhesion of Muscovy, Transylvania, Moldavia, Wallachia, and even the Shah of Persia. While Contarini sent home his report and while the Venetian Senate undertook to debate the Habsburg proposals, Linz and Rome turned their attention to Hungary and Poland. It seemed advisable to make at least one attempt to win back Magyar sympathies: Thököly, for all his personal ambitions, had enjoyed a mass following, and the Imperial government may have realized dimly how much German rule was hated in Hungary. An amnesty commission was established, and although Innocent advocated no mercy for Thököly personally, Leopold insisted on framing the proclamation to include everyone who would submit. Issued on January 12, 1684, the decree promised respect for the decisions of the Sopron Diet of 1681 and assured retention of personal property. All that was necessary was to appear in Bratislava by the end of February and render homage. The effect in western Upper and Lower Hungary was good, but there was little response from the East where only the force of arms could be determinative. The reaction of the rebels was probably influenced to some degree by the actions of Michael Abafi, who was afraid to join the Emperor until the latter had liberated Belgrade.[66]

Confirmation of the relationship to Poland was relatively easy despite various obstacles both at home, where there was lingering anti-Sobieski sentiment, and in Poland, where the offended Queen and the fractious magnates intrigued. The papal diplomats had meanwhile settled the sensitive issue of the King's involvement in Hungarian affairs. The prestige of the royal victories and news of other gains in Podolia and (albeit temporarily) Moldavia were also positive factors and overshadowed the serious Polish loss of life. Above all, the concept of the Holy League was fully in keeping with Sobieski's own goals, was, indeed, in part his own brainchild. In January Austro-Polish military discussions over the forthcoming campaign began in Warsaw, and it was evident that Poland would join the gradually ripening coalition. The key to the latter was of course Venice, and during the early weeks of the new year its senators carefully weighed the pros and cons of renewing hostilities with the Porte. This time the Republic would not have to fight alone as during the long, enervating Cretan contest. The Pope was offering financial help, and growing crusading enthusiasm in all of Europe seemed to portend further assistance. Neutrality might even endanger the possessions along the Dalmatian coast. Marco d'Aviano, who had come to the Lagoon City, participated in the discussions with considerable effect. On January 28 Contarini was able to inform the Austrians that his masters had given their assent. The details were hammered out in a series of conferences, and on March 5 the Venetian, Polish, and Habsburg plenipotentiaries affixed their signatures to the finished document of union in the presence of Buonvisi, proxy for the Pope—the official Protector and Guarantor of the agreement. Although Muscovy did not join until 1686 and although the plans for Persia's involvement proved far-fetched, the Holy League was born. With the later assistance of contingents from various German states (including even Brandenburg) and with numerous individual volunteers from many other lands, it would lead to the permanent shattering of Ottoman dominion in East Central Europe.[67]

The Truce of Regensburg

The great enterprise was temporarily jeopardized, however, during the spring of 1684, and Buonvisi still had to suffer several months of agonizing uncertainty. Leopold's assumption that it would eventually be possible to hammer out a tolerable truce with France was cast into serious doubt by developments in the Lowlands. The roots of the new crisis stretched back to December of 1683. Spain, proudly obdurate in the years of her worst national degradation, would not even hear of Louis' most recent terms and went so far as to declare war on France (December 11). The Sun King concluded that further coercion was necessary. Luxembourg City was treated to a heavy bombardment at Christmastide, and French soldiery ravaged the countryside in Brabant and the Waas region of Flanders. Nevertheless, the Bourbon monarch continued to avoid the risks that more extreme measures would have entailed. He did not allow his men to attack the fortified "Barrier" cities where the Prince of Orange's troops were stationed. As Charles II of England was more or less under Louis' control and since the other allies of Spain and the Northern Netherlands were involved elsewhere, the most likely catalyst for any joint action against France seemed to be the States General. No matter how peace-minded the influential Amsterdammers were, it was again necessary not to push too hard: d'Avaux's delicate negotiations could easily be upset. (Of course there was also danger, once more, of causing a turn-about in Austria.) Not only did the French King extend his time limits on several occasions, but on February 17 he further relaxed his conditions. Now Madrid, as well as the Empire, could have a twenty-year truce, which meant retention of only the Luxembourg reunions, not including the capital. At precisely the same moment the Dutch were plunged into a crisis that almost verged on civil war. William accused several Amsterdam deputies of treason for having consorted with d'Avaux, whose mail the Prince had intercepted and deciphered. The passionate Stadholder, who was still trying to ram through his supplementary levy, thereby made the mistake of pressing too hard and by early April was beginning to lose adherents. Amsterdam's plausible argument that war was untimely, and republican fear of Orangist monarchism made his position all the more untenable.[68]

The French ruler, apparently sensing his advantage, decided to raise the ante. In latter April he took to the field with his troops for a regular siege of Luxembourg City,[69] which was not then considered a part of the Barrier and the reduction of which was not likely to alienate Amsterdam. The result was another period of acute international tension. The Austrians, who had been trying vainly to get Brandenburg's backing for a stronger nogotiating stand, now had to consider whether they should send regiments westward after all. Waldeck was bending every effort to create a strong pan-German army. The Circle forces would not suffice alone. The Bavarians hesitated, waiting to see what Leopold would do; they neither sent their units eastward as planned, nor moved toward the Rhine. The Emperor ordered Count Kaunitz back to Munich in late May in an effort to prod Max Emmanuel into action in the West. Still, the Habsburger was unwilling to commit his own men, stating that his decision would depend upon what the United Provinces and the other Associates did. Again cause and effect were intertwined. At the same time the French made another show of force by ruthlessly bombarding Spain's friend, Genoa. Buonvisi, close to despair, turned all his eloquence upon Leopold, dragged in Bishop Sinelli and Marco d'Aviano, and had his own counterpart in Paris, Ranuzzi, seek (uselessly) to influence the Sun King. Meanwhile Vauban was giving new proofs of his vaunted skills: Luxembourg fell on June 7, whereupon the French army moved menacingly toward Trier and the Palatinate.

For the Emperor a settlement was now only a question of timing. Not unaffected by ecclesiastical oratory; unable to count upon the Great Elector, not to mention Hannover, Sweden, and the States General; apprised of huge, new Turkish military preparations—he apparently concluded that a two-front war was impossible. The final straw was the complete collapse of the Stadholder's faction in the United Provinces. On June 29 the Dutch signed a convention with France, in which they agreed to work for Spanish acceptance of a truce. Louis would keep his reunions, plus Luxembourg and three small border seigneuries; all of Flanders would be evacuated. If Madrid did not agree, the Dutch would remove their garrison troops and provide no assistance at all to their allies. The French ruler consented to undertake any further military action that might be necessary outside of Belgium. On August 2 the Imperial resident in the Hague informed the States General that because of the Turkish danger Leopold would accept the truce, for himself, the Empire, his allies, and especially the Burgundian Circle and Genoa by virtue of authorization from His Catholic Majesty. All that was needed was for France's king to empower his minister in Germany to make a treaty. The formal, twenty-year Truce of Regensburg was signed on August 15, 1684. Spain, in defeat even less willing to deal directly with France, later signified its acceptance of the separate agreement negotiated and signed for it by Austria. While Louis was thus able, ultimately, to secure all that he had sought from Kara Mustafa's invasion of the Habsburg realms, the

victory would prove ephemeral in most respects. Leopold's calculation
that a final removal of the Ottoman threat would give him the strength to
repel his life-long Western foe would stand the test of time.[70]

D. The Siege in Historical Perspective

It is a commonplace that there are no sharp lines of division in history,
but surely there are points at which human affairs begin to change
direction perceptibly. There are also milestones, such as Austria's shift of
diplomatic-military emphasis between September of 1683 and August of
1684, at which one may pause to look ahead and gaze backward. Of
course, the same bend in the road affects the lives of the individuals who
helped lay out its course, and so the ultimate fate of the agents of
Vienna's salvation warrants consideration too.

The popular hero of the hour was clearly Starhemberg, upon whom all
manner of congratulations, honors, and pecuniary rewards were heaped.
Important military tasks still lay ahead of him, but, as noted before, he
had reached the high point of his career. His colleague in tribulation,
Kapliřs, also received due recognition, but the strains of the siege had
been too much for the septuagenarian, who survived but three years.[71]
Cardinal Kollonitsch, whose earlier involvement in the premature assertion of royal authority in Hungary had led to an eclipse of influence, was
once more prominent and a kind of ascendant star: his voice would be
heard again in matters relating to a thoroughly liberated and hence more
malleable Magyardom. His clerical confrère, Sinelli, had only two more
years in which to intrigue at Court. Conceivably, the latter's demise
weakened the position of Hermann who was toppled from power, in part
as a result of papal diplomatic efforts. The fall of the War Minister
(1687) was linked to an alleged correspondence with the perennially
negotiating Thököly, whose own credit among his fellow countrymen
declined over the years to the vanishing point.[72] The erstwhile "Prince
and Lord of the Partium" died at İzmir, a piteous semi-prisoner of the
Turks, in 1705, having outlived his wife, Helena, by only two years.
Another captive of the Porte, although only until the spring of 1684, was
the inquisitive Marsigli, whose scientific career was yet to unfold.

A particularly glorious albeit relatively short future was reserved for
the Duke of Lorraine (~1690), the conqueror of Buda (1688). His
humiliations and self-effacement in 1683 were thus destined to be compensated. Equal, if not greater military reknown was to be the lot of the
impetuous Ludwig Wilhelm, "der Türkenlouis," who would also prove
his skills in action against the armies of France. The overly-ambitious
Maximilian Emmanuel, on the other hand, would earn little honor and
less profit from the renunciation of ties to his father-in-law, Leopold, in
the War of the Spanish Succession. John George and Prince Waldeck,
preoccupied as they were with the Ludovican menace, doubtlessly wel-

comed the War of the League of Augsburg, but early death was to deny them the satisfaction of personally experiencing the frustration of their adversary. Innocent XI and Cardinal Buonvisi would see the first great victories of the Holy League, but their last days would be clouded by the division of Christianity's resources in the third war against the Sun King. The hypnotic Marco d'Aviano was to have another sixteen years of spiritual ministrations to an aging Emperor, who would pass away in 1705 amidst the climactic struggle to contain France. Borgomanero, too, was not to witness the final triumph of the Grand Alliance although he would live long enough (~1695) to assist in the penultimate anti-French enterprise, Of all the persons involved in the relief of Vienna the one to whom the future truly belonged was the as yet little-known Eugene.

If Kara Mustafa's assault upon Austria provided a professional début for the most brilliant general of the first decades of the eighteenth century, it also produced the circumstances under which he and the state he served were to rise to the forerank of continental politics. To be sure, the chief results of the Ottoman defeat were hardly apparent at once, and one must distinguish between less weighty immediate and more momentous long-range effects.

The short term consequences concern badly battered Vienna and gutted Lower Austria. As indicated, the recovery from Turkish depradations was slow and painful.[73] The government, of course, was not insensitive to the great economic suffering and did take certain measures, such as a moratorium on internal tariffs, to alleviate matters. An interesting reflection of the inequitable social circumstances of the time is the apparent fact that the nobility and allied privileged elements were able to recoup their losses more quickly than were others. Vienna's City Council complained vigorously about the abusive advantages of individuals associated with the Court (officials, servants, purveyors, and craftsmen) and about exploitation by religious orders, but the burghers could obtain only a partial remedy of their "gravamina." There is also evidence that the restrictive and monopolistic guilds helped impede a prompt reparation of damage. The one undertaking executed with relative dispatch was the reconstruction of Vienna's defenses. The battle-field clean-up commenced almost immediately with the aid of prisoners. The citizens were called upon to assist in the restoration of the works but, as could have been expected, responded insufficiently. *Robot* laborers from Lower Austria and troops were brought in, and, under Starhemberg's forceful direction, the job was finally done (May, 1684) .[74]

One may also safely assume that the financial burden of uninterrupted hostilities contributed to the tardy rebuilding process. At the same time, however, the War of the Holy League was logical and historically necessary if the Archhouse was to reap full rewards from the sacrifices of 1683. Only by eradicating Turkish power in East Central Europe—a goal not attained until the Treaty of Karlowitz in 1699—could the dynasty and its peoples be assured of tranquil internal growth. Only with the permanent removal of the age-old Islamic threat could the eastern provinces begin to develop in earnest. Only then could agriculture, commerce, and industry provide the material foundation for that remarkable cultural *essor,* which was the High Baroque of the Caroline Era.[75] Perhaps it is not going too far to say that Belvedere Palace and St. Charles' Church are in the last analysis an outcome of the Grand Vezir's aggression since a tree which has been radically pruned may eventually produce a more luxuriant foliage.

The political repercussions of the siege were no less remarkable. The first dividend from the subsequent fighting in Hungary was the accrual of strength which enabled Leopold to afford a two-front war from 1688 onward. The same accumulation of new resources, compounded over a longer period, allowed his immediate successors to transform Austria into a great power—"Das Werden einer Großmacht" in the words of Oswald Redlich.[76] Doubtlessly, the gigantic struggle against the Porte, taken up so unwillingly in the days of Kara Mustafa, was the crucible of the now much-lamented multi-national Habsburg Empire.[77]

Another issue which deserves to be raised when examining the meaning of 1683 for Austria (and for Europe) is historiographic. The tendency from the end of the First World War to 1945 was to see in the campaigns against the Turks an early revelation of Greater German striving, a flowering of German national sentiment despite the lasting setbacks of the Thirty Years' War and despite (or because of) the bafflements of the age of French hegemony. Since the re-establishment of the Republic of Austria a diametrically opposite viewpoint has prevailed, especially in writings of a semi-popular nature emanating from official or quasi-official sources. There seems to be a deliberate effort to discover and underline any indications of Austrianism in past centuries and deliberately to ignore evidence of common German feeling. Hence, it is instructive to note that seventeenth-century accounts sometimes refer to the victory over the Turks with such phrases as "teutscher Heldenmuth." The word "Austrian" does not appear often and when it does it is generally in a dynastic sense or in contrast to "Franconian" or "Bavarian." In short, the men of the time appear to have taken their *Deutschtum* more or less for granted, to have had a latent awareness of community with other speakers of their tongue, which is of course an entirely different thing from either of the above-mentioned extremes.

Probably each generation rewrites history. In view of the current movement toward European integration it would seem appropriate to regard Vienna's deliverance (and the War of the Holy League) as an international endeavor. A majority of the troops may have been Teutons, but the overall character of the allied armies was polyglot. Moreover, the fruit of their exertions was not only national—Magyar liberation and German penetration into the Balkans—, but supranational—the creation of Imperial Austria. Another unifying feature was religion. Despite the sixteenth-century schism and intellectual stagnation, Christianity continued to inspire the masses. While the Pope's call for a crusade contradicted the *Zeitgeist,* it did not lack an echo altogether. Ironically, the last refrain of Mediaeval ecclesiastical universality heralded the birth of the secular catholicity of the Dual Monarchy.

If the siege was so significant for the future, it is equally fitting to ask why it failed. Eight distinct factors—each of which, if different, could have brought about the opposite result—stand out. That time—Kara Mustafa's arrival at Vienna one week too late—was critical seems obvious. Without the delay, caused by both geographic distance and sheer fortuity,[78] the city most likely would have been his. Lorraine's cool-headed behavior in managing the Austrian army after the initial ups and downs in Hungary was a second element. Had the field forces been destroyed, succor would have been impossible. Similarly crucial was the rôle of Starhemberg and the professional soldiery. The presence of Rimpler among the defenders and his supplementary works should also be recalled. A fifth reason was the unstinting financial and diplomatic support of the Curia. The arrival of auxiliary contingents, accelerated by the Imperial foreign service, was another indispensable component of victory. No less decisive was the *Ser'asker's* incompetence as a field commander. The failure to fortify the Wienerwald and internal maladministration were crippling liabilities. The Muslim leader simply did not understand the cardinal principle of generalship: namely, that wars are not won by taking cities but by smashing armies. Finally, the organizational, technological, and tactical inferiority of the Turkish military establishment, at least with respect to pitched battles on open terrain, requires emphasis.[79]

Clearly, then, the Porte's defeat was not inevitable. However, the Grand Vezir's (presumptive) larger undertaking of conquest and permanent dominion was almost certainly foredoomed. A comparison of the static socio-economic situation of the contemporary Ottoman Empire with conditions in Central and Western Europe should suffice to prove its futility. Western civilization was not saved at the Battle of the Kahlenberg, as the commemorative plaque on St. Leopold's Chapel proclaims. It was only the Emperor who had been redeemed—and the embryonic Habsburg realm of a later day. Had the city fallen into Muslim hands even for a short time or had the relief army been vanquished, the beneficiary to a lesser or greater extent would have been the Most Christian King. In the former case Louis would most likely have been able to secure the reunions ten months sooner, and further French encroachment upon the Rhineland would have been greatly facilitated. In the latter case, it is probable that Leopold would have been rejected, if not actually deposed, and thus pre-eminence in the *Reich* would have passed into Bourbon hands. Crowned or uncrowned, the Gallic monarch would have enjoyed for a while at least, the allegiance of Central Europe. Thus, at the utmost, a Turkish victory could have made France the arbiter of the continent.

Bibliography and Footnotes

Abbreviations

AGS —Archivo General de Simancas (Valladolid)
AKTA—*Akta do dziejów króla Jana III*ᵍᵒ *sprawy roku 1683°*
AöG —*Archiv für Kunde österreichischer Geschichtsquellen*
CHP —*Cambridge History of Poland*, London, 1950
FRA —*Fontes rerum austriacarum*
HHSA—Haus-, Hof- und Staatsarchiv (Vienna)
KA —Kriegsarchiv (Vienna)
MAE —Ministère des Affaires Étrangères (Paris), archives
MKA —*Mitteilungen des Kriegsarchivs*
MIöG —*Mitteilungen des Instituts für österreichische Geschichtsforschung*

Select Bibliography

Bibliographical Aids

Forst de Battaglia, Otto, critique of Walter Sturminger's bibliography in *Deutsche Literaturzeitung*, Vol. 78 (1957), pp. 423–426. The reviewer has appended a long, supplementary list, especially of titles in Eastern European languages.

Sturminger Walter, *Bibliographie und Ikonographie der Türkenbelagerungen Wiens 1529 und 1683*, Graz-Cologne, Böhlau, 1955.

Vansca, Max, "Quellen und Geschichtsschreibung," *Geschichte der Stadt Wien*, Vol. IV/1, Vienna Alterthumsverein, 1911, pp. 1–108. On pp. 40–77 the author gives an exhaustive analysis of the printed sources relating to the second siege.

Unpublished Sources

AGS, "Sección del Estado," fascicles 3922, 3923, 3924, 3925, 3926.

HHSA, "Lothringisches Hausarchiv," carton 96.

Kreutel, Richard, unpublished portion of German translation of Turkish sources (see "Kreutel" under Printed Sources).

Kriegsarchiv (Vienna), "Feldakten 1683;" Protocol of Court War Council 1683.

MAE, "Turquie: Supplément 1679–1684."

(See also Preface, pp. vii–viii).

Printed Sources

Benaglia, Giovanni, *Außführliche Reiß-Beschreibung/ Von Wien nach Constantinopel/ Und wieder zurück in Teutschland*, etc., Frankfurt, Wagnern, 1687. A vivid description of the Ottoman scene.

Cantemir, Demetrius (Dumitru), *The History of the Growth and Decay of the Othman Empire*, translated from the Latin MS by N. Tindal, London, 1733–1734. Cantemir (1673–1723), the Turks' satellite Prince of Moldavia, should be used with circumspection.

Dalérac, F. P., *Polish Manuscripts: or the Secret History of the reign of John Sobieski, The III. of that Name, K. of Poland . . .* , London, Rhodes et alia, 1700. The author makes himself sound more important than he probably was, but he provides a host of sometimes illuminating, sometimes misleading details.

Dupont, Philippe, *Mémoires pour servir à l'histoire de la vie et des actions de Jean Sobieski III. du Nom Roi de Pologne,* published after the MS by J. Janicki, Warsaw, 1885. Recollections, long after the events, of a close associate of Sobieski; in part a reply to personal attack by Dalérac.

Dyakowski, Nikolaj, *Dyaryusz Wiedenskiéj okazy r. 1683,* Kraków, Czecha, 1861. Not a diary despite the title; the sometimes mendacious reminiscences of a young ensign at least thirty-five years later; plausible in places.

G. V. Ghelen, *Kurtze. . . . Erzelung Der. . . . Belagerung. . . . Wie auch. . . . Entsetzung Römisch -Keyserlicher Residentz-Stadt WIENN,* Vienna, 1684 (?). Written, printed, and published by a well-educated, socially prominent, Flemish-born nobleman; contains otherwise unrecorded facts.

Glaubwürdiges Diarium und Beschreibung dessen, was Zeit wehrender türckischer Belägerung der Kayserl. Haupt- und Residentz-Stadt Wien vorgangen, etc. (anonymous but "von einem Kayserl. Officirer, so sich von Anfang bis zu End darinnen befunden"), Vienna, n.p., 1683. A first-rate source, the unknown authorship notwithstanding; obviously put together as events occurred.

Hocke, Nicolaus, *Kurtze Beschreibung Dessen, Was in wehrender Türckischer Belägerung der Kayserlichen Residentz Statt Wienn Vom 7. Julij biss 12. Septembris dess abgewichenen 1683. Jahres / sowohl in Politibus & Civilibus, als Militaribus passiret,* Vienna, Voigt, 1685. Somewhat caustic account of a high Viennese civil servant. Fundamental.

Kluczycki, Franciszek, *Akta do dziejów krola Jana III^{go} sprawy roku 1683°, a osobliwie wyprawy wiedeńskiej wyjaśniającę,* Kraków, Akademii Umiejętnosci Krakowskiej. 1883. Judicious, compendious selection of archival materials; a *sine qua non.*

Kochowski, Wespazyan, *A.M.D.G. Commentarivs belli Aduersùm Turcas ad Viennam & in Hungaria,* Kraków, Gorecki, 1684. Work of a royal PR writer but not without verisimilitude.

Kreutel, Richard, *Kara Mustafa vor Wien: das Türkische Tagebuch der Belagerung Wiens verfaßt vom Zeremonienmeister der Hohen Pforte,* Graz, Vienna, Cologne, Verlag Styria, 1955. See Chapter Five, footnote 88.

Kunitz, Georg Christof, *Diarium, Welches Der am Türckischen Hoff und hernach beym Vezier in der Wienerischen Belagerung gewester Kayserl. Resident Herr Baron Kunitz eigenhändig beschrieben,* etc., Vienna, n.p., 1684. Brief but informed report from inside Turkish camp.

Laskowski, Otton, "Relacja wyprawy wiedeńskiej," *Przegląd Historyczno-Wojskowy,* Vol. II (1930), pp. 156–170. An anti-Sobieski polemic with a few details of interest; probably stems from the Crown Referendary Krasiński.

Marczali, Henri, "Il Conte di Frosaco, Francesco Provana: Relation du siège de Vienne," *Revue de Hongrie,* Vol. III (1909). Comprehensive description, in the form of two long letters to a friend, by a front-line officer; fresh and convincing. See also Chapter Seven, footnote 77.

Menčik, Ferdinand, "Ein Tagebuch während der Belagerung von Wien im Jahre 1683," *AöG,* Vol. 86 (1899), pp. 205–252. A somewhat sketchy glimpse of events from inside Leopold's court by an Imperial functionary, Count Ferdinand Bonaventura Harrach.

Rauchbar, Johann Georg von, *Leben und Thaten des Fürsten Georg Friedrich von Waldeck,* 2 vol's, Arolsen, Speyer, A. Halm, 1882. For all practical purposes Waldeck's own memoirs.

Ruess, Johann, *Wahrhaffte und gründliche Relation Über Die den 14. Julii Anno 1683 angefangene / den 12. Septembris aber glücklich auffgehobene Belägerung der Kays. Haupt- und Residentz-Stadt WIEN,* Vienna, Ghelen, 1683. Partly plagiarized (from

Glaubwürdiges Diarium) but still important first-hand testimony of a minor municipal official.

Rycault, Sir Paul, *The History of the Turks Beginning with the Year 1679* . . . *Until
the End of the Year 1698 and 1699*, London, Clavell and Roper, 1700. A balanced depiction of the Turkish scene by a resident English diplomat.

Sauer, Augustin, *Rom und Wien im Jahre 1683*, Vienna, K.K. Hof- und Staatsdruckerei,
1883. Supplements Kluczycki.

Stöller, Ferdinand, "Neue Quellen zur Geschichte des Türkenjahres 1683," MIöG,
Ergänzungs-Band XII, Heft I (1933) . See Chapter Seven, footnotes 28 and 77.

Vaelckeren, Johann Peter von, *WIENN von Türcken belägert / von Christen entsetzt*,
Linz, Rädlmeyer, 1684. Author was the official court "Historiographer;" best single
source. A contemporary English edition is expurgated.

Watzl, Hermann, *Flucht und Zuflucht: Tagebuch des Priesters Balthasar Kleinschrott*,
Graz-Cologne, Böhlaus, 1956. Lively memoir of a humble secular cleric; tells of the
ravishment of Lower Austria.

SECONDARY WORKS

Camesina Albert, *Wiens Bedrängnis im Jahre 1683; Wien und seine Bewohner während
der 2. Türkenbelagerung 1683*, Wien, Alterthumsverein, 1865. The pioneering
scholarly work; still of some use; invaluable illustrations.

Forst de Battaglia, Otto, *Jan Sobieski, König von Polen*, Einsiedeln-Zürich, Benziger,
1946. See Chapter Two, footnote 12.

Klopp, Onno, *Das Jahr 1683 und der folgende grosse Türkenkrieg bis zum von Carlowitz
1699*, Graz, Verlag Styria, 1882. Excellent for the international scene; anti-Prussian
coloration.

Koehler, Kurt, *Die orientalische Politik Ludwig's XIV; ihr Verhältnis zum Türkenkrieg
von 1683*, Leipzig, privately printed, 1907. Indispensable for background of diplomatic
maneuvering in Turkey.

*Das Kriegsjahr 1683: nach Akten und anderen authentischen Quellen dargestellt in der
Abteilung für Kriegsgeschichte des K.K. Kriegs-Archives*, Vienna, k.k. Generalstab,
1883. Despite slipshod footnoting, a handy guide.

Mansberg, Karl Wilhelm Frh. von, *Der Entsatz von Wien am 12. September 1683*, Berlin,
Rathenow, 1883. A superb technical study by a Prussian staff officer.

Newald, Johann, *Beiträge zur Geschichte der Belagerung von Wien durch die Türken
im Jahre 1683*, 2 Vol's, Vienna, Kubasta and Voigt, 1883–84. An archivalist's critique
and correcture of bicentennial publications; essential.

Renner, Victor von, *Wien im Jahre 1683*, Vienna, Waldheim, 1683. Official commemorative work of the Viennese City Council; a mine of detail; lacks footnotes but based on
documents and generally reliable.

Wentzcke, Paul, *Feldherr des Kaisers: Leben und Taten Herzog Karls V. von Lothringen*,
Leipzig, Koehler & Amelang, 1943. Pan-German flavor but scholarly.

Notes

N.B. The first citation in *each* chapter indicates the exact location of the original
footnote containing full bibliographical data.

Preface

1. The most extreme claims are made in J. B. Morton's elegant biography, *Sobieski,
King of Poland 1629–1689* (London, 1932) : "He saved Europe outside the walls of
Vienna, and blasted the last Turkish dream of planting the crescent on St. Peter's at
Rome, and making the Christian princes dependents of the Porte" (p. 2) ; and "Thus
was Vienna relieved, and all our inheritance saved by the sword of the Polish king" (p.

200). Yet even some first-rate historians have made the same error or have come close to doing so. E.g., G. N. Clark in *The Seventeenth Century,* London, 1945, pp. 178–179; and R. R. Palmer in his superb textbook *A History of the Modern World,* New York, 1965, pp. 189–190.

2. Richard F. Kreutel's *Kara Mustafa vor Wien:* and Hermann Watzl's *Flucht und Zuflucht* (see Bibliography).

3. See Bibliography.

Chapter One

1. Josef Kraft, "Ein Bericht über die Türken bei Perchtoldsdorf im Jahre 1683," *Heimatjahrbuch 1938 der Pfarre Mauer bei Wien,* Mauer bei Wien, 1938, p. 92. Practically the whole of the Wienerwald was reserved for the imperial nimrod. For the peasants, however, hunting represented a great material burden: they could not kill marauding game and had to suffer the damage caused by riding parties. Ann Maria Leitich, *Vienna Gloriosa,* new edition, Vienna, 1963, p. 124.

2. It is not possible to determine exactly which route the Emperor took through the Inner City; he may also have followed the road around it, outside the moat (Ringstrasse of today). The sources are contradictory.

3. Ferdinand Menčík, "Ein Tagebuch während der Belagerung von Wien im Jahre 1683," *AöG,* Vol. 86, pp. 211–213; Christian Wilhelm Huhn, *Nichts Neues und Nichts Altes,* Vienna, 1717, pp. 13–14; Franciscus Wagner, *Historia Leopoldi Magni Caesaris Augusti,* Vol. I, Augsburg, 1719, p. 588; Victor von Renner, *Wien im Jahre 1683,* Vienna, 1883, pp. 225–226; Johann Newald, *Beiträge zur Geschichte der Belagerung von Wien durch die Türken im Jahre 1683,* Vol. II, Vienna, 1884, pp. 22–23.

4. Eucharius Gottlieb Rinck, *Leopold des Grossen Röm. Käysers wunderwürdiges Leben und Thaten,* Leipzig, 1708, p. 41. Rinck, Protestant but Imperialist, wrote more objectively than Wagner, the officially subsidized Jesuit apologist.

5. Rinck, p. 143.

6. *Ibid.,* p. 167; Anonymous, *The Life of Leopold late Emperor of Germany,* London, 1706, p. 384; this book was translated into German by D. Johann Burchard Mencke with only slight corrections in name spelling and the addition of unessential facts; often it is incorrectly regarded as Mencke's own work; (for an evaluation of these sources, see Nana Eisenberg, "Studien zur Historiographie über Kaiser Leopold I.," *MIöG,* Vol. 51 (1937), pp. 359–413); the Venetian Ambassador Morosini (1674) *FRA,* 27, "Relationen der Botschafter Venedigs," p. 144; the French envoy Sèbeville, as quoted in Gaetan Guillot, "Leopold I et sa Cour," *Revue des questions historiques,* Vol. 81, pp. 416–417.

7. *Ibid.,* p. 416.

8. Anonymous, p. 387; Rinck, p. 315; Venetian Ambassador Molin (1661), *FRA,* p. 48.

9. Anonymous, p. 387.

10. Esaias Pufendorf (Swedish minister to Vienna), *Bericht über Kaiser Leopold, seinen Hof und die österreichische Politik* 1671–1674, Leipzig, 1862, p. 59.

11. Rinck, pp. 96–126; *passim;* A. F. Pribram and M. L. von Pragenau, "Privatbriefe Kaisers Leopold I. an den Grafen F. E. Pötting 1662–1673," *FRA,* zweite Abteilung, Vol. LVI (1903), xvi–xxi; Leitich, pp. 77–105, *passim;* Hugo Hantsch, *Geschichte Österreichs,* new ed., Vol. II, Graz, 1962, pp. 132–133.

12. Guillot, p. 424.

13. Rinck, pp. 93–95; Molin, *FRA,* p. 48; Pribram and Pragenau, xxv–xxviii.

14. Venetian Ambassador Veniers (1692), *FRA,* p. 311.

15. Pufendorf, p. 58.

16. See footnotes 4 and 6.

17. Morosini, *FRA,* p. 144.

18. Venetian Ambassador Contarini (1685), *FRA,* p. 249.

19. Venetian Ambassador Corner (1690), *FRA,* p. 276.

20. Maria Heyret, *Pater Marcus von Aviano,* Munich, 1931, p. 372. This study, unfortunately the only full scale biography of Marco d'Aviano, is poorly organized and wordy. The author's credulity is matched only by her bigotry toward Protestants, whom she regularly labels "the heretics." Heyret performed a greater service later (1937) in

publishing the correspondence of the monk and the Emperor (Vol. II of this work).

21. Cf. Oswald Redlich, *Weltmacht des Barock: Österreich in der Zeit Kaiser Leopolds I.*, 4th ed., Vienna, 1961, pp. 49, 89.

22. Cf. Anna Coreth, *Pietas Austriaca: Ursprung und Entwicklung barocker Frömmigkeit in Österreich*, Vienna, 1959. Leopold supported the activities of the Flemish-born, Spanish Franciscan, Bishop Cristobal Rojas y Spinola, author and proponent of a plan for Church union (see Samuel J. T. Miller and John P. Spielman, Jr., *Cristobal Rojas y Spinola, Cameralist and Irenicist*, Vol. 52, Part 5 of the "Transactions" of the American Philosophical Society, Philadelphia, 1962). In the last analysis the Emperor's actions must speak for his convictions. His support of the Bishop seems to have been only lukewarm, while his Hungarian policies and expulsion of the Viennese Jews were decisive moves. He was also unwilling to permit the exercise of the Evangelical faith by persons in the capital who had begun to frequent the chapels of the foreign diplomatic representations.

23. Franz von Krones, *Geschichte von Osterreich*, Vol. III, Vienna, 1878, pp. 567–568, 571, 631.

24. Reinhold Lorenz, "Reisen des Kaisers Leopold I. und des Kurfürsten Max Emmanuel im Türkenjahr 1683," MIöG, Vol. 53 (1935), p. 297.

25. Guillot, "Leopold I, les Hongrois, les Turcs," *Revue d'histoire diplomatique*, Vol. 25, pp. 419, 429.

26. Anonymous, p. 386.

27. Onno Klopp, *Das Jahr 1683 und der folgende grosse Türkenkrieg bis zum Frieden von Carlowitz*, Graz, 1882, p. 29.

28. ". . . essercitate nell' arte della pace, i tumulti della guerra furno in lui necessità più ch' elettione . . . ," Veniers, FRA, p. 311; "No Prince that had so much a Disinclination to War was ever so much involved in it . . . ," Anonymous, p. 386.

29. The Archduchy, Bohemia, and Hungary were re-united with Inner Austria in 1619 and with Upper and Further Austria in 1665. Note that the Archduchy and Inner Austria jointly constituted Lower Austria in the larger sense. This concept, however, ceased to be meaningful after 1564. Redlich, p. 7.

30. Henry F. Schwarz, *The Imperial Privy Council in the Seventeenth Century*, Cambridge (Mass.), 1943, pp. 1–189, *passim*.

31. *Idem.*

32. John B. Wolf, *The Emergence of the Great Powers*, New York, 1951, p. 136; E. C. Helbing, *Österreichische Verfaßungs- und Verwaltungsgeschichte*, Vienna, 1956, pp. 231–239, 266–267. This is not to say that the Leopoldine age witnessed no progress at all in central control to the intermediate and local levels. Vienna did manage to inch its way forward unsystematically by installing its officials alongside those of the estates and the nobles as the opportunity might arise. Friedrich Walter, *Die theresianische Staatsreform von 1749*, Vienna, 1958, pp. 11–12.

33. The latter seventeenth-century aristocrats (apart from the Magyars) should not be regarded as convinced, intentionally obdurate, and aggressive opponents of central government. Their obstructionism local in scope, more likely stemmed from a traditionalist frame of mind and from a simple lack of imagination. Moreover, certain of them were the first to develop a group or class consciousness of a specifically Austrian state. Many individual, so-called "court nobles" (*Hofadel*) served the government (administration, army, Church) alongside legally-trained, bourgeois-descended officials (*Beamtentum*), accepting its goals and working industriously to increase its power. Lobkowitz (see below, p. 28) stands out as the prime example of this type. Cf. Joseph Redlich, *Das österreichische Staats- und Rechtsproblem*, Vol. I, Leipzig, 1920, pp. 22–25; O. Redlich, p. 25.

34. *Ibid.*, p. 17.

35. Walther Hubatsch, *Das Zeitalter des Absolutismus*, Braunschweig, 1962, p. 117; Robert Kann, *A Study in Austrian Intellectual History*, New York, 1960, pp. 27–34. The potential physical strength of the monarchy was of course recognized by the mercantilists and other sharp-sighted contemporaries (e.g., Hörnigk's famous *Österreich über Alles wenn es nur will* of 1684). Rinck's commentary (p. 191) bears repeating: "Es mangelt der österreichsichen Monarchie sonst gantz und gar nicht an der krafft und würde der Kayser auch an armeen, denen an bezahlung und unterhalt nichts abgehen

dörffte, der größte Monarch von Europa seyn, wenn die kammer in ordnung gienge."

36. Kann, pp. 34–39. The interpretive problems of the Austrian Baroque era are so complex as to preclude meaningful discussion within a brief context.

37. The Turks copied certain courtly habits of the Magyar nobility. Many developed a taste for the wine that was prohibited them by their religion, and there was even a little intermarriage. Otto Zarek, *Die Geschichte Ungarns*, Zürich, 1938, pp. 344–345.

38. Gyula Szekfü, *Der Staat Ungarn*, Stuttgart, 1918, pp. 73, 75; Zarek, pp. 307–308; C. A. Macartney, *Hungary: A Short History*, Chicago, 1962, pp. 69–70; Charles d'Eszlary, "L'Administration et la vie urbaine dans la Hongrie occupée par les Turcs au cours des XVIe et XVIIe siècles," *Ibla, Revue d'instituts des belles-lettres arabes*, XX (1957), pp. 351–368.

39. Lajos Fekete, *Türkische Schriften aus dem Archiv des Palatins Nikolaus* Esterházy, Budapest, 1932, xxiii–xlii.

40. William McNeill, *Europe's Steppe Frontier*, Chicago, 1964, pp. 20, 50–51; Emil Lengyel, *1000 Years of Hungary*, New York, 1958, pp. 70–72. The Habsburg side of the border was protected by a number of large, relatively modern fortresses: Győr (Raab), Komárno, Nové Zámky (Neuhäusel), Oradea (Nagy Varád, Großwardein), Karlovac (Karolyvaros, Karlstadt), and Radkersburg (after the loss of Kanizsa). In addition there were numerous small castles, belonging both to the crown and to individual magnates, not to mention many moated, palisaded blockhouses (*Palanken*), similar to the stockades of the American Wild West. This defense line was originally maintained by the taxes and the *robot* (corvée) of the surrounding estates and farms, called *Porten*. Upon the arrival of a Turkish raiding party, the latter were supposed to provide the "Portal Militia," organized by the comitat, in order to supplement the regular garrisons. If an aristocrat could muster fifty horsemen by himself, he was entitled to serve under his own flag (*Banderium*) in the so-called "Nobles' Insurrection." If he could not, he joined the comitat's contingent as an individual fighter. When the danger had passed, the soldiers returned to their forts, the nobles to their manors, and the peasants to the plow. By the beginning of the seventeenth century this system was beginning to break down. The cost of maintaining the regular garrisons proved to be too much for Hungary alone, and the greater part of the burden was ultimately taken over by the estates of the Habsburg hereditary lands. The Austro-Germans and Magyars unfortunately failed to recognize their interdependence. The Hungarian aristocrats increasingly neglected their fiscal and service obligations, and the peasants were largely forced to carry on alone. For a long period the Habsburgs kept the garrisons understrength. During the Thirty Years' War, namely, money and troops were required elsewhere. The remaining troops, naturally discontented and unruly, degenerated into a real plague for the surrounding countryside. Despite some effort toward improvement after the Treaty of Westphalia, the Hungarians could not basically reform the existing structure. Vienna thereupon concluded that it should continue to rely mainly on its own professional forces, whom the Magyars regarded as "foreigners" (*miles extraneus*). These soldiers, whose discipline was not of the best, were held to be tools of the Austrian government for depriving the estates of their "liberties" and for the imposition of an absolutist régime. The Protestants, of course, resented their presence even more strongly than the Catholics. H. Pirchegger, F. M. Mayer, R. F. Kaindl, *Geschichte und Kulturleben Österreichs*, 5th ed., Vienna, 1958, p. 189; O. Redlich, pp. 159–160. The Croatian-Slavonian frontier constitutes a special story, well-treated by Gunther E. Rothenberg (*The Austrian Military Border in Croatia*, Urbana, 1958).

41. Fekete, p. 41; Macartney, pp. 70–72. The case for the horror of the Turkish occupation is strong, but there were a few positive factors (apart from those noted in the text) of a psychological, literary, musical, horticultural, and culinary nature. For example, the Central European delicacy, *Palatschinken* (a kind of jam-filled pancake) is thought to be of Ottoman origin. Cf. Robert Gragger, "Türkischungarische Kulturbeziehungen" in *Literaturdenkmäler aus Ungarns Türkenzeit*, Berlin, 1927, pp. 1–32. The classic account, now a little outdated, of the Turkish period is Franz von Salomon's *Ungarn im Zeitalter der Türkenherrschaft*, Leipzig, 1887.

42. Denis Sinor, *History of Hungary*, New York, 1959, p. 161.

43. Ladislaus Freiherr Hengelmüller von Hengervar, *Franz Rákóczy und sein Kampf für Ungarns Freiheit,* Vol. I, Stuttgart and Berlin, 1913, pp. 4–5.

44. The estates were poorly equipped to defend their autonomy because of decentralization. While in the sixteenth century they still resorted to constitutional means of resistance, in the seventeenth they chose physical opposition (not illegal, for that matter). Hungarian parliamentarianism really functioned only within the comitat. Szekfü, pp. 81–92.

45. The Venetian Ambassador Molin (1661), quoted in Heinrich Kretschmayer, *Die Türken vor Wien: Stimmen und Berichte aus dem Jahre* 1683, Munich, 1938, p. 27.

46. *Cf.* Oscar Jászi, *The Dissolution of the Habsburg Monarchy,* new ed., Chicago, 1961, pp. 43–55.

47. An Hungarian-speaking ethnic group of disputed origin; largely peasants.

48. G. Müller, *Die Türkenherrschaft in Siebenbürgen,* Hermannstadt (Sibiu, Rumania), 1923, pp. 5–70, *passim.*

49. Hengelmüller, p. 18; McNeill, pp. 100–101; Georg Stadtmüller, *Geschichte Südosteuropas,* Munich, 1950, pp. 278–281.

50. "Partium regni Hungariae dominus" was a title conceded to John Sigismund Zápolya by Emperor Maximilian II in 1570. It referred to an area which at that time comprised only four comitats: Bihar, Kraszna, Central Szolnok, and Maramureş (Máramaros), all situated in the mostly mountainous terrain along the uppermost stretches of the Tissa (Tisza), Someşul (Szamos), and Crişul Repede (Sebes Körös) Rivers. "Partes adnexae" was a synonym. The phrase, of Mediaeval origin and initially applied to the whole region east of the central Tisza and Temes Rivers, also came to be used in a more general sense: i.e., simply to indicate lands outside the traditional borders of Transylvania. With the latter State's expansion into the northeastern Alföld and adjacent piedmont under Bocskay, Bethlen, and George Rákóczy I the term once more took on a rather broad territorial meaning: e.g., in 1645 when the Habsburgs were forced to renounce control temporarily over seven other comitats (Bereg, Ugocsa, Szatmár, Szabolcs, Zemplén, Abaujvár, and Borsód). In 1648 upon the accession of George Rákóczy II, five of these reverted to Vienna's control. The new Prince kept Szatmár, Szabolcs, the fortresses of Mukachevo (Munkács), Sáros Patak, and Tokaj, as well as Bihar, its eastern neighbor of Zarand, Kraszna, Central Szolnok, and Maramureş. In 1664 Bihar and Zarand (Oradea and Jenö region) went directly to the Porte and Szatmár and Szabolcs back to the Crown. The Seven Comitats, however, soon became the scene of the Kuroczok-Labanczok struggle and later fell under the control of Thököly, would-be "Lord of the Partium," who also strove to obtain the comitats of the neighboring, largely Slovak mountain country (the Tatra and Slovak Ore Mountains), from which he himself originated. (See footnote 90 and pp. 33–35). The Partium was most recently divided after the Second World War and now belongs, variously, to Czechoslovakia, the Ukrainian S.S.R., Rumania, and Hungary. Krones, Vol. III, pp. 281, 545, 596; Sinor, p. 164; Macartney, p. 78; and Redlich, p. 164.

Another expression for the lands in question that can lead to confusion is eastern "Upper Hungary." In its original sense "Upper Hungary" signified all territory to the north of the Danube whereas its counterpart, "Lower Hungary," was used for the region to the south. In the eighteenth century, however, Vienna saw fit to alter the geographical orientation of the two names from north-south to east-west. The former practice seems more appropriate, both historically and physiographically (Krones, Vol. I, pp. 473–474).

51. Ladislas Makkai, *Histoire de Transylvanie,* Paris, 1946, pp. 238–246.

52. *Ibid.,* p. 240; Sinor, p. 199; Zarek, pp. 335–336. (Sinor and Zarek are based on Hungarian sources and show an equivalent bias.) Like the fortress troops (see footnote 40), Montecuccoli's field army was irregularly paid and difficult to control. Krones, p. 487. Looting in a friendly country was apparently a still common phenomenon in the seventeenth century, above all in the East.

53. Hugo Hantsch, pp. 30–32; O. Redlich, pp. 171–172.

54. Max Immich, *Geschichte des europäischen Staatensystems,* Munich and Berlin, 1905, pp. 50–51; Adam Wolf, *Fürst Wenzel Lobkowitz,* Vienna, 1869, p. 122.

55. When the Hungarian Estates met in 1662, the Protestant party, concerned mainly

with religious complaints, counted upon Zrinyi's support. They also demanded, even more vehemently than the Catholics, the removal of the German garrisons (see footnote 40).

56. However, it should be noted that Zrinyi, too, was a creditable military thinker who put his ideas to paper. Salamon, pp. 363–366. For Zrinyi, see also Sinor, pp. 199–200; Zarek, pp. 336–337; and Krones, p. 591.

57. Hungarian historians sometimes hold that Montecuccoli deliberately permitted the Turks to seize Zrinyivár, as an act of personal vengeance against the Ban. The two men were enemies because of an anonymous pamphlet of Zrinyi which attacked Montecuccoli's published defense of the 1662 campaign and which ridiculed the Italian. See Eugen Csuday, *Geschichte der Ungarn*, Vol. 2, Steinamanger (Szombathely, Hungary), pp. 130–131, 136. However, the failure to relieve the rather primitive fortress was more likely due to strategic considerations.

58. A "Roman month" was a fixed sum granted the Emperor for military purposes. The term derives from the imperial expeditions to Italy in the Middle Ages.

59. The actual battlefield is located around the village of Mogersdorf (after 1920 in the Austrian province of Burgenland). The size of the allied force involved was so small because of previous losses (disease and fighting) and detachments made elsewhere.

60. For a detailed account of the battle and the preceding campaign see H. von Zwiedeneck-Südenhorst's Pan-German flavored *Deutsche Geschichte im Zeitalter der Gründung des preussischen Königtums*, Vol. I, pp. 243–253; Immich (p. 53) gives a bibliography. See also O. Redlich, p. 599; Georg Wagner, "Raimund Montecuccoli, die Schlacht and der Raab und der Friede von Eisenburg (Vasvár)," *Österreich in Geschichte und Literatur*, Vol. VIII, No. 5 (May, 1964), pp. 201–221—a diffuse but informative, source-based account; Rudolf Kiszling, "Die Schlacht bei Mogersdorf," pp. 222–225; Walter Hummelberger, "Der 1. August 1664 bei St. Gotthard," Truppendienst, 4 (1964), pp. 309–312; and Kurt Peball, *Die Schlacht bei St. Gotthard-Mogersdorf 1664* ("Militärhistorische Schriftenreihe," No. 1), Vienna, 1964.

61. Krones, p. 561. The Sultan, however, was obliged to send a gift in return and did so in a most munificent manner. Regarded from the Austrian standpoint, this exchange clearly represented an improvement over the previous situation (i.e., since Zsitva Török) in which the Emperor paid a kind of tribute. Now he and the Padishah were juristic equals. See Georg Wagner, "Der angebliche Türkentribut nach der Schlacht bei Mogersdorf 1664," MIöG, Vol. LXXII (1964), pp. 409–441. Wagner, whose inability to organize his material is apparently irremediable, also attempts, less successfully, to show that Reniger was a skilful diplomat. Leopoldov arose on the western bank of the Váh opposite the now Turkish palank of Hlohovec (Freistadl-Galgócz) which R. W. Seton-Watson (*History of the Czechs and Slovaks*, Hamden, Conn., 1965, p. 134) has confused with Nové Zámky (Neuhäusl).

62. O. Redlich, pp. 190–193; Hantsch, pp. 34–35; Krones, p. 599; Immich, pp. 52–53; Pribram and Pragenau, p. 225.

63. The marriage to Margareta Theresa took place December 12, 1666. The Empress died, however, in 1673. Leopold's second wife died in 1676. He married Eleanora the same year. Krones, p. 563.

64. See above, p. 11.

65. To the Hungarians, Leopold's act seemed illegal and unconstitutional. Cf. Csuday, p. 141.

66. There exists a rather naive study of Grémonville by Franz Scheichl (*Bretel von Grémonville*, Berlin, 1914). The volume at least has the advantage of providing a compilation of the printed references. See the critique by H. von Srbik in MIöG, Vol. 37 (1917), pp. 521–523; see also I. Hudiță, *Histoire des relations diplomatiques entre la France et la Transylvanie au XVIIème siècle*, Paris, 1927, pp. 202–237.

67. *Raggvaglio historico della gverra Trà l'Armi Cesaree, & Ottomane dal principe della ribellione degl' Vngari sino al fine del mese d' Ottobre dell' Anno 1683*, Venice, 1683, pp. 3–4. (Author unknown.)

68. Pribram and Pragenau, pp. 157–158. Leopold regretted Tattenbach's death sentence but felt he could not have one brand of justice for Hungarians and another

for Germans (*ibid.*, pp. 202–203). Nádasty's participation was something of a blow for the Emperor because he held the magnate in personal esteem. The sovereign wrote in a letter to Lobkowitz: "Pauper Nádasty requiescat in pace; habe schon 2 Messen vor ihn gehört" (Max Dvořák, "Briefe Kaisers Leopold des I. an Wenzel Euseb Herzog in Schlesien zu Sagan, Fürsten von Lobkowitz," AöG, Vol. 80 [1894], p. 494). Hungarian authors are wont to complain of the illegality of the trials which took place in the Archduchy, not in the Kingdom. However, Leopold did have some legal foundation for his procedure. The accused were also Imperial nobles; Nádasty held property in Lower Austria, while Zrinyi and Frankopan were soldiers. Still, the main reason probably was that a trial in Hungary would have necessitated the convoking of the estates and most likely would have resulted in an acquittal, Hengelmüller, p. 36.

69. The most recent and exhaustive study of the conspiracy is E. Lilek, *Kritische Darstellung der Ungarisch-Kroatischen Verschwörung*, 4 volumes, Celje, 1928–1930. See also Reinhold Lorenz, *Das Türkenjahr 1683*, 3rd ed., Vienna, 1944, pp. 104–121; Krones, pp. 600–616; O. Redlich, pp. 196–212; and Georg Wagner, "Der Wiener Hof, Ludwig XIV, und die Anfänge der Magnatenverschwörung," *Mitteilungen des österreichischen Staatsarchivs*, Vol 16 (1963), pp. 87–150. Wagner dates the beginning of the conspiracy from the fall of 1663 (*ibid.*, pp. 94–95).

70. Zwiedeneck-Südenhorst, p. 474. It is impossible, within the scope of this book, to examine the difficult question of absolutism. Suffice it to say that I use the term in the sense of its readily demonstrable practical manifestations: i.e., the drive to establish state power on a rational, centralized basis. While monarchical aspirations were probably a progressive force in European history, it does not follow by any means that the estates were a negative factor. *Cf.* Fritz Wagner, *Europa im Zeitalter des Absolutismus*, Munich, 1959, p. 3.

71. Zwiedeneck-Südenhorst, 475. See Wolf, pp. 230–234, for a discussion of the corruption in the financial administration.

72. Sinor, p. 203. While it is true that in later days *Schlamperei* was believed to temper despotism, it should be remembered that absolutism was an innovation for seventeenth-century Hungary.

73. Zwiedeneck-Südenhorst, p. 375; F. M. Mayer, H. Pirchegger, *Geschichte Österreichs mit besonderer Rücksicht auf das Kulturleben*, Vol. II, 3rd ed., 1909, p. 207.

74. "Ich will aber mich der Occasion bedienen und in Hungern die Sachen anderst einrichten." Pribram and Pragenau, p. 84. To what extent Lobkowitz, rather than Hocher, was the driving force of the new absolutism is hard to say. This question and that of Leopold's precise viewpoints certainly deserve a thorough monographic investigation. Such a study would contribute much to a knowledge of European absolutism in general. Hans Sturmberger's *Ferdinand II und das Problem des Absolutismus* (Vienna, 1957) has already provided an analysis of this kind for the preceding era. The book shows that while Counter Reformatory Catholicism (Jesuitism) was a powerful impulse, other elements (divine right concepts of Mediaeval origin, contemporary political theory based on Roman law, "Machiavellian" *raison d'état*) also influenced imperial actions.

75. Wolf, pp. 340–343. The documents pertaining to the pacification of Bohemia in Ferdinand II's time were fetched from the archives and studied for precedents. *Ibid.*, p. 343.

76. Pufendorf, p. 76.

77. Redlich, p. 220; Mayer-Pirchegger, p. 208; Krones, p. 618. Szekfü (pp. 94–95) holds that Western Hungary's Catholicism was a fact of great consequence, leading to a deep rift in the emotions of Hungarians. The split between the anti-Habsburg Protestants of the East and the pro-royal Westerners seemed irreparable. The latter were in a sense caught between the hammer and the anvil. Convinced they could gain autonomy without resorting to the legal right of resistance, hoping for an understanding with Vienna, they were scorned by the Easterners and distrusted by the government. They were the real "Greater Hungarians," desiring reunification under the constitutional ruler. They also bore the major burden of holding off the Turks. It may also be that the towns of Western Hungary, like Upper Hungary contained important Protestant and German elements, which became alienated from the monarchy as a result of

the persecutions. Hans Tschanny's *Ungarische Chronik,* a contemporary account published in Pest in 1852, reflects such a viewpoint.

78. Redlich, p. 219.

79. It would, nevertheless, be erroneous to assume that the Protestants were completely blameless. The Protestant Rinck writes: "Endlich aber haben die evangelischen Ungarn, absonderlich dero geistliche, mit ihren hitzigen verfahren nicht wenig zu ihrem unglück contribuiret. Es ist diese nation ihrer natürlichen hitze öffters ergeben, es mag solche nun der catholischen oder evangelischen religion zugethan seyn." (p. 178).

80. Twenty-six were ultimately turned over to the Dutch admiral, Michael de Ruyter. See Anonymous, *Sufferings of the Protestant Ministers,* London, 1676, pp. 1–8. For the field operations of the Jesuits, see Franz von Krones, "Zur Geschichte Ungarns (1671–1683) mit besonderer Rücksicht auf die Thätigkeit und die Geschicke des Jesuitenordens," in AöG, Vol. 80 (1894), pp. 353–457. It is again noteworthy that many of the Jesuits were themselves Magyars.

81. Pufendorf, pp. 50–51.

82. Hengelmüller, p. 40; Renner, p. 14; Zwiedeneck-Südenhorst, p. 476; Krones, p. 619.

83. In Western Hungary, however, the religious persecutions continued. Tschanny (p. 26) tells of further restrictions upon the Protestants of Sopron (Ödenburg) in 1678. Bishop Kollonitsch took a personal hand in prohibiting divine services and ousting the Evangelical city government.

84. Sinor, p. 203; Krones, *Geschichte,* p. 623; Csuday, p. 162; Redlich, pp. 225–227. The cruelty shown by the opposing sides was unique, so it would seem, only in its increased frequency of occurrence over "peacetime." The anonymously-written work, *Ungarischer oder Dacianischer Simplicissimus* (originally published in 1683, reissued by Johann Seitz in Leipzig in 1864), which is apparently a first-hand account of conditions in the region during the 1650's, contains a detailed description of the kind of civil justice meted out in the city of Košice (Kaschau, Cassovia). Criminals were dispatched not only by flaying and impalement but also by the rack and by interment. It may be noted, parenthetically, that the successful performance of an impalement (i.e., keeping the victim conscious as long as possible) required a considerable degree of expertise (see the stylistically brilliant depiction of Ivo Andrić in *The Bridge on the River Drina,* New York, 1959, pp. 46–52). Another technique of execution was to slash a man's skin into ribbons, bind him in a freshly-drawn horse hide and leave him to cure in the summer sun. Decapitation was reserved for women and gentle persons. Lesser crimes were also punished drastically: the Košice city fathers forced a burgher who had offended their official dignity to eat human faeces. The psychological implications of such barbarous chastisements (formerly practiced in all parts of Europe) surely merit investigation.

85. Hudită, *passim* but especially p. 277ff.

86. Csuday, pp. 163–165.

87. Hudită, p. 325.

88. Niclos Bethlen, "Mémoires," Vol. VI of *Histoire des Troubles d'Hongrie,* Paris, 1680, pp. 266–267.

89. Hudită, p. 371.

90. Spiš was a German ethnic island in what is now Slovakia (former Hungarian comitat Sáros); it was situated in a valley just southeast of the High Tatry, leading out into the Great Alföld.

91. Hengelmüller, pp. 42–43, footnote 3; Krones, pp. 626–627.

92. To some Magyars Thököly is a patriot, however misguided, merely because he fought the Habsburgs. For this attitude see Ignaz Acsády, *Der Entsatz Wiens von der Türkenbelagerung im Jahre 1683 und die Befreiung Ungarns vom Turkenjoche bis zum Frieden von Karlowitz,* Budapest, 1909, p. 36. Csuday (p. 170) is more critical.

93. *Raggvaglio,* pp. 1–2.

94. Klopp, p. 80.

95. "Il lui donna la meilleure éducation qu'il pût, dans les lieux où les habiles gens sont rares, & où toute l'occupation de la noblesse consiste à aller à la chasse & à faire

bonne chère. Ce que lui a pû être de plus grand usage, c'est la coûtume d'aller à cheval, que l'on prend parmi les gens de qualité, depuis l'enfance." Anonymous ("Le Clerc"), *Histoire de Emeric de Tekeli ou mémoires pour servir à sa vie*, Cologne, 1693, pp. 7–8. (The volume's tone is sympathetic to Thököly). Redlich (p. 229), basing himself upon Dávid Angyal (*Késmárki Thököly Imre 1657–1705*, Budapest, 1888), states, on the contrary that the Kuroczok leader was trained by good teachers and well-read. He was also an accomplished linguist, speaking fluent Magyar, Latin, German, and Turkish (Johann Mailath, *Geschichte der Magyaren*, Vol. III, Regensburg, 1853, p. 333). Undoubtedly, Calvinist schoolmasters and divines maintained a certain level of literacy among the leaders, at least, of their flocks. However, the circumstances of Thököly's youthful life were chaotic. His education was probably of a very basic order. Yet as a result of his skill as a writer and orator, he may have appeared more learned than he was. Even the linguistic attainments are not so singular in an area as ethnically complex as Eastern Europe's "shatter belt." Certainly, he had no time for the broadening, cosmopolitan, grand-tour type of training that the young Sobieski enjoyed.

96. Stephen Thököly's great wealth—confiscated by the Imperial government until Imre was able to return to the area with his own army—placed his son in the magnate category. A study of the complicated religious and sociological aspects of the rebellion would be extremely useful. See p. 32 and footnote 84.

Chapter Two

1. Roland Mousnier, *Les XVIᵉ et XVIIᵉ siècles*, Vol. IV of "Histoire générale des civilisations," Paris, 1961, p. 127. The Polish army is discussed in Chapter V, pp. 182–187.

2. *Ibid.*, p. 128; J. Rutkowski, "The Social and Economic Structure in the Fifteenth and Sixteenth Centuries," CHP, p. 447.

3. Mousnier, p. 128.

4. A. Brückner, "Polish Cultural Life in the Seventeenth Century," CHP, pp. 557–569, *passim;* W. Tatarkiewicz, "Polish Art in the Seventeenth Century," CHP, pp. 570–578.

5. Oskar Halecki, *A History of Poland*, London, 1961, p. 153; William H. McNeill, *Europe's Steppe Frontier: 1500–1800*, Chicago, 1964, p. 116.

6. *Ibid.*, pp. 121–123.

7. Cf. Chapter XIII of the CHP.

8. E. Hanisch, *Geschichte Polens*, Bonn-Leipzig, 1923, p. 232.

9. Otton Laskowski, *Sobieski, King of Poland*, Glasgow, 1944, pp. 63–74.

10. *Ibid.*, pp. 75–88.

11. Although the title as quoted dates from a document of 1679, Kiev, Smolensk, and Chernigov were no longer in Polish hands. By the Treaty of Andrusovo, Russia had acquired the right of occupation. The Poles were compelled by circumstances to consent regularly to the renewal of the arrangement. See also pp. 54–55.

12. Otto Forst de Battaglia, *Jan Sobieski: König von Polen*, Einsiedeln-Zürich, 1946, pp. 9–91, *passim*. It is fortunate that a scholar of the caliber of Forst de Battaglia (of Polish descent, despite his name and Austrian nationality) has written a biography in a Western European language, thus making available the results of almost all non-Communist Polish research on the topic. Forst de Battaglia is, *mirabile dictu*, simultaneously sympathetic and objective toward his subject. He has also contributed a chapter to the CHP (no. XXIV, pp. 532–556), which summarizes many of the points of his gracefully written book. It would be desirable for the latter to appear in English, equipped with the scholarly apparatus promised for a later date in the German edition. Laskowski is not quite so valuable because of a certain adulatory tendency but is still worthwhile because of detailed military accounts and occasionally penetrating political insight.

13. Description of the "Abbé F.D.S." reprinted in Morton, (see Preface, footnote 1), p. 277.

14. N. A. de Salvandy, *Lettres du Roi de Pologne Jean Sobiesky à la Reine Marie Casimire Pendant la Campagne de Vienne*, etc., Paris, 1826, p. 49. (Cf. *Akta*, p. 363, for Polish original).

15. Forst de Battaglia, CHP, p. 539.

16. The idea, however, does not originate from the present century. Cf. Jan Chelmecki, *König Johann Sobieski und die Befreiung Wiens*, Vienna, 1883, p. 8. Morton has done much to foist the fable upon the English-language reading public.

17. Halecki, p. 171. Halecki's views (which do not ignore the Christian motivation in Sobieski) are presented at somewhat greater length in "Polens Anteil am Entsatz Wiens," in the *Marco d'Aviano Festschrift*, Vienna, 1933, pp. 22–41.

18. Salvandy, p. 177. (Cf. *Akta*, p. 511).

19. Morton, p. 277.

20. Philippe Dupont, *Mémoires*, etc., Warsaw, 1885, p. 234.

21. Salvandy, pp. 29–33. (Cf. *Akta*, p. 343).

22. *Ibid.*, pp. 8–9.

23. *Ibid.*, pp. 81–82.

24. F. P. Dalérac, *Polish Manuscripts*, etc., London, 1700, p. 47.

25. S. Rubinstein, *Les Relations entre la France et la Pologne*, Paris, 1913, p. 5.

26. Forst de Battaglia, CHP, pp. 555–556.

27. *Ibid.*, p. 537.

28. Forst de Battaglia, *Jan Sobieski*, p. 73.

29. *Ibid.*, p. 55; Laskowski, pp. 88–89.

30. Forst de Battaglia, CHP, p. 536; *Jan Sobieski*, p. 65.

31. Laskowski, pp. 93–94.

32. This attitude is best exemplified by Count Jean Hamel du Breuil in "Sobieski et sa politique de 1674 à 1683," *Revue d'histoire diplomatique*, VIII (1893), pp. 481–527; and VIII (1894), pp. 56–74. A fascinating example of a completely erroneous interpretation of historical documents.

33. The remainder of the account, unless otherwise noted, follows Forst de Battaglia, *Jan Sobieski*, pp. 69–125.

34. It is not entirely clear why Louis remained as stubborn in this matter as he did. Cf. Kurt Koehler, *Die orientalische Politik Ludwig's XIV.; ihr Verhältnis zum Türkenkrieg von 1683*, Leipzig, 1907, p. 45.

35. Zhuravno is today a town of 3500 to the southwest of Lvov. Sobieski checked a vastly superior Turkish army there for twenty-three days before the signing of the armistice.

36. The rebels had actually toasted him as king at a banquet and had sworn fealty. Louis XIV was quite cool toward the whole project. Cf. Hamel's account (p. 509), a summary of the relevant document in the French archives.

37. A Silesian dukedom for her father was part of the bait.

38. It should be recalled that Sobieski had defeated both Lorraine and the Palsgrave in 1674.

39. See below, p. 103.

40. Why he did is not entirely certain. Perhaps one reason was that he was loathe to support a nobles' *Fronde* against a crowned and consecrated colleague, whether an elected monarch or not.

41. Even at this early date Sobieski was endeavoring to get backing for a crusade, as, e.g., his relations with distant Portugal show. Cf. Luis Ferrand de Almeida, *As Cortes de 1679–1680 e o Auxilio a Polonia para a Guerra Contra os Turcos*, Coimbra, 1951.

42. Hans Übersberger, *Rußlands Orientpolitik*, Vol. I, Stuttgart, 1913, pp. 1–24, *passim*. For the problems of the Ukrainian revolt, see C. Bickford O'Brien, *Muscovy and the Ukraine from the Pereislavl Agreement to the Truce of Andrusova*, Berkely, 1963.

43. *Ibid.*, p. 30; Anatole G. Mazour, *Russia: Tsarist and Communist*, Princeton, 1962, pp. 86–87; McNeill, pp. 144–146.

44. Walter L. Wright, *Ottoman Statecraft: the Book of Counsel for Vezirs and Governors of Sari Mehmed Pasha, the Defterdār*, Princeton, 1935, pp. 22–25.

45. *Ibid.*, pp. 26–28.

46. *Ibid.*, pp. 30–38.

47. See below, pp. 187–197.

48. The Phanariotes, who were descended from important Byzantine mercantile

families and whose name derives from the Istanbul quarter which they inhabited, were also drawn to coöperation with the Turks because of their antipathy to the Roman Catholic Church which, as one manifestation of the Counter Reformation, had become increasingly active upon traditionally Orthodox preserves. Rudolf Tschudi, "Die osmanische Geschichte bis zum Ausgang des siebzenten Jahrhunderts," Vol. II of the *Neue Propyläen-Weltgeschichte*, Berlin, 1941, p. 595. These Greeks held important administrative posts, both in Istanbul and in the satellite states of Moldavia and Wallachia. They were extremely useful to the Turks because of their commercially-acquired linguistic and managerial skills. They also monopolized the high offices of the Church. Leften S. Stavrianos, *The Balkans Since 1453*, New York, 1959, pp. 270–272. The most prominent Phanariote of the latter seventeenth century was Kara Mustafa's Grand Dragoman (translator and secretary), Alexandros Mavrokordatos.

49. Wright, pp. 59–60.

50. E.g., the Defterdâr whose reformist work Wright has translated; and Kutshi Bey, a confidant of Murad IV, who wrote a memoir (1630) analyzing the reasons for the Empire's decline (Tschudi, p. 597).

51. Stanford J. Shaw, "The Ottoman View of the Balkans," *The Balkans in Transition* (ed. by Charles and Barbara Jelavich), Berkely, 1963, pp. 57–80.

52. Cf. Stavrianos, pp. 124–134; the relevant literature is cited here.

53. See Chapter One, footnotes 40 and 41.

54. P. Rycault, *The History of the Turks Beginning With the Year 1679 . . . Until the End of the Year 1698 and 1699*, London, 1700, preface: McNeill, *op. cit.*, p. 42. McNeill holds that the limits to expansion imposed by geography favored the development of hereditary land-owning since there were no new countries for the warriors to conquer. Thus the vigor of the military class declined, and the Sultan's own power was simultaneously compromised. Formerly the Ottomans had exploited marginal areas; now they began to milk the interior of their domains. *Ibid.*, pp. 26–65.

55. *Ibid.*, pp. 132–139.

56. Fekete, xxii–xxiii.

57. Nicholas Jorga, *Geschichte des osmanischen Reiches*, Vol. IV, Gotha, 1911, pp. 75–76.

58. Tschudi, p. 595.

59. Moldavia and Wallachia played a relatively insignificant, peripheral rôle in the events of 1683. However, the two vassal principalities benefitted politically, for a short time at least, from the Turkish defeats of the latter seventeenth century. Prince Stefan Petriceicu went over to Sobieski after Khotin and talked about a rebellion of the enslaved Balkan peoples and a joint campaign of the Christian powers. Utopian as such a scheme was for that day and age, the plan continued to crop up and influenced Sobieski in his unfruitful, post-1683 military operations. It is also noteworthy that the Transylvanian Rumanians resisted Abafi's pro-Magyar-rebel policies and coöperated with the pro-Austrian, Catholic faction. (Abafi was a Calvinist himself.) They were supported by Prince Serban Cantacuzeno of Wallachia. The Prince, although Phanariote-descended (see footnote 48) was Rumanianized and became the leader of his country's national opposition to the pro-Turkish Greek upper class. Although forced to provide the Turks *corvée* at Vienna in 1683, he sympathized with the besieged and even managed to aid them a little. In later years, basing himself upon Poland, Austria, and Russia in turn, he was temporarily able to maintain a degree of independence from the Porte. However, after Peter the Great renounced his Ukrainian ambition, the Rumanians were again firmly yoked to the Turkish cart. Istanbul placed the thoroughly reliable Mavrokordatos family in charge (1716). O. Brunner, "Österreich und die Walachei während des Türkenkrieges 1683–99," in MIöG, Vol. 44 (1931), pp. 265–272. For a more complete analysis of the geopolitical and socio-economic factors in sixteenth- and seventeenth-century Moldavia and Wallachia, see McNeill, pp. 48–49, 88, 103–111, 125–141. The two territories are of considerable importance to the author's thesis that Eastern European history in the Early Modern era constitutes a process of division of agricultural lands, previously organized as interstitial political entities, between the three great bureaucratic empires, Turkey, Russia, and Austria.

60. See above, p. 23.

61. Leopold von Ranke, *Die Osmanen und die spanische Monarchie im XVII. und XVIII. Jahrhundert*, Leipzig, 1887, p. 74.

62. M. Brosch, *Aus dem Leben dreier Großvesire*, Gotha, 1899, p. 142.

63. Giovanni Benaglia, *Außführliche Reiß-Beschreibung*, etc., Frankfurt, 1687, p. 66. The author was the secretary of the special Austrian peace mission to the Porte in 1682–83.

64. Brosch, pp. 143–144.

65. P. Alderson, *The Structure of the Ottoman Dynasty*, Oxford, 1956, pp. 55–56.

66. Joseph Freiherr von Hammer-Purgstall, *Geschichte des osmanischen Reiches*, Vol. III, Pest, 1835, p. 594.

67. Brosch, p. 137.

68. Jorgas, p. 135.

69. *Ibid.*, pp. 136–137.

70. Brosch, p. 147.

71. Jorgas, p. 167.

72. See above, p. 25.

73. Dorothy Vaughan, *Europe and the Turk: A Pattern of Alliances 1350–1700*, Liverpool, 1954, pp. 252–254.

74. *Ibid.*, p. 265.

75. Ambassador Nointel demanded the "right of the stool," which was customarily set up for diplomats at interviews with the Grand Vezir, placed on the *same* level as the latter's pillows and not at the foot of the steps leading up the dais (i.e., the "sofa"). The ambassador was actually knocked down physically from the sofa. He thereupon withdrew, taking his presents with him, and was later placed under house arrest. Von Hammer, p. 695.

76. Koehler, pp. 61–64.

77. *Idem.*

78. Klopp (footnote 27, Chapter One), pp. 58–59.

79. Koehler, pp. 64–71.

80. Nicolò Barozzi and Gugliemo Berchet, *Le relazioni degli stati europei: lettre al Senato dagli ambasciatori veneziani nel secolo decimosettimo*, "Turchia," Ser. V, Venice, 1871, p. 308.

81. Von Hammer, p. 692.

82. Barozzi and Berchet, p. 309.

83. His seraglio included 1500 *odalisques*, the same number of slave girls, and 600–700 black eunuchs. Franz Babinger, *Encyclopedia of Islam*, Leyden, 1927, p. 755.

84. Barozzi and Berchet, p. 260.

85. Von Hammer, p. 670.

86. Barozzi and Berchet, p. 260.

87. Copy of a document sent by Civrano to Vienna, AGS, 3923.

88. Barozzi and Berchet, *idem.*

89. Dalérac, p. 59; Dupont, p. 122. The assertion about capitulation, for which there is no confirmation in Turkish sources, is highly dubious. *Cf.* Chapter Eight, footnote 78.

90. Demetrius (Dumitru) Cantemir, *The History of the Growth and Decay of the Othman Empire*, London, 1734–1735, pp. 304–305.

91. See Chapter Seven, footnote 17.

92. Related questions are how to determine: 1.) the date of his private decision to attack the Habsburgs; and 2.), when he made up his mind to attempt the seizure of Vienna. It may never be possible to give positive answers in either instance although there is more information with which to work in the latter case. (See below, p. 152.) The Grand Vezir's interest in an Austrian war goes back in any event to at least 1676. *Cf.* Klopp, p. 51. How he first became aware of the possibility of conquest is also very uncertain. Morosini implies that the Dutch (not the French) are to be held responsible, noting that, with almost criminal negligence, they presented the Sultan atlases of Europe. Mehmed IV, Kara Mustafa, and the Grand Dragoman Mavrokordatos are said to have studied this material closely (Barozzi and Berchet, p. 209). Perhaps commercial jealousy colored the Venetian envoy's views.

Chapter Three

1. Heinrich Kretschmayr, *Geschichte von Venedig*, Vol. III, Stuttgart, 1934, pp. 362–373, *passim*.

2. Alfred von Arneth, *Prinz Eugen von Savoyen*, Vol. I, Vienna, 1858, p. 26.

3. Kretschmayr, pp. 373–386, *passim*. Venetian cultural achievements were not as noteworthy as in the past, but the age was by no means barren in this respect (e.g., Longhena and Monteverdi).

4. Max Immich, *Papst Innocenz XI. 1676–1689*, Berlin, 1909, p. 4.

5. Vilmos Frakñói, *Papst Innocenz XI und Ungarns Befreiung*, Freiburg im Breisgau, 1902, p. 21.

6. Klopp (Chapter One, footnote 27), p. 41.

7. Leopold von Ranke, *Die römischen Päpste*, Berlin, 1941, p. 432.

8. Ludwig von Pastor, *History of the Popes*, Vol. XXXII, St. Louis, 1940, pp. 12–13.

9. Frakñói, p. 22.

10. Pastor, p. 16.

11. *Ibid.*, pp. 17–29, *passim*.

12. Von Ranke, p. 432; Immich, p. 14.

13. F. X. Seppelt, *Papstgeschichte von den Anfängen bis zur Gegenwart*, Munich, 1940, p. 253.

14. For a discussion of the difficulties of the Baroque as an historical period, see Kann, (Chapter One, footnote 35), pp. 1–4, 42–49.

15. Frakñói, pp. 16–17.

16. Heyret (Chapter One, footnote 20), pp. 1–284, *passim;* "Marco d'Aviano. Ord. M. Cap. Eine Festschrift," in *Österreich: Kultur und Religion*, Vol. III, Vienna, 1933, p. 9.

17. Heyret, *idem*.

18. Prince Adalbert of Bavaria, *Das Ende der Habsburger in Spanien*, Vol. I, Munich, 1929, pp. 17–20; J. H. Elliott, *Imperial Spain*, New York, 1963, pp. 359–367; R. Trevor Davies, *Spain in Decline*, London, 1957, pp. 141–142.

19. No secondary studies seem to exist either. Aside from the numerous ambassadorial dispatches in the Simancas Archives, comments in the Venetian *Relazioni*, and other scattered references, the only material I have been able to locate is a handful of not very informative personal letters in the *Archivio di Stato* of Modena. The *Archivio segreto estense*, Vol. I, Rome, 1953, pp. 120–121, contains a listing of these records. The biographical data are from Pompeo Litta, *Famiglie celebri italiani*, Vol. II, Part 2, Milan, 1825, plate XIV, and from various Simancas documents. The title derives from the town and fief of Borgomanero just to the west of Lake Maggiore. (Possibly local depositories hold something of interest.) The one thing that is fairly certain is that the Marchese was generally short of cash. His reports to Madrid make frequent mention of a "lack of means." On June 17, 1684, for example, he writes he cannot live in the completely ruined embassy and, being in a state of "extreme necessity," does not have the money for its repair. The Council of State did manage to send him the requested funds, however. In 1686 he submitted a petition to King Charles, in which he pointed to his many services, diplomatic (he had also represented Spain in London) and military, adding that the income from his own estates was shrinking and requesting that he be granted a position that would indemnify him for everything. The monarch replied by according him the Vice-Royalty of Galicia, i.e., an absentee living. While it is possible that Borgomanero exaggerated his distress in order to get the amounts he really required, the bankrupt state of the Spanish fisc can scarcely be gainsaid.

20. Philippe Sagnac and A. de Saint-Léger, *La prépondérance française 1661–1715*, 3rd ed., Paris, 1949, p. 693.

21. E.g., H. A. Wakeman, *The Ascendancy of France 1598–1715*, 4th ed. (21st impression); first published in 1893.

22. Sagnac and St. Léger, p. 57.

23. Albert Guérard, *France*, Ann Arbor, 1959, pp. 173–175.

24. Most recently, for example, by Mousnier, (Chapter Two, footnote 2), p. 297.

25. *Extraits des Mémoires du Duc de Saint Simon*, preface by Louis Bertrand, Paris, 1929, pp. 226–227 (Vol. II).

26. Gaston Zeller, *Les temps modernes: de Louis XIV à 1789*, Pt. Vol. III of Renouvin's "Histoire des relations internationales," Paris, 1955, p. 9.

27. Guérard, p. 177.

28. His involvement in the Turkish attack proves this. Cf. David Ogg, *The Seventeenth Century*, 8th ed., New York, 1960, pp. 226–227.

29. W. F. Reddaway, *A History of Europe: 1610–1715*, London, 1962, p. 228.

30. Mousnier, pp. 166ff.

31. John B. Wolf, *The Emergence of European Civilization*, New York, 1962, p. 236.

32. Mousnier, p. 171.

33. Frederick L. Nussbaum, *The Triumph of Science and Reason: 1660–1685*, New York, 1953, pp. 79–85.

34. Reddaway, p. 269.

35. E. Préclin and V. Tapier, *Le XVIIᵉ siècle*, Paris, 1943, p. 236. This work contains a summary of the military improvements of Louis' reign and cites the specialized literature (see especially p. 245).

36. Ogg, p. 223.

37. Jacques Pirenne, *Les grands courants de l'histoire universelle*, Vol. III, Neuchâtel, 1948, pp. 8–9.

38. E. Lavisse, *Histoire de France*, Vol. III, Part 1, Paris, 1911, p. 68.

39. Schönborn intended the League to serve as a balance for preserving the existing order in the Holy Roman Empire, which he believed to be threatened more by Austria than by France. Max Braubach, "Vom Westfälischen Frieden bis zur französischen Revolution," in Bruno Gebhardt's *Handbuch der deutschen Geschichte*, Vol. II, Stuttgart, 1955, p. 211.

40. A. F. Pribram, "Beitrag zur Geschichte des Rheinbundes von 1658," *Sitzungsberichte der kaiserlichen Akademie der Wissenschaften*, CXV (1887), pp. 94–196, *passim*.

41. Zeller, p. 18.

42. Koehler (Chapter Two, footnote 34), p. 60.

43. Braubach, p. 222.

44. The appearance in 1667 of a brochure written by a Parisian publicist on the alleged justice of Louis' claims to the Empire also agitated the Germans and caused the King much embarrassment. Zeller, pp. 28–30.

45. Author, *inter alia*, of the famous *Bouclier d'État*, a rejection of Louis' theses concerning the Spanish Netherlands. Lisola's eloquent warnings and his diplomatic activity eventually had considerable effect. See A. F. Pribram, *Franz Paul Freiherr von Lisola (1613–1674) und die Politik seiner Zeit*, Leipzig, 1894, esp. pp. 351–365.

46. Leopold's peace of mind was greatly disturbed. Ogg, p. 238.

47. Not only did Leopold recognize the rights of his Spanish sister-in-law, but he was now bound to stand idly by for several years while the French king became increasingly aggressive. Hantsch (Chapter One, footnote 53), p. 37.

48. Schönborn now turned toward the Emperor without actually becoming anti-French. Braubach, pp. 224–225.

49. Louis provided a degree of assistance to the Dutch in their 1665–67 war with the English.

50. Bernhard Auerbach, *La France et la Saint Empire germanique*, Paris, 1912, stresses the intensity of German public opinion during the war and lists the relevant monographs (pp. 184–185).

51. Veit Valetin, *Geschichte der Deutschen*, Vol. I, Stuttgart, 1947, p. 225.

52. Wilhelm Treue, "Wirtschafts- und Sozialgeschichte vom. 16. bis zum 18. Jahrhundert," in Gebhart, pp. 412–415. Perhaps an overall forty percent of the country-dwellers vanished, the victims of violence, famine, and disease. Large groups of people fled their home areas (although other places benefitted from their settlement). *Ibid.*, p. 415. The question of the physical effects of the war remains highly controversial. Robert Ergang (*The Myth of the All-Destructive Fury of the Thirty Years War*, Pocono Pines, Pa., 1956), who forcefully presents the case for the "revisionists," believes that future research will show the total population loss to have been under one-third (*ibid.*, p. 27).

53. Hajo Holborn, *A History of Modern Germany*, Vol. 2 (New York, 1964), pp. 24–26.

54. Treue, p. 416.

55. Many princes, especially Lutherans, influenced by mercantile thinking, Biblical studies, and fiscal, economic-pedagogical, and military considerations, became involved in manufactories themselves. *Ibid.*, pp. 382–383.

56. *Ibid.*, pp. 408–409.

57. Kann, pp. 31–34. While German mercantilism was primarily oriented toward the continent, rather than seaward, it did recognize the impossibility of economic autarchy and was somewhat aware of the significance of agriculture even before the advent of the Physiocrats. On the other hand, it did not become a formally organized discipline until the eighteenth century. *Ibid.;* Treue, p. 409.

58. Holborn, pp. 36–39.

59. In literature, apart from the romancier, Grimmelshausen, only poetry stands out, and the poets (Opitz, Dach, Albert, Fleming, Gerhard, Klaj, Gryphius, Hoffmannswaldau) are distinguished more by felicity of expression than by profound or original thought. Drama is represented principally by Gryphius, remembered far more for what he tried to accomplish than for what he did. (Richard Newald, *Die deutsche Literatur vom Späthumanismus zur Empfindsamkeit* [Vol. V of De Boor and Newald's "Geschichte der deutschen Literatur"], Munich, 1951, p. 293.) In sculpture only Andreas Schlüter comes to mind, and he is a late arrival. In painting one is at a loss to mention a single important name. Architecture does not begin to flower until the turn of the century, and even then Italian influence is significant. Music is active and vital but also strongly under the Italian imprint. Only the organists—and they come late—are worthy of independent note. In science and philosophy Otto von Guericke and Leibnitz stood by themselves, for Kepler really belongs to the sixteenth century. Political theorists like Pufendorf and Seckendorf hardly rank alongside such giants as Locke and Hobbes. German scholars themselves, confronted with selecting the places of honor in the standard national biography, *Die Grossen Deutschen* (ed. by Hempel, Heuss, and Reifenberg, Berlin, 1956), have accorded the seventeenth century fewer entries than any other from the sixteenth onward.

60. See Newald (Chapter One, footnote 3), II, p. 6, for a good example of *Kanzleideutsch*.

61. It may be argued, however, that the decentralization of German political life was not altogether harmful. The resultant appearance of a large number of capital towns created provincial intellectual centers that stood in sharp contrast to the barrenness and sterility of smaller cities and towns in England and France. Wilhelm Treue, *Deutsche Geschichte von 1648 bis 1740* (No. 40 of the "Sammlung Goschen"), Berlin, 1956, p. 6.

62. Miller and Spielman, (Chapter One, footnote 22), do not state this explicitly, but their study leads one to infer it.

63. Ernst W. Zeeden, "Das Zeitalter der Glaubenskämpfe," Gebhardt, p. 199.

64. G. Barraclough, in his now classical study, *The Origins of Modern Germany*, Oxford, 1946, p. 383, somewhat overstates his case in this regard, as well as in other matters relating to the latter seventeenth century.

65. Bernhard Erdmannsdörffer, *Deutsche Geschichte vom Westfälischen Frieden bis zum Regierungsantritt Friedrich des Grossen*, Vol. I, Berlin, 1893, pp. 26–48.

66. *Ibid.*, pp. 48–51.

67. The failure of the Reichstag was variously interpreted during the nineteenth century: either according to the pro-Prussian, Little German approach (Droysen), which blamed the Emperor; or according to the anti-Hohenzollern, Greater German viewpoint, which held the estates responsible. Treue, *Deutsche Geschichte*, pp. 29–31.

68. The current trend among German and Austrian historians is to stress the territorial state as the true locus of political reality in the latter seventeenth century. This contrasts with the brilliant but overly-intellectualized, Pan German orientation of Reinhold Lorenz (*Grundlegung des Absolutismus*, Vol. III-3 of Leo Just's "Handbuch der deutschen Geschichte"). Lorenz, a pupil of Srbik and product of the *Wiener Schule*, was dismissed in 1945 from the University of Vienna where a Roman Catholic viewpoint has since prevailed.

69. Gerhard Oestreich, "Verfaβungsgeschichte, vom Ende des Mittelalters bis zum Ende des alten Reiches," in Gebhardt, pp. 351–352.

70. Frederick William's achievements are brilliantly presented in Part III of F. L. Carsten's *Origins of Prussia*, Oxford, 1953.

71. Erdmannsdörffer, pp. 56–75, *passim.*

72. *Ibid.*, pp. 65–85, *passim.*

73. Salvandy (Chapter Two, footnote 14), p. 33.

74. Rinck (Chapter One, footnote 4), p. 252.

75. Krones (Chapter One, footnote 23), p. 641.

76. Erdmannsdörffer, *idem.*

77. *Ibid.*, pp. 171–172, 185–192; Johann Georg von Rauchbar, *Leben und Thaten des Fürsten Georg Friedrich von Waldeck*, 2 vol's, Arolsen, Speyer, 1882, *passim.*

78. "Markgraf Hermann von Baden," *Allgemeine deutsche Biographie*, Vol. 12, Leipzig, 1880, pp. 120–122.

79. Otto Flake, *Türkenlouis: Gemälde einer Zeit*, Baden, 1937, p. 38.

80. G. A. Kittler, "Georg Rimpler, kaiserlicher Obristleutnant und Oberingenicur im Türkenkrieg 1683," *Zeitschrift für die Geschichte des Oberrheins*, 99 (1951), p. 169.

81. Flake, p. 143.

82. Venetian Ambassador Contarini (1685), FRA (Chapter One, footnote 6), p. 250.

83. Flake, p. 65.

84. "Ludwig Wilhelm von Baden," *Allgemeine deutsche Biographie*, Vol. 19, Leipzig, 1884, p. 485.

85. Rinck, p. 452.

86. Venetian Ambassador Veniers (1692), FRA, p. 314.

87. Erdmannsdörffer, pp. 65–85.

88. See below, p. 127.

89. Philipp Bogislav Chemnitz ("Hippolitus a Lapide"), an anti-Habsburg, Swedish-subsidized publicist, asserted, in a rather superficial treatment, that the Reich was a princely aristocracy. Veit Ludwig von Seckendorf's orientation was Imperial. While author of a book of practical hints for territorial rulers, he rejected the concept of their absolute authority. By all accounts, the most thorough and original of German political thinkers was Pufendorf. Not only did he develop an intellectual rationale for princely despotism, based upon his own exposition of natural law, but he depicted the Empire as an historian should: as it had unfolded over the ages. His "monster" metaphor, however famous, was not the most remarkable thing about his work, which, above all, represented a fresh and independent view of conditions. Recognizing that the Reich was a hybrid of monarchy and confederacy, he maintained that one could only make the best of things and work for coöperation and harmony. Erdmannsdörffer, pp. 52–54; Stephen Skalweit, "Political Thought," Chapter Five of the *Ascendancy of France*, Vol. V of the "New Cambridge Modern History," Cambridge, 1961, pp. 110–114.

Chapter Four

1. See Sir George Clark, *War and Society in the Seventeenth Century*, Cambridge, 1958, Chapter One, "War as an Institution."

2. Hungary was a market for the exchange of diseases. From the East came spotted fever; from the West, amoebic dysentery. Franz Laifle, "Die Seuchen während der Belagerung von Wien und während des letzten Türkenkrieges," *Archiv für Hygiene und Bakteriologie*, Vol. 119 (1937), p. 74.

3. Richard Kralik, *Geschichte der Stadt Wien*, 2nd ed., Vienna, 1926, pp. 218–219; Wiener Altertumsverein, *Geschichte der Stadt Wien*, Vol. VI, Vienna, 1918, pp. 260–261. It is difficult to establish even an approximate number of deaths. The figures vary between 8,000 and 140,000. The former number is based upon research in the Vienna City Archives by a painstaking, modern scholar, Gustav Gugitz, while the latter derives from a list in the archives of the Harrach family. The discrepancy probably can be explained by the fact that the corpse bearers were paid according to the number of bodies they carried and were allowed to report the sums by themselves. Thus the

second estimate is far too high. Gugitz, on the other hand, does not include the suburbs (the area outside the fortifications), the records of which were destroyed during 1683; there were perhaps another 4,000 victims there. The total population of Vienna at the time is unknown. In 1702 both city and suburbs are said to have had 80,000 inhabitants. The first census, in 1754, listed 175,460 persons. Assuming that the 1702 estimate is correct and that Vienna by that time had recovered its losses from the plague—the number of civilian dead in the siege was minimal—, the proportion of deaths to population would have been 15%, still a high figure. The disease also swept through the countryside where, of course, most people lived. (Based on correspondence with Dr. Walter Sturminger.) For the relevant literature see Gugitz' *Bibliographie zur Geschichte und Stadtkunde der Stadt Wien*, 5 vols, (Vienna, 1949–1962), numbers 1860, 3758, 9130, 9158, 9163, 9189, 9197, 9209, 9211.

4. Borgomanero's letter, Vienna, July 31, 1681 (to the *Consejo del Estado*), AGS, 3922.

5. See below, p. 111.

6. Rákóczy died a natural death in 1676; he and Helena had been married for ten years.

7. Renner (Chapter One, footnote 3), p. 42; Lorenz, (Chapter One, footnote 69), p. 145.

8. Frakńoi (Chapter Three, footnote 5), pp. 27–46.

9. *Ibid.*, pp. 42–48. Montecuccoli helped in the effort to topple Sinzendorf. Cf. Klopp (Chapter One, footnote 27), p. 76.

10. Forst de Battaglia (Chapter Two, footnote 12), p. 125.

11. *Ibid.*, p. 126; Laskowski (Chapter Two, footnote 9), pp. 123–124.

12. Forst de Battaglia, p. 128.

13. It is hard to understand why Sobieski agreed to sending so incompetent a person. Can he himself have realized that the time was not yet ripe and, while wishing to accommodate public opinion, have deliberately sent somebody who would fail? Did he have to accept Radziwiłł for diplomacy's sake (i.e., domestic political considerations) or did he simply miscalculate?

14. It will be recalled that Zierowski planted the first two of these ideas in Maria Kazimiera's head earlier (see above, p. 53). To Vienna, however, such suggestions appeared presumptuous; only later, in more dangerous circumstances, was it willing to consider them and, even then, solely as bait (see below, p. 159).

15. Forst de Battaglia, pp. 130–132; Laskowski, p. 124; Klopp, pp. 73–74.

16. Forst de Battaglia, p. 129.

17. See Chapter Two, footnote 41.

18. Forst de Battaglia, pp. 130–131; Laskowski, p. 124.

19. Frákńói (p. 41) favors the Pope and Forst de Battaglia (p. 126), Sobieski.

20. Immich (Chapter Three, footnote 4), pp. 16–17.

21. Pastor (Chapter Three, footnote 8), pp. 43–45. It is possible that Paolo also indirectly influenced Sobieski. The friar had contacts with Polish diplomats in Constantinople, to whom he bared his scheme. Forst de Battaglia, pp. 127–128.

22. Immich, p. 18; Pastor, p. 45.

23. *Ibid.*, pp. 69, 74.

24. W. Platzhoff, "Ludwig XIV, das Kaisertum und die europäische Krisis von 1683," *Historische Zeitschrift*, Vol. 121 (1920), p. 398.

25. Zeller (Chapter Three, footnote 26), p. 57.

26. *Ibid.*, pp. 57–58.

27. Braubach (Chapter Three, footnote 39), p. 233.

28. E.g., Onno Klopp and Gustav Droysen.

29. Braubach, p. 233.

30. Richard Fester, *Die armierten Stände und die Reichskriegsverfaßung 1681–1697*, Frankfort a.M., 1886, pp. 41–43.

31. Koehler (Chapter Two, footnote 34), pp. 71–75; Klopp, p. 70.

32. Renner, p. 45.

33. *Ibid.*, p. 46.

34. Forst de Battaglia, pp. 132–135.

35. *Ibid.*, pp. 136–139.
36. *Ibid.*, p. 139; Koehler, p. 49.
37. Rubinstein (Chapter Two, footnote 25) , p. 9.
38. Forst de Battaglia, p. 140.
39. *Ibid.*, p. 141.
40. Koehler, pp. 48–49.
41. Zeller, pp. 58–59; J. Schoetter, "Le Luxembourg et le Comté de Chiny depuis le traité de Nimègue . . . ," *Section Historique de l'Institut Royal Grand Ducal de Luxembourg*, Vol. XII, Luxembourg, 1880, pp. 296–297.
42. Wagner (Chapter One, footnote 70) , p. 94.
43. Immich (Chapter One, footnote 54) , p. 107.
44. Klopp, pp. 77–78. David Ogg, *England in the Reign of Charles II*, Vol. II, London, 1963, pp. 584–594.
45. Auerbach, (Chapter Three, footnote 50) , pp. 211–212.
46. Klopp, pp. 70–71.
47. Koehler, pp. 75–77.
48. Guillot (Chapter One, footnote 6) , pp. 431–435, *passim*.
49. Ludwig Baur, "Berichte des hessen-darmstädtischen Gesandten Justus Eberhard Passer an die Landgräfin Elisabeth Dorothea," AöG, Vol. 37 (1867) , p. 309.
50. Redlich (Chapter One, footnote 21) , pp. 230–233.
51. *Ibid.*, pp. 233–234.
52. Renner, p. 50. For the meaning of the terms "Partium" and "Upper Hungary," see Chapter One, footnote 50.
53. Forst de Battaglia, pp. 149–150; Auerbach, pp. 216–218. The French tactic of expansion in the Spanish Netherlands had two facets: 1.) an exhumation of ancient, feudal suzerainties; and 2.) a unique interpretation of the Nijmegen Treaty. The former device applied to Luxembourg, the latter to Flanders, but each was relevant to the other. The Sun King began with the second region (via the Tournai Chamber) . He asserted that villages and areas which his army had occupied during the late war—the restoration of which the Treaty did not expressly mention—belonged to him even though his troops had evacuated them in the meantime. The claims, which included Alost and the old town *(bourg)* of Ghent, amounted to a major portion of Flanders and would have left both Ghent and Brussels geographically untenable. (The decrees were left unexecuted, probably because of the Dutch and their sensitivity over the "Barrier.") The militarily helpless Spaniards protested vigorously. Louis XIV replied that he realized that their communications would be hampered and that he would consider counter-proposals. He was, in effect, mounting a false attack in order to divert attention from his true goal, Luxembourg.
The Metz Chamber undertook the genuine attack in April, 1681, by claiming and occupying the County of Chiny, within the confines of the Duchy of Luxembourg, as a "dependency" of the Metz Bishopric. Spain accepted its loss (July) in order to placate the French and to preserve the bulk of Flanders. Certain territories along the meanders of the Meuse (Namur) as well as the County of Virton (Luxembourg) were yielded simultaneously. However, as stated in the text, the French immediately proceeded to seize almost all that remained of Luxembourg as "dependencies" of Chiny. The discussions at Kortrijk, where the French formally advanced their claims for Flemish lands on August 4 in order to be able to demand "equivalencies" (i.e., Luxembourg) were now deliberately dragged out by the Spanish—a reversal of the situation in 1680. In November, 1681, the French exerted further pressure by initiating a partial blockade of Luxembourg City and, the next month, by tightly investing it (see below, p. 131) . They claimed the fortress capital in return for their own earlier military withdrawal from Kortrijk, despite the fact that in this case the Treaty specifically obligated them thereto. Henri Martin, *Histoire de France*, Vol. XII, Paris, 1858, pp. 585–586; Hermann Kaufmann, *Die Reunionskammer zu Metz*, Metz, 1899, pp. 206–207; *La Grande Encyclopédie*, Vol. X, Paris, 1890, p. 380; *Mémoires de Saint Hilaire* (Vol. II of "Sources de l'histoire de France") , Paris, 1916, pp. 4–6; Schoetter, pp. 258ff; Pieter Geyl, *The Netherlands in the Seventeenth Century*, Pt. 2, London, 1964, p. 163.
Casale, too, was a matter of concern for Madrid. Although not Spanish, its control by

France threatened adjacent Milan and environs, which were. Borgomanero's correspondence for this period is replete with references to Spain's north Italian holdings where, of course, his personal patrimony was also situated.

54. See footnote 4.

55. Klopp, pp. 90–91.

56. ". . . hasta aora no hay noticia cierta de las circumstancias, aunque certisima de la perdida, que ha causado aqui consternación grandisima, pues ademas de la perdida misma, que estan considerables, se pondera, y con razon, el desprecio que hace el Rey Xptmo. del Empor. y del Imperio, dando por preliminar de la Conferencia de Francfort, un golpe tan considerable a toda Alemania, que es un casso que jamas se habra oydo. . . ." Borgomanero's letter, Sopron, October 9, 1683, AGS, 3922.

57. ". . . . y habiendo anoche llegado el Baron de Saponara que viene de tratar con el, presto sabremos lo que puede esperar, pero como aun no ha tenido audiencia de Su Magd., mas sobre este particular, sino es que dentro de ocho dias executara el Conde Alberto Caprara su jornada a Constantinopla, creyendo que deteniendose tendria mejor suceso en la Porta su negociación llegando despues del ajuste de Ungria. . . .". Borgomanero's letter, Vienna, January 1, 1682, AGS, 3922.

58. *Ibid.*

59. Koehler, p. 50.

60. Forst de Battaglia, pp. 142–144. The actions of Louis' representatives in Poland were but one example of French diplomacy. Taken by itself, it obviously gives no grounds for revising C. G. Picavet's conclusion that the French Foreign Service, its half-formed character notwithstanding, was superior to that of other countries (*La diplomatie française au temps de Louis XIV*, Paris, 1930, pp. 118–119). Indeed, Picavet himself points out (pp. 203ff) that diplomacy by bribery sometimes failed to pay off. Moreover, if Béthune, Forbin-Janson, and Vitry behaved in a *gauche* fashion, Guilleragues in Constantinople and other Ludovican envoys comported themselves with considerable skill. It is nonetheless clear that Saint Simon's estimate of Béthune (quoted in *ibid.*, p. 77) requires correction.

61. The Poles had actually concluded an offensive alliance with the Tsar, who was to supply an army of 20,000 infantry. Sobieski appears to have conceived of the agreement as the beginning of a pan-European enterprise. His envoy in Spain stated that the King hoped to win many victories with the aid of the princes of Christendom, including His Catholic Majesty. Discussion of the Council of State, May 29, 1681; letter of the Abbé Dini, May 10, AGS, 3922.

62. Forst de Battaglia, pp. 144, 146–147.

63. Laskowski, p. 126.

64. Forst de Battaglia, p. 149.

65. Rubinstein, p. 54.

66. See above, p. 117.

67. *Ibid.*, p. 215; Fester, pp. 31–37.

68. ". . . que es a quien ellos en todos sus papeles cargan, de que quiera por su proprio interes volver a la guerra para alojar en el Imperio, y por este medio despues oprimirle, hablando tambien aqui en este tono el Ministro de Francia [Sèbeville] al del Suecia, al del Palatino, y al del Brunswicg. . . ." Borgomanero's letter, Sopron, December 4, 1681, AGS, 3922.

69. Oestreich (Chapter Three, footnote 69), p. 335.

70. To precisely what extent the 1681 law was responsible for 9,000-odd Circle troops in the relief army is unclear except in the case of Swabia where the Duke-Administrator created two new companies, about 400 men (Karl Linnebach, *Deutsche Heeresgeschichte*, Berlin, 1935, p. 260). The recruitment of the Franconians and the Bavarians, who constituted the bulk of the Circle forces, was probably due more to the personal efforts of Waldeck. Still, the new measure provided a useful legal foundation and psychological stimulus.

71. Fester, pp. 44–45.

72. Michael Doeberl, *Entwicklungsgeschichte Bayerns*, Vol. II, Munich, 1928, pp. 87–93; Sigmund Riezler, *Geschichte Bayerns*, Vol. VII, Gotha, 1913, pp. 258–263; Michael Strich, *Das Kurhaus Bayern im Zeitalter Ludwigs XIV und die europäischen*

Mächte, Vol. II, Munich, 1933, pp. 389–409. The Eisenach project was ultimately frustrated by the refusal of the Vatican to grant the necessary dispensation, in which decision Buonvisi had some hand (Riezler, p. 262). The Nunzio apparently hoped that Austro-Bavarian nuptials would facilitate a political linkage against the Turks. It seems likely that Max Emmanuel quickly reconsidered the idea—actually in the air ever since the early 1670's—of espousing Maria Antonia, for the next spring (1682) he sent a certain Canon Preysing to Austria to initiate his wooing (see below, p. 146).

73. Georg Schnath, *Geschichte Hannovers,* Vol. I, Hildesheim-Leipzig, 1938, pp. 133–186.

74. J. A. de Mesmes, Compte d'Avaux, *Négociations de Monsieur le comte d'Avaux en Hollande: 1679–1684,* Vol. I, Paris, 1752, p. 162; Immich, *Geschichte etc.,* p. 108; Onno Klopp, *Der Fall des Hauses Stuart und die Succession des Hauses Hannover,* Vol. II, Vienna, 1875, p. 337.

75. Johanna Oudendijk, *Willem III Stadhouder van Holland, Koning van Engeland,* Amsterdam, 1954, p. 151. The conventional view of William is given by G. N. Clark (*The Later Stuarts,* 2nd ed., London, 1955, p. 100); there is also the self-seeking interpretation of Lucile D. Pinkham (*William of Orange and the Respectable Revolution,* Cambridge, Mass., 1954).

76. Klopp, *der Fall etc.,* pp. 238ff.

77. Borgomanero's letter, Linz, April 10, AGS, 3922. In pursuing his aims the Spanish ambassador was no less loathe to use bribery than any other diplomat of the day. He suggested to his unfortunately bankrupt government that a gratuity be sent to Strattmann, the Imperial representative in Regensburg, whom he regarded as very useful to the Spanish cause.

78. "Copia de Memoria q el Marqués de Burgomayne presente a Su Magd. Cessa. tocante a la unión con Inglaterra," AGS, 3923. In this document Borgomanero also mentions contacts with English friends, "good Parliamentarians." On August 1 in London the Dutch and Spanish ambassadors (then Citters and Ronquillo), plus some Englishmen, had pressed their Austrian colleague, Count Thun, on the same subject (Klopp, *der Fall etc.,* pp. 341–342). Presumably, Borgomanero was in contact with them, possibly even with William.

79. Accompanying letter of Borgomanero, Sopron, August 20, 1681, AGS, 3922. Ogg, (pp. 600–601, 614–615), cites Louis XIV's lack of concern over Charles' possible enmity (which the author interprets as a deprecation of English military strength) and the French ruler's personal mistrust of his Stuart colleague. The reason for the orally-concluded treaty was the Sun King's supposed wish to alleviate the status of persecuted English Catholics and to assure the Catholic succession. A Gallic desire for English neutrality cannot have been a factor. The latter viewpoint is not convincing. The terms of the agreement (made with Barillon) did, after all, clearly imply non-involvement. It is also fairly safe to assume that Louis knew that England—whatever its physical weaknesses—could serve as the catalyst for a coalition of France's continental foes (see below, p. 143). It is likewise difficult to believe that the preservation of English neutrality was not a consideration when the French sovereign allowed Charles to extract another million (see below, p. 131) and, ultimately, when (as Ogg asserts) he gave up the Luxembourg enterprise altogether because of Charles' intervention (see below, p. 143). As for Charles himself, there were other reasons apart from the domestic political dilemma for refusing to commit England to the anti-French cause. No immediate British national interest was involved; continuing prosperity could be assured by avoiding foreign entanglements; the navy, the country's only practicable weapon, was momentarily in poor shape. Clark, pp. 109–110.

80. See footnote 56.

81. See footnote 77.

82. Immich, *Geschichte etc.,* pp. 108–109.

83. A report of the Spanish minister in Regensburg, dated December 13, 1681, and forwarded to Madrid by Borgomanero on January 18, 1682, AGS, 3922. The reference in the document to the "Most Serene Elector" could mean Cologne or Trier as well as Brandenburg. The question is not crucial since Berlin was the center for the spreading of French propaganda in Germany anyway.

84. Borgomanero's letter, Sopron, December 4, 1681, AGS, 3922.

85. Ogg, p. 622; Klopp, *der Fall etc.,* pp. 357–360. Borgomanero claimed that his influence kept Thun in England with instructions to work for Spain (letter of August 20).

86. Borgomanero's letter, Vienna, August 27, 1681, AGS, 3922.

87. Koehler, pp. 79–82.

88. Klopp, *der Fall etc.,* p. 396. This is not to say that Louis was entirely uninterested in the Imperial crown. Cf. Platzhoff, p. 395.

89. Koehler, pp. 82–84.

90. *Ibid.,* p. 86.

91. Klopp, *Das Jahr 1683* etc., pp. 90–91.

Chapter Five

1. Klopp (Chapter One, footnote 27) , pp. 88–89.

2. Guillot (Chapter One, footnote 6) , p. 435.

3. Krones (Chapter One, footnote 23) , p. 569.

4. See above, pp. 97–98.

5. These are the names that the Spanish ambassador mentions most consistently in his correspondence of 1682.

6. Krones, p. 631.

7. *Ibid.,* p. 569: Guillot, p. 431; Guillot, "Leopold I., les Hongrois, les Turcs,"*Revue d'histoire diplomatique,* Vol. 25 (1911) , p. 435.

8. Since the Prince was close to Sèbeville and was a pecculator, one might be tempted to suspect bribery. However, there is presently no documentary evidence of this; Borgomanero does not even raise the charge. Perhaps Schwarzenberg ought to be given the benefit of the doubt. The circumstances of his death possibly give some indication as to the sincerity of his convictions. See below, p. 163.

9. Borgomanero's letter, Vienna, January 15, 1682, AGS, 3923.

10. The other Court and administrative figures, either from honest persuasion or from self-interest, seem to have supported the partisans of Spain, at least at the beginning of the year. These persons included: Austria's Nijmegen delegate and Hocher's successor, the very competent Theodor von Strattmann; the second Nijmegen representative and later Burgrave of Bohemia, the gifted Ulrich Kinsky; the War Commissar (logistics) , Count Seifrid Breuner; the former President of the Imperial Court Council, Count Ernst von Öttingen; the Stadholder of Lower Austria, Quirin Jörger (a particularly candid fellow who composed an eight volume memoir, suppressed at Leopold's request) ; the tough field administrator, general and later War Commissar (of Neapolitan birth) , Count Anton Caraffa. Members of the so-called Old Guard, i.e., more venerable advisers, were the then-Burgrave, Count Valentin Martinic; and the Bohemian Court Chancellor, Count Johann Nostic. Also of long-standing influence were the Jesuits, of whom Borgomanero complained. Leopold had two personal favorites, although these men were not necessarily powerful: Counts Ferdinand Harrach and Gundacker Dietrichstein. Other courtlings were Count Maximilian Dietrichstein (later Lord High Steward); Count Ferdinand Waldstein (later Grand Chamberlain) ; and Prince Ferdinand Schwarzenberg, the hero of the plague. Other individuals of somewhat lesser stature were: Bishop Kollonitsch; Count Wolfgang Rosenberg, Principal Commissar of the Emperor at Regensburg and Abele's successor as Treasurer; Count Kašpar Zdenko Kapliřs; and some minor Privy Councillors, Count Christoph Schaffgotsch and Barons Dorsch and Bartholdi. The two Counts Mansfeldt might also be mentioned: the one a regimental commander, sidekick of the Duke of Lorraine and later high official; and the other ambassador in Paris and Madrid, successively. The two Italian brothers, Counts Enio (the general) and Alberto Caprara (the *internuntius*) should not be forgotten either. Rüdiger von Starhemberg and the Duke of Lorraine were also prominent at this time. Krones, *passim;* Klopp, p. 120.

11. Borgomanero's letter, Vienna, January 15, 1682, AGS, 3923. The ambassador advised Caprara, before the latter's departure, to keep an eye on the activity of certain Spanish subjects from Messina, who were in the pay of the Porte.

12. Borgomanero notes on several occasions during 1682 the financial strains caused by the Istanbul mission.

13. Renner (Chapter One, footnote 3) , pp. 52–53; Klopp, pp. 105–107.

14. *Ibid.*, p. 99.

15. Borgomanero's letter, Vienna, March 27, 1682, AGS, 3923.

16. Borgomanero's letter, Wiener Neudorf, June 18, 1682, AGS, 3923.

17. Letter of March 17; Klopp, p. 111; Renner, pp. 53–54; Acsády (Chapter One, footnote 92) . Sophia Bathory Rákóczy had recently died. Apparently Leopold's consent still carried some material, legal, or psychological value. In any event, the official permission did not arrive until after the marriage ceremony (letter of June 18) .

18. Renner, pp. 54–55.

19. Salim Necati, "Die Zweite Belagerung Wiens im Jahre 1683," *Militärwissenschaftliche Mitteilungen,* Vol. 64 (1933) , p. 661; Redlich (Chapter One, footnote 21) , p. 242. Some Turkish help was accorded Thököly in 1681 but was of such a local nature as to be scarcely distinguishable from the border warfare of normal "peacetime" years.

20. Rauchbar (Chapter Three, footnote 77) , pp. 206–207.

21. Borgomanero's letter, Vienna, July 14, AGS, 3923.

22. *Idem.*

23. Renner, pp. 55–56.

24. Borgomanero's letter, Vienna, July 30, AGS, 3923. This account of the reason for the city's fall differs from the traditional view, according to which Thököly gained entrance through trickery (see Klopp, p. 123) . Borgomanero adds that the captured fortress was of poor quality and that its loss would not have been so serious save for the prestige factor. In this same connection I see no reason to accept the Venetian contention (final report of Contarini, 1685, FRA [Chapter One, footnote 6], pp. 27, 242) that the fortresses of Upper Hungary were deliberately left weak in order that Thököly might take them. They seem to have been undermanned primarily because of the troop concentrations in Germany, against Louis, and in West Hungary, opposite the army of the *Beylerbey*, İbrahim Pasha. There were simply not enough men to go around, especially since Borgomanero was doing his best to keep as many units as possible on the Rhine (see footnote 52) . On the other hand, it is possible that the Austrian army did not strike back as vigorously as it might have for fear of provoking the Turks, of whom a peace agreement was still hoped.

25. Renner, p. 56.

26. Borgomanero's letter, Vienna, May 7, 1682, AGS, 3923.

27. Borgomanero's (second) letter, Vienna, July 30, 1682, AGS, 3923.

28. Klopp, pp. 170–172. Borgomanero's letters show that Klopp makes too much of the idea that Vienna came to this decision because it was ignorant of the degree of Kara Mustafa's determination to wage war against Austria. By 1682 the Habsburg Court can have had little doubt about his intentions.

29. Koháry was thrown into a dungeon but released upon the ultimate reconquest of the area. Renner, pp. 56–57; Klopp, pp. 123–125.

30. Acsády, pp. 5–6; Necati, pp. 123–125.

31. Renner, pp. 57–58; Necati, p. 662. For the title "Prince of Central Hungary," see Chapter Seven, footnote 19.

32. Le Clerc (Chapter One, footnote 95) , p. 134.

33. Acsády, pp. 5–6.

34. Borgomanero's letter, Vienna, September 24, 1682, AGS, 3923.

35. Borgomanero's letters, Vienna, October 8 and 22, 1682, AGS, 3923.

36. Kollonitsch was still at work on November 23, closing schools in Sopron and expelling a pastor. Baur (Chapter Four, footnote 49) , p. 357.

37. Renner, pp. 64–65; Klopp, p. 37.

38. Forst de Battaglia (Chapter Two, footnote 12) , pp. 151–152.

39. *Ibid.*, pp. 152–154.

40. *Ibid.*, pp. 154–156.

41. Forst de Battaglia (p. 156) makes one of his rare errors in stating that Thököly was made King of Hungary on August 10.

42. Frakñói (Chapter Three, footnote 5), p. 67. Buonvisi also greeted a suggestion that the Church mediate between Vienna and the rebels. However, Thököly's demands in ecclesiastical matters seemed so extreme that the Cardinal, no ecumenicist, was forced to take a very reserved attitude. The Hungarian's duplicity eventually turned the Churchman into a determined enemy.

43. Borgomanero's letter, Vienna, September 10, 1682, AGS, 3923. Klopp, p. 163, asserts that continuing uncertainty as to the goal of the Porte's military preparations— Austria *or* Poland—galvanized action in the latter nation.

44. Borgomanero reported that Leopold told him that he knew positively that Sobieski wanted this, and that the Polish king was also counting upon his support for Jakób's succession. Maria Kazimiera later demanded that a pension be added to the collar. The Spanish ambassador pushed the Austro-Polish negotiations as much as he could, ". . . . hasta llegar a ser impertinente para que no pierda Tpo., pues la flema con que van aqui en todo me tiene desesperado. . . ." Letter of September 10. The *Consejo del Estado* immediately gave its consent for the fleece (Deliberation of October 20, AGS, 3923).

45. Forst de Battaglia, pp. 156–159; Koehler (Chapter Two, footnote 34), pp. 51–56; Klopp, p. 165; Charles Gérin, "Le Pape Innocent XI. et el siège de Vienne d'après des documents inèdits," *Revue des questions historiques*, Vol. 39 (1886), p. 64.

46. Klopp, *Der Fall* etc. (Chapter Four, footnote 74), pp. 358–362. See Chapter Four, footnote 53.

47. Klopp, *das Jahr 1683 etc.* (Chapter One, footnote 27), pp. 95–96, 103–104; Platzhoff (Chapter Four, footnote 24), p. 406; Ogg (Chapter Four, footnote 44), p. 623; Immich (Chapter One, footnote 54); Geyl (Chapter Four, footnote 53), p. 163; cf. Chapter Four, footnote 79.

48. Klopp, *der Fall etc.*, pp. 37–375.

49. Borgomanero's letter, Vienna, March 27, 1682, AGS, 3923. The Spanish ambassador's tone in this document seems to indicate that he himself was unsure about his government's intentions.

50. The Spanish attempted to use the occasion of the Imperial accession to the agreement for forcing the Dutch to help them in Luxembourg. Their plan centered upon the fact that Leopold's joining depended upon Spain's doing likewise. While the Imperial minister in the Netherlands signed without waiting for the Spanish to do so, he apparently added a codicil stating that Imperial ratification would not ensue unless the States General aided Spain. Whether the Dutch were in fact influenced by this ploy in their decision to back Spain on Luxembourg is hard to say. In any case, Louis did give up the blockade, and Spain adhered to the Tractate in May. Borgomanero's letter, dated February 12, 1682 (no place indicated); letter of Don Balthazar de Fuenmayor, dated the Hague, February 25; deliberation of the *Consejo del Estado,* March 25; all AGS, 3923. Charles II of England excused himself from joining by stating that Brandenburg would have to do likewise—which convinced Vienna of his future uselessness. Borgomanero's letter.

51. Klopp, *das Jahr 1683 etc.*, p. 119.

52. Borgomanero's letter, Wiener Neudorf, May 21, 1682, AGS, 3923. The size of the projected Rhine army is not entirely clear. Klopp (*ibid.*, p. 119) says that the southern wing was to have a total of 30,000 men, the central segment 20,000, and the northern part 20,000 (Brunswickers). Borgomanero speaks of 16,000 Brunswickers *and* Saxons for the north. By July the course of events in Hungary forced Vienna to hold back 8,000 of the 13,000 troops it was sending westward (to join the 13,000 already there). However, the 3,000 cavalry promised Waldeck for completing the 20,000 men of the center were sent. (Borgomanero's letter, Vienna, July 14, 1682, AGS, 3923). Moreover, on August 27 Borgomanero succeeded in keeping the Duke of Lorraine from being shifted to Hungary (with which decision the Duke himself was allegedly in agreement). The ambassador argued that the Duke's transfer would discourage the Empire—which would assume that the rest of Austria's Western army would soon follow, leaving it at the mercy of the French. Thököly might well have found his progress in Upper Hungary more difficult if Lorraine had been present. (Borgomanero's letter, Vienna, August 27, 1682, AGS, 3923.)

53. Sinelli himself went to work to scrape up the funds, taking the matter out of the less-capable hands of Rosenberg. (Borgomanero's letter, Vienna, May 21, 1682, AGS, 3923.)

54. Rauchbar, p. 207.

55. Paul Wentzcke, *Feldherr des Kaisers: Leben und Taten Herzog Karls V. von Lothringen,* Leipzig, 1943, pp. 182–183, 403.

56. Riezler (Chapter Four, footnote 72), pp. 259–263.

57. Strich (Chapter Four, footnote 72), pp. 499–501.

58. Schnath (Chapter Four, footnote 73), pp. 231–234.

59. Borgomanero's letter, Vienna, April 23 and May 7, AGS, 3923 (two separate communications on the latter date). This information negates Strich's belief that the Elector was not aiming for marriage to Maria Antonia as early as 1682.

60. Strich, pp. 497, 503–504.

61. Schnath, p. 190.

62. Borgomanero's letter, Vienna, April 9, 1682, AGS, 3923.

63. See below, pp. 163.

64. Borgomanero's letter, Vienna, July 14, 1682, AGS, 3923.

65. *Ibid.,* August 27, 1682.

66. *Ibid.,* August 28, 1682.

67. *Ibid.,* September 9, 1682.

68. *Ibid.,* November 19 and 25, 1682.

69. *Ibid.,* October 22, 1682.

70. The festivities included balls, ballets, and sleighing parties. Although officially prohibited on January 19, they seem to have continued for a while. On the other hand, the most important ministers had begun to remove their furniture by New Year's. (Baur [Chapter Four, footnote 49] pp. 364–365).

71. Borgomanero's letter, Vienna, December 31, 1682, AGS, 3923.

72. *Ibid.,* October 22, 1682 (second letter).

73. *Ibid.,* December 31.

74. A fifth factor may have been the influence of certain Westerners in Istanbul. See footnote 90.

75. Klopp, *Das Jahr 1683 etc.,* pp. 110, 114. (Largely verbatim from Caprara's reports.) Also see above, p. 62.

76. See above, p. 71.

77. Contarini, FRA, p. 244; see also Chapter Two, footnote 90.

78. See also Chapter Seven, footnote 17.

79. Klopp, p. 110.

80. Cantemir (Chapter Two, footnote 90), pp. 295–296.

81. *Ibid.,* p. 296.

82. Klopp, p. 113.

83. Necati, p. 662.

84. Cantemir, pp. 296–297. Many of the author's allegations about the *degree* of the Sultan's coöperation do not sound credible.

85. Koehler, pp. 89–98. Koehler holds that the Sultan was not convinced of the wisdom of the enterprise until this point. Cantemir's version has Mehmed persuaded from a very early date, presumably from the beginning of the year at least. Necati, who writes from the Turkish sources, places the Janissary intrigue *after* the arrival of Caprara, noting that the Padishah listened favorably to the *Internuntius.* Logically, Kara Mustafa could have made the demand for Győr, reported by Caprara on June 23, either before or after getting his master to agree to it as a precondition to peace. (Caprara himself noted the Sultan's peaceful disposition, information echoed in Borgomanero's letters). Thus, the most that one can say is that the Turkish sovereign was probably converted to the idea of war sometime between Caprara's first audience (June 4) and the time of Guilleragues' declaration. If, for the sake of argument, one were to accept Cantemir's view that the Sultan was long predisposed in favor of the Grand Vezir's plan, then he must have hidden his true sentiments, either because of the domestic opposition or in order to confuse the Austrians (or for both reasons).

86. Necati, p. 662.

87. Contarini, p. 224. Cantemir also adhered to this view; see footnote 84.

88. The first major Turkish source for 1683, as well as for the background of the previous year, is the eyewitness diary, "Vikayi-i-Beç," of the anonymous Master of Ceremonies of the Ottoman Court. It exists in two manuscript copies, one in London and the other in Istanbul, and has been translated into German and annotated by Richard F. Kreutel. However, only that portion of the work concerning the siege and its aftermath has been printed (Preface, footnote 2). Closely related to the diary is the "History of the Weapons Bearer" (*Silâhdar tarichi*) of Fyndyklyly Mehmed Ağa, a seventeenth-century Turkish scholar. This book, published only in 1928 (Istanbul), contains the bulk of the former volume, plus supplementary material which seems to reflect first-hand knowledge but which lacks any indication as to origin. The relevant parts of this latter writing have also been published in German by Kreutel as indicated. For the unpublished parts of "Vekayi-i-Beç" and the untranslated section of the Silâhdar's ("Silihdar" is the Turkish version of an originally Iranian word) study I have relied upon MS materials kindly placed at my disposal by Dr. Kreutel. There is also a Turkish monograph, Cevat Üstün's, *1683. Bin altiyüz seksen üz Viyana seferi* (Istanbul, 1941), but it is said to offer little improvement over Necati. One other source, if not directly Turkish at least written from a more or less Turkish viewpoint is the "Historiai Alexandrou Mavrokordatou" (the Grand Dragoman) published by E. Hurmuzaki in *Documente privitoare la istoria Românilor*, Vol. XIII, pp. 3ff.; and by Otto Brunner, "Eine osmanischen Quelle zur Geschichte der Belagerung Wiens 1683," *Mitteilungen des Geschichtsvereines der Stadt Wien*. Vol. V (1925), pp. 32ff. While meager in comparison to the diary and lacking independent revelations, it is not without value with respect to details and as corroboration of the Ceremony Master's testimony.

89. All of the above information derives from the Silâhdar. A. N. Kurat in the "Ottoman Empire under Mehmed IV," *New Cambridge Modern History*, Vol. V, p. 513, suggests that Mustafa Efendi was deliberately made to share the blame for the Turkish failure.

90. Civrano mentions the activity of a certain Don Giuseppe Marebese of Messina, who is said to have conferred frequently with the Ottoman ministers and to have received gifts from the Grand Vezir. The Italian renegade is also supposed to have provided Kara Mustafa with fortress plans and to have insinuated that the Turks could succeed easily in everything (footnote 24). It may be noted that Italian and French technicians were later (allegedly) present with the Turks at Vienna. Then there were the cartographic donations of Dutch merchants (Chapter Two, footnote 92). It is likewise possible that French Jesuits and Capuchins, anxious to maintain the ecclesiastical prerogatives of their nation within the Ottoman Empire (protectorate over all Christians), supplied some incitement. (Klopp, pp. 99–101). Lastly, the Vezir may have been encouraged by persons associated both with Thököly and the Porte—either separate from or in conjunction with the Magyar leader. There is a secret intelligence report (reprinted in Klopp, pp. 200–202) from Buda in the Vienna archives, which mentions the Capuchin engineer, Ahmed Bey, a certain Mustafa Bey, and Thököly's agent, Paul Szepey, as being responsible for agitating Kara Mustafa.

91. Koehler, p. 91.

92. See above, p. 135.

93. Klopp, p. 128.

94. *Ibid.*, pp. 114–116. The Silâhdar stresses Komárno alongside Győr. See below, p. 206.

95. *Ibid.*, pp. 124–127, 139–140. For Mehmed IV's attitude, see below, p. 223.

96. Borgomanero's letters, Vienna, December 3, 16, and 31, AGS, 3923.

97. Renner, pp. 170–171.

98. Borgomanero's letter, Vienna, January 14, 1683, AGS, 3923.

99. *Idem.*

100. Borgomanero's letter, Vienna, March 25, 1683, AGS, 3924.

101. Borgomanero's letter, Vienna, May 4, 1683, AGS, 3924.

102. *Idem.* See also Chapter One, footnote 50.

103. Renner, pp. 173–181.

104. Newald (Chapter One, footnote 3), I, pp. 84–88.

105. Renner, p. 175; Klopp, pp. 179–180. The plans were supposedly made by Ahmed Bey at the time of the last rebel peace mission to Vienna (see above, p. 140).

106. Renner, p. 173; and Klopp, pp. 179–180 (for Caprara and Kunitz); Cantemir, p. 300 (for Thököly). Cantemir spoke personally with Thököly many years later. The old man denied that he had been responsible for the attack, laying the blame for the story at the feet of the Grand Dragoman, Mavorokordatos, who was supposedly trying to exculpate himself after the débâcle and the fall of his patron, Kara Mustafa. Several high Ottoman officials, witnesses of the events in question, corroborated Thököly's testimony, says Cantemir. Klopp (pp. 192–193) suggests that if one is to accept Thököly's somewhat dubious word at face value, it may be that by the time of his personal meeting (June) with Kara Mustafa he had developed second thoughts about a siege, having guessed that the Vezir was only trying to use him as he was trying to use the Vezir. (The Silâhdar has nothing to say about encouragement by Thököly).

107. Renner, pp. 179–180.

108. It was also argued at the time, not very convincingly, that Thököly was pushed forward by his lieutenants, who were unwilling to make peace with Leopold since the end of fighting would deprive them of the chance to become rich from booty. Mailath (Chapter One, footnote 95), p. 334.

109. Forst de Battaglia, pp. 159–166.

110. Ibid., pp. 166–177, 175; Rubinstein (Chapter Two, footnote 25), pp. 131–132; Franz Kluczycki, König Johann III im Feldzug gegen die Türken, Kraków, 1883, pp. 18–20. It is apparent that the victory in the Diet is not to be credited primarily to Pallavicini, Zierowski, and Waldstein, as, e.g., Hantsch (p. 47; Chapter One, footnote 11) maintains.

111. Forst de Battaglia, pp. 171–175; Frakńói, pp. 70–74; Borgomanero's letter, Vienna, March 25, 1683, AGS, 3924.

112. Kluczycki, p. 22; Laskowski (Chapter Two, footnote 9), p. 128.

113. Forst de Battaglia, pp. 176–179.

114. Borgomanero's letter, Vienna, June 17, 1683, AGS, 3924.

115. Frakńói (p. 75) overstresses the influence of the Nunzio by claiming that Sobieski's shift was mainly the result of the Italian prelate's admonitions and cash support.

116. The relevant documents are collected in Augustin Sauer, Rom und Wien im Jahre 1683, Vienna, 1883. For the Persian plan see above, p. 108.

117. Von Pastor (Chapter Three, footnote 8), pp. 164–165, 216–217.

118. Frakńói, p. 77. It appears impossible to calculate the precise amount of papal subsidies.

119. See below, p. 208.

120. Immich (Chapter Three, footnote 4), p. 20.

121. Ibid., pp. 21–27.

122. Schnath, p. 190. Hannover never received more than 50,000 talers from Leopold. Ibid., p. 220.

123. Strich (p. 517) plays down the anti-French character of the treaty a little more than necessary.

124. Borgomanero's letter, Bratislava, May 8, 1683, AGS, 3924; May 21 and June 3.

125. Klopp, der Fall etc., pp. 380–381.

126. Ibid., pp. 386–387; letter of the Marchese de Grana (governor of the Spanish Netherlands) to the Consejo del Estado, May 19, AGS, 3924.

127. Borgomanero's letter, Bratislava, May 9, 1683, AGS, 3924.

128. The case for blackmail seems strongest, for the Austrian ambassador to Spain, Count Mansfeldt, delivered several scarcely-veiled threats to Prince Don Vincente de Gonzaga of the Consejo (two memorials, Madrid, May 9, 1683, AGS, 3924). On June 8 the Count resumed his pressure by stating that promises based upon such vague and remote things as the arrival of the treasure fleet or the ecclesiastical tithes of Spanish Italy (destined by the Pope for Sobieski), were insufficient, adding that the Spaniards ought to take the cash from royal household funds. In return, said Mansfeldt, the Austrians would provide a written declaration of the support they would render against

Louis. (Deliberation of the *Consejo del Estado,* Madrid, July 1, 1683, AGS, 3924.) (Note: letters between Vienna and Madrid took about one month.) On the other hand, there are grounds for suspecting an underhanded manipulation of Schwarzenberg. On February 10 the Austrians made an oral statement in Regensburg, similar to the authorization (*Poder*) of April. Borgomanero, hearing of this, betook himself to Königsegg on March 10 and was assured that the Emperor contemplated no separate negotiations; on April 8 the ambassador wrote home that Leopold was remaining firm. The Spanish diplomat did not become alarmed until the latter part of April, when he learned of the drafting of the *Poder* and received only evasive answers from Königsegg (now apparently leaning to the Schwarzenberg viewpoint) . (Letters of April 8 and May 9, Vienna, AGS, 3924) . Possibly, Königsegg, who had belonged to Borgomanero's party as late as October, 1682 (see above, p. 148) but who was always in need of money, had sold out to the French. His whole behavior during 1683 is open to question. See A. H. Berma, "Doppelspionage im Türkenjahre 1683," MIöG 17/18 (1965) , pp. 1–23, esp. pp. 22–23. Finally, the three possibilities discussed in the text need not be mutually exclusive.

129. Borgomanero's memorial of May 2, 1683, AGS, 3924.

130. Renner, p. 71.

131. Guillot, p. 437.

132. Borgomanero's letter, Vienna, June 8, 1683, AGS, 3924.

Chapter Six

1. Theodore Ropp, *War in the Modern World,* new ed., New York, 1962, pp. 11–15.

2. Karl Linnebach (Chapter Four, footnote 70) , pp. 94–95.

3. Like many political institutions, Austria's standing army evolved gradually from practical requirements, and so it is impossible to speak of any exact birthdate. Still, it appears that the incipient period lasted over a century, the ultimate origins dating back to the final third of the sixteenth century. The idea itself had been propagated as early as 1526. Eugen Heischmann, *Die Anfänge des stehenden Heeres in Österreich,* Vienna, 1925, pp. 223–224.

4. Oskar Regele, *Der Hofkriegsrat,* Vienna, 1949, pp. 11–12.

5. *Ibid.,* pp. 13–50, *passim.* There were, of course, periods in which the distribution of military authority was not quite so widespread. Montecuccoli and Eugene, for example, were able to concentrate more power in their own hands than was Charles of Lorraine.

6. Alphons Wrede, *Geschichte der k.u.k. Wehrmacht,* Vol. I, Vienna, 1889, pp. 29–30.

7. *Ibid.,* pp. 34–35. At one point Montecuccoli appears to have succeeded in making the regiment and the battalion (at that time a more or less contiguous battlefield formation) equal in size (1280 men) . However, regimental staffs were too expensive to maintain, and in 1670, in order to spread money further, the regiment was increased to 2040 men. Renner (Chapter One, footnote 3) , p. 92. In his memoirs Montecuccoli presupposes a 1500 man regiment. Since it was still too large for his battalion, he advocated detaching four large squares of musketeers to serve with the cavalry. This would enable a commander to reduce the length of the front by one square. Montecuccoli (who was not convinced that firepower was becoming more effective) feared that if the sleeves of musketry at the side of the pike were too broad, they would be torn to pieces, thus leaving a gap through which enemy horse might penetrate. Raimondo Montecuccoli, *Mémoires,* Strasbourg, 1735, pp. 35–36.

8. Anton Dolleczek, "Monographie. . . .", p. 59. The flintlock, known for decades prior to its adoption, was more expensive (4½ florins per piece) than the matchlock (3 fl.) , which apparently explains the lateness of adopting it. Matchlocks were made in Wiener Neustadt by a specially imported, government supervised band of Belgian craftsmen, who also produced the lighter wheelock carbines and pistols used by the cavalry and dragoons. The matchlock was also manufactured in Steyr and bought in Belgium directly. In 1699 the contractors were given the job of converting all remaining weapons of this type. There were a few flintlocks, mostly carbines and pistols, as well as the costly and more complicated wheelocks, in use in 1683 since the cavaliers had the option of purchasing their weapons abroad. *Ibid.,* pp. 59–61.

9. Henry Marczali, "Il Conte di Frosasco, Francesco Provana: Relation du siège de Vienne," *Revue de Hongrie,* Vol. III (1909) , p. 55.

10. Walter Hummelberger, "Die Türkenkriege und Prinz Eugen," in *Unser Heer,* Vienna, 1963, p. 70.

11. The Venetian ambassador mentions that at the Kittsee military review (early May) the spectators were endangered by bayonets flying off when the muskets were fired, the troops having forgotten to remove them from the barrels beforehand. Klopp (Chapter One, footnote 27) , p. 189. Moreover, Dolleczek (p. 53) says that the Austrian troops at the siege of Buda in 1686 were equipped with plug bayonets as well as the even earlier, insertable broad-bladed hunting knife (*Charnier-bajonett*) . The bayonet was neither a particularly new, nor a uniquely French (nor Dutch, nor English) invention. The knife that could be stuck into the bore appears to have been known in Germany in the fifteenth century and the socket type in the sixteenth (August Demmin) , *Die Kriegswaffen,* Berlin, 1893, pp. 831–834.

12. Herbert Patera, *Unter Österreichs Fahnen,* Vienna, 1963, p. 71.

13. *Feldzüge des Prinzen Eugen von Savoyen,* Series I, Vol. I, Vienna, 1889, p. 223. The "Spanish Rider" was put together from a number of individual "swyne's feathers." The latter device, also known in England (see Charles Ffoulkes, *Arms and Armament,* London, 1945, pp. 70–76) was a musket rest with the protruding upper part of the hook sharpened for piercing purposes. Detached from its wooden pole, the metal section apparently also served as a bayonet, at least in Montecuccoli's day. Dolleczek, p. 53; Ffoulkes, p. 74.

14. Hermann Meynert, *Geschichte der K. K. Österreichischen Armee,* Vol. I, Vienna, 1852, p. 180; *Feldzüge,* pp. 214–215; Hummelberger, pp. 72–74.

15. Wrede, Vol. III/1, p. 1.

16. *Ibid.,* pp. 6–7.

17. *Ibid.,* p. 8; *Feldzüge,* p. 227.

18. Wrede, Vol. IV/1, p. 1.

19. See below, p. 234.

20. *Ibid.,* pp. 6–7.

21. Anton Dolleczek, *Geschichte der österreichischen Artillerie,* Vienna, 1887, pp. 149–152; see also Peter Miethen, *Artillerie recentior praxis,* Frankfurt-Leipzig, 1684.

22. The charts are adapted from Dolleczek, pp. 153–156. I have translated the German *Schlange* ("snake") as "culverin," but in the case of the German *Columbrine* I have merely restored the original Spanish form, *colubrina* (Latin *colubra,* also meaning "snake") . This is necessary because the German words represent somewhat different guns and the English rendering of *colubrina* is also "culverin." Likewise, one should note that Austrian guns, which have names that are the same as, or similar to, those used in England and America, do not necessarily correspond to the latter in dimensions. (*Cf.* Albert Mauncy, *Artillery Through the Ages,* Washington, 1949, p. 35.) The heavier pieces listed in the first chart were intended for siege work, specifically for blasting walls, either at a distance or, for greater accuracy, at point-blank and below. During the Thirty Years' War even bigger guns, as for example, the hundred pound double carthoun, were used for this purpose, but the enormous weight of such weapons posed almost insuperable transportation problems. Thus, after 1648, they began to drop out of use. In the case of unusually stout walls, mining produced the same effects with greater practicability. Chambered pieces served against buildings and personnel inside a besieged place. The Dutch-invented, highly mobile howitzers (German *Haubitze* from the Czech word for "sling" or "catapult") , were still a relatively recent innovation: there were only two kinds available in 1683. The blunt-nosed, one-to-three-foot-long mortars, mounted on a base plate at a 45 degree angle, were far more common but by no means as easy to shift about. While the howitzers were not used for the support of troops in the field until the time of Frederick the Great, the smaller model mortars, developed so successfully by the Dutch Baron Menno van Coehoorn, could be stuffed with hand grenades and fired against the advancing enemy ranks. Because of the steep elevation, chambered pieces (their heavier projectiles notwithstanding) could match the range of (less elevated) guns of the same weight. As with the latter, the closer the target was located, the greater the accuracy. Mortars and howitzers, however, would

have to be placed farther forward than guns equally heavy because the destination of their missiles, behind a city's circumvallation, was more remote.

23. Dolleczek, pp. 155–173.

24. *Ibid.,* pp. 179–195. *Mordschlag* sometimes means a petard also.

25. *Ibid.,* p. 197; Wrede, p. 37. According to Wrede the following tools were taken into the field: entrenching shovels, axes, knives, petards, forges, bridge matériel, rope, string, torches, lanterns, iron, nails, wheels, rims, winches, stools, cooking equipment, horseshoes and nails, hand grenades, leather buckets, ladders, pick-ax heads, mantlet linen, fireworks, petard canisters, axles, shafts, anchors, quoins, assault ladders, melting pans, coal, saltpeter, turpentine, camphor, colophonium, quicksilver, arsenic, wax, oakum, hemp, linseed oil, tree sap, felt, sieves, candles, excavation baskets, soil-bags, forks, chains, candles, scythes, fodder, lubricating grease, chassis, saddles, sheet copper, and iron nails for half carthouns and falcons.

26. See Chapter One, footnote 39.

27. Wrede, Vol. V, pp. 10–12.

28. Christian Wilhelm Huhn, *Nichts Neues und Nichts Altes,* Breslau, 1717, p. 15.

29. See below, p. 237.

30. Gunther Rothenberg; see Chapter One, footnote 40.

31. See below, p. 208.

32. FRA (Chapter One, footnote 6), p. 188.

33. In addition to the opportunities for graft listed above (which were open to the captains), there were the traditional, profit-rich rights of higher officers: sale of commissions and promotions, fees for granting permission to marry or to go on leave, kickbacks from merchants, and wartime booty. Wrede, pp. 66–67. As for pay (which varied considerably), the scale for the period 1672–1696 was as follows (infantry only):

Colonel	450 fl.	Ensign	38
Lieutenant Colonel	120 (*sic*)	Sergeant	20
Captain	140	Corporal	12
Lieutenant	40	Private (1)	7½
		Private (2)	6½

Cavalrymen of the rank of captain and below received somewhat higher salaries. The food maintenance costs of 13 foot regiments (1672) came to 1,547,762 fl.; 12 cavalry to 1,068,768 fl.; and two of dragoons to 170,975. Recruitment funds for four new infantry regiments amounted to 138,240; three cavalry to 161,460; and one of dragoons and one of Croats to 70,200. Meynert, pp. 170–173. It should be noted that the cost of maintenance was deducted from the soldier's pay. Moreover, even the remaining portion, which was supposed to be handed over in cash, was frequently months in arrears not only because of the officers' corruption but also because of the often bankrupt status of the Court Chamber.

34. *Feldzüge,* pp. 300–341, *passim;* Hummelberger, *passim.*

35. Patera, pp. 292–295.

36. The Bavarian army was of a particularly high caliber. Interesting is the fact that it adopted the French practice of peacetime maneuvers. The thorough exercise held during the fall of 1682, in which emphasis was placed upon the build-up of firepower, proved to be timely. Strich (Chapter Four, footnote 72), pp. 482–491. The Saxon army was also quite modern. Hannover, in a particularly difficult international situation, likewise developed its military sinews. The advanced status of the Great Elector's war machine is a matter of common knowledge. The Circle forces, on the other hand, suffered much from the decentralized character of their sponsors and can hardly be considered a standing army. Waldeck was in any event a general of no especial aptitude.

37. Available studies do not agree on the precise depth of the Swedish square or on the number of ranks firing simultaneously. Still, it was certainly shallower than Maurice's file of ten and, with better muskets, could produce even more rapid volleys. *Cf.* C. R. L. Fletcher, *Gustavus Adolphus and the Thirty Years' War,* new ed., New York, 1963, pp. 126–127, 188ff.; C. V. Wedgewood, *The Thirty Years' War,* London, 1944, pp. 297–298.

38. Meynert, pp. 155–156; Henri Bernard, *La Guerre et son évolution à travers les*

siècles, Vol. I, Brussels, 1955, pp. 145–149; Hans Delbrück, *Geschichte der Kriegskunst im Rahmen der politischen Geschichte,* Vol. IV, Berlin, 1920, pp. 182–183. Montecuccoli's memoirs also contain interesting material on this subject.

39. Hummelberger, p. 70.

40. Delbrück, p. 205; Dolleczek, pp. 227–234, 248.

41. *Ibid.,* pp. 234–235.

42. Dr. Walter Sturminger, typescript of lecture on Charles, p. 21.

43. Wentzcke (Chapter Five, footnote 55), pp. 1–63, *passim.*

44. *Ibid.,* pp. 64ff.

45. *Ibid.,* p. 168.

46. *Ibid.,* p. 371.

47. J. de la Brune, *La Vie de Charles V, Duc de Lorraine et Bar,* Amsterdam, 1716, pp. 444–445.

48. Wentzcke, p. 374.

49. Brune, p. 445.

50. Wentzcke, p. 379.

51. It does not seem necessary to say much about the Lithuanians, who did not participate in the relief of Vienna. While their troops did get as far as Upper Hungary in support of Sobieski, the damage which they caused—their indiscipline was even worse than the Poles'—appears to have outweighed the psychological value of their movements. Cf. Dalérac (Chapter Two, footnote 24), p. 124.

52. Anton Dolleczek, "Die polnische Armee im XVII. Jahrhundert," *Österreichische Militärzeitung,* XXIV (1883), pp. 107–110; Dalérac (Chapter Two, footnote 24), p. 7.

53. Dolleczek, pp. 111–114.

54. *Ibid.,* pp. 115–119; Marjan Kukiel, "Das polnische Heer 1683," in *Marco d'Aviano Festschrift* (Chapter Three, footnote 16), pp. 47–48. Montecuccoli, p. 17; Dalérac, pp. 14–20. The armament of the Polish forces varied so much that the description given should be regarded only as approximate.

55. Beda Dudik (ed.), "Pater Berhard Brulig's Bericht über die Belagerung der Stadt Wien im Jahre 1683," *Aög,* 1850, pp. 430–432. Brulig's description of the Polish infantry and dragoons is more favorable than that of Dalérac (p. 93) and of Bernard Connor, Sobieski's English private physician (*History of Poland, in several letters to persons of quality,* London, 1698, Letter VI, pp. 3, 13). Despite personal damage inflicted by the Poles, the former's tone is also more objective.

56. Dolleczek, p. 121; Dalérac, p. 3.

57. Dolleczek, pp. 121–123; K. W. Freiherr von Mansberg, *Der Entsatz von Wien,* Berlin, 1883, pp. 48–55. Mansberg asserts (p. 55) that the *pancerny* thought themselves too good for any tactical function save charging in line of battle.

58. Dolleczek, pp. 123–125.

59. J. Deny, "Timar," *Encyclopedia of Islam,* Vol. IV, Pt. 2, Leyden, 1929, p. 769. After the reforms of Count de Bonneval in the 1720's two further corps were added, the *tulumbacı* (firemen) and *mühendı* (engineers). The traditional, classical order of the *kapu kulu* was composed of *seven* branches: those listed above (save the *lâğuncı*) plus the *toparabcı* ("gun drivers," i.e., artillery train), the *bostancı* (a praetorian guard always kept in Istanbul) and the *acemi oğlan* (see below, p. 190). The last two bodies are sometimes accounted part of the Janissaries, which illustrates well the great difficulty of trying to write meaningfully of the organization of the Ottoman army. The details of the massive source material available (collated somewhat indiscriminately, in Turkish, by Uzun Unzunçarşili) are quite confusing. The problem is made all the worse by interchangeable nomenclature and still unclarified abbreviations. The subject cries out for a systematic, logical, chronologically arranged survey—a job, probably, for a team of researchers rather than just one historian.

60. Stavrianos (Chapter Two, footnote 48), pp. 86–87.

61. Deny, p. 769; Ferdinando Luigi Marsigli, *Stato Militare Ottomano,* the Hague, 1732 (in French also in same volume), *passim;* Kreutel (Chapter Five, footnote 88), pp. 182, 184.

62. They were as follows: 1.) absolute obedience to officers; 2.) full accord and perfect union; 3.) abstinent behavior; 4.) adherence to Saint Haci Bektaş' principles of

piety; 5.) recruitment only by the *devşirme* and from prisoners of war; 6.) if needed, capital punishment only in a special, privileged form; 7.) seniority in promotions; 8.) punishment only by Janissary officers; 9.) guaranteed retirement; 10.) no beards; 11.) no marriage; 12.) no practicing of a trade or profession; 13.) residence in barracks; 14.) time to be utilized for training and exercise. Ahmed Djevad Bey, *État militaire ottoman*, Istanbul, 1882, pp. 55–56. The admission of ethnic Turks was not, of course, a primary cause of Janissary decline but rather a secondary one and, simultaneously, an effect; i.e., the manifestation of the clash between the *devşirme* class, deprived of its pristine vigor since becoming an hereditary interest group, and the old-aristocracy of Turkish rayah (see above, pp. 58–61).

63. They included the *kulkâhyaşı* ("governor of the servitors"); the *seymen başı* ("chief of the dog-keepers," constituting with the former and the Aga the three Janissary generals); the *zagarcibaşı* ("chief of the hunting-dog-keepers"); the *samsuncubaşı* ("chief of the bulldog-keepers"); the *turnacubaşı* ("chief of the crane-keepers"); and the *başçavuş* ("chief provost" or "chief army messenger"). Nahoum Weissmann, *Les Janissaires*, Paris, 1964, pp. 38–39.

64. *Ibid.*, p. 30.

65. *Ibid.*, *passim*; Djevad Bey, pp. 157–159; Meynert, pp. 118–123; *Feldzüge*, p. 554; Kreutel, p. 183.

66. Weissmann, pp. 46–48; Djevad Bey, pp. 172, 231. Bey, who examined relics in the Janissary supply dépôt, mentions a number of other weapons, both short and long range. Among the latter were sling-shots, hatchets, and catapults. Among the former were bludgeons, battle axes, flails, forks, lances, sickles, boathooks and halberds. Bey also distinguishes between sabers, rapiers, broadswords, and scimitars. There is no sure way of telling to what extent these older type weapons were used in 1683, but museum displays of booty in Western countries indicate that they certainly were not absent from the scene.

67. *Feldzüge*, p. 557; Meynert, pp. 124–125. Weissmann errs in stating that all the Porte's *sipâhi* were heavy cavalry.

68. Leo Barbar, "Zur wirtschaftlichen Grundlage des Feldzugs der Türken gegen Wien im Jahre 1683," *Wiener staatswissenschaftliche Studien*, Vol. 13, Heft I, pp. 1–46 (lists twenty different categories of service for Christians); Denis, p. 769; Stavrianos, pp. 86–87. Denis claims that the territorial *sipâhi* were better disciplined than their Portal colleagues, but this is hard to believe since the former were "reserves" and the latter "regulars." The impression one gains from the Turkish sources for the events of 1683 is also the opposite.

69. J. C. G. Hayne, *Abhandlung über die Kriegskunst der Türken*, Berlin, 1783, pp. 29–30; Montecuccoli, pp. 345–346; *Feldzüge*, pp. 559–60, 628.

70. E. Petrach, "Zur Geschichte und kunsthistorischen Würdigung der Türkenbeute des Markgrafen Ludwig Wilhelm," *Zeitschrift für Geschichte des Oberrheins*, Vol. 100 (1952), pp. 566–691, *passim*.

71. *Idem*.

72. In speaking of Ottoman horrors it is well to remember Christian bestiality during the Thirty Years' War or the murderous ferocity of the Puritans in Ireland. To be sure, in the former case, it was the unusual length of the conflict with an attendant breakdown of almost all social order that led to atrocities on so broad a scale. In the latter instance, as with the Ottomans, religious fanaticism bears much of the blame. In any event, Western European wars were waged with *relative* gentleness in the latter seventeenth century. The experience of the first four decades may well have been traumatic.

73. Hayne, pp. 38–55; cf. Montecuccoli, pp. 260–261.

74. *Feldzüge*, pp. 565–568. The authors overstress the insufficiency of the Turkish supply system. There is evidence to indicate that in 1683 at least careful preparation were made. (See Barbar *loc. cit.*; Montecuccoli, pp. 208–209; and Viktor von Renner, "Türkische Urkunden den Krieg des Jahres 1683 betreffend nach den Aufzeichnungen des Marc' Antonio Mamucha della Torre," *Jahrbuch des Leopoldstädter Gymnasiums*, Vienna, 1888).

75. *Feldzüge*, p. 568.

76. *Ibid.*, pp. 569–570; Hayne, pp. 208–209; Montecuccoli, *passim.*
77. *Feldzüge,* p. 594; Weissmann, pp. 47–48, 52.
78. Benaglia (Chapter Two, footnote 63) , p. 141.
79. *Ibid.,* p. 140.

Chapter Seven

1. Kreutel, MS (Chapter Five, footnote 88) ; Necati (Chapter Five, footnote 19) , pp. 663–664.
2. *Idem.*
3. Benaglia (Chapter Two, footnote 63) , p. 68ff.; Cantemir ([Chapter One, footnote 90], p. 299) asserts that it was the pavillions of the Sultan and Kara Mustafa that were overturned.
4. Benaglia, p. 100ff.; Constantin Jireček, *Die Heerstrasse von Belgrad nach Constantinopel,* Prague, 1877, pp. 113ff.
5. Kreutel, MS; Necati, pp. 664–665.
6. Rycault (Chapter Two, footnote 54) , p. 99.
7. *Idem.*
8. Georg Christof Kunitz, *Diarium, etc.,* Vienna, 1684, p. 6.
9. E. Veress, "Il Conte Marsili in Ungheria," *Corvina,* Vol. XIX–XX (1930) , p. 27.
10. Benaglia, p. 122.
11. Kreutel, MS.
12. Veress, p. 19. The figures for the Tatars and the Rumanians derive from Kunitz, p. 6, the Court Master of Ceremonies, and the relevant Austrian source (which gives a slightly higher count than the first two; see footnote 14) .
13. For the Magyars, see Chapter Nine, footnote 5.
14. The estimates of the Austrians (who first saw the Turks at Győr when the latter were at their fullest strength) , while somewhat contradictory, tend to support a relatively low, overall total. Some of the Imperials maintained that there were 100,000 enemy "hommes de guerre"; others held that there were 150,000 and still others said only 80,000 if one subtracted the separately encamped Tatars. What made any compilation hazardous was the fact that the Turkish tents were arranged in a very irregular manner. (François Le Bègue, "Le Journal de la première campagne de hongrie en 1683," in Ferdinand Stöller, "Neue Quellen zur Geschichte des Türkenjahres 1683," *MIöG,* Erg.-B XXIII, Heft I (1933) , p. 75) . Other contemporary estimates are of dubious value. According to second-hand information that the Austrians received from Venice and Rome there were supposed to be some 200,000 of the foe. Le Bègue's final estimate, 300,000, while probably correct with respect to several individual contingents, also seems greatly inflated. The breakdown is as follows: a.) 240,000 warriors, including 8,000 Egyptians, 37,000 Janissaries, 30,000 Istanbul *sipâhi,* 24,000 Tatars, 6,000 Wallachians, 6,000 Moldavians, and the rest feudatories; b.) 32,000 artillerymen, miners and engineers; and c.) 30,000 "gens de vivres." (*Ibid.;* "Récit du Secours de Vienne en l'Année 1683," in Stöller, pp. 16–17) . The impossibly high figure of 400,000 given in the Austrian army's own study, *Das Kriegsjahr 1683* (Vienna, 1883) , p. 53, is obtained by adding to Le Bègue's final calculation a rough guess of 100,000 for Thököly's bands and the camp followers. (For analysis of le Bègue as a source, see footnote 28.)
15. Klopp (Chapter One, footnote 27) , pp. 182–184; Montecuccoli (Chapter Six, footnote 7) , pp. 209–210.
16. Necati, p. 666; Klopp, pp. 190–192; Renner (Chapter One, footnote 3) , pp. 184–196. Caprara, after many adventures, reached the Imperial lines near Tulln on August 10 (Benaglia, p. 134) .
17. According to the Silâhdar (Kreutel, MS) . The Turkish historian also reports that Mustafa Efendi argued that the electors would then recognize Thököly as emperor; Kara Mustafa, enriched by Vienna's treasures, would be able to use Thököly as a tool; would be covered with glory both in the now and in the hereafter; and could spend the rest of his life in peace. This information supports the assumption that the Grand Vezir was driven forward not so much by greed as by the need to secure his own position. The Silâhdar does not corroborate Cantemir's assertion that Kara Mustafa was seeking to establish his own sultanate. See above, p. 71.

18. See Chapter Five, footnote 106.

19. Whether one should use the word "King" rather than "Prince" is difficult to determine. The Turkish sources refer to Thököly unequivocally as *qral*, but the Magyar leader's Latin pronouncements and coins bear the humbler title of "Princeps." Presumably Thököly was simply taking care not to offend the sensibilities of his fellow Hungarians, who, after all, had not elected him to royal office. A related question is what territory was connected with the Turkish appointment. In the fall of 1682 the Turks linked Thököly with their own particular concept of "Central," i.e., eastern Upper Hungary. After Osijek, both the rebel and his new suzerain seem to have thought of Hungary in a more general way.

20. Kreutel, MS; Necati, p. 666; Klopp, pp. 192–193.

21. According to the Silâhdar (who was not personally present). The diary of the Court Master of Ceremonies gives no details of the meeting.

22. Klopp, p. 194.

23. Lorenz (Preface, page i), p. 197.

24. The reasoning is Dr. Kreutel's (letter, October 8, 1964).

25. Necati, p. 668.

26. *Das Kriegsjahr 1683*, pp. 12–22; Wrede (Chapter Six, footnote 6), p. 30.

27. Newald (Chapter One, footnote 3), I, pp. 48–82; Sauer (Chapter Five, footnote 116), pp. 10–11; Renner, pp. 96–110; V. Zahn, "Das Jahr 1683 in Steiermark," *Mitteilungen des historischen Vereines für Steiermark*, Vol. 31 (1883), pp. 67–117. The cash sums mentioned above and elsewhere are hardly meaningful today. Hence a few comments about money and its value in the seventeenth century are appropriate. When cited in figures, the florin or gulden, constituting 60 kreuzers, does not represent a real gold or silver coin but only an accounting unit that remained unchanged from the sixteenth century until 1857 when the decimal system was introduced. The actual pieces used were various kinds of thalers and ducats. In keeping with the complexities of economic growth and finance, their precious metal content, reckoned in "accounting florins," gradually lessened while the number of kreuzers, into which they, too, were divided, increased. In 1682 the (accounting) florin was the equivalent of .9442 grams fine gold or 14.834 grams pure silver. The thaler was then made up of 102 kr. and the ducat of 219 kr. (A. F. Pribram, *Materialien zur Geschichte der Preise und Löhne in Österreich*, Vol. I, Vienna, 1938, *passim*.) A rough idea of purchasing power at this time may be gained by comparing the army pay scale (Chapter Six, footnote 33) with the following prices, which obtained in Vienna before the inflation of the siege: 1 lb. of beef cost 3½ kr.; 1 lb. of veal, 4 kr.; 1 lb. of pork, 5 kr.; 1 lb. of mutton, 3½ kr.; 1 lb. of bacon, 8 kr.; a brace of small chickens, 8 kr.; a capon, 45 kr.; 3 lb. of bread, 2 kr.; 1 lb. of fresh butter, 10 kr.; 1 lb. of plain cheese, 6 kr.; 1 lb. of rice, 9 kr. (A pound was slightly more than the current U.S. standard.) Food prices were apparently moderate in terms of income (although not for the poorly paid recruit). Manufactured goods seem to have been far more expensive. A pair of shoes, for example, cost a whole thaler. The City Council paid 160 fl. for a hammered silver wedding cup presented to the burgomaster's daughter. (See Renner, *op. cit., passim;* and Albert Camesina, *Wien und seine Bewohner während der zweiten Türkenbelagerung*, Vienna, 1862, pp. 37–38).

28. *Das Kriegsjahr 1683*, pp. 19–22, presents (with but one exception) only the favorable aspect of Austria's war preparations. The three contemporary accounts in Ferdinand Stöller are far more critical, especially with respect to the condition of Vienna's fortifications (e.g., p. 12). Two of them, the "Récit" and the "Journal," were written by a Lorraine bureaucrat, ducal confident, and personal witness of the events described (i.e., Le Bègue). While they are the best records available for military operation, their utilization presents certain difficulties. The "Récit" is a defense of Charles' management of affairs, written later in the year; the "Journal" seems to be a somewhat more spontaneous work. Sometimes the two versions supplement each other; sometimes they are contradictory. In the latter case, it is not always possible to determine which is more likely to be correct. Is the "Récit" merely a correction in light of more accurate later knowledge, or does it change the original to make the Duke look better? (The third source is discussed in footnote 77).

29. "Récit," pp. 11–12; "Mémoire Badois" (Hermann of Baden), *Akta*, pp. 631–632.

30. Georg Kittler, "Georg Rimpler, Kaiserlicher Obristleutnant und Oberingenieur im Türkenkrieg," *Zeitschrift für die Geschichte des Oberreheins,* Vol. 99 (60), Heft 1, 1951, pp. 139–189, *passim.* A second article of Kittler ("Neue Beiträge zur Beurteilung Georg Rimplers, etc.," *MIöG,* Vol. LXIV [1956], pp. 25–33) presents a plan and a detailed discussion of the Győr fortress, which, when completed, was most formidable.

31. No single English word can convey the exact Magyar meaning of either the Rábaköz or the Szigetköz. "Köz" is an island in the specific sense of terrain that lies *between* rivers. It is thus not quite the same as the German "Aue" (see Chapter Nine, footnote 29). "Sziget" is an island as the word is more generally understood, i.e., ground surrounded by water. "Schütt" is not as difficult a term. It is Middle High German for "inundation" and, in a slightly different form *(Schutt),* Modern High German for "detritus," especially fluviatile (alluvium). "Csalló" is merely the Magyar name for the Malý Dunaj. The "Golden Garden" was another (German) designation for the area, which suffered a disastrous flood as recently as 1954. For the appearance of the Rábaköz in 1683, see the reproduction of one of Count Marsigli's maps in E. Lovarini, *La schiavitù del generale Marsigli sotto i Tartari e i Turchi,* Bologna, 1931, pp. 141–142. For the problem of Lake Neusiedl see Andrew Burckhardt's exemplary monograph, *Borderland: a Historical and Geographic Study of Burgenland, Austria,* Madison, 1962, pp. 15–16.

32. E. Lovarini, *Autobiografia di Luigi Ferdinando Marsigli,* Bologna, 1930, pp. 36–41.

33. "Récit," pp. 12–13; "Journal," pp. 55–60.

34. The "Récit" places the meeting on May 9, the "Journal" on May 7. The former apparently confuses the final, decisive meeting (May 9) with the preliminary one (May 7). There also appears to have been an even earlier session at Bratislava on May 5, at which Marsigli's latest map was used (Newald, p. 89; Lovarini, *Autobiografia,* p. 41).

35. "Journal," p. 60.

36. Renner, pp. 179–180.

37. "Récit," p. 14; "Journal," p. 61. Apparently the Court War Council (May 9), contrary to Lorraine's staff (May 7), preferred Nové Zámky since Leopold's instructions carry this implication ("Mémoire Badois," *Akta,* p. 632).

38. Lovarini, *La schiavitù,* pp. 142–144; *Autobiografia,* p. 42.

39. "Journal," pp. 63–67; HHSA, Lothringisches Hausarchiv (carton 96, folio 390), mss. 227, 232, Le Bègue's letters of May 27 and June 13 to Monsieur Canon (a Ducal functionary in Vienna). Charles apparently first doubted the wisdom of attacking Esztergom upon being informed—erroneously—that the Turks had crossed the Drava in force. Even after obtaining more correct intelligence, there were other good reasons for desisting (lack of forage, endangered supply route, proximity of Turkish reinforcements at Buda). "Journal," p. 67. Hermann claims that the Duke's own generals had forewarned him of the difficulties ("Mémoire Badois," *Akta,* p. 633). Lorraine's reasons for proceeding to Nové Zámky were: a.) to preserve the Emperor's reputation by not wasting the three-week interval before the expected arrival of the main Turkish force; b.) news that the Turks were still on the far side of the Drava; c.) the more isolated site of Nové Zámky; d.) relative safety because of favorable potamic relationships; e.) Nové Zámky's outmoded works; f.) the place's strategic importance; and g.) the possibility of help from Schultz in case of an attempt at relief by "part" of the Ottoman field army. *Idem.*

40. The intriguing in Vienna continued. Lorraine's main source of support continued to be the "faction of the three Eleanoras." Leopold's wife, who believed Charles to have the support of a majority at the Court, nevertheless advised him to send someone of stature to present his case, and the Duke himself was anxious to have his viewpoint explained in the "gazettes." HHSA, mss. 236, 234, two letters of Canon to Le Bègue of June 13 and Le Bègue to Canon, June 19.

41. *Ibid.,* mss. 228, 229, 230, 232, Le Bègue to Canon June 8, 9, 10, 13. Leopold's letters, written in Italian with gold ink and preserved alongside the Le Bègue material *(ibid.,* mss. 15–63), are further examples of the practically illegible Imperial scrawl. These documents also cover the months of July, August, and early September but become increasingly briefer as the ruler's involvement in military affairs lessens—a

development which itself may partly be due to the events of May and June. See below, p. 312.

42. *Ibid.,* mss. 231, 232, 233, Le Bègue to Canon June 12, 13, 18; "Récit," p. 13; "Journal," pp. 70–75. Hermann's own account ("Mémoire Badois") naturally takes the Duke severely to account.

43. Lovarini, *Schiavitú,* pp. 12–14; *Autobiografia,* p. 43. Hermann and Lorraine also disagreed on the details of defending Győr. The War Minister, whose belief in the subordination of field forces to fortresses did not go so far as to require support when the odds against the exposed troops seemed overwhelming, favored the Szigetköz in order to have a guaranteed route of retreat. Charles, who did not believe in Győr's capacity to resist a full-scale onslaught from all but one direction (which would be the case if Hermann's plan were followed) held that Turkish numerical superiority could be compensated by facing the enemy on the *equal-length* front which his own dispositions would assure. Le Bègue, at any rate, failed to recognize that the Badener's predilection for fortresses was subject to rational limitations. This is clear from his sarcastic observation: "et En tout cecy je vois le maxime que jay ouy dire de tout le monde fort boulversé scavoir que les armees doivent estre pour la deffense des pays et des places et non pas exposer les places et les pays pour l'armée." *(Sic).* HHSA, ms. 235, Le Bègue to Canon, June 21. Initially the Duke had toyed with another idea. Afraid that the Turks would be able to entrench themselves easily on the glacis, he began to build outworks there for the field army (i.e., *east* of the Rába, whose mouth watered the moat). But the covered way and the palisading were unfinished, and so the idea proved impractical. "Journal," pp. 73–74.

44. "Auff dises abziehen von Neuheyssl seyn die maisten Vngern von Lager heymb nach hauss gangen. Vnd haben kein Vertrauen mehr zu den Teutschen gehabt. Die Kartollischen vnterdessen haben sich greulliches Trowort Verlauten Lassen, wie man die Vungern sambt den Lutherischen wirt auss rotten." Tschanny (Chapter One, footnote 77), p. 69. See also Chapter One, footnote 39.

45. "Journal," p. 72.

46. Bruck initially resisted the enemy assaults, but, as the number of the foe increased, its position became untenable. It seemed the better part of wisdom to ask Thököly (rather than the Grand Vezir) for protection. In return for non-molestation the population had to send supplies to the Turkish encampment at Vienna, including at one point 200 chickens, 100 geese, 10 turkeys ("Gallos Indiacos"), 800 eggs and 300 lb. of onions for Kara Mustafa's own kitchen. Kurt Holter, "Türkische Urkunden für Bruck a. d. Leitha aus dem Jahr 1683," *Unsere Heimat,* Vol. IX (1936), pp. 268–269.

47. Esterházy's letter is printed in its Latin original in Freiherr Philipp von Diersburg Röder's *Des Markgrafen Ludwig Wilhelm von Baden Feldzüge wider die Türken,* Vol. I ("Urkunden"); Karlsruhe, 1839, pp. 10ff. and, in German translation, in Klopp, pp. 195–197. Kalmán Thaly, *Az 1683-iki taborzás történtéhez* ("Concerning the History of the 1683 Campaign"), Budapest, 1883, convincingly defends the Magyar loyalists against unfair criticism from Austro-German writers.

48. The "Journal," p. 75, mentions swimming and fording only, but there is no evidence that all the bridges were destroyed.

49. Lovarini, *Schiavitú,* pp. 60–63, 144–170; *Autobiografia,* pp. 43–45.

50. Gaetan Guillot, "Un témoin italien de la guerre des Impériaux contre les Turcs 1683," *Revue d'histoire diplomatique,* Vol. 28 (1914), pp. 163–164.

51. Both the "Récit" (p. 16) and the "Journal" (p. 75) speak of Austrian regiments being "dans le Rabau," but it is unlikely that they had penetrated deeply, since Marsigli, who was not far away at that time, makes no mention of them. Indeed, the Italian notes that a plea to the Duke for help, brought the reply that *repeated* orders from Vienna prevented the sending of Germans (Lovarini, *Schiavitù,* pp. 60–61). Apparently, even if the lateral bridge across the swamp had been ready, direct authorization from the Emperor would have been necessary, the approach of the main Turkish force notwithstanding.

Moson (Wieselburg) and Magyaróvár (Ungarisch-Altenburg) were separate towns in 1683 but have since grown together.

52. "Journal," p. 77; "Récit," p. 18; Marczali, O. von Uechtritz Steinkirch, *Heinrich*

Tobias Freiherr von Hasslingen: ein Beitrag zur Geschichte der Befreiung Wiens im Jahre 1683, Breslau, 1883, p. 21. Leslie left the Szigetöz on the fifth because the Turks had sent a strong detachment across the Rábca. He was apparently worried about his own cavalry-less position and fearful that the enemy march upon Vienna had begun. He withdrew to the Velký Ostrov Žitný. The Duke thereupon decided to build two bridges across the main Danube opposite and below Bratislava in order to communicate with Leslie's units and to reoccupy the Szigetköz, should Vienna order such a move. The events of the seventh put an end to these plans. "Journal," pp. 76–77; Newald, Part II, pp. 18–19. The Court remained unhappy about the separation of the infantry and cavalry, fearing that the largely ungarrisoned capital would be overrun by the Turks before its own army could be reunited. Letter of Borgomanero, July 18, AGS, 3925.

53. "Journal," p. 78; "Récit," p. 19; Marczali, p. 45. Hermann ("Mémoire Badois," *Akta,* pp. 637–638) accuses Lorraine of mismanaging the encounter and claims that the baggage ought not to have been sent forward since confusion could thus have been prevented. However, considering the proverbial "fog (in this case, dust) of war" Charles seems to have acted wisely.

54. Kittler, p. 190, is unfair to Charles when he asserts that there was no need for the Austrians to withdraw from Győr since the enemy flanking movement was only by "weak" forces. Turkish sources (Kreutel, MS) indicate that it was the whole enemy vanguard, some 28,000 men. It is also clear from Le Bègue's account that the Duke did not fall back because he was *sure* that the Turks were heading from Vienna.

Another, somewhat different interpretation of Lorraine's retirement has been that he was merely adhering to the principles of his own mentor, Montecuccoli, a man who believed in avoiding battle until the prospects of victory were certain (Lorenz, p. 198). Whether or not one accepts this view, it is clear that the situation of July 1683 was atypical. It did not fit the customary, *Western*-oriented military mold of the latter seventeenth century, an age of relatively small, highly trained, expensive-to-maintain professional armies. The normal strategy of exhaustion, the policy of evading risks while endeavoring to wear down one's opponent, was simply not applicable to the events in question. The usual presuppositions—that both participants aimed for the same object, that their forces were roughly equal, that they behaved like gentlemen— were missing in an Eastern theatre of operations. The Turk was bent upon achieving complete annihilation with one massive stroke; see above, p. 195.

55. Cf. Max Braubach, *Prinz Eugen von Savoyen,* Vol. I, "Aufstieg," Munich, 1963, pp. 80–85. Eugene was contemplating going to Austria already beforehand (whereby Borgomanero probably also played a role).

56. "Journal," p. 78; "Mémoire Badois," *Akta,* p. 638.

57. Cantemir, pp. 303–304, mentions a second council of war and claims that Kara Mustafa's decision to march upon Vienna was prompted by the news that the Emperor had fled, that the city was in confusion, and that it was necessary for the Grand Vezir to work up the Janissaries in order to strengthen his case. Neither the Silâhdar, the Court Master of Ceremonies, the Grand Dragoman (Alexandros Mavrokordatos; Chapter Five, footnote 88), nor Kunitz have anything to say about this. The story is also unlikely because of chronological difficulties. (Cantemir's account of the earlier meeting also conflicts with the sources from inside the Ottoman camp.)

58. Kreutel, MS; Necati, pp. 668–669; Renner, p. 246.

59. Kreutel, MS; Necati, pp. 669–670; Renner, p. 217.

60. Kreutel, MS.

61. Kreutel (Preface, footnote 2), pp. 24–29.

62. *Ibid.,* p. 28.

63. Renner, pp. 112–113.

64. *Ibid.,* pp. 113–115. Recatholicized Vienna was well garrisoned by religious. In the Inner City alone there were eleven houses, of which three were Jesuit. There were also seven female convents. For the laity, there were confraternities, of which the most famous was the Brotherhood of the Dead. E. Tomek, "Die Bedeutung Wiens als Vorort der Christenheit in den Türkenkriegen," in Othenio Abel, *Wien: sein Boden und Geschichte,* Vienna, 1924, pp. 269–282.

65. Renner, pp. 117–118.

66. *Ibid.,* pp. 123–133.

67. *Ibid.,* pp. 133–140.

68. Baur (Chapter Four, footnote 49), p. 361.

69. See below, p. 318.

70. Renner, pp. 140–152.

71. Ludwig Eberle, "Wien als Festung 1530–1740," *Geschichte der Stadt Wien,* Vol. IV-1, Vienna, 1911, p. 218.

72. The huge sums of money required came from different sources: from the City, from the Imperial and Provincial Estates, from special local taxes and duties (including an entrance fee to town), from various German cities, from rich merchants, from the Church, from excise taxes and fines. *Ibid.,* pp. 276–277.

73. *Ibid.,* pp. 219–229.

74. Dalérac, p. 63.

75. Marczali, p. 65.

76. Of Vienna's bastions, only one remains in faintly recognizable condition today. It is the *Mölkerbastei,* directly across the Ring Boulevard from the New University. There is also a visible remnant of the old courtine in the street still called the *Dominikaner-bastei* ("The Preacher"). The memory of six other bulwarks is preserved in the form of street names. The fortifications system as such was demolished in 1858. In its place arose the lovely Boulevard, which runs, roughly speaking, along the former line of the counterscarp and the inner margin of the glacis. A fragment of the old moat lies behind the New Hofburg.

77. "Relation du siège de Vienne par un officier de la garnison," Stöller, p. 128. Contrary to Stöller's identification of the author as a certain Lt. Col. Hoffmann, it is almost certain that the "Relation" stems from the Count of Provana (Marczali). The style, the framework of the narrative, even whole sentences are the same. (Marczali's "Relation" derives irrefutably from the Count).

78. The cunette, a ditch dug in the moat itself, was intended to force the foe to dig even deeper and thus to hit ground water. It was also useful for receiving the débris from any breach, thus preventing the enemy from using the former as a ladder to mount an assault.

79. "Relation," p. 128.

80. Kittler, p. 192.

81. The individual stakes were about eight feet long and eight to nine "fists" thick. They were not round but flat, like cricket bats. The space between them was large enough for a man to pass through. Similar obstacles were *fraises,* which protruded from ravelin scarps. François, Comte de Pagan, *Les fortifications du Comte de Pagan,* Paris, 1689, pp. 48–49.

82. It could hold 35–40 men. *Grosses, vollständiges Universal-Lexicon,* Vol. V, Leipzig-Halle, 1733, p. 676.

83. A fausse-braye was a low wall lying in front of the courtine in the moat. It helped to defend the latter after the enemy had succeeded in lodging himself upon the covered way. *Idem.*

84. Kittler, pp. 193–194.

85. *Ibid.,* pp. 194–196.

86. Camesina, p. 206; Klopp, p. 206; and (most strongly) *Das Kriegsjahr 1683,* pp. 130–131; take the unfavorable view. Newald's rebuttal (I, pp. 19–44, 99–100, 105–109), while proving that the Austrian government *began* to take appropriate action well in advance, does not show that the measures were either sufficient or completed in time.

87. The minister of Hesse-Darmstadt recorded in December that several hundred unemployed people had been put to work on the walls. In March he noted that construction was once again underway with the help of the rural population (*robot*). Baur, *passim.* Newald (footnote 86) lists other steps.

88. Marczali, pp. 50, 57. Other eyewitness critics of Vienna's defenses include: Le Bègue ("Récit" and "Journal," pp. 20, 79); Starhemberg (letter of July 11, 1683, quoted in Klopp, p. 206); the French ambassador (Marius Vachon, "Un deuxième centenaire: la France et l'Autriche au siège de Vienne en 1683," *La Nouvelle Revue,* Vol. 23 [1883], p. 947); Contarini (FRA, XVVIII, p. 240); a soldier participant, Huhn

([Chapter One, footnote 3], p. 20) ; and the semi-official historian of the siege, Johann Ruess (*Wahrhaffte und gründliche Relation, etc.*, Vienna, 1683, p. 4). The most mordant comment of all came from an anonymous, yet credible sounding siege veteran, probably of English nationality: "Yet whenever they suffer themselves in such a state to be surprized for the future, they are accountable to their own follies for neglecting the Means, for they are not always to expect God should work by Miracles." *The present state Of The German and Turkish Empires. . . . Together with Memoirs OF the siege of Vienna By an Emminent Officer in that city*, London, 1684, p. 89.

89. Kittler, p. 193; "Récit," p. 20; Renner, pp. 157–163. The Count of Provana (Marczali, p. 47) suggests that the reason the government did not really expect an attack upon Vienna was that it could not conceive of the Turks advancing without first having taken Komárno and Győr.

90. Newald, pp. 19–44, 105–107, *passim;* Baur, p. 359; *Das Kriegsjahr 1683*, p. 131.

91. Nicolaus Hocke, *Kurtze Beschreibung* etc., Vienna, 1685, pp. 221–230. There were many more guns in the dépôt that were not even used, over 800 altogether if one is to believe the Count of Provana (Marczali, p. 50). The existence of this reserve greatly facilitated the defense.

92. Dolleczek (Chapter Six, footnote 21), pp. 252–271.

93. Klopp, pp. 227–228; Kreutel, pp. 141–143; Dalérac, p. 65; Marczali, p. 50.

94. Baur, p. 353.

95. Alois Veltze, "Das Kriegswesen," *Geschichte der Stadt Wien*, pp. 160–168.

96. Hocke, pp. 23–33.

97. Veltze, pp. 185–197.

98. *Ibid.*, pp. 202–213.

99. Gustav Gugitz, "1683 und die Bürger Wiens: Legende und Geschichte," *Unsere Heimat*, Vol. 25 (1954), pp. 108–120; Newald, I, pp. 129–140, 159–172.

100. Andreas, Graf Thürheim, *Feldmarschall Ernst Rüdiger Graf Starhemberg, Wiens ruhmvoller Vertheidiger*, Vienna, 1882, *passim*.

101. The following excerpt from a letter to his cousin, written during the disastrous Austrian siege of Buda in 1684, is illustrative of his self-righteous tone (as well as of contemporary Austro-German and the Count's errant orthography) : "Und dued noch alle zeid das widerschbill dessen was ich einrate. Dises ist die lezte campagnia die ich mache unter dem commando eines anderen, denn der keiser und kein mensch kann mihr aufdragen, das ich die reputation, so ich mid so grosser mie erworwen, durch anderer leid feler und capricien verlieren solle und mihr hernach imputiren lassen, was andere gedann hawen." Victor von Renner, "Vertrauliche Briefe des Grafen Ernst Rüdeger (*sic*) von Starhemberg an seinen Vetter den Grafen Gundacker von Starhemberg aus den Jahren 1682–1699," *Wiener Communal-Kalendar und Städtisches Jahrbuch*, 28 (18), 1890, p. 156.

102. Rinck (Chapter One, footnote 4), p. 41.

103. Venetian Ambassador Veniers (1690), FRA, p. 315.

104. See footnote 101.

Chapter Eight

1. Baur (Chapter Four, footnote 49), p. 381.

2. Newald (Chapter One, footnote 3), II, pp. 20–22; Renner (Chapter One, footnote 3), pp. 218–219; cf. Chapter Five, footnote 52. W. Pillich, "Die Flüchtung der Schatzkammer, des Archivs und der Hofbibliothek aus Wien im Jahre 1683," *Mitteilungen des österreichischen Staatsarchivs*, Vol. X (1957), p. 137, gives a slightly different version.

3. Baur, p. 387; Watzl (Kleinschrott), (Preface, footnote 2), *passim*. The beating of the Jesuits aroused satisfaction, as did the siege itself, among the Calvinists of far-away New England, who regarded the events of 1683 as God's just vengeance upon the House of Habsburg. Vaughn, Dorothy M., *Europe and the Turk: A Pattern of Alliances 1350–1700*, Liverpool, 1954, pp. 271–2.

4. Newald, I, pp. 93–94.

5. Menčík (Chapter One, footnote 3), pp. 218–219; Borgomanero's letter, Linz, July 18, AGS, 3923; Renner, p. 224; Leopold to Waldeck, Vienna, July 7, HHSA, "Kriegsarchiv," fasc. 210.

6. Renner, pp. 224–225.

7. Johann Peter von Vaelckeren, *WIENN von Türcken belägert / von Christen ent-setzt*, Linz, 1684, pp. 9–10.

8. Johann Ferdinand Fischer, *DIARIUM* (of the siege), Regensburg (no date; evidently 1683–1684) , p. 2.

9. Huhn (Chapter One, footnote 3) , p. 11.

10. Marczali (Chapter 6, footnote 9) , p. 51. ". . . dans le temps même ou il paroissoit que sa perte étoit inévitable ses habitants dormaient dans une indolente sécurité. A l'égard des paysans qui s'y étoient refugié il y en eut beaucoup que se tirent de la misère en prenant parti dans les troupes ce qui aidoit à les soutenir." *Ibid.*, p. 179.

11. Baur, p. 384.

12. Hocke (Chapter Seven, footnote 91) , pp. 1–2; Newald, I, p. 96; II, pp. 23–28. Nineteenth-century Czech nationalism led to the making of extreme claims for Kapliřs. See Josef, Freiherr von Helfert, *Der Chef der Wiener Stadt-Vertheidigung 1683 gegen die Türken*, Prague-Leipzig, 1883.

13. *Ibid.*, pp. 3–5; Newald, I, pp. 97–98; "Récit," "Journal" (Chapter Seven, footnote 14) , pp. 20, 29; Joannes Constantius Feigius, *Adlers-Krafft oder Europaeischer Helden-kranz*, etc., Vienna, 1685, p. 18.

14. Hocke, pp. 6–7; "Journal," p. 79; anonymous, *Glaubwürdiges Diarium, etc.*, Vienna, 1683, p. 5; J. P. Kaltenbeck, "Belagerung Wiens durch die Türken 1683: Bericht eines Augustinermönchs," *Österreichische Zeitung*, Vol. I, (1835) , p. 107.

15. Pillich, pp. 138–147.

16. Newald, I, pp. 107–113; II, pp. 36–52.

17. G. V. Ghelen, *Kurtze . . . Erzelung* etc., Vienna (?) , 1684, p. 4; Marczali, p. 55; Huhn, p. 22; Renner, p. 245; "Récit," p. 21.

18. Hocke, p. 13; "Journal," pp. 79–80; Newald, I, p. 114.

19. Kreutel (Preface, footnote 2) , pp. 32–33.

20. Newald, I, p. 114, footnote 1.

21. *Das Kriegsjahr 1683* (Chapter Seven, footnote 14) , pp. 137–138; Hocke, pp. 15–16.

22. *Ibid.*, p. 24; "Récit," p. 20, Huhn, p. 33; Newald, I, p. 115–116; *Das Kriegsjahr 1683*, p. 48; O. v. Uechtritz-Steinkirch, op. cit. (Chapter Seven, footnote 52) , pp. 21–22.

23. Newald, I, pp. 119–120. For a more favorable view of clerical participants, see L. Hartmann, "Die Wiener Jesuiten während der Türkenbelagerung 1683," *Die Reichs-post*, March 28, 1933, pp. 18–19.

24. Vaelckeren, p. 28; Ghelen, p. 5; Hocke, p. 35.

25. *Ibid.*, p. 36; Feigius, p. 28; Vaelckeren, p. 30; Hummelberger (Chapter Six, footnote 10) , pp. 80–81; "Relation" (Chapter Seven, footnotes 28, 77) , p. 129.

26. Ruess (Chapter Seven, footnote 88) , pp. 10–11.

27. Huhn, pp. 55–56.

28. Marczali, p. 58. See also footnote 34.

29. Kreutel, pp. 30–31; Klopp, pp. 221–223. Ahmed Bey allegedly, had advised against an attack upon the weakest point of all, the bastions opposite the spit of land where the Wien River and the Danube Arm converge: the danger of a sudden torrent in the former stream seemed too great. Such a gamble would probably have paid off, however.

30. Kunitz (Chapter Seven, footnote 8) , p. 6. Kunitz subtracted the 10,000 unarmed Rumanians and 20,000 Tatars, who were also present at Vienna. See above, p. 204.

31. The sources conflict as to the date of the ultimatum and the manner of delivery. The fourteenth seems most likely. The text may be found in Georg Jacob, "Türkische Urkunden," *Der Islam*, Vol. VII (1917) , pp. 281–286.

32. It is not clear from the sources whether the cannonade began on the fourteenth or the fifteenth.

33. Kreutel, pp. 141–143.

34. *Glaubwürdiges Diarium*, pp. 6–7; *Das Kriegsjahr 1683*, pp. 154–155; Klopp, pp. 223–224. Many Viennese believe that the Trautson Palace was the location of *the* Grand Vezirial tent, the idea apparently being based upon a misleading sentence in Renner (p. 277) . A contemporary plan of Rimpler's fellow Saxon and colleague, Daniel Suttinger, does indeed show *a* tent at this spot, but the fancy *pavillion* was clearly located "auf der Schmelz," as is apparent from other drawings of the time and from the context of Kreutel. Had Kara Mustafa set up his main tents so close to the trenches he would also have been within range of cannon fire from the city.

35. Vaelckeren, pp. 21–22.

36. "Relation," p. 130; *Glaubwürdiges Diarium,* p. 8.

37. Hocke, p. 41.

38. *Das Kriegsjahr 1683,* pp. 158–160 (date given here incorrect) ; Kreutel, pp. 36–37; "Récit," "Journal," pp. 21–22, 81; Huhn, pp. 52–54.

39. Vaelckeren, p. 34; Hocke, p. 34; Ghelen, p. 10; Kreutel, pp. 37–38.

40. Marczali, p. 60; Kreutel, p. 40; "Relation," p. 130; anonymous, *Das Geängstigte und wider erquickte Wien,* Vienna, 1683, p. 2.

41. "Relation," pp. 130–131.

42. Hocke, p. 51.

43. Marczali, p. 60.

44. "Relation," p. 131; Hocke, p. 61; Vaelckeren, p. 73; Newald, II, pp. 65, 75–77. Lacy may have been an ancestor of Maria Theresa's general, Count Franz Moritz Lacy (Lascy) , but I have had no occasion to research the question. Can he have also been the author of the anonymous account quoted in footnote 76?

45. Kunitz, p. 6; Kreutel, pp. 52–53; Vaelckeren, p. 41; Huhn, p. 47.

46. Kunitz, p. 7; Kreutel, p. 47; Hocke, p. 68; "Relation," p. 131. Heider was later released.

47. Marczali, pp. 63–64; "Relation," pp. 131–132; Kreutel, pp. 58, 62.

48. *Ibid.,* pp. 60–63, 67, 68; "Relation," p. 132; Vaelckeren, p. 48 (cf. Renner, p. 297) ; Newald, I, p. 140.

49. "Relation," pp. 132–133; Hocke, p. 106; O. von Duncker, "Drei Berichte aus dem belagerten Wien 1683," MKA, Vol. VII (1893) , pp. 269–270.

50. *Ibid.,* pp. 60, 75, 80, 109, 153; Ruess, pp. 39–49.

51. Renner, pp. 339–341.

52. *Ibid.,* pp. 341–346.

53. Hocke, p. 188; also quoted by Renner, p. 346.

54. *Ibid.,* pp. 346–353.

55. *Ibid.,* pp. 353–360. Renner indicts only the Jesuits (see footnote 23) .

56. Laifle (Chapter Four, footnote 2) , *passim.*

57. Hocke, p. 162; also quoted by Renner, p. 361.

58. Laifle, *passim.*

59. Renner, pp. 364–375.

60. Hocke, p. 135; Ruess, p. 33.

61. Huhn, p. 110; also quoted by Renner, p. 372.

62. Walter Sturminger, "Die Kundschafter sur Zeit der zweiten Türkenblagerung Wiens im Jahre 1683," *Festschrift zur Feier des zweihundertjährigen Bestandes des Haus-, Hof-und Staatsarchivs,* Vol. II, pp. 349–369.

63. Vaelckeren, p. 64.

64. "Relation," p. 134. The countermines also had air-holes to the surface, which actually made them dangerous for the city. They could have been used by the Turks as a direct route into town. Marczali, p. 190.

65. "Relation," p. 134.

66. *Ibid.,* p. 177.

67. J. B. de Rocoles, *Vienne Deux-fois assiegée par les Turcs MDXXIX & MDCLXXXIII & heureusement déliverée,* Leyden, 1684, pp. 269–270.

68. Marczali, pp. 179, 181; "Relation," p. 134; Ghelen, pp. 19, 37.

69. Kreutel, *passim;* Kunitz, p. 9; Laifle, pp. 71–73; Klopp, p. 236; Ruess, p. 85.

70. Kreutel, pp. 85–86; *Das Kriegsjahr 1683,* p. 242; Kunitz, p. 11. The cross is reproduced in Camesina (Chapter Seven, footnote 27) . p. 135.

71. Rocoles, p. 285.

72. Kreutel, p. 92; "Relation," p. 135; Marczali, p. 182; Duncker, pp. 270–272. The Austrian miners, however, were not a complete failure. The various sources do record some successes, both in exploding their own devices and in discovering and disarming those of the foe. The operations were supervised by a regular officer, a certain Captain Hafner, who came forward when he saw how badly the civilians were doing. Cf. *The present state Of The German and Turkish Empires* (Chapter Seven, footnote 88) , p. 84.

73. "Relation," p. 136; Marczali, p. 185, Renner, p. 325.

74. "Relation," p. 136; Marczali, p. 186.

75. *Idem.*

76. *Ibid.*, p. 194. Kunitz (p. 15) states that the reason for the vigor of the Turkish assaults from September 5 onward was that the enemy had received information to the effect that Starhemberg had only 5,000 men left, that he needed help badly, and that there was a lack of harmony between him and the citizens, who might have resolved to surrender if the attack on the fourth had lasted longer. This intelligence was derived from "the servant of an Armenian doctor" who had left Vienna with a packet of letters. The source does not specify whether the man came into the Ottoman camp voluntarily or whether he was taken captive. The latter possibility seems more likely since Marsigli, corroborating Kunitz, says: ". . . nell' animo del Visire gonfio di superbia accertato (intesi a dire) da un constituto, che fece nella persona d'un captivo, che Vienna fosse a momenti per rendersi . . ." Veress (Chapter Seven, footnote 9), p. 30. In any case, it seems that the person involved was the courier Seradly who disappeared while on his way to the Duke of Lorraine (Sturminger, p. 353). Klopp (p. 248) went so far as to opine that he might have been a special peace delegate of the City Council, a view earlier examined and convincingly rejected by Newald (II, pp. 198–203). Yet even though Klopp is wrong in this instance, there are no grounds for automatically discounting the information given the Turks. There is other indirect evidence of the existence of at least one disloyal or wavering faction within the city. At the beginning of the siege some Viennese, irritated at Leopold's supposed desertion, are said to have spoken of paying homage to Thököly (Vauchon, p. 78). After the Battle of the Kahlenberg, Sobieski noted that Starhemberg was not on good terms with the magistracy (although it is possible that this was due only to the overall poor performance of the militia and burghers). A much more explicit source is the anonymous author of *The present state Of The German and Turkish Empires.* According to him, "this business of the Ravaline had so frightened our Citizens, that some of them began to murmur, and to say that Starhemberg would sacrifice them all to the fury of the Turks; that it was full time to make some agreement with the Enemy; that if he deferred it too long, they should have no Quarter given them; that it was the Emperor's interest in this juncture of Affairs (since better could not be hoped for) to consider the Garrison of Vienna as able to do good service to the Empire and save it from the Turkish fury, provided the compaction were in time."

The commanding general is asserted to have quashed this seditious talk by means of a proclamation threatening the death penalty (pp. 19–20). The same story was current among other contemporaries (cf. Klopp, p. 249, footnote 2), and it cannot be discredited simply because it is not found in the Viennese sources. It should be noted that when the question of Viennese loyalty was first raised by Klopp in 1882, a storm of protest ensued (cf. Karl Uhlirz, "Die neueste Literatur über das Jahr 1683," *MIöG*, Vol. V, Sonderheft 2 [1884], p. 6). Nevertheless, there has never been a convincing refutation of the case for suspecting, at the least, irresolution. Newald's attempt to ascribe the weakheartedness primarily to newly-naturalized burghers and refugees is devoid of documentation, and his argument does not necessarily follow by logic. It is at best an only partly valid explanation.

77. "Relation," p. 137; Marczali, p. 191; Hocke, p. 180; Ghelen, p. 51; Ruess, p. 41; Vaelckeren, pp. 78–79. The Count of Provana ("Relation" and Marczali) speaks of the first action as having taken place on the eighth. The other sources assign it to the sixth and mention a second action on the eighth (although they disagree as to whether there were one or two mines). The diary of the Ottoman Court Master of Ceremonies has no entry for the sixth but speaks of an assault on the eighth as having caused the most casualties (Kreutel, p. 100).

78. *Idem.;* Vaelckeren, 86; Marczali, pp. 194, 196. Redlich (Chapter One, footnote 21), p. 255, claims that even before this time Kara Mustafa could have conquered Vienna if he had only mounted a second assault at some other point along the circumvallation (i.e., a second set of approaches). The numerically weak defenders could not have resisted successfully in two places at once. This theory, which merits the closest scrutiny, was already current in more extreme form immediately after the siege. Dupont (Chapter Two, footnote 20, p. 122, says: "Il est certain que Vienne dut son salut à l'avidité sordide du visir, qui comptait de profiter seul des richesses

renfermées dans cette place, ce qui l'empecha pour s'en rendre maître de profiter de ses grandes avantages par un assaut général." Dalérac (Chapter Two, footnote 24), p. 59, is even more explicit: "He was informed of the Riches shut up within the City, and fearing to lose them during the Pillage, if his Army took it by assault, he moderated their efforts and slackened their Attacks to oblige the Town to come to a Capitulation, with which all the Officers upbraided him, for by this means he gave the King of Poland time to arrive. . . ." A similar tale is related by Cantemir: "For being persuaded, that the city could not escape falling into his hands [anyway], he would not suffer it to be closely blocked up on all sides, and the Turkish soldiers to attack the breaches everywhere with equal vigour, but orders them daily to assault in small parties only, that the garrison being exhausted with continual watching and loss of men, might be obliged to surrender the castle." Cantemir adds that the idea of prolonging the siege arose from the early successes of the Ottoman troops and Kara Mustafa's plan of establishing an autonomous realm of his own in the West by means of the supposed treasures stored in Vienna (Cantemir [Chapter Two, footnote 89], pp. 304–307). The Silâhdar, too (Kreutel, p. 159), was a proponent of this view, stating in particular that the Grand Vezir prevented a heavier artillery bombardment. Finally, Klopp also, in somewhat variant form, is an adherent of this thesis. He suggests that the Grand Vezir, enheartened by the admissions of Seradly (footnote 76), refrained from making an all-out assault in hope of receiving a surrender offer from the burghers (p. 248). All of these statements suffer from internal flaws which, in part, reflect insufficient acquaintance with the actual circumstances of the siege. In the first place the initial Austrian resistance—the defense of the counterscarp—lasted an unusually long time and was overcome by the Turks only at heavy cost. Secondly, it is apparent that the erection of siegeworks around the whole enceinte (if that is what Cantemir means by the phrase "closely blocked up") would have been extremely difficult if not impossible. Even if one assumes that the Turkish army had enough laborers for such an operation, the *lâğuncı* would have encountered flooded or very swampy terrain in any sector apart from the one actually chosen, as Dalérac himself admits (p. 56). Opportunities for mining would have been even more limited. The Ottoman siege artillery, insufficient even for the task assigned it, would scarcely have sufficed for a more extensive undertaking. Clearly, no general storm could have been attempted without effecting breaches through mining or cannon fire. As for the Löbl and Palace Bastion area, one cannot say positively whether more vigorous assaults, in particular a simultaneous effort against both bulwarks, would have brought success. It appears that the Turks were in a position to break through only in the final days of the siege when the approach of the relief army had already caused them to divide their forces. Moreover, the impression afforded by both the Austrian sources (Kunitz says so outright) and the Turkish siege diary is that the Ottoman warriors really did exert themselves to the utmost until after September 8. In short, there are solid reasons for questioning the assertion that Kara Mustafa consciously neglected to employ his full strength. On the other hand, there is no cause for rejecting summarily the idea that the Ottoman leader coveted Vienna's riches or even that he desired to establish a principality of his own. Such goals seem fully in accordance with what is known about the conditions of his previous career. (It is therefore also possible that he eased the artillery bombardment of the town as distinct from its defenses.)

79. "Relation," p. 138; Marczali, p. 195.

80. *Idem.*

81. Huhn, p. 206.

82. Josef Kraft, "Schaden und Wiederaufbau in Niederösterreich nach der Türkenbelagerung Wiens," *Arbeiterfreund-Kalender* 1934, pp. 51–57; Watzl, *passim;* Newald, II, p. 93.

83. Perchtoldsdorf retains its administrative autonomy.

84. Watzl (pp. 205–209) seems most convincing as to the number of dead. See also Josef Kraft, "Ein Bericht . . ." (Chapter One, footnote 1) and Adam Latschka, *Die Türken in Perchtoldsdorf im Jahre 1683*, Vienna, 1883. The decision to surrender appears to have been evoked by the gradual appearance of more of the enemy, including Turks, and by a shortage of munitions. However, the reports are somewhat contradictory.

85. Kreutel, p. 38.

86. See below, p. 208.

87. One noteworthy side effect of the Turco-Tataric incendiary rage is the fact that many persons who are descendents of seventeenth-century Lower Austrians can trace their ancestors back only to the fall of 1683 when the clergy returned to their ash-strewn quarters to take up anew the task of record keeping. Cf. Watzl, footnotes 3, 5, p. 213.

88. "Récit," p. 23. For the Vezirial table, see Chapter Seven, footnote 46.

89. *Idem;* see Ubald Kostersitz, "Das Chorherrnstift Klosterneuburg 1683," in S. Brunner, *Ein Chorherrnbuch*, Würzburg-Vienna, 1883, pp. 315–325.

90. See Paul Tobner, *Leben und Wirken des Abtes Matthäus III. Kolweiss von Lilienfeld*, Brno, 1883.

91. Cf. Romuald Gumpoldsberger, "Melk in der Türkennoth des Jahres 1683," in *Jahresberichte des k.k. Ober-Gymnasiums zu Melk 1883*.

92. Cf. D. Schmolk, "Das Chorherrnstift Herzogenburg," in Brunner, *op. cit.*

93. Watzl, pp. 62–82.

94. V. Kraus, "Herzogenburg und Umgebung während der Türkennoth," *Blätter für Geschichte von Niederösterreich*, Vol. II (1886), pp. 186–200. Other places in the "Quarter Above the Vienna Woods" that held out were Tulln, Traismauer, Göttweig Monastery, Lembach, and Schloss Wald. Newald, I, p. 157.

95. Several miles upstream from Pitten Castle stands an imposing bluff, equipped with artificial ruins and known as the "Turkish Drop-off" (*Türkensturz*). Related not to 1683 but rather to Suleiman the Magnificent's campaign of 1532, it is the subject of various, especially colorful folk legends.

96. Kraft, "Schaden und Wiederaufbau . . . ," p. 53.

97. Karl Kirsch, *Burg Forchtenstein*, Vienna, 1958, *passim*. However, 150 militarily-inept peasants who ventured forth on a sortie were slaughtered.

98. Klopp, pp. 217–218. The gutted castle was never rebuilt. Its jagged ruins serve to attract tourists today.

99. *Das Kriegsjahr 1683*, pp. 74–79, 313–318.

100. Newald, I, pp. 76–82, gives a detailed documentation of the inadequacies.

101. *Ibid.*, pp. 149–159.

102. See below, p. 4.

103. Watzl, footnote 16, p. 224; Newald, II, p. 92; KA, "Kay: Hof- Kriegs- Canzley Regist: Protocollum 1683," pp. 258, 389, 490. Since many, perhaps most of the War Archive's individual records are missing, the Protocol, made up of summaries, is a prime source.

104. H. Kunnert, "Das Burgenland im Türkenkriege 1683," *Burgenländische Heimatblätter*, Vol. II (1933), pp. 157–167.

105. Anonymous, *Curiöse Denckwürdigkeiten des österreichischen triumphirenden Adlers*, Nürnberg, 1683, appendix.

106. A. Schachinger, "Die Neubesiedlung nach der Katastrophe des Türkenjahres 1683," in *Der Wienerwald: eine landeskundliche Darstellung*, Vienna, 1934, p. 308.

107. Kraft, "Schaden und Wiederaufbau . . . ," p. 55.

108. See C. A. de Martelli, *Relatio Captivo-redempti*, Vienna, 1689, for a vivid account of the tribulations of these prisoners. One must of course distinguish between the unenviable lot of the captives of the Ottoman army and those Christians shipped to Turkey and turned over to civilian control. Doubtlessly Western writers have greatly exaggerated the "horrors" of the latter fate.

109. Karl Toifel, *Die Türken vor Wien im Jahre 1683*, Prague-Leipzig, 1883, pp. 260–261.

110. Kraft, *passim;* Schachinger, p. 334.

Chapter Nine

1. See above, p. 262.

2. See above, p. 253.

3. "Récit" (Chapter Seven, footnote 14), pp. 22–33.

4. Lubomirsky and Schultz had not actually joined at the Váh. The three-and-a-half

understrength Polish regiments (about 2,000 men altogether) were only underway when the Austrian general was ordered to Vienna. The bulk of these mercenaries, however, were apparently present in time for action at the Prater bridgehead on July 16 (see above, p. 262); their commander arrived four days later. "Journal" (Chapter Seven, footnote 28). As for the towns enumerated, the list given in *Das Kriegsjahr 1683* (Chapter Seven, footnote 14), p. 80, is incomplete and has been supplemented here with others mentioned by the Turkish sources.

5. The figures relating to Kör Hüseyin Pasha's army are fairly certain since both the Austrian and Turkish sources agree. It was made up of men from Eger and Oradea. Kreutel, MS (Chapter Five, footnote 88); Kreutel (Preface, footnote 2), p. 147. The force also included at the start men from Timişoara, Jenö, and Nové Zámky, but they appear to have been detached before the advance to Bratislava. The strength of Thököly's contingents is uncertain: the Austrians speak of twenty thousand, the Turks of ten. I have split the difference. It should be noted in passing that Thököly's followers were also serving in western Hungary, and thus the *overall* total can well have been around 20,000.

6. The Austrian position at the bridges after July 16 consisted not only of the fort on the north shore but also of emplacements on the two bigger islands, a fact that is apparent from Le Bègue's remark ("Journal" (Chapter Seven, footnote 14), p. 81 that only the two small bridges were burned that day, and from a later reference ("Récit," p. 31) to the existence of "our old trenches" on the islands. One cannot say precisely when the destruction of the two larger spans took place although it was apparently just prior to the army's departure for the Morava and Bratislava ("Récit," p. 24). It would seem that the final withdrawal from the Prater on the 16th did not cause Charles to give up immediately the idea of returning to Vienna (or indeed communicating with it) via the bridges. However, it did not take long for him to conclude that a recrossing in the face of enemy resistance was unfeasible (cf. Le Bègue's report to Sobieski, *Akta,* p. 230). The adoption of the plan to relieve the city by marching across the Wienerwald (see below, p. 288) signified this recognition. Then, when it became necessary to leave the area in order to counter Thököly, the further existence of the structure constituted a serious liability: it could also be used by the Turks for a foray into Lower Austria. That even the remnants of the bridge represented a great danger later became evident (see below, p. 294).

7. "Récit," p. 24; "Journal," pp. 83–84; Röder von Diersburg (Chapter Seven, footnote 47), pp. 39–40; *Akta,* pp. 204–205. (The source indicated by the last citation, an anonymous Polish account, erroneously places the council before the walls of Bratislava.) Ludwig Wilhelm gave himself all the credit for getting the army to go beyond the Morava. It is a measure of Lorraine's own qualities as a leader that he was willing to hear the arguments of a rather brash subordinate and, without being offended, weigh them on their merit. The same self-effacing qualities are evident in the Duke's dealings with Sobieski.

8. *Das Kriegsjahr 1683,* pp. 85–86; "Récit," pp. 24–27; "Journal," pp. 85–86; Röder von Diersburg, pp. 42–44; anonymous account, *Akta,* pp. 204–205.

9. Kreutel, pp. 150, 154. The anonymous Polish account sheds supplementary light here. It indicates that there was opposition in the Duke's staff to an open field encounter but that Lubomirsky and Ludwig Wilhelm succeeded in overcoming the negative arguments. It again appears as if the Duke himself let both sides speak before issuing orders. The Turks, according to this version, withdrew because they had already sent back their artillery park, while the Imperials pulled back to the Morava because of a lack of forage. Other interesting remarks concern the looting of Polish soldiers and the slaughter of all, save distinguished prisoners. *Akta,* pp. 204–208. As for the poor performance of the Magyars, it should be pointed out that Thököly did his best to maintain regular military discipline—as is apparent from a stringent penal code issued by him. See Gustav von Gömöry, "Ein Strafedict Emmerich Thököly's aus dem Jahre 1683," MKA, Jahrgang 1883, pp. 212–215.

10. *Akta,* pp. 192–195.

11. "Récit," p. 28.

12. There is no written record of Taaffe's instructions. They can only be inferred

from Leopold's reply (footnote 19) and from a later message despatched by Lorraine (footnote 15). Apparently the Count suggested that a force of 30,000 men would be large enough for the job. Cf. Anna Maria Trivellini, *Il Cardinale Buonvisi, Nunzio a Vienna,* Florence, 1958, p. 65.

13. Court War Council Summary, July 17 and 20. *Akta,* p. 180.

14. Forst de Battaglia (Chapter Two, footnote 12), pp. 190–191.

15. Camesina (Chapter Seven, footnote 27), "Anhang," p. cxcviii. That he was to suggest a relief independent of the Poles may only be inferred from his written instructions.

16. Newald (Chapter One, footnote 3), I, pp. 127–128.

17. Court War Council, July 18. *Akta,* p. 175. Passau also began to take measures of its own for the collection of bridge materials. The government was fortunate, moreover, in having competent engineers on hand—transferred earlier from the Rhine garrison thanks to Starhemberg's forethought. Newald, p. 157.

18. The burghers of Tulln, protected by a wall and a moat, had managed to fend off the Tatars who were in control of most of the plain during the first half of the campaign. It is not possible to determine at precisely what point the place first received professional military aid or whether the sending of the latter represented a deliberate attempt by Charles to lay the groundwork for a second bridgehead. All that is certain is that the Duke was contemplating building a bridge there as early as July 31 (Lorraine to Sobieski, July 31, *Akta,* p. 216) and that the boats were being made ready by August 5 (Le Bègue to Sobieski, *Akta,* p. 230). By August 9, when the Turks released Count Caprara nearby, there was a regular garrison, consisting of one cavalry squadron and one company of foot. Benaglia (Chapter Two, footnote 63), pp. 254ff. Presumably, these troops were a detachment from Dünewald's corps and had been present for some time already. The town itself is of great antiquity, being mentioned in the *Nibelungenlied* as one of the way stations on Kriemhild's voyage to King Etzel. It also possesses a Romanesque charnel-house (*Karner*) of considerable architectural merit.

19. Newald, I, p. 176. Leopold's negative response to the early relief suggestion may have been evoked, in part at least, by Buonvisi. See Trivellini, p. 66.

20. Pálffy's instructions, *Akta,* pp. 201–202.

21. "Récit," pp. 25–26.

22. It is conceivable that the Großenzersdorf false alarm was a rebel stratagem.

23. "Récit," p. 28; "Journal," pp. 88–89. Drunkenness appears to have affected Lubomirsky's men, too, although not at this point (anonymous account, *Akta,* p. 209). The part of Lower Austria in question—a fertile land that much impressed the Poles—is still dotted with vineyards. The soldiers doubtlessly slaked their thirst with the famous "Green Veltliner," a white wine from the Steinberg near Zistersdorf, and with the good growths of Poysdorf and Mistelbach.

24. "Récit," p. 27; "Journal," pp. 91–92. Since he was a Prince of the Empire, entitled to the predicate "Altesse," it was quite proper for Lorraine to correspond directly with men such as the Elector of Saxony or the Duke of Lauenburg—individuals with whom he was also personally acquainted (cf. Newald, I, p. 128).

25. *Ibid.,* p. 158; Court War Council summary, Aug. 10–17, *Akta,* p. 264; "Journal," p. 92. Tulln appears to have been under serious consideration as early as July 31 (see footnote 18). Nussdorf and Klosterneuburg were also discussed (Newald, footnote 6, p. 157), but the proximity of the enemy ruled out any Viennese or near-Viennese location (Le Bègue's report). See also footnotes 35, 37.

26. "Journal," p. 92.

27. Taaffe's letter to his brother, August 17, 1683, *Akta,* pp. 267–268.

28. "Journal," pp. 92–94; "Récit," p. 28; Lorraine to Sobieski, August 11, *Akta,* pp. 243–245; Court War Council summary, August 19–20, *ibid.,* p. 275; Rauchbar (Chapter Three, footnote 77), p. 254. For contents of the August 11 letter, see below, p. 306. The August 16 letter is apparently preserved only in Le Bègue's summary.

29. In seventeenth century German an *Aue* was a meadow surrounded (and/or dissected) by a small watercourse, i.e., an islet. Since the regulation of the Danube, which took place by stages in the latter part of the nineteenth century, the region has

been somewhat drier. Today it is an attractive wild life preserve, pierced by bicycle paths.

30. "Récit," pp. 28–29; "Journal," p. 94.

31. Menčík (Chapter One, footnote 3), p. 236.

32. "Journal," pp. 94–95.

33. Menčík, p. 234. The decision was made on August 16 and was contingent upon the agreement of Sobieski and other leaders. The Court War Council not only accepted Lorraine's reasoning about the use of infantry but concluded that forage and victuals could be supplied (some locally and the rest by river) more easily than in the devastated region opposite Bratislava. The Wienerwald approach also left open a more secure route of retreat in the even of necessity. "Mémoire Badois," *Akta,* p. 644. The proponents of the Bratislava plan, however, did not give up, and it was clear that the matter would be settled definitively only upon the arrival of Sobieski. Letter of the Marchese di Pucci, August 18, *Akta,* p. 269.

34. Rauchbar, p. 255. The same charge against Lorraine was levelled by di Pucci (footnote 33). In all likelihood, it was Hermann and his clique who twisted Lorraine's tentative suggestions into a charge of irresponsible recklessness. See "Mémoire Badois," *Akta,* p. 695.

35. Sobieski himself after his arrival in Austria concluded that there had been no reason "to fear that they would undertake anything before we arrived" (letter of September 4 to Marysieńka, *Akta,* p. 346). On the other hand, Charles' desire to place himself on the south side of the river prior to the Poles' advent may indicate that he wished to be in a position to advance independently in case of dire necessity. As for the numerical contribution of the Poles, see footnote 71.

36. This is the interpretation given by Stoye (Preface, p. i), pp. 183–189, who also leads one to believe that the Duke suffered from acute nervous anxiety. While the Duke's actions do show that he was more troubled about the situation than Passau, his concern would certainly seem to have been justified by the tenor of four letters smuggled out of Vienna, particularly the last (*Akta,* pp. 255–256). Charles' mistrust of the administrative capacities of Hermann and his probable awareness of the ponderous nature of the Austrian bureaucracy can hardly have served to allay his worries. (There is good evidence that Charles was nervously upset in late May and early June; whether this state continued is pure speculation.)

37. The Silâhdar (Kreutel, p. 154) claims that Kör Hüseyin Pasha was reinforced with only 300 Tatars, but Le Bègue's account of the Battle of the Bisamberg (footnote 41) makes it appear as if the actual number were considerably higher. Kunitz, (Chapter Seven, footnote 8), p. 10, also reports the dispatch of a much larger contingent (10,000). The Silâhdar is also probably mistaken in asserting that Kör Hüseyin Pasha learned from prisoners that the Austrians had already left the Morava, since the Turkish decision to depart was allegedly made on August 14—a date at which Charles was still demonstrably encamped at Angern. Conceivably the prisoners told the *Beylerbeyi* that the Duke intended to move upstream.

38. Kreutel, pp. 154–155.

39. "Récit," p. 29; Lorraine to Sobieski, August 26, *Akta,* pp. 305–306. It is conceivable that the Duke was correct in surmising that the maneuver was intended to draw him away from Tulln. The Silâhdar's statement that its purpose was the transfer of Kör Hüseyin Pasha's men to the main Ottoman army does not absolutely preclude such a possibility. Despite his surface reaction, Kara Mustafa may well have given some credence to Kör Hüseyin Pasha's warning. One may argue further that if the Grand Vezir had merely wanted the force from Upper Hungary to rejoin him, it could have traversed the river elsewhere. See also footnote 42.

40. Kör Hüseyin Pasha was joined by some foragers (*seymen* and *gönüllü*) from the main army, who came over by boat (Kreutel, p. 88). There were perhaps 500 of them (Taaffe to brother, August 25, *Akta,* p. 299). They suffered the misfortune of failing to relocate their skiffs when they retreated.

41. "Récit," pp. 29–30; "Journal," pp. 95–96. The Silâhdar's account of the battle (Kreutel, pp. 155–158) is not, I think, completely reliable. He asserts, e.g., that the enemy—numbering 80,000, completely surrounded the Muslims. He does, however,

inform us that the Duke's use of infantry (dragoons presumably) and light field pieces was very effective.

42. "Récit," p. 51. Whether as a diversion or solely as a means of transfer (or both), it seems likely that the new structure was intended for the use of the remnants of Kör Hüseyin Pasha's detachment, which Kara Mustafa (vainly) ordered up to Vienna a second time (Kreutel, pp. 90–91, 159). For the Rumanians, see above, p. 294.

43. Menčík, AöG, pp. 213–219. The confusion of these weeks is particularly apparent in the gaps and disordered entries in the Protocol of the Court War Council (Chapter Eight, footnote 103).

44. Menčík, AöG, pp. 219ff; KA, Protocol, p. 179 and *passim;* Renner (Chapter One, footnote 3), pp. 381–382; Newald, II, pp. 53–62. Grain turned out to be an item of great scarcity because of the Tatar raids, and by August the Emperor was trying to get it from Germany himself. KA, *Feldakten 1683,* Vol. 8, Fasc. IX/6, No. 64/65. It is not clear whether the Bishop's demand was ever satisfied.

45. Braubach (Chapter Seven, footnote 55), p. 91; Heyret (Chapter One, footnote 20), p. 287; Menčík, p. 236. A Czech poem of 1683 asserted: "A good shepherd sacrifices himself for his flock; a hired one deserts his sheep and flees." Walter Hummelberger, "Wehen und Klagen in den österreichischen Landen," *Wiener Geschichtsblätter,* Vol. 16 (76), 1961, p. 351.

46. H. Staudinger, *Das Kur-Bayerische 2. Infanterie-Regiment Kronprinz 1682–1683,* Munich, 1882, p. 73; *Das Kriegsjahr 1683,* p. 234.

47. Menčík, AöG, pp. 237ff; KA, *Feldakten,* No. 58/59, 106/107; KA, Protocol, pp. 206–210. The Franconians were also reluctant about leaving the Rhine exposed to the French. Rauchbar, p. 247.

48. The original Danish-Brandenburg scheme went back to the summer of 1682. Louis, still unwilling to break entirely with his ally of the Dutch War, did not support it then. However, various indications of a possible pro-Imperial reorientation of Hohenzollern policy caused him to change his mind and encourage the plan. The French ambassadors then overextended themselves in making commitments in Copenhagen and Berlin. The King, to whom the whole affair was merely a tactical gambit and who was interested primarily in isolating Brunswick-Lüneberg, refused to back them. The Great Elector was incensed. The whole affair is illustrative of Louis XIV's failure properly to handle the traditional French *barrière de l'est* policy. A. Lossky, "Louis XIV, William III and the Baltic Crisis of 1683," *University of California Publications in History,* Vol. 49, Berkeley-Loss Angeles, 1954, p. 73.

49. Anonymously-written account of Saxon involvement (source-based) in Raumer's *Historisches Taschenbuch,* Dresden, 1848, pp. 226–232.

50. *Ibid.,* pp. 232–235; P. Hassel, Count Vitzthum von Eckstadt, *Zur Geschichte des Türkenkrieges 1683,* Dresden, 1883, pp. 53–113, *passim;* K. G. Helbig, "Kurfürst Johann Georg III. in seinen Beziehungen zum Kaiser und zum Reich 1682 und 1683," *Archiv für Sächsische Geschichte,* IX (1871), pp. 92–98.

51. *Ibid.,* pp. 98–104; Raumer, pp. 235–263; Hassel-Vitzthum, pp. 113–136. John George originally aspired to supreme command of *all* the allied forces, basing his claim on the text of his alliance with Austria. Lamberg wrote to him that this clause applied only to a bilateral, not a multilateral situation. The Elector, who exercised the honorary function of Imperial Vicar, then lowered his sights to obtaining command of the forces from the Empire, which idea Leopold rejected because of the probable negative reaction of Max Emmanuel and Waldeck. Upon learning of the Emperor's refusal (at Teplice), the Saxon still insisted that he retain control at least of his own troops. Helbig, pp. 96–100. It has been argued (Hassel-Vitzthum, p. 111) that John George was thinking merely of avoiding divided command—the ill effects of which he had observed in the Dutch War—, but it is hard to believe that personal ambition and prestige considerations, the hallmarks of the territorial ruler, did not also play a rôle.

52. Schnath (Chapter Four, footnote 73), p. 52.

53. H. Prutz, *Preussische Geschichte,* Vol. II, 1900, pp. 249–250, 268–270; Lorenz (see Preface, p. i), p. 248. Prutz relates Rébénac's further arguments.

54. The terms included cession of the Silesian principalities of Liegnitz, Brieg, and Wohlau; recognition of the Habsburg claim to Jägerndorf in return for 200,000 thalers;

the same amount from Spain; and 300,000 from the Netherlands. These conditions were not too different from ones brought back by Lamberg on an earlier visit to Berlin (June). The main change was that Frederick William was no longer willing to take an anti-French stand at the Regensburg Diet. The rapid shifting of his viewpoints during 1683 is also apparent from the fact that he considered a Habsburg alliance for a short while in January, 1683. Klopp, pp. 264–267. (Klopp, a Hannoverian, unable to forget the Welf grievances of 1866, must be used with caution here.)

55. *Ibid.*, pp. 277–278; *Urkunden und Aktenstücke zur Geschichte des Kurfürsten Friedrich Wilhelm von Brandenburg*, Vol. XIV-2, Berlin, 1891, p. 1107 (pp. 1091–1103 contain the text of the aborted agreement).

56. Text of *Scriptum* and nuntial reports of April 18, *Akta*, pp. 80–88; Laskowski (Chapter Two, footnote 9), pp. 129–130; Forst de Battaglia (Chapter Two, footnote 12), p. 182.

57. Cf. Dupont (Chapter Two, footnote 20), p. 83.

58. Forst de Battaglia, p. 183; Zierowski documents, *Akta*, pp. 102–103, 110; Jan Wimmer, *Wyprawa wiedeńska 1683*, Warsaw, 1957, p. 73; Wespazyan Kochowski, *A.M.D.G. Commentarius belli Aduersùm Turcas ad Viennam & in Hungaria*, Kraków, 1684, p. 12; Kluczyski (Chapter Five, footnote 110), pp. 24–25; Dalérac (Chapter Two, footnote 24), pp. 72–73. Martial enthusiasm was not absolutely universal, however. Kochowski (p. 11) reports that soldiers enlisting in Lubomirsky's regiments were pitied as marked for death.

59. Some of the Polish foot were without swords and pikes and had to be equipped by the King himself. Sobieski to Marysieńka, August 31, *Akta*, p. 327.

60. Relevant documents in *Akta*, pp. 105–150; cf. Forst de Battaglia, p. 183; Sauer (Chapter Five, footnote 116), p. 44; Dalérac, p. 47.

61. Nuntial reports, *Akta*, pp. 150, 161–162, 170–171, 185–186. The Poles believed that the Muscovites were waiting to see the outcome of the first fighting before committing themselves.

62. F. de Bojani, *Innocent XI: sa correspondance avec ses nonces*, Vol. III, Roulers, 1912, p. 689. The Imperial request for support along the Váh seems all the more justified in light of the fact that there was as yet no sign of the 4,000 cavalry promised by Sobieski.

63. See Dupont, pp. 81–82, for a reflection of Polish sympathy for the rebels. As for strictly material interests, peace between Leopold and Thököly would clearly have permitted the Poles to recommence later the pursuit of their own particular objectives in Podolia. In a more immediate sense it was desirable because it would secure the position of Kraków (vulnerable to attack from Upper Hungary upon the departure of the Polish army for Austria). Fortunately for Sobieski, Thököly himself was exposed to the rear. The rebel had property along the Polish frontier; his wife and family were also within easy reach at Mukachevo. He was also obliged to pretend at least to be serving the Turks in the West. The result was an informal bilateral neutrality compact (August 9), probably expedited by a threat of Sobieski against Helena. Dalérac, pp. 74, 122.

64. Laskowski, p. 132. It is noteworthy that the Emperor was now *asking* Sobieski to come rather than—as the day before—the latter volunteering to do so. Another indication of Austrian pleading is Buonvisi's notation of July 9: "si é spedito in Polonia per solicitare l'uscita del Ré al nostro soccorso." De Bojani, p. 690. On the other hand, there seems little reason for accepting the oft-cited claim that Leopold personally begged John III to come. This belief derives from Dupont's undocumented assertion that when Count Caraffa arrived in the royal camp (at Bytom, August 19) he carried an epistle, handwritten by the Emperor, which stated that since the Polish army could not arrive in time, the King's appearance alone would suffice. Dupont, p. 126. Dupont may possibly be thinking of a letter actually sent by Lorraine (*Akta*, p. 306).

65. Court War Council notation, July 5, *Akta*, p. 164; de Bojani, pp. 695–697; Laskowski, pp. 132–134; Diary of Prince Jakob, *Akta*, p. 617; Sobieski to Frederick William, July 19, *Akta*, pp. 176–177.

66. Sobieski to Lorraine, July 22. *Akta*, pp. 187–189: Sobieski to Lorraine, July 25,

Akta, p. 198; Lorraine to Sobieski, July 31, *Akta,* pp. 216–220; Lorraine to Sobieski, August 5, *Akta,* pp. 229–331.

67. Nuntial report, August 12, *Akta,* p. 249.

68. Sobieski to Lorraine, August 6, *Akta,* pp. 223–233.

69. *Akta,* pp. 248–250, 229–231; Sobieski to Lorraine, August 11, *Akta,* pp. 243–245. How many men remained in Poland is not entirely clear. Wimmer (p. 50) speaks of 7,000, not counting the tardy Lithuanians and missing Cossacks. It is also uncertain how many troops of the "Old Army"—the original 12,000 man force—remained close to the Turkish frontier in Podolia, their normal cantonment. Hence, it is likewise difficult to say how far preparations for the southeastern offensive had progressed by the time it became necessary to alter directions. The "Old Army"—as indicated—had been brought up to authorized strength, but the little evidence available indicates that the overall mobilization was somewhat behind schedule.

70. *Akta,* p. 249. Pallavicini (the nunzio) does not specify whether his figures, obtained from Jabłonowski, also include Sieniawski's advance guard, which is elsewhere said to have counted 8,000 men ("Journal," p. 72). However, the prelate's secretary, writing on August 18, does (Sauer, p. 38).

71. Dalérac, p. 47. 18,000 seems a reasonable estimate insofar as it also represents the total of Polish forces mentioned by Le Bègue (12,000 horse, 3,000 foot and 3,000 men kept in Lower Austria. "Récit," pp. 32, 34). If one were to include Lubomirski's corps, the total would be 19,500–20,000—a figure that corresponds with the sum of combatants given in the most recently published Polish source (O. Laskowski, "Relacja wyprawy wiedeńskiej," *Przegląd Historyczno-Wojskowy,* Vol. II [1930], p. 163); and with the estimate of the Turks themselves (Hurzumaki [Chapter Five, footnote 88], p. 14). An Imperial document in the Baden archives provides further support for this conclusion: it specifies 20,000 Poles (Röder von Diersburg, p. 31). The French ambassador speaks of 14,000–15,000 men, meaning presumably the forces participating in the relief action (Newald, I, p. 90), while an Imperial officer in Silesia put the total force at even less, 16,000 (*ibid.,* p. 85). The weight of evidence is thus against the Saxon estimate of 26,000 (*Das Kriegsjahr 1683,* p. 236). I likewise see no good reason to accept Wimmer's estimate (p. 27) of 27,000. It is based upon muster rolls which were apparently even more inflated than those of the Austrian army, surely more than the ten percent Wimmer is willing to concede. The only way in which one could possibly raise the Polish total (the official Polish account—Kochowski, p. 24—mentions 24,000) would be to make some rough estimate for infantry units which did not arrive in time to take part in the Battle of the Kahlenberg. On August 29 Sobieski ordered Jabłonowski to hurry up with the hussars and the "rest of the army," *leaving behind* the infantry (*Akta,* p. 319). A contemporary chronicle, which describes the Polish march through Moravia (see Chapter Six, footnote 55), notes that the Polish foot passed through every day until September 26. (The Lithuanians got only as far as Upper Hungary and that after the lifting of the siege.) Indeed, the number of Polish infantrymen before the battle was so small (3,000) that Sobieski had to ask for Imperials to be mixed with them (see below, p. 318). Finally, Kochowski (p. 29) also admits that the battalions of new recruits arrived rather late. The reason for this tardiness was of course not merely their inability to travel as quickly as cavalrymen but also the greater financial difficulties encountered in raising and equipping them.

72. It is impossible to tell whether Sobieski was delayed primarily because of the effort to organize the march or because of the entertainment he had to accept.

73. Diary of Martin Katski, Polish artillery commander ("Prefect"), *Akta,* p. 580; diary of Prince Jakób, *ibid.,* pp. 618–619; Lorraine to Sobieski, August 7, *ibid.,* p. 235; Lorraine to Sobieski, 15 August, *ibid.,* p. 255; Lorraine to Sobieski, 19 August, *ibid.,* pp. 273–274; Sobieski to Lorraine, 24 August, *ibid.,* p. 295; Lorraine to Sobieski, 25 August, *ibid.,* p. 298; Sobieski to Marysieńka, 25 August, *ibid.,* pp. 301–302; Newald, II, pp. 88–89. The encampments of the Polish army, which for the most part appear to have been set up at some distance from larger centers of habitation in order to prevent damage to the local population, were in the following places: August 22, Gliwice; August 23, Rudowa; August 24, Piotorwice; August 25, Dvorce and Hof; August 26,

Olomouc; August 27, Vyskov; August 28, Kovalovice; August 29, Modric; August 30, Drnholec; August 31, Oberhollabrunn (Prince Jakob's diary).

74. See above, p. 185. The Silesian officials, of whose activity there remains a plethora of evidence in the *Akta*, seem to have done a much better job in helping the Poles along. See Nikolaj Dyakowski, *Dyaryusz Wiedenskiéj okazy r. 1683*, Warsaw, 1861, p. 7. (My references are to a ms. German translation preserved in the *Feldakten 1683* of the Viennese Kriegsarchiv) ; and Dalérac, p. 125.

75. Lorraine wrote again on the 21st, including Starhemberg's letter of August 19; on the 26th and the 28th, including messages from Vienna of the 27th. The letter of the 26th is especially indicative of the Duke's tact in dealing with Sobieski: Charles states that the King's name will alone suffice to liberate the city. *Akta*, pp. 281–283, 305–306, 310–313. Sobieski sent further notes to Lorraine on the 24th, 28th, and 29th. That of the 28th was in reply to the Duke's of the 26th, that of the 29th to the Duke's of the 28th. *Akta*, pp. 295–296, 313–315, 317. There is no record of the King's response to Charles' communication of the 21st. By now of course the interval between letters was shorter, and news was no longer cold upon arrival.

76. Sobieski to Marysieńka, August 29, *Akta*, pp. 317–320; *ibid.*, August 31, pp. 238–331; Prince Jakób's diary, *ibid.*, p. 619; "Journal," p. 97.

77. Rauchbar, pp. 259–261; Sobieski to Marysieńka, September 4, *Akta*, pp. 348–350; "Journal," p. 98.

78. It will be recalled that the Court War Council had already opposed the plan, and it may be presumed that Lorraine and Sobieski, who were more or less of the same mind about the matter in their correspondence, had discussed it beforehand. No other source supports Dupont's assertion (p. 130) that the King had to impose the idea upon most of the other generals, who allegedly wanted to take a more circuitous route (across the Wienerwald not at the Kahlenberg but further south). Interestingly, Hermann of Baden (*Akta*, pp. 645–646) tries to take the credit for the Kahlenberg decision.

79. Rauchbar, pp. 261–263.

80. "Journal," p. 98; "L'ordre de bataille," *Akta*, pp. 333–335; anonymous Polish letter, *ibid.*, pp. 348–350. The *ordre de bataille* allegedly drawn up by Sobieski does not correspond to the final arrangements used but rather to the plan adumbrated in the anonymous letter. If it is genuine, it was probably no more than a preliminary sketch, greatly modified as a result of the discussions at Stetteldorf. To be sure, Sobieski as commander-in-chief was responsible for the ultimate drafting of the plan.

81. Menčík, p. 243.

82. See footnote 64.

83. Trivellini, p. 67. Buonvisi's original opposition was based on the argument that since the Emperor in no case would be permitted to get any closer to the army than two leagues, it would be undignified for him to go; because of the obligation of presenting gifts, the trip would also be costly. By the end of the month the nunzio was against the plan because of the ceremonial question: i.e., which ruler should proffer his hand first. Whether Buonvisi recognized the real issue at stake—formal command—is unclear; presumably he did. De Bojani, pp. 712, 747–749.

84. Borgomanero's letter of August 13, AGS, 3925.

85. Leopold to Sobieski, September 7, *Akta*, p. 351. Leopold told Buonvisi that he had also written a second letter to Sobieski, stating that the last-named ought not to wait for the Imperial party, that John III should continue to march vigorously toward Vienna, that the Emperor would leave the direction of the army and the glory to the King and had asked the generals to do the same. De Bojani, p. 740. The letter, if actually sent, clearly did not placate the Polish ruler.

86. Menčík, pp. 239–247.

87. *Ibid.*, pp. 247–250.

88. In 1688 d'Aviano claimed that he had twice calmed the wrought-up Sobieski, from which it has been inferred (Klopp, p. 297) that the prospect of Leopold's coming caused the King to threaten to go home. At the least the padre's presence had a soothing effect upon the mutually jealous leaders: the records of all participants speak appreciatively of him.

89. Uechtritz-Steinkirch (Chapter Seven, footnote 52), pp. 12–13, 22–23; Rauchbar, pp. 259–260; "Journal," p. 98.

90. *Ibid.*, pp. 98–99; "Récit," p. 32; Rauchbar, pp. 259–260; "Prefect," *Akta*, pp. 386–387; Sobieski to Marysieńka, September 9, *ibid.*, p. 359; Dupont, p. 132. Even in Tarnowskie Gory, Sobieski had been embarrassed about his infantry. Dalérac, pp. 123, 125.

91. "Prefect," *Akta*, pp. 389–390; "Récit," p. 32; "Journal," pp. 99–100; Rauchbar, pp. 264–265. There is some contradiction between Le Bègue's *ordre de bataille* and other versions based upon the report of the Saxon engineer Suttinger (*Das Kriegsjahr 1683*, pp. 238–239). The main discrepancy is that the latter speak of the three wings as consisting of: a.) an Imperial-Saxon left; b.) a Bavarian-Franconian *corps de bataille, including* Sachsen-Lauenburg; and c.) a Polish right. Le Bègue's version seems preferable because it more or less accords with Waldeck's (Rauchbar, p. 267). How many (three or four) lines of battle there were is also difficult to determine, but the question may be irrelevant because the terrain was really too rough to permit full-fledged text-book schemes.

92. See footnote 88.

93. "Récit," p. 33; "Journal," pp. 100–101; Sobieski to Marysieńka, September 12, *Akta*, pp. 373–375; "Prefect," *ibid.*, p. 390; Kochowski, p. 27; Rauchbar, pp. 265–266; Mansberg (Chapter Six, footnote 57), pp. 61–62.

94. The place of the meeting cannot be determined with certainty; it may have been on the road rather than in Weidling.

95. The term "Kahlenberg" in the seventeenth century appears to have been used both for the whole crest of the Wienerwald and for its first prominence, the present "Leopoldsberg," directly above the Danube. Confusion is easy since today's Kahlenberg—known in the past as the "Schweinsberg," "Sauberg," and "Josefsberg"—is the *second* peak before the Danube.

96. Figures on the overall size of the army vary. It probably consisted of well over 70,000 men, but detachments had to be left behind in northern Lower Austria and at Tulln. See "Récit," p. 34.

97. "Prefect," *Akta*, pp. 390–391; "Récit," pp. 34–35; "Journal," p. 101; Rauchbar, p. 268; Mansberg, p. 63. Dupont's claim (p. 134) that the only guns present were those brought up by the Poles is not only contradicted by Le Bègue but also illogical by virtue of the longer route and rougher terrain followed by Sobieski's men.

98. Sobieski to Marysieńka, September 12, *Akta*, p. 375; "Prefect," *ibid.*, p. 391; Wimmer, pp. 111–112; Rauchbar, p. 268; Dalérac, pp. 90–91; Dupont, pp. 133–135. The lower courses of the creeks now flow through tunnels mostly. The area itself is built up almost solidly to the base of the Nussberg.

99. "Journal," p. 101; Dupont, p. 135; Sobieski to Marysieńka, September 12, *Akta*, p. 374.

100. Kreutel, pp. 90–91, 99–101, 159.

101. Cantemir (Chapter Two, footnote 90), pp. 308–310.

102. Some Turkish units had been encamped in the space between Hernals and Döbling from the beginning of the siege, but not really contiguously and not in great numbers. The bulk of the forces, before this time, appear to have been concentrated in the area to the rear of the approaches (Penzing-Breitensee-Hernals). An exact demarcation of the lines of the camp is impossible, contemporary maps being somewhat contradictory.

103. Marsigli, *Stato militare* (Chapter Six, footnote 61), p. 120. While Kara Mustafa's failure to take advantage beforehand of the gully-marked, naturally-defensive terrain between Vienna and the Wienerwald was a grievous error, it bears remarking that the construction of rearward-facing lines was a military technique not yet customary among the Turks.

104. Vaelckeren (Chapter Eight, footnote 7), pp. 85–87; Ruess (Chapter Seven, footnote 88), pp. 42–44; Hocke (Chapter Seven, footnote 91), pp. 183–194; Ghelen (Chapter Eight, footnote 17), pp. 53–55; Kreutel, pp. 101–106.

105. Exact records exist only for İbrahim Pasha's right wing, which counted 28,400

men (*ibid.*, p. 131). The center and the left, to judge from the general statements in the Turkish sources, were probably somewhat smaller. Without the Rumanians and the Tatars, the Ottoman army at Vienna originally encompassed roughly 90,000 men. According to Kunitz (p. 7), it suffered 30,000 dead by August 12. While this number sounds too high when compared to the defenders' own estimates of Turks killed in individual actions, a final overall figure of this size (including deaths from wounds and disease) is probably not unlikely. With İbrahim Pasha's 13,500 men from Győr, the Turkish army would thus have included around 73,500 men (again not including the Rumanians and Tatars), of whom perhaps 10,000 may be assumed to have been left in the trenches. The famous Turkish muster list (Kunitz, appendix), supposedly made for the Grand Vezir on September 7 and found in his tent on September 13, gives a grand total, including auxiliaries, of 174,500. It is puzzling. In certain instances it matches exactly the figures given for the units of İbrahim Pasha's command by the Court Master of Ceremonies; yet in other cases it is greatly exaggerated. It is clear, however, that this mysterious roll, the original of which has never been found, also lists contingents stationed in Hungary (e.g., Thököly and Abafi) and some that are not mentioned elsewhere. It apparently represents original, theoretical strengths. The individual commanders, for personal, selfish reasons may have wished to deceive the Grand Vezir, although it is difficult to see how he could have been unaware of the great losses already suffered.

106. Marsigli, pp. 120–121; Kreutel, pp. 114–118.

107. There is no way of telling whether the battery was placed on the right or on the left flank of the Kahlenberg. Cartographically, the left would seem more logical.

108. "Mémoire Badois," *Akta*, p. 647; "Récit," p. 37; Camesina, footnote 1, p. 129; Mansberg, p. 88; *Aufrichtige und Unpartheyische Relation von der Victoria der Christen . . . zur Vertheidigung der Sächsischen Tapfferkeit*, no place and date of publication but by internal evidence probably written by the engineer, Daniel Suttinger, pp. 5–7.

109. While the Silâhdar (Kreutel, pp. 106–107) describes the *Ser'asker*'s post as being an artillery-protected place where he could observe action on the right (hence only the Türkenschanz), he also speaks later (*ibid.*, p. 109) of the Grand Vezir's suite fighting the Poles at the same place. The Grand Dragoman provides the apparent key to the riddle by stating that his master faced the Polish *left* wing (Hurzumaki, p. 15). In all probability, the left side of the *Türkenschanz* opposed Sobieski's men, but the rest of the position clearly faced Sachsen-Lauenburg and Waldeck. The latter, in any case, asserts that his troops assaulted the hill "worauf der Grossvezier stand." Rauchbar, p. 269.

As for the Mass ("Récit," p. 8), controversy has long raged whether the ceremony took place at St. Joseph's (Kahlenberg) or at St. Leopold's (Leopoldsberg). A plaque still affixed to the latter church asserts its claim; the Polish curate of the former volubly defends his building as the site. The evidence is in favor of the good father. St. Joseph's is mentioned by Le Bègue (*ibid.*, p. 36), Dupont (p. 136) and, at least by inference, Prince Jakób (*Akta*, p. 621). Dalérac and lesser contemporary relations appear to be the source of the former view. Whether Charles was present at the service is unclear: Dupont says so, Le Bègue implies not. Dalérac speaks of "all the generals." Tradition has it that Sobieski served as acolyte, that d'Aviano preached a fiery sermon, and that the King dubbed his son a knight. This seems unlikely. There may be some confusion with a Mass and penetential divine service held by d'Aviano at Tulln on the Feast of the Virgin's Birth (September 8). Heyret. pp. 291–292. See R. Herle, "Der Streit um die Türkenmesse," *Die Warte*, Vienna, January 10, 1953.

110. Dalérac, p. 92. See footnote 125, first paragraph.

111. Laskowski, pp. 144–145; Forst de Battaglia, p. 213 (cites a rather generally-couched statement of Brandenburg's envoy as evidence).

112. Wimmer, p. 112. For the passage in Sobieski's letter, see *Akta*, p. 375.

113. Wentzcke, pp. 214, 219; Hantsch (Chapter One, footnote 11), pp. 49–51; Newald, I, p. 79; F. R. von Weihs-Tihany, *Belagerung und Entsatz von Wien 1683*, Graz, 1933, p. 43; "Récit," p. 36.

114. Rauchbar, p. 268.

115. See footnote 125, second paragraph.

116. It is impossible to determine the exact location of the fence.

117. Hocke, p. 97; Vaelckeren, pp. 88–89; Kochowski, p. 30; "Mémoire Badois," *Akta,* p. 647; "Récit," p. 38; *Relation,* p. 7; Mansberg, pp. 90–91.

118. "Récit," p. 38.

119. The various sources conflict somewhat as to the hours. I have relied principally upon the "Prefect" and Le Bègue who seem to fit together fairly well.

120. "Récit," p. 38; Mansberg, pp. 91–95.

121. "Prefect," *Akta,* pp. 591–593; Wimmer, pp. 116–118; Dalérac, pp. 95–96; Kreutel, p. 108; Kochowski, p. 36; Dyakowski, p. 20; cf. Anton Dolleczek, "Die Entsatzschlacht vor Wien am 12. September 1683," *Organ der Militärwissenschaftlichen Vereine,* Vol. 26 (1883) , p. 165.

122. "Prefect," *Akta,* p. 594; Dyakowski, pp. 18–19; Dalérac, p. 96; "Récit," pp. 38–39; "Journal," p. 102.

123. Dupont, p. 137; Dalérac, pp. 96–97. The standard in question was taken by the Poles and sent off to the Pope shortly thereafter. Cf. Camesina, pp. 78ff.

124. "Récit," p. 39; "Journal," p. 102; Raumer, pp. 278–279.

125. "Prefect," *Akta,* pp. 494–495; Kochowski, p. 30; Dupont, p. 138; Prince Jakób, "Diarium," *Akta,* p. 625; see Forst de Battaglia, pp. 218–219; see Dolleczek, p. 166; see Mansberg, pp. 103–105. Dalérac (p. 97) and, less explicitly, Dupont (p. 137) assert that their master commanded Lorraine to support the final Polish attack, thus giving the monarch credit for overall direction of the assault. (See above, p. 323.) None of the strictly Polish sources (including the King himself) raises this claim, and above all there is no mention of John III suggesting the German swerve into the northern sector of the Turkish camp. It is possible that Sobieski asked the Duke to put pressure on the Ottoman right wing while the Polish hussars were still in trouble or that an order to advance was sent *after* Charles had already begun to penetrate into Oberdöbling.

As for the immediate cause of the Turkish rout, there is not only the evidence of the admittedly partial Le Bègue but also of three other sources, two Ottoman and one Western. The Silâhdar (Kreutel, pp. 113, 115) , whose attitude toward Kara Mustafa is by no means uncritical, emphasizes the Beylerbeyi's flight as the reason for the defeat. So does the Grand Dragoman (Hurzumaki, p. 15) . The Count of Provana asserts that the Duke "fit une telle bonne disposition que l'aile droite des Turcs fut contrainte de prendre la fuitte, ce que mit le roi de Pologne en état de pousser l'autre aile des Turcs qui luy étoit opposée, en fit que le victoire se déclarat entièrement pour nous." Marczali (Chapter Six, footnote 9) , p. 41. The Prefect, too, at least indirectly, emphasizes the rôle of the Christian left (*Akta,* p. 594) . Finally, it is clear from a map study that the retreat of the Turkish right inevitably exposed the center and left. On the other hand, there can be no question that İbrahim Pasha served as a very convenient scapegoat. It is undeniable that the Grand Vezir's own negligence and the advent of the Poles on his left, which led him to weaken fatally the already battle-worn right, were essential preliminaries to the Christian victory.

126. Dalérac, p. 100. The author is incorrect in stating that Jabłonowski (a political adversary of the King) and *all* of the Polish reserves were uninvolved in the battle. As indicated, the Palatine's role was important, and to carry it out he also had to call upon his second and third lines ("Prefect," *Akta,* p. 595) .

127. Rauchbar, pp. 269–270; Kochowski, pp. 37–38; Kreutel, pp. 108–109; Hocke, p. 197; "Journal," p. 139; Dalérac, pp. 99–100; Laskowski, "Relacja . . . ," pp. 164–165. Two streets near the Türkenschanz Park of today are named to commemorate Waldeck and Max Emmanuel. Rimpler is similarly honored nearby. There is a Sobieskiplatz, a Karl Lothringergasse, and a Graf Starhemberggasse but no street for Elector John George, which may reflect enduring spite over the difficulties associated with obtaining Saxon help in the first place.

Epilogue

1. Laskowski, "Relacja. . . ." (Chapter Nine, footnote 71) , pp. 164–165.

2. *Idem;* Sobieski to Marysieńka. September 13, *Akta,* p. 377; "Prefect," *Akta,* pp.

596–597; "Mémoire Badois," *ibid.*, p. 648; Dupont (Chapter Two, footnote 20), p. 138; Dalérac (Chapter Two, footnote 24), p. 100; Vaelckeren (Chapter Eight, footnote 7), p. 93; Dyakowski (Chapter Nine, footnote 74), p. 22. Dupont says that the Poles began to plunder only in the morning, but the others, insofar as they give a time at all, indicate that it was during the night.

3. Sobieski to Marysieńka, September 13, *Akta*, pp. 377–378; Kreutel (Preface, footnote 2), p. 110; Hocke (Chapter Seven, footnote 91), p. 198; Rauchbar (Chapter Three, footnote 77), p. 270. For the question of the flag, see Chapter Nine, footnote 123. Kollonitsch also made off with Turkish documents which, unfortunately, have disappeared (Renner [Chapter One, footnote 3], p. 439).

4. Kochowski (Chapter Nine, footnote p. 58), pp. 38–39.

5. Ghelen (Chapter Eight, footnote 17), p. 60; Vaelckeren, p. 89; Kreutel, p. 110; Wagner (Chapter One, footnote 3), p. 616; "Specificarum Rerum inventarum in Castris Turcicis pro Armamentatio," Austrian National Library, Codex 12775.

6. Some suburbanites, despite the loss of the wine, were able to raise the cash for rebuilding: they sold off food stores the Turks had left in their cellars. Feigius (Chapter Eight, footnote 13), p. 83.

7. Hocke, pp. 205–206; Ghelen, p. 62.

8. Anonymous (Chapter Seven, footnote 88), pp. 49–50.

9. *Ibid.*, p. 50. The Silâhdar (Kreutel, p. 166) asserts that 10,000 of his wounded and sick compatriots were struck down, but, as with many of his other figures, the statement does not have the ring of accuracy.

10. Anonymous, p. 50; *Genaue und eigentliche RELATION Dessen, waß nach glücklichem Entsatz Der Stadt Wienn / Biß zum 15.(25.) Septemb. weiters passirt, etc.*, Regensburg, 1683, p. 10; Hocke, p. 203; *Das Kriegsjahr 1683* (Chapter Seven, footnote 14), pp. 261–263; Veress (Chapter Seven, footnote 9), p. 33; see also Chapter Nine, footnote 105.

11. Le Bègue, "Journal" (Chapter Seven, footnote 14), p. 103; "Récit," p. 40; Marczali (Chapter Six, footnote 9), p. 197.

12. *Ibid.*, p. 198.

13. *A letter from the King of Poland to his Queen, etc.*, "Translated from the Cologne Gazette, Octob. 19, 1683," London, 1683, n.p.

14. Hocke, p. 203; Vaelckeren, p. 94; Ghelen, p. 61; Feigius, p. 64; "Récit," p. 40; "Journal," p. 103; Prince Jakób, "Diarium," *Akta*, p. 623.

15. Sobieski to Marysieńka, September 13, *Akta*, pp. 379–380; Sobieski to Charles II, September 13, AGS, 3925. The latter document goes on to propose a crusade. If offered aid, Greece, Albania, Macedonia, Bulgaria, Dalmatia, Wallachia, Moldavia, and other Turkish provinces will rebel against the Porte.

16. *Die weitberühmte Und Wohl ausgebaute Türckische Bad-Stube / So vor Wienn 1683. ist geheitzet worden*, (?), 1683.

17. Hocke, p. 202; "Récit," p. 40; "Journal," p. 103.

18. Wagner, p. 616; Ruess (Chapter Seven, footnote 88), p. 48; Vaelckeren, p. 96; Rauchbar, p. 271; "Journal," p. 103.

19. *Ausführlicher Bericht Wegen erhaltener Christlichen Victori wider die Türcken, etc.*, Vienna, 1684, n.p. John George sent back (from Klosterneuburg) a letter in which he excused himself because of "indisposition." Raumer (Chapter Nine, footnote 49), p. 286. The real causes of his sudden departure were by no means clear to contemporaries and have remained a puzzle to historians. The well-informed Venetian ambassador, Contarini, wrote of Electoral opposition to the anti-Protestant policies in Hungary (which possibly reflected a reluctance to remain involved in an operation which could change from an anti-Turkish to an anti-Thököly crusade), annoyance over greater deference paid to Max Emmanuel of Bavaria, the heavy losses suffered by one regiment, and the Poles' monopolization of the booty. Cited by Klopp (Chapter One, footnote 27), p. 219, footnote 1. The Saxon himself claimed in a later letter to Sobieski (*ibid.*, p. 318) that political conditions in northern Europe necessitated his return. The King, for his part, thought the reason was Leopold's failure to express adequate thanks. Sobieski to Marysieńka, September 17, *Akta*, pp. 395–396. A modern writer has suggested that it

was continuing resentment over the Emperor's unwillingness to foot the bill for the Saxon army, a belief that the main job had already been accomplished, and financial troubles at home, as well as the northern situation. Hassel-Vitzthum (Chapter Nine, footnote 50), p. 168. If one may believe a Swedish diplomatic report from Vienna, however, the most important factor was wounded self-esteem (thus partly confirming Contarini). While mentioning the uncooperative attitude of the Bohemian Estates, the document (which the Spaniards somehow obtained) asserts flatly that the main reasons were that the "Catholics had employed all kinds of means to prevent said Elector from coming in person to the relief of Vienna" and that, even worse, the Imperial Court had shown few signs of respect, especially insofar as the Saxon troops were reviewed after everybody else. AGS, 3925 (no date, but received November 1).

20. Sauer (Chapter Five, footnote 116), pp. 129–140, 145–146; Sobieski to Marysieńka, September 17, *Akta*, p. 397; Newald, II (Chapter One, footnote 3), p. 113, footnote 8. Buonvisi, whom the ministers had succeeded in keeping in Linz, argued in a letter that the "right hand" ought to be conceded not just to any king but certainly to "un Rè bravo, che ha abbandanato il proprio regno et è venuto a liberar Vienna, questi Stati e tutta la Christianità dall' imminente schiavitudine," Sauer, p. 146.

21. E.g., Laskowski (Chapter Two, footnote 9), pp. 226–235.

22. Sobieski to Marysieńka, September 17, *Akta*, p. 398; Prince Jakób, "Diarium," *Akta*, p. 623; Forst de Battaglia (Chapter Two, footnote 12), pp. 226–235.

23. Sobieski to Marysieńka, September 17, *Akta*, pp. 399–408; "Perfect," *ibid.*, pp. 496. The cemeteries of the Inner City were already filled with the dead of the siege. Likewise the chaòtic conditions in the immediate post-siege period made prompt dispatch of supplies impossible. While the Polish wounded could have been taken into Vienna (the Bavarians were), fear of their unruliness may well have acted as a deterrent. (Sobieski's sensitivity at Schwechat may have been heightened *beforehand* by these incidents.)

24. Klopp (Chapter One, footnote 27), pp. 321–322; Dyakowski, pp. 25–26. The two main Austrian accounts of the meeting (Hocke, p. 210; Vaelckeren, pp. 99–100) give no hint of a lack of cordiality but were of course quasi-official publications issued at a time when memories of the unpleasant repercussions were still fresh. Other contemporary reports reflect the negative impression made by Sobieski's rather abrupt departure. (Jabłonowski was given the job of showing the rest of the Polish troops to the Emperor.) E.g., Marczali, p. 198; "Journal," p. 104.

25. Dyakowski, p. 26; Sobieski to Marysieńka, September 21, *Akta*, pp. 418–419; Dalérac, p. 100; Laskowski, "Relacja . . . ," p. 165; Sobieski to Charles II, September 13, AGS, 3295. Dalérac and the author of the "Relacja," a Jabłonowski partisan, allege that Sobieski insisted on staying because of selfish, personal (i.e., dynastic) interests. This was true, but only within the framework of his broader ideals for Poland.

26. Sobieski to Marysieńka, September 17, *Akta*, p. 395; "Journal," p. 104; Rauchbar, pp. 271–273.

27. "Journal," p. 105; "Récit," p. 41. In the "Récit" Le Bègue claims that a further alternative was to seize Parkan, but this seems like the benefit of hindsight. The idea appears, rather, to have emanated from Sobieski on the spot. See below, p. 350.

28. Sobieski to Marysieńka, September 21, *Akta*, pp. 415–418; Rauchbar, p. 271; "Journal," pp. 105–107; "Récit," p. 41. It might be argued that the allied army could have gotten underway sooner and more intact if Leopold had not showed up at all. Cardinal Buonvisi thought so (quoted in Forst de Battaglia, p. 236). Possibly the Saxons would have stayed, but logistical preparations would still have caused considerable delay.

29. Mavrokordatos (Chapter Five, footnote 88), p. 15.

30. Veress, pp. 30–31; Count Taaffe to the Earl of Carlingsford, September 27, *Akta*, p. 420.

31. Veress, pp. 31–32. The Grand Dragoman (Mavrokordatos, p. 16) says that the attack was a false alarm and that the Transylvanians were the first to flee.

32. "Journal," pp. 106–107; Veress, p. 32; Dalérac, pp. 372–373; a Necati (Chapter Five, footnote 19), p. 684; Mavrokordatos, p. 16.

33. It is not clear to what extent Lorraine, personally, was an advocate of Nové Zámky although Sobieski's letters make it clear that it was the preferred objective of the Germans from Vienna onward. The Duke had burned his fingers there before.

34. "Journal," pp. 107–111; "Récit," pp. 42–43; Sobieski to Marysieńka, September 28, *Akta*, p. 423; Sobieski to Marysieńka, October 7, *ibid.*, p. 433. Interestingly, both Dupont and Dalérac, on the one hand, and Le Bègue, on the other, claim (mendaciously) for their respective masters the merit of having devised a plan *beforehand* to seize Parkan and then to use the bridge to capture Esztergom.

35. "Journal," p. 111; "Récit," p. 43; Marczali, p. 278; Dalérac, pp. 139–140; Sobieski to Marysieńka, October 8, *Akta*, pp. 450–451.

36. "Journal," pp. 111–112; "Récit," p. 42; Wimmer (Chapter Nine, footnote 58), pp. 128–129; Sobieski to Marysieńka, October 8, *Akta*, p. 451; Marczali, p. 279. The belief that the Ottoman forces on the north shore were small was based on interrogation of prisoners. Dyakowski, p. 29.

37. "Journal," p. 112; "Récit," pp. 43–44; Sobieski to Charles II, Parkan, October 10, AGS, 3925; Sobieski to Marysieńka, October 8, *Akta*, pp. 451–454; Laskowski, "Relacja . . . ," p. 166; Dalérac, pp. 140–145. Dyakowski, p. 28, blames the King for the loss of the dragoons.

38. Count Taaffe to the Earl of Carlingsford, October 10, *Akta*, p. 461; Marczali, p. 285; Dalérac, pp. 146–147; Sobieski to Marysieńka, October 8, *Akta*, p. 453; "Journal," pp. 112–113; "Récit," p. 44; Dyakowski, p. 31. Figures for the Polish dead vary from 500 to 3000. I have taken Taaffe's and the Grand Dragoman's as a mean.

39. Dalérac, pp. 147–148; Dupont, p. 154; Necati, p. 685.

40. See above, p. 294.

41. "Journal," p. 113, 115; "Récit," pp. 44–45; Marczali, p. 285. The "Récit" asserts that Germans were mingled with the Polish wings to provide stiffening, but this cannot be confirmed. Figures for the Ottoman forces vary. Polish sources give greater totals than the Austrian (which are followed here).

42. "Journal," pp. 113–114; "Récit," pp. 45–46; Marczali, p. 287; Dupont, pp. 154–155; Dalérac, pp. 149–152; "Prefect," *Akta*, p. 605; Count Taaffe to the Earl of Carlingsford, October 10, *ibid.*, p. 462. Dupont and Dalérac contradict the others in certain respects but sound less convincing. The King did not describe the battle at all in his next letter home, which gives further grounds for questioning the two Frenchmen.

43. Again the figures can only be approximate.

44. "Journal," pp. 114–116; "Récit," p. 46; Marczali, pp. 287–288; *Das Kriegsjahr 1683*, pp. 291–292; Dalérac, pp. 152–153; "Prefect," *Akta*, pp. 605–608; Count Taaffe to the Earl of Carlingsford, October 10, *ibid.*, p. 462. Sobieski and Jabłonowski squabbled over retention of the two pashas, supposedly worth a rich ransom. The King gave in, and the Grand Hetman held the pair for a decade. The money he eventually got from Turkey did not cover the heavy costs of keeping his "guests" in state. Dyakowski, p. 33.

45. Mavorokordatos, pp. 17–18; Necati, p. 686.

46. "Journal," pp. 115–116; "Récit," pp. 47–48; *Das Kriegsjahr 1683*, p. 294.

47. "Journal," pp. 117–118; "Récit," p. 48. Herberstein was not strong enough to oppose the Turkish crossing at Osijek and withdrew in the face of Ottoman detachments sent his way. Mavorokordatos, p. 17.

48. *Idem;* "Récit," p. 50; Dupont, p. 148.

49. "Journal," p. 119; "Récit," pp. 49–50; Sobieski to Marysieńka, October 17, *Akta*, pp. 485–486; Dalérac, p. 156.

50. "Journal," pp. 119–122; "Récit," pp. 50–52; Dupont, pp. 158–159; Marczali, pp. 288–291; Mavrokordatos, p. 17; *Das Kriegsjahr 1683*, p. 303.

51. "Journal," pp. 122–124; "Récit," p. 52; Fraknói (Chapter Three, footnote 5), pp. 79–84; Forst de Battaglia, pp. 239–240.

52. "Journal," pp. 124–125; "Récit," pp. 52–53.

53. *Ibid.*, p. 53; "Journal," pp. 125–126; Dalérac, p. 177; Sobieski to Marysieńka, November 27, *Akta*, pp. 388–389; Sobieski to Marysieńka, December 6, *ibid.*, pp. 364–365.

54. Forst de Battaglia, pp. 247–248; Dalérac, pp. 174–180; "Récit," pp. 53–54; *Das Kriegsjahr 1683*, pp. 311–313.

55. Cantemir (Chapter Two, footnote 90), pp. 491–492; Guilleragues to Louis XIV, Pera, December 10, 1683, MAE, "Turquie: Supplément 1679–1684." Conceivably, Thököly, fearful of punishment by Kara Mustafa, lent his voice to those advocating the Grand Vezir's downfall. Klopp, p. 376.

56. Cantemir, p. 493; Rycault (Chapter Two, footnote 54); Guilleragues to Louis XIV, MAE.

57. Kreutel, pp. 103, 121–123, 184; Rycault, pp. 133–134; Guilleragues to Louis XIV, Pera, March 28, 1684, MAE.

58. See above, p. 162.

59. Auerbach (Chapter Three, footnote 50), pp. 225–226; Gérin (Chapter Five, footnote 45), p. 140; Immich (Chapter Three, footnote 4), pp. 30–31. The Emperor did designate three commissioners, but the text was published only on August 24; the Diet accepted the French offer on September 1. French troops entered Hainault in mid-August. Borgomanero's memorial to the Emperor, August 27, 1683, AGS, 3925.

60. Frakňói, p. 87; Gérin, p. 142; proposals made by Count Mansfeldt (ambassador to Paris) were apparently inspired by the nunzio Ranuzzi. Borgomanero to Madrid, Linz, October 8, 1683, AGS, 3925; Borgomanero to Madrid, Linz, October 9, 1683, AGS, 3925 (two letters); Klopp, pp. 341–342 (text of Kunitz letter).

61. Klopp, p. 361; Frakňói, pp. 77–85; D'Avaux (Chapter Four, footnote 74), I, pp. 222–223, 374–375. Even before the October 20 conference Leopold indicated which way he was leaning, for earlier in the month he sent his approval of the Diet resolution of September 1 (footnote 59). Auerbach, p. 227.

62. D'Avaux, pp. 328–330; Klopp, p. 367.

63. *Ibid.*, pp. 362–363; Rauchbar, II, pp. 285, 289, 323; G. von Antal, V.C.H. de Pater, *Weensche Gezantschapsberichten van 1670 tot 1720*, Pt. I (1670–1697), The Hague, 1929, pp. 370–371.

64. Klopp, pp. 364–366; Borgomanero to Madrid, Linz, November 20, 1683, AGS, 3925; Borgomanero to Madrid, Linz, January 13, 17, 18, 1684, *ibid.*, 3926; Leopold to Charles II, Linz, December 28, 1683, *ibid.*, 3926.

65. See above, p. 148.

66. Klopp, pp. 371–374; Redlich (Chapter One, footnote 21), p. 269.

67. Laskowski, pp. 164–165; Frakňói, p. 86; Forst de Battaglia, pp. 260–261; FRA (Contarini), II, pp. 227, 246. Papal money appears to have provided the impetus for the latter operation (De Bojani [Chapter Nine, footnote 62], p. 882), which also reflects Sobieski's far-ranging strategic concepts. For the details of Venice's accession, see Kretschmayr (Chapter Three, footnote 1), III, pp. 340–343.

68. D'Avaux, II, pp. 79–113 (*passim*), 121–124, 184–192, 195–215, 281–294; Geyl (Chapter Five, footnote 53), pp. 163–168.

69. The siege of Luxembourg City was a considerable undertaking. The garrison was reduced from 4000 to 1700 men, and the French are said to have lost 6000. The fall of the fortress evoked much enthusiasm in France. Schoetter (Chapter Four, footnote 41), pp. 300–301.

70. D'Avaux, II, pp. 318, 322–333; Strich (Chapter Four, footnote 72); "von Antal and de Pater," pp. 377–378; Borgomanero to Madrid, Linz, May 27, AGS, 3926; Frakňói, pp. 102–103; Immich, pp. 36–37; Braubach (Chapter Three, footnote 39), p. 236; D'Avaux, III, pp. 257–258; Auerbach, pp. 228–230. Borgomanero was realistic enough by now not to ask for Austrian troops but merely for pressure upon Bavaria (memorial of April 26, 1684, AGS, 3926). While Linz did send seven regiments in late June and while the Bavarian and Circle forces also mobilized, the Emperor had already made up his mind, and the moves served only to provide leverage for the final dealings in Regensburg. Redlich, pp. 271–272.

71. The town councillors and the surviving troops were also requited in various lesser ways. Cf. Renner, pp. 442–446.

72. The Protocol of the Court War Council (KA) contains a number of references to the allegations against Hermann.

73. See above, pp. 283–284.

74. Renner, pp. 452–453, *passim*.

75. Hantsch ([Chapter One, footnote 11], p. 51), in an overly-enthusiastic resumé of the siege's consequences, gives the erroneous impression that victory resulted in an immediate efflorescence of everything Austrian.

76. Oswald Redlich, *Das Werden einer Großmacht: Österreich von 7100–1740,* 4th ed., Vienna, 1961.

77. See Preface, p. viii–ix.

78. My reference here is to the apparently heavier than normal precipitation in Rumelia and Serbia in late March and April of 1683. (The region is usually characterized, meteorologically, by May–June rains and a relatively dry winter and early spring). The adverse weather slowed down the Ottoman march, and, so it would seem, high waters held up completion of the Osijek bridge. See above, pp. 203, 205.

Index

437

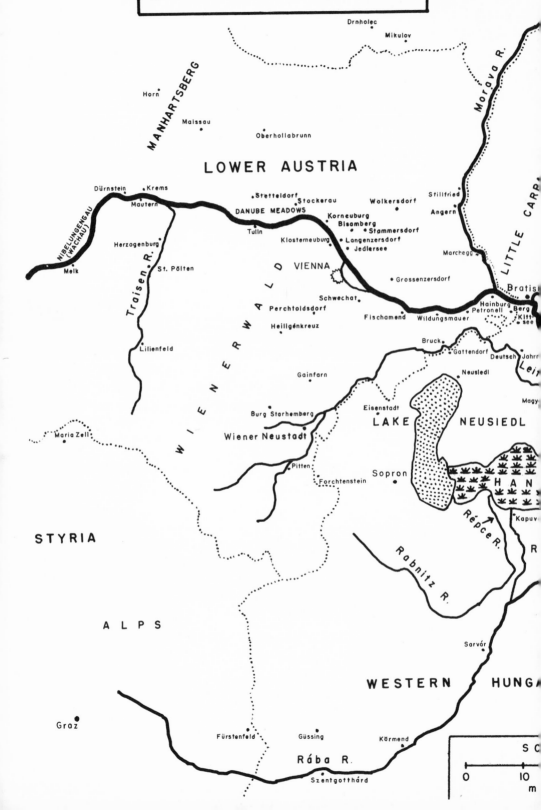

Theater of Operations
Summer-Fall of 1683

Drnholec
Mikulov

MANHARTSBERG

Horn

Maissau

Oberhollabrunn

LOWER AUSTRIA

Dürnstein • Krems
Mautern
NIBELUNGENGAU (WACHAU)
Melk

• Stetteldorf Stockerau
DANUBE MEADOWS
Tulln
Korneuburg
Bisamberg
Klosterneuburg • Stammersdorf
• Langenzersdorf
• Jedlersee

Wolkersdorf

Stillfried
Angern

Marchegg

LITTLE CARP

Morava R.

Herzogenburg
Traisen R.
St. Pölten

WIENERWALD

VIENNA

• Grossenzersdorf

Bratis

Schwechat
Perchtoldsdorf
Heiligenkreuz

Fischamend
Wildungsmauer
Hainburg Berg
Petronell Kitt
see

Lilienfeld

Bruck
Gattendorf Deutsch Jahr
Neusiedl Lei

Maria Zell

Gainfarn

Burg Starhemberg
Wiener Neustadt

Eisenstadt

LAKE NEUSIEDL

Magy

Pitten
Forchtenstein

Sopron

H A N

STYRIA

Kapuv

Répce R.

R

Rabnitz R.

A L P S

Sarvár

WESTERN HUNGA

Graz •

Fürstenfeld
Güssing
Körmend

Rába R.

Szentgotthárd

S

0   10
m